A New Introduction to Sociology

Mike O'Donnell, Ph.D.

Foreword by Tony Marks

HARRAP

First published in Great Britain 1981
by Harrap Limited,
19-23 Ludgate Hill, London EC4M 7PD

Reprinted: 1981; 1982 (*twice*); 1983

ISBN 0 245-53647-7

Filmset by Elliott Brothers and Yeoman Ltd, Liverpool
Printed in Great Britain by Mackays of Chatham

Contents

(A detailed list of contents precedes each chapter)

Foreword

Dr O'Donnell has produced a book with two important characteristics which differentiate it from many volumes designed to serve a similar readership.

First, he has 'come clean' in relation to one of sociology's most thorny and persistent dilemmas: he does not attempt to claim objectivity in the manner of authors of many introductory texts. Indeed he states his own ideological and political preferences clearly. His evident humanistic concern with a variety of social issues gives the book an urgency which challenges the reader to clarify her or his own thoughts. This does not mean that the book is consciously partisan in terms of the myriad of related issues of value which permeate sociology. Like many conscientious social scientists, he offers a full and generally sympathetic account of approaches which he finds less satisfactory.

As an experienced teacher and examiner of sociology at GCE advanced level, Dr O'Donnell is familiar with the demands of existing syllabuses, and this is reflected in the text. It is, nevertheless, clear that the volume's usefulness embraces much more besides. The 'A' level courses in sociology administered by the various examining boards and the revision of those syllabuses should be well served by *A New Introduction to Sociology*. It is pleasing to see a number of newer syllabus topics discussed here. Chapters on urbanisation, community and development, age and generation, race, and social policy and problems ensure that the book's coverage is very comprehensive. Introductory courses in higher education ought to be made more stimulating and comprehensible than they often are.

A particularly interesting feature of the book is the author's analysis of the common ground as well as the differences between the various sociological perspectives, Dr O'Donnell's exploration of the bedrock principles of sociology culminates in a final chapter in which he argues that the various sociological perspectives share a number of concepts, and that a 'unified sociological paradigm' or perspective is a feasible possibility. In summarising and partly synthesising a variety of recent works which reflect a concern for the reconstruction and reintegration of sociological theory, he captures a rising trend within the discipline. As a result, *A New Introduction to Sociology* stands out from purely perspectives-oriented textbooks as a distinctive and even original contribution to the introductory literature of the subject. It presents the perspectives not as the essence of sociology but, critically, as various contributions to the creation of a more fully developed discipline which nonetheless still awaits mature accomplishment.

The other major advantage contained in this book which students and teachers should note is the explicit and sustained attempt to make sense of empirical material – often of an historical and/or cross-cultural nature – in terms of sociological theories. The ability to be theoretically informed is a distinguishing characteristic of the better students in introductory courses in sociology of all kinds. It enables students to advance from simply 'knowing facts' about a particular society at a particular time, to contexting these in a framework which indicates how apparently discrete items might be linked. This is the very stuff of sociology or, indeed, of any social science. *A New Introduction to Sociology* is designed to facilitate this process and for this reason alone it is to be welcomed. I am no longer faced with several hundred 'A' level scripts each year. If I were there is little doubt that this book would make that task more rewarding. More importantly students and teachers are likely to derive insight and stimulus from *A New Introduction to Sociology*. Its publication is a welcome event.

TONY MARKS
*Formerly Chief Examiner
GCE 'A' Level Sociology,
Associated Examining Board*

How to Use this Book

I decided to write this book some years ago in order to meet a frequently stated need. At conferences up and down the country, teachers often expressed frustration that a sociology textbook did not exist which introduced theory, method *and* empirical findings in relevant areas at a level appropriate to teenagers. Not all these teachers were social science specialists, and I suspect they also needed such a book themselves: they, perhaps, are the 'secret' audience for this work, which is intended as a simple and comprehensive introduction to sociology. Its major audience is the sixteen plus age group, and it is primarily their needs which have guided the level of language and content. I hope, however, that the book will be of use also to students in higher education.

In the last two years some useful introductions to sociological theory have been published, but the need for a textbook of this kind is as great as ever. Indeed, with the new AEB syllabus coming into operation in 1981, it is perhaps even greater. The requirements of the JMB syllabus have also been closely borne in mind. I am, nevertheless, wholly convinced of the value to the contemporary student of a comparative educational perspective: as a result, there is a constant comparative and historical 'refrain' in this book which should make it useful to students following the London and Cambridge syllabuses. There is, in any case, a slight convergence in all four courses of study, with 'development' making a welcome appearance as a topic in the revised AEB programme.

'Topics' in sociology are, to some extent, arbitrary and overlap greatly. There is no need to read this book in any particular order: chapters and sections are self-contained. The index is an essential part of the book. Some themes are followed through several chapters and the index sign-posts where. In addition, ample cross-references are given within chapters. This may seem cumbersome, but textbooks exist to provide information, not to look pretty. It must be stressed again, however, that the book is written chiefly for the student beginning an 'A' level course at 16 and finishing it at 18. Accordingly, the early chapters are relatively simple, though not to the point of excluding material required by the various syllabuses. As a comparison of national results in other 'A' level subjects shows, sociology is a difficult option, not the easy one it is often assumed to be. Sections E and F are, therefore, written at a level which will enable a good student, who reads them conscientiously, to get the grade he or she deserves. Such a student should be able to understand these chapters unaided; others will probably need guidance. The six sections, A to F, cover the six terms of a two-year 'A' level course. Section F is very brief, to allow time for revision before the examination. The sections are presented to allow for the best cumulative understanding of the subject: where a chapter has a relatively high theoretical content, this is indicated by putting the word 'theory' in brackets following the chapter title.

Bias and uncontrolled subjectivity are always spoilers and the reader must guard against them; I also ought to say where I myself stand both sociologically and politically. Sociologically, I cannot conveniently place myself squarely within a single major perspective: a combination of conflict-structuralism and interpretive perspectives seems to me to offer the best possibility of a coherent understanding of society. As I make clear in the last chapter, I take no joy in the theoretical fragmentation currently characterising sociology, and I make some suggestions towards a single unified sociological paradigm. By all means let the thousand flowers bloom, but let us arrange them in some sort of order. Politically, I am a libertarian socialist. This may explain why the themes of democracy and equality recur through the various chapters of this book. I have kept in mind, however, that a textbook should present all relevant information and opinion with absolute fairness. I hope that, if I had not stated my own opinions and values, they would not otherwise have been too obvious.

Finally, this textbook is not a substitute for doing sociological research. It is quite true that 'you cannot find out about society from a book.' You must go out and examine it for yourself, with the sociological tools you have at your disposal. All I aspire to do in these pages is to guide you on the way.

MIKE O'DONNELL, *September 1980.*

Acknowledgements

I would like to thank Anne Vellender for typing, correcting and, sometimes, improving this book. My thanks also to Dorothy Montague for the typing she did. Caroline Riddel and Gina Garrett gave constant advice and encouragement: it can be truly said that 'without their help this book would not have been written'. I am very grateful to Howard Newby for his advice on Chapter 7, Stan Cohen for his detailed comments on drafts of Chapters 16 and 17, and Tom Bottomore for looking over the chapters on stratification and politics. Through vigorous debate and criticism, Jim Pey has helped to clarify my presentation of educational sociology, for which I am now grateful. Tony Marks gave helpful advice over a range of matters. My thanks also to Helen Huckle and Diana Giese of Harrap for their editorial guidance. All the above have improved this book but I must accept its remaining flaws as entirely my own. Finally, my apologies to friends, especially the Lankaster family, whom I have seen rather less since I started writing this book.

MIKE O'DONNELL

Section A **Perspectives: Theory and Method**

How to Use this Section

Students often begin a textbook with the feeling that they must carefully read it from cover to cover. That is not the spirit in which to approach this section.

The intention here is both to *introduce* the theory and method of sociology and to provide a *point of reference* for theory and method to which the students can return as necessary for fuller information about given points. Thus, if you come across a reference to Marxism in Chapters 3 or 4 and want to check back to Marxist theory in general, then, using the index if necessary, it would be a simple matter to refer to the relevant pages in Chapter 1. Similarly, if you meet a reference to the method of enquiry known as *participant observation* in a later chapter, you might want to return and re-read the detailed description of it in this section. So, the initial way to approach this section is to read it for a *general impression*. Get a 'feel' for how sociologists go about their work rather than trying to learn in detail about it. At a later point, possibly about half-way through the course, it will be necessary to give closer study to Chapter 2, though, by then, the contents of Chapter 1 will probably have already been fully absorbed.

We can liken sociology to a mansion full of variety of valuable things. At the moment, you are outside the mansion and will remain so for a short time. In front of you lies a map and some implements used in the construction and decoration of the building. Examining these things may be less interesting than touring the house but being familiar with them helps in appreciating it. Understanding the blueprints and implements used in any enterprise or craft is bound to deepen our know-

1

ledge of it. In the case of sociology, Chapter 1 *(perspectives, theory)* can be thought of as 'the map' of the subject and Chapter 2 *(theoretical concepts, methods)* can be regarded as 'the tools of the trade'. Some will spend longer studying Chapters 1 and 2 at this stage than others. This does not matter, but every one should at least read Chapter 1 now.

Beyond this section lies the varied *content* of sociology. This includes information and analysis of the family, race, deviance and so on. Every subject can be divided into the way people go about doing it (theory-method) and what they find (content). Subjects are often presented to the general public only in terms of their content – it is assumed that only 'the expert' can 'do' them. By contrast, this book attempts to present the content of sociology, to describe how to practise the discipline and to examine the relationship between the two. The final chapter of this book deals with many of the issues raised in this section at a higher level.

1 The Making of Sociology: Sociological Theory and Method, Part 1

Why Study Sociology?

Sociologists, like Socrates, the Greek sage, are sometimes accused of corrupting youth. This accusation is usually based on a vague anxiety that they have the power to implant dangerous and subversive ideas in the minds of the young. It is almost as if they are regarded as sorcerers who can charm others from the paths of virtue. Indeed, within education something resembling 'witch hunts' of sociologists do occasionally occur when attempts are made to undermine the prestige and influence of the subject. Like Socrates, sociologists are inclined to defend themselves by replying that their aim is not to corrupt, but to enlighten – not just the young but anybody who will listen and take part.

But 'enlightenment' is perhaps a pompous way of putting it. What sociology can do is to provide the means or the tools to understand society better than would otherwise be likely. To understand society better is to know a little more about what is happening to you, thereby, perhaps, gaining more control over your own life. For example, to appreciate how and why advertisers try to persuade you to buy their products – especially the leisure and fashion products popular in the teenage market – arms you against exploitation. Similarly, to know why qualifications are worth less in the job-market than they used to be, should help you to evaluate your own prospects more clearly.

There are many other important ways in which sociology can improve your understanding of your own life. It can show you how society works, including how people manage to get along with one another. It may help you to be more independent and avoid being manipulated by others. Perhaps that is what the opponents of sociology really mean when they say it is corrupting. They may prefer that you conform without understanding why you do: that way, life is easier for those in power, who are reassured in their own opinions. For students who require a practical as well as an intellectual motive for studying sociology, the subject provides a useful background for training in many careers, as will become apparent during the course of this book.

Understanding yourself and society better will not happen, magically, in a moment. Learning any worthwhile skill takes some time. But the early stages of learning are usually the worst. Take learning to ride a bicycle or to drive a car: there is no need to describe how frustrating and demoralising both can be. But they are worth it in the end. So is sociology.

The Continuing Importance of Marx, Durkheim and Weber

You will probably have noticed that so far I have indicated some of the things that sociology can do for you without quite defining the subject. Nor do I intend to do so immediately. A better way of approaching the discipline is firstly to appreciate some of the problems sociology attempts to analyse. This is where *Marx* (1818–1883), *Durkheim* (1858–1917), and *Weber* (1864–1920) are relevant. They were among the first to look at society in what we have come to think of as a specifically sociological way. Far from being out of date, their work and influence is greater now than it ever was. To say no more, Marxism as a method of understanding how society works and as a way of life has captured half the world.

The continuing relevance of the work of these three 'founding fathers' is a result of two things. First, some of the problems they attempted to understand are the same as, or similar to, major problems of today. Second, the frameworks of social analysis and explanation or *sociological perspectives* that they worked out have not been replaced by anything better, although they have been greatly developed and modified.

The early nineteenth century was a period of rapid change every bit as great as today's. Industrial and political revolutions, sometimes known as the 'dual revolutions', tore apart the fabric of society. The agricultural revolution forced peasants off the land, and the industrial revolution provided jobs for them in the cities. Often, the new industrial workers – and, at first, these included women and children – lived and worked in conditions of squalid exploitation. By contrast, the manufacturing, commercial and financial middle class prospered in an industrial boom. The traditional landed aristocracy also generally thrived, partly because of its great hereditary wealth and power, and partly because many of its members managed to 'get in on' industrial expansion.

Politically, the new middle class struggled successfully to share power with the aristocracy. In Britain, it managed to acquire the vote and other political rights without revolution, but France and other European countries experienced almost a century of political turmoil. As the century progressed, the claims of the working class for political rights and social justice

5

were more and more strongly asserted. Europe was swept by revolution in 1848. In this, the working class and its supporters played a prominent part. Marx himself participated in an unsuccessful uprising in Germany in that year.

Marx, Durkheim and Weber were interested in and wanted to understand the major changes that were occurring in Europe during their own time. Even though they were of different nationalities, Marx being German, Durkheim French and Weber Austrian, the scale and scope of change was such that they were confronted by much the same problems. Our interest arises from the fact that our own period is a direct continuation of theirs and society today can be partly explained by past events and developments. Ours is an industrial, urban society in which, at last, the working class and women have political rights, but in which class conflict is by no means dead. The nineteenth century was a battleground between the old regime and the new, the traditional and the modern. Along with the study of class relations, the contrast and conflict between the traditional and the modern remains an axial consideration of sociology. Britain is still cloaked in tradition: witness the continuation of the monarchy and the House of Lords. Further, the conflict between traditional, rural society and modern, industrial society has been partly 'exported' from Europe to the wider world, in which the developing countries are the new battleground. Marx, Durkheim and Weber's writings are of relevance to all these matters.

But the founding fathers of sociology wanted to do more than just tell the tale of their times and perhaps offer a few unsystematic interpretations of events. They went deeper than that in their search for explanations and, in doing so, created the foundation of a new discipline, sociology. Separately, they attempted to develop ways of examining society and social change which would account not only for how their own societies functioned and changed but which would explain the nature and functioning of society itself. They believed that a scientific approach would assist them greatly in this enterprise. Indeed, perhaps they put too much faith in science, and many sociologists have since argued that, as well as being affected by society, men also help to create it – perhaps to a greater extent than Marx and Durkheim, though possibly not Weber, allowed. In their faith in science, the founding fathers reflected the spirit of their period. Charles Darwin's exciting new scientific theory of evolution seemed to offer a biological explanation of the origin of man and Marx, Weber and Durkheim sought to explain social life in similarly scientific terms. They were aware, however, that human consciousness and creativity raise issues that do not occur in the non-human sciences and we return to these later. Marx and Durkheim, in particular, built up distinctive perspectives or general models of how society works. Since their deaths, other perspectives have been developed within sociology, some of which address themselves more specifically to the problems of the individual in modern society. We mention these shortly. In what immediately follows we will tend to emphasise the differences rather than the similarities between the perspectives of Marx, Weber and Durkheim. However, we attempt to convey the common central concerns of sociology by examining their perspectives in the form of answers to a number of fundamental sociological questions. Sociology is better understood as a series of questions on the nature of society with no set answers, than as a set of agreed findings.

Sociological Theory: Structural and Interpretive Perspectives

At this stage, all that we mean by sociological theory is the body of ideas, tested and untested, making up sociological thought.

We can best understand the disagreements among contemporary sociologists, many of which have their roots in the thought of Durkheim, Marx and Weber, by examining some basic questions of sociological theory to which, in one way or another, all three gave answers. It would not be possible to construct an adequate sociological perspective without answering the following questions, although other major questions could also be asked:

1 **How is society constructed?**
2 **How does society 'operate' or function?**
3 **Why are some groups in society more powerful than others?**
4 **What causes social change?**

5 Is society normally in orderly balance or in conflict?
6 What is the relationship of the individual to society?
7 What is the primary purpose of sociological study?

The different (though not entirely different) answers given to these questions by Durkheim, Marx and Weber helped to produce three distinct traditions of sociological thought or perspectives: *Functionalism* which owes much to Durkheim, *Marxism* (Marx), and *Social Action Theory* (Weber). We will examine separately these three traditions and the answers they give to the above questions of theory. All three of these sociological perspectives are *structural* in nature. Structural sociology is primarily concerned with how society affects individual and group behaviour, rather than with how individuals and groups create society. Thus, the sort of issue a structural sociologist would be interested in, is how the class and family background of an individual (the individual's *social-structural position*) affect his chances of doing well at school and getting a good job. Functionalism is referred to as *consensus* structuralism because it emphasises the central role that agreement (consensus) between people on moral values has in maintaining social order. Marxism and Social Action Theory, on the other hand, stress *conflict* in society rather than consensus. It is a further crucially important feature of the structuralist theories that they tend to seek scientific or *positivist* explanations of social behaviour.

Interpretive sociology, in contrast to structuralism, is primarily concerned with how individuals and groups create, find meaning in, and experience society, rather than in how society affects them. Examples of the kind of matters that have interested interpretive sociologists are what it 'feels like' to be labelled a 'criminal' or 'mad' or, simply, 'not very bright' at school work. Interpretive sociology is, in part, a reaction against the scientific or positivist approach associated with the structural perspectives. We further explain interpretive sociology later in this chapter. Immediately, we describe the structural sociologies of Functionalism, Marxism and Social Action Theory by reference to the seven key questions stated above. It can be seen that the answers given to the questions by the various perspectives differ, sometimes to the point of contradiction.

Structural Perspectives: Functionalism: Consensus Structuralism: Durkheim

1 How is society constructed?

Society or the *social system* is constructed of various *institutions*, the most basic of which is the family. A social institution is a group of people organised for a specific purpose (or purposes) – the nuclear family, for example, is organised in order to produce and rear children. As societies develop, the number and complexity of social institutions increases. This process is referred to as *differentiation*. The civil service and industrial corporations are examples of complex, modern institutions. They developed, respectively, from the King's adviser and small-scale cottage industries.

Institutions are grouped together into four sub-systems:—
a Economic (factories, offices)
b Political (political parties)
c Kinship (families)
d Cultural and Community Organisations (schools, churches)

2 How does society 'operate' or function?

Functionalists consider that society 'operates' in a way comparable to the functioning of a biological organism. This comparison is referred to as the *organic analogy* (or *organismic analogy*). So social institutions function in combination with one another and for the benefit of society as a whole just as the various parts of the human body function in relation to one another and to the whole body. For example, schools function in relation to work because they prepare people for work. And, like the human body, society is more than the sum of its individual parts.

Although the *structure* and *functioning* of society can be separated for the purpose of theoretical consideration, in reality they are inseparable. Obviously, a society or organisation has to exist (have structure) before it can do anything (function).

3 Why are some groups in society more powerful than others?

The question of power in society has tended to interest Marxists and *social action theorists* more than functionalists. The latter tend to assume that *it is practically necessary that some individuals and groups be more powerful than others, because only a limited number*

9

can take important decisions. Thus, they argue that there must be leaders in organisations and in society, otherwise there would be chaos.

4 What causes social change?

According to functionalists, *social change occurs when it is functionally necessary for it to do so.* For example, in modern societies educational systems tend to expand because such societies require a more literate and numerate population than less advanced societies.

Change may occur through adaptation or integration. Adaptation occurs when an existing institution readjusts to meet new needs – as in the example given in the last paragraph. Integration occurs when a society adopts a new element and makes it part of itself. Thus, a society may successfully integrate (or fail to integrate) a group of immigrants.

Functionalists tend to think of change as *evolutionary,* (gradual) not *revolutionary.*

5 Is society normally in orderly balance or in conflict?

Functionalists consider that order and equilibrium (balance) are normal to society. Disequilibrium (civil war, for example), is an abnormal social state. They compare disequilibrium in society to sickness in a living organism.

The basis of social equilibrium is the existence of *moral consensus.* Moral consensus means that everybody, or nearly everybody in a society shares the same values. Thus, a high level of consumption of goods might be a value in American society, but not in many economically and technologically more 'primitive' societies. As we shall see in a later chapter, functionalists stress the importance of the effective teaching of social values in maintaining order and conformity. The role of parents and teachers in passing on values to the younger generation is stressed.

6 What is the relationship of the individual to society?

Functionalists regard *the individual as formed by society* through the influence of such institutions as the family, school and workplace. They leave little room for the view that the individual can significantly control his own life, let alone change society. Durkheim stated that, for him, the individual is the point of arrival, not of departure. In other words, in his view sociology is not about the individual. As we shall see, not all sociologists agree with this.

7 What is the primary purpose of sociological study?
The primary purpose of sociology is to *analyse and explain the normal (and abnormal) functioning of society*. This involves studying the relationship of the different parts of society to one another, and of the parts to the whole. Thus, the relationship between education and work is studied but so, too, is the (necessary) contribution of both to the functioning of the social system as a whole. Durkheim insisted that sociologists should discover and explain the relationship between *social facts*, just as natural scientists do with physical facts.

Marxism (Conflict Structuralism I)

1 How is society constructed?
According to Marx, *society is constructed from classes. In all societies except the most simple, there are two major social classes. It is people's relationship to the means of production that determines which class they are in.* The most powerful class is that which owns the means of production (land, factories) and the least powerful is that which has to sell its labour in order to make a living. In capitalist society (a society based on a private enterprise economy), the *capitalist class* or *bourgeoisie*, as Marx called it, is the ruling class and the *working class* or *proletariat*, the subordinate class. In other words, in his view, business controls labour.

2 How does society 'operate' or function?
In Marx's view *society operates mainly through class conflict. Each class normally pursues its own interest, and this brings it into conflict with other classes.* In particular, he argued that in capitalist society the bourgeoisie and proletariat are fundamentally opposed. This point is developed and explained later.

3 Why are some groups in society more powerful than others?
For Marx, class is the basis of power. *Some classes are more powerful than others because they own more property and wealth, and this*

11

gives them the means to defend and keep what they hold. Unlike functionalists, Marx did not consider that this state of affairs is inevitable and necessary. He believed that socialism could achieve a more equal sharing of power, property and wealth.

4 What causes social change?
Social change occurs as a result of class conflict. Class conflict is the dynamo of history. In the later middle ages, there was conflict between the landed aristocracy and the rising bourgeoisie, and in capitalist society the major conflict is between the bourgeoisie and the proletariat. The victory of a new class introduces a new historical period. Thus the rise of the bourgeoisie introduced the *capitalist epoch.*

5 Is society normally in orderly balance or in conflict?
Society is in a state of fundamental conflict between the classes. Marx recognised, however, that periods of social order and equilibrium can occur, in which class conflict is temporarily submerged. He argued that such periods benefit the rich and powerful more than others.

6 What is the relationship of the individual to society?
There are two major schools of thought amongst Marxists about the relationship of the individual to society, and these reflect an ambiguity in Marx's work itself. One tradition of Marxist thought tends to see *the individual as powerless to affect either his own life or that of others.* Those who hold this view regard class conflict and socialist revolution as inevitable regardless of what any single individual may do. Some Marxists, however, see a much greater role for the individual in society even though they still see the prime source of individual identity as coming from class membership. (Chapter 20, pp. 575-8).

7 What is the primary purpose of sociological study?
The purpose of sociology is *to describe, analyse and explain class conflict.* Nearly all Marxists also want to change the world in a Marxist direction.

Social Action Theory (Conflict Structuralism 2): Weber

1 How is society constructed?

Society is created through social interaction. Social interaction is the behaviour of people consciously relating to one another. In the process of interaction, people form institutions. Although people create institutions such as schools, factories and churches, these institutions in turn influence people. This is partly because pressure exists to observe the rules and procedures of institutions.

Weber felt that Marx overemphasised the importance of class groupings. He recognised that classes are important but considered *political parties* and *status groups* (social and friendship groups) to be further powerful and important forces in society, not necessarily dependent on class (as Marx contended they essentially were). This major point of difference between Marx and Weber is explained fully in Chapter 8. Weber also stressed the power of large organisations or *bureaucracies* over the life of the individual.

2 How does society 'operate' or function?

Again, Weber's answer to this question shows his keen awareness of both the individual's influence on society and of society's influence on the individual. On the one hand, he stresses that *the ideas and feelings people have do sometimes inspire action and affect history.* For example, he argued that certain powerful and dynamic figures, or *charismatic* leaders as he called them, such as Christ and Napoleon, really can change the course of events. On the other hand, he realised that *most people's lives are formed and limited by the society they live in, and particularly by the immediate institutions they come in contact with, such as schools and places of work.* He was personally concerned that large-scale institutions of modern societies (factories, government bureaucracies for example) would limit the scope of individual freedom and creativity. It seems to worry Weber more than the strict functionalists that many people are no more than 'small cogs in large machines' as far as their work is concerned.

3 Why are some groups in society more powerful than others?

Power is one of Weber's central concepts. He combines elements of consensus and conflict sociology in his treatment of this matter. He agreed with the functionalists that for society to function efficiently some people have to have more power than others. He pointed out that *in modern bureaucratic organisations (the civil service, for example) there are always more powerful people at the top, and less powerful people at the bottom; that is, bureaucracies are organised hierarchially.* But Weber also accepted with Marx that those groups that do gain a powerful position in society tend to use it primarily in their own interest. Thus, in medieval society the king and nobility used power for their own ends, even though they may also have sometimes used it for the general good as well.

4 What causes social change?

Weber considered that social change can occur for many reasons, or, more technically, his analysis of social change was *multifactoral. Ideas, new inventions, war, the rise and fall of power groups, influential individuals and other factors all contribute to, and are part of, historical change.* In insisting on the possible variety of causes of change, Weber wished to distinguish his position from that of Marx, whom he thought overemphasised class conflict as an explanation for change.

5 Is society normally in orderly balance or in conflict?

The issue of equilibrium and conflict in society is posed to contrast functionalism and Marxism and is of less central concern to social action theorists. Weber considered that society is not normally either in balance or in conflict – the state of society varies from case to case. *A society may be untroubled for centuries and then be plunged into decades of turmoil. Weber preferred to study specific cases rather than make sweeping generalisations about what is 'normal'.*

6 What is the relationship of the individual to society?

The relationship of the individual to society is of central importance in social action theory. Although Weber fully realised that individuals are affected by social institutions such as the family, school, the workplace and the mass media, he did not consider analysis of the operation and effect of these influences to be the only or primary purpose of sociology. It is more important, in his view, *to understand the meanings that individuals experience in their own social lives than simply to analyse what 'causes' or 'influences' them to act as they do.* Although Weber appreciated that individual social action is uniquely experienced by the social actor he still felt able to *generalise* about *social action,* because in practice there are widely-shared patterns of social behaviour. For instance, people may act *rationally, emotionally* or *idealistically,* and it is possible to categorise and generalise their actions accordingly. Despite Weber's emphasis on *interpreting* the quality and potential variety of individual experience and meaning, he was, therefore, committed to scientific sociology. Nevertheless, although we have termed him a *conflict structuralist* in this section, he was also a founding father of interpretive sociology. The interpretive approach has become popular, and has developed in a number of forms in the twentieth century.

7 What is the primary purpose of sociological study?
The purpose of sociology is *to understand and explain the meaning of social action and interaction.*

Interpretive Perspectives: Phenomenological Approaches: Symbolic Interactionism and Ethnomethodology

The meaning of the above terms is much simpler than their length and clumsiness might suggest. The sociological approaches they describe are all primarily concerned with *the interpretations and meanings that actors in social situations give to events* rather than imposing interpretation and meaning on them by use of scientific or mathematical techniques such as statistical analysis. Thus, it is how *you*, the student, are experiencing school (bored? interested?) rather than merely *what is supposed to be happening to you* (being taught Maths or Geography) that the phenomenologist tries to discover. (As we shall see, this approach requires different research methods from traditional, scientifically-oriented sociology). We will use the terms *phenomenology* and *interpretive sociology,* more or less interchangeably, to cover sociological perspectives of this kind. Sometimes, too, we will employ the term *interactionism* to refer to the same approach. These terms do have specific roots, but within general sociology they are virtually synonymous. Phenomenology has its origin in the philosophical approach of Edmund Husserl (1859–1938). Alfred Schütz (1899–1959) took Husserl's central point that interpretation must be based on the meanings of actors, and applied it to sociology. *Symbolic interactionism* and *ethnomethodology* are the major examples of perspectives that can be grouped under the broad heading of phenomenology (or interpretive sociology).

We will defer more detailed consideration of symbolic interactionism until Chapter 3. This is because the symbolic interactionist perspective is best introduced within the specific context of socialisation. Indeed, the founding father of symbolic interactionism, the American, George Mead (1863–1931), was as much a psychologist and philosopher as a sociologist. He was very interested in the processes by which children are integrated into, and learn to participate in, society.

Although Mead's approach was quite different from Weber's he shared certain underlying concerns. Firstly, both believed that society is the product of social interaction and that social action has meaning in so far as human beings intend it to have. Thus, Mead cited *language* as the prime example of meaningful communication, but he believed that most aspects of human social behaviour bear the stamp of *conscious purpose*. This is true of comparatively unimportant actions such as deciding not to go to school or work on a particular day, and of important ones such as assassinating a Prime Minister. Secondly, both Weber and Mead considered that it was a major part of the social scientist's task to understand the purpose and meanings of social action.

Despite his widespread influence, Mead himself wrote comparatively little. Since the Second World War, symbolic interactionism has been developed by a number of sociologists, mainly American. It is largely through its application to crime and deviancy theory that symbolic interactionism has recently progressed (for details, see Chapters 16 and 17). Interactionists argue that *it is part of the sociologist's task to understand the point of view and experience of, say, the criminal, the juvenile 'delinquent' or the football 'hooligan', as well as of the authorities that label these people deviant.* They insist that it is not the sociologist's role to decide what is right or wrong in society, but rather to understand how the power to decide operates and how decisions about what is, and is not, deviant affect people.

Ethnomethodology is an attempt to describe *how individuals make sense of their social experience.* This is a rather different emphasis from the concern of symbolic interactionists with *shared meaning.* Indeed, ethnomethodologists point out that different individuals can experience the same situation and yet give a quite different *account* of it. We can illustrate this with the example of witnesses at a car crash. All have their 'story' to tell and all may very well be telling the 'truth' – but it is the truth as they see it. One witness may blame the driver of the blue saloon, another the driver in the red sports car, yet another may find fault with a pedestrian and so on. Now, undoubtedly this tendency to relate and interpret the same situation differently does widely exist. To take another example, you might very well find that the account that two students give of the same class or lecture is quite different not only in the way they evaluate it, but also in terms of the sort of occasion it was, and the nature of the events that took place. What ethnomethodologists seek to do is to explain how individuals arrive at their accounts of events. Further, they argue that sociological accounts of events are essentially no different from the commonsense accounts that everybody makes of them. In that sense, everybody is his or her own sociologist. Ethnomethodologists try hard to 'see beneath the surface' of their own societies – they believe that only by taking *nothing* for granted will they see more clearly how people behave. (Chapter 20, pp. 580–1).

The variety of social life means that generalisations are dangerous and ethnomethodologists, in contrast to structuralists, tend to prefer small-scale, detailed and specific studies. Thus, they would rather study crime in a single area than, say, national criminal trends. Later, we examine just such a study by the American criminologist Aaron Cicourel (Chapter 17, pp. 479–80). Finally, ethnomethodologists issue a warning to sociologists themselves. Given that sociologists, too, have their own 'commonsense' values and beliefs, it is important that they be critically aware of this when doing their work. If not, confusion can result – as Cicourel and Douglas show in Chapter 17.

Sociological Perspectives and Values, Personal and Political

So far, we have described the sociological perspectives as though they are nothing less than attempts to describe the social world exactly as it is. To varying degrees this is the intention of some sociologists. The substantial differences between the perspectives, however, indicate that they are *a combination of the way given sociologists perceive the social world and its actual 'reality'*. The perspectives differ because sociologists perceive society differently. To some extent this is inevitable although sound sociological research can establish some theories to be, to various degrees, correct, and others not. Here we will avoid the question of *why* sociologists perceive the social world differently and instead concentrate on the practical question of *what kind of values (or, bias) tend to influence them to perceive the world in given ways.* The student needs to know this. In reading a person's work, it often helps to be aware of what his values and beliefs are. Fortunately, it is easy to show, in a broad way, what values tend to underly the major sociological perspectives.

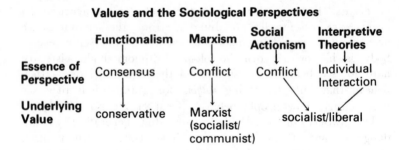

Values and the Sociological Perspectives

	Functionalism	Marxism	Social Actionism	Interpretive Theories
Essence of Perspective	Consensus	Conflict	Conflict	Individual Interaction
Underlying Value	conservative	Marxist (socialist/ communist)	socialist/liberal	

The above diagram contains great oversimplifications, but if it enables you to get an early 'feel' for the perspectives, and to appreciate that they represent different viewpoints, not just 'collections of facts', it will have done its job. Functionalists are often conservative although most live in countries (notably the United States and France) in which no party called Conservative exists. It is therefore easier to think of their conservativism as personal, rather than specifically political: crudely, they are

18

'conservative types'. The link between Marxist sociology and Marxist politics is much more direct. Jibing at arm-chair theorists, Marx said 'philosophers have tried to understand the world, the point is to change it'. Probably all Marxist sociologists want a more communist and socialist world, though they may disagree about precisely what such a world would be like. The link between the remaining perspectives and values, political or personal, is extremely loose indeed. Nevertheless, a number of sociologists, whose work we shall, in due course, discuss, seem to have turned to Weber's social action theory in order to find a conflict perspective other than Marxism. A.H. Halsey and David Lockwood are among them. Politically, such writers often tend towards socialism, but would not want to call themselves Marxists. Interpretive sociology often reflects a highly individualistic and liberal view of social life. The term 'liberal' here means a stress on personal freedom and creativity. Such an outlook does not easily translate into political terms, but often interpretive sociologists are libertarian – that is, they identify with civil and political rights and the right to be personally 'different'. In Britain, work reflecting a fusion of Marxist and interpretive perspectives has recently appeared.

Sociological perspectives are not merely collections of opinions that 'float in the air', relatively untouched by what actually happens in society. *Perspectives are bodies of theories and concepts which must, as far as possible, be tested against the findings of research.* Sociology is extremely rich in its research methodologies – as, indeed, it needs to be – given the complex nature of its subject matter, human beings.

2 The Making of Sociology: Sociological Theory and Method Part 2

Theory, Method and the Perspectives

Whereas the last chapter was concerned to present the major sociological perspectives, this one is mainly devoted to describing the concepts and methods of sociological research. Now that you have a general blueprint (or blueprints) of the subject, we concentrate on how it is done at the practical research level. Basic sociological research methods are not difficult to understand, and you may well want to do some research yourself.

However, it is important to start this chapter with an awareness of the links between perspectives, theories and methods. We consider sociological theory and method under two headings: the *scientific* or *positivist*, and the *interpretive*. These divisions flow directly from those adopted in the previous chapter to describe the perspectives: functionalist, Marxist and social action perspectives tend to adopt a more scientific approach and symbolic interactionist and ethnomethodological perspectives an interpretist one.

Before separately analysing scientific and interpretive theory and methods, we must present some terms that occur throughout sociological practice.

Theories and Concepts

Concepts are general ideas or generalisations. They are necessary to describe types of phenomena (objects, physical or mental). 'Car' and 'House' are concepts, because they describe a type or category of object and have an abstract or 'ideal' existence in our minds and in verbal communication. Two sociological concepts are 'class' and 'role'. It can be seen from these examples that concepts are infinitely variable in the scope of what they represent. Without concepts specific to the discipline, it would be impossible to practise sociology or for sociologists to communicate effectively about their discipline. Along with research

21

methods, concepts are the basic tools of the trade. Nevertheless, sociologists sometimes disagree about the precise meaning of a given concept. Fortunately, however, their disagreements about concepts are probably less than those about general perspectives. An example of a difference in conceptual usage is the term 'role'. Functionalists tend to describe roles as socially given 'things', behavioural patterns that *have* to be performed, whereas interpretive sociologists stress that roles can be 'played' (or interpreted) differently by different people. Thus, functionalists tend to see the role of worker as one in which a job is done, whereas interpretive sociologists try to understand the worker's individual responses to, and feelings about, the job. The notion of a role as a 'thing', on the one hand, and as a part to 'play', on the other, encapsulates the difference between scientific and interpretive perspectives.

The key concepts used in this book include social structure (social division as well as integration); interaction; power and authority; culture and ideology; community and alienation. You probably already have some idea of what these concepts mean and we will define them in more precise sociological terms in relevant contexts later. The point to grasp here is that these concepts are part of the essential substructure of sociology. For example, 'what is the *structure* of society?' is the first sociological question we asked in the last chapter. The concept of structural stratification or division provides the conceptual framework for Chapters 8 to 13 and the concepts of interaction and culture recur throughout this book (in addition Chapter 19 is devoted to cultural issues).

The above concepts are commonly used as analytical tools by all sociologists. For example, Robert Nisbet uses three of them – community, alienation and power (or, more precisely in his terms, authority) – as what he calls 'unit ideas' in sociology. In this author's view, Nisbet's illuminating work, *The Sociological Tradition*, is flawed by its failure to include structure, particularly structural conflict, as a unit idea or fundamental concept of sociology. So sociologists can disagree about the relative importance of the various concepts. Other important concepts, many related to the above, are introduced throughout this book.

Theories are propositions about the relationship between specified phenomena. They may be *unproven* or, on the basis of research or testing, *proven*. An example of a theory is that educational attainment correlates with (is closely linked to) social class origins. By now, research has virtually proved this theory. We will discuss how theories are 'researched' and tested shortly. Concepts play a part in the construction of all theories. Take, for instance, Marx's theory of class conflict, which combines the concepts of class and conflict. In isolation, concepts explain nothing; it is only in their concrete application to the analysis of problems that they become useful.

We will now examine the relationship between theories, concepts and perspectives. It helps to think of *the perspectives as made up of bodies of related theories and concepts.* Thus, Marxism contains concepts and theories such as class, class conflict and many others which, together, help to make up the perspective. Concepts of consensus, integration, adaptation and others characterise functionalism. Those of meaning and interaction are commonly found in phenomenology. It is perhaps too sweeping to think of disposing of a whole perspective by 'proving it wrong', but theories and concepts associated with given perspectives must be open to testing. Thus, despite the tendency of given perspectives to use some concepts more than others, the major sociological concepts are the 'common currency' of the discipline.

Although interpretive sociologists do produce theories, they tend to be rather less concerned with testing them than structural sociologists. Often description and understanding are the limited but not easily achieved goals of interpretive sociologists.

Explanatory and Descriptive Research: A Precise Distinction?

Explanatory research seeks to explain why something happens. An example would be an attempt to find the causes of levels of educational attainment. *Descriptive research is aimed at finding and presenting facts (for example, about poverty) or at describing social processes (for example, how a gang operates).* We need to be wary, however, of the distinction between explanatory and descriptive work both in principle and in practice. To describe 'the facts' involves selecting what is and what is not important. Facts do not choose themselves. By implication, therefore, some interpretation is implied in selection. In practice, most researchers prefer to take the responsibility of interpreting their own findings. Peter Townsend, for instance, in his book on poverty in Britain presented massive factual findings on the subject, but he also included explanations of why it occurs. Researchers are usually in the best position to explain their own findings – if left without guidance, others may misunderstand or misuse them. We now turn to the problem of sociological method.

Scientific Sociology

Science

This section offers a simple introduction to the nature of science. More problematic issues are considered in the final chapter of this book. *Science is concerned with the accumulation of verifiable (capable of being proved true) knowledge.* It has traditionally used two methods: *observation* and *experimentation*. For reasons outlined below, laboratory experimentation is often considered the most accurate and, therefore, ideal method of testing a theory. In practice, all the sciences also use observation. Biologists observe, record and attempt to explain aspects of organic life. The same applies to astronomers in respect of their field of enquiry. It is important that observations are precisely and accurately made. To establish the truth of an observation, it helps to repeat it. Sociologists make full use of observation but very little of the laboratory experiment. Instead, they have developed a battery of methods of their own. How these compare to the laboratory method we consider below.

Scientific research of an explanatory kind often involves *establishing whether the scientist's initial idea or hypothesis is true or false. The research is the means by which the hypothesis becomes a proven theory.* Thus, we can very simply present the process of explanatory scientific enquiry in three stages:

1 The generation and formulation of a hypothesis (unproven theory)
2 Testing the hypothesis by research (method)
3 Analysing the data and researching a conclusion (proven theory)

The most common method used by natural scientists such as chemists or physicists to test a hypothesis is the laboratory-controlled experiment. We discuss this method now because the precise findings it gives and the relative lack of its use in sociology are often cited to undermine its scientific claims.

The Laboratory Experiment

Natural scientists, like social scientists, often want to measure the effect of one 'thing' on another. A biologist might want to measure the effect that being deprived of light has on the growth of a plant; a sociologist might want to measure the effect of class background on educational attainment. Let us see how a biologist might set up his experiment. He may hypothesise that light deprivation will slow growth, but is not sure by how much. He is likely to use two plants that for reasons of precise comparability are as similar as possible. One will be deprived of light and the other (the control) will not. Here we must introduce the concept of a *variable*, something that varies. Relevant variables that can affect plant growth are moisture, heat, soil quality and, of course, light. All other variables apart from light must be *held constant* between the two plants. This means that both plants must receive the same amount of moisture, heat and so on, but not, of course, light. If this were not so, it would be impossible to tell whether light variation or some other variable accounted for the difference in growth. Another way of putting this point is that the conditions in which the experiment takes place must be *controlled*. In this experiment, light is referred to as the *independent variable* (because it is assumed to be the causal factor, not the affected factor, in the experiment) and growth is the *dependent* variable (because it is affected by the independent variable). The biologist can calculate the result of the experiment by measuring the difference between the plants. He will then be able to confirm, discard or rephrase his original hypothesis in more precise theoretical terms. A reliable and valid experiment is *repeatable* and so its findings are open to further *verification* (proof). A repeatedly verified experiment adds to the growing body of scientific knowledge.

Bearing the above in mind, we now turn specifically to the problem of how sociologists pursue their own discipline. We divide this into two sections. The section on scientific sociology is itself divided into the production of original or primary data and the use of existing or secondary data.

Scientific Sociological Methods 1

The Systematic Production of Original Data (Primary Research)

a THE EXPERIMENT Despite the popularity and undoubted usefulness of the laboratory method in the natural sciences, it is almost never used in sociology. The reasons are both practical and moral. Two major practical problems may be noted. Firstly, the kind of processes sociologists study, such as the effect of family background on educational attainment, often occur over too long a time-span to be artificially 'set up' and observed in a laboratory. Secondly, people would not behave as they normally do in such an artificial environment. Psychologists are often better served by the laboratory method because they tend to study very specific and limited aspects of *individual* behaviour. Any moral objection to experimentation involving humans must depend on the nature of the particular experiment. For instance, most social scientists would find it morally abhorrent to test by laboratory experiment the effects of, say, extreme and prolonged overcrowding on human social behaviour. Such experiments were conducted by the Nazis during the Second World War and were widely condemned as being against natural law. Biologists and psychologists, however, are able to experiment with animals in this way without, apparently, greatly offending public opinion. Scientists experimenting with plants and inanimate matter do not, of course, face the same moral issue.

Sociologists have, however, used experimental techniques in broader, if less controlled contexts than the laboratory. Many of these, such as testing the effects of media violence or sex on attitudes and behaviour have tended to be psychological rather than sociological in nature (see Chapter 19). When testing the effects of such material it is helpful to set up a *control group* (a group not to be exposed to the material) as well as an *experimental group*. The control group should be as similar as possible to the experimental group, so that any differences in attitude or behaviour that develop after the experimental group has, for example, seen the films the effect of which the researcher wishes to test, can be reliably attributed to that fact.

The sociologists 'laboratory' could be said to be society itself. He wants to study how people actually behave, not how they might behave in a laboratory. But scientific concepts such as the concept of the variable have been of immense use in educational and other social research. Further, in examining the relationship between variables (say, a social class variable such as parental income and educational attainment), sociologists, often use mathematical and statistical techniques. This, however, applies to the *processing* rather than the *production* of data. To produce data, scientifically-inclined sociologists typically use social survey rather than experimental methods. We now discuss this method of data production.

b THE SYSTEMATIC PRODUCTION OF ORIGINAL DATA BY USE OF QUAN-TITATIVE METHODS Quantitative methods are virtually synonymous with *the social survey*. When a sociologist wants to produce his own statistical data, he invariably conducts a social survey. Social surveys are not used only for academic social research, however. They are used by the government (for example, the Census), in market research (for example, to test public response to a new product), and in public opinion research (for example, election polls). Used properly, the social survey is one of the most useful tools produced by social science.

It is helpful to think of a social survey as being undertaken in three stages:
1 *The Selection of a Sample*
2 *The Collection of Information from the Sample*
3 *The Processing of the Information*
A census is a survey of the whole of the group or *population*, as it is technically termed, that the sociologist is interested in. He usually has neither the time nor the money to conduct a census. He must therefore, obtain a *representative* sample. As M. D. Shipman ironically remarks, monkeys caged in a zoo are unlikely to provide data to explain the behaviour of humans. There are two basic types of samples: the *purposive* (or quota) sample and the *random* (or probability) sample. A *purposive sample* is one selected for its appropriateness by the researcher himself. Thus, when John Goldthorpe, David Lockwood and their colleagues wanted to study the affluent (well paid) manual worker, they selected a group of workers in Luton, because it is a prosperous town likely to contain the kind of workers they were looking for. This was a good choice because it ensured that the sample chosen was representative of the group Gold-

thorpe *et al.*, were interested in (for a fuller account of their research see Chapter 9, pp. 243–7). A bad choice would have been a depressed area of high unemployment such as the dockland area of the East End.

A *random sample* allows each member of the group being sampled an equal chance of being selected. Thus, a sample of fifty students from a total of five hundred could be randomly selected by putting the names of the whole group into a hat and drawing out fifty. It is more usual, however, to take a *systematic sample*. This involves selecting names at regular intervals, depending on how big the sample is to be. In the case of our 500 students a school or college list could be used from which every tenth name would be selected up to the five hundredth to get a sample of fifty. The same technique could be used in the case of electoral registers or other lists appropriate to particular areas of research.

Sometimes the population or target group chosen for survey is *stratified*, or divided, into separate groups to facilitate specialised study. Thus, if 75% of a population is immigrant and 25% non-immigrant, it can be divided into two strata of the same percentage proportion. It is then possible to survey the strata either randomly or by the quota method (in which the choice of respondents lies with the researcher or interviewer).

Once the sample has been selected, and if the sociologist has decided what questions he wishes to ask, the survey can be implemented in a variety of ways. Which way is chosen to implement the survey will have an effect on the extent and the quality of the sample *response*. However, the researcher would be foolish to rush into the full-scale survey at this stage. Instead, it is desirable to test systematically the various features of the survey design by means of a *pilot study*. This is not a haphazard process. C. A. Moser and G. Kalton compare it to the final dress rehearsal of a play – a lot of work has preceded it. The analogy breaks down only in that a pilot-study is on a smaller scale than the main survey, but contains all its essential features. Thus in a questionnaire survey, a pilot study should establish which questions elicit imprecise (or angry) answers.

We can now consider problems relating to the main survey. Generally, the least satisfactory way to adminster a questionnaire (list of questions) is through the post. The possibility of large numbers being lost or ignored is considerable. Response rate can be improved if either the researcher or an assistant visits the places to which the questionnaires have been sent. This also enables difficult or misleading questions to be explained (though in a well-designed questionnaire, there will not be any). Alternatively, the questionnaires may be personally presented either at the respondents' front doors, or even in the street. In such circumstances, however, answers may not always be well thought out. Sometimes the best alternative is to deliver a questionnaire personally, explain its contents, and arrange to pick it up at a later date.

The completely formal interview technique with standardised questions and restricted answer-options in which the interviewer merely records the answers, is sometimes adopted for ease of quantification. The more standardised the answers (a choice of 'yes' or 'no' would be the most standardised), the simpler it is to quantify them for analysis – possibly with the help of a computer. Sociological data that is to be processed by a computer must be able to be given a numerical value. This means it must be possible either to quantify it (for example, 20 'yes's', 80 'no's') or to *codify* it. To codify means to put something into numerical form for the purpose of statistical analysis.

A problem with formal interviews and, indeed, with questionnaires is that respondents often feel frustrated that they cannot elaborate on or qualify their answers. At worst, they may consider that their real 'feelings' have not been expressed at all. In such cases, a respondent may give angry, silly or humorous answers, and so invalidate (as far as the researcher is concerned) the findings. Many researchers accept that feelings and subtle shades of opinion cannot adequately be expressed in statistical form and for that reason informal and unstructured interviews are sometimes preferred (see below).

The problems faced by social survey researchers in achieving scientific precision are considerable. Things can go wrong at the sampling stage if the sample selected is too small or unrepresentative, at the stage when information is collected, or, finally, at the various stages of processing, analysing and interpreting information. The random sample is always subject to the laws of chance: a small unstratified survey of a black ghetto could always 'catch' the few whites living there and only a disproportionately small number of blacks.

Even so, social survey methods of investigation have become

steadily more sophisticated and a well designed survey can expect to overcome all these problems. But even a successful survey can only achieve a limited amount compared to a scientific experiment. The difference in the kind of results achieved by the experimental and social survey methods is as much a function of the difference in the subject matter (non-human/human) of science and social science as in the methods themselves. A successful social survey will give an accurate measurement of attitude and opinion *at the time the survey is conducted*. A fact of life that sociologists have to live with is that once surveyed, human beings change their minds and chemicals do not. It would, however, be misleading to give the impression that social surveys never discover repeated patterns of human behaviour. They do. For instance, every large-scale survey on voting behaviour has shown that the working class in Britain *tends* to vote Labour and the middle class *tends* to vote Conservative. In particular, social surveys have been able to show how given variables *tend to influence* human behaviour. Thus, a number of independent surveys have shown that the variables of maternal interest in a child's education and the material quality of the home *tend* greatly to affect a child's educational performance. *Longitudinal* surveys (studies over a period of time) can be used to monitor the effect of a given variable or group of variables over a period of time. The famous television survey *7 Up* is an example in point. A group of children from different social backgrounds have been interviewed at regular intervals of seven years (so far, the group has been interviewed at seven, fourteen and twenty-one). It is quite clear that *social class* has had a great effect on the life of these children and particularly on their educational career and cultural opportunities. Social surveys, can, then, help to establish regularities or *tendencies* in human behaviour, but not social scientific laws. Taken together, established tendencies provide a basis for the cumulative (gradually increasing) development of social scientific theory and knowledge, just as scientific experiment and law provides a similar basis for science.

We need, finally, to establish a connection between the large or *macro* level theorising and research of the structuralists, and the more limited or *micro* research of social surveys. Social survey methods can provide means to test aspects of general structural theory. Thus, the hypothesis, at one time unconfirmed, of many sociologists that a disadvantaged social class background is likely to affect adversely the life opportunities of even an intelligent child has now been confirmed by many social surveys. Whilst it is true that the confirmation of this hypothesis could have been predicted by commonsense, this does not apply to many of the *detailed* findings of these surveys.

It can be said that social science research as a whole is faced with two categories of problems. Firstly, there are a variety of difficulties associated with the design and implementation of research and the analysis of findings. Secondly, there are problems that arise from the unpredictable nature of the subject matter itself – human beings. Underlying both these difficulties is a third: the fact that the social scientist is himself an example of the species he is researching into. We discuss in a later chapter the problems of bias and lack of perspective that this can produce. Despite these problems, however, logical and rational methods of procedure are available to 'scientifically-minded' social scientists. If these fall short of producing results comparable to those obtainable in a laboratory, they are still far better than mere guesswork.

Scientific Sociological Methods 2

The Systematic Use of Secondary (Existing) Material

There is, of course, a vast fund of existing information about human society available to the sociologist. This includes historical documents, contemporary records and statistical sources. Weber and, particularly, Durkheim, offered detailed guidance about how secondary material can be properly used by sociologists. As the material already exists, neither quantitative nor qualitative methods are needed to produce it. If anything, this means that it must be used even more critically and carefully than freshly produced data.

Both Durkheim and Weber advocated the use of the *comparative method as an alternative to the experimental method*. Thus, in trying to explain the rise of capitalism (the private enterprise economic system) in certain European countries, Weber found it useful to compare conditions in these countries with China. As both the Chinese and the Europeans were relatively advanced technologically Weber was able to deduce that some factor other than technology was likely to have triggered capitalist development in Europe. After extensive comparative research he concluded that those countries or areas in which the Calvinist religion was strongly established were predisposed to develop capitalist economies. (Chapter 19, pp. 538–9).

The *historical method* is often closely linked with the comparative. Indeed, Weber's previously mentioned study of the rise of capitalism was historical as well as cross-cultural (comparing more than one culture or society). Sociologists, like historians, are interested in explaining social change and development. Durkheim actually went as far as trying to classify societies according to their 'stage of development'. Although his scheme is not widely used now, it is good practice, when comparing societies, to be aware that they may be at a different developmental or evolutionary stage. In Chapter 8, for instance, stratification (the division of society into different social layers) is described in traditional (pre-industrial) and modern (industrially developed) societies. Even a general framework such as this imposes some order and coherence which otherwise would not exist on sociological material.

Durkheim, Marx and Weber all hoped that by systematic study of an historical and/or comparative kind they would be able to demonstrate *regularities* in the operation of society. *A regularity meant that a recurrently causal relationship between two factors was established.* For example, Durkheim believed that his research on suicide established a causal connection between high suicide rates and low levels of community support and identity (or low levels of community *integration* as he referred to it). Again, given that the laboratory is closed to the sociologist, disciplined, comparative social research provides an alternative way of establishing regular patterns of social behaviour. Both Durkheim and Marx were extremely optimistic that they would be able to establish a high level of causal explanation of social events. Let us follow Durkheim further in his attempt to do this in respect of his explanation of suicide.

Durkheim wanted to find out what causes suicide. Or as he put it, he wanted to discover what *social facts* cause suicide. For reasons already given, the laboratory method was not open to him. He could hardly experiment with people using in turn a number of variables (isolation, loss of income and so on) to see which made them commit suicide! Indeed, he could not control in any way the social conditions in societies whose suicide rate he wished to compare. All he could do was compare the official suicide rate in various societies and observe what *seemed* to be the most frequent factor which correlated with a high rate of suicide. This is exactly what he did. We examine his methods and findings and various criticisms (mainly from an interpretive standpoint) in Chapter 17, pp. 469–72. The general point to note here is that Durkheim sought to establish the causal relationship between social facts such as community integration and suicide. Although social scientific research methods have greatly improved in the half-century since Durkheim's death, they still do not produce results that are as precise, repeatable and which provide so sound a basis for prediction as those of the natural sciences.

Max Weber also offered an original contribution to sociological method with his concept of the *ideal type* which he also used widely in comparative research. An ideal type has nothing to do with ideals or perfection in, for instance, the religious sense. *An ideal type is merely a theoretical model which is made up of the typical characteristics of the species or general category that it represents.* Thus, Weber gave an ideal type definition of *bureaucracy* (large-scale, modern organisation) which contained such characteristics as hierarchy (top to bottom structure of authority); appointment on the basis of experience and qualifications; promotion through merit and vertical (top to bottom) lines of communication. What is the use of such an ideal type model? The answer is that ideal types, like other concepts, help to guide and structure research, particularly comparative research. By knowing *precisely* what he was looking for, Weber was able to describe, analyse and compare the similarities and differences in the growth of government bureaucracy in a number of different countries. Like any sociological model and concept, ideal types must be tested against social reality – they are of little use if they are imprecise. Once tested, they help the sociologist to arrange his findings in an orderly and meaningful way, as did Weber's ideal type model of bureaucracy.

One of Weber's better known applications of the ideal type is to the concept of social action (see Chapter 1, p. 15). Among his major types of social action were the rational, the emotional and the idealistic. His typology of action was useful in the systematic or, broadly, the scientific study of human behaviour.

Obviously, the rational action of a bureaucrat will be different from the idealistic action of a freedom fighter and to be able to categorise them helps analysis. Weber did not consider that his interest in the meaning of action prevented the scientific study of it and its consequences. Indeed, this was his prime concern.

Marx also attempted to study society as scientifically as possible. However, his concern was not to establish factual correlations, as was Durkheim's, but to develop what he thought of as a scientific theory of society. Among his major theoretical concepts were class and class conflict, and we shall see that he used these in combination with other concepts to build-up a theory of how capitalist society (society with an economy based on private business) operated and changed. There is widespread disagreement about how scientific Marx's sociological approach is. A particular problem is that Marx himself was openly critical of capitalist society and wanted to change it. His motives were as much political as analytical and this has brought the charge of bias against him. A fuller perspective on these matters will be presented in the course of the book (see especially Chapter 20, pp. 575–8).

At this point we must add another name to the trinity we have just been considering. It is that of Auguste Comte (1798–1857), who is often considered to be the first genuine sociologist. He believed that man's behaviour can be explained by the laws of 'cause and effect' in the same way as the behaviour of matter. This approach is known as positivism. Comte argued that positivistic sociology would eventually provide a complete explanation of human social life. Today, positivism is widely regarded as a narrow approach to science. To a greater or lesser extent, however, the founding fathers were all positivists. Comte had a major influence on his fellow countryman, Durkheim, who was thoroughly committed to the positivist approach. Indeed, Durkheim dedicated himself to the study of the relationship between social facts and to their effect on man. Of the founding fathers, Weber was perhaps the most modest in his expectations of the level of scientific precision, explanation and prediction that sociology could achieve. He thought it could establish regular patterns of causal connections but rarely, if ever, social laws. Marx is still thought by some to have discovered the laws of social change but, for all his insight, we can take it that his claim is far too optimistic.

34

Comte equated the positivist approach with science itself, but a broader definition of science is simply that it is the systematic pursuit of knowledge. This definition includes both the observational and interview methods of sociology discussed below but as these have, in addition, the particular purpose of interpreting meaning rather than merely explaining behaviour, we treat them separately.

Interpretive or 'Qualitative' Sociological Methods

There are three types of interpretive or qualitative methods of sociological research: the *in-depth interview, non-participant observation and participant observation. These methods are employed in order to observe accurately and record faithfully the quality of social experience that the social actors themselves feel.* Their purpose is to provide description and human understanding rather than causal explanations. As we shall see, in some instances, these methods come closer to artistic rather than scientific forms of understanding social behaviour. It hardly needs to be said that qualitative methods and interpretive theory complement each other. Given that precise observation is an acceptable scientific research method, *qualitative research can also be considered scientific.* Certainly, it can add to our stock of knowledge about human social behaviour. Perhaps the point to emphasise, however, is that it is the *quality* of human experience rather than its causes that interpretive sociologists wish to explore – though the two motives are frequently combined.

The In-depth Interview

The in-depth interview is often lengthy, sometimes extending to several hours. Frequently, *several separate interviews with the same person or group will be necessary,* as was the case with Elizabeth Bott's study of twenty families of varied class background. In-depth interviews are usually unstructured, though the interviewer will generally have a clear idea of the ground that needs to be covered and can gently direct the interview accordingly. Often the researcher will have a schedule of questions corresponding with areas to be covered in the interview, as did Hannah Gavron in her interviews with ninety-six housewives, the results of which were published in her study *The Captive Wife.*

Nevertheless, as has commonly been recognised by social scientists, the main value of this type of interview is that it provides the respondents with the opportunity to say what *they* want rather than what the interviewer might expect. This intention contrasts strongly with the much more limited aim of the formal interview. The major danger with the unstructured interview is that the interviewer will unduly influence the respondent. This is particularly likely, if the interviewer has strongly preconceived ideas about what his findings might be.

Non-participant Observation

Non-participant observation involves the sociologist in an exclusively observational role in relation to the subject of his research. At least, that is the theory. In fact, however, one of the earliest examples of the use of observational technique showed how difficult it is for the researcher to remain entirely separate from his subject. This was in Elton Mayo's Hawthorne Experiment of 1924. Mayo and his team were asked to examine the effects of various changes in working conditions on the productivity of the work force at the Hawthorne factory. Mayo found that virtually any change in working conditions – even those that made conditions worse than they were originally – seemed to result in an improvement in productivity! At last, he was forced to conclude that what caused the improvement in production was the presence of the research team itself. It must have stimulated the workforce to greater efforts! The Hawthorne experiment provides a strong warning to sociologists to be aware of the effect they themselves can have on their findings. Taking their cue from Mayo's experience, some sociologists have preferred to 'factor out' the effect of their own presence by observing their subject matter secretly. (Chapter 15, pp. 410–11).

Participant Observation

Participant observation involves the sociologist taking part in the social events which he seeks to describe and understand, so that he may do so more effectively. It is a more commonly used method than non-participant observation and has been particularly widely employed since the nineteen sixties by interactionists and ethnomethodologists. The origins of participant observation within social science go back, however, to the earlier part of this century. It was in anthropology that participant observation

36

became popular. It was employed, in particular, by Bronislaw Malinowski and Margaret Mead (see Chapter 13 for further reference to Mead's work). One of the societies that Malinowski examined was the Trobriand Islanders of the Western Pacific. Malinowski used participant observation for the same purposes as more recent sociologists. He wanted to 'grasp the natives' point of view', to 'realise (their) vision of the world' and observe them 'acting naturally'. To do this he had to remain with them for over a year. In order for the participant observer to give people the opportunity to adjust to his presence and to show a typical range of behaviour, he must often be prepared to spend lengthy periods of time with them. It is crucial for the participant observer to win the confidence and acceptance of the people he is studying if they are to behave naturally.

More recent participant observational studies have often been of specific subcultures. In particular, there have been a large number of participant observational studies of gangs and other youth subcultural groups. One of the earliest and most influential of these was William Foote Whyte's *Street Corner Society*. Whyte studied a gang in a poor, largely Italian immigrant part of Chicago. He described himself as 'seeking to build a sociology based on observed interpersonal events'. The following quotation from Whyte states a major justification for the participant observational approach:

> As I sat and listened, I learned the answers to questions that I would not even have had the sense to ask if I had been getting my information solely on an interviewing basis.

In other words, participant observation teaches the social scientist what questions to ask as well as providing some of the answers.

A more recent study of a gang is James Patrick's *A Glasgow Gang Observed*. Keeping his identity as a researcher secret, Patrick joined a Glasgow gang. The result is a fascinating study of gang behaviour and particularly of gang hierarchy and ritual. But was Patrick justified in keeping his identity secret? According to the author's own account, the members of the gang did not think so and would happily exact revenge on him for misleading them. No general moral rule can be laid down on this question of privacy: each sociologist must make his own judgement on the matter.

The very involvement that is the basis of the deepened insight that participant observation can give, may itself become a disadvantage. Again, William Foote Whyte puts the issue well when he states that although he began as a participant observer, he ended up as an 'observing participant'.

If the sociologist comes to identify strongly with the subject of his research, his account may be biased and offer little in the way of a general contribution to the research area. Ronald Frankenburg, himself the author of a celebrated participant observational study of life in a Welsh village, has usefully suggested three stages of research for the participant observer. Each of these stages involves a different degree of involvement with the subject matter. Firstly, the research project must be set up – a relatively objective process. Secondly, the sociologist becomes subjectively (personally) involved with those he wishes to study. Thirdly, he withdraws to consider and assess his experience and findings.

The relatively small amount of space given to explaining interpretive methods of research should not mislead the student into thinking that they are less important than scientific methods. This is a matter for each sociologist to decide for himself or herself. It happens that interpretive methods are best understood in the context of specific pieces of research. In addition to those examples mentioned above, several more are included in later chapters (see especially Chapters 6, 15 and 16).

The Relationship Between Theoretical Perspectives and Method

Having established that a simple and typical connection exists between theoretical perspectives and method, we must now introduce qualifications.

Firstly, the relationship between general theoretical perspectives and applied sociological method is, in practice, much looser than might be expected. This is especially the case in respect of the structural perspectives. A major reason for this is that the various sociological perspectives are so *general* that it is virtually impossible conclusively to prove or disprove them by testing their content in research. Thus, functionalists have been able to maintain their view about the 'normality' of social order and consensus, and Marxists have held their position on social conflict partly because it is not feasible to mount a survey wide enough in scope to prove one or other view correct. Further, propositions of this degree of generality are both likely to have some basis in fact and so it is easy to select evidence to support either of them. Whether we like it or not, therefore, general theory tends to have a life of its own!

This may sound very unsatisfactory. Surely, sociology is concerned with proving things about society and not just disagreeing about them? It is certainly true that if investigation does strongly suggest that a particular proposition of general theory is incorrect, then it should be discarded. It is, however, helpful to look at the sociological perspectives in a different light from this. Here we come to a further explanation for the loose connection between sociological theory and method, and one which perhaps does partly justify what might otherwise seem too flabby a relationship. Instead of regarding theoretical perspectives merely as something to be proved or disproved, it can be more useful to think of them as a *guide* to examining and understanding society. The perspectives can help the sociologist to order his concepts and direct his detailed research. Thus, because of the nature of their respective perspectives, Marxists typically direct their attention to class conflict whereas functionalists are more interested in how harmony and consensus are produced in society. In studying industrial relations a Marxist would regard tension and dissatisfaction at work as normal, whereas a functionalist would consider them to be 'dysfunctional' (the opposite of functional). The perspectives literally do give perspective, context and overall meaning to detailed research. Regarded in this way, the various perspectives provide wide-ranging models or, to use a more technical term, *paradigms* within which sociologists can arrange and make overall sense of their concepts and research. Nevertheless, in those areas in which the perspectives basically contradict each other the effort to reconcile them should continue.

There is a second reason for qualifying the clear connections between theory and method described in the first paragraph of this section. Although, as previously stated, a strong tendency exists for specific perspectives to be associated with complementary methods, this relationship is by no means invariable. In particular, much of the best of what would be broadly categorised as interpretive sociology is, more precisely, something of a theoretical and methodological mix. Stanley Cohen's book, *Folk Devils and Moral Panics,* contains elements of interpretive and structural analysis and employs both quantitative and qualitative research methods as well as a technique termed *content analysis* which has elements of both (for an analysis of this work see Chapter 17, pp. 463–4). *Content analysis involves examining what is contained in, say, various newspapers or media programmes to determine their interest in and treatment of a particular issue.* Thus, to choose an obvious example, the *News of the World,* contains a high percentage of material on sex and crime (which it appears to disapprove of). Another work that employs a variety of theoretical perspective and method is Paul Willis's *Learning to Labour: How Working Class Kids Get Working Class Jobs.* Willis employs observation, participant observation and taped interviews and interprets his material from within a Marxist perspective which still manages to do justice to the feelings and opinions of the 'lads' he is writing about (see Chapter 5, pp. 114–5). Students should not, therefore, feel either overwhelmed by the variety of sociological theory and method or that they must work rigidly within the boundaries of perspectives.

'Doing' Sociological Research
It is no doubt the purpose of a textbook to describe and explain rather than to inspire. Nevertheless, perhaps enough interest has been raised to suggest the possibility that the student should attempt to do some of her or his own research. By far the best way to find out the advantages and disadvantages of a particular research method is to try it. Indeed, someone embarking on research for the first time will probably find that he learns more by trying to construct a well designed piece of research than from the results themselves. If original research is attempted, it is only fair that selected 'guinea pigs' should not be unduly inconvenienced. For obvious reasons, more students have been the subject of research than probably any other single group. Yet sociology students should think twice before deluging their particular school or college with questionnaires. When faced with a sudden outbreak of questionnaires, the patience of staff and other students can wear thin. This does not help the rate or quality of response! Most local communities offer opportunities to carry out research which challenges the

student to think more widely than school-based research and relieves the school of the burden of too much enthusiastic attention from would-be sociologists. Research into certain areas, such as attitudes to local public amenities, could be positively useful. If well done, such a piece of research might deserve to be published in the school magazine, if not the local press.

Guide to further reading and study

Rather more advanced coverage than the above – really second year sixth form level – is provided by several articles on *theory and method* in Meighan, Shelton and Marks, *eds, Perspectives on Society* (Nelson, 1979). Chris Brown's *Understanding Society* (John Murray, 1979), is also to be recommended as an introduction to theory. Other collections of readings on theory are generally more suited to students in higher education. Nevertheless, given the high standard and competitiveness of 'A' level nowadays one of the more comprehensible of these is worth mentioning. Cuff and Payne, *eds, Perspectives in Sociology* (Allen and Unwin, 1979) covers the various perspectives in greater detail than is necessary at 'A' level, but for those students who are prepared to stick with it, it clears up many problems that often remain obscure and confusing at 'A' level. Unfortunately, only Meighan *et al.* of the above books makes any systematic attempt to explore the relationship between theory and method.

A very useful, clear and comprehensive book on *method* is M. D. Shipman's *The Limitations of Social Research* (Longman, 1981). Emphatically for the more advanced student only, is Bell and Newby, *eds, Doing Sociological Research* (Allen and Unwin, 1977). This collection of readings tends to the anecdotal (the sociological equivalent of 'travellers tales'), but for those who have thoroughly grasped the basics, it illustrates well the variety of sociological methods available and the part that personality and human relations can play in research. Otherwise, the student is best referred to the methodological appendices of some of the better known recent works of sociology published in popular paperback editions in Penguin, Pelican, Paladin or other almost equally cheap and accessible labels. The section 'Appendix: How the Research was Done', in Young and Willmott's famous study *Family and Kinship in East London* (Pelican, 1962) is strongly recommended. This study employed a variety of social survey techniques, interviews and participant observation. Although quite different in style and content, Stanley Cohen's *Folk Devils and Moral Panics* (Martin Robertson, 1981) also contains an appendix which succinctly and clearly describes a wide range of sources of data used by the author. The late Hannah Gavron's appendices on method to *The Captive Wife* (Pelican, 1970) is recommended as a guide to the advantages and pitfalls of the interview method. The place to find brief descriptions of sociological method is at the back of books of original sociological research. If the student dislikes what he finds, there is no shortage of alternative choice.

Questions

A selection of questions on theory and method from Past 'A' Level Papers will be found at the end of Chapter 20. The following questions are more suitable for students *starting* an 'A' level course, and don't require essay-length answers.

1 What were some of the questions about society that interested Durkheim, Marx and Weber? Are they still of interest to us?

2 Can society be usefully compared to a living organism? Criticise this analogy from other perspectives.

3 Compare and contrast Marxist and social action sociological perspectives.

4 In what sort of research situations might you prefer qualitative to quantitative methods?

5 What are the major links between the theoretical perspectives and research methods?

Section B **Self, Socialisation and Society**

How to Use this Section

As with Section A, the reader is urged to use this section as is convenient. The concepts of socialisation and culture examined in Chapter 3 fascinate some, but others find them rather theoretical. After a dose of theory in Section A, some may prefer to move straight into Chapter 4 and return to Chapter 3 later – perhaps after finishing the section on education. Nevertheless, if adhered to, the order of this section will reveal a logical progression. In any case, Chapter 3 should be read in order to understand the theoretical background.

This section begins with the smallest conceivable social unit, the individual, and ends with an analysis of global relations, specifically, those between the industrialised and non-industrialised world. It is the links between the individual or self, and society, that is our constant theme. In order to bring into focus the effects of society on the individual, and the way in which the individual makes sense of society, we use the concept of culture, particularly class culture.

Broadly, the plan of the section is *to proceed from the micro-level of self and family through an examination of the educational system, to a consideration of the major macro-issues of social order and change at the level of both national and world society.* The initial theme of self and socialisation carries us through the whole section. It is important not to let the individual be 'blotted out' as we begin to review the influence of ever larger institutions – family, community, the educational system, national and international bodies – on him. To let this happen would be – to risk a pompous phrase – a form of sociological alienation. Society does not exist as an abstraction. Contrary to Durkheim, it is not an entity, still less a 'thing', nor can it 'do' anything. It is perhaps not even desirable to think of society as 'made up of' people. People are not bricks in a wall. People make society and if this is the basis of their freedom it is also a burden of responsibility for them. If it is possible to forget these things when considering only our own relatively stable society, it is difficult to do so when surveying the West's uncertain relationship with the Third World.

3 Self, Socialisation and Culture (Theory 3)

Socialisation

We now consider how the individual becomes a member of society. Inevitably, much of this chapter will be about the formation of the person by society – by family, school, work, and class – but there is a growing emphasis within sociology upon the ability of individuals to control, in some measure, their own lives. Obviously, most members of society will not expect to leave a substantial mark upon it, but many do have the reasonable hope of living their lives largely as they want to. This chapter will stress the possibility of personal control and creativity in social life as well as analysing the powerful social or cultural forces that affect the individual and which sometimes hamper, as well as help, self-expression.

Culture is a central sociological concept and we will concentrate on it here. The fundamental role of culture in shaping individual behaviour is easily demonstrated although, of course, the essential biological basis for human development must first exist. *Culture is everything that is learnt and created through social interaction.* Just how much is learnt through culture can be illustrated by the following examples of individuals who, by chance, avoided cultural influence. There are a few cases of children growing up 'in the wild' with apparently very little human contact and, as a result, their behaviour was virtually devoid of cultural formation. One such case is that of 'the Wild Boy of Aveyron', and another involved two young girls, 'the Wolf Children of Bengal', who were discovered when they were two and eight years old, respectively. The common features of these cases make it clear how much of what we take for granted as 'normal' human behaviour is, in fact, the product of socialisation. Both the 'Wild Boy' and the 'Wolf Children' were readily comparable to animals in their behavioural habits. Their 'uncleanliness', 'uncouth' eating habits, and nakedness were relatively superficial matters: the basic aspect of culture that they lacked was *language*. Their powers of communication were, therefore, acutely limited.

Interactionists and other *interpretists* regard language as the basis of human culture. Language is the major means of communication in all complex societies and, to a slightly lesser extent, in most pre-literate ones as well. Because it proved impossible to develop the language skills of any of these children beyond the learning of a few words, none of them became fully a part of society. It seems that if a person fails to develop basic language skills at an early age, his capacity to do so decreases thereafter. A recognition of the importance of language in the process of socialisation and as a communication medium is central to the symbolic interactionist perspective. However, first we look at socialisation from a specifically functionalist point of view.

Socialisation: Values, Norms and Roles: Functionalist Perspective

According to functionalists, socialisation is the process by which a person learns to behave in an acceptable manner within a society or group. It refers to the way in which the *values* and *norms* (standards and rules) of the society or group become part of the individual's own way of feeling and thinking. This process is referred to as the *internalisation* of these values and norms and through it the individual becomes part of a given culture. Functionalists consider that for society to operate smoothly individuals must be socialised into the general *consensus* of (agreement about) values, norms and behaviour. In their view, inadequate socialisation can lead to disruptive and deviant (abnormal) behaviour: if everybody 'did their own thing' there would be chaos. Socialisation usually occurs first within the family but continues throughout life in school, at work, through friends and via the communications media. These institutions are referred to as *agents of socialisation.*

We will deal briefly with values here, as they are a central concern of a later section in this chapter. A *value* indicates the attitudes and behaviour approved of in a given society. The values of loyalty, honesty and respect for human life are common to most societies. As we illustrate later, however, other values are more variable. Functionalists consider that there must be consensus (agreement) on basic values within a society if it is to function well.

The term *norm* is broader than rule or even standard, and includes informal as well as formal understandings and expectations about what is acceptable and required behaviour. A law is an example of a formal norm and many organisations and clubs have more or less formal norms. Despite the ever mounting pile of legislation and the increase in bureaucratic rules characteristic of advanced countries, most social behaviour is still guided mainly by informal custom, convention and expectation rather than by laws and formal rules. For instance, there are no laws about how to behave at dinner parties or about how students should conduct themselves in the classroom but people usually 'know' how to behave in these contexts; or, if somebody does behave outrageously at a dinner party or in a classroom, he likewise usually 'knows' that he is doing so. It is not necessary for these normative guides to be written down. Norms can be thought of as 'lying between' values and roles. Values underpin norms in the sense that they provide the basis of specific behavioural roles. Thus, the value of honesty perhaps affects the normative behaviour of, say, accountants and shop assistants, in a very specific way, because they deal with other people's money. We examine the link between norms and roles shortly.

Norms are often more flexible in less formal situations. By contrast, legally controlled situations theoretically 'admit of no exceptions'. An eccentric dinner party guest may 'get away with it', but the eccentric thief nevertheless is a thief, and will normally be treated as such. Even in informal situations, there is a limit beyond which an individual cannot go without incurring some kind of social censure (disapproval). One of the most comic episodes from modern fiction, an incident in Kingsley Amis' *Lucky Jim*, illustrates what happens when the limits of tolerance are breached. The occasion was rather a formal one. Jim, a young academic at a provincial university, was required to give a lecture to a large audience of teaching staff and students. The lecture was meant to be a public demonstration that he could make the grade in his profession. Already disillusioned with his job and apprehensive at the thought of having to give the lecture, Jim prepared for his ordeal by getting thoroughly drunk. His resulting performance, which included a routine in which he mimicked several senior professors, ensured that a reason was shortly found for his dismissal. Jim might have got away with the irreverent joke or two, but a series of mimickings took him beyond the bounds of tolerance.

In addition to values and norms, the concept of *role* is very important in functionalist theory. A role is the part a person is expected to perform within a given institution, for example, mother/son in a family, teacher/pupil in a school. A role is governed by norms that are generally considered to apply to the given situation – for example, responsible and caring behaviour is expected of teachers. Along with other functionalists, Parsons stresses that roles have to be *learnt*. It is only by watching, listening and being taught that we learn to play roles.

It is necessary to emphasise that functionalists consider that people are not only socialised to think in certain ways but also to feel certain things: often these two processes occur together. Thus, a child may be made to feel guilty about an action – say, stealing – and he may also receive a rational explanation about why he should not steal. As Freud observed, childhood socialisation often continues to have a powerful hold in later life precisely because the individual has become emotionally as well as rationally committed to certain patterns of belief and behaviour. Moral, religious, political and social customs and behaviour of various kinds, acquired in childhood, can resist contrary influences in later life. In this way, a person of humble origins, who has become rich, may prefer not to adopt a 'posh' (in his view) accent because he has always felt such an accent to be 'snobbish'. The same person may also cling to working class political beliefs, such as supporting trade unions or voting Labour. He may even retain some working class leisure habits, such as going to football matches (though usually, the place from which he watches the game will change). Similarly, someone who has been brought up to be strongly religious may continue to practise his religion out of habit or because it 'feels right' to do so, rather than because he genuinely believes in it. Other alternatives of behaviour are, of course, possible: the above examples are chosen merely to illustrate the potential power of socialisation.

The leading functionalist, Talcott Parsons, points out that rewards and punishments are used to persuade people to conform but reason may also be used. A child, rewarded with a lollipop for 'good' behaviour, is said to receive *positive reinforcement,* and one punished with a slap, *negative reinforcement.* Conduct that is rewarded usually comes to be regarded as virtuous and that which is punished as wrong. From the point of view of the smooth functioning of society, it is not important whether an individual conforms through fear, desire for reward,

49

or reason: what matters is that he conforms.

Perhaps Parsons insufficiently stresses that, as a child grows older and his reason develops, there is the possibility of rethinking the values, attitudes and norms he has been socialised into. The opportunity to do this is a very valuable one and does not come equally to everybody – to some perhaps not at all. A broad and undogmatic education, or simply the acquisition of wider experience, can help to make an individual rethink his early values and beliefs. That some people should do so is no doubt necessary if society is to change and develop; although, by the same token, if everybody did so, the smooth functioning of society would be adversely affected.

Primary and Secondary Socialisation

American sociologist, Charles Cooley (1864–1929), distinguished two types of socialisation: *primary* and *secondary*. These two forms of socialisation are defined partly in terms of the particular groups or 'agencies' in which they occur. Primary groups are small, involve face-to-face relationships and allow the individual to express his whole self, both feelings and intellect. The family, peer groups of close friends and closely-knit groups of neighbours are primary groups. Within these groups the individual learns, by personal experience, of the primary ideals such as love, loyalty, justice, and sharing. Freud emphasised that the first few years of a person's life – those usually spent amongst primary groups – are the most important in forming the framework of his character. Secondary groups are larger, more impersonal, more formally organised, and exist for specific purposes. Secondary socialisation involves learning how to organise and conduct oneself in formal contexts and how to behave towards people who have different degrees of status and authority. The school is the most important example of an agency of secondary socialisation, but all formal organisations influence their members to some degree and, to that extent, can be included within this category. Trade unions and professional associations are relevant examples: membership is granted to the individual on the assumption that he will conform to the beliefs, aims and regulations of the organisation. In allowing the organisation to affect his behaviour in this way, the individual necessarily accepts a socialising influence on his conduct. In addition to primary and secondary groups, the mass media – the press, radio, television, the cinema, records, tapes and various other forms of communication which comprise it – plays a socialising role whose effects we will consider in more detail later.

The distinction between primary and secondary socialisation parallels that between *informal* and *formal* socialisation. Informal socialisation usually takes place as a part of everyday activity: it affects us unconsciously and must be distinguished from the formal acquisition of specific skills such as reading and writing. In primary socialisation, certain values and customs will be formally taught to a child (formal socialisation) but much else will be informally 'picked up' by *imitating* parents, siblings, and other children.

The infant peer group is a strong and informal agency of socialisation, especially around the age of three or four when the child begins to achieve a slightly fuller understanding of what the world is like beyond his own family. Through interacting with others of his own age, he discovers what other children regard as 'normal', and whether he and his own family correspond to what is generally acceptable. When a child is, or feels he is, different, anxiety and sometimes personal crisis can follow. Thus, at this stage of life, not having a father or mother, or being a member of a racial minority, can be a matter of painful social adjustment to a child. Problems are made worse if the 'difference' causes him to be rejected and persecuted by his peers.

In addition to acting as an informal agency for the enforcement of conformity, the peer group can also provide comfort, support, and identity for the individual when the pressures and demands of home, school or work become 'too much'. Peer groups exist throughout life as a 'haven' and as a basis for the organisation of play and leisure activities. As well as being based on age, peer groups are often divided according to gender. With the tension of sexuality removed, the peer group can seem a more relaxing and uncomplicated refuge than it might otherwise be.

The Increasing Importance of Secondary Socialisation in Modern Societies

Cooley noted a change in the nature of socialisation from traditional to modern societies. In traditional societies, most socialisation takes place informally, and within primary groups. In traditional societies, even the acquisition of specific skills, such as hunting or cooking, tend to be 'picked up' in the course of everyday life, rather than formally taught. Of course, the life of the group also has a formal aspect – usually concerned with religious or military ritual. As Durkheim noted, these ceremonial occasions have important socialising effects. From a sociological point of view, ceremonial ritual functions mainly as a means of focusing community feeling and strengthening group identity.

Although primary socialisation remains of fundamental importance, modern societies are characterised by a great variety of formal institutions in which secondary socialisation takes place. The school is where the most important stage of secondary socialisation occurs. In Britain, as in other advanced societies, the period spent at school is long, and influential in the formation of character: attendance at school from the ages of five to sixteen is, in effect, compulsory. As well as the formal academic curriculum of varied subjects, much *informal* learning and socialisation takes place. For instance, a child learns to co-operate with his peers and to accept authority, not merely because he is told to do so, but by imitating others and so acquiring a set of habits seen as socially necessary. What a child learns in this way is sometimes referred to as the *hidden curriculum*.

Cooley considered the growth of formal educational institutions, such as schools and colleges, as part of a general process by which the modern world has become increasingly organised for specific purposes. With the development of industrial society, first work, and then education were separated off from the rest of life: they became organised in a more formal and impersonal way. To 'fit into', say, a large school or factory, the individual has to adopt a self-controlled and unemotional mode of behaviour suitable for fulfilling his or her role. As a child goes to school, he is expected increasingly to adopt impersonal, goal-oriented behaviour (for example, to try and pass examinations) and at work, too, 'things have to be done' which may be of no personal interest to the employee. In complex, modern societies, it is necessary that people acquire the discipline to do essential tasks, whether these are interesting or not. As we shall see in more detail in due course, this discipline is first learnt at school and then applied later at work.

Both Cooley and Parsons noted that in modern societies it is expected that deeply-held personal feelings will be expressed primarily in the family and other 'private' contexts whilst the 'public' area, including the educational and economic systems, requires rational, controlled behaviour. This clear division between public and private life was much less a feature of pre-industrial communities where socialisation, learning, work, family and community life tended to merge into one another. As a result, the difference in the individual's behaviour in the public and the private spheres tended to be less, and because of his lack of differentiation, the individual could 'be himself' more often – precisely in the popular meaning of that term. In any case, in small-scale traditional communities, the opportunity for a private life scarcely existed: 'everybody knew what everybody else was doing'. We examine the contrast between traditional and modern communities in Chapter 7 and, to some extent, in the next chapter, pp. 85–91.

Cooley has often been viewed as a forerunner of the symbolic interactionist perspective but we have also noted that his analysis is partly compatible with that of the functionalist, Talcott Parsons.

Socialisation, Culture and the Development of Self: Interactionist Perspective

So far, we have stressed the power of institutions such as family, school, the peer group and the work place, to form values, attitudes and norms: this involved an emphasis on *structural influences*. In turn, we now examine the process of socialisation and development of self from a specifically *interactionist perspective* and with close reference to the work of the American social psychologist, George Mead. He describes two general stages in the development of the self: the *play* and *game* stages. Prior to these stages the child's relationship to others is one of imitation without conscious awareness of the meaning of actions.

At the play stage, the child begins to try out certain familiar roles such as parent, teacher or doctor. The child's 'let's pretend to be . . .' is a powerful in-built learning device. It is, however, a limited one. At this stage, the child does not see beyond individual roles to a more generalised view of social situations. He or she only attempts to perform the roles of certain *significant others* seen at first hand or perhaps through the media. It is as if in the early stages of learning a play, the child 'gets to know' some leading parts but has little sense of the 'plot' as a whole.

The game stage involves virtually a double progression. Firstly, in Mead's words, 'the child must have the attitude of all the others involved in that game' or situation. Perhaps children play team games so badly because they have not fully developed an awareness of the various roles in the team or a competent way of fitting in with other roles. Gradually, the child becomes more socially aware, not only at games, of course, but in other group situations such as meals and outings. However, the full development of self depends not only on the awareness of all other roles in a situation but on the further ability to realise that the group, community or society *as a whole* 'exercises control over the conduct of its individual members.' In this sense, Mead refers to the group as a whole as the 'generalised other'. Only in so far as the child learns to take the attitude of the other does he become a full member of society. Essentially, Mead is saying the same thing as Parsons. Both recognise the need for the child to learn 'the rules of the game' or of society. Crucially, Mead gives more emphasis to the capacity of the individual to '*play* the game' actively and creatively. This is apparent in the aspect of his thought to which we now turn and which complements the above.

Mead divided the self into the '*I*' and the '*me*'. The 'I' is the active part of the self whereas the 'me' is passive, that is, the 'me' is the part that others (significant and generalised) act upon (see diagram, p. 55). Cooley used the term 'looking-glass self' to describe how we see an image or get an impression of ourselves through the responses of others. As the individual becomes aware of the 'me', he or she is also able to act upon him or herself, by controlling it. As Mead put it, the individual becomes an object to him or herself. More than Cooley, Mead wanted to stress that the 'I' can control or direct the self not only to conform but to act independently. As he put it: 'The "I" gives the sense of freedom, of initiative'. Mead noted that the dynamic 'I' often dominates over the conformist 'me' in highly creative people such as artists and brilliant sportsmen but that we all have moments of originality (or, at least, moments that feel original). In providing a framework of analysis in which the social actor could, indeed, be conceived of as *acting*, often unpredictably and with uncertain consequences, Mead made an outstanding contribution to social science.

The Self

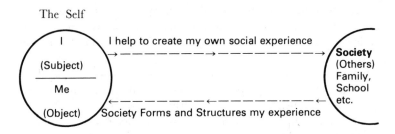

Symbolic Interactionist Model of Socialisation (and social experience generally).

Mead's awareness of both the constraints on (controls and limits) and creativity of, social interaction is apparent in his analysis of language – a central feature of symbolic interactionism. Language is the major vehicle of social communication. Its purpose is to express meaning. Of necessity, the young child is, at first, only the object of linguistic communication, but gradually begins to use language for his or her own purposes. Mead strenuously rejects the notion that language is simply a matter of imitation (except, he concedes, in the parrot). Nearly all the meanings that an individual could want to express are available in the stock of words of most languages but, even so, scientists and poets operating at the limits of available meaning and language do create new words and linguistic forms. That is what language is for: to provide meaningful symbolism. When necessary, new verbal symbols are created. Because the main concern of symbolic interactionists is with meaningful communication they have a primary interest in language. Interactionists frequently stress that (by means of language), people *negotiate* the various social roles they are expected to play. This means that they bargain with others, often those in authority, about how exactly they will perform them. This suggests the further concept of *negotiated order*. For example, certain students or workers may be able to 'get away with' doing less work than others because, over time, they have managed to establish or 'negotiate' a lower level of performance with whoever is in charge. Others may also try to do so but for some reason fail. Order exists but it reflects the complexities and negotiations of interaction. Similarly, interactionists note that different individuals *interpret* the same role in different ways. Roles are seen as less binding than functionalists suggest. Thus, as a glance around your classroom or lecture hall will verify, the role of student can be interpreted in many different and contrasting ways.

Before concluding this section, we need to be clear about how interactionists approach the analysis of social institutions. For them, an institution is not a 'thing' separate from the people that make up its structure, but is considered as the product of interaction; this is true of the family, the school, the peer group. Indeed, any institution can be viewed as the product of the interaction of the people of whom it is composed. As we shall see when we examine specific topics, such as education and work, this perspective is extremely fruitful. It can, however, be criticised as incomplete. Interactionists persistently disregard the very real power of institutions to mould and limit individual and group action. This criticism is developed at some length in the conclusion to the chapter on Deviance and Social Control (Chapter 17).

The nature of modern symbolic interactionist theory is well illustrated by the metaphors interactionists use to describe social life. Erving Goffman has compared social interaction with the dramatic action of a play, and Eric Berne, the founder of transactional psychoanalysis, entitled one of his books *Games People Play*. For Goffman, the main difference between acting in a play and 'acting' in life is that there is more scope for role interpretation in life itself; nor is the social actor tied to a formal script but can improvise freely. He recognises that social change greatly depends on such original and creative 'improvisation'. Yet, the essential similarity between drama and life remains and Goffman adopts a *dramaturgical* model of social interaction. Social life, like a play, is 'made up': it is a human construction that has the meaning and 'reality' that human beings give it.

Socialisation, Social Consensus and the Social System: **Functionalism**

We have already described how the individual learns social values, norms and roles. In this important section, we will describe the attempt of Talcott Parsons to build these concepts into a fully developed model of how the *social system* and its *sub-systems* work. We conclude the section with an analysis of the place of *value consensus* in Parson's model, because this is the basis of his whole scheme. It will be recalled that in Chapter 1 we said that functionalists frequently divide the social system into four sub-systems: the economic, political, kinship and cultural/community. Various institutions make up these sub-systems within which people play given roles. Below is a diagram of Parsons' model of society as a social system:

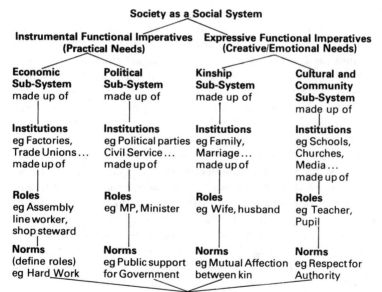

Society as a Social System

Instrumental Functional Imperatives (Practical Needs)		**Expressive Functional Imperatives (Creative/Emotional Needs)**	
Economic Sub-System made up of	**Political Sub-System** made up of	**Kinship Sub-System** made up of	**Cultural and Community Sub-System** made up of
Institutions eg Factories, Trade Unions... made up of	**Institutions** eg Political parties Civil Service... made up of	**Institutions** eg Family, Marriage... made up of	**Institutions** eg Schools, Churches, Media... made up of
Roles eg Assembly line worker, shop steward	**Roles** eg MP, Minister	**Roles** eg Wife, husband	**Roles** eg Teacher, Pupil
Norms (define roles) eg Hard Work	**Norms** eg Public support for Government	**Norms** eg Mutual Affection between kin	**Norms** eg Respect for Authority

Norms (and whole system) Supported by Fundamental Values such as Loyalty

The above model implies a relationship between individual needs and the needs (or *functional imperatives*, as Parsons calls them) of society. The fulfilment of needs is seen as a two-way process: the individual and society contribute to each other's welfare (or survival). In order to understand this relationship, we must explain further Parsons' understanding of how the four sub-systems or *institutional orders* function. We can then 'fit' the individual and social group into the model. The economy is concerned with what Parsons refers to as *adaptation*. By this he means that man must adapt to the material world in order to survive. This need was mainly fulfilled by hunting and farming in primitive society, although modern economies are much more complex. The term adaptation is a familiar one in biology and its use here is an example of the application of the organic analogy that characterises functionalist sociological theory. The theory of evolution rests partly on the view that natural organisms adapt to survive. The political sub-system is concerned with *goal-attainment:* that is, establishing the main purposes for which a society strives, and attempting to persuade people that these purposes are worthwhile. Thus, in a party democracy like Britain, one political party may pursue the goal of achieving better-equipped armed forces, whereas another may pursue that of better social services. In theory, the parties argue about these goals and the public decides between them. Parsons calls the imperatives of adaptation and goal-attainment *instrumental functional imperatives* but we can refer to them as the practical needs of society.

The kinship and cultural/community sub-systems fulfil functional imperatives or needs of an expressive (creative/emotional) rather than a directly practical kind. It is essential to realise, however, that these needs are catered for in a way that supports, not hinders, the functioning of the social system. These needs are *pattern maintenance/tension management* (kinship) and *integration* (cultural/community sub-system). The family helps to maintain the pattern and stability of society through socialising individuals into socially acceptable values, norms and roles. It also 'manages' tension in the sense that it is the institution in which people often feel most free to express their feelings. Integration refers to the means by which people are persuaded to conform to society's expectations. It is carried out by such cultural organisations as schools, churches and the media.

Integration can be said to be the result of successful socialisation and, as we have seen, the three latter institutions are all involved in socialisation. The needs fulfilled by the kinship and cultural/community sub-systems are referred to by Parsons as *expressive* because they are concerned primarily with personal and cultural matters.

Parsons also considers that the social system is underpinned or supported by the fundamental values shared by society's members. We turn to this central aspect of his thought now.

The Social System, Culture and Values

Functionalists, like interactionists, fully recognise the importance of the concept of culture in understanding how society operates. The transmission of culture (its passing on from generation to generation) is necessary for society to survive. For functionalists this is largely achieved through the socialisation of the individual into acceptable values, norms and roles. Cultural values are at the heart of this process and we examine them now.

a Fundamental Values Common to all Societies

Even in these days of supra-national movements, such as Pan-Africanism and the Common Market, the nation-state is still the largest frame of reference to which most people relate with any frequency and intensity. For most modern people, their nation *is society,* although tribal man identifies with no larger unit than his tribe. All societies expect their members to have certain basic values. For example, a citizen is required to be loyal, patriotic and obedient to his country's laws. To use Parsons' terms, these *fundamental values underpin the social system and without them it could not function.* Parsons' emphasis on values is directly derived from Durkheim, who first developed the notion of moral consensus which we explained in Chapter 1. Basic values are learnt both formally and through informal socialisation. Often the latter is more effective. We hardly need to be told to be patriotic when every day the media assumes that we already are. The importance of basic national values is illustrated by the dignity, and even sanctity, with which national symbols are held. Thus, as Durkheim noted, in tribal society the totem pole represents and focuses socially approved feelings,

59

as does the flag, the King or President, and national football team in a modern society. These symbols often have a 'not to be questioned' quality about them – which is not to say that they are never, in fact, questioned.

b Values Particular to a Given Society
Parsons considers that, in addition to the values that societies have in common, each society also has its own characteristic values and also a particular national culture of its own. If we compare, say, the United States and the Soviet Union in this respect, the point will become clearer. Certain functionalists have argued that the United States is characterised by the values of individual liberty and achievement. The value of aggressive, individual achievement is embodied in the national folklore of the United States: the phrase 'from log-cabin to White House' (the Presidency) captures this myth precisely. Many American children are socialised into the belief that 'anybody can make it if they try hard enough' – if not quite to the Presidency, at least to respectable middle class prosperity. On the other hand, the Soviet Union has certainly cultivated the values of material equality to a greater extent than was done in Tsarist Russia and probably more than it is cultivated in the United States today. Just how attracted the majority of the Soviet people are to the notion of material equality is not clear to the outside observer, but the simple life-style of national leaders such as Lenin and, later, Khruschev, can be seen as an attempt to popularise egalitarian attitudes.

It is worth adding that national character *stereotypes* (popularly-believed models) can be linked with the concept of cultural values. Examples are the notions of the 'sensuous' French, the 'reserved' English, the 'discipline-loving' Germans and the 'emotional' Latins. How far these cultural stereotypes actually exist is a matter for empirical investigation but, to the extent that they do, they are necessarily reproduced through socialisation and, particularly, through the family. Anyone who has observed a gesticulating, talkative, tactile Latin family will recognise that there is at least some truth in the concept of national character.

Nationally, specific values as well as universal ones help to keep a given society together and to give that society its particular character. People are expected to orientate their behaviour in accordance with socially accepted values. Functionalists refer to all the major values that serve to unify a society as its *central value system*, and in a smoothly functioning society there is a national consensus around these central and fundamental values. Thus, in the United States, functionalists consider that there is a consensus about the values of individual liberty and achievement – though whether they are right is questionable. According to functionalists, the opposite of value consensus – value dissensus – is a sign of social dysfunction and disorder. An example would be if large numbers of United States citizens attempted to practise equality as understood by Communists.

Socialisation and Social Class: **Conflict Perspective**

Although Marxists do not use the same terminology, they agree with functionalists that central values serve to keep society together. In particular, the French Marxist *structuralists*, Louis Althusser and Pierre Bourdieu, stress the capacity of society to mould people into conformity and so to reproduce itself through the generations. Beyond this, however, there is little agreement between sociologists of the two perspectives. As we have seen, Marx considers societies, particularly capitalist societies, as fundamentally divided rather than unified. Any unity and consensus that exists is, therefore, of a false kind and likely to be in the interest of the rich and powerful, and not of the poor and powerless. Marx argued that the working class is often misled into being loyal, patriotic and obedient to a society in which it is exploited. To the extent that this is so, they accept what he called the *ideology* (ideas, values and justifications) of the rich and powerful. Such conformity in the midst of inequality was, for him, a sign that the working class had been duped. (For more on this see Chapters 5, 8 and 17). Here, however, we want to concentrate less on the way working class people are socialised to conform, and more on the potential for conflict that class socialisation can produce. Many non-Marxists as well as Marxists recognise this potential though perhaps the latter stress it most. Further, it is worth remarking that whereas socialisation provides a means for introducing a fairly full description of functionalist social systems theory, it does not

61

provide a basis to introduce adequately Marxist class theory. This is because the latter is based on an analysis of people's relationship to the means of production, and this we fully examine later.

Class membership is not simply a matter of having a certain kind of job or a given level of income. The very position people have in the work place affects their behaviour, values and beliefs. Traditionally, working class people tend to work and live close together and to build a common neighbourhood *culture*. Docking and mining neighbourhoods are classic examples. Middle class people, too, though often less involved in their immediate neighbourhood, tend to live near one another and to associate mainly with each other. On a day-to-day basis, class experience is a more important frame of reference than society or nation. Initially, class socialisation and the class *identity* it produces occur within the family and are usually reinforced by the peer group and at work. Class socialisation is rarely conscious: indeed, many adults think about class very little and might not even be sure which class they belong to. Nevertheless, just as income and education correlate with class so, too, do certain cultural values and norms. In pursuing this point we will consider first the working class, then the middle class, and finally the upper class. Because class culture is distinct from the general culture of a society, it is sometimes referred to as class sub-culture. We prefer to use the term class culture, however, and to reserve the term sub-culture for smaller groupings. Goldthorpe and Lockwood's diagram on working and middle class perspectives should be a helpful reference point in considering class culture and is printed on the next page. However, it is too general to be anything more than that.

a Socialisation: Working Class Culture

Members of traditional working class communities often had an 'us' and 'them' attitude to life. On the one hand, family and neighbourhood life was strong and intense whilst, on the other, treatment of the middle class, such as employers and doctors, might be courteous, but they were considered to belong to a different social world. Working class *solidarity* (collective group-support) was expressed economically through the trade unions and politically through the Labour Party. Most people born into the working class stayed there, and probably only a minor-

An Ideal-type Comparison of Working Class and Middle Class Beliefs, Values and attitudes

	Working-class perspective	*Middle-class perspective*
General beliefs	The social order is divided into 'us' and 'them': those who do not have authority and those who do. The division between 'us' and 'them' is virtually fixed, at least from the point of view of one man's life chances. What happens to you depends a lot on luck; otherwise you have to learn to put up with things.	The social order is a hierarchy of differentially rewarded positions: a ladder containing many rungs. It is possible for individuals to move from one level of the hierarchy to another. Those who have ability and initiative can overcome obstacles and create their own opportunities. Where a man ends up depends on what he makes of himself.
General values	'We' ought to stick together and get what we can as a group. You may as well enjoy yourself while you can instead of trying to make yourself 'a cut above the rest'.	Every man ought to make the most of his own capabilities and be responsible for his own welfare. You cannot expect to get anywhere in the world if you squander your time and money. 'Getting on' means making sacrifices.
Attitudes on more specific issues	*(on the best job for a son)* 'A trade in his hands'. 'A good steady job'.	'As good a start as you can give him'. 'A job that leads somewhere'.
	(towards people needing social assistance) 'They have been unlucky'. 'They never had a chance'. 'It could happen to any of us'.	'Many of them had the same opportunities as others who have managed well enough'. They are a burden on those who are trying to help themselves'.
	(on Trade Unions) 'Trade unions are the only means workers have of protecting themselves and of improving their standard of living'.	'Trade unions have too much power in the country'. 'The unions put the interests of a section before the interests of the nation as a whole'.

Source: *Goldthorpe and Lockwood*, reprinted in Butterworth and Weir *The Sociology of Modern Britain*, p. 317.

ity expected or tried to become one of 'them'. To try to do so was to risk community, and particularly peer group, disapproval. 'Think's 'e's posh', or 'snob' are among the politer descriptions that might be aimed at the would-be upwardly-mobile working class child by his less ambitious peers – though some support for 'bettering yourself' could also be found. Particularly in the past, but still now, working class people expected one another to accept their lot and to 'muck in' and get along with others in the same position. From the point of view of the welfare of the group, this makes good sense, although to the ambitious individual it must often seem cruel. Working hard in the evening in order to do well at school or at work is a middle class rather than a working class habit. For the working class, leisure tends to be for pleasure, an attitude referred to as *short-term hedonism* (a desire for immediate pleasure) by social scientists.

Patterns of child rearing have become generally more permissive but there is evidence that working class mothers use reason less than middle class mothers in socialising their children, and, instead *tell* them what to do, often with little explanation why. Sometimes this approach is supported by the threat or, more rarely, the actuality, of physical punishment. This kind of socialisation can produce a mistrust of authority. In extreme cases, it may create a tendency towards authoritarianism: that is, a fear of the authority of others and a tendency to exercise one's own authority harshly. For whatever reason, it certainly seems true that a relatively larger number of working class rather than middle class boys have strained relations with authority figures – notably teachers and, in a minority of cases, the police. For instance, working class children often appear to 'size up' a teacher in terms of 'weakness' or 'toughness'. They then act accordingly! A teacher who is considered to be 'in control' will be feared and respected, whereas one who is not can be given a very rough time indeed. A disorderly classroom harms pupils (as well as teachers), yet it is quite consistent with the experience of many working class children to want to test authority before accepting it. In practice, school often 'goes wrong' for working class children both in terms of socialising and formal learning. These processes cannot easily take place without a stable educational environment.

The observations made in this section apply to the traditional manual working class. This group, however, is in numerical decline. Traditional working class neighbourhoods have often been 'cleared' and their former inhabitants have either been re-housed elsewhere or, in the case of a significant minority, have bought their own houses. What are patterns of working class socialisation like in new housing estates, high rise flats, or new towns? There is surprisingly little detailed work in some of these areas, but we do know much about the difficulties experienced by those families 'left behind' in the inner city. In general, there is agreement that community has declined and that the family has become more isolated but still more vital to the life and happiness of its members. These, and other points, must await development in later chapters.

b Socialisation: Middle Class Culture

In contrast to the attitudes of solidarity of the traditional working class, the middle class tend to see the social structure as a ladder which an individual can climb up, or slip down, depending on his own effort and intelligence. Middle class children tend to be socialised to believe that they can 'make it' if they try. Success is usually defined in terms of educational and career achievement. In order to achieve long-term success and security, middle class children are urged by their parents and teachers to make short-term sacrifices. A major sacrifice is to stay in and do homework rather than to go out and have a good time. This kind of behaviour involves *deferred gratification* (putting off immediate pleasure for future gain) which is the opposite of short-term hedonism. Another way of stating this difference between middle and working class socialisation is that middle class children are taught to be *future-oriented,* whereas working class children are allowed to be *present-centred.* Perhaps the main reason for the greater educational success of middle class children is that teachers are consistently and actively reinforced by parents in their demands for hard work from children, whereas such support is rarer from working class parents. When they do give support, however, it can be as effective as that of the middle class parents.

As indicated above, reason and persuasion, rather than mere authority or force, are the means often adopted by middle class parents to control and socialise their offspring. The use of reasoned argument by parents no doubt helps the child to develop the ability to reason himself, an obvious advantage for school and career. The high level of interest that middle class parents (especially mothers) take in the upbringing of their children has a number of positive effects. 'Shared interests' means more communication and this results in the child improving his vocabulary and use and comprehension of language. It also means that he is exposed to a flow of ideas and images that should expand and stimulate his own intellect and imagination: all this amounts to a considerable 'cultural' advantage. The low-key, often relaxed, quality of parental authority in the middle class home helps the child to adapt more willingly to authority in other contexts. He is less likely than the working class child to expect conflict with authority. Indeed, in the long run, he will probably expect to assume a measure of authority himself. Finally, it is worth pointing out that the lower middle class is often considered to be socialised into values of respectability and conformity. This prepares them for their subordinate positions at the lower levels of the white collar hierarchy (see Chapter 9 pp. 238–42).

c Socialisation: Upper Class Culture

We know more of how the children of the upper class are socialised at school than within the family. The nature of socialisation in private boarding schools, to which the children of the rich are often sent for their education, builds upon what has already occurred within the family. Today, as in the past, the upper class often have their young children tended by paid help and educated in a private nursery school or by a private tutor. From an early age, therefore, the upper class child often spends a relatively long time separated, physically and emotionally, from his parents. Thus, the child learns independence and, because of the emotional self-control that separation from his parents involves, he may even acquire a tough edge to his character. Whereas the working class boy may be tough and rough, the upper class boy, thanks to the socialisation he receives, is likely to be tough and smooth. These qualities may well assist him if and when he assumes a leadership role as an adult.

Typically, an upper class boy will be sent to a private preparatory ('prep') school at seven or eight, then, at thirteen, to a public school, or, if he fails to qualify for entry, to a less prestigious private school. (Roughly speaking, public schools are better known and established than private schools). The yearly fees at most public and private schools are about the same as an unskilled manual worker's annual take-home pay. Although fee-paying boarding schools are becoming increasingly co-educational, upper class girls are likely to spend more of their childhood and youth at home and are often educated in private day schools. Today, equality of the sexes is more of a reality at all levels of society, and the number of 'finishing' schools which produce socially well-appointed but academically under-educated 'ladies', whose main aim is to make a good marriage 'catch', is in decline.

The demanding and competitive régimes of most boys' public schools – plenty of 'prep' (homework), sport, and firm discipline – establish and strengthen qualities of self-control, application and hard work. Pupils have to learn to take orders but they know that ultimately, they are very likely to exercise considerable authority themselves. The prefect system gives early experience of leadership and the public school ethos provides the basis for an easily ridiculed but often formidable character type. The Combined Cadet Force (CCF), popular in private schools, further illustrates the kind of socialisation upper class children often receive. Its stated aim is:

> To provide a disciplined organisation in a school so that boys and girls may develop powers of leadership by means of training to promote the qualities of responsibility, self-reliance, resourcefulness, endurance and perseverance and a sense of service to the community.
>
> (*Guardian*, May 19, 1980)

By contrast, the Army Cadet Force, for non-public school boys, seems to be training followers, not leaders. Its aim is:

> To develop among its members . . . qualities of good citizenship and the spirit of service to Queen and country.   (*Ibid.*)

As Polly Toynbee, author of the *Guardian* article, remarks: 'Leadership for the upper crust and service and citizenship for the proles.'

In conjunction with the immense material and social advantages of belonging to the upper class, a public school education and training can give a child of even less than moderate intelligence every chance of maintaining, if not improving upon, the

67

high socio-economic position he has had the good luck to in-herit. Another feature of public school socialisation strengthens this likelihood further: in the absence of family, the peer group takes on an especially important role in schools. Friend-ships made at public school can provide a basis for a self-help 'club' in later life. The notion of the 'old boy network' is not merely a music hall joke although, perhaps because of its informal and rather inaccessible nature, neither has it been the subject of detailed sociological research. The best way to know about it is to be part of it, and that kind of subjective experi-ence is more often recounted in novels or memoirs than found in sociological works.

At this point we present a summary of functionalist and class conflict perspectives on socialisation in model form. It is, of course, no more than a partial guide.

As we have seen, all of us are socialised and re-socialised throughout life. The family, peer group, school and work situa-tion affect our values, ideas and behaviour profoundly. So, too, does that modern creation, the mass media. Nation and class are major frames of reference that affect socialisation, as are gender and race. The only justification for such scant reference to these matters here is that they are considered in detail later.

Few of us like to think that we are little more than the pro-duct of our socialisation: the programmed robots suggested by cruder functionalist models. Yet, the individual must be aware of the power of socialisation if he is to make relatively free and informed choices for himself. Often individuals seem to prefer the ease and security of conformity to the challenge of choice, almost regardless of what it is they are conforming to. At times, human nature seems disconcertingly plastic. In this cen-tury of totalitarianism, we have seen how easily manipulated are the minds and wills of entire nations. If people are to become independent, patterns of socialisation are needed that enable them to think for themselves, rather than to tell them what to think.

Guide to further reading and study

Literature dealing with aspects of socialisation is listed at the end of chapters dealing with specific topics: Chapter 4 (The Family), Chapter 5, (Education), Chapter 12 (Generation).

Functionalist model of Socialisation, stressing conformity

Central Values (loyalty, patriotism)
Symbols of Unity (monarch, totem species)

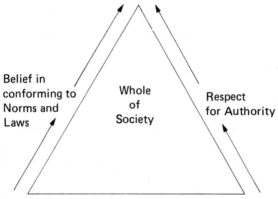

Belief in
conforming to
Norms and
Laws

Whole
of
Society

Respect
for Authority

Concentrates on norms and values that unite society

Class Conflict model of Socialisation, stressing conflict

Recognises existence of 'central' values as Ideology
in the interests of the Upper/Middle Classes

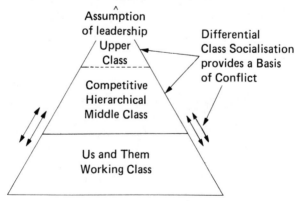

Assumption
of leadership

Upper
Class

Differential
Class Socialisation
provides a Basis
of Conflict

Competitive
Hierarchical
Middle Class

Us and Them
Working Class

Socialisation provides a basis of conflict as well as consensus

There is no further need to study socialisation in a general way at this stage but for those with a strong comparative interest in the theme, Margaret Mead's works are recommended (see Chapter 13's reading guide).

Questions

NB: The standard of these questions is intentionally well below 'A' level.

1 Write a paragraph each on primary and secondary socialisation.

2 Write a paragraph each on four agents of socialisation.

3 Write a page on each of the following:
    (a) Socialisation and Consensus
    (b) Socialisation and Class

4 The Family and Community

The Family: Definition of Terms

There are two basic family systems: the *nuclear* family and the *extended* family. A nuclear family is comprised of mother, father and child/or children, whether natural or adopted. The nuclear family is also sometimes referred to as the *conjugal* family. Usually, members of a nuclear family share the same household. The extended family consists of the nuclear family and at least one relative living in the same household. The extended family is also sometimes referred to as the *stem* family. The classic extended family in Britain was a couple, their eldest son, and his wife and children living in the same household. It is helpful, however, to broaden our conception of the extended family. Often relatives such as grandparents or elderly aunts live near a given nuclear family and participate in fairly intense social interaction with it. It is useful to think of such a situation as an *extended family type structure*. We also include various communal structures within this broad description. *Kinship* is social relationship based on real or assumed (adopted) consanguinity (blood relationship).

Different forms of marriage affect family structure. *Monogamy* allows one wife to one husband and is usually the only legally permitted form of marriage in societies in which the Christian tradition has predominated. *Polygamy*, which allows a person to have more than one spouse is common in some traditional societies. Polygyny, where a man has more than one wife, is more common than polyandry, where a wife has more than one husband. The former is common in some tribes but is also practised by some modern Muslims. It also occurs as a result of Mormon religious belief, particularly in the North American State of Utah. Polyandry occurs as a matter of practicality in

72

parts of Tibet. It operates as a form of birth control in poorer regions. However many husbands a woman has, she is limited by nature to a certain number of children.

Perspectives on the Family

For many, the family seems a familiar and comfortable institution. It can be a 'haven in a heartless world', a refuge from the impersonality and stress of work or school.

Sociologists have never accepted as adequate this simple and romantic view of the family. They have always considered that the influence of society penetrates deeply into the family and some have argued that the family, in turn, can substantially influence society. Nevertheless, until quite recently the sociology of the family occupied a predictable niche in sociology. Broadly speaking, the literature dealt with the functions of the family in relation to society as a whole or to the various social subsystems. The functionalist approach has now been challenged from various directions. Even so, functionalist analysis of the family provides perhaps the clearest and easiest to understand application of this perspective.

a **Functionalist**

Functionalists regard the family as an important 'organ' in the 'body' of society. It is what the family 'does' or the functions of the family that most interest them. George Murdock, an early functionalist, considered the four basic functions of the family to be the sexual, the reproductive, the socialising and the economic. Although these functions can evolve, he considered them to be 'universal'.

We can take *sex* and *reproduction* together. According to functionalists, marriage and the nuclear family provide the best opportunity for the socially controlled expression of the sex drive. More importantly, they provide the necessary institutional stability for the reproduction and nurture (bringing up) of children. The bringing up of children requires considerable time and effort: human maturation takes longer than that of any other species relative to life-span. To be brought up effectively, children usually require the help of more than one person (for practical if not emotional reasons). In most societies the two people who produce a child are expected to take responsibility for its upbringing. Family work is usually divided into domestic and economic. Practical commitment to children based on shared involvement and responsibility exists in polygamous as well as monogamous marriages. In polygamous Muslim societies a man is not expected to marry more wives and produce more children than he can afford.

To argue that the nuclear family is a socially useful institution is not to say, as some functionalists do, that it is biologically necessary and inevitable. Margaret Mead seems correct in contending that the nuclear family is *culturally created*, not *biologically given*. Comparisons with similar species by no means provide conclusive evidence, but males of other primates often do not remain with the female they have made pregnant. The fact that the human male usually does so is probably because this arrangement conveniently provides a secure context for the lengthy child-rearing necessary to our species. Another pointer in this direction is the fact that whilst many societies have allowed considerable sexual freedom before marriage, the widespread tendency is to curtail or abolish it afterwards. This, again, is a question of practicality not biology: it focuses energy and attention on spouse and children and, in particular, prevents the male from having more children than he is able to look after. Historically, the taboo (social disapproval) on sex outside marriage is a protective device for children and, to that extent, the human species. This argument loses much of its practical, if not emotional, force, however, in the age of the pill.

The family's role in laying down the basis of culture through socialisation is universally stressed by functionalists, as seen in Chapter 3.

The basic *economic* function of the family is to provide food and shelter for its members. In pre-industrial societies many families produced much of what they consumed. Now, individuals work for wages but the family remains an important unit of consumption of industrially produced goods.

As explained in the first chapter, functionalists see each social institution in terms of its role within its own social subsystem and in terms of its relationship to society as a whole. The model below illustrates this point in respect of the modern family.

74

The Interchange between the Nuclear Family and the Functional Sub-systems of Society

Nuclear Family	Wages Labour Goods Family Assets	← → ← →	Economy
Nuclear Family	Leadership Loyalty Decisions Compliance	← → ← →	Polity
Nuclear Family	Support Group- Participation Identity Adherence	← → ← →	Community
Nuclear Family	Specification of standards Acceptance of standards Approval Conformity	← → ← →	Value System

Source: Adapted from *Bell and Vogel,* 1960.

The figure is very simple to interpret. It shows that the family gives 'something' to and gets 'something' from each sub-system. Take the example of the economy. The family provides labour for which its members get paid. Money is then 'recycled' back into the economy through the purchase of goods which the family needs and through family savings. Thus, the family is seen as both dependent on and contributing to the economy. It is the same with the political system. In return for loyalty and obedience (compliance), family members get leadership from politicians (however confusing this may sometimes be!). From the community comes support and identity in return for participation and commitment (adherence). The only aspect of the model that might cause difficulty is calling the fourth sub-system the value system, rather than kinship. The family is, of course, part of the kinship system and reflects and passes on the values of society. Other institutions are involved in value socialisation, but the family's role is primary.

Despite great recent criticism of functionalist analysis, this model has a certain commonsense usefulness. However, as D. H. Morgan points out, Murdock's analysis suffers from a failure to consider whether other institutions could take over the functions he associates with the family, but later functionalists such as Parsons have explored this issue. Further, Murdock rather too readily assumes that the nuclear family functions harmoniously. More contemporary functionalists, N. W. Bell and E. F. Vogel, as well as radical phenomenologists R. D. Laing and David Cooper, have shown that the modern family can contain frightening tensions. Recent functionalists, however, still tend to assume a 'fit' between the nuclear family and society as a whole, even though they may concede that it may be internally under stress. Arguably, they are overinfluenced by the harmony implicit in the organic analogy in making this assumption. We examine functionalist analysis of how the family has 'adapted' to the 'needs' of industrial society in a later section (Chapter 4 pp. 85–91).

b Marxist and other Class-based Analysis of the Family

Marxists also adopt a structural perspective on the family. They do not, however, regard the nuclear family as a universal feature of human society, but put it in the particular context of capitalist society and, particularly, the class nature of that society.

Friedrich Engels' (1820–1895) *The Origin of the Family: Private Property and the State*, remains the starting point for most Marxist analysis of the family and of gender relations. Engels examines the emergence of the nuclear family and male dominance in an historical context. He hypothesised that in the nomadic stage of man's social development there was a substantial measure of sexual equality. Neither exclusive sexual possessiveness nor much private property existed. People and things were held in common although mothers had an immediate involvement with young children. Gradually, the male sphere of activity became more specialised and distinct: cattle breeding, mining and trade were added to their primary responsibility of hunting. This leads to the central point of Engels' argument. As men acquired greater control over wealth and property, they sought means to ensure that it stayed within their personal possession and was passed on to their offspring.

To do this they had to know who their offspring were! This meant that the free sexual relations of the horde had to be replaced by monogamy, and a system of inheritance based on blood introduced. In a male-dominated society, the eldest male was established as inheritor. The state, also male-dominated, gave powerful legal support to male control over the family, women and private property. Thus, in Engels' analysis, the growth of private property and male dominance evolved together.

As Rosalind Delmar puts it, the major contribution of Engels was to assert 'women's oppression as a problem of history, rather than of biology.' She uses the word 'assert' rather than 'prove' because the details of Engel's historical account are thought to be wrong. The precise historical truth on this issue is probably beyond proof but the point to appreciate is that Engels concluded that as the monogamous nuclear family and female subordination had developed historically *they were capable of being changed.* This is the basis of Marxist and most socialist analysis of the family. The opposite view, that the sexual division of labour which consigns the woman primarily to the home and the man to economic labour, is founded on the analysis that such an arrangement is biologically rooted and virtually immutable (unchangeable). It is the basis of the more crude functionalist analysis of the nuclear family.

Although the patriarchal (male-dominated) nuclear family pre-dated capitalist society, Engels, and Marx too, considered that it fitted the needs of capitalism particularly well. Capitalist society was based on the accumulation of private wealth and property mainly controlled by men. Accordingly, a patriarchal family structure linked to a system of primogeniture (in which the eldest son inherits) suited it very well. Primogeniture was primarily of significance among the upper and middle classes: the working class had little to pass on anyway. Marx and Engels did argue, however, that capitalism provided a limited opportunity for women to escape domestic bondage by finding employment outside the home and thus acquiring an independent source of income. Even so, they considered that, ultimately, the liberation of women depended on a change of social system from capitalism to socialism. Private property would then be abolished and the organisation of child-rearing and socialisation would be a matter for the community as a whole to determine.

More recent Marxist and socialist writers – particularly feminists – have tended to be sceptical of the supposed improvement in the status of women that more direct involvement in the economy brings. Blackburn and Stewart point out that women often play the kind of 'service' role in the work situation which can be regarded as an extension of their low domestic status rather than an improvement on it. Further, Engels has been somewhat criticised for a 'waiting for the revolution' approach to the solution of gender exploitation. Contemporary Marxist and socialist feminists such as Juliet Mitchell and Ann Oakley tend to be much more diligent than he was in the search for immediate improvements in gender relations towards that larger end (see Chapter 11, pp. 288–90 where non-Marxist feminist perspectives on gender are also discussed).

Some Marxists regard the sexual possessiveness of marital partners as just one expression of the possessive and, in their view, selfish, individualism of capitalist society. Marx himself claimed that marriage 'is incontestably a form of exclusive private property'. The female 'gives' sex in return for the economic security her husband provides. She gets the worst of the arrangement because she is the more dependent. Engels suggested that her position is one of glorified prostitution. Perhaps the cultural stereotyping embodied in such phrases as 'she's a real gold-digger' and 'she's out to get her man' bear out the view that the economic dependency of women under capitalism can undermine their dignity.

Marxists consider that the family can socialise children to conform, even though, in the case of the working class, it is against their interests to do so (see Chapter 3 pp. 62–6). On the other hand, experience of exploitation can produce feelings critical of the system among the *proletariat* (working class) and these may also be passed on through the family as well as through workmates and friends. As we shall see, Marxists generally consider that the socialising and other functions of the nuclear family could, at least, be pared down and done more effectively by other institutions such as state nurseries.

It would be wholly wrong to think that only Marxists are aware of the major influence of class on family life and, especially, of the way the family socialises children to 'belong' to a particular class. On the contrary, since the war a vast body of largely empirical work has contributed to our knowledge of the links between family and class. The writings of A. H. Halsey and J. W. Douglas are examples. Through the research of these and other scholars we later study the relationship between family, education and class, and that section (Chapter 5, pp. 109–18) should be regarded as a direct continuation of this chapter. Indeed, class pervades not only the family but virtually all aspects of social life. The experience of class, however, begins in the family.

Is the Nuclear Family Universal or can it be Replaced?

The Debate between Functionalists and Marxists

We must now put to the test the partly conflicting functionalist and Marxist claims about the family. We do so mainly by examining various attempts to modify the family along broadly socialist lines and by discussing a celebrated example of a society which did not appear to have a nuclear family, the Nayar case.

Although Murdock's arguments are now regarded as oversimple, modern functionalists still accept that the nuclear family is universal. They, of course, recognise the widespread existence of the extended family but see the nuclear family as its essential core. Literally, the extended family is an *extension* of the nuclear family. The same argument is applied to polygamous families. One person may make several marriages but each separate coupling and offspring is regarded as a nuclear family.

Two quite distinct arguments are presented to support the contention that the nuclear family is universal. Firstly, the universality of the nuclear family is seen as a result of its unique practicality and usefulness in meeting certain basic human needs. A few functionalists take this to the point of claiming that man is biologically predisposed towards the nuclear family. Secondly, the accumulation of historical and cultural material is taken to show that, as a matter of empirical fact, the family is universal. We now examine these two arguments in turn.

We have already discussed the first argument: that the family is universal because it is functionally necessary. In the next section we look at how these functions have evolved – particularly under the impact of industrialisation. Here it only needs to be added that functionalists stress that it is only the family which *combines* the four basic functions mentioned above. Other institutions can perform some of them but only the family is so effectively *multi-functional*. The basic functions of the family are to a greater or lesser extent concerned with one matter – the maintenance and regeneration of the species – and it is efficient and convenient that they should be integrated into a single institution.

A useful way to test the second functionalist argument that, as a matter of *fact*, the family is universal, is by finding and evaluating possible alternatives to it. This we do below.

The Nayar Case

It can be argued that the Nayars of Malabar offer an example of a society in which the nuclear family did not exist. Until about the mid-nineteenth century, when their traditional social system began to break up under the impact of the British, the Nayar produced and reared children without the aid of the nuclear family. No direct institutional link existed between sex and reproduction and the rearing of children. Once a woman had undergone a sexual initiation ritual, she could have sexual intercourse with any man she wished. As a result, paternity was often uncertain. In practical terms this did not matter, as the mother's brother, not the natural father, was responsible for looking after her and her offspring. When this was not possible the next nearest male relatives on the mother's side were responsible.

The Nayar case is surely an exception to the familiar nuclear family pattern. Kathleen Gough's point that a special and socially recognised tie existed between a woman and the man who first initiated her sexually does not affect the argument at all. The 'couple' certainly did not constitute the basis of a nuclear family in that the nuclear 'unit' had no continuous social existence. Further examination shows, however, that there was a sound functional reason for the Nayar form of child-rearing. The Nayars were a very warlike people. The women were able to assist each other during the frequent absences of the men, and in the event of one male relative being killed, there would still be others left to provide for the woman and her children.

The Nayar system of child-rearing was, then, *functionally well adapted* to the needs of that particular society. Regarded thus, it is quite consistent with functionalist perspectives about the need of children for a stable social environment. Perhaps this is more significant than the literal fact that the Nayar case does represent a rare exception to the 'universality' of the nuclear family.

The Kibbutzim

There have been few attempts in modern society to abolish the nuclear family outright but many efforts to replace it partially by other institutions or to merge it within a larger extended family-type structure. Perhaps the best known attempt to supplement the family by providing alternative institutions to assist parents with childrearing is the Israeli *Kibbutzim*. In the early days of the Jewish settlement in Israel, the Kibbutzim stressed the collective values of the whole community against the more concentrated, limited, and, it was thought, selfish ties of the family. It was also part of the beliefs (or ideology) of the movement to release women from child-rearing and to enable them to have as much time for work and leisure as men. Young infants were taken to special Children's Houses after only a short time with their parents. They grew up together and were looked after by specially trained nurses (or metapalets) and teachers. They were allowed to see their parents for a few hours only each day, and slept in the Children's Houses and not their parents' residence. Women were therefore free to do any work on the same terms as men. Gradually, these patterns are changing: the separation between parents and children is less complete; in many Kibbutzim, children return to spend the night at their parents' flat, and women are more involved than men in traditionally feminine roles such as working in the communal kitchen or laundry.

Despite this partial return to nuclear family norms, the Kibbutzim still thrive and are now well beyond the experimental phase. It is significant that children of the Kibbutzim and adults from Kibbutzim backgrounds are as psychologically well adjusted as others. Not unexpectedly, however, many have acquired values that express the importance of the group rather than individual achievement. The charge by Bruno Bettelheim that adults brought up in the Kibbutzim lack the capacity for leadership has not been found to be true, however. It does seem, therefore, that the role of the family in rearing children can be successfully reduced, as long as other *effective* institutions exist to do the job.

The Sixties Commune Movement

A much less organised effort to breach the limits of the nuclear family was the commune 'movement' of the late nineteen sixties. Communes of one kind or another have existed for thousands of years – religious communities are one example – and will no doubt continue to exist, although they have a tendency to be short-lived. An interesting example of communal idealism which illustrates the fragility of the movement was the plan of the poets Wordsworth, Coleridge and Southey to establish a *utopia* (perfect society) in miniature on the banks of the Sussquehannah River in the United States. Like most people's dreams of returning to nature this one, too, remained a dream although Wordsworth and Coleridge did go to live in the more accessible English Lake District.

The ideological theorising which inspired many of the communes of the nineteen sixties was rarely as well thought out as that of the Kibbutzim pioneers. Ideas of 'togetherness' and of 'sharing things, feelings and experience' were enough to persuade thousands of young people, at one time or another, to spend a few weeks or months in a commune. Others pursued the ideal of alternative living more rigorously and attempted to live self-sufficiently, practising communist principles in respect of property. In many communes nuclear families or, quite often, single-parent families simply fitted in – sometimes benefiting from the help that single adults or childless couples gave them with their children. In others, more organised attempts to bring up children communally occurred and in such cases these arrangements were often consciously thought of as alternatives to the nuclear family. Likewise, serious attempts were sometimes made to share the burden of domestic work equally between men and women.

Even at its peak in the late nineteen sixties the commune movement was never more than a marginal challenge to conventional family structures. The nature of modern society tends strongly to undermine the extended family type structure of communes. Geographical mobility – often caused by occupational change – is so great that the chances of the same group of people finding it convenient to stay together over a long period are small. Unless modern society itself breaks down and we return to a more localised agricultural pattern of living, communes seem likely to remain peripheral. Yet, for certain groups, especially students and young, unmarried adults, communal living can offer an enjoyable and practical social framework. It is also not uncommon for groups of one-parent families to live either together or close to one other in order to benefit from mutual cooperation and assistance.

Similarly, the relatively few examples of homosexual or lesbian 'families' are best seen as an accommodation to circumstances by an interested minority, rather than as a challenge to the nuclear family. Research evidence indicates that children brought up by a couple of the same sex are no more likely to be homosexual than children raised by a heterosexual (sexually mixed) couple. Again, this suggests that other institutions besides the nuclear family are capable of bringing up children successfully.

The Soviet 'Experiment'

There has been only one attempt by a government seriously to undermine the nuclear family. This happened in the Soviet Union in the period immediately following the Revolution of 1917. Marriage, divorce and even abortion were made available on almost a casual basis. The ideological inspiration behind this attempt to undermine the family was the Communist ideas of Marx, Engels and Lenin. They considered that in capitalist societies the family both expressed and helped to perpetuate the unequal and repressive nature of the system itself. In particular, they considered that the domination of husband over wife in the family reflected that of the capitalist manufacturer over the wage-labourer in economic and social life. But it was not simply ideology that motivated the Communist revolutionaries. Practically, they wanted to release more women from domestic toil to enable them to assist in reconstructing the country's economy which had been badly damaged by revolution and civil war. To help achieve this, communal facilities were established for bringing up children, though at first these were quite inadequate.

In the mid nineteen thirties, the government substantially changed major aspects of its policy towards the family. In 1935 a new law was passed, making parents legally responsible for the misbehaviour of their children. In 1936 much stricter marriage and divorce legislation was passed. This was partly because the previous approach had helped to produce considerable social problems, including a high rate of infant mortality and neglect and juvenile delinquency. In addition, the government was now keen to increase the birth rate and this was thought to require a stable family structure and fewer abortions. It is significant, however, that a progressively extending network of maternity homes, nurseries and kindergartens was also established both to assist population expansion and to allow women more freely to enter and remain in the labour force.

As Professor Bronfenbrenner says, conditions were so unstable in post-revolutionary Russia that it would be unwise to regard the Soviet experiment to undermine the family as a serious test of whether it is possible for a society to do without the family. Nevertheless, certain less general conclusions do suggest themselves. Firstly, the Soviet experiment again makes it obvious that the crucial functions concerning the reproduction, nurture and socialisation of children, traditionally fulfilled by the family, cannot just be left to chance. If the family does not perform them, then some other institution or institutions must. Secondly, where adequate alternative institutions are established, they can, at least in part, replace the family. The Soviet Union, and indeed other Communist countries, have recognised the need for planned alternative facilities for child-rearing if the traditional functions of the family are to be reduced. The Soviet Union, East Germany and China are much better equipped with nursery and pre-school facilities than Britain. In addition, the Soviet Union runs a state system of boarding schools which bring up millions of children and so frees their parents, particularly their mothers, from the need to do so.

It is clear that the nuclear family is outstandingly well-equipped to perform the basic functions of the reproduction and rearing of children although in many traditional societies it only functions efficiently as part of an extended kinship system. It is historical fact that in almost every society the nuclear family has been the basic social unit. It is equally obvious from the above comparative cultural survey, however, that it is possible to reduce the functions of the family as long as additional supportive institutions are established. Whether any government or given group of people wants to increase or reduce the role of the family in society is a question of *judgement* and *value*. As such, it is beyond the strict limits of sociological consideration. Those who wish to maintain or extend the role of the nuclear family and ensure its prestige as a social institution often do so because they value the strength and intensity of the personal relationships that they believe characterise it: the husband-wife and mother-child relationships are perhaps especially valued. By contrast, many Communists and other radicals consider that the nuclear family is a narrow institution which fosters selfish individualism and helps to maintain the corrupt capitalist system. In particular, they argue that the family prevents women from fulfilling their true personal and social potential.

The Family and Community in Britain from Pre-Industrial to Modern Times

It used to be thought that the extended family was typical in pre-industrial England and that the nuclear family became predominant as a result of industrialisation. It was argued by Goode and Parsons that the industrial economy requires a more mobile population and that this tends to break up extended families; in particular, the urban, industrial areas drew in younger people. Historical and sociological research has shown this to be too simple a view. Nevertheless, as Edward Shorter and others argue, this new knowledge need not fundamentally change our perception of the difference between local community life in pre-industrial and modern times. Even though family structure has changed less than was thought, its relationship to the wider community has changed. We will divide our study of changes in the family into three historical phases: the pre-industrial, the early industrial and the modern.

1 The Pre-Industrial Family
Peter Laslett has shown that, in fact, the nuclear family was the norm in pre-industrial Britain and other research strongly suggests that the same was true for North America. It is quite likely, however, that the extended family was more common in continental Europe, at least in the East. One important excep-

tion to the nuclear family norm existed in Britain. It was usual for the eldest and inheriting son and his family to remain in his parents' home. This was to mutual benefit: the ageing parents could receive help from their eldest son who was able to live in and look after the property he would eventually inherit. Although other children usually moved out of the parental home at marriage, they normally lived close by.

An interesting suggestion emerging from the new research on the family further refutes the functionalist view that the nuclear family was the result of industrialisation. Harris argues that the very fact that non-inheriting children had to make their own way in the world helped to provide a mobile labour force and to foster the values of hard work and achievement necessary for capitalist activity. Seemingly, it was not necessary for the family to 'adapt' greatly to the early industrial society as functionalists maintain. On the contrary, the single inheritance system may have helped foster industrialisation. The same system of inheritance exists in Japan and may have had a similar effect.

Talcott Parsons has emphasised the multi-functional nature of the pre-industrial family. Whereas the modern nuclear family typically receives much assistance from the state in performing its basic functions, the pre-industrial family had to be more self-sufficient. At times of crisis, considerable help was often provided by kin and neighbours. If this help was essentially informal, it was also expected and needed.

Then, as now, the family was the major institution of sex, reproduction and nurture. As far as socialisation was concerned, the family, supported by church and community, taught traditional behaviour and morality. For the great majority, there was no formal schooling and most could neither read nor write. Skills, including farming skills, were normally learnt through practical application, usually under the watchful eye of family or kin. The major economic function of most families was to produce enough for their members to survive – if possible, comfortably. The better off and more successful produced a surplus which could then be sold in market towns – mainly for consumption by the urban minority. The function of *job-placement* was more often performed by the family in pre-industrial times, than now. This means that older members of the family would frequently place younger members in work.

Whatever the precise size and structure of the pre-industrial family, Edward Shorter seems to be right when he suggests that both kin and community had greater control and influence on individual and nuclear family life before the nineteenth century, than now. This observation fits in with the functionalist view that family and community 'did' more for their members then than today.

2 The Early Industrial Family

With industrialisation and the movement of population to the towns, major changes began to take place in the functional relationship of the family to society. But just as sociologists have exaggerated the extent of the extended family in the pre-industrial past, so they have often over-stressed the speed and extent of the change to the nuclear family in industrial, urban areas. Obviously, if the nuclear family was the predominant form *before* industrialisation, there could hardly have been a massive shift towards it *after* industrialisation. There is some evidence that in industrial working class areas the extended family was, in fact, more common than in rural areas. This was the pattern found by Anderson in his research into households in the cotton-manufacturing town of Preston and a rural area near-by, in the mid-nineteenth century. Peter Willmot and Michael Young's famous study of working class family life in Bethnal Green in the nineteen-fifties showed the strength of extended family type structures at that time and it is likely that this pattern had existed for several generations. The usefulness of extended family type structures to the working class in the nineteenth century is apparent. Older women could help out domestically when the younger married ones went out to work. Kin arriving from the rural areas would often stay with relatives, not only out of immediate necessity but in the hope of picking up tips about jobs or even getting a specific recommendation and placement. Extended families in contemporary immigrant communities play much the same role.

There were also sound personal and social reasons for middle class families to stay close together in Victorian England. In particular, the old still depended on their kin for help and companionship. The welfare state is a twentieth century phenomenon. Quite often, the large, three-floor Victorian middle class house was the home of three generations.

Despite the considerable amount of evidence that there was no marked change from the extended to nuclear family form as a result of industrialisation, it is likely that *over a long period of time*, say, from the early nineteenth into the twentieth century, the *further* development of the nuclear family at the expense of the extended occurred. As Goode and Parsons stipulate, this was partly the result of the geographical mobility that a free labour market tended to stimulate. As the service sector increased and people with specific educational qualifications were demanded, it became more likely, particularly for the middle class young, to leave their home locality to work elsewhere.

Even so, the pattern painted by modern scholarship is of more continuity between pre-industrial and early industrial family structure and life than has been previously noted. The extended family and supportive community was often needed as much in industrial areas and dockland as it had been in rural areas. The middle class Victorian septuagenerian had no more taste for living alone than had the aged country gentry. The real change in family and community life occurred much closer to our own time.

3 The Modern Family

a CHANGING FUNCTIONS The twentieth century, our third period for consideration, has seen substantial changes in the size of the family and in its relationship to society. Largely as a result of improved methods of birth control and the resultant decrease in the fertility rate, families tend to be much smaller than in Victorian times. A family of four, parents and two children, has become typical of both the working and middle classes. Change in family size has probably had as much effect on family life as any supposed change in family structure. Nevertheless, it can be said that the post-Second World War period is the one in which the nuclear family has overwhelmingly predominated over the extended. Indeed, in 1979, the majority of households contained only one or two people – a fact which suggests that even the nuclear family is suffering some fragmentation. According to functionalists such as Talcott Parsons, the modern nuclear family has adapted to fulfil more *specialised* functions. Finally, the relationship of family to community has changed.

The basic functions of the modern nuclear family remain

those that the family has traditionally fulfilled. To a greater or lesser extent, however, all four functions have been modified. As the basic functions have tended to be reduced, the family has, arguably, acquired a still greater role in personal and emotional life. There has been a parallel decline in the involvement of the local community with the individual. Often there is a wall of privacy between family and neighbourhood community.

For the majority, marriage is still the main outlet for sexual activity and some consider it to be the only morally acceptable one. Many others, however, no longer exclusively associate sex with marriage. Michael Schofield's work shows a growth in permissive attitudes to sex before marriage among young people. In America the Hite Report suggested that many women no longer regard sexual expression exclusively in terms of their marital relationship. If marriage is not as exclusively the outlet for sexual expression as in the past, is still provides the most popular basis of companionship and mutual assistance.

Reproduction still occurs predominantly within a two-parent family context despite a noticeable increase in illegitimacy in recent years. There has been a corresponding rise in the number of children taken into local authority care, but most of these still received early nurture and socialisation within some sort of family situation, however unstable.

The state has come increasingly to intervene in child socialisation, particularly from the age of five when children usually start school. Even infants and, for that matter, unborn children can benefit from a variety of advice and assistance available from central and, sometimes, local government sources. A state system of pre-school nurseries is not, however, provided in Britain and the responsibility for early child-care and socialisation falls more squarely on the family than in the Communist countries of Eastern Europe. Functionalists stress the continuing central importance of the family as the agency of primary socialisation. Here they are not merely referring to informal socialisation, which functionalists have always seen as necessary to passing on the values and norms of society, but to formal teaching too. Fletcher notes that more teaching and learning take place in the family now than in the past. We live in a complex world in which the three 'r's' are necessary rather than optional. Many parents play a large part in teaching these and other skills.

The protection and assistance traditionally afforded by kin and community is now commonly provided by the state. Muriel Nissel goes so far as to say that: 'Supplementary benefit, not the family, must remain the safety net for people faced with poverty.' The National Health Service plays a major role here. So, too, do the contributory national insurance schemes covering sickness and unemployment payments and the social security system which, as its name implies, is supposed to be the ultimate 'security' against poverty if all else fails. Some have seen the apparent loss of the family's welfare function and its assumption by the state as an example of the growing impersonality of the modern world. Even caring for one's fellow man has been taken over by 'big brother.' Strugglers are assisted by salaried social workers rather than friends. This is too simple a view. Firstly, the welfare state provides many services, including necessary medical services to the poor, that people would not otherwise obtain. Secondly, help from family and friends does and, indeed, should supplement and overlap that provided by the welfare state. The state cannot usually supply the human and emotional support that people undergoing material or emotional crisis often need, although many social workers make remarkable efforts to do so. The administration of social security payments has, however, often been obtusely bureaucratic – hardly a bracing recipe for 'clients' often already dispirited and suffering.

The family is rarely now a unit of economic production, although it is an important unit of consumption. Many goods, such as refrigerators, washing machines, and three piece suites are manufactured largely for the family market. It hardly needs to be said that, without this market, there would be economic collapse. In addition, families collectively produce and maintain the labour force. Finally, the investment of family money in banks, building societies, unit trusts and stocks and shares provides necessary loan capital for industrial investment.

Talcott Parsons emphasises the importance of the contemporary family in 'stabilising' the adult personality. It provides a relatively secure and personally meaningful context for self-fulfilment, in contrast with the frequently stressful and impersonal nature of work. Parsons considers that the family has shed some of its less necessary functions and has adapted to become more specialised in two tasks: that of socialisation, and 'tension' or emotional management. Marxists are sceptical of this claim and, as we shall see when we examine the evidence for stresses on the family. They are not without ammunition for their cause.

b PRIVATISATION Michael Young and Peter Willmot make some interesting observations on changes in family roles and relationships in their book *The Symmetrical Family*. Much of what they say continues and develops earlier British research on the family, including their own. In the nineteen fifties, for instance, Elizabeth Bott found that, on the basis of an admittedly small sample (twenty families), working class spouses tended to divide tasks sharply whereas the opposite applied to the middle class. Thus, she describes these as, respectively, *segregated* and *joint conjugal* role relationships. Willmott and Young found that, by the time they did their research in the early nineteen seventies, joint conjugal role relationships had become quite common among the working class, too. For one thing, far more women had joined men in the labour force. So impressed were Willmott and Young by this development that they used the term 'symmetrical' in the title of their book to indicate the trend to greater role sharing. Feminists have strongly criticised Willmott and Young for exaggerating this trend and we shall air their criticisms later (see Chapter 11, p. 297).

Willmott and Young also echo a point made about family life by John Goldthorpe and David Lockwood in their 'affluent worker' study. Goldthorpe and Lockwood noted a tendency towards family – rather than community – based social life both among their main sample of affluent manual workers and the smaller, control group of white collar employees. Spouses spent time together inside the home rather than in visiting friends and neighbours. Goldthorpe and Lockwood termed this trend the *privatisation* of family life.

There are several reasons for the development of the privatised nuclear pattern of living. An underlying factor is the movement of population caused partly by the operation of a free labour market and government policy to disperse population from the declining inner city areas. This has undermined community and extended family type social networks. Important, too, is the massive post-war boom in home-based, leisure consumer items such as televisions and hi-fi's. Many married people, as well as aspiring to a high material standard of living, have great expectations of their marital relationship as well. Unlike many Eastern societies in which marriages are arranged by parents, Western societies allow people to marry for love and romance. Even after the first flush is over, couples tend to expect and demand much of each other, both in terms of everyday companionship and deeper emotional and physical commitment. With this in mind some commentators have referred to modern marriage as *companionate marriage*.

Christopher Lasch, a radical American intellectual, gives a depressing view of the nuclear family in capitalist society. He puts quite a different value on family consumerism and even on the marital relationship from that of functionalists. He argues, as do many Marxists, that the family market is manipulated by capitalist advertisers and producers. People are persuaded to buy the 'latest' item even when they neither need nor want it: this spending keeps the wheels of the capitalist economy turning. The stresses of a materialist society which lacks deeper spiritual or human values shows in marriage – and divorce. For Lasch the family in 'bourgeois' society has ceased to be a private refuge. Its walls have been breached by relentless waves of media propaganda, its members are awash like flotsam in an uncaring sea. We look more closely at these and like observations in the following section.

c FAMILY, CLASS, CULTURE AND COMMUNITY Middle and working class cultures remain distinct despite the invasion of almost every home by the consumer durables of the 'mass' market. Here we further explore differences between working and middle class cultural and community life or 'social networks', to use Margaret Stacey's term.

Already Richard Hoggart's painstakingly detailed description of traditional working class life in Leeds has a curious old fashioned snap-shot quality. But the fact that traditional working class community is breaking up does not mean it never existed. Some recent commentators, failing to find thriving working class communities of the kind described twenty years ago by Willmott and Young and by Hoggart seem almost to assume that the whole phenomenon is a romantic fiction.

Coates and Silburn's generally excellent study of the lower class St Anne's district of Nottingham falls a little into this trap. The fact that they find St Anne's to be a fragmented community does not mean it was always so. As they, in fact, well illustrate, the decline of community was due partly to urban renewal policies – a factor also emphasised by Willmott and Young in their Bethnal Green study well over a decade previously.

Apart from those working class people who have chosen to leave inner city areas, many had to leave because of compulsory clearance orders and were offered public housing elsewhere. This was part of a national plan (which had considerable local variations) to divert industry and population away from the inner cities, which could then be used as the location for office blocks, major shops and stores, and as the centre of the leisure and entertainment industry. Public housing makes up well over a quarter of residential property, and generalisations need to be made carefully. However, a consensus has emerged, which includes even their original designer, that high rise flats have been a failure as a major means of providing cheap mass-accommodation. Incidents such as the collapse of the Ronan Point block, and the suicide jump from her high-storey flat of a depressed Birmingham mother, with her baby, have created the worst publicity, but myriad problems of design and functioning, such as block entrances leading out into garbage zones or lifts perpetually breaking down, have provided a daily diet of irritation and frustration for thousands. Nevertheless, it is, of course, a major contribution that the material conditions of living provided by many of these developments are vastly superior to that of the old-fashioned terraced houses they have often replaced. But this improvement can be achieved equally in smaller, low rise developments or still other kinds of accommodation at less cost to communal life. As potential communities high rise flats have limited possibilities. Living off the ground is not conducive to shared activity and most corridors in high rise flats do not provide an environment that encourages friendly conversations with neighbours. Even Frank Lloyd Wright's imaginative idea of high rise developments as 'vertical streets in the sky' with various shops, facilities and meeting places strategically scattered on all levels to facilitate interaction and communication seems expensive and artificial, though clearly the concept is an improvement on the human filing cabinets that some blocks have become.

Working class housing estates make up most of the rest of public housing. These are often located on the outskirts of urban areas and replace traditional, more centrally situated housing. Living conditions on post-war, mainly working class housing estates vary from almost as bad as in the worst of the high rise flats to very good indeed. John Stedman's estate at Corby and the prize-winning Handley Green development at Laindon, near Basildon, are spacious, well-designed and attractive. But in general, people have to travel to work from public housing estates and shopping, too, can require a journey. The separation of these basic functions is not conducive to an integrated community life in the old style. A seldom remarked-on effect of the decrease in the fertility of working class mothers is that fewer children exist to establish inter-family social links and this must further reduce the numbers of friends within the neighbourhood. Community centres, which are a feature of some recently established estates, often fail to draw people together for leisure activities though teenagers do frequently use them. Even so, the streets and open areas of estates are often preferred by adolescents – especially by 'tougher' boys. Perhaps it is through their activity and that of younger children who still like to 'play out' that we see a glimpse of at least one continuous strand in the pattern of working class neighbourhood life.

Despite the complexity of the overall picture, most middle class owner occupiers still tend to live in suburban neighbourhoods. The term suburban neighbourhood can cover a wide spectrum from, for instance, areas of inter-war semi-detached property, with upper working as well as lower middle class residents, to areas of high status, often detached property occupied mainly by professional, managerial and business groups. Generalisations therefore need to be cautious.

In dormitory suburbs, the very fact that people live and work in separate places is not conducive to the development of integrated community life. But if work is not a shared activity as in a mining or docking community, it can provide a conversation topic for middle class people who already know each other or want to get to know each other. 'What do you do?' is a favourite opening question at middle class dinner parties. Though social life in the immediate suburban neighbourhood is less intense than in a traditional working class community, networks of friends and acquaintances tend to be spread more widely. The middle class are more ready to join clubs and associations requiring commitment to activity beyond the immediate neighbourhood. For instance, middle class parents are more likely to participate in organisations and activities concerning their children's educational welfare such as Parent-Teachers Associations or school open days.

The privatisation of middle class family life is highly compatible with extended friendship networks and relative lack of involvement in the immediate neighbourhood. Social life is more organised and friends are not expected to 'pop in and out' as they might do in a traditional working class neighbourhood. A telephone call can courteously pave the way for a visit but it can as easily do instead if one of the parties is occupied. Privacy and control of time can be virtually a necessity if work brought home from the office and children's homework is to be properly done. The home, with all its modern amenities, can serve as a place of almost self-sufficient retreat.

Mutual concern with children is what brings middle class people most readily together. In their book about the Canadian suburb of 'Crestwood Heights', Seeley and his co-authors argue that the major institutional focus of the community is on child-rearing. Interfamily social life is organised, mainly by mothers, around this central concern from the time when turns are taken to give children's tea parties, to when offspring depart for higher education. At this point the female parent often returns to work.

Despite the above contrasts, family and community life is more similar across the middle and working classes than, say, fifty years ago. Then, the majority of the working class was forced to live in rented accommodation. Now, the majority live in public housing and an increasing proportion own their own houses. Indeed, a majority of families in Britain now own their own homes. This fact, in combination with the movement out of the urban areas means that the suburban ideal cuts across class lines to a considerable extent. A house of their own out of town, is what most families seem to want and many have already achieved it. Add to this the even more general processes of family privatisation, consumerism and, more controversially, symmetrical gender role-playing already noted and a very real *convergence* in family life-style between, particularly, the lower middle and upper working class is apparent. Yet, as we shall see throughout the book, class and status differences still divide these groups and even more, those groups at the social extremes.

Stresses on Marriage and the Modern Family

The evidence that the modern family is under considerable stress is substantial, though whether things are now 'worse than they were' is, like all such generalisations, highly debatable. The rise in the divorce rate is the most striking indicator of family stress. It is important to note, however, that many thousands of broken marriages end in separation rather than divorce. The divorce figures, therefore, underestimate the extent of family and marriage break up. In 1966, 47,000 divorces were granted. In 1977, the figure was 170,000. For every three to four marriages there was one divorce. Children were involved in the majority of divorce cases. A detailed picture of the *rate* of increase in divorce can be seen from the table below.

The Increase in the Divorce Rate* 1951–1977

1951	1961	1966	1971	1972	1973	1974	1975	1976	1977
2.6	2.1	3.2	6.0	9.5	8.4	9.0	9.6	10.1	10.4

*The *Divorce Rate* is the rate of divorces per thousand married population.

Source: *Social Trends,* 1980.

Indicators in respect of child welfare also suggest that the family is not fully coping. In 1976, the number of children in local authority care passed 100,000 and has since remained at about this figure. It has frequently been shown that the majority of boys in care develop antisocial behaviour patterns but it was thought that girls were damaged less. Recent research suggests, however, that girls in care are also often profoundly disadvantaged. In 1979 'the year of the child,' the number of 'latch-key' children was declared by a concerned charity to be at a record figure – well in excess of 600,000. Whoever is to 'blame' for this, the many thousands of unsupervised children in the five to fourteen age-group involved in road accidents gives pause for thought on the matter. Physical cruelty to children by parents is, of course, a minority problem and occurs relatively less often in Britain than in the United States and Germany. Nevertheless, at a conservative estimate, upwards of 3,000 incidents of baby battering occur in Britain each year, of which about 10% result in death. A still more emotional issue is that of abortion. Opinions vary from the view that it is a murderous way to escape from parental responsibility to the conviction that only a woman has 'the right to choose' whether or not to have a child. The 1967 Abortion Act made abortion on the National Health relatively easy to obtain. As a result abortions went up from 50,000 in 1969 to 111,000 in 1973. The total dropped slowly to 103,000 in 1977 and rose again to 112,000 in 1978. It is too early to say whether the 1978 figure indicates a new trend upwards, and whether attempts to change the law to make abortion more difficult to obtain will succeed. Finally, the steady increase in juvenile delinquency since the War and the more recent steep increase in heavy drinking among the young is considered by some to be partly related to the breakdown of family authority. Others, however, would see these factors as symptoms of a much wider crisis of social values and norms.

Is it possible that there is an underlying crisis in the family which explains the above, admittedly mixed, though generally depressing, collection of facts? We will start answering this question by examining the causes and some consequences of divorce.

Divorce: Reasons for and Implications of the Increase

a CHANGES IN CULTURAL ATTITUDES Changes in cultural attitudes towards marriage have created a climate of public opinion in which it has been possible to pass laws which have made it increasingly easy to opt out of marriage. The long-term background to the erosion of marriage as a permanent and binding commitment is the decline in formal religious belief. Marriage is less often seen as a sacred, spiritual union, but more as a personal and practical commitment which can be abandoned if it fails. This attitude to marriage has resulted in a series of changes in the law, making the grounds for divorce less strict and the administrative procedure for obtaining it less complicated and time-consuming (in 1977 it became possible to get divorced by post in some circumstances). The Divorce Law

Reform Act of 1969 (actually implemented in 1971) established that it was enough merely to prove 'irretrievable breakdown of marriage' to obtain a divorce. The 'irretrievable breakdown of marriage' was made the sole cause for it. The phrase is general enough to be interpreted to include virtually all conceivable reasons for divorce. Although there was an increase in the divorce rate following the Act, it would be crude to think of the Act as 'causing' this increase. Deeper reasons for it must be sought in the broader cultural factors mentioned above. Viewed in longer perspective, the statistical trend is that of a gradual increase in divorce with occasional sharp jumps when enabling legislation was passed. In addition to the 1969 Act, another such instance was the 1949 Legal Aid Act which enabled women seeking divorce to obtain financial assistance in doing so.

As well as the decline of religion, another cultural factor that explains the fragility of modern marriage is the rise of individualistic and romantic values that have replaced the traditional values referred to in the previous paragraph. The question of romantic marriage must be seen against the background of a steady decline in family and community control of choice of partner, courtship and marriage. Traditionally, couples married (or had their marriages arranged) for down-to-earth material reasons such as, to take a middle class example, joining two family estates or businesses together. Courtship was supervised closely, if more or less informally, within the community. For a period of about two hundred years, however, people have been increasingly marrying whom they want rather than whom they are told to. As Edward Shorter points out, the danger in marrying for mainly romantic reasons is that when romantic love and attraction disappear, so, too, might marriage.

A further factor to consider in relation to our own time is the sexual revolution of the post-Second World War period. The pill provided a safe opportunity to have sexual relations with more than one person after marriage as well as before it. However much most people say they disapprove of such behaviour, more and more seem to be indulging in it (though needless to say reliable statistics are not available on so personal and sensitive a matter).

Edward Shorter suggests that the underlying factor which ultimately explains why so many marriages now end up in the divorce courts is the nature of capitalist industrial society itself.

Capitalism broke up traditional communities and set their populations 'free', in the limited sense that they could come to towns and compete for work. But they were free also from traditional family and community control, freer in personal and sexual relations with whom they wished. In the long-term, this freedom evolved into the virtual right to choose and, within ever more generous limits, get rid of one's spouse. Of course, there is a price to pay for this freedom, particularly in terms of anguish and, frequently, material deprivation to children of broken families. There is, however, evidence from several sources that children with divorced parents show fewer signs of mental stress and delinquent behaviour and have a better adjustment to their parents than children from intact but unhappy homes. It seems that keeping an 'empty shell' marriage together 'for the children's sake' can backfire. The wide belief that divorce is 'bad for' children cannot, then, be simplistically accepted.

b PROBLEMS OF INTER-PERSONAL COMMUNICATION A cluster of other factors – most of which are fairly self-evident – correlate with divorce. Partners who are dissimilar in culture, social background, or religion, or who are of very different age are more prone to divorce, as are those who marry young and may still be developing personally and emotionally. Barbara Thomas and Jean Collard in a recent publication, *Who Divorces*, suggest that for these and other divorced couples a common underlying problem is often poor inter-personal communication. Consistent with Willmott and Young, they note that the small conjugal family has increasingly become the principal and, sometimes, sole source of deep emotional expression, and that this can put a strain on the marriages of those who have communication problems.

c THE CHANGING STATUS OF WOMEN Some observers associate the increase in divorce with the changing status of women. The female share of divorce petitions has generally outnumbered that of men in both Britain and the United States, and recently there has been a striking increase. In Britain the female share was about seventy per cent in the late nineteen seventies. It may be that, as more women have entered the labour market, they have acquired the necessary economic independence to opt out of an unsatisfactory marriage if they choose to do so. Further, going to work also enables them to meet more prospective partners than if they remained full-time housewives. Interestingly, according to the U.S. Bureau of Census Report (1972), better-paid female divorcees are more likely to delay remarriage or remain single than are low-paid ones. Whether women will be able to maintain their limited gains in the contracting labour market of the early eighties remains to be seen.

FAMILY AUTHORITY Among the mixture of facts used to illustrate the supposed decline in parental authority within the modern family, the increase in juvenile delinquency is often mentioned. Specifically, the charge made is that the family is failing to act as an effective agency of social control. This accusation however, could equally be made against the schools and police. The causes of juvenile delinquency must, therefore, be sought in the wider society rather than in the failure of any single institution such as the family. This we do in Chapter 17. Here, it need only be said that the more permissive and democratic ideals of the post-war period reduce the credibility of physical punishment as a means of maintaining control both within the family and within society. Reason may often be preferred to force as a matter of principle and humanity, but it is an instrument that takes time and patience and, unfortunately, is no more guaranteed to succeed than cruder methods of control. Similarly, there are no easy solutions to the problems of children that arise because their parents divorce or because both work. Socialists want more state aid for the family so that, in particular, women can go to work in peace. Conservatives generally would like to see families (and particularly mothers) resume what they feel to be their traditional responsibilities to children more fully.

ABORTION The abortion issue highlights the extent to which matters relating to the family and especially the role of women within it are politically, socially and morally sensitive. On the day these lines are being written, massive demonstrations and counter-demonstrations for and against a bill to curb the availability of abortion, as laid down in the 1967 Act, are taking place in London. Some see the bill as a first step in an attempt to restore traditional family stability and responsibility.

Others consider that, to the extent that it forces women to have children they do not want, it will have the opposite effect. For the modern world, moral disagreement and confusion characterise matters relating to the family as they do so much else.

THE DYNAMICS OF FAMILY VIOLENCE: RADICAL PSYCHIATRY One of the cult figures of the nineteen sixties was radical psychiatrist, Ronald Laing. His analysis of the family illustrates aspects of the phenomenological perspective. His primary concern is with the 'self' but he does not separate the life of the self from that of others. For him 'madness' is not a personal deficiency but must be interpreted as a way of making sense of experience. Thus, he spoke of schizophrenic families rather than schizophrenic individuals – if the self is forced into fantasy escape it is because there is something to escape from. Although Laing's primary focus of analysis is the micro level of group interaction, the tension and psychological 'violence' he sees in family life persuaded him to look at the wider world:

> Concerned as I am with this inner world, observing day to day its devastation, I ask why this has happened.

If he finds an answer to this question it is that the violence of the outside world – the Vietnam war was particularly in his mind – fuses with and reinforces the potential for violence within us. Corpses on a dead television screen are unreal, but slowly we learn not to care about them or each other, or the human consequences of what we do. The family cannot cope with all this or give it meaning. He suggests that for some, personal madness is a retreat from 'madness out there.' This recalls the pained cry of poet Allen Ginsberg: 'I have seen the best minds of my generation driven mad.'

David Cooper, a colleague of Laing's, goes beyond the latter in taking explicitly political attitudes. His approach owes much to Marx, but, unlike him, Cooper wants to abolish the family itself – at least, as a hard and fast biological unit. Cooper's basic criticism of the family in bourgeois society is the peculiarly limiting and constraining role it plays:

> The child, in fact, is taught primarily not how to survive in society but how to submit to it. Surface rituals like etiquette, organised games, mechanical learning operations at school replace deep experiences of spontaneous creativity, inventive play, freely developing fantasies and dream.

101

That, perhaps, is the nub of Cooper and Laing. They want a freer, less repressive society – always provided that what is freely expressed is love rather than selfishness or hate. Cooper's belief that spontaneous, 'wanted' relationships should take preference over biological and legal bonds is what leads him to attack the traditional family.

In retrospect, Laing and Cooper's contributions have been less in the directly social and political dimension of their work than in nudging their sizeable audience, particularly among young, educated adults, further in the direction of experimental permissiveness in relationships, not only with children, but with each other. To that extent they are not entirely out of tune with the genial liberal advisor on childrearing of the fifties, Dr Spock – although they might regard that comment as an attempt to bury rather than praise them.

Another commentator on the family, anthropologist Edmund Leach, seems to capture the essence of the above criticisms of the family in his own description of it as 'a prison.' Although Leach intends the analogy to be derogatory there is a sense in which the family must inevitably constrain the individual. Society itself is also sometimes compared to a prison and for the same reason: it limits total freedom. If functionalists accept the need for social control too uncritically perhaps the radical psychiatrists underestimate the potentially dangerous as well as positive effects of its absence.

IS THE FAMILY BREAKING UP OR MERELY CHANGING? We have examined impressive evidence of stress on the family. This does not mean that the family is breaking up, or to use David Cooper's more dramatic word, 'dying.' Marriage remains highly popular. Well over ninety per cent of the population gets married. Moreover, the remarriage rates of divorcees are high, both in Britain and the United States, where three quarters of divorced women and five sixths of divorced men remarry. At current remarriage rates in Britain, nearly one in five born around 1950 will have been married twice by the time they are fifty. True, statistics from the United States and Sweden show that more young people are living together for quite lengthy periods than previously, but most established couples do eventually get married. So stress on the family is not necessarily equivalent to family break-up.

When people divorce they are giving up a particular partner, not the idea of marriage. In any case the majority of the population still does not get divorced but remains committed, more or less happily, to one partner for life. If present trends continue, however, a large minority will experience a different marital pattern from the traditional one. This pattern has been called *serial monogamy*. This means having more than one spouse, but at different times. Less frequently, individuals have more than one family.

The above change can give little obvious comfort to those who favour the extended family type structures. The modern family is typically small and second families especially so. No satisfactory general alternative to the nuclear family seems to exist. The nature of modern society works against extended family structures – attractive though these may be in principle. A less mobile, more localised society would no doubt produce a family system woven into kin and community but, for the moment, that is not the kind of society we have. Nevertheless, the minority pattern (serial monogamy) just described does not seem an especially functional social adaptation. Rather, it represents what a large number of people seem to want or, at least, accept as sometimes necessary regardless of considerable inconvenience. A United Kingdom survey in 1977 found that as many as sixty per cent of young people considered that divorce was something that might happen to them. So a recognition of the potential impermanence of marriage and even family commitment is now part of our cultural outlook.

If marriage and the family remain very much alive, the radical criticisms of them nevertheless deserve to be taken seriously. Edmund Leach has drawn attention to the often huge gap between the ideals of family and marriage and reality. In particular, women are often sold misleading images of romance and motherhood through the media, and suffer much when hard truth dawns. It may even be that the ideal of exclusive love of one person for life is selfish, restricting and, in the modern world, unlikely to be achieved. Of course, insecurity and emotional emptiness in relationships are no replacement for personal romance and love. An alternative might lie in less possessive and wider relationships of the kind communal movements aspire to but find so difficult to attain. Here, however, we have left sociology for moral speculation.

Guide to further reading and study

Relatively few books can be recommended to the student to be read early in the first year, even on this topic. Mary Farmer's *The Family* (Longman, 1979) is clear, readable and comprehensive. The second edition is up to date in its summary of relevant research. D. H. Morgan's *Social Theory and the Family* (Routledge and Kegan Paul, 1978) is demanding, but clear and comprehensive. Despite these qualities, the first year student would hardly be expected to read it from cover to cover. Ronald Fletcher's *The Family and Marriage* (Penguin, 1973, third edition), gives a straightforward functionalist analysis of the family. Sidney Peiris's 'The Family – a Marxist View' in Meighan, *ed, Perspectives on Society* (Nelson, 1979) is useful. A brief account and critique of Engels' *The Origins of the Family* is contained in Juliet Mitchell and Ann Oakley, *eds, The Rights and Wrongs of Women* (Penguin, 1976). Michael Young and Peter Willmott's three books on the family are all worth dipping into, even if the time is not available to read them fully. They are all historically-based accounts of the changing structure of the family. *Family and Kinship in East London* (Pelican, 1969) is a classic study of the decline of the traditional, working class extended family. *Family and Class in a London Suburb* (Mentor, 1967) is its companion volume, with a major focus on the middle class suburban family. Their more recent, *The Symmetrical Family* (Penguin, 1975) is the broadest in scope and traces the development of the family from preindustrial times to the present day. For those who want to read further about the Kibbutzim 'alternative,' there is Bruno Bettelheim's rather critical *The Children of the Dream* (Paladin, 1971). A full bibliography of feminist literature on the family is given at the end of Chapter 11.

Past Questions

(Questions on Gender Roles are at the end of Chapter 11).
1 Examine the view that the family as a social institution is dying. (AEB, 1977).

2 Discuss whether the nuclear family is an essential component of the organisation of any society. (JMB, 1978).

3 How might a sociologist account for the popularity of marriage in societies which have a high rate of divorce? (JMB, 1979).

4 Examine the view that families, which in pre-industrial times were units of production, are now increasingly units of consumption. (AEB, 1979).

5 Education

The Relationship of the Educational System to Society

This chapter and the next should have personal relevance to all students who read them. The educational system claims a large portion of your life – a minimum of eleven years and probably thirteen or more, given that you are reading this book. It is certainly worth knowing what the educational system is 'doing' to you.

A major issue in the sociology of education is that of equality, particularly why working class children *generally* attain less (in terms of examinations) than middle class children of similar measured intelligence. For instance, J. W. Douglas compared the attainment level of high ability students from different social backgrounds and found that success at 'O' level was directly and very strongly correlated with class: 77% of upper middle, 60% of lower middle, 53% of upper working and 37% of lower working class were successful. He found the difference between intelligence and attainment was even greater among pupils of less measured intelligence from a similar wide range of social backgrounds. Social class, then, makes a substantial contribution to academic attainment. A number of sociologists, including the American, Jencks, have raised another important question of educational inequality. They argue that even when children of different social backgrounds do achieve similar levels of attainment, their life-chances, in terms of careers and acquiring wealth, are not equalised as a result: higher classes still do better.

Both functionalists and Marxists agree that education socialises people 'into' society by formal and informal processes. Because Marxists are opposed to capitalist society, however, they are highly critical of the ways in which young people are socialised to conform to it. Functionalists tend to take conformity for granted as normal. A third perspective occurs within educational sociology. It is a distinctly liberal one and reflects the reforming political orientation (inclination) which, as we noted in Chapter 1, characterises some sociologists. Liberal sociologists take their stand on the principle that everybody should have equal educational opportunity, even though they accept that fair competition will still result in inequality in examination results, and in career opportunities and rewards. Nonetheless, they want equality at the starting line, not at the finishing tape. The attempt to achieve the limited goal of equal opportunity has involved much political campaigning and legal change. The abolition of the 11+ examination in many areas owed something to the analyses and efforts of liberal sociologists. Both Marxists and liberals see the source of inequality of educational opportunity in socio-economic background differences, but liberals tend to be much more optimistic that this inequality can be reduced by reform at the educational level itself, whereas Marxists argue that real change in the educational system requires a much more fundamental change in the structure of society. Thus, if there were more equality of income and if workers had more control of the places they work in, they would be able to afford to keep their children at school longer and also pass on greater confidence and experience to them.

The above perspectives should be regarded as 'ideal-type' descriptions rather than labels: reality is usually more complex than any description of it. Sociologists do not like being neatly labelled, any more than anyone else does. For instance, many functionalists take a liberal attitude to educational reform. Similarly, some Marxists carefully support certain educational reforms, even though these do not go as far as they might like. There are, also, other strands in the sociology of education as important as the ones so far mentioned. These include the interactionist perspective, and a growing body of work on the curriculum (school courses) itself. We return to these later.

1 Education, Socialisation and Cultural Reproduction:

Durkheim and Marx

Both Durkheim and Marx fully understood that in order to survive, societies need to socialise their young to accept dominant norms and values. If the existing culture is not passed on, it must die. The contemporary French Marxist, Pierre Bourdieu, has stressed the same point in referring to the need of capitalist society to 'culturally reproduce' itself. Reflecting the realities of his time, Marx himself concentrated relatively more on the role of religion in reinforcing cultural conformity whereas present day Marxists see a greater role for education. Interestingly, some of the major contemporary contributions to the sociology of education owe substantial debts to both Marx and Durkheim: this is particularly true of Althusser and Bourdieu.

We begin with Durkheim partly because of the importance and detail of his work in this area and partly because of his continuing influence. The following quotation illustrates how great he considered the power of education over the individual to be:

> . . . each society, considered at a given stage of development,
> has a system of education which exercises an influence upon
> individuals which is usually irresistible.

Although Durkheim considered that the individual can hardly resist the effect of the educational system, his own historical studies of educational systems show that he also regarded the educational system itself as open to wider social influences. Basically, it must pass on society's values. For example, he argued that the competitive examination system came about precisely because modern society is itself individualistic and competitive. He contended that such a system would have been positively dysfunctional (disruptive) in the middle ages, when people generally inherited their social status. For the aristocracy to have to compete with others to maintain their social position would have risked overthrowing the whole social order so such an idea was not entertained.

We need to give more practical illustration of what Durkheim meant by the role of the educational system in producing con-

109

formity. Most obviously, teachers 'tell' pupils formally what to do. Formal socialisation can cover a great deal, such as telling pupils how to eat, dress and speak, as well as what values they should hold. Durkheim particularly emphasised the role of ritual in forming patterns of behaviour and in reinforcing values. Thus, school assemblies might involve rituals in which national patriotism is expressed and strengthened. He was also aware of the less obvious or 'unconscious' ways in which pupils are socialised. For example, schools are very hierarchical institutions (power is concentrated in the hands of a few people), and it is precisely because hierarchy is assumed to be beyond question that children come to accept it as inevitable. They learn that some people, such as headmasters, can command more respect, politeness and obedience than others and, as a result, they are prepared to accept the same situation in society generally.

Althusser, Bourdieu and Bernstein

The Marxist structuralists, Althusser and Bourdieu, have absorbed much of Durkheim's approach to analysing education, as well as that of Marx. It is worth explaining briefly how this dual influence has come about. Durkheim was, of course, French. His influence was passed on to Althusser and Bourdieu partly through a philosopher called Lévi-Strauss, the founder of a school of thought known as *structuralism*. An important aspect of structuralism is that by *unconsciously* (without conscious awareness) learning ways and structures of thought, feeling and behaviour, people 'automatically' carry on the culture into which they have been born. Really, this is to say little more than that people are socialised to conform, except that it emphasises the extent to which this process occurs unconsciously. Now, the socialisation of the unconscious mind has been stressed by Durkheim and, via Lévi-Strauss, it surfaces again in the work of Althusser and Bourdieu. It is to their work that we now turn.

It must be remembered that although Althusser and Bourdieu reflect the influence of their compatriots, Durkheim and Lévi-Strauss, they are also Marxists. Marx's thought, therefore, figures prominently in their writings. Following him, Althusser considers that the functioning of the educational system is largely determined by the needs of the capitalist socio-economic

110

system. As far as the working class is concerned, this means that it must also be socialised to accept its position in the class system and the kind of work it has to do. It is the second of these points which we concentrate on in this section – we examine the first in detail shortly. What must be grasped is that, to Althusser, the educational system serves the needs of capitalism. Bourdieu has made a specialist study of education in capitalist society and, particularly, in France. It is in his writings that we see most clearly the convergence (coming together) of certain concepts of Marx and Durkheim.

Whereas Durkheim emphasised that certain aspects of a common culture (for example, patriotism) are passed on to all members of a society, Bourdieu concentrates on how middle and working class cultures are reproduced. He analyses particularly the role of the educational system in this process. Like Althusser, he argues that schools are middle class institutions, run by middle class people (teachers), in which, in general, middle class pupils succeed. Working class culture does not fit well into the demands of such an educational system. In support of his case, he is able to point to substantial empirical evidence to show that both in the United States and the Western European countries, middle class children tend to achieve better qualifications and to get better jobs than working class children of equal measured intelligence. He explains this further by use of the term *cultural capital*. He argues that because the educational system is middle class, middle class children come into it better equipped to do well. Their values, attitudes and behaviour correspond more closely with teachers' expectations and the demands of the examination system than those of working class children who, in that sense, suffer a cultural deficit (see Chapter 3, pp. 61–8 for a general view of class cultural differences). This observation does not mean that Bourdieu has a low opinion of working class culture, but that he regards it as largely non-academic. For instance, a working class novelist is a contradiction in terms because any such person who writes a novel employs middle class patterns of thought and expression and therefore starts to become middle class.

The work of Basil Bernstein on class culture is highly complementary to that of Bourdieu. Bernstein is particularly noted for his contribution to the analysis of the relationship between class and language. He has suggested that working class children speak in what he calls a *restricted code* and middle class children in an *elaborated code*. This means that the former tend to talk about particular cases or examples whereas the latter express themselves more conceptually and are more inclined to make abstract generalisations. Thus, a working class child will understand from concrete experience what it means to be 'diddled' or 'done' by paying too high a price in a shop or supermarket, but he will be less prepared than the middle class child to understand and talk about, say, the concept of the inequalities of the capitalist system. According to Bernstein, this is not just a matter of unfamiliarity with the relevant vocabulary – although this must play a part – but it is due, more fundamentally, to lack of practised competence in elaborated (or conceptual) codes of thought.

Bernstein's hypothesis has been criticised by the American sociologist, William Labov, amongst others. Labov interviewed a number of black working class children and found that, once they felt confident and at ease with him, they were perfectly capable of expressing themselves in abstract conceptual terms, albeit in dialect rather than standard English. Interestingly, from the point of view of the effect of research method on findings, Labov stresses the importance of establishing an interview situation in which the subjects can behave normally. He suggests that formal interviews can sometimes have the opposite effect and produce misleading data. In defence of Bernstein, it still remains quite possible that middle class children have more practice in conceptual thought and expression. Further, to take Labov's point at face value, differences of dialect, whether based on race or class, would tend to disfavour working class children and to favour middle class children in communicating with middle class teachers. Both points are acceptable within Bourdieu's broad capital-deficit model of cultural reproduction. He himself relates his scheme to the whole range of cultural expression: it is not just the language and modes of thought but also the style and manners, sentiments and forms of emotional expression of teachers that accord better with those of middle class children. For example, behaviour that seems 'nice and well-mannered' to a middle class child may seem 'posh and snotty' to a working class child. Neither view is more correct than the other, but the former provides a more stable basis for a productive school relationship than the latter.

Bourdieu regards the examination system primarily as a formal and ritual ('ceremonial') occasion, of which the already reproduced cultural ascendancy of the middle class child is ratified and *legitimised* (made to seem generally just and acceptable). The 'success' of middle class children and the 'failure' of working class children is certified. The examination system is not a fair competition although it *seems* to be as there is a surface appearance of neutrality. Because it is accepted as fair by the middle and working class alike, it serves to legitimise (justify) what Bourdieu regards as the fundamentally unequal process of cultural reproduction. As a result, the middle class is generally considered to have earned its superior rewards and status and the working class, likewise, to have gained its deserts. Bourdieu sums up the means by which this 'illusion' is achieved in the term *symbolic violence*. It is a powerful phrase and it means that the middle class cultural ascendancy and privilege is conserved and reproduced not by physical force but by a commanding superiority in the field of communication – particularly language. Thus, expertise in manipulating cultural symbols and forms such as literature, art and logic in a way acceptable to the middle class is a weapon in the class struggle, whether consciously used as such or not. Untrained and inexperienced in this skill, working class children are often over-awed and 'mystified' by it. The almost physical sense of injury and loss undoubtedly suffered by many working class 'failures' perhaps justifies Bourdieu's savage metaphor of symbolic violence. At any rate, to him, it provides the answer to the question of how working class people are ideologically persuaded to fit into their often boring and relatively unrewarding roles.

Bourdieu has been criticised both by more orthodox Marxists and by liberals. Of the former, Raymond Boudon argues that Bourdieu overstresses the cultural or, as he calls them, the primary effects of stratification to the point of virtually ignoring the secondary, or material and practical, effects. Boudon considers the secondary effects more important. These affect older working class pupils, who may find that they simply do not have enough money to stay on at school, or who may leave school just because their friends do. Boudon gets qualified support from the British sociologist, A. H. Halsey, whose refutation of Bordieu we turn to shortly.

Bourdieu and his colleague, Althusser, are also sometimes accused of a mechanical or deterministic view of cultural reproduction. Bourdieu, in particular, is arraigned as a 'cultural determinist.' (This is not a simple issue and the student need not worry if he or she fails to understand it here. We return to it in Chapters 19 and 20). Basically, the charge of determinism means that Bourdieu is thought to believe that class culture is inevitably passed on from generation to generation, changing only in response to deeper developments in the economic substructure (or base) of society. Thus, he would recognise that changes in economic production, such as wide scale automation, might affect the way of life and the educational training of working people but, or so the accusation goes, he would not allow the possibility that working class people could change their own social position or cultural awareness outside the framework of such technological and socio-economic development. This charge seems broadly to be valid, although in defence of Bourdieu, he does allow that the educational system (and the cultural system generally) can operate in a 'relatively autonomous' (free) way. In other words, teachers, artists and other intellectuals and creative people have some freedom of thought and action. Bourdieu makes two major qualifications of this, however. First, such 'autonomy' does not ultimately change the class system; indeed, it may even provide a safety valve for it. Second, teachers and artists, like other people, are in any case socialised 'into' the class system and, consequently, most unlikely to think beyond it. Such freedom as exists is, therefore, very limited for most individuals. Althusser's position is similar to that of Bourdieu, although he uses different terminology to present it. We return to him in a later chapter (Chapter 19).

How Working Class Kids Get Working Class Jobs: An Observational Study

Paul Willis' book is entitled *Learning to Labour*, but its real concern is manifested in its sub-title: *How working class kids get working class jobs*. Willis describes a harsh collision between the tough working class 'lads' who are the subject of his study and the highly middle class world of the educational system. The 'lads' seldom even begin to struggle for examination success which not only requires a kind of mental discipline foreign to their experience but is unlikely to be of much use in the kind of manual jobs most of them expect to get. The lads tend to find the conformist behaviour of the 'lobes', as they call more hard-working pupils, a matter for mockery and amusement.

The school experience of the lads fails significantly to alter the course of their lives. Schools are middle class institutions in that they are run by middle class people (teachers) and because success in them requires conformity to middle class values, such as academic commitment, and middle class goals, such as a career. Comparing the lads to the lobes, Spansky, one of the lads, says:

> I mean, what will they remember of their school life? What will they have to look back on? Sitting in a classroom, sweating their bollocks off, you know, while we've been . . . I mean look at the things we can look back on, fighting on the Pakis, fighting on the JA's (Jamaicans). Some of the things we've done on teachers, it'll be a laff when we look back on it.

School seems to be good for a 'laff' and not much else. Judging by the following reactions of the lads to a lecture on the need for discipline at school and work, they obviously see little connection between school and the type of work they will do.

> *Spansky*: He makes the same points all the time, Fuzz. He's always on about if you get a job, you've got to do this, you've got to do that. I've done it. You don't have to do none of that. Just go to a place, ask for a man in charge, nothing like what he says.
> *Joey*: It's ridiculous . . .

Paul Willis notes that in later years, some of the 'lads' do come to regret their failure to realise that education did offer a possible escape from life as a manual labourer. But to what extent does the school system give the 'lads' a fair chance? Basically, Willis sympathises with their spirited rejection of the label of 'failures'. He appreciates, far more than Bourdieu seems to, that, in terms of their own class position, their way of life makes sense. It does so because most of them will, in fact, remain working class.

A. H. Halsey's Critique of the Theory of Cultural Reproduction

A. H. Halsey is one of the leading post-war British sociologists. His recent work draws heavily on a survey study of social change in Britain between 1913 and 1972, known as the Oxford Mobility Study. The original sample was of 10,000 men between the ages of 20 and 64.

Before describing the points on which Halsey differs from Bourdieu, it is important to be clear on their fundamental points of agreement. They are at one in stressing and lamenting the fact that many working class children do not reach anything approaching their full educational potential and, therefore, get jobs below their capacity. Both want to change this situation, although they have different views about how this might be done (see next chapter).

A substantial and important point of emphasis, rather than a total disagreement, divides Halsey and Bourdieu. To explain this, we need first to introduce the difference between material and cultural factors affecting educational attainment. Material factors are physical and environmental, such as the standard of housing, clothes and food. Virtually, they amount to 'the things money can buy.' Cultural factors refer to less tangible matters of values, norms and attitudes. We have already seen that Bourdieu argues that it is the possession of 'cultural capital' which accounts for the educational success of middle class children; school merely plays a part, albeit an important one, in the reproduction of cultural advantage. In his major work, *Origins and Destinations*, with A. F. Heath and J. M. Ridge (1980), Halsey tends to emphasise material rather than cultural factors in explaining class differences in educational attainment. He makes a number of points. Firstly, drawing on data from the Oxford study, he shows that there has been a substantial and progressive tendency for children to improve on the formal educational attainment of previous generations, and that even in state selective schools (mainly grammar schools selecting at 11), the 'overwhelming feature' was that the majority of pupils came from social backgrounds in which neither parent had an education of grammar school quality. Clearly, therefore, these first generation 'selected-school' pupils could not have inherited their cultural advantage from parents who did not have it to pass on.

A second point in Halsey's case is his critique of Jackson and Marsden's *Education and the Working Class,* a piece of research that seems to support Bourdieu's thesis. Out of a sample of 88 working class boys who went to grammar school, Jackson and Marsden found that a much higher number (34) than would have been expected purely on the basis of chance, came from 'sunken' middle class backgrounds. By 'sunken' middle class, they mean working class families with middle class relatives or families whose head had previously owned a small business. Halsey's data, however, forces him to work with a slightly different definition of sunken middle class; even so, his findings lead in the opposite direction from Jackson and Marsden's. His evidence is that the relative chances of obtaining selective education declined for those from educated backgrounds, and that this was true of the sunken middle class as well as others. The group of middle class children that *did* benefit disproportionately from selective education did not have selectively educated parents, and so could not have inherited cultural capital in this way. Finally, although Halsey fully accepts that working class children are educationally disadvantaged, he makes much of the fact that those who did get places at grammar school *and* survived there to take 'O' levels did almost as well as children from middle class backgrounds. The problem, of course, as Halsey recognises, is that relatively few working class children got into grammar schools in the first place.

Although Halsey emphasises material rather than cultural factors in explaining the educational under-attainment of working class children, he is not conclusive on the issue. Indeed, he has to concede that class cultural, as well as material factors, may account for the fact that, under the tripartite system, a much higher proportion of middle class children sat 'O' levels. Disadvantage took effect particularly at the 11+ examination which prevented a large number of able working class children, as well as 'border-line' children from all classes, from obtaining an academic education.

Halsey is aware of the need to take into consideration the change in the secondary system from tripartite to comprehensive in explaining the relatively low attainment of working class children. In doing this, he uses the terminology of Raymond Boudon, who categorises the educational effects of class stratification into the primary and the secondary. As interpreted by Halsey and applied to British education, primary effects are cultural and material differences that hamper educational success in early schooling, and secondary effects are those that govern performance at secondary school level. Halsey suggests that, under the tripartite system, primary effects probably predominated, but that with the widespread abolition of the 11+ examination and the introduction of comprehensive education, secondary effects may be more potent. Their operation could well prevent the improvement in educational opportunity and attainment of working class children that comprehensivisation was widely expected to bring about (see next chapter).

Halsey stresses that class is 'a major' factor affecting educational attainment, but he avoids sweeping generalisation in favour of closely reasoned argument supported by detailed evidence. The following quotation, taken from one of his reviews, perhaps reveals his complex spirit:

> Life, including the life of the . . . examination room, is understood better by gamblers than by mechanistic theoreticians. The dice are loaded – by class, by sex, by date of birth and even, perhaps . . . by genes. Among these, the force of class is a major one: it affects deeply the structure of opportunity. The force of stratification is still wider and deeper. But neither make it possible to deduce automatically the fate of particular individuals.

2 Education, The Economy and the Preparation of a Labour Force

The preparation of a labour force requires not only the teaching of specific skills, such as the three 'R's,' typing or computing, but also the more general socialisation of individuals to accept the discipline of work and, to some extent, their own likely place within the occupational structure. We will begin this section by presenting a functionalist perspective on these points, and then introduce Marxist and liberal refutations.

Functionalism, Occupational Selection and Social Mobility
Talcott Parsons gives a highly functionalist description of how he considers the educational system operates in relation to the

occupational structure. He suggests that elementary (primary) schools sort out pupils according to their general level of ability (capacity), that secondary schools establish the more specific abilities and, accordingly, direct some to work and others on to further education:

> Very broadly we may say that the elementary school phase is concerned with the internalisation in children of motivation to achievement. The focus is on the *level* of capacity . . .
>
> In approaching the question of the types of capacity differentiated, it should be kept in mind that secondary school is the principal springboard from which lower-status persons will enter the labour force, whereas those achieving higher status will continue their formal education in college, and some of them beyond.

Parsons, then, believes that the educational system actually does what is generally claimed for it – that is, selects people according to their ability and qualifies them accordingly. He and other functionalists tend to assume that there is a rough correspondence between individual intelligence, individual attainment (a pupil's measured performance) at school, and the job he eventually gets. Parsons sees the allocation of occupational status on the basis of 'achievement' as strongly characteristic of modern capitalist societies and particularly of the United States. More traditional societies allocated people to occupations on the basis of 'ascription' (by birth). Ralph Turner also considers that genuine and intense competition operates in the American educational system through comprehensive high schools, and he calls the resulting social mobility (movement up and down the social scale) 'contest' mobility. By contrast, he regards mobility of talented lower class children in Britain as 'sponsored' – through the grammar school system. This distinction, made in the nineteen fifties, has been blurred as a result of comprehensivisation in England and Wales. In any case, Turner's argument is severely weakened by the fact that he failed adequately to consider that lower social class membership substantially hinders social mobility in both countries.

The Relationship between Functionalism and the Hereditary View of Intelligence

It is clear that the functionalist case rests on whether intelligence, academic attainment and occupational position do, in fact, correlate strongly with one another. In particular, if intelligence and occupational status do not correlate strongly, then the functionalist model is largely discredited and the possibility must be examined that other factors are more relevant in determining occupational status. The functionalist position has recently acquired support from the work of a number of psychologists on both sides of the Atlantic though, as these scholars are not sociologists, it would be misleading to think of them as functionalists when their work merely complements the functionalist position. In Britain, Hans Eysenck is the foremost of these and, in the United States, Arthur Jensen and Carl Bereiter have been prominent. Before briefly summarising their major points, something must be said about what is meant by intelligence. Intelligence refers to general cognitive ability, or the ability to reason, comprehend and make judgements. It is produced by heredity and environment. Psychologists do not agree on the precise relative importance of these two factors: some put the influence of heredity as low as 50%, whilst others put it at 80%, or even slightly higher.

As one might expect, those psychologists who consider that intelligence and occupational status strongly correlate, estimate the hereditary element of intelligence at the high end. The 'high-estimate' viewpoint received a blow when it was demonstrated that the methodology of Sir Cyril Burt, on whose work the hereditarian case partly rested, was unscientific. Nevertheless, the debate continues. The psychologists who stress heredity – we may call them 'the hereditarians' – explain the fact that the children of parents of high occupational status also tend to achieve similar status in terms of their relatively higher level of inherited intelligence. The same applies, in reverse, to people of low social origin. Of course, although the hereditarians argue that there is a strong link between the level of intelligence of parents and children, they accept that this correspondance is not complete. For the minority of less intelligent middle class children and more intelligent working class children, the possibility of downward or upward mobility, respectively, occurs by reason of the level of their intelligence. The hereditarians regard the fact that there is only a fairly small amount of long-range upward or downward mobility in either Britain or the United States as evidence for, not against, their argument. Like functionalists, the hereditarian psychologists consider that the educational system 'does its job.' It qualifies people according to their ability and directs them towards appropriate occupations.

Marxism, Occupational Selection and Social Mobility

To date, the major refutation of the above argument comes from the American Marxists, Herbert Bowles and Samuel Gintis. We will present their refutation first and then describe the broader theoretical context of their position. On the basis of detailed statistical analysis, Bowles and Gintis show that, in the United States, the probability of obtaining economic success is considerably greater for those born of parents of high socio-economic status than for those of high intelligence. Put plainly, socio-economic background is generally a much more significant factor in obtaining economic success than is intelligence. They show that a man born in the bottom decile (tenth) in terms of socio-economic background has only 4.2% probability of being in the top fifth of income distribution, whereas a person born in the top decile in terms of socio-economic background has a 43.9% probability of being in the top fifth of income distribution as an adult. That this extreme inequality of outcome is due to socio-economic background and not to the differential distribution of intelligence is shown by a further sophisticated statistical calculation. This calculation is hypothetical (rests on supposition) and demonstrates how income *would* be distributed *on the basis of measured intelligence only*. Because the general level of measured intelligence is somewhat higher for those born into higher socio-economic backgrounds, those born into the top decile have, in this hypothetical model, a *marginally* better chance of reaching the top fifth of income distribution than those born into the bottom decile on the basis of 'the genetic inheritance of I.Q.' (Bowles and Gintis). Those born in the bottom decile would have an 18.7 probability of being in the top fifth in income, and those born in the top decile a 21.4 probability on the basis of differences in intelligence alone. These figures are so far from the actual patterns described above that we have to agree with Bowles and Gintis' insistence on the unimportance of I.Q. and the prime importance of socio-economic background in explaining economic success. The best hope for obtaining high income, then, is to be born into a high socio-economic background. As Bowles and Gintis say succinctly: 'The power and privilege of the capitalist class are often inherited, but not through superior genes.'

Another American, Christopher Jencks, has also written with authority in this area. He sums up the matter effectively when he writes that although the heredity-environment argument is likely to rage indefinitely, the best evidence

> ... does not, however, suggest that variations in cognitive skill account for much of the inequality among American adults.
> There is nearly as much economic inequality among individuals with identical test scores as in the general population.

Jencks further points out that schools themselves cannot make an unequal and hierarchial society equal. For that to happen, income, wealth, cultural opportunity and status would have to be more equally distributed. This observation is obvious but nonetheless true.

It is a strength of Bowles and Gintis's case that they use their opponents' data on the relationship between heredity and intelligence. Other authorities also see this relationship as less strong than Jensen and Eysenck do and point out that not only does the relative level of educational attainment of a child vary over time but so do scores in intelligence tests. Indeed, it is actually possible to prepare successfully for intelligence tests, so they can hardly be regarded as neutral instruments of measurement. J. W. B. Douglas, whose work we refer to above, regards intelligence tests in this more sceptical light. He argues that scores achieved in them, as well as academic performance, are considerably influenced by social background.

A Reformer's Response to Marxists and Functionalists: A. H. Halsey

Halsey rejects what he sees as the pessimism of Marxists and the conservatism of many functionalists. Yet, in arguing that educational reform can facilitate upward mobility from the working class, he has to work hard with the facts produced by his own research and that of his colleagues. The data he presents in *Origins and Destinations* largely confirms the established view that in Britain, as in America, the offspring of the middle class have a very much greater chance of remaining middle class than the offspring of the working class have of becoming middle class, (over six times greater, depending on precisely how middle and working class are defined). What is more, this situation did not substantially change between 1913 and 1972. What *did* happen is that because of the expansion of the service sector and the contraction of the industrial sector of the economy, more middle class jobs became available. All classes benefited, but the working class did *not* do so any more than others. Indeed, in the years following the immediate post-Second World War period, it did relatively less well.

In the face of such evidence, Halsey is determinedly hopeful rather than optimistic. He conceded that, so far, the middle class has benefited proportionately more from the expansion of state education than the working class, but he argues that this would be unlikely to continue if *further* expansion took place. Given that middle class youth is now largely catered for, an additional increase in educational opportunity would be bound to benefit the working class. He also hopes that as (and *if*) the comprehensive system becomes better established, it will reduce class inequalities in education. His own research, however, does not provide data on whether or not this is happening (see Chapter 6). The section of Halsey's book on future educational policy is, inevitably, more speculative than the rest of *Origins and Destinations*. Perhaps its implied corollary is that, in his view, there is, in any case, no practical alternative to reform.

Marxism, Economy, Education and Class

Marxists do not consider that the educational systems of advanced capitalist societies effectively and fairly match people to jobs. They believe that education in capitalist society contributes to the continuance of the class system and class inequality; in particular, it reproduces a labour force which is socialised to accept its lot and has, in any case, no adequate alternative means of survival. By 'socialised' we mean that the majority of working class children who 'fail' academically tend to accept their own 'failure' and the 'success' of most middle class children as legitimate. The fact that a small minority of working class children do 'make it' helps to foster the illusion that the educational system is fair and 'neutral,' and a highly unequal society presupposes that most children will fail academically and fill the lower occupations. In a sense, these matters become 'facts of life' for them, although, for many, an underlying sense remains that circumstances could be different.

123

Like Bourdieu, Bowles and Gintis give many examples of how social relationships in the educational system echo those of the economic system and thus prepare children for working life. They stress especially that educational institutions, like factories and offices, are intensely hierarchical. Like workers, pupils are expected to obey authority and have little or no control over the content of their work. This results in a feeling of non-involvement in, or *alienation* from, work. Only a minority of mainly middle class children go on to experience relative freedom and responsibility in study: fewer still are educated for leadership.

The American Marxist, Harry Braverman, has expanded interestingly and controversially the analysis that, far from being primarily involved in teaching working class children specific occupational skills, it is one of the hidden functions of schools to prepare children for the tedium of work (by being tedious themselves!). Braverman's critique, however, is more complex than this suggests and deserves fuller presentation. He sees the educational system as subordinate to the economic, but not, perhaps, as might be anticipated. He makes a powerful argument that most unskilled, semi-skilled and even many so-called skilled manual and non-manual jobs can be done with little or no skill at all (see Chapter 14). He therefore eliminates occupational training as a major function of education for the majority. Indeed, it is true that most jobs at these levels are learnt at work itself, not at school. He agrees that the three basic communication skills of reading, writing and arithmetic are learnt in schools, but he considers these to be necessary in the general context of modern life, rather than specifically at work (where, of course, they also help!) Braverman's thesis is supported by estimates that in Britain between two and five million adults are not fully literate; yet they obviously manage to do their jobs, despite this handicap. He also differentiates between the kind of work just described and professional, managerial and other work of a similar level, for which lengthy training is necessary. Some critics have suggested that even with these occupations, the length of time spent in studying in institutions could be profitably shortened. Thus, Robert Dore suggests that engineers could be well trained through a combination of supervised experience 'on-the-job' and part-time or short, full-time courses.

What, then, are the functions that Braverman thinks schools do perform? He considers that they socialise and 'child mind' whilst parents are at work. He points out that the raising of the minimum age for compulsory education has coincided with the increase in the numbers of working mothers. His comments on the relationship between educational expansion and the rate of unemployment are interesting and are echoed by the British social historian, Harold Silver. They both claim that, in the nineteen thirties, this relationship served to reduce unemployment amongst the young by removing large numbers of them from the job market. In addition, it provides jobs in teaching and administration for many thousands of middle class people. The increase in those staying on for further education in Britain during the late nineteen seventies and early eighties similarly 'mops up' some of the unemployed. However useful or not qualifications may be, the pursuit of them occupies the time and energy of young people. Significantly, provision has been made increasingly for less qualified sixteen year olds, who are the weakest in the job market, to stay on in education. Braverman's rather exaggerated remark that 'there is no longer any place for the young in society than school' refers to the role of schools generally, but it has a particular application to those of school leaving age.

Braverman not only argues that few job-specific skills are learnt in pre-sixteen education, but also that the 'qualification paper-chase' is in itself unnecessary and futile. Whilst there is empirical support for the first position, the second depends very much more on point of view. It is true, however, that pupils and the general public are sometimes unaware of the extent to which the job-market value of qualifications has become substantially less now that more people have them at all levels. To take two examples, teacher training and librarianship; the GCE qualifications required for entry into both these courses have risen. This does not guarantee that the people now entering them will be better than in the past or that they will do the job more effectively, but they will appear more impressive on paper. Braverman suggests that employers use qualifications as a screening device to ensure a minimum quality of entrant and, to maintain the same standard over time, they tend to adjust their requirement upwards. He cites some interesting survey evidence from Berg that there is now chronic over-qualification

125

in many areas of unemployment, particularly at the clerical level. Berg's data also showed that over-educated employees tended to do a worse job, and to be more dissatisfied than the less well qualified.

Although the functional relationship between the educational and economic systems in Britain and America is, in some respects, rather obscure, its importance should not be underestimated. Modern nations require, at the least, a highly educated minority, particularly in the areas of scientific and technological research, and a generally literate and numerate population. Accordingly, education is a major item of government expenditure in all such societies. Some critics have suggested that the educational system in Britain ought to be more closely directed to serve the needs of the economy. In many other countries, the government insists on closer control: the Soviet Union is an example. Its planned economy is dependent on the government's knowing in advance the number, quality and variety of skills of the country's labour force. Japan is another country that has had a recent tradition of centralised planning in education: its 'economic miracle' would not have been possible without the efficiency of its educational system. Great emphasis is placed on the development of mathematical and scientific skills; although this has achieved results, it has often been at the price of putting extreme pressure on teenagers.

Factors influencing Educational Attainment

The various factors that influence educational attainment are interconnected and, to a greater or lesser extent, social class, including class cultural experience, probably always plays some part in an individual's educational career. The factors we discuss here are social class and culture, intelligence, the quality of schools, gender and race. The educational policy of central and local governments also plays a role in providing the resources for educational success (or failure), and that issue is dealt with in the next chapter.

1 Social Class, Class Culture and Intelligence
As the above points have been discussed extensively in previous sections of this chapter, they need only to be briefly reviewed

126

here. There is a virtual consensus among sociologists that social class has a major effect on educational attainment, although a number of functionalists and 'hereditarian' psycologists give greater emphasis to intelligence which they argue, or sometimes appear to assume, is overwhelmingly (about 80%) hereditary. There is a growing debate among those sociologists who stress the influence of social class on educational achievement about the relative importance of cultural and material factors. It may be, as Halsey himself implies, that it is simply not possible to separate the two entirely. In any case, the family is seen as the primary medium through which class factors, cultural and material, are focused, with the school taking an important secondary role. Despite current debate, Morrison and McIntyre's summary, published in 1971, of cultural and material aspects of home environment, which researchers had consistently found related to academic success, remains a useful check-list:

1 Parental Attitudes to Education
2 Educational Level of the Home
3 Family Size (it is generally an educational disadvantage to be a member of a large family)
4 Quality of Maternal Care of Young Children
5 Material Prosperity of the Home
6 Social Disorganisation
7 Abnormal Family Background (for example, a 'broken' home)

Working class children are more disadvantaged than middle class children in respect of the first six factors, (though family size is of much less significance, as a general tendency for families to be smaller was apparent in the nineteen seventies). The seventh factor is increasingly likely to affect children of all social backgrounds, owing to the rapid rise in the divorce rate between the mid nineteen sixties and late nineteen seventies. It is worth adding that the precise way in which each of the above factors influences educational attainment varies, not only between the classes, but from individual to individual.

The two tables printed below summarise differences in educational qualifications by social class and by sex. The differences between the educational qualifications of the sexes has diminished somewhat amongst younger people, but the data given below presents a useful overview of the total population. The degree to which higher social classes are better formally

Highest educational qualification by social class, males, Great Britain (percentages*)

	Social class (R.G. (S.E.)70)						
	1	2	3	4	5	6	All
Degree or equivalent	53	8	7	0.3	0.1	0.2	5
Higher education below degree	20	10	12	2	0.5	—	5
G.C.E.† A level or equivalent	10	9	10	4	2	1	6
G.C.E.† O level or equivalent, or C.S.E.§ grade 1	7	20	20	12	6	3	13
C.S.E.§ other grades/ commercial/apprenticeship	1	8	8	16	7	4	10
Foreign and other	5	4	4	3	3	1	3
None	3	41	39	63	81	90	57
Social class of sample	5	14	19	41	16	6	100

*Percentages over 1 rounded
†G.C.E. = General Certificate of Education
§C.S.E. = Certificate of Secondary Education

Highest educational qualification by social class, females, Great Britain (percentages*)

	Social class (R.G.(S.E.)70)						
	1	2	3	4	5	6	All
Degree or equivalent	(21)	4	3	0.5	0.1	—	2
Higher education below degree	(1)	11	11	0.7	0.4	—	6
G.C.E. A level or equivalent	(2)	3	3	2	0.5	—	2
G.C.E. O level or equivalent, or C.S.E. grade 1	(4)	11	19	8	5	1	12
C.S.E. other grades/ commercial/apprenticeship	(1)	8	14	8	4.	2	9
Foreign and other	(2)	5	4	2	2	0.4	3
None	(3)	60	46	79	88	96	66
Social class of sample	0.6	4	50	8	28	9	100

*Percentages over 1 rounded
( ) Actual numbers, too small for conversion to percentages
(Devised from table 4.7, General Household Survey 1972 1975)
Source: Ivan Reid, *Social Class Differences in Britain,* 1977, pp. 168–9.

qualified is very marked. Compare, for instance, the data on degrees and social class.

2 Schools, 'Labelling,' and Cultural Reproduction

We have already seen how the Marxists, Bourdieu and Bernstein, see the educational system as a middle class agency which helps to reproduce middle class cultural ascendancy. A number of interactionists, in Britain and America, have reached similar conclusions. Their theoretical focus is, however, in some cases narrower than that of the Marxists, and their method of research, likewise, is on a smaller scale and largely participant-observational.

A pioneering study in this area is David Hargreaves' *Social Relations in a Secondary School*. The secondary school in question was an all boys' secondary modern school in which Hargreaves took on the participant observational role of teacher. His study was concerned with the factors *within* the school context which contribute to the creation of two sub-cultures, 'the academic and the delinquescent.' He emphasises how academic streaming greatly affects the membership of these two sub-cultures. Those who were placed in the lowest ('E') stream were the most likely to become part of the delinquescent (or delinquency-prone) sub-culture, whereas those in the 'A' stream tended to conform. Hargreaves attributes the formation of these peer-group sub-cultures directly to the school's policy of streaming which, he claims, results in an increasing feeling of inferiority on the part of the lower stream boys as they progress into the third and fourth forms. We can, then, conveniently think of the streaming process as a form of *labelling* which, in this instance and presumably often, has unintended consequences. It must be said that other sources show that social class factors mediated through the home and neighbourhood also contribute to the formation of youth peer-groups, although these were beyond the practical limits of Hargreaves' research.

Colin Lacey's *Hightown Grammar* is a precise parallel study to that of Hargreaves, concerned with the effect of streaming in a grammar school. His findings complement those of Hargreaves and he adds the observation that when frustrated expectations at school coincide with problems at home, 'the worst cases of emotional disturbance occur.'

In Paul Willis' study, *Learning to Labour*, the role of the school, including the labelling of working class 'lads' and the formation of what he calls *anti-school sub-cultures*, is put in a much wider socio-economic context. In pointing out that the academic failure of the 'lads' provides new recruits to manual labour, and so helps to maintain the capitalist system, Willis shows himself to be a structural sociologist as well as a detailed ethnographer (a social scientist who studies cultural activity through detailed observation).

Like Willis, Nell Keddie draws on both interactionist and structural perspectives in her detailed examination of how cultural reproduction occurs in the classroom through the labelling process. She argues that sometimes intelligent working class children may be labelled, or mis-labelled, stupid because of 'troublesome' behaviour. This label can become a 'self-fulfilling prophecy,' if the child accepts it and loses the motivation to compete academically. Keddie distances herself, however, from Bourdieu and Bernstein by rejecting any implication that working class culture is inferior: she refers to this view as 'the *myth* of cultural deprivation.' She argues that the educational system should build on working class culture rather than ignore or repress it – a view that Bernstein himself accepts as having clarified his own position. One problem is that nobody has yet explained in detail what a curriculum based on, or even substantially reflecting, working class culture might be like, or how it would help working class children to function better in capitalist society (if, indeed, that were its aim). The way of life of the 'lads' seems to defy the limits of any curriculum outside that imposed by the experience and discipline of work. We return to these issues in our discussion of educational policy in the next chapter.

3 The Quality of Schools

A piece of research which contrasts markedly with those described in the previous section is that of Michael Rutter *et al.*, *Fifteen Thousand Hours*. Rutter's methods were highly empirical and statistical and both his methods and his findings have attracted strong criticism, but he has stood by his main conclusions. *Fifteen Thousand Hours*, published in 1979, summarised several years' research into the performance of twelve inner London secondary schools. The aim of the research was to discover why some schools 'succeeded' and others did not. The team looked at four factors: attendance, academic achievement, behaviour in school, and the rate of delinquency outside it.

Rutter found that schools obtained very varied ratings on all the above counts, even when difference in social class background and intelligence in intake was allowed for. Those schools that scored well on one factor tended to do well on others. What, then, on Rutter's evidence, makes for a successful school? Pupil performance on the above four points is associated with a certain school 'ethos' of which sound teaching and professional behaviour is the keynote. Teachers who are punctual, well-organised, patient, encourage pupils, share extra-curricular activities with them, and can inspire by example, are likely to get the best from pupils. Whatever the teacher's style and values, consistency helps. This applies as much to senior staff as to junior, and Rutter adds that an established system of rewards and punishments improves pupils' performance. Because some schools were successful on all four points, the researchers sought an underlying reason. These successful schools varied in their approach from the traditional to the progressive but the researchers concluded that what they had in common was a consistent commitment to their own values and rules. This consistency created an atmosphere or ethos that was secure and purposeful and in which effective work could take place and good human relationships prosper.

Fifteen Thousand Hours was initially well received both by the press and by many influential academics. Like many books that elicit such a response, it clarified and built upon a body of sentiment that had been growing for some time. In the mid-nineteen seventies, a concern for academic standards and quality in education, which had been simmering for some time, rose to the surface. The Bennet Report of 1976, comparing various kinds of teaching methods in primary schools found, amongst other things, that whatever method of teaching was used, the ability, experience and commitment of the individual teacher was a crucial variable. Formal and informal teaching methods could both be successful – *provided* that they were done well. Again, themes of consistency and commitment are stressed.

We can divide Rutter's critics into those who attack the quality of his research in its own terms and those who argue that, in addition to the limitations of his methodology, he also asks inadequate, if not wrong, questions. Of the former, several are especially concerned with the limitations of his statistical method. Amongst these, particularly, are Anthony Heath and Peter Clifford of Oxford University, who argue that the effect on performance which Rutter attributes to secondary school factors might well have been caused by the carry-over effect of primary schooling or by the interest of parents. In brief, Rutter has not controlled for the various non-school factors that are well known to affect children's school attainment.

The second group of Rutter's critics put their criticisms of his methodology within a broad critique of his whole theoretical approach. Michael Young rejects the assumption that social relations in school can be adequately understood on the basis of a model that assumes value consensus within the school. He finds it inconceivable that a school could 'function' or be properly analysed without reference to class, gender and racial divisions. To him, it is ludicrous to applaud consistency without raising the question of 'consistency in the pursuit of what purposes?' Rutter's answer to Young was that his research was only concerned with school performance in relation to the four factors mentioned above.

A further criticism of the report is that it tells us nothing about the fate of the children when they leave school. Rutter does not even present data on the question of whether, because children in some schools do better in public examinations than others, their occupational prospects are improved – a point which cannot be assumed, given that most of the children in the study were highly disadvantaged and that even 'the examination successes' were moderate by national standards.

Perhaps Rutter cannot be condemned for asking a particular set of questions, but clearly these questions are limited in scope and context and, to judge by the current state of debate, the answers to them require to be treated with caution. Even so, it is worth recalling in the heat of argument that, if interpreted cautiously and in the light of other relevant data, Rutter's findings appear neither startling nor particularly original. Writing in 1968 of lower manual working class pupils, J. W. Douglas said:

> Although (they) . . . are at a disadvantage relative to the middle class in all types of school, those at schools with a good record are far less handicapped.

132

4 Gender

Despite the changes that the women's movement has helped to bring about, certain social roles in our society tend to be allocated to men and others to women. It still remains true that, in a family context, the man is expected to be the 'main breadwinner' and the woman to take care of her home, even if she also works outside it. This division of labour, based on sexual difference, has become more blurred but it remains strong.

Education plays a major role in preparing males and females for their traditionally different social roles and therefore helps to maintain a division of labour based on sexual differences. The table (p. 128) shows how relatively ill-equipped woman are, in terms of formal qualifications, to compete with men. This is especially true of working class women. Why is there such inequality of educational attainment between the sexes? At the most obvious level, girls tend to study subjects such as needlework or home economics which will help them either in housework or in certain 'female' occupations, rather than subjects such as woodwork or technical drawing which are considered 'more suitable' for boys. Although it is now illegal, under the terms of the 1975 Sex Discrimination Act, for schools to discriminate on grounds of gender in offering school subjects, advice and guidance often steer pupils in predictably traditional directions. As long as society as a whole tends to assume that the pattern of a person's life is largely determined by sexual identity, this is, perhaps, inevitable. It is the 'hidden curriculum' of sexist assumption rather than formal discrimination that operates against girls.

In an interesting article, 'Why are there so few women scientists and engineers?', Tessa Blackstone and Helen Weinrich-Haste offer some detailed analysis of female under-achievement in education. They argue that girls 'learn' to under-achieve. In particular, there is some evidence that parents and teachers expect and even demand academic success for boys, but not so much for girls. They point out the problem of sex *stereotyping* in which girls are expected to do certain kinds of subjects and boys others. At the most general level, sciences are sometimes thought of as hard, masculine subjects concerned with physical realities, and the arts as the opposite. They mention clear evidence that stereotyping has more powerful effect in mixed than in single-sex schools. In the latter, girls are more likely to choose and do well in maths and sciences. It seems that the very presence of boys has a negative effect on girl pupils' (and perhaps teachers') educational expectations. At least, this is so in England. Research on the comparative educational performance of West Indian boys and girls suggests that the strength of the matriarchal family tradition in the West Indies and amongst West Indian immigrants in Britain seems to give the girls a positive and 'coping' attitude to work, including school work, and they do better than West Indian boys.

It is in the context of 16-plus education that gender disadvantage becomes strongly apparent. At 'O' level, the number of passes achieved is roughly the same for both sexes even though there is a predictable concentration in different subject areas. At 'A' level, considerable inequality of achievement is obvious. In 1973, boys achieved a total of 189,000 passes compared to 139,000 for girls (Meighan). Further inequalities are more marked at degree level. In 1976/77, there were 43,000 male graduates and only 23,000 female graduates – although this gap is decreasing slowly. Further, the great majority of graduates in law, science and mathematics-degrees which tend to lead to careers in better-paid professions – are men. Women still tend to be concentrated in arts, education and social science departments. When we look at the situation of non-advanced courses in further education, the picture is quite different. About as many females as males are involved in a wide variety of non-advanced courses in major establishments of further education (*Social Trends*, 1979). Post-16 education for women is, then, generally at a lower level than for men. We can suggest two reasons why this is so.

Firstly, society as a whole, including many, if not the majority of women, has lower career expectations of women than of men. This inevitably means lower educational expectations as well. As we shall see later (Chapter 11), these lower expectations are fully reflected in career as well as educational performance. Although individual teachers may dislike this situation, schools in general probably reflect society on this issue. Secondly, and very importantly, the structure of society still supports a division of labour in which men are the 'main breadwinners' and women look after the children and home. As we shall see in Chapter 11, there have been significant but not fundamental changes in this situation. Again, the educational system tends to mirror dominant attitudes on gender. Blackstone refers to the 'caution and lower aspirations' girls show in their career choices. If this is 'realistic' in terms of the way society is, then, perhaps, the challenge is to change further the dominant social attitudes towards gender, and not merely the educational system that reflects them. It may be that the cliché, 'education cannot change society,' applies as much to gender as to class inequality.

5 Race

The problem that race presents in education is vividly shown in the table below.

Percentage of Pupils fully educated in the UK placed in Upper Quartile on transfer to Secondary School
(in the Inner London Education Authority)

	English	Mathematics	Verbal reasoning
West Indian origin	9.2	7.4	7.2
Asian origin	19.3	20.2	21.2
Indigenous	25.0	22.9	19.8

Source: Alan Little, 'Schools and Race', in *Five Views of Multi-Racial Britain*, 1978, p. 61.

The performance of children of Asian origin is comparable to those of indigenous or British origin and does not, therefore, constitute a major problem. The performance of children of West Indian origin is much worse than that of both the other groups and does, therefore, constitute a considerable problem. Comparably low performances have been found for black children in the United States. The evidence of the school performance of West Indian children is not all depressing, however. A study by the National Children's Bureau showed a noticeable improvement in the achievements of *second generation* British West Indian children, although they remained below Asian and British. There is also some evidence that the secondary school performance of West Indian children is relatively better than their primary school performance. One very limited survey of school leavers in five multi-racial inner-city schools shows that

135

West Indian boys and, especially, girls achieved results that were generally better than those of English boys and girls. The author of this research, Geoffrey Driver, attributes the success of West Indian girls to the strength derived from the matriarchal tradition in Jamaica and carried over, out of practical necessity, to England. A major problem with Driver's research is that he does not control for social class variables and it may be that he is comparing groups of white and black children of different socio-economic background. In any case, he himself counsels against generalising from his research and we must pitch our discussion on wider and more pessimistic findings.

For those who consider that black people are genetically less intelligent than Caucasian (Indo-European) people, no problem is presented by the evidence of their comparatively low achievement. Jensen, for instance, believes that the fact that negroes score, on average, 12 to 15 points less on general intelligence tests than whites is a clear indication that they are innately substantially less intelligent. From his point of view, the kindest course would be to accept this and to cease trying to make them achieve levels of academic attainment that are generally beyond them. A variety of arguments can be cited against Jensen's view, but here we will concentrate exclusively on the environmental factors which might affect the performance of blacks in attainment and in intelligence tests.

The first environmental factor to consider is the child's home and family. A disproportionate number of immigrant families relative to the indigenous population live in old, often inner city houses which lack basic amenities. Partly because of the stresses brought about by slavery, the black family in the United States, the West Indies, and now Britain, tends to be less stable than that of whites or Asian immigrants. In particular, there is a higher proportion of one-parent families among West Indians than the indigenous population. We know that children from one-parent families are often the most disadvantaged of all. Another cultural heritage from the West Indies is the stricter, 'power-based' discipline of many West Indian homes. It has often been noted that this is poor preparation for the liberal climate of many British schools. Sometimes, when West Indian children do not find the authoritarian form of discipline they expect, they threaten the orderly running of classes and even schools.

A further example of clash between West Indian sub-culture and indigenous culture is language usage. The school is the major arena (one might almost say 'battlefield') in which this clash occurs. The difference between the form of English used by most West Indians and 'standard' English is great enough to cause some difficulty in communication between West Indian pupils and their (mainly) white teachers. This difficulty is often seen in terms of a language 'problem' of the West Indian students rather than one caused by cultural differences between pupils and teachers. In fact, the form of English used by most West Indians is a *dialect* of English, containing grammatical features which reflect various West African languages. Thus, *'he stand still'* and *'six boy'* are usages that occur regularly in the writing of West Indian children. A further point is that black sub-culture in both Britain and, especially, the United States has been extremely rich in the production or reworking of words. Thus, 'pop' words like 'hippie,' 'cool' and 'high' have their origin in black sub-culture. Sometimes black teenagers employ their distinctive linguistic forms and vocabulary deliberately to cut themselves off from white society which they feel has, in any case, rejected them. Given the above circumstances, it is not surprising that black children generally perform less well than whites on vocabulary tests.

The problems Asian pupils have in learning English as a second language have been recognised and, to some extent, met. It is only recently that the extent of the difficulties facing West Indian pupils has been appreciated and measures to accommodate them started. In fairness to Jensen, his case does not rest primarily on the fact that blacks perform worse on vocabulary tests than whites. The evidence is also that blacks score lower on tests of non-verbal reasoning – a major aspect of general intelligence tests. N. J. MacKintosh's response to Jensen is that non-verbal reasoning may itself be an ability which develops better in some environments than others. Groups that lack experience in the sort of abstract thinking measured by non-verbal reasoning tests might be expected to do worse at them.

Finally, there is much disturbing evidence that the *self-image* of many West Indian children is low. Low self-esteem undermines the learning process. In trying to do something, it certainly helps to believe that it can be done. Often, West Indian children appear to have lost confidence in their ability to succeed educationally. In the course of research in the Southern United States, Robert Coles noted that the drawings of black children contained some strange features. They tended to picture themselves as small, dowdy and, sometimes, with various features missing, whereas they portrayed white children in a large and positive way. Even the weather and landscape on the pictures depicting the white children were better! More recently, Bernard Coard came across a similar phenomenon in Britain (*Urban Education*, 1971). No doubt black self-image is undermined partly by the depressing position of blacks historically (since slavery), and in most present-day industrial societies. In addition, teachers themselves can unwittingly damage the confidence of black children. A particularly harmful example would be to decide prematurely that a West Indian child is 'not academic' and to place him in a bottom stream, although there are many less obvious ways of slighting a child than that.

We have not, in this section, refuted Jensen's arguments about black intelligence directly nor in the highly technical terms in which he presents them. Instead, we have simply described the alternative possibility that environment and cultural interaction (between black and white) produce profound problems likely to affect the attainment levels and, quite possibly, 'intelligence' scores achieved by black pupils. Until these problems have been more fully understood and fairly and sensitively accommodated, there can be no serious talk of black inferiority. Indeed, to do so might seem more like an example of further ideological discrimination than of scientific observation.

Sociology, Ideology and Policy

The recurrent issue in this chapter is that of wasted potential. The relative under-achievement of many working class children, girls and young blacks needs more than analysis: it begs for solution. Such is the strength of feeling generated by these issues that opinion and values always threaten to break through the posture of objectivity and scientific neutrality adopted by some researchers. Sociologists have, of course, every right to

138

support their values and beliefs with research findings provided that they do so with honesty and with appropriate caution. In the next chapter we examine some practical educational policy issues in which sociologists have been much engaged.

Guide to further reading and study

Sorting through the vast literature on the sociology of education for material to recommend to 'A' level students still at an early stage in their course is rather like looking for a needle in a haystack. Certainly, this is an area in which the teacher needs to have a range of carefully-graded and representative (of the perspectives) handouts. Two textbooks that might be recommended to first year higher education students are M. D. Shipman's *The Sociology of the School* (Longman, 1975) and Ivan Reid's *Sociological Perspectives on School and Education* (Open Books, 1978), but these had better wait until the second year of an 'A' level student's course. Shipman's book is characteristically clearly written and simply presented.

There are many collections of readers covering the area. Two or three of the best of these, used selectively, would provide examples of writings from most relevant perspectives. Deservedly popular is the Open University's set book, *School and Society* (Routledge and Kegan Paul, 1971). The articles and extracts are mostly very short. Interpretive perspectives are especially in evidence but other approaches are also represented. Another excellent book of short, varied articles published by Routledge is *Education and the Urban Crisis* (1977), edited by Frank Field. These reflect practical problems and issues rather than sociological perspectives. Frank Musgrove's *School and the Social Order* (John Wiley, 1980) gives an abrasive review of the state of educational sociology and perhaps marks an upturn in an already discernible reaction against the extremes of phenomenology. Like Halsey's *Origins and Destinations* (Clarendon, 1980) it is a tome for the library rather than the classroom. The latter can be referred to as a sophisticated example of empirical research as well as for its actual findings. There is nothing at our level on Bourdieu's interesting contribution to educational sociology which is one reason why I have given a fairly full analysis of his work here.

Education is an area which provides a ready opportunity for first-hand research for students and teachers. It offers perhaps the best opportunity of all topics for a research practical.

Past Questions

1 'The primary function of education is to transmit the values of society to a new generation.' Discuss. (AEB, 1978)
2 Examine the relationship between education and social stratification. (AEB, 1975)
3 Critically examine the view that informal relations between pupils are a means of coping with a meaningless formal curriculum. (JMB, 1977)
4 Girls, blacks and the lower working class are less successful in the education system than boys, whites and non-lower working class children. Select *one* of these pairs (e.g. girls/boys, blacks/whites, working class/non working class) and explain their relative 'success' or 'failure.' (AEB, 1976)

6 Social Problems and Social Policy with Particular Reference to Education and Health

Sociology, Social Problems and Social Policy

A social problem is a matter that causes difficulty, inconvenience or distress to a group or to the public at large. Poverty, racial conflict, and educational underattainment are social problems. No doubt the reader can think of many more. *A social policy is a course of action or plan to deal with a social problem or problems.* Sociologists can assist policy makers (usually, politicians) by precisely *identifying* and *explaining* the causes of given social problems. The word 'precisely' is operative here. Virtually everybody knows that there is some poverty, racism and educational underattainment, but in order to develop adequate policies to deal with these problems, governments, and often voluntary agencies (non-government bodies concerned with social problems) need to have hard data about them, and convincing explanations of their causes. This section seeks only to present the main links between sociology, social problems and social policy. Several chapters, including those on stratification (poverty), race, and gender deal with specific policy issues. We also examine some educational problems and the problem of health in terms of policy solutions later in this chapter.

The distinction between identifying and explaining social problems directly parallels that between descriptive and explanatory research made in Chapter 2. The government itself is by far the major collector, user and supplier to others of descriptive or statistical information not only on social problems but on most other matters of our national life. Most major government departments have large research staffs which collect and *collate* (categorise and compare) statistics relevant to their area. The Home Office, for instance, produces and publishes statistics on the administration of justice, criminal and penal matters, immigration, and other areas in which precise information is vital for policy formulation. Top civil servants in the Home Office and other departments are involved with policy creation at a much more important level than collecting statistics (not, in itself, a specifically sociological skill). They advise ministers. In the Home Office and, particularly, in the Department of Health and Social Security, a proportion of civil servants have a background or competence in the social sciences.

A more familiar, though not necessarily a greater, influence on social policy, is the work of sociologists based in institutions of higher education, particularly the universities, and other high status research establishments such as Political and Economic Planning (PEP). Sometime their work is directly funded by a government department. Thus, the PEP report on race relations of 1977, which we examine later in this book, was partly funded by the Home Office. The first major PEP report in

1967, greatly influenced the content of the 1968 Race Relations Act. The research contained in the 1977 report had already been published in more technical form between 1974 and 1976 and this, likewise, influenced the 1976 Race Relations Act. Relations between government and academic researchers do not always run smoothly. Sometimes a change of government presents a problem if the incoming and outgoing governments have a different attitude to a given problem. A. H. Halsey recounts how the Educational Priority Area projects were set up with the support of Anthony Crossland, the Labour government's Secretary of State at the Department of Education and Science, and closed down shortly after the election of a Conservative government in which Margaret Thatcher was at the DES. It is clear that Halsey feels that the EPA projects were hardly given the time and resources to develop their research side adequately.

Much sociological research that appears to have implications for social policy is not directly funded by, or otherwise linked with government. If having completed his research, the sociologist then wants to draw policy conclusions from it, he is faced with the problem of publicising (as well as publishing!) his findings and opinions. Peter Townsend found himself in this position after the publication of his massive study of poverty in 1979. He gave many talks and public lectures not only to 'advertise' his data but to 'educate' opinion about what policies he believes are necessary to reduce or abolish poverty and excessive inequality. His recommendations, which were based on the view that a socialist reconstruction of the nation's economic and social life is necessary, had no chance of convincing the incumbent Conservative government. His hope was to persuade the Labour party to adopt more radical policies on poverty and inequality.

The last example shows that when a sociologist draws practical policy conclusions from his findings he is, in fact, entering the arena of politics. It is perfectly reasonable to do this but it is equally important for the sociologist to recognise that sociology and politics are *not* the same thing. *Sociology is about understanding society whereas politics (including taking decisions on social policy) is about how society should be 'run.' Sociology describes and explains, politics prescribes and implements and it is vital to recognise the difference.* As we have seen, the two activities can and do have

143

a meeting point but the urgent need of politicians for solutions should never persuade the sociologist to distort or over-simplify his findings merely to 'fit in' with the political beliefs of others or, for that matter, with his own.

Education: Problems and Policy

Given the power that education is thought to have to change people and society, it is not surprising that it has frequently been an area of intense public and political debate. Many adults may be generally indifferent about social and political matters, but most care about their children's education. Quite a lot care enough to do something about it if they feel action is necessary. Education is always potentially a 'hot' issue, both locally and nationally. Despite this, it did appear that the major issues in respect of primary and secondary education had been largely settled by the Butler Education Act of 1944. There was a sizeable political and public consensus behind this Act. It stated the government's commitment in principle to providing an educational system which enabled each person fully to develop his or her abilities. In pursuit of this objective, local authorities were required to organise education in three progressive stages; primary, secondary and further (most post-school education *excluding* higher education, which was based mainly on universities). Although this was not specifically laid down in the Act, most, though not all, local authorities divided secondary education into grammar, secondary modern and technical schools. This threefold division became known as the *tripartite system*. Grammar schools were for more 'academic' children and secondary modern schools for virtually all the rest. Nationally, only a very small percentage of students went to technical schools which provided practical, vocationally-oriented courses. Most local authorities used an 11+ examination to select pupils for specific types of schools. Very few offered grammar school places to even as much as thirty per cent of their secondary intake and many offered far fewer.

The three problems and related policy debates which we deal with below must be understood in the above educational context. Of course, the broader social context is also relevant, particularly the class nature of British society. It became clear in the nineteen fifties and early sixties that the educational system as it had developed under the 1944 Act was not ensuring equality of opportunity between social classes and was failing to bring out the potential of many children, particularly those from disadvantaged backgrounds. Halsey's early work with Floud and Martin, and Jackson and Marsden's study already referred to were significant sociological contributions to this growing awareness. The major issue at secondary level focused on the 11+ exam and the system to which it paved the way.

The alternative secondary school system suggested by opponents of the tripartite was the *comprehensive system*. The comprehensive debate is our first policy issue. Secondly, we consider efforts made to compensate children from 'disadvantaged' social backgrounds *before* they entered the educational system. The aim here was to try to put to rights the cultural imbalance that young lower working class children were thought to suffer from. Thirdly, we look at a still growing debate about the content of the school curriculum. This debate has partly been stimulated by the relative failure of educational reform – including, so far, comprehensivisation – significantly to improve the relative performance of working class children.

The Comprehensive Debate

The major criticism against the tripartite system, put forward by the Labour party, was that the 11+ examination discriminated against working class children. Research showed that relatively few working class children passed the exam, even among those who were of comparable intelligence to successful middle class children. But so difficult was the 11+, that inevitably many middle class children also failed it. Unless their families could afford to send them to private school, these children, too, had to share the common fate of 'failures' – and 'failure' *was* the term used. An educational system that had many more 'losers' than 'winners' was likely to cause widespread resentment. It was not long before specific and detailed arguments against the tripartite system began to be presented. Criticism also focused on the content of the exam itself, as well as on the divisive effects of the tripartite system. Some authorities cast doubts on the validity of the aptitude and attainment tests frequently used in the exam. In local authorities in which teachers' reports were also used as a basis of selection, it was an easy matter to suggest that unfair and subjective judgement might decide a child's future. 'Deciding a child's future at eleven' was at the nub of the debate: eleven was widely considered to be too early to determine this issue. A child might have an 'off day' during the 11+ examination period; might not realise the importance of the exam, or be a 'late developer' ... For those who accepted them, these arguments suggested the alternative to tripartite of a non-selective or comprehensive system of secondary schooling. Those who favoured comprehensivisation did so because they believed that it would remove the damaging and unfair stigma of 11+ 'failure.' Further, by enabling pupils of different social backgrounds to mix with each other, it was thought that a cultural 'rub-off' effect would occur, of particular benefit to working class children. The Labour government elected in 1964 issued Circular 10/65 inviting those local authorities which had not yet done so – still, in 1965, the large majority – to draw up schemes for comprehensive education. By the end of 1978, just over eighty per cent of state secondary education was organised along comprehensive lines although some observers seriously doubt whether much more than sixty per cent are 'genuinely' comprehensive.

In assessing the performance of the comprehensive system, it must be realised that the term comprehensive covers many different types of schools. The Leicestershire system, for instance, involves separate institutions for the 11 to 14 age group and for the 14 to 18 age group. More typically, South East Essex has 10 schools for 11 to 16 year olds which 'feed into' a single-site sixth form college. Despite the growing popularity of the sixth form college and of other '16+' colleges, the most common form of comprehensive is still the school for 11 to 18 year olds.

More important in judging whether a school is genuinely comprehensive is its internal system of academic organisation. These vary widely. Some schools 'stream' pupils rigidly – 'tripartite under the same roof' as their critics would say – whilst others use mixed ability teaching for most, if not all, classes. Many would say the former are not really comprehensive. Similarly, pastoral or tutor systems (concerned with general pupil welfare and discipline) can vary greatly in quality.

146

Tutor groups which contain children from a variety of social and, where relevant, racial backgrounds are closest to the comprehensive spirit.

It is still early days to compare the academic results produced within comprehensive and tripartite education areas. The occasional foolish and misleading comparison in recent years of results in socially quite different areas has not helped. Sounder general assessments remain much the same as John Eggleston's of 1975. He summarised the evidence available to the effect that the results from comprehensive schools and the aggregated (added together) results of secondary modern and grammar schools in similar areas were about equal. Precisely the same conclusion was reached by a report published by the National Children's Bureau in 1980. The NCB survey gains greatly in authority because of its *longitudinal* nature. Whereas other studies simply compare attainment levels in a group of comprehensive and grammar/secondary modern schools at a single time, this study examines relative performance at the time of entry (11) and at 16. Its basis of comparability is therefore much stronger. 8,700 children, some of whom went to grammar or secondary modern schools and others to comprehensives, were tested at the ages of 11 and 16. It was found that those in the latter group did as well as children of similar ability in the former group. High ability children in comprehensives did as well in mathematics and reading tests as those of equivalent attainment at 11 who went to grammar schools. The least able seemed to do rather better in comprehensives than in secondary moderns. Despite these generally reassuring findings, the fact that the comprehensive system has not yet brought about a clearly demonstrable improvement in the performance of working class children relative to middle class children is certainly a disappointment to its supporters. A firmer conclusion on that point, however, must wait until the system is widely established on a stable basis, and the disruptive effects of reorganisation on pupils, parents and teachers have passed.

A controversial early study by Julienne Ford on the effects of the greater social mixing that the comprehensive pastoral and (sometimes) academic systems promote, produced findings that were not encouraging to supporters of comprehensivisation. In the three schools where Ford made her case study, she found than an attempt had been made to achieve social mixing through the pastoral system by placing children of different social backgrounds in the same form and house, whereas academic groupings tended to reflect class divisions more sharply. Ford found that it was the academic group which generally provided the basis for friendship. Middle class children, who were a majority in the upper academic groupings, tended to associate with one another, and the same applied to the working class children in the lower academic groupings. It must be noted, however, that a single limited study does not provide a valid basis for generalisation though it can certainly alert people to the problems that can arise in a given type of institution. Ford herself points out that the achievements of comprehensivisation can better be assessed by detailed longitudinal studies (of which the NCB survey is an early example).

In the absence of really convincing evidence against it, the comprehensive system is not likely to be abandoned because of minor defeats in a war of facts about results. Less tangible and measurable characteristics of the system are also important. In our less formal and less status conscious age, the separation of children at 11 on a hierarchical basis would be repugnant to many simply in terms of basic values and feelings. Further, the comprehensive system at least allows teachers (and parents) to work with children of a greater variety of social backgrounds and ability in the same institution. Under the tripartite system this was less possible. In that sense, the comprehensive system is potentially a more flexible instrument of policy. As we shall further illustrate, however, those who expect education to 'change society' may have to look elsewhere for a more reliable tool. Even Halsey, a committed reformer, says: 'Education('s) . . . capacity is essentially not to create but to recreate society.' To achieve fundamental social change, if that is the aim, more than educational reform is needed.

Compensatory Education: An Example of the Principle of Positive Discrimination

The principle behind compensatory education is to provide additional educational or education-related help to those who are socially disadvantaged. Given the obvious goodwill and apparent commonsense behind such a policy, it is perhaps surprising that it has proved to be so controversial in practice.

Like many recent progressive initiatives in post-war education and social work, compensatory education was first tried in the United States. There, the major motive was to compensate those who had been deprived for racial reasons, whereas in Britain, the focus has been on compensating for general social disadvantage (though in the inner cities this has included large numbers of black and brown people). Neither country has adopted educational policies to compensate females for the historical disadvantage they have widely experienced.

As early as 1956, a 'demonstration guidance project' was established in New York, to provide extra educational support for intelligent children of the deprived racial minorities. It was reckoned a success and similar programmes followed but with the difference that they included the whole ability range. In 1965, the Johnson government included a 'Head Start' programme in its policies of social reform. As its name suggests, the purpose of 'Head Start' was mainly to prepare disadvantaged minority children for school by giving them special pre-school help.

Assessments of Head Start vary. The principle criteria used in the follow-up studies in evaluating success were gains in I.Q. and improvement in academic performance. On both counts the results of the *initial* follow-up studies were disappointing. I.Q. gains tended to be short-term, and there was little difference in attainment between the Head Start children and others of similar background. The hereditarians in the nature-nurture debate have cited this as evidence that intelligence and even educational performance cannot be significantly improved by 'environmental engineering.' Others have viewed the matter differently. Hunt argues that some schemes in the Head Start programme were inappropriate to the needs of the children they were supposed to help. Apparently, the curricula adopted often *assumed* considerable competence in the verbal and numerical skills that it was the object of the programmes to teach! This was because available curriculum material reflected the needs and attainment of middle class children who normally had virtually exclusive access to pre-school education. Several better designed pre-school programmes have, in fact, achieved lasting gains. A prominent feature of some of these has been the close involvement of the children's mothers, but Bereiter and Engelmann report several successful projects not involving direct maternal participation. Frequently, these involved a special stress on developing linguistic skills. A later (1976–77) and more comprehensive follow-up of Head Start by Lazar and Darlington showed an average reduction of academic failure in project children of 36.4%. It must be noted, however, that their findings were based on better pre-school projects, and not from a random sample of Head Start projects. They are not, therefore, representative of the whole original Head Start population.

In a useful review of the evidence relating to Head Start, Harry McGurk adds a cautionary note. He points out that both mothers and children often got considerable pleasure out of Head Start schemes and increased their confidence as a result of being involved in the programmes. This is important in itself. As McGurk says, our society professes other values than simply improving I.Q. scores.

The Educational Priority Area (EPA) programme, has been Britain's major effort in the field of compensatory education. The EPA's embodied the principle of *positive discrimination* (that extra help should be given to the socially disadvantaged) advocated by the Plowden Report of 1967. The EPA projects were set up by the Labour Secretary of State for Education and Science, Anthony Crossland. They were located in London, Birmingham, Liverpool and the West Riding of Yorkshire. On the basis of their exploratory work, they recommended positive discrimination, especially in the form of pre-schooling, in their report to government in 1971. Plowden aside, the main propagandist and theorist of positive discrimination in Britain has been A. H. Halsey. The policy of positive discrimination has not been short of critics however and we will briefly review their comments before returning to Halsey's defence.

First is a powerful criticism of the *limited scope* of positive discrimination based on analysis initially put forward by Barnes and Lucas, but later reiterated by Peter Townsend. They correctly point out that although particular areas of geographical concentration of poverty do exist, the majority of the poor are scattered throughout the country and outside these areas. As a result, positive discrimination can miss the needs of the majority and serve as a smokescreen for penny-pinching by government. Barnes and Lucas refer to the 'ecological fallacy' underlying the EPA approach: a policy that is generated through area analysis rather than the needs of specific social groups.

The above observations partly provide the basis for a more fundamental criticism by Townsend. He argues that policies of positive discrimination tend to be merely cosmetic whilst the real causes of disadvantage and poverty remain untouched. In his view, these causes are national in scope and structural in nature. He demands industrial, employment, housing and land policies which will radically redistribute wealth and systematically reduce, if not abolish, poverty. In order to illustrate his point, he draws on the experience of an exercise in positive discrimination outside education, the Community Development Project. In particular, the Coventry CDP group argued that in the face of national or, even, international factors which affected the local context in which they worked, they could do relatively little. For example, a few community workers could not deal with the consequences of thousands being thrown out of work as a result of a recession in car production. They contended that only a national policy of economic redevelopment and social justice could cope. This kind of analysis has received distinguished support from the American, Christopher Jencks, in his book *Inequality*.

Basil Bernstein's controversial article, 'Education cannot Compensate for Society' (1970), was concerned with the cultural aspects rather than socio-economics of positive discrimination. The essence of his criticism is that compensatory education implies that working class culture is in some sense inferior. The policy implications of this are to direct attention away from the quality of schools and curricula towards supposed inadequacies in working class families. Bernstein suggests that is the wrong emphasis. He argues that it is more important to put right the mainstream of the educational system than to over-concentrate on marginal 'compensatory' reforms. He argues that curriculum reform is needed to take into account the way working class children live their lives – the 'conditions' and 'contexts' of their culture should affect everyday education as much as do those of the middle class. Bernstein is surely correct in this central point. Educational change that does not affect the central curriculum is likely to be of only peripheral influence. On the other hand, there is no reason why both major reform and special help for the acutely disadvantaged should not occur.

A. H. Halsey has consistently defended compensatory education against its critics. The starkly assertive title of an article he published in 1980 is 'Education can Compensate,' and it is clearly intended as a reply to Bernstein's piece of ten years before. He especially emphasises the reassuring American evidence of Lazar and Darlington. He stresses that, given enthusiasm and careful organisation, a pre-school programme of compensatory education can be a 'crucial weapon' of government policy. He fully accepts, however, that the mainstream of the educational system must also be fair and effective as well. Thus, he continues passionately to support comprehensive education. For their part, his Marxist critics continue to wonder whether educational reform can significantly help the disadvantaged in the absence of fundamental social and economic change.

Radical Policy for Curriculum Change: The Sociology of Educational 'Knowledge'

Halsey seems to accept that the educational system will remain a competitive 'feed' into a competitive society but wants to ensure that competition occurs on equal terms for everybody. This involves state help for the socially and, therefore, educationally disadvantaged. The work of the authors we now discuss is much more critical both of what is learned in schools and of the society for which schools socialise pupils than is Halsey's. They point out that, even if equality of opportunity were achieved, the outcome would still be unequal, as long as people are rewarded unequally both materially and in terms of status. Here we concentrate on their analysis of school curriculum and assessment and their suggestions for change.

We normally assume that the educational system tests us. This section puts the boot on the other foot. We seek to ask some testing questions about the nature of the education or the knowledge acquired in schools. Which subjects are considered more and which less important? Who decides the order of priority? Who succeeds and who fails in this system? Who decides the winners and losers and on the basis of what criteria? Does the existing educational system smother alternative approaches to education and knowledge? If so, why? To answer these questions fully would require another book. Here we will simply try to show why they are important. To do so we must look again at the social context in which education occurs.

The idea that the content of education and the style in which it is presented always reflect the culture within which it occurs, has recently been explored by several sociologists. Because it examines the social influences on school curricula this field of study is sometimes referred to as *the sociology of educational knowledge* (for a full discussion of the sociology of knowledge see Chapter 20 pp. 564–70). The sociology of educational knowledge and the sociology of knowledge in general seek to show that what we learn and take for granted in some way reflects the society in which the learning takes place and is therefore culturally *relative* (relative to society). The attempts of Bourdieu and Bernstein to show that schools tend to reflect middle class cultural forms and style, rather than those of the working class, are a relevant example. A major contribution to research in this area is the collection of readings in *Knowledge and Control*, edited by Michael Young. In his introduction, Young cites a study by Gay and Cole which seeks to illustrate further the socially relative nature of knowledge. Two groups of culturally very different people, a number of illiterate Kpelle adults and a group of American overseas volunteers, were given the same two problems to solve. First, they were asked to estimate how many cups of rice could be obtained from a bowl of rice and, second, to sort out in three different ways eight cards with various numbers of red or green geometrical symbols on them. The Kpelle did very much better on the first test and very much worse on the second. Neither group could be considered mathematically superior on this test: each group applied mathematical skills more effectively in a context familiar to it. Yet, we can be sure that the Kpelle would 'fail' the mathematical tests conventionally used in Western schools just as the volunteers would falter if making everyday practical 'mathematical' calculations in Kpelle society. Perhaps immigrant children 'fail' in British society because they are often tested about unfamiliar things in unfamiliar ways (see the Bernstein/Labov controversy in the previous chapter). A particularly ludicrous example of cultural insensitivity was noted by a Nigerian teacher in a mission school in his country. The story books from which the children learned English often contained titles such as *The Starling, the Farmer's Friend*. The point is that starl-

153

ings are not indigenous to Nigeria and knowledge of them would be irrelevant to the needs and experience of young Nigerians. Assuming that the radical critics are correct (and we have seen that some disagree with them), why is it that educational systems in advanced capitalist societies cater so sparsely for the culture of working class and racial minorities? One explanation is that middle class educationalists simply do not know much about non-middle class culture. This would not be surprising – sociologists themselves have not yet fully and convincingly explored the vast field of comparative class and ethnic culture. A more frequent reason given by these critics for the middle class domination of curricula is that the relative success of middle class children and failure of working class children in public examinations 'rubber stamps' or, more technically, *legitimates* class inequality. Certificates seem to prove the objectivity of a system that is essentially unfair and exploitative.

A growing number of more detailed studies have begun to appear which attempt to demonstrate that the content and organisation of curricula serve to perpetuate the social system as it is. A particularly interesting article is Geoff Whitty's 'Teachers and Examiners.' Whitty criticises the extent to which public examinations are often taken as an 'absolute' standard by which merit and effort are judged. He also comments on the concern among some employers, senior academics and others, at the appearance of a small number of teacher-based modes of assessment. Yet, it does seem that a teacher who has known a student for two or more years should be able to make a better assessment than an examiner who sees perhaps just three hours of not very typical work, written under conditions of considerable stress. We are forced to ask why, given its considerable imperfections and unpleasantness, the traditional form of examination continues to dominate. Again, most of the radical critics mentioned above, such as Young and Whitty, would reply that the traditional examination system helps to perpetuate the inequalities of our society.

The examination system itself can be fitted easily into the critique of the educational system and class culture already presented. The following are some commonly made points. Firstly, the upper and middle class are disproportionately the winners in competitive examinations. Secondly, those who lose, predominantly children from the working class, learn to accept for the future the label of 'failure.' Given that our society is very hierarchical, this can be regarded as functional (if not, from the radical point of view, desirable). Thirdly, to sit a series of demanding examinations is to submit to a ritual of conformity which 'breaks' the young person into society. Rebellion, in the form of refusing to take exams is an option, but 'the system' exacts a heavy penalty by refusing the acceptance and rewards that accompany conformity and conventional success. Fourthly, although the examination system is often confused with education itself, a moment's reflection will show that a competition involving little more than a random mix of memory-work, some comprehension and, usually, ability with the written word, is very narrow in scope. It hardly allows for an adequate expression and assessment of such important qualities as, for instance, research skills, interest in, and commitment to, the subject, ability to co-operate with and motivate co-workers, or of diligence and stamina over a long period. These criticisms, however, do not wholly apply to the growing number of examinations partly assessed on projects, coursework, practical work and oral tests. Fifthly, there are bureaucratic reasons for continuing with the present system. It is centralised, cheap, and easy to administer and those who currently run it have a vested interest in keeping it as it is. Finally, it should be noted that what the educational system is *said* to do and what, according to the above account, it actually *does*, are very different. This is the gap between *ideology* (that everybody has an equal chance to succeed) and *practice* (some have a better chance than others). Ideology, therefore, serves to justify or legitimate the system. This does not mean that ideology involves conscious deception. On the contrary, the more people who believe it – whether they benefit from the system it justifies or not – the more effective it is.

As yet, Marxist and other radical educational thinkers have produced rather fewer fully-developed alternative curriculum schemes than might be expected. Understandably, this may be because they are sometimes caught between their opposition to 'the system' as it is and the practical need many feel to work within it for change. However, a full-scale proposal for an alternative national system of assessment based on schools rather than examination boards has been offered by Tyrrell Burgess and Elizabeth Adams. The process begins at the end of the third year when all students make a summary of their existing skills and attainment, and of their interests and aims. They then state how they wish to develop in the next two years and, in combination with a tutor and parents, produce a plan of educational activity to achieve their goals. This 'negoti-ation' phase is important, because it allows adults to ensure that the curriculum contains certain essential activities (Maths and English would generally be considered as such) yet enables the pupil to state his or her interests and choose certain options. Thus, freedom and responsibility are balanced. Exter-nal assessment would come from interested, involved and com-petent people from the community – including teachers from other schools. There are many possible variations on this scheme, some of which are already tried in schools.

Burgess and Adams' proposals answer most of the criticisms commonly made of the examination system but they do not, of course, constitute an alternative system of education. Jane Tor-rey comes closer to satisfying the Marxist critique of education and cultural reproduction when she argues, in the case of American blacks, that curricula should be based on their own subculture. Black speech patterns would be the normal medium of classroom environment and standard English taught almost as if it were a foreign language. Similarly, black cultural and historical experience would be emphasised. It is very doubtful whether the difference between Bernstein's elaborated and restricted codes (even if his analysis is valid) provides the basis for a similar experiment in class linguistics. Nevertheless, the principle that children should be enabled to understand, inter-pret and express their own social experience seems sound. If taken too far, however, this could lead to a formalised system of educational 'apartheid' based on class. A balance must be struck between enabling children to understand their own social experience and providing the skills and knowledge they need to operate most effectively in a wider society.

Access to a wide range of skills and knowledge is, according to Ivan Illich, the key to real education. His complaint is that at present schools systematically fail to provide this. They are so cut off from society and so organised around academic sub-ject specialisms, that many teachers themselves lack basic prac-tical skills. The constraints of formal teaching mean that many teachers are unable to respond to children's need for daily information and advice about, say, house or vehicle repairs, personal health, their relationships, social and political matters, the publication (through print, video or whatever) of their own views, and a range of other practical and theoretical matters. Instead, teachers and students rely on 'experts' to do almost everything for them or, if they learn to do things for themselves, it is often not in school. So Illich wants much more interchange between school and community. He would like to see the divide between mental and manual labour bridged – so that the former could be better and more widely understood, and the latter become again more dignified. Thus, like President Nyerere of Tanzania, he would have teachers in the fields and farmers in the classroom – so that they could learn from each other. Underlying Illich's educational critique is the view that work in modern societies has become so fragmented and specialised that it is often meaningless. A few people – the experts – know more and more about less and less but the majority know less and less about less and less – because the routine nature of production and office work does not require them to know more. He believes that educational change will not occur unless a wider social transformation also takes place, including a restructuring of the system of production to involve people more meaningfully in work.

We have included this discussion of radical thought in curriculum change in the policy section because the radicals are concerned to *do* something. Nevertheless, it could have appeared in the previous chapter either as a perspective on the way the educational system operates, or as part of our examination of the factors that affect educational attainment. This reflects the fact that radicals are moving towards a general critique of the educational system rather than simply offering odd criticisms. Some Marxists, including Althusser, have suggested that the above critics 'blame' teachers rather than the class system for the injustice perpetrated by the educational system. This criticism may have had some truth in it in the early nineteen seventies, but very little now. Indeed, many of the radical critics are Marxists although their Marxism is often buttressed by insights from phenomenology, ethnomethodology and even anthropology. Most fully realise that their detailed critique of the educational system must be married to an analysis of the socio-economic system.

Education: Ideals and Practicalities

The 1944 Education Act states that the aim of the education system should be to enable each individual to develop his or her capacities to the full. That is the ideal. In practice, neither the tripartite system nor any other system of education has provided this opportunity for *every* member of society. The cost and organisational difficulty of so doing has proved a universal deterrent but perhaps, too, lack of real belief and commitment has prevented a serious attempt being made even to approximate to this ideal. At the most, some societies have given great opportunities for self-expression and development to a few. These have often been the children of a privileged elite who could afford to provide their children with the best education available. More recently, state education has established a narrow ladder of ascent for some more able working class children and offered more limited education to others. But how much talent and potential still remains unexpressed? Halsey estimates that on the basis of *measured* intelligence, about 6,000 working class boys a year or about 500,000 between 1913 and 1953 did not receive the education they merited. He understates matters when he describes much wastage as 'hardly trivial.' If we assume that class affects measured intelligence, as Halsey does not in his calculations, then it becomes possible to adjust his figures upwards – how much depends on the estimated effect of class on measured intelligence.

Although the working class may suffer most from educational under-achievement, others may also fall short of their potential. To appreciate this, it will be helpful to refer to the work of the humanistic psychologist, Abraham Maslow. He presents a comprehensive theory of human needs and motivation which we can conveniently relate to education. He argued that man's behaviour is centred upon a series of needs which can be arranged as a hierarchy. These are:

1 Physiological Needs, for example, food
2 Safety or Security Needs, for example, shelter
3 Social Needs, for example, human interaction
4 Esteem or Egoistic Needs, for example, status
5 Self-actualisation Needs, for example, the expression of a personal talent or creative ability

Most people probably think of education as a way of preparing themselves for a job, so that they can meet basic needs (1 and 2). Rather fewer seriously hope to get high status jobs (4). Social needs (3) are naturally expressed and developed in schools and other educational establishments as they are in all institutions. Here, our major interest is in education and self-actualisation (5).

The educational system allows mainly, though not exclusively, for the development of academic potential. Nevertheless, many are unable to benefit fully from the academic opportunities that are, theoretically, available. Further, academic self-expression is often narrowly defined as 'what is needed to do well in an examination.' This approach can smother liking and flair for a subject as well as, possibly, stimulate it. It is undoubtedly true that education has provided more opportunities for self-expression in the arts and sport since the Second World War. The possibility for expansion in this area remains great, however. This is especially obvious if we remember that in certain areas, such as music or soccer, shortage of teachers or resources can result in the less talented not being given an opportunity at all for tuition or organised self-expression. 'Third teams' are notoriously undersupervised, and music departments are usually too understaffed to cater for slow learners. Despite the dedication of many teachers, the ideal of self-fulfilment often falters in application to those of moderate or little talent. Further, opportunities for extending educational opportunities to adults remain unexploited and yet they are often the most enthusiastic and appreciative of learners. Certainly, the space and much of the teaching expertise exists to answer to their needs and wants.

Despite the rhetoric, the truth is that education has not primarily been organised on the principle that the individual should be given the opportunity to develop his capacities. In practice, the need to provide a literate, numerate and conforming labour force has predominated over the ideal of personal and collective self-actualisation. If this repression of potential was necessary in the past for societies to survive, it is less necessary now. In the advanced societies, it is no longer essential for people to be socialised to submit to the tyranny of boring toil to the point where their awareness of a better life is stunted. This is because, over the period of the last hundred years, leisure time has greatly increased and work time has proportionately diminished. Even though some tedious work remains, people now have the time to do much else besides. The computer revolution means that it is likely that this potentially liberating trend will continue and possibly accelerate. In these circumstances, education for leisure rather than merely for work becomes not only possible and desirable, but sensible. (See also Chapter 14, pp. 401–2, for the development of this theme).

Health: Biological or Social Issue?

This brief introduction to the sociology of health concentrates on three issues: the relationship between biological and social aspects of health; the differences in health between the social classes; and the social factors relating to organisation of health in Britain.

First, we must disentangle the *biological* from the *social* basis of health. You were probably not surprised to find education used to illustrate social issues. It is common knowledge that a disadvantaged social background may hamper educational performance. But health, surely, is unambiguously a biological problem. We 'become' ill or we 'are' ill, sometimes, even we 'make' ourselves ill, but about the fact of illness little doubt is expressed. Even 'psychological' illnesses are presumed to have certain identifiable 'symptoms' which both describe 'the problem' and suggest remedies or cures.

But matters are more complex than these familiar, taken-for-granted assumptions allow. Certainly, there is a solid organic basis to certain diseases of physical deterioration and bodily malfunction (it would be misleading to deny this) but beyond this, ambiguities reflecting various cultural interpretations of 'symptoms,' occur. Thus, in comparative study of the treatment of various ethnic groups in Boston, Irving Zola found that in cases where no organic basis for illness was discovered, Italians were consistently diagnosed as having some psychological difficulty such as personality disorder or tension headache, whereas Irish and Anglo-Saxon were usually diagnosed as having nothing wrong with them. Zola suggests that doctors were able to prise symptoms out of the more voluble and dramatic behaviour of the Italians in a situation in which illness was being looked for.

It is precisely in the area of 'psychological illness' that

ambiguity and variety in recognising and interpreting symptoms is most apparent. Most vividly, in the Soviet Union individuals may be treated for 'mental illness' who, in the West, are regarded as among the most highly motivated and aware people. The language of medicine and particularly psychiatry does provide a battery of labels with which to dismiss ideas or behaviour that we do not like. Roger Gomm gives two such examples from the United States which would be amusing if it were not for the human suffering they involve. The first case concerns a sudden change of definition by the American Psychiatric Association about the status of homosexuality as 'sick' or acceptable behaviour. For a long period it was defined as a disease. Then a vote of the Association determined that it was not. Of course, this 'decision' reflected a much more gradual change in cultural attitudes to homosexuality – which precisely illustrates the point that 'disease' can be produced through cultural definition as well as biological disorder. Gomm's second example concerns the supposed disease of 'Drapetomania' which only afflicted black slaves. It was 'discovered' by a psychiatrist, Samuel Cartwright, from the deep southern state of Louisiana; he published a paper on it in 1851. The major symptom of 'Drapetomania' was running away, and this could be cured by the apparently imcompatible treatments of beating slaves to their knees if they failed to retain a submissive posture, and by being kind and humane to them. This is a particularly obvious case in which medical terminology is used as part of an ideology of social control. Flight from, or opposition to, social repression is seen as sickness. There is no shortage of modern examples of the same thing, as the files of Amnesty International, the major voluntary agency concerned with the repression of civil liberties show.

We need, therefore, to look at the social interpretation of health in the widest possible context. How disease is regarded within a culture is a major factor in determining the treatment of it. In the advanced industrial countries, the predominant model or paradigm of health is the *bio-medical* one. In other words, disease is seen as the deterioration or breakdown of organic processes – such as occurs in the case of cancer or heart arrest. Our whole medical system is still geared to curing disease *after* it has developed.

An alternative model or paradigm of health has long attracted a minority in the West and has recently gained strength. It is that health is the product of diet, exercise and, to some extent, mental outlook. It is undoubtedly a more positive approach to health and puts the emphasis on *prevention* rather than cure. Signs of its growth are apparent in the jogging 'movement' and in the appearance of at least one health food shop in most towns. In theory it is easy to reconcile the dominant bio-medical paradigm and what we can call the 'healthy living' approach and, no doubt, some individuals do so by using professional medicine only when it seems organically necessary to do so. But in practice the two approaches do not have equal status within our culture. This can be illustrated by the fact that not long ago an interest in natural or health foods was widely regarded as slightly crackpot and even now, jogging still attracts mockery. This sort of semi-humorous rejection of a movement is a sure sign that it challenges the way the majority 'normally' look at the issue under question.

Another illustration of the continuing predominance of the bio-medical paradigm is the dependency of many patients and doctors on drugs or other 'scientific' preparations for treatment. It is almost as if doctors are regarded and regard themselves as health 'mechanics' – a little adjustment of the machine and it will 'go again.' There lurks behind this approach both the core cultural assumption that applied science can explain and cure everything and the massive commercial power of the major international drug companies who bombard doctors and the television screen with advertisements for their preparations. Whether the doctors or the companies or neither are 'in control' of all this is a point for debate. Radical commentators such as Klass (1975) and Heller (1977) would argue that the massive vested interests of the drug companies in profitably marketing their products gives great support and impetus to a drug-based system of health treatment, regardless of its real merits. The extreme opposite of this approach is to be found in attitudes commonly expressed within Hindu philosophy. Health is seen as a product of a harmonious relationship to the total environment – spiritual and material. This belief and the way of life based on it is so remote from dominant Western assumptions as to be almost incomprehensible within the terms of our culture.

A final point on cultural attitudes to health is the loose distinction sometimes made between disease and illness. Disease is a bio-medical condition, and illness is the way people respond to it. Put otherwise, disease is the objective reality and illness the subjective way of dealing with it. It is variation in the latter that is the starting point to the sociology of medicine as we have been discussing it above. Let us take a final example of differential response to the same underlying organic condition, this time at the individual level. Mass screening tests show that many people are in some way clinically ill without defining themselves as such. Others, technically more healthy, 'feel' themselves to be ill. Often being declared 'ill' is the process of a 'negotiation' between doctor and client, rather than a mere function of organic ailment.

The second matter to consider is the relationship between health and social class. This an aspect of *epidemiology*, which is the study of the distribution and causes of disease and injury. By now, you will appreciate the need to effect a working definition of disease as a necessary preliminary to assessing its distribution by social class. Here we adopt the self-definition of respondents in answer to the question posed by the General Household Survey of 1972 (which equates disease and illness): 'Do you suffer from any long-standing illness, disability or infirmity?' Responses show that the lower the social class the higher the rate of long-standing illness (see table below). Answers to the further question: 'IF YES Does (it) limit your activities compared with most people of your own age?' show a similar general trend (see table). This suggests that either the severity of long-standing illness is greater among the working class or that it is less effectively treated – or, most likely, both. There is an abundance of other evidence that the quality of health correlates with social class. The question is, why?

Rates per 1,000 reporting (1) long-standing illness, (2) limiting long-standing illness, by social class

| | Social class (RG(SE)70) | | | | | | |
	1	2	3	4	5	6	All
Long standing illness	130	168	192	192	265	317	206
Limiting long-standing illness	65	90	104	113	162	208	121

Source: Ivan Reid, *Social Class Differences in Britain,* 1977, p. 109. (adapted from *General Household Survey,* 1972).

163

The general answer is that the material and cultural conditions of working class life are less conducive to health than those of the middle class. A minority of the lower working class still live in housing conditions in which damp and cold are threats to health – particularly for the old and children. A detailed study of class and diet by Richard Wilkinson produced startling results. For example, per head, the poor eat 56% less fruit, 28% fewer fresh green vegetables and 31% less carcass meat than the rich. They eat much more sugar, cereal products and potatoes. Poverty may be the major underlying cause of less rich diet, but lack of knowledge about what a healthy and balanced diet consists of must also contribute. A further explanation of the relative ill-health of the working class is that the conditions in which they work are often worse than those of the middle class. The General Household survey shows that the rate of reported absence in social class 6 is almost 5 times greater than in social class 1. No doubt in addition to illness and injury, alienation from tedious work is a contributory factor. Another point is that the privileged access of the rich to private medicine must be to their advantage although doctors are often curiously coy about saying that private medicine is generally 'better' than state medicine.

Perhaps surprisingly, evidence also shows that the middle class has benefited more from the NHS than the working class. Until recently, there was doubt about this but the authoritative government-sponsored report, *Inequalities in Health* (1980) is quite clear on the matter. It is true that this and other studies show that the working class use the National Health Service more often than the middle class, but not as much as might be expected *relative to need*. A second point is that there is a tendency for middle class patients to receive better quality treatment from the NHS because the availability and quality of care tends to be superior in middle class localities. J. T. Hart further attributes this to the greater ability of the middle class to negotiate for the services they want, though he admits that the statistical basis of his argument is slight. More precise statistical evidence is supplied by Ann Howlett and John Ashley, albeit on a small scale. They found that teaching hospitals which are recognised to be among the best, tended to admit a substantially larger proportion of middle class than working class men for treatment of enlargement of the prostate gland.

Simply, then, middle class patients were somehow being referred to hospitals in which superior treatment might be expected. Two limitations of their study is that they do not prove their assumption of superior treatment by the teaching hospitals, and that they fail to offer an explanation of how selection takes place. However, it seems likely that this is just one instance of the general middle class bias that the previously mentioned report, *Inequalities in Health*, finds to characterise the NHS.

The above considerations no doubt constitute some of the reasons why social class differences in mortality and illness have widened in post-war years. Rather like the national system of education, the NHS has not brought about greater equality. Further, the general improvement in the health of the nation that has undoubtedly occurred this century can be attributed largely to the conquest of contagious disease and improvements in public hygiene rather than to the health service. This is clearly shown by the fact that the major increase in life expectancy occurred well before the NHS was set up.

Finally, we examine some social factors relating to the organisation of health in Britain. We have already referred to the power and interest of drug companies in maintaining a system of treatment based largely on drugs. Here, we discuss bureaucratic and professional aspects of the health system. Ivan Illich is surely correct to see the position of doctors in the context of the tendency of certain services (such as teaching and accountancy) to be increasingly organised within bureaucratic structures. Doctors play the role of 'experts' within the larger 'health machine.' In principle, they, rather than clients decide what 'label' to give specific illnesses. They then pass the client 'down the line' to, say, the chemist or a hospital. Two aspects of this process merit comment. First, is the power to 'label.' Talcott Parsons was perhaps the first to see illness as a form of deviance from the norm – albeit of a more acceptable kind than, say, crime – which society needs to label and deal with. Illich and Thomas Szasz are much more suspicious of labelling. They ·see it as a virtual invitation to the client to avoid positive responsibility for dealing with his or her own condition and, more sinisterly, in the case of mental 'illness,' as a potential threat to the liberty of the individual who in certain circumstances could be committed for treatment against his or her will (for an analysis of Erving Goffman's account of the labelling process in an asylum see Chapter 15, pp. 418–19). A second point, is that, like any other large organisational structure, the National Health Service produces vested interests. An alternative system of medicine to that operated by the NHS would threaten a vast range of interests, from the Chairman of the international drug company Roche, to the jobs of junior staff nurses. For that reason it would be powerfully opposed.

Alternative, largely non-bureaucratic and non-professional systems of medical treatment do exist. Indeed, in parts of the Third World less expensive systems, operated by less qualified people are the only option available. Thus, in China and Tanzania large numbers of 'barefoot doctors' work as a tier of medical service at the grassroots, below a small elite of highly trained medical practitioners. They treat for basic illness and immunise against contagious disease. An element of community medicine is built into this approach and these medical workers are based in specific areas and are known personally to most of those they work for. Their role is seen as educational and preventive as well as curative. This may be medicine on the cheap but it is based on principles that the West could well learn from. Indeed, without remotely suggesting that the NHS, as presently constituted, be dismantled, the *Inequalities in Health* report does argue for more community-based health care. In particular, it puts forward the need for more ante-natal and post-natal care (death at birth and in the first few months of life is relatively high in Britain); better child health services; free school meals for all children, and better home help and nursing services for the disabled. The emphasis on child health is based on the well founded belief that illness in childhood can cast a long shadow forward into adulthood. These and other policies suggested in the report were given a lukewarm reception by the Conservative Social Services Secretary, Patrick Jenkin (the Working Group on Inequalities in Health had been set up under a Labour government in 1977). The major objection was that they would cost too much to implement. The Working Group had anticipated this response by suggesting that most of the reforms could be financed by money saved from abolishing the married man's tax allowance for all married men with no dependants – a worthwhile sacrifice in their view. Like all policies, those suggested by the Working Group involve issues of value, choice and priority.

Guide to further reading and study

W. D. Birrell *et al, ed, Social Administration: Readings in Applied Social Science* (Penguin, 1973) is recommended for the breadth of its coverage. In particular, it contains a useful article by F. Laffitte, 'Social Policy in a Free Society' which introduces various definitions of social policy. David C. Marsh, *ed, Introducing Social Policy* (Routledge and Kegan Paul, 1979) is also comprehensive, and contains a section on education and health policy. For a controversial and committed examination of the area see Mike Simpkin's *Trapped Within Welfare: Surviving Social Work* (MacMillan, 1979). By contrast, W. E. Baugh's *Introduction to the Social Services* (Unwin, 1977) is meticulously factual and presented in a thorough, 'text-bookish' way. Roger Gomm's article 'Social Science and Medicine' in Meighan, *ed, Perspectives on Society* (Nelson, 1979) is very useful, because it illustrates how to use sociology to understand what might *seem* a non-sociological problem: health. A good general reader is D. Tuckett and J. M. Kanfert, *eds, Basic Readings in Medical Sociology* (Tavistock, 1978).

Questions

1 Examine the relationship between Social Policy and Sociology. (Specimen Question for 1982 AEB syllabus)
2 'Social Science provides neutral information for benevolent policy makers.' (Specimen Question for 1982 AEB syllabus)
3 What can sociologists contribute to an understanding of programmes of compensatory education? (AEB, 1976)
4 'The social distribution of 'good health' closely reflects the social distribution of wealth and income.' Discuss. (Specimen Question for the 1982 syllabus).

7 Community and Urbanisation; Development and Population (Theory 4)

In this section we have so far moved through progressively
larger areas of personal experience – first, primary (family)
then, secondary (education). This chapter reverses this procedure and examines some of the major factors that affect not
just personal but also national and global life. Its perspective is
predominantly structural. Topics analysed are the nature of
traditional and modern societies; urbanisation; development and
underdevelopment; and, finally, population and related problems. Class is an underlying reality behind all these themes.
We refer to it continually but do not deal with it specifically
until the next section.

From Rural Community to Urban Society

There have, of course, been great changes in Western society in
the last two hundred years. Crudely, we can say that Western
society has moved from the traditional to the modern. Poorer
societies – nearly all of them in the southern hemisphere – are
today going through a similar process of change even though
many are trying to control, interpret or even resist it in their
own way. What we seek, therefore, are concepts and theories
that explain and illuminate this near-universal pattern of
change.

The shift from traditional to modern is probably the most
fundamental development in world history. Raymond Aron, the
French sociologist, remarked that it was not until he visited
India that he realised that the significant division in the world
was not between communism and capitalism but between the
modern, industrially-advanced states and those which remained
industrially underdeveloped. Over-simplified or not, this comment at least helps to knock aside the cultural blinkers which
often obscure the way Westerners see the world.

Community Defined
It is frequently observed that over the past few centuries there
has been a 'loss of community.' This comment is often ex-

pressed with the sentiment that, in a human rather than material way, life was better 'then' than 'now'. Before any assessment of the validity of this feeling can be made, we must be clear about what is meant by community. Three major usages can be discerned.

1 The term community is employed to describe *locality* (*a given geographical area as a basis of social organisation*). Thus, a traditional rural village where people are born, live and die close to each other fits this usage.

2 Community is used to refer to a *local social system or set of relationships that centre upon a given locality*. Margaret Stacey suggests that, from a sociological point of view, it is the concentration of relationships, rather than the geographical factor that matters. Stacey would prefer to drop the term community in favour of *local social system*. This has the advantage of implying nothing at all about the nature of relationships in a locality but simply designates them as the topic for study.

3 Community is also used to describe a *type of relationship* which produces a strong sense of shared identity. This usage does not depend on physical whereabouts or even on people having met each other. Thus, it is possible to refer to the Catholic or Jewish community in a neighbourhood, town, country or, even, throughout the world. The Argentinian nation had every appearance of being a community at the moment of their team's World Cup Final victory of 1978. In fact, their President referred to the popular involvement in the team's progress as 'an experience in collective unity.' Similarly, this author recalls a newscaster's comment after Manchester United won the European Cup in 1968 that 'this was not only a victory for Manchester United fans but for the British people as a whole.' As Howard Newby points out it is 'loss of community' in terms of shared identity and accompanying experiences that accounts for much of the usage of the phrase.

We will consider how useful and accurate the notion 'loss of community' is when we have reviewed the major literature comparing traditional and modern society.

Ferdinand Tönnies and Emile Durkheim: Gemeinschaft/Gesellschaft and Mechanical/Organic Solidarity

Tönnies and Durkheim sought to understand the change from traditional to modern society. Their major writings on this matter were published before the turn of the century and their focus was European rather than global. Nevertheless, their theories have influenced more recent thinkers, particularly those of a functionalist perspective, who have had a major interest in world development.

Tönnies in *Gemeinschaft and Gesellschaft* (1887), and Durkheim in *The Division of Labour* (1893), contrast the social life of traditional rural communities with that of rapidly developing, industrial urban areas. On the one hand, they stressed family and community as sources of identity and support and, on the other, their relative weakness in the urban context where a more individualistic and impersonal way of life was developing. Tönnies used the terms *gemeinschaft* and *gesellschaft* to describe this broad sweep of social change. *Gemeinschaft* means community and *gesellschaft* can be translated either as society or association. He considered *gemeinschaft* relationships to involve the whole person and to be typical of rural life. Because people related more *fully* to each other, and not simply in respect of their specific functional roles (shopkeeper, policeman, teacher), greater mutual involvement and caring existed, and so a stronger community was formed. Thus, a policeman was not merely somebody who did a given job but a friend or, at least, an acquaintance who had a *general* concern for the order and welfare of the community. The difference is summed up in the admittedly rather exaggerated and idealised contrast between the 'friendly, village bobby' and the modern, panda-car policeman.

Gesellschaft relationships are seen as associations or transactions for practical purposes, with little informal content. Thus, a policeman appears on given occasions and for specific purposes; otherwise, in our privatised and individualistic society, he is likely to be considered as 'nosey' or 'interfering.' Terms that are virtually interchangeable with the rather cumbersome phrases *gemeinschaft* and *gesellschaft* relationships are, respectively, *holistic* (full) and *segmental* (partial) relationships. Tönnies used his key terms not only to describe relationships but also organisations. *Gemeinschaftlich* ('community-like') organisations such as the church are stronger in traditional societies, whereas *gesellschaftlich* organisations, such as big businesses, are stronger in modern societies. Churches have a moral and emotional influence, whereas businesses predominate in the practical and economic spheres. These examples illustrate the deep change perceived by Tönnies from the moral/emotional quality of traditional life to the practical/rational quality of modern life.

Durkheim's analysis in *The Division of Labour* concentrated rather more systematically on the problem of how societies achieve social order and cohesion or, to use his term, social *solidarity* than did Tönnies. Nevertheless, his terms *mechanical* and *organic* solidarity overlap and complement Tönnies' *gemeinschaft* and *gesellschaft*. He described solidarity in traditional societies as *mechanical* and in industrial societies as *organic*. Mechanical solidarity is the product of a uniformly accepted and strictly enforced system of belief and conduct and is facilitated by a small, homogeneous (similar) population. Classically, it occurs in primitive or traditional societies in which everybody shares the same religiously inspired beliefs and habits. In such societies, a person would not think of rejecting the moral consensus: personal fulfilment and identity are gained by identifying with the whole group and not through a separate sense of individuality, as to a large extent they are in modern societies. A different basis of order and cohesion – organic solidarity – develops as societies become more complex. Organic solidarity is a product not of common beliefs but of shared material interests and practical *interdependence*. To understand this, we must first describe what Durkheim meant by the division of labour. The *division of labour* means that work is broken down into specialised tasks performed by different people. It is a particular feature of modern society, and assembly-line production may be considered the prime example of it. Organisationally and humanly, the division of labour divides men but it also makes them more dependent on one another. Thus, a single group of workers, say, toolsetters, can bring an assembly-line to a halt by taking disruptive industrial action. Interdependence is broader than this example might imply and encompasses the whole of a modern society – a strike in the gas or electricity industries might bring other forms of industrial production to a halt. Durkheim himself succinctly reconciles the paradox of increased job or role specialisation with increased solidarity:

> This (organic) solidarity resembles that which we observe among
> the higher animals. Each organ, in effect, has its special
> character and autonomy; and yet the unity of the organism is as
> great as the individuation of the parts is more marked. Because

> of this analogy, we propose to call the solidarity which is due to the division of labour, 'organic.'

Although Durkheim commented on the strength of organic solidarity, he felt that the ultimate stability of modern society depended on finding a new *moral* basis of solidarity in addition to practical interdependence. He argued that without moral and normative consensus in society, people tend to suffer from *anomie* – a sense of normlessness or lack of moral guidance to behaviour. In such circumstances, deviant activities such as crime and suicide tend to rise. We examine Durkheim's theory of anomie and deviance in greater detail in Chapters 16 and 17

The work of Georg Simmel, (1858–1918), echoes many of the sentiments of Tönnies and Durkheim. More than they, he attributed most that is characteristic of modern life, including 'lack of community,' almost solely to the growth of the city. His stress on the impersonality and isolation of city life parallels Durkheim's concern with anomie. Simmel's particular interest in the effect of the urban environment on the individual – eloquently expressed in his essay 'The Mind and the Metropolis' – places him as much within the tradition of social psychology as sociology. This essay and his work on dyads (two people) or tryads (three people) have led some to claim him as a founding father of interactionism, which is the sociological perspective that gives most attention to individual psychology.

Yet Simmel also had a strong sense of structure, as his analysis of the characteristics of urban life shows. He designated urban life as *rational* in the sense that it involves quick, logical and calculating reactions. This is because of the many practical, money-based relationships that city life depends upon. He contrasted this to the slow, habitual quality of rural life. Quite simply, he argued that the mind became more agile in the city through sheer overstimulation. Crudely, we could say that he gives academic clothing to the popular stereotypes of 'city slicker' and 'country bumpkin.' There is no doubt, however, that like Tönnies and Durkheim, Simmel is on the side of what he sees as a receding rural past, rather than the emerging urban present. He regards the blasé and reserved attitudes necessary to cope in the city as poor change for the involvement and community of rural life, despite the greater material wealth and cultural sophistication of the city. Within it, the values of the market-place so predominate that people often

173

treat others as things or mere bearers of commodities and services. Like Durkheim, Simmel had great influence on the Chicago School of urban sociologists, whose work we consider shortly.

Several comments and criticisms can be made about the community/society model. Firstly, it is suffused with conservative romanticism about the past. As a result, it tends to minimise the *repressive* nature of traditional community and perhaps exaggerate its satisfying aspects. Secondly, the model largely disregards class conflict, or reduces it to the level of mere 'disequilibrium' in society. There were immense differences in wealth, power, life-style and prestige between people before the industrial revolution, as well as after it. The fact that the privileged position of the nobility was sanctioned by custom, tradition and religion never *did* convince all the peasantry that such glaring inequalities were either natural or justifiable. Thirdly, a bi-polar or two part, model of change is too simple. Durkheim himself constructed a more complex scheme of comparative change but rather than describe this in detail now, we will go on instead to consider more recent and, often, more complex, theories of order and change.

Talcott Parsons' Pattern Variables

Parsons' attempt to analyse the transition from traditional to modern society owes something to both Durkheim and Weber. His lists of pattern variables (which categorise *pairs* of contrasting values and norms) can be regarded as an expansion of Durkheim's mechanical-organic axis of comparison. Accordingly, we can present them as follows:

Pattern Variables 'A': characteristic of Traditional Society

Ascription: The status etc. a person is given at birth, for example, king

(Role) Diffuseness: relationships are broad or gemeinschaftlich (see above)

Pattern Variables 'B': characteristic of Modern Society

Achievement: The status a person acquires through his own efforts, for example, a soccer star

(Role) Specificity: relationships are for specific purposes or *gesellschaftlich* (see above)

Particularism: people treat each other in a *personal* way, so a farm-labourer asks 'the squire' to give his son a job	*Universalism:* the same rules, principles or laws apply to everybody equally, as in appointing a person to a post in the civil service
Affectivity: the expression and satisfaction of emotions is felt to be important, so criminals are publicly punished so that the community can express its vengeance	*Affective Neutrality:* the affective or emotional side of man is controlled so that it does not interfere with 'the job in hand', so a bereaved person must control his grief rather than share it with colleagues
Collective Orientation: shared interests are most important, for example, with the family or community	*Self-Orientation:* individual interest is most important, as in the pursuit of personal success even if it distances an individual from his family

At this stage, it is enough thoughtfully to read through Parsons' pattern variables paying as much attention to the examples as to Parsons' tongue-twisting terminology itself. Having presented his pattern variables as a contrast between traditional and modern society, we must, in fairness, immediately complicate the picture. First, Parsons fully recognised, as did Tönnies and Durkheim, that there can be considerable overlap between the two types of society. Indeed, it makes sense to think in terms of a graded rural-urban *continuum* (development) of which pattern variables 'A' and 'B' are extreme poles, which, in practice, are more likely to appear together in various 'mixes.' Further, he considered that though modern society is more rational and affectively neutral, people do, of course, have feelings which they need and want to express. These feelings or *expressive functional imperatives,* as Parsons rather gruesomely called them, find their main outlet in the kinship and cultural community sub-systems (see Chapter 3). Still, what we want to emphasise here is the continuity of Parsons' model of societal types with those of Durkheim and Tönnies. As such, it hardly does more than offer a useful comparative check-list for locating given societies on a traditional-modern continuum. Thus, a primitive tribe would 'score' high under 'A', a modern state high under 'B', and an industrially developing country, such as Saudi Arabia, would show a mix. We will further evaluate Parsons' pattern variable model in the section on *development* later in this chapter.

The Urban and Community Studies of the Chicago School of Sociology

The Chicago school of sociology established an international reputation between the two world wars. Durkheim was a major influence on the urban sociology for which the school became renowned. This showed itself in two ways: first, in the clean cut contrast made between rural, 'folk' society and urban society and also in the use of the organic analogy to describe the processes of urban life.

Louis Wirth followed Durkheim closely in making a firm distinction between rural and urban society. He defined the city in terms of three fundamental features: population *size, density* and *heterogeneity* (Wirth, 1938). These characteristics meant that though the city dweller would experience more human contacts than the rural inhabitant, he would also feel more isolated because of their emotionally 'empty' nature. Social interactions typical of the city, those required to obtain goods and services, were seen by Wirth as impersonal, *segmental* (narrow in scope), superficial, transitory, and usually of a purely practical or instrumental kind. These kinds of interactions were referred to as *secondary* contacts. Wirth considered that secondary contacts had increased at the expense of *primary* contacts, that is total relationships involving emotional as well as practical content, such as those within a family. Like Durkheim, Wirth saw a partial solution to individual atomisation in the rise of voluntary associations, representative political institutions, industrial organisations and other collective or corporate organisations. However, he too did not think these provided the quality of emotional self-expression characteristic of primary group relations.

It is in the work of another urban sociologist of the Chicago school, S. W. Burgess, that we find the most faithful application of functionalist theory to the physical and social development of the city. Burgess describes urban processes 'as a resultant of organisation and disorganisation analogous to the anabolic and katabolic processes of metabolism in the body.' More usually, Burgess draws on plant ecology rather than human biology as a model for understanding urban processes. He writes of 'urban ecology' almost as if it is an impersonal and natural phenomenon, rather than man-made and susceptible to control.

Burgess presents a model or, as he referred to it, ideal construction, of the tendency of urban areas to expand radially from the central business district. The centre circle of the series of concentric circles in the model is the main business area. Next comes the zone of transition containing the slums and ghettos of the lower working class and immigrant groups. This zone is also characterised by cheap hotels and lodging houses and the easy availability of drink and sex. Other descriptions of this zone used by Chicago sociologists still sometimes employed are 'twilight zone' and 'zone of deterioration.' Later we shall look in some detail at the analysis of lower class 'deviance' within this zone, developed by sociologists at the University of Chicago (Chapter 17, pp. 457–8). The next zone contains the homes of more successful and respectable working class people: it is an area of escape from the ghetto. Beyond are the higher class residential areas which make up the next zone. Finally, there is the commuter zone interspersed with countryside and farmland and merging into predominantly rural areas.

In his own day, Burgess' model was far from universally applicable – even in the United States. Since the Second World War, residential patterns have become still further complicated, particularly in countries such as England and Holland, where public housing projects have often been built outside the central urban zones. As a guide to the physical location of particular social groups and as a way of understanding why these groups inhabit particular areas, Burgess's work is inadequate. It does make the point, however, that social groups are cut off from one another both spatially and in their way of life or culture. Other urban sociologists, including Hoyt, have argued that a sectoral model provides a more accurate description of the patterns of neighbourhood layout. More recently, B. T. Robson's carefully researched study of residential patterns in Sunderland found

177

that Hoyt's model applied closely to the south of the city and Burgess', somewhat less precisely to the north.

Sociologists now consider other issues to be more important than the relationship between space and residential patterns as such. One such issue is to explain how physical and spatial environments affect people's social and cultural opportunities and the nature and quality of their interactions. We can refer to this type of analysis as *socio-spatial*. A further sociological concern is to identify the factors that enable some social and ethnic groups to live in 'desirable' neighbourhoods and which force others to live in slums. A major criticism of the sociologists of the Chicago school is that they largely ignored this problem. Their work is descriptive rather than explanatory. Instead of examining how the free-market system in land and property affected socio-spatial systems, they assumed these effects to be 'natural' and therefore did not analyse what caused them. Because they did not adequately examine how the control of wealth and power affects residential patterns and community life, their work can be said to be clearly limited by their own belief in, or ideological commitment to, capitalism. As with Tönnies, Durkheim and Parsons, what they took for granted masks vital issues of social justice both in relation to what might be considered a fair distribution of material resources (property ownership) and in respect of the differential availability of cultural opportunities (educational facilities) between people living in different areas. The Chicago school failed to refine and develop significantly the thinking of their mentor, Durkheim. In addition to the points made above, they underestimate both the survival of the community in the city and the ability of people to develop means of self-expression other than within primary groups. It is to the issue of 'loss of community' that we now turn.

Criticisms of the 'loss of community' thesis

The works we have so far discussed have been at the level of 'grand theory.' Perhaps the best way of testing the ideas presented in them is by means of the community study. Of course, it is impossible to go back and examine at first hand what community was once like but, at least, the persistent stereotype that community has declined can be measured against real cases. In addition, the world offers many examples of traditional as well as modern communities and these can be studied for comparative purposes. Our first case-study is of just such a kind.

SOME CASE STUDIES In the nineteen thirties, Robert Redfield published a study of social life in Tepoztlan, a Mexican village. He found a stable, well-integrated and harmonious community. In 1949 an account of the same village appeared, written by Oscar Lewis. He discovered a tense, divided and distrustful community. It seems highly probable that some of the apparent 'change' lay in the eyes of the beholder rather than in the social life of the people of Tepoztlan. More precisely, the two researchers approached the village with different expectations and theoretical perspectives: Redfield was predisposed to find community, and Lewis was conscious of the degradation that poverty can produce in traditional societies. Howard Newby, who has a keen eye for the relationship between sociologists' personal values, their choice of theoretical and methodological approach, and their ultimate 'findings,' describes the discrepancy between the reports of Redfield and Lewis as 'unnerving.' It reminds us that, despite sociologists' impressive battery of research apparatus, they, like others, sometimes end up seeing what they want to see. With due caution, therefore, it can only be said that Lewis further opened up the doubts about the *gemeinschaftlich* qualities of traditional communities.

Studies of urban life, however, have raised questions about the *gesellschaft* side of the comparative model. Herbert Gans' *The Urban Villagers* describes the lively, 'village-like' ethnic and working class communities of Boston's West End and New York's Lower East Side. The individual is seldom isolated, but supported by informal groups of family, kin and friends. We have already referred to Willmott and Young's Bethnal Green study which was published in 1957. Some seventy years after Tönnies mourned the passing of community, Willmott and Young found a thriving community in an inner city industrial area. They emphasise especially how 'mum' figures are at the centre of local interactions, functioning as combined information exchanges and transit-depots. The key link in the traditional working class extended family is the relationship between mother and daughter. This continues when the daughter is married because of the likelihood that the newly married couple

179

will live close to the female's family of origin or, in the early days of marriage, actually in her parents' home. Traditionally, men spent much of their leisure time separately from women in pubs and Working Men's or Labour Clubs. This pattern of segregation has long been breaking down, though there are still public bars in some areas where 'respectable' women would not drink, even in male company. Although there are enthusiastic exceptions, watching and playing football is largely a male monopoly and this is even more true of the declining sports of dog-racing and 'pigeon fancying.' As looking after the home is now quicker and easier, older working class women often turn to bingo to pass the time. Working class children of all ages tend to be left to get on with their own lives much more than middle class children and 'playing out in the backs' or 'on the streets' can be a major activity until well into adolescence, especially for boys. Any 'mischief they get up to' is likely to be met with rougher parental justice than a middle class child would normally expect to receive. Traditional working class community is woven in a web of 'talk' and 'gossip' and in the passing of time together in ways more or less amusing or practically useful. There are reserved areas of personal and family privacy but the whole is or was, essentially open, collective and social.

The waning of the above pattern of life might be regarded as a second phase – and, perhaps, a more genuine one – in 'loss of community.' Already Richard Hoggart's painstakingly detailed description of working class life in Hunslet has the quality of an old snapshot about it. But the fact that traditional working class community is breaking up does not mean it never existed. Some recent commentators, because they no longer find thriving working class communities of the kind described twenty five years ago by Willmott and Young and by Hoggart, seem almost to assume that the whole phenomenon is a romantic fiction. But one of the reasons for chronicling traditional working class life was an awareness of its imminent decline.

Coates and Silburn's excellent study of the lower working class St Anne's district of Nottingham falls somewhat into this trap. The fact that they find St Anne's to be a fragmented community does not mean it was always so. As they well illustrate, the decline of community was due partly to urban renewal policies – the effects of which had been emphasised by Willmott and Young in their Bethnal Green study well over a decade before. By 1970, St Anne's was a classic example of a working class community in decline. We attempt to explain the causes of the widespread decline of working class community later (but see also Chapter 4).

Another development that has undermined any simplistic rural-urban contrast is the fast growth of commuter villages. In *Urbs in Rure* (The City in the Countryside), R. E. Pahl draws our attention to the commuter invasion of rural areas. Some villages are almost wholly occupied by people who work elsewhere. Pahl has also written of the culture clash between indigenous village inhabitants and commuters. The irony is that in their search for community, commuters sometimes destroy what they are looking for. Other studies have shown that class division, business rationality and many of the problems of isolation and anomie frequently associated with urban life also occur in rural Britain.

In addition to the above case studies, it is worth recalling that historical enquiry has also thrown doubt on notions of traditional community, at least in so far as they depended on the predominance of the extended family (see Chapter 4).

SOME GENERAL POINTS OF CRITICISM OF 'THE LOSS OF COMMUNITY' THESIS The empirical data discussed in the previous section provides a tentative basis from which to make some general criticisms of the 'loss of community' thesis.

Firstly, it is an oversimplification. At both 'ends' of the continuum we have found evidence to contradict the model. Secondly, a related point: the model seems to underestimate the capacity of people to rebuild community in new circumstances after the break-up of their old communities. Thirdly, the *ideological* limits of the model need to be criticised. It is characterised by conservative nostalgia. As a result, it tends to miss or minimise the unpleasant aspects of traditional society. From this limited perspective, a crucial theoretical flaw emerges – which brings us to our fourth point. The model has no use for class or class conflict in the analysis of community life. It takes as a 'given' the capitalist system instead of examining how this system shapes social life. More recent work has sought to rectify this imbalance. Indeed, it has tended to argue that it is

181

precisely what the above critics ignored – capitalism and resultant class divisions – that account for the lack of community which so concerned them. Before examining these conflict-based approaches, however, we will briefly review the new towns movement in Britain which, among other things, represented a 'search for' better communities than had developed in the urban environment of industrialism.

THE NEW TOWNS: AN EXAMPLE OF 'THE SEARCH FOR COMMUNITY' The New Town concept, first popularised around the turn of the century by Ebenezer Howard, was an attempt to plan social idealism into reality. Howard's 'bread and roses' idealism aimed at providing the city dweller with improved housing in less crowded neighbourhoods with conveniently available facilities, but he also advocated sacrosanct agricultural areas around the town, and wanted to erode class barriers by introducing socially mixed neighbourhoods. Welwyn Garden City, one of the early new towns (1920), probably came closest to the fulfilment of Howard's dream but more recent new town developments tend to have been less ambitiously conceived. Notwithstanding the inevitable crop of mistakes and complaints there is no doubt that, in terms of basic amenities provided, the new towns are a vast improvement on what they replaced. One woman in Milton Keynes said: 'It's like being in paradise compared to where I used to live.' There is no doubt, despite her choice of metaphor, that she was thinking in terms of such things as an upstairs bathroom, spacious lounge, perhaps central heating, and having a toilet which belonged to her own house and which worked properly. Against the backcloth of inner city decay (which we examine shortly), the New Towns represented a substantial improvement in the standard of life of most who moved to them. Nevertheless, contrary to what is often imagined, only a small percentage of migrants from the inner city have gone to New Towns. Crucially, from the point of view of the decline of the inner city, these have often been skilled or semi-skilled workers and their families.

As an attempt to tinker with the class system by introducing 'socially balanced' neighbourhoods, the new towns have been less successful. A useful piece of research in this area is B. J. Heraud's *Social Class and the New Towns* – a detailed study of social class in Crawley. One of Heraud's crucial findings is that movement out of the originally mixed social class areas was usually to social-class defined communities. This was especially true of middle class families. The original balanced areas tended to become socially more working class whereas the middle class moved into the new subsidised housing areas. As Heraud points out, however, the commitment of the town's Urban Development Corporation to social balance seemed to weaken progressively, and it is possible that a more sustained experiment would be more successful.

In the middle nineteen seventies, as the total population went into slight decline and it became clear that the inner cities were, if anything, under- rather than over-populated, New Town developments have tended to slow down or be abandoned. Stonehouse, which was to have been near Glasgow, and the planned central Lancashire New Town, reputedly to have been named Red Rose, will probably stay on the drawing board. It may be that this slackening in momentum will provide opportunity to adjust to, and improve on, the changes that have already taken place.

The New Towns, therefore, have provided materially better communities than elsewhere, but not socially very different ones. In particular, they, too, are characterised by class division. Given that they exist in a predominantly capitalist society, this is probably inevitable.

Conflict-based Models of Urban-rural Analysis: Some Major Points

a THE SOCIAL EFFECTS OF CAPITALISM It is not only Marxist critics who find the ultimate cause of both urban and rural inequality and decay in the nature of capitalism, but the roots of such an analysis are certainly to be found in the writings of Marx and, his colleague, Engels. Unlike Durkheim and Tönnies, Marx's starting point for understanding society was not community or lack of it, but class. Marx believed that national and international community would be part of a socialist world but he did not consider that such community was possible under capitalism: competition and class conflict prevented it. Only *within* classes did he consider that community and *solidarity* (a sense of unity and mutual support) were normal, although he fully recognised that the capitalist ruling class would seek to produce a 'false' sense of national community so as to reduce class conflict and consolidate its own interests (see Chapter 3).

The contemporary Marxist, Manuel Castells, contextualises his analysis of urban life within a broad critique of capitalism. He sees almost every aspect of urban life as a spin-off from the capitalist system's need to have a readily-available pool of workers concentrated in the city. Because the education, housing and maintenance of these workers is not generally a profitable business, it is left to government to provide them. Sufficient resources are rarely allocated for these purposes. Castells sees the inefficiency and inadequacy of the welfare state and the dissatisfaction this produces as a potential weakness and conflict point in the 'system.' For Castells, there are no isolated problems of urban life: mothers inconvenienced through lack of nursery facilities, homelessness, and environmental negligence, are all explicable mainly in terms of a system concerned with private profit rather than public need. Thus, when a large national or multinational corporation decides to close a plant in a given area, the social effects can be enormous. For example, thousands became unemployed when Courtauld's closed down in Skelmersdale. After a few days an event like this ceases to be news, but the effect on people's lives can last for years.

A brilliant, if controversial, exploration of the relationship between the capitalist economic system and its social effects is John Rex and Robert Moore's *Race Community and Conflict*. Specifically, they examine how the *housing market* operates. In particular, they wanted to know why coloured immigrants occupied a disproportionate number of old, run-down inner city houses (either as tenants or, less often, as owner-occupiers) and relatively few council houses. The answer given was their weakness in the housing market. Low income often prevented them from obtaining mortgages and the length of residence requirement disqualified them from council housing (though this now applies to far fewer immigrants than when Rex and Moore wrote). Rex and Moore's theoretical framework perhaps owes more to Weber than Marx. Like Castells, however, their perspective is socio-economic rather than narrowly social. Recently, Rex has given more attention to the position of coloured immigrants in the job market and educational system, as well as in the housing market (see Chapter 12, p. 317).

b THE SOCIO-SPATIAL EFFECTS OF CAPITALISM The separation here of
the social and socio-spatial effects of capitalism is purely for the
purposes of presentation and in recognition of the fact that the
use of space has been of particular interest to sociologists in
recent years. Clearly, the amount and quality of space people
occupy and otherwise enjoy is a major feature of their social
life. The spatial question is, therefore, essentially a social rather
than a physical issue as far as we are concerned. 'Space' is
rather an abstract word, but what is meant is that identifiably
different groups of people occupy different 'bits of territory'
within a given society. Thus, as we saw, coloured immigrants
are over-represented in inner-city areas as, for that matter, are
poor whites. The middle class predominates in suburbia,
although, as Herbert Gans has shown, this is something of an
oversimplification as far as the United States is concerned.
What sociologists seek to do is to explain *why* some groups
occupy *more* and *better* space (both environmentally and in terms
of amenities) than others. Put as simply as possible, why do
some people live in bigger and better houses and less crowded
and more attractive neighbourhoods than others?

The answer given to the above question by the social geog-
rapher, David Harvey, is the same as that offered by Castells
and by Rex and Moore. The problems associated with the city
– housing, environmental decay, poverty, crime – are not
caused by the city as such, but by the way the socio-economic
system affects the city. In other words, the problems are *societal*
rather than essentially urban in nature. It is the unequal way
in which the employment, housing and consumer markets work
nationally (and *internationally*) that is the main cause of these
problems. Logically, therefore, these problems can also occur
outside the urban environment in places where the capitalist
system favours some at the expense of others. As we have seen,
R. E. Pahl's appropriately titled *Urbs in Rure* makes exactly this
point: high-income commuters and 'second-house' weekend vis-
itors introduce new class divisions and material and status inequalities into rural society. Raymond Williams, however, makes
the point that class divisions, including the glaring juxtaposition
of ostentatious wealth and humiliating poverty, have long been
a feature of rural life. He stresses that the capitalistic development of agriculture has often been as hard on the peasantry as
industrial development has been on the urban proleteriat.

Indeed, originally it was partly because the peasantry were dispossessed of their land by the agricultural revolution that they spilled into the cities in search of work. This sort of systematic socio-economic analysis is far from either the static concentric circles model of Burgess, or the simple rural-urban continuum of Tönnies.

c CLASS AND GROUP CONFLICT IN THE URBAN CONTEXT: CAPITAL, POLITICIANS, PLANNERS AND CITIZENS We now discuss the urban context in terms of groups which have power and those which have little or none. The groups we will consider are businessmen, politicians, miscellaneous 'gate-keepers' and the citizenship as a whole. These groups live and work within the limits of the capitalist system but they also contribute to the creation and changing of that system. The most important of these groups is the fourth and, accordingly, we devote more space to it.

Businessmen have power to affect the lives of other people. Investment provides work and a basis for prosperity, and lack of it causes unemployment and social hardship. The fact that we tend today to think of business in terms of large national and international companies and institutions may make economic power *seem* more impersonal, but the effects of it are real enough. If Henry Ford were to decide to switch car production to a European or American factory, there is relatively little that British Ford workers could do about it. It is true that trade unionists are beginning to respond to the international nature of many large companies by organising internationally themselves, but they often lack the resources and experience to do so effectively. In any case, the harsh truth is that, if private enterprise declines, withdraws or fails to invest in a given area, that area tends to decline socially as well as economically. The poverty and social deprivation of parts of the North East during the depression of the interwar period vividly demonstrates this.

National and local politicians are a second group whose power affects others. As elected representatives of the people, their policies ought to benefit the public though this does not always seem to happen. Let us look at local government first. Joe Chamberlain, as mayor of Birmingham in the eighteen sixties, was an early urban reformer who successfully sought to

186

improve the public amenities and standard of health of his city. His achievements were a model for other local politicians concerned with the standard of public amenities in their areas and were the prelude to great advances in civic provisions. Not all local authorities, however, have matched what he helped to inspire. Theoretically, government should be 'above' sectional interest and seek to serve the common good. This involves placing checks and controls on the activity of business. There is always a danger, however, that government may favour business 'development' at the expense of others. Sometimes it even happens that the immense revenues controlled by local authorities which are the practical basis of their power and patronage are mis-spent. Much of the design and construction of public works such as the building of roads and houses is contracted out by local authority officials to private companies of builders and architects. Inevitably, this sometimes leads to corruption. An example is the case of T. Dan Smith, the leading politician on Newcastle's Labour-dominated Council in the early nineteen seventies. Smith was found guilty of giving contracts to architect John Poulson in return for bribes and favours. Such clear-cut cases of corruption are rarely proven but sometimes Council contracts do seem to favour the interests of commercial developers rather than the public. After the Second World War, most working class people as well as most politicians believed that a new Council residence was worth the destruction of their old house. Now, doubt and suspicion have not infrequently come to replace trust and optimism.

A third 'group' which has power in the city is made up of planners, architects, state and local authority bureaucrats, welfare workers, and managers of banks and building societies. We include them together mainly as a matter of convenience. The important thing that these various people have in common is that their decisions can profoundly affect the lives of ordinary citizens. Because of this power they are sometimes referred to as 'gate keepers'. They can open or close the door to valuable resources such as public housing, social security payments and help from the social services. More than that, some of these agencies have great power to interfere in, and even radically change, the course of people's lives. Payment of social security will often be made dependent on a visit from an investigator who will ask a range of questions that in normal circumstances would be regarded as constituting an invasion of privacy. In some circumstances, investigation can continue in a secret and lengthy manner. Social security 'fiddling' is, understandably, not popular with the majority of the public and so the pryings of officialdom tend to be grudgingly accepted in this area by the tax-paying majority.

Planning policy, by contrast, is an example of bureaucratic power that has frequently provoked widespread condemnation. With the support of the politicians who employ them and who often depend on them for detailed advice, planning officers can make use of wide legal powers to require people to quit their houses which can then be destroyed. A number of key positions which regulate access to various resources controlled by private enterprise ought also to be mentioned here. In particular, money lending institutions of various kinds, notably banks and building societies, can make decisions that affect people's lives radically. For instance, acquiring a mortgage may mean the difference between independence, security and comfort for a family and the opposite. Yet often a remote 'expert' will assess a mortgage claim on the basis of prescribed rules with little idea, or perhaps even thought, about the human consequences of his decision.

We now discuss the most important group mentioned above, the citizenship as a whole. Actually, the phrase 'citizenship as a whole,' like 'the average man,' hides more than it reveals. What we really want to talk about are the varied individuals and groups who live or work in urban areas. For many of these people – and this is one of the most important observations in this book – the problems they have faced in the postwar period have caused them to adjust their practical understanding of democracy. Classically, democracy in Britain involves voting for a representative with, perhaps, occasional communications thereafter. Increasingly, people have become more aware of the possible conflict between their own interests and the policies of government and its official representatives. Sometimes the 'threat' seems to come from an alliance of government and business. Let us give an example.

Bridgtown is a small suburb of the town of Cannock in Staffordshire. In 1976, the Bridgtown Redevelopment Inset Plan stated that 'the redevelopment of the area for industrial purposes will ultimately necessitate the removal of all residential

188

property.' The opposition to this plan in the 1,500-strong community was considerable, and much of it was challenged through the Bridgtown Residents' Action Group. A newspaper report quotes one particularly uncompromising resident, a Mr Tart, as follows:

> 'They'll have to carry me out of here. I'm staying.'

Another observed:

> This place was built because of industry, we have learned to live with it. There is no need to mow us down.

In response to the opposition, the chief planning officer produced the circular argument that the development of more industry in Bridgtown would lead to a further deterioration in the district as a residential area and that it was therefore in the best interests of the residents to be rehoused over a period of years.

It would take much more space than is available here to establish the merits of this conflict. What is important is to appreciate the organised response to a perceived threat of members of the Bridgtown community. Although their roles are not examined in the above brief account, it is clear that industrialists – who would supply some of the resources for 'development' – and politicians – who have the power to pass the plan into law or not – are as deeply involved as the planners in the conflict. Although the Bridgtown example is a particularly graphic case of community power politics, similar conflicts are reported almost daily in the press.

Communities are created and recreated in a crucible of power. Decisions taken by businessmen, politicians and planners affect the lives of individuals and communities. C. Wright Mills sought passionately in his writings to make people aware of the relationship between 'private' troubles and 'public' or political issues. It is largely in an attempt to control, or at least to influence and make more accountable, the above powerful groups that community action movements began rapidly to develop in the nineteen sixties. These movements vary widely in kind and purpose. Tenants' Associations are concerned with practical matters of self and group interest such as rents and living conditions. They bear a similar relationship to community life as do trade unions to work: they aim to protect the interest of their members. More *ad hoc* groups may organise around an issue affecting a particular local area at a given time. An example from the provinces is the protest group in Preston's suburb of Ashton, which organised against a plan to drive a road through an avenue of birches in Haslem Park.

Where an issue is general rather than local – such as homelessness – a movement with a wider geographical base of support may develop. For instance, there were some 30,000 estimated squatters in the Greater London area in 1977, many of whom received some assistance from the London Union of Squatters. Their case was that London's many homeless should be matched with the even greater number of empty residential properties in the area. Against this is the legal argument that they do not own the property they squat in and the administrative one that they should wait their turn in the official queues for public housing.

Many community groups in poor areas have been built up partly by the efforts of young middle class activists. If this is a necessity for the existence of some groups, it is also invariably their weakness. Whatever the strength of their idealism, middle class activists can rarely afford to stay in deprived areas for a long period. Accordingly, some seek employment as community workers in voluntary or statutory (government) agencies in order to continue their work of trying to organise the poor and to channel what resources they can in their direction. (For further information on community movements, see Chapter 17).

It can be argued that the community movements of the past two decades represent a revival of a sense of local community. Perhaps the challenge is to transform their necessarily self-defensive nature into more positive channels. There are some signs in this direction. A number of local authorities allow their tenants to paint and decorate their houses within generous limits. Some local social services pay untrained 'community people' to 'keep an eye on' older residents. For such changes to become widespread would mean that 'we' rather than 'they' would need to take much of the day to day responsibility for neighbourhood life. Whether people want to dilute the 'privatised' pursuit of happiness for such involvement is a moot point.

The Inner City: An Example of Conflict Analysis

This section is about the inner city not as a physical entity but as the focal point of the activity of groups of people, the most powerful of whom are probably businessmen, politicians and top civil servants. Sometimes these groups act in concert and sometimes in conflict, but their major decisions affect the lives of the rest of us. More abstractly, we want to show how the capitalist system operates on the inner city – always bearing in mind that government can try to act as a checking or, to use Galbraith's term, *countervailing power* to control business as well as to smooth its path.

Since the Second World War the inner city or, more precisely, the inner city ring (the area *around* the business centre) has been inhabited by low income groups and beset by social problems. Once-thriving manufacturing areas were hit by the decline of such staple industries as docking, shipbuilding, textile production and heavy manufacturing. Manchester, Liverpool, Glasgow, Belfast, Newcastle and Inner London all developed 'inner city problem areas.' For instance, the break-up of traditional working class community in East London (see above, Willmott and Young) was due to the decline of the docks and the associated service and distribution trades. In addition, advanced technology and large scale industry made the craft industries and other small scale production units of the East End obsolete and uncompetitive. People moved out in droves. Between 1961 and 1971, almost 100,000 people left the single borough of Tower Hamlets. Those that remained in inner London were drawn, disproportionately, from the old, socially disadvantaged, unskilled and semi-skilled workers. They were joined by coloured immigrants who were prepared to do unskilled and semi-skilled work in the inner city of a kind that many whites wished to avoid.

It would be quite misleading to 'blame' individual businessmen for the above situation. Many of them also suffered as a result of the decline of Britain's traditional industrial base. The point to pursue is a quite different one. It is that when capitalism falters or fails – even if only in the process of change rather than collapse – it is incapable of rectifying the resultant adverse social consequences. The capitalist system works on profit, not philanthropy, and when it fails it is left to the sometimes reluctant hand of government to pick up the pieces.

We now look more closely at occupants of the inner city (and in part, the centre city) to show that class factors like income and education mean that people in the same geographical zone lead radically different lives. Inner city occupants can be divided into various disadvantaged groups: immigrants, 'cosmopolites,' and some members of the upper class. We have already explained why the disadvantaged and immigrants are disproportionately represented in the inner city, and we will have much more to say about them later (see Chapters 10 and 13). 'Cosmopolites,' to use Gans' term, include students, artists, writers, musicians, entertainers as well as other intellectuals and professionals. Though some may be quite poor, this is not the definitive feature of life that it is for disadvantaged groups: for them the city is meaningful because it provides opportunity for self-expression and experience. The fact that different social groups can live in close physical proximity, yet socially in different 'worlds', is still better illustrated by reference to the very rich who keep a town residence (often in the centre rather than inner city) as well as, often, a country home. A member of the upper class may live a stone's throw from a poor community but is sealed off from its occupants by wealth, privilege and power. The urban environment may be the physical limits of the poor man's world but the rich man is much more geographically mobile: he can escape to the 'country' or abroad, almost at will. On the whole, the upper class do not live or spend time in the countryside to seek community except in some cosmetic or whimsical sense. Their residences are usually well secluded from those of nearby inhabitants, although traditionally-minded landed aristocrats and gentry may still pride themselves on being 'part of the local community,' however cushioned their position may be by privilege and by the deference afforded to them. In fact most of these, like the nouveaux riches who have bought into rural real estate, tend to have friends of similar social status who, in the nature of things, are unlikely to live close by. The upper class, however, can afford to travel and visits and meetings are easily arranged. Friendship networks are likely to be national or international and may seem to have an unreal, 'starry' quality to those outside the charmed circle. Members of the upper class know each other but others only know of them. Recently, upper middle and middle class people have bought property in some previously working class areas in the inner city. This process is sometimes referred to as 'gentrification.' It has added to the jigsaw-like quality of the social patterns of residence of many of Britain's cities.

The role of national government in helping to create the above social and demographic (population distribution) patterns is important. In the post-war period, government and industry co-operated to disperse industry and population away from the old industrial areas. The new town movement was part of this policy. The centre and inner city zones were redeveloped as office and service areas. Some of the new housing, including high rise flats and large estates, was of poor quality and design. 'Living in the sky' made community virtually impossible and caused families great practical problems. Even so, the new housing was generally a material, if not an aesthetic, improvement on what was left undemolished of the old inner city housing stock. Most of this came to be occupied by those groups who, for reasons already mentioned, did not participate in the new 'out of city' expansion. Welfare state expenditure tends to be relatively high in inner city areas although this is a palliative, not a solution to the basic problem. Various government schemes have been adopted to encourage the economic development of these areas. As in similar schemes in the United States, money has tended to disappear without much seeming to happen. Perhaps this is because the basic economic and planning trends described above tend to be 'inevitable.'

The above account of the inner city is intended to illustrate the inequalities and potential conflict caused by the capitalist system. Whether government is seen as the handmaiden of capitalism or the saviour of its 'victims' is a matter for personal assessment, but what is undeniable is their mutual involvement in inner city processes.

The *gemeinschaft-gesellschaft* model is not adequate to analyse rural and urban social life. The 'loss of community' thesis has some basis in that there has almost certainly been a decline in the *local* basis of relationships but divisions of class, power and status characterised traditional societies as they do modern. Simply to see modern urban life in terms of lack of community is to ignore the major economic and political forces that structure social life. It is towards an understanding of these forces that recent 'urban' sociology has tended to be directed. As a result, 'urban' sociology has often become national or even international in scope. What happens in Calcutta today may well have been decided by the United Nations or World Bank in Washington yesterday.

Development and Underdevelopment

Terms and Issues

The concept of social *development* from the traditional to the modern was implied in the evolutionary theories of Durkheim and Tönnies. It is the term now generally used to describe the same transition in respect of countries in the non-industrialised world: underdevelopment refers to lack of industrial development. For obvious reasons, some find that these terms imply a superiority on the part of the 'developed' over the 'underdeveloped' nations. 'More developed' and 'less developed' is a common alternative usage as is 'developed' and 'developing.' As J. K. Galbraith suggests, the terms rich and poor nations are probably the simplest and truest. The terms First, Second and Third World are useful. The First world is the United States and Western European capitalist democracies, the Second World is the Soviet Union and its communist bloc allies, and the Third World is the poor or relatively poor countries.

Breakdown of employment in selected countries:—

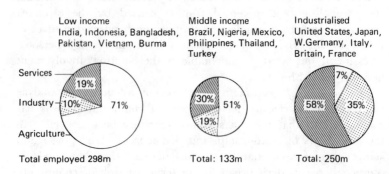

Low income
India, Indonesia, Bangladesh, Pakistan, Vietnam, Burma

Middle income
Brazil, Nigeria, Mexico, Philippines, Thailand, Turkey

Industrialised
United States, Japan, W.Germany, Italy, Britain, France

Services — 19%
Industry — 10% 71%
Agriculture

30% 51%
19%

7%
58% 35%

Total employed 298m

Total: 133m

Total: 250m

Levels of Development

Note. The percentages refer to levels of employment in given economic sectors.

Source: *The Economist,* February 24, 1979, p. 32.

We need to extend the above description of the economic and political divisions of the world. Not all countries fit neatly into a developed/underdeveloped categorisation. The diagram above shows three groups of countries at different levels of development on the basis of income and predominant type of production (agriculture, industry, services). A large service sector is a sign of advanced industrial development; such economies, like that of the United States, are sometimes referred to as *post-industrial* or *post-modern*. The diagram also gives population data. The major point to note here is that the poorest countries tend to have relatively larger populations.

Perhaps the most difficult countries to fit into a development perspective are the oil-rich nations of the Middle East. Their industry is often not modern with the exception of oil production, their culture is frequently an uneasy mix of the traditional and modern, and the services many of their inhabitants enjoy, especially the elites, are post-modern in quality. What is not in doubt is that their oil gives them great power.

Power is a central concept in understanding the 'modern' world. Fierce competition for influence, if not always control, exists in various parts of the world between the major communist nation, the USSR, and the major capitalist nation, the USA. Not all communist nations support the USSR, nor do all capitalist nations support the USA. These *non-aligned* nations include India (capitalist) and China (communist). The model below usefully combines economic and political divisions of the world though it does not give details of alignment and non-alignment.

	Developed	Underdeveloped
Communist	USSR EASTERN EUROPE NORTH KOREA	CHINA, VIETNAM, CUBA
Capitalist	USA, EEC, JAPAN, AUSTRALIA, SOUTH AFRICA	CAPITALIST THIRD WORLD eg INDIA

Why does development matter? Selfishly, it is important because Britain is a world wide trading nation and 'depends' on other countries for raw materials and markets – including,

195

increasingly, the developing world. Less selfishly, the major practical and cultural issues in the contemporary world are undoubtedly global in nature. Poverty is the major material issue and we examine it further in Chapter 11. Poverty is largely about trying to feed and clothe people, so it is intimately linked to population increase. The final section of this chapter in part deals with population and poverty in the Third World and, to that extent, is a direct continuation of this section.

Environmental and ecological issues are also of global concern. The reduction of poverty depends on the development of the world's food and energy resources, but this should not occur at the expense of the environment or of the ecological (natural) processes that produce the balanced conditions in which life can exist. In particular, the development of nuclear and/or other forms of energy casts a shadow over the last part of this century. The malfunctioning of the nuclear energy plant on Three Mile Island and the subsequent finding that birth abnormalities doubled in the immediate proximity reminds us of the potential dangers of nuclear energy.

We now turn to some cultural issues that arise from development. History shows us that people from different cultures tend to distrust and exploit one another (though not always or completely). In the recent past, the balance of power and of exploitation has been heavily on the side of the West (for an illustration of this point, see the opening section of our chapter on Race – Chapter 13). Exploitation has been given a crude edge by the common assumption among Westerners that their culture is superior to others. Not surprisingly, as ex-colonial nations regain their independence and self-confidence, they frequently reject certain aspects of Western values and culture and seek for themselves positive forms of cultural expression and meaning. Sometimes these take the form of a reassertion of traditional values and behaviour, as in Iran, or the adoption of socialist or Marxist beliefs as a new ideological basis on which to re-organise the country. China, Tanzania and Zimbabwe are examples here. Certain countries, such as Kuwait, which, to varying degree, seek to retain traditional identity, also adopt certain convenient capitalist institutions and values.

As the last point indicates, the material and cultural aspects of development are not, in reality, separate. Within the limits of its own history and circumstances, each nation or 'bloc' of nations attempts to decide the identity it wants to 'develop.' The word 'develop' is used with an intentional double-meaning here. Development is not something that simply happens in a material sense: still less is it merely imposed by international agencies like the World Bank or International Monetary Fund (in its loan-making capacity). It also involves *acts of conscious creation*. Mao, Castro of Cuba, and Julius Nyerere of Tanzania have all consistently sought to guide their newly free nations to a fresh identity, and to articulate what that identity might be. In his own way, the Ayatollah Khomeini has attempted to do the same.

Modernisation Theory (Functionalist Approach)

It is now widely considered that the functionalist-inspired, modernisation theory of Talcott Parsons, Walt Rostow and others offers too simple a model for the understanding of the problems of development and underdevelopment. Yet, despite its limitations, it is of great interest as an application of this type of theory. It is also helpful from a descriptive, if less from an explanatory, point of view.

It is worth reiterating that Parsons' pattern variables model is useful as a *general* pointer to the differences between traditional and modern societies. We now proceed to Parsons' *explanation* of how the change from the traditional to the modern takes place. Functionalists tend to describe change in terms of *evolutionary adaptation. The social system seeks to retain equilibrium even when adapting to change, although a major change may cause social equilibrium to settle at a different level.* Parsons uses the term *dynamic* or *moving equilibrium* to describe this process. Thus, a country may absorb the impact of industrial and agricultural technology and, after some social change and unrest, may settle down to the more complex equilibrium of a relatively advanced society. Perhaps contemporary Brazil – 'half' modern, 'half' traditional – is such a society. When countries adapt to external (or *exogamous*) factors, like the influx of 'foreign' technology and expertise, their institutions change. Thus, their banking systems may become more complex. This process is referred to by Parsons as *differentiation* and when it occurs on a large and extensive scale, as it does in the change from traditional to modern society, the term *structural differentiation* is used.

Parsons' model has some descriptive value but is severely limited. First, it assumes that societies will all 'develop' in the same direction, from traditional to modern. This is an important application of what is termed *convergence theory* which makes precisely this assumption (see Chapter 10, p. 274). He is so confident of this that he even introduces a 'half-way house' in the form of an *intermediate stage*. Actually, it is not certain that all societies either can or will want to proceed with modernisation. Because of their over-population, Third World countries need labour intensive, not machine intensive, development and if this occurs a quite different social structure may develop from the one we, in the West, are used to. Secondly, Parsons is inclined to exclude from his scheme the external causes of change in traditional societies in so far as they relate to political and ideological factors such as imperialism, colonisation and economic and human exploitation. As so often in his thinking, everything is a bit abstract and impersonal. Thirdly, and continuing the theme of impersonality, Parsons tends to forget that *people* have some choice in creating the kind of society they want – it is not simply a question of *institutional* adjustment and differentiation. Parsons' conceptualisation of choice and motive is cramped by what was referred to earlier as his 'oversocialised' conception of man.

Walt Rostow, an economist, argues that societies fall into five categories of economic development. These are

1 *The Traditional Society*
2 *The Pre-conditions for Take-off*
3 *The Take-off*
4 *The Drive to Maturity*
5 *The Age of High Mass Consumption (modern society).*

Without going into unnecessary detail, Rostow's stages simply represent the varying degrees to which the values and institutions of Western capitalism are accepted and adopted by underdeveloped societies. His model of convergence is cruder than Parsons' and, in particular, he greatly underestimates the extent to which sections of the same societies may be at quite different 'stages of development,' varying from the feudal to the modern. It is arguable that Parsons' analysis could be refined to accommodate the criticisms made of it, but Rostow's model is so openly biased to capitalistic forms of development that it smacks of propaganda. For example, he went so far as to call Communism a 'disease of transition.'

Underdevelopment (Dependency) Theory

A number of more recent writers have produced an alternative theory of development – even though they do not, of course, agree on all points. The Marxist-influenced or Neo-Marxist, Gunder Frank, was among the first to attack modernisation theory. Instead, he suggested a theoretical approach which paid more attention to the problems and aims of underdeveloped countries and which also analysed what he termed 'the world-embracing system' of capitalism of which both the under-developed and developed countries are a part (a point we explain in a moment). These two points set development in a wholly different context from that discussed above. Indeed, Frank's determination to 'put the Third World first' leads him to prefer the term 'the sociology of underdevelopment' to that of the 'sociology of development'. He points out that the gap between the wealth of the developed and underdeveloped nations is growing and that by no means all Third World countries seem destined to develop: some stagnate or even 'underdevelop.'

It is his second point, however, that has found a more potent echo in the work of other writers. The relationship between Western capitalism and the underdeveloped countries is now commonly seen in terms of imperialism and economic exploitation. It is true that the formal political-legal framework of empire has gone but economic *dependency* remains. Often Third World countries depend almost wholly for 'non-aid' income on a single major crop or commodity such as sugar (Cuba), sisal (Tanzania) and copper (Zambia). If these fetch a poor price on the world market, the whole social life of these countries is affected. The basis of dependency lies in the exploitation of Third World resources by the developed countries for use in the production of manufactured goods some of which are exported to the Third World but most of which are sold in the home markets. This unequal relationship is sometimes referred to as *metropolis-satellite* and *core-periphery*. Wallerstein has interestingly suggested that the nature of the world economy is *more* capitalistic than the internal economy of many capitalist countries. This is because the state is able to intervene within the national context to counterbalance the power of capital (big corporations). As there is no world government, there is no major organisational force to check the power of multi-national corporations. In *this* sense, they are responsible to no power greater than themselves. National governments do, of course, have a general legal authority over the businesses within their boundaries but often, in the case of Third World countries, they know that unless they provide the conditions that multi-national corporations want, the latter may decide against trade and investment and without this there may not be development. Partly because they are overwhelmingly funded by American and Western European money and attach stringent conditions to loans, international aid agencies like the World Bank cannot really be considered to right this balance of power. Indeed, they do not seem concerned to do so. On the contrary, sometimes Third World countries find themselves locked in an 'ideological' conflict with development agencies. At the time of writing, Julius Nyerere of Tanzania is insisting that the 'strings' (such as less public spending) that the International Monetary Fund is attaching should not interfere with the policies of egalitarian socialism that he is committed to following.

The most convincing criticisms of neo-Marxist analysis of development have been partial rather than total. John G. Taylor, a sympathetic commentator, argues that the sociology of underdevelopment offers an explanation of why under-development occurs – the more capitalist intervention, the less development – but it has not produced a *positive* theory of development. To argue that Third World countries should avoid *dependency* on capitalist powers – whether corporate or national – does not tell them what they should do. An important point which, oddly, is seldom clearly made in the relevant literature is that, as well as Western influence, Soviet money, expertise and ideology is playing an increasing role in world development and politics generally. Cuba survives largely on Soviet 'aid.' Some of the emerging African nations, such as Angola, also have close links with the Soviet Union. Elsewhere, socialist countries seek greater independence by balancing off Soviet and Western aid. As we said above, the world presents a very mixed picture in both economic and political terms. There is great instability and, at times, everything seems 'up for grabs.' This is certainly a period when people need to reflect carefully on the values and institutions they and their countries stand for and seek to extend.

Population, Social Policy and Planning

Demography – the study of population statistics – is of vital contemporary concern because of the rapid increase in the world's population, particularly since the end of the Second World War. According to the best estimates, the world population was 2,500 million in 1950, 4,300 million in 1977 and is likely to be more than 6,000 million in the year 2000. In other words, the world's population will have much more than doubled in fifty years. Most of this increase has occurred in the poorer countries of the world. The brute questions are – does the world have the resources to provide at least a minimally adequate standard of living for these people and, if it has, is there a sufficiently high level of international co-operation and humanitarian commitment to mobilise them? The 0.4% of their gross national product devoted to aid in 1980 by the rich Western nations hardly seems to constitute this kind of effort. The target of 0.7% suggested for 1985 by the Brandt Commission on the Third World is not expected to be achieved. It is easy for us to forget that famine, drought, disease and warfare are still 'natural' ways of controlling population in much of the world.

It would be a great practical help if world population increase slowed down or stopped. In this respect, the history of the advanced industrial countries offers some hope: most of them, including Britain, have gone through three stages of population development. First is a long period of very gradual population increase. Secondly, a period of very rapid increase occurs during industrialisation and, thirdly, population size becomes stable, with minor fluctuations either way. We will use Britain to examine the basic concepts and patterns of population development and some associated problems of social planning. This is not only a convenient but also an appropriate choice, in that Britain is very representative of advanced industrial countries in this matter. We then return to consider the global dimension of population.

Three major factors affect population size: the *birth rate*, the *death rate* and the *rate of migration*. The migration rate is the difference between immigration and emigration. The birth rate is the number of live births per 1,000 of the population in a given year, and the death rate the number of deaths per 1,000 of the population. The death rate in Britain has fallen steadily throughout this century, although at 11.5 it is unlikely to fall much further unless there is a major medical breakthrough in the areas of heart disease or cancer. Like the death rate, the birth rate has been subject to a long-term downward trend from the mid-Victorian period but there have been significant variations in this pattern, notably the post second world war baby 'boom' and the ensuing drop (1965–1977). The reason for the decline in the birth rate is that people have both wanted to reduce family size and, because of improved methods of contraception and more easily available abortion, have been able to do so. The decrease in the number of children born per 1,000 women of childbearing age is referred to as a decline in the *fertility rate*. Contrary to what is often thought, rather more people emigrate from Britan than immigrate to it: between 1968 and 1977, just over half a million more people left than entered.

The concept of *dependency ratio* is central in understanding the relationship between population and policy making. The dependency ratio is the proportion of people out of work (and dependent) against those in work. The dependent population is, therefore, mainly made up of children and the retired. Although the dependency ratio is now falling slightly and is likely to continue to do so until about the year 2000, it rose sharply between 1931 and the early nineteen seventies. In 1931, the dependency ratio was 5:10 and in 1974, 7:10 – a very substantial increase. It is perhaps fortunate that the gross national product about doubled over the same period. There are two major reasons for the increase in the dependency ratio. Firstly, children remain at school longer. The main cause of this was the raising of the school leaving age in 1972 and the increase in the proportion of children staying on in education after 16. Secondly, not only did the total number of old people generally increase, the number of *very* old did so enormously. Between 1951 and 1977 the number of old people over 85 more than doubled to over 450,000. The increase of dependents in both these areas required a corresponding increase in national spending on education and social security.

Speculation about future population trends and the likely consequences for government policy is notoriously liable to inaccuracy. Nevertheless, some tentative policy projections can be made on the basis of existing *firm knowledge* about past population trends. The birth rate in the relevant two periods tells us that the number of children in schools is going to continue to decrease in the nineteen eighties (the number of children under 15 has been falling since 1975) and that the number of people reaching retirement age in the last 20 years of the century is, with one major and some minor fluctuations, going to drop. These trends are due, respectively, to a decline in the birth rate of over a third between 1964 and 1977 and a previous drop between 1914 and 1932 – with the exception of the usual post-war 'bulge'.

Predictably, the effect of the decline in the birth rate between 1964 and 1977 first affected primary schools. Policies of closure or amalgamation, later to be applied to secondary schools, were adopted by some local authorities. There was a severe cut-back in the number of teachers to be trained. Teacher unemployment increased as did the number of teachers on short-term contracts. In 1980, the Conservative government decided to cut back the educational budget by 6% over four years in anticipation of a decline in the school population of over 13% in the same period – to considerable accompanying unrest in the teaching profession. The root cause of this situation – a low birth rate – is unlikely substantially to change despite the slight rise between 1977–79. Of course, if the planners are wrong and there *is* a sustained rise in the birth rate *and* more young people stay on at school (perhaps because of rising unemployment), then the educational system may suddenly be without sufficient teachers, buildings and equipment. That is the problem with 'futurology' – the experts can rarely anticipate all relevant variables. We will not pursue our second major example of the effect of population change on policy as the position of the elderly is fully discussed in the final section of Chapter 14, pp. 354-7.

It would be convenient if the neat balance by which the newly born replace the dead in Britain were repeated in the underdeveloped world. For several reasons this is not at all the case. On the contrary, unless policies are employed to prevent it, the world's population will boom to 10 billion before the end of the next century with 9 out of 10 living in today's developing nations. The way in which the birth and death rates have spiralled down together in the West has not been repeated in the underdeveloped world. The introduction of better medicine, agricultural technology and nutrition has reduced the death rate but there has not been a corresponding drop in the birth rate. This is partly for practical and partly for cultural reasons. Generally, it is easier to get medicine and food to people than to teach them contraceptive techniques. Cultural attitudes in predominantly agricultural societies traditionally tend to favour large families. Historically, large families were an investment against isolation and want in old age, but now they are a prescription for poverty. Whatever, the practical and cultural difficulties, however, a solution to the population 'problem' is necessary if world poverty is to be abolished or even significantly reduced.

Guide to further reading and study

Camilla Lambert and David Weir's *Cities in Modern Britain* (Fontana, 1975) is a very good general reader on community and urbanisation. The 'Community' section in Weir and Butterworth's *The Sociology of Modern Britain* (Fontana, 1976) contains some useful extracts. Ronald Frankenberg's *Communities in Britain* (Penguin, 1967) is a good general introduction to community theory and also gives a survey of major community studies including Frankenberg's own participant observational study of a Welsh village, where he joined the local football club (albeit on the administrative rather than the playing side!) Colin Bell and Howard Newby's *Community Studies* covers much European and American, as well as British Material. Ray Pahl's *Whose City? And Further Essays On Urban Society* (Penguin, 1975) is a helpful selection from the author's work. Particularly recommended is a comprehensive collection of readings edited by John Raynor and Elizabeth Harris *The City Experience* (Ward Lock Educational, 1977). A useful reader of short extracts from Castells, Gorz and other Marxists or radicals is John Cowley *et al, eds, Community or Class Struggle* (stage 1, 1977).

Research into a community problem – perhaps with an interventionist intention (with a view of doing something about it) – might well appeal to many students. To do this successfully from an academic point of view requires considerable planning.

Raymond Williams' *The Country and the City* (Paladin, 1975) has a penultimate chapter which compares rural-urban problems within countries to the relationship between the underdeveloped and developed world. This chapter, at least, is worth reading. The 'Society Today' section of *New Society* (April 17, 1980) gives a useful 'sub-'A' level' introduction to development. Peter Worsley's *Modern Sociology* (Penguin, 1978) contains a collection of readings on this issue. R. K. Kelsall's *Population* (Longman, 1975), is a standard introduction to the area.

Past Questions

1 'Sociological analyses of the city as a social unit suffer from inadequate attention to political conflict in cities.' Discuss (AEB, 1976)

2 Critically assess the view that urban life is characterised by role specific relationships whereas in rural life role diffuse relationships predominate. (AEB, 1978)

3 Many cities have 'problem areas' near the centre. Why is this? (AEB, 1979)

4 To what extent are sociological theories concerning social change useful for understanding changes in contemporary society? (JMB, 1977)

5 Give a critical assessment of theories of development and underdevelopment

6 What is the relationship between population 'explosion' and social order and change?

Section C **Stratification**

How to Use this Section

The thematic unity of this section is too obvious to be laboured: it is that of *stratification*. The six chapters specifically about stratification are the cornerstone not only of this section but of the whole book. The major stratificational divisions of class, gender, race and generation drive wedges between the lives of us all. The study of them is essential to our understanding of the structure and operation of our society and of our own social experience. Chapters 9 to 13 deal with the main areas of stratification; the other, Chapter 8, is a simple introduction to the basic theory of the area. Because although stratification explains so much about society it, too, must be explained. Definitions of class differ, but the immediate origins of stratification lie in the relationships people have to economic production and in the way work is organised. For this reason, Chapter 9 begins with a review of recent economic development in Britain, and its effect on stratification.

The ground covered in the first three chapters of this section is necessary to any advanced course in sociology. Most syllabuses, however, would allow for selection in the areas of gender, race and generation.

8 Introduction to Stratification (Theory 5)

Definition and Importance of Stratification

Stratification is the division of a society or group into layers. In modern societies the most important of these layers is social class. As was explained at the beginning of the previous chapter, class must be understood within the economic context of society. This point is further pursued below. Stratification occurs in almost infinite variety: height, weight, physical attractiveness, prowess at sport, academic attainment can all be used as a basis for stratification although they might be relevant only in specific contexts – height, for example, in selecting a basketball team.

The division of society into layers, or *strata* (stratum – singular), as they are more frequently called, is often compared to geological formation. But to compare social stratification to layers of rocks, one on top of each other, suggests more rigidity in social structure than is usually found. If we remind ourselves that the relationship between geological strata can shift and change, the simile begins to tell us more about the dynamic relationship between social strata. Further, just as in certain cases, where there is extreme tension between geological strata, an earthquake can erupt and change the structure of the land, so, too, extreme social conflict, in the form of revolution or invasion, can overturn social orders.

It would be a small-minded contemporary sociologist who failed to recognise wider units of stratification than those within the nation-state: most conspicuous is the division of the world into rich and poor nations. As we saw in the previous chapter, the wealthy nations are themselves divided into two major blocs – the Soviet, and United States/Western European blocs. These two blocs vie for influence in the poor or Third World, using as their means both 'aid' and, in some cases, military intervention.

The term social *differentiation* is often found in the context of stratification, although it has a wider application. *Differentiation refers to that which makes an individual or group separate and distinct:* thus differentiation provides a basis for categorisation and comparison. For instance, within class strata, occupation, income, and education provide criteria for differentiation, classification and comparison. Given adequate data, it is possible to place every individual in a given class within the social class structure – that is, to differentiate individuals and groups from one another.

We will introduce the concept of *social mobility* only briefly here, as a full section will be devoted to it in the next chapter. *Social mobility refers to movement either up or down the social hierarchy to a different social status or position.* In industrial society this is usually brought about by occupational change.

Stratification in Pre-Industrial Societies

There are two major reasons for comparing traditional, or pre-industrial, forms of stratification to industrial, class-stratified society. Firstly, traditional societies continue to exist in what we arrogantly call 'the modern world'. Indeed, even those societies, which are the most basic and 'under-developed' continue to survive in parts of Africa, Australia, South America, and elsewhere. There are many areas of the world in which the traditional and the modern come into contact and, invariably, conflict. Thus, the modernisation programme of the Shah of Iran, aided by Western expertise and technology, so enraged traditional Muslim believers (not least over the question of female emancipation) that a popular backlash developed which forced him to leave the country in early 1979, and threw into doubt the future direction in which the country would move. As we shall briefly consider later, the recent history of India can also be seen in terms of the coming together of the traditional and the modern – often with conflicting results.

A second reason for surveying forms of stratification in traditional societies is that a comparative perspective may enable us to see more clearly what the origins and causes of stratification are. This enquiry implies the additional question: is stratification universal – does it occur in all societies? The answer, in turn, prepares the way for what is, in a sense, the 'sixty-four thousand dollar question' about stratification: is it inevitable? We attempt to answer this question in Chapter 11, pp. 280-3.

Estate and Caste Societies
Estate systems date back to the ancient Roman Empire, but the

European feudal system may be taken here as the most relevant example of this form of stratification. In an estate system, the people of the various strata were identified by the rights they had and the duties they were expected to perform. These rights and duties were enforceable by law or by military might. At the top of the feudal hierarchy in medieval England were the king, nobility and clergy. The gentry, free tenants, and serfs followed in order of descent. A most important right, from the king's point of view, was that of being able to summon the nobility to provide soldiers for him. This was established when they took their oath of allegiance to him. It was generally believed that the feudal system was 'sanctioned by Almighty God'.

In general, there were therefore strong legal barriers against social mobility in estate systems. Exceptions could occur, however. The king could ennoble a given individual. The church provided an avenue of social ascent for some able individuals – as, indeed, it was intended to do. The growth of a powerful commercial and industrial class, and with it the increasing demand for economic and political rights, contrary to feudal law and practice, eventually undermined the feudal system in Europe. Even so, its influence lingers on – perhaps most conspicuously in the survival of the House of Lords.

Another form of stratification is the *caste system*. A pure caste system is a form of stratification rooted in religious belief, involving rigid ranking according to birth, and restrictions on occupation and marriage. The Hindu caste system of India comes closest to matching this definition. The term 'caste' has also come to be used more widely to refer to any hereditary and exclusive social group. In caste societies, social mobility is open to groups but not to individuals. This is because every individual, from the highest to the lowest, is considered to be divinely predestined to fulfil the role into which he has been born. In India, the caste system has been undermined, but by no means destroyed, by Western influence: caste and class exist uncomfortably side by side.

Sometimes more change took place in estate and caste societies than was officially admitted. A major reason why estate and caste societies seem rigid and unchanging is that those groups who benefited from the *status quo* did not want to accept or sometimes even acknowledge change. They managed

210

to persuade themselves and, to a remarkable extent, the 'lower orders' as well, that society was best at it was. The sociologist, however, must not be so foolish as to accept their biased view of reality. The powerful and privileged may not want change, but they cannot finally prevent it from taking place. In England, for instance, the feudal order came under growing pressures over a period of several hundred years before a distinctly new 'bourgeois', or industrial middle class order, was established, in the course of the nineteenth century. Not surprisingly the monarch and much of the nobility resisted this challenge to their power and advantage.

Stratification in Industrial Societies

This section is mainly concerned with describing the theories of stratification put forward by Marx and Weber. Much briefer mention is made of Durkheim's contribution. This is because, as we saw in Chapter 7, Durkheim and other functionalists are much more concerned with social solidarity than with social class. Important mention is made of the elite/masses theory of the Italian sociologist, Mosca. We also present a number of attempts to stratify people on the basis of occupation, of which the most widely used is the Registrar General's occupational scale. Finally, a working model of class stratification is put forward in which I attempt to pull together elements from some of the previously described models.

Marx's Theory of Stratification (Class Conflict)

THE ECONOMIC ROOTS OF CLASS CONFLICT Marx argued that conflict between social classes is inevitable because of their different relationships to the means of production. This much has already been explained. Here, we will describe Marx's theory of stratification mainly in relation to modern capitalistic society. To recap briefly, in capitalist society the two major classes are the capitalist, or *bourgeoisie,* and the industrial working class, or *proletariat.* As far as Marx was concerned, estate and caste societies were just as much class stratified societies as are capitalist societies. The landed nobility of feudal Europe and the wealthy higher castes of traditional India he simply regarded as ruling classes. He considered as mere convenience (or as mere ideology) their claims that their social position was divinely sanctioned – whether they recognised this themselves or not.

In Marx's view, class conflict, rooted in the economic realities of differential relations to the means of production, flowed into every aspect of social life, including work, politics, education, family and religion. With particular reference to capitalist society, let us analyse what he meant by conflict in the economic context a little further before describing how it operates in other areas. Marx contended that those who own the means of production always try to make a profit on the commodities (goods, services) produced by those who work for them. The lower the wages paid, the higher the profits made by the capitalist. The difference between the wages and the price of commodities (goods, services) produced by those who work for the capitalist class, Marx called *surplus value*. The interest of the capitalist class is to maximise surplus value and thus increase profits. Marx's contention, that the economic relations of production produce the framework for social relations, is aptly illustrated by the startling facts of economic inequality. Even in our own day, the richest 1% own over 25% of personal wealth and the bottom 80% rather less than 20%. In Marx's time inequality was even greater. He and his friend, Engels, commented bitterly on the low wages, poor housing, insanitary living conditions, and lack of medical care of the working class (see Engels' *The Condition of the English Working Class*, 1844).

THE BASE AND SUPERSTRUCTURE In order to explain how Marx considered class conflict operates, it will be helpful to introduce a simple, two part classification of the social system which he put forward – the division of society into the *base*, and *superstructure*. In effect, we have already described what Marx meant by the base: it is the economic system and the bi-polar (two part) class system that economic relations produce. The superstructure refers to all other major aspects of society, such as politics, education, intellectual and religious life and so on. Marx argued that the base influences and even determines the nature of the superstructure, although there is much argument about how complete he considered this determination to be. He certainly thought that class relations are lived out in all major areas of social activity. The superstructure can be roughly divided into the *state* (government, civil service, judiciary) and *ideological institutions* (e.g. the educational system, the church, the media).

Marx considered that, in a capitalist society, control of the state is in the hands of the economically most powerful class, the bourgeoisie. This does not mean that he thought that capitalists and businessmen held all, or most, of the top positions in politics, civil service, or in the legal profession themselves. He meant that the power of the bourgeoisie as controllers of wealth and production is so great that it limits the power of other groups effectively to act against the capitalist system and the capitalist class. For Marx, therefore, economic power is the key to political power: the economically most powerful class is also the ruling class. We will examine in detail, later, Marx's controversial analysis of the relationship between economic and political power (Chapter 18, pp. 514-16).

Marx is as clear and consistent, within the terms of his own analysis, about the relationship between class and ideology as he is about that between class and state. He believed that, in any age, the ruling ideas (the predominant and most generally accepted) are those of the ruling class. For example, in the feudal period most people believed that the monarchy was, in some sense, divinely approved. A Marxist would argue that this idea became widespread because it suited the practical interests of the monarchy that it should be. If people believed that the monarchy was 'hedged in with divinity' they would be more likely to respect and accept it. Today, when the monarchy is no longer powerful, few believe that it is a divinely inspired, rather than a purely human, institution. The same analysis is applicable to 'bourgeois' ideology. Marx described the ideology of the capitalist class as *bourgeois liberalism* or *bourgeois individualism*. As far as he was concerned, this meant little more than the liberty of the bourgeoisie to pursue private gain and wealth. Bourgeois ideology, like bourgeois society, emerged out of feudalism. In feudal society people were expected to keep to their station and there was legal restraint on individual initiative, particularly in the area where the bourgeoisie most wanted it – the economic. The bourgeoisie achieved their aims through parliamentary pressure, refusing to pay certain taxes, and by civil war. Marx pointed to socialism, which emphasised collective action and greater material equality, as an alternative to bourgeois liberalism. In his analysis of the spread of bourgeois ideology to other sections of the population besides the capitalist class, he was particularly concerned to explain how some sections of the working class came to adopt a bourgeois liberal ideology rather than socialism, which he considered to be more in their interests. How modern Marxists consider people are socialised to conform has already been described in Chapters 3 and 5, and we examine this issue further in Chapters 18 and 19.

CONFLICT AND CHANGE So far, our account has tended to stress Marx's analysis of how the ruling class establishes and maintains its position. We know, however, that he considered *change* and *conflict* to be at the heart of the social process. He argued that the position of the working class in the economic structure placed it in conflict with the capitalist class. Trade unions are the organisational means by which the working class seek higher wages and better working conditions. Marx also stressed the need to establish a revolutionary party of the working class, with socialist and communist ideals. He observed several *contradictions* and developments in the capitalist system which, he felt, would promote the rise of revolutionary class consciousness. A major contradiction in the capitalist system which he suggested was that, in order to make as much profit as they could, the bourgeoisie would pay as low wages as possible to the working class and thus *emiserate* them (make their situation miserable). The precise meaning of Marx's so-called *emiseration hypothesis* is the subject of scholarly debate, but we can take it that he expected the working class to suffer economic exploitation, and that this would provide a stimulus to revolutionary discontent. This has not happened in capitalist society and may well never do so.

In retrospect, Marx's analysis of the contradiction that can develop between the *relations of production* (the formal and legal framework governing the relations of workers and capitalists) and the *forces or means of production* (machinery/technology), seems a more important and lasting contribution to sociological theory. He meant that technological developments can make out of date, and so help change, the relationships of social classes to one another, even to the point where the established system breaks down. (A clear example of technological change producing profound, if not 'break-down' social effects, is apparent in our own time in the impact of the micro-chip 'revolution'.) Marx argued that the capitalist class itself rose to power because it controlled *capital* (money) and productive machinery, and that these became even more important than the old basis of wealth and power – *land*. A revolution in both the forces and relations of production constituted a change in the *mode of production*, a term encompassing both concepts. Marx believed that the development of large-scale production would eventually make it a reasonably simple matter for the working class to take over control of industry, if they were to consciously organise to do so.

A factor that facilitated the development of working class consciousness of its own power and interests was that its members were increasingly crowded together in urban areas and factories. This gave them the opportunity to react collectively to collective grievances and to organise against them. Marx expected that the factors promoting the creation of revolutionary consciousness among the working class would prove stronger than those persuading them to accept capitalist society. He did not, however, assume that this would happen without the conscious efforts of committed individuals and groups to bring about change and revolution.

OTHER SOCIAL GROUPS (PETIT-BOURGEOISIE, PEASANTRY, LUMPEN-PROLETARIAT) So far, our analysis of Marx's account of social class in capitalist society has referred to only two social classes: the bourgeoisie and the proletariat. This fairly reflects Marx's own emphasis. Nevertheless, he recognised the existence of other groups. He referred to small businessmen and, sometimes, to professionals as *petit-bourgeois*. He considered that, as the conflict between the bourgeoisie and the proletariat developed, the petit-bourgeoisie would be forced into one side or the other of the class struggle. At the bottom of the social stratum are two further groups: the *peasantry* and the so called *lumpen proletariat*. Marx considered that, in an industrial and urban society, the peasantry would become smaller, less powerful and less relevant to the central class conflict of the capitalist order. The lumpen proletariat refers mainly to the unorganised working class: it includes those in low-paid and irregular employment and those who, for one reason or another, are virtually unemployable. Many of these are poor. Marx rightly considered that the lumpen proletariat was much less powerful than the industrial proletariat.

We will deal with various criticisms and revisions of the above aspects of Marx's class analysis in the appropriate parts of this book. Conveniently, Max Weber addressed himself fully to several important issues raised by Marx, and it is to Weber's analysis of stratification that we now turn. Before doing this, those looking for a summary of recent developments in Marxist thought will find it in Chapter 20.

Max Weber: Power and Stratification

CLASS, PARTY AND STATUS For Weber, as for Marx, the public life of a society is largely concerned with *power conflict*. Whereas Marx saw stratification and power conflict in terms of an exclusively class-model of society, Weber described two additional dimensions of stratification – *party* and *status*. Weber used these terms to refer to three separately distinguishable but greatly overlapping areas of stratification: the economic (class), the political (party), and the social (status). It is much easier to differentiate these factors in theory than in practice, but Weber was keen to distance himself from Marx's view that party and status are merely functions of class.

Although Weber did not attach the absolute importance to class that Marx did, he still considered it to be a most important aspect of stratification. He differed from Marx, however, on the precise definition of class, making a distinction between *economic class* and *social class*. He defined economic class as a person's situation in the economic market; both the commodity market (buying/selling) and the employment market (providing or seeking jobs). Social class includes economic but, in addition, members of the same social class share similar chances of social mobility (thus people from a low social background would tend to have a poor chance of upward mobility). Members of a given social class, therefore, share a common socio-economic situation. This difference in the definition of class led to a fundamental disagreement between Weber and Marx about the class structure of capitalist society.

CLASS: THE 'WHITE COLLAR CLASS' Weber described four major
social classes. He agreed with Marx that the most powerful
class in capitalist society is that of the owners of property and
wealth – the upper class. Again, like Marx, he recognised that,
in rare cases, education could provide entry to the upper class
from lower down the stratification hierarchy. He also agreed
with Marx that a second class, the petit bourgeoisie, was likely
to become of less importance and that the growing strength of
the third group, the manual working class, gave it great potential importance. Contrary to Marx, however, Weber gave great
emphasis to what he considered was a distinct and numerically
expanding class: propertyless white-collar employees. He referred to them as 'technicians, various kinds of white-collar employees, civil servants – possibly with considerable social differences depending on the cost of their training.' It is Weber's
view of the role and importance in capitalist society of this
class that fundamentally distinguishes his class analysis from
that of Marx who was far more interested in the industrial proletariat. Weber regards white-collar employees as middle class.
What distinguishes their market situation is that they sell mental or intellectual labour and skill rather than manual. In general, these skills are rarer than manual skills; thus the market
situation of the middle class tends to be stronger than that of
the working class. Obviously, this applies to some more than to
others: it is more true of a top civil servant than of a clerk.

PARTY (POLITICAL POWER) We now consider Weber's view of the
role of parties in the stratification system. As we have seen,
Marx contended that economic control was the source of political power in capitalist society. Weber disagreed. He regarded
political power as a distinct dimension of stratification and not
merely as a function of economic factors.

In contrast to Marx, Weber did not regard political democracy as mere 'window dressing', designed to obscure the fact
that the capitalist class had the real decision making power and
influence. He felt that once the working class had won the
vote, it could be used as a powerful lever to achieve social
change. He considered that policies such as nationalisation,
redistributive taxation, expansion of the welfare state and public
education, adopted by political parties supported by the working class, could help to provide new economic and social

217

opportunities for the working class. For Marx, of course, these policies were no substitute for socialist revolution and 'real' change.

Weber insisted that, although economic factors could certainly affect political ones, the reverse was also true. For instance, the policy of nationalisation favoured, in some degree, by most European Socialist parties of Weber's own day, was likely to have profound economic consequences. In the chapter on political sociology (Chapter 18), we will look much more closely at the relationship between economic and political power. For the moment, it is enough to be aware of the major issues involved in Marx and Weber's 'great debate' on power.

STATUS (SOCIAL PRESTIGE) A status group provides a shared life style or similar level of social prestige for its members. Status is symbolised in *patterns of consumption* and habits of behaviour. Thus, to give three examples: wearing a bowler hat, sticking pins through one's nose and dressing in smart 'mod gear' are status symbols of (some) businessmen, punks and mods respectively. *Ascribed* status is the status a person is born with, and *achieved* status is acquired during the course of life. Weber argues that ascribed status rapidly declined as a means of access to economic and political power in modern societies. In the political area, for example, the titles and functions of royalty and aristocracy have generally become of symbolic significance only – they are certainly no longer an automatic passport to national or local leadership. Similarly, he regards economic and career opportunities as increasingly open to competition. He can be criticised for not considering sufficiently whether this 'free' competition is, in fact, equally open and fair to all classes. He perhaps did not fully realise that the decline of status and the rise of class meant that one form of inequality replaced another.

Later we will apply the concept of status to the analysis of both race and youth. Here, however, we will draw our detailed example of status stratification from traditional society, because Weber considered that status stratification is strongest in this type of society. He argued that the Hindu caste system was (and to some extent remains) a form of status stratification which helped the upper castes to control society and led to the exclusion from wealth and privilege of the lowest castes, particularly the 'untouchables', who were considered to be outside the caste hierarchy. It must be said that, despite the efforts of recent Indian national leaders to discredit caste taboos against the untouchables, traditional attitudes persist strongly, especially in rural areas. In 1978, a young British educated Indian doctor, who happened to be an untouchable, felt that to return home to practise a calling forbidden to his group might mean persecution and even death. He was willing to risk this martyrdom, not only to provide needed medical skills, but also to undermine what he saw as repressive traditional beliefs. It would be difficult to find a more vivid example of the operation of status distinction.

It needs to be said again that Marx regarded status distinctions primarily as a function of class stratification. Certainly, the overlap between the three dimensions of stratification – which Weber himself stressed – is particularly obvious in the case of status. In modern societies, an individual's status is usually derived from his economic or class situation. The wealthy generally adopt the status symbols they can afford, as do other groups. Even though Weber accepted this, he also believed that the chain of causation can operate in the other direction: status group membership can give access to economic and political power and advantage, as he argued it did in the caste system. Later, we further examine Weber and Marx's disagreement about the importance of the concept of status in the context of our analysis of race and youth.

Although Weber is rightly seen as a conflict theorist, he deliberately set out to qualify Marx's extreme stress on conflict. He argued that party and status identities could cut across class lines and thus blur the edges of class conflict. In rejecting Marx's polarised analysis of the class structure and replacing it with a more finely graded version, he attempted to undermine further Marx's theory of stratification. Yet, the basis of Weber's perspective *is* power-conflict. Throughout society he sees individuals and groups competing for power and control and the wealth and prestige that often accompanies them. In this fundamental matter, he and Marx were in agreement.

Durkheim and Stratification

Durkheim, like later functionalists, regarded stratification as necessary and universal. He assumed that very important or particularly demanding social roles would naturally be allocated more status and rewards than would less functionally important ones. Thus, even in relatively unstratified primitive society, the power, duties and wealth of, say, a chief or medicine man would differentiate him from others.

Partly because Durkheim tended to take stratification for granted, he did not give it the detailed analysis that we find in Marx and Weber. It is only in the work of the later functionalists, Talcott Parsons and, notably, Davis and Moore, that we find fuller justification of the view that stratification is necessary and universal. We examine functionalist arguments about stratification and the reply of a number of conflict theorists to them at the end of Chapter 10.

Durkheim himself regarded the problem of social solidarity and stability as more important than that of stratification (see Chapter 7, pp. 172–3). His analysis of stratification tends to become subsumed in this more urgent concern. Stratification stresses the divisions and conflicts in society and this was not the emphasis Durkheim wished to make. For him, it was normal for society to function harmoniously just as it was normal for the human body to do so. Indeed, in a most interesting reference to class conflict, he stated that 'nothing comparable to this can be observed in the (biological) organisms.' It is worth adding that, like Weber, he considered that social mobility could moderate class conflict.

The Concept of Elite in Stratification Theory

The concept of a governing elite was partly developed as an alternative to Marx's ruling class theory. *A governing elite is a group of people who rule.* Whereas Marx argued that the basis of the power of the ruling class is economic, elite theorists contend that the power of the ruling elite (as they prefer to call it) may be primarily military, political, economic, or whatever. As originally presented by Pareto (1848–1923), elite theory was undemocratic. He argued that although elites 'circulated' (replaced each other in power), an elite ruling during a given period was generally unrepresentative of the people it controlled. Mosca (1858–1941) argued, however, that it is quite possible for elites to exercise power in a representative and democratic way – as he believed they did in parliamentary democracies. Mosca was the first to distinguish systematically between the elite and the mass (the rest) – a framework of analysis that has been influential not only in political sociology, but also in cultural analysis. To some extent, the term 'masses' was intended to supersede 'classes' – again with the intention of presenting an alternative to the Marxist model of society. Although elite/ masses theory has not been primarily developed by functionalists, Mosca's version would be acceptable to most.

Social Class and Occupation: The Registrar General's Scale

THE USES AND LIMITS OF CLASS SCALES DETERMINED BY OCCUPATION
The Registrar General has the unenviable task of categorising over 20,000 occupational titles into five social class categories. The occupations included below are merely amongst the most common examples:

Typical Occupations by Social Class

Social Class	Examples of Occupations Included
I Professional etc.	Accountant, architect, chemist, clergyman, doctor, lawyer, surveyor, university teacher
II Intermediate	Aircraft pilot or engineer, chiropodist, farmer, nurse, police or fire-brigade officer, school teacher
III Skilled non-manual	Clerical worker, draughtsman, sales representative, secretary, shop assistant, telephone supervisor, waiter
III Skilled manual	Bus driver, butcher, bricklayer, carpenter, cook, electrician, miner (underground), railway guard, upholsterer
IV Partly skilled	Agricultural worker, barman, bus conductor, fisherman, machine sewer, packer, postman, telephone operator
V Unskilled	Kitchen hand, labourer, lorry driver's mate, messenger, office cleaner, railway porter, stevedore, window cleaner

Whereas Marx defined class in terms of a person's relationship to the means of production and Weber defined it in terms of a person's market position, most recent attempts to construct detailed hierarchies of stratification have been based on occupation. In Britain, the best known of these is the Registrar General's scale of social classes. Social class scales based on occupation tend to reflect the thinking of Weber more than Marx, although Marxists have found it quite possible to use certain information categorised within this framework. In the next section, we discuss in detail the problem of constructing a single, simple and easily applied model of class stratification from among the various existing models.

On the basis of what criteria does the Registrar General classify occupations by social class? Occupations entered in a given class are, as far as possible, of comparable general standing in the community, although changes in classification have occurred from time to time. Educational and economic factors are of great importance in deciding to which class a particular occupation is allocated, although income itself is not of overriding importance. It is true, however, that in order to guess a person's income or educational attainment the single most useful piece of information to know is his social class. To put it in more technical terms, the three factors *correlate* strongly. In 1971, the division of social class III into non-manual and manual was officially adopted. This may have misled some into thinking that the classes above III non-manual are also non-manual, and vice-versa for manual. In fact, only class I is exclusively non-manual and class V exclusively manual. Classes II and IV are mixed, although the former is predominantly non-manual and the latter predominantly manual. It is also worth noting that persons whose basic occupational status is class IV or V, but who are of foreman or managerial status, are allocated to class III (foreman and manager, class V occupation), or II (manager, class IV occupation).

In official surveys, married women and dependent children are allocated to the class of their husband or father. The majority of married women are not in full-time work and of those who are, few are in occupations of higher status than those of their husbands. To a considerable extent, therefore, class categorisation by male occupation reflects a family based social system. There are those who feel that this system of classification illustrates and underlines the inferior position of women in British society. This is a point we will return to later.

Although the Registrar General's scale is the most widely used, others exist. Indeed, a government department, that of Employment and Productivity, uses two different occupational classifications in its research and publications. Another classification widely used by sociologists (other than the Registrar-General's) is the Hall-Jones scale. A criticism of the scale is that the sample of opinion that Hall and Jones used in helping them to construct it was biased towards the middle class. As this illustrates, the difficulties in establishing a sufficiently objective basis for occupational classification are considerable. We will discuss one of these problems later – the fact that 'objective' and 'subjective' social class do not always coincide. The scale adopted by the National Survey of Health and Development is worth mentioning because it was not based solely on occupation. As well as occupation, the educational and social class background of the father and mother was considered relevant in determining the class of the children involved in the survey. Finally, the important study of social mobility made at Oxford University (1972) adopts a complex definition of occupation based on comparing the market and work situations of various groups (see Chapter 9, pp. 255–7).

THE USES AND LIMITS OF CLASS SCALES DETERMINED BY OCCUPA-TION Simply to know a person's class suggests a very great deal of other information about him or her. Ivan Reid, in his useful book *Social Class Differences in Britain* (1977), does not overstate the case:

> We can state that middle class people, in comparison with the working classes, enjoy better health; live longer; live in superior homes, with more amenities; have more money to spend; work shorter hours; receive different and longer education, and are educationally more successful; marry later in life; rear fewer children; attend church more frequently; belong to clubs more often; have different tastes in the mass media and arts; are politically more involved – to mention only a few examples.

Much of this book is concerned with the operation of social class in specific contexts such as the family, education, and work. It would be quite wrong, however, to think that class predetermines the nature of family, education, work or any other experience in a crudely causal way. As will become clear, we often do not know precisely how class differences operate. Merely collecting facts about class will not necessarily tell us why the facts are as they are. Sometimes, of course, empirical data does suggest explanations about the nature of the internal relationship between facts. That numbers of the upper class tend to send their children to private schools is obviously related to the fact that they can afford to do so. Yet, even here, we cannot say wealth *causes* the upper class to send their children to private school: indeed, some do not.

Sometimes 'the facts' do no more than supply ammunition for theoretical argument. Many of the more interesting questions about social class do not lend themselves readily to simple, factual proof. Examples of such questions are: is class conflict inevitable? Why do large numbers of lower class people conform to societies in which they are relatively deprived? Do schools reduce or increase the influence of class factors on educational attainment? There is certainly an empirical element in the answer to all these questions, but considerable theoretical construction is also required to provide adequate answers to them. In addition, as well as quantifiable facts, it is necessary to know something about the everyday life or culture of classes and groups before presuming to generalise about them.

Stratification and Culture
All the sociologists referred to in this chapter would agree that the work a person does tends greatly to affect his way of life or culture. For a start, occupation largely determines income which, in turn, determines what we can buy, including the size and quality of our house, car and other consumer items. Work influences our choice of friends and, as we have seen, leisure habits. In fact, the long list of class correlatives (factors associated with class) on the previous page vividly illustrates how class affects almost all aspects of cultural life.

Marx sees a particularly strong connection between class and culture (Chapter 3, Socialisation and Class). Marxists often use the term *class culture* to refer to the way of life – physical and mental – and behaviour typical of a given class. The Marxist historian, E. P. Thompson, defines the concept in terms of human experience, not as a collection of statistical correlations.

The following quotation from Thompson deserves a close reading:

> The finest-meshed sociological net cannot give us a pure specimen of class, any more than it can give us one of deference or of love. The relationship must always be embodied in real people and in a real context. Moreover, we cannot have two distinct classes, each with an independent being, and then bring them *into* relationship with each other. We cannot have love without lovers, nor deference without squires and labourers. And class happens when some men, as a result of common experiences (inherited or shared), feel and articulate the identity of their interests as between themselves, and as against other men whose interests are different from (and usually opposed to) theirs. The class experience is largely determined by productive relations into which men are born – or enter involuntarily. Class-consciousness is the way in which these experiences are handled in cultural terms: embodied in traditions, value-systems, ideas and institutional forms. If the experience appears as determined, class consciousness does not, We can see a *logic* in the responses of similar occupational groups undergoing similar experiences, but we cannot predicate any *law*. Consciousness of class arises in the same way in different times and places, but never in just the same way.

Weber did not think that culture was quite so closely connected with class as do Marxists. Indeed, he often used the term *life-style* rather than culture, which has a deliberately more individualistic sound to it. For him, the working class person with middle class values, friends and leisure pursuits is a relatively common exception requiring no special explanation. People develop their own cultural habits which can easily cut across class lines. For Weber, a middle class pigeon fancier or a working class member of a yacht club would be within the predictable range of human variety. He tended to refer to groups of people with similar life-styles, such as members. of a youth sub-culture, as *status groups*.

Functionalists, including Durkheim, tend to regard it as the major role of culture to unite rather than to divide society (see Chapter 3, Socialisation and Social Consensus). In particular, Durkheim was concerned to bridge the rift between capitalist and worker. He suggested that they join together for mutual benefit in industrial associations. As we have seen, he also regarded the educational system as a means for socialising children into cultural conformity. Marx regarded this process as ideological exploitation.

Towards a Working Usage of Class

This framework is in addition to, and not instead of, those already referred to. We will later discuss the merits of established theories of stratification in the light of recent social change, but meanwhile an easy and uncontroversial reference point for the understanding of class is necessary. Detailed though the Registrar General's scale is, it does not provide an adequate basis for theoretical analysis of class. In particular, it cannot be used to understand either the upper class or the poor. The framework offered here is as follows:

Upper class
Upper middle class
Lower middle class
Upper working class
Lower working class
The poor

As we shall see, the four classes between the upper class and the poor are defined, quite conventionally, in terms of occupation. The upper class and the poor, however, are defined in terms of their wealth and income (or lack of them). This definition can be justified in respect of the upper class, because it is largely inherited and otherwise unearned wealth, rather than occupation as such, which is the more important to its members. Wealth is the basis of the privileged cultural life and status of the upper class, although it is possible to be rich and yet excluded from it on the basis of, say, lack of connections, education or social graces.

Whether the upper class approximates to Marx's bourgeois or capitalist 'ruling' class is a matter for analysis in due course (see Chapter 18, pp. 514–19). It needs, finally, to be noted that many members of what we have termed the 'upper class' appear as 'middle class' in some official occupational scales. Our contention here, however, is that it makes more sociological sense to consider, say, a millionaire school master first as a millionaire and then as a school master.

Our description of the upper and lower middle class is taken from A. H. Halsey, with the difference that what is called here 'the upper middle class' he refers to as 'the middle class'. The upper middle class, then, is composed of professional, managerial, and administrative occupational groups and higher technicians. The lower middle class is composed of non-manual employees, small proprietors, self-employed artisans and also lower grade technicians and supervisors of manual workers who might be thought of as a 'blue collar elite.' Halsey describes the working class as 'industrial manual workers and agricultural workers whether skilled, semi-skilled or unskilled.' We will take the line between skilled manual workers and those 'below' them as the rough divide between the upper and lower working class.

Who, then, are the poor? The following groups are particularly liable to poverty: the old, the low paid, the unemployed, the chronically sick and disabled, and one-parent families. A disproportionate number of immigrant families is also poor. It will be obvious why we do not follow the convention and categorise this group according to occupation. Many of them do not have a regular occupation, and some do not have an occupation at all. Whether the poor can correctly be called a 'class' is to some extent an academic point. They are a group of several millions identified by the common experience of poverty. There can be no argument that they merit separate consideration in the stratificational hierarchy, although we must remember to examine the possibility that the reasons why some people are poor may be related to the reasons why others are very rich.

No claim is made here that the above usage of class would satisfy the sociological purist, or even that it is internally consistent. The student should, however, find it comprehensive and useable until such time as he decides for himself which theory or combination of theories about stratification he finds most convincing.

Class and Other Forms of Stratification

It is not intended here to return to the debate between Marx and Weber on whether stratification is best viewed exclusively in class terms or should include party and status as well. Rather, the aim is to remind the reader briefly that other forms of stratification exist besides class; amongst which gender, generation, and race are considered to be the most important in modern society. Superficially, these three categories can be seen as forms of status stratification. Male and female, young and old, black and white are allocated different degrees of status, apparently on the basis of sex, age, and racial differences. In fact, in all three, class cuts across, although it does not obliterate, the lines of status differentiation. For instance, a working class woman may find it easier and more practicable to make common cause with working class men than with middle class women – even though all women may be victims of discrimination on grounds of their sex. A young, middle class white person may have much more in common with his parents than with a working class 'street kid'. A black labourer may identify with his workmates of all colours and find little in common with the 'black bourgeoisie'. The relationship between these forms of stratification and class is a matter for careful consideration later in this book.

Guide to further reading and study

Tom Bottomore's *Classes in Modern Society* (Allen and Unwin, 1966) is highly recommended as a brief, succinct introduction to class stratification. His *Elites and Society* (Penguin, 1964) has the same virtues, although the topic is perhaps better pursued in detail under political sociology, later in the course. Ivan Reid's *Social Class Differences in Britain* (Open Books, 1977) is certainly not a theoretical introduction to stratification theory, but is an excellent collection of empirical data about class differences. The Fontana Modern Masters series has titles on *Marx* (David McLellan), *Weber* (Donald MacRae) and *Durkheim* (Anthony Giddens). Anthony Giddens's *The Class Structure of the Advanced Societies* (Hutchinson, 1973) is too useful not to mention, but it is demanding reading.

For questions on Class Stratification see the end of Chapters 9 and 10.

9 Class Stratification in Britain

The Issues

For the sake of simplicity, this chapter and the next have been broken down into syllabus oriented sub-sections, but it is important not to lose sight of the central theme of social equality. We examine stratification primarily in Britain but also, more briefly, in a wide comparative context. As far as Britain is concerned, the major issue explored is whether it has become a more or less equal society since the last war. This involves looking at changes in class structure, class culture and in the rate of social mobility. The first two are analysed together as part of our examination of each class, and the third separately – but they are all part of the same general inquiry. The data presented enables us to answer the future question of whether Britain remains a deeply class-divided society – as it certainly has been historically. An issue that is particularly discussed is whether post-war affluence and certain other factors have resulted in a decline of traditional working class attitudes and culture. Is it true that 'we are all middle class now' or that 'there is no such thing as class any more'? Finally, it is essential to remember that whereas Marxists regard political and status issues as rooted in class, for Weberians these are relatively separate aspects of stratification. We allude to these two perspectives on a number of occasions in this chapter, although both the political and status aspects of stratification are discussed fully elsewhere.

At this stage, we need only distinguish two basic concepts of equality: the *socialist* and the *liberal*. Ironically perhaps, neither means *absolute* (complete) equality. Socialists do characteristically believe, however, that there should be a substantial degree of *material* equality (for example, in income and housing) and that this will partly pave the way to equality of cultural opportunity. Only a minority of socialists are Marxists, but Marx's own epigram on this issue has wide appeal: 'from each according to his ability, to each according to his need'. The Marxist ideal of a classless society need not be taken to imply complete equality although Marx certainly considered that there would be much greater material equality in communist than in capitalist society. This is rather general but it is probably safe to say that most socialists and, certainly, all Marxists, favour a greater degree of material equality than exists in Britain today.

Marxists consider the achievement of stable equality to be dependent on the abolition of the major forms of private property (for example, private enterprise) but other socialists, including many members of the British Labour Party, tend to favour a mixed economy (part nationalised, part private) and rely on redistributive taxation and heavy government expenditure on public services to bring about greater equality. They further contend that the public provision of better material and cultural services such as libraries and educational facilities will provide equal cultural opportunity for all. This is, of course, quite different from saying that, given equal cultural opportunity, people will express themselves in the same way; that is an absurd idea.

The liberal view of equality is that every individual should have equal opportunity to *compete* for wealth, power and status. This view was developed by Adam Smith and John Stuart Mill among others, and took firm hold in the nineteenth century. It has tended to appeal, in varying degrees, to politicians across the three major parties. The outcome of such competition would almost certainly be a society of great inequality – but, at least, it would be an inequality based on *merit*, not inheritance and privilege (which conservatives defend). It is possible to test whether equal opportunity does exist by examining the rate of social mobility and the extent to which the talented rise and the untalented fall. This we do later. In practice, most modern liberals would wish to reduce even 'natural' inequality resulting from 'fair' competition. They would do so by a limited redistribution of wealth, mainly through taxation. The 'middle-of-the-road' liberal and 'middle-of-the-road' socialist meet halfway between the two philosophies of equality.

The Economic Context of Class Change

Economic and occupational change is the background against which developments in the British class system must be understood. It is worth summarising these changes here: since about 1900 there has been a steady expansion of the service sector and a parallel growth of female employment; there has been a move from small to large-scale production and corresponding expansion of bureaucracy (large, hierarchical organisations), and a growth in public corporations at the expense of small-scale private businesses. Class is produced primarily in the work

231

situation and changes in the class system can only be understood in the context of economic and occupational change. This summary statement is intended to include the Marxist view that changes in the means of production (for example, technology) will affect class relations. For instance, a rapid increase in automation could affect the class position of millions. Class is not, however, exclusively defined in terms of work. Class consciousness (awareness of class identity) and class culture are part of class although they cannot be properly analysed without reference to the economic and occupational structure within which they are generated. For that reason, class structure and culture are considered together. For the purposes of presentation, social mobility is considered separately, although in reality it is also inextricably intertwined with class structure. Movement up or down the social structure is bound to change it.

The importance of the effect of changes in the occupational structure on class is worth pursuing in more detail. These developments also have profound implications for gender relations because they have changed the working and domestic lives of both sexes. The following chart shows the number of people working in different sectors of employment from 1960 to 1978. The two charts show the industries in which men and women work, and how the numbers in each group of industries have changed over time.

One of the most important developments in the occupational structure has been the increase in the number of women employed in the service sector; a massive 2¼ million since 1960. We give this development fuller analysis in a separate section (Chapter 12 pp. 301-4), and make only brief comment here. There has also been a less spectacular increase of male employment in the service sector: by half a million. Overall, therefore, it is the expansion of the service sector that is the outstanding feature of change in the structure of employment since 1961. Other data shows that a remarkable 71% of the *increase* in service sector employment between 1961 and 1975 occurred in the areas of central and local government, although the economic cuts of the late nineteen-seventies and early eighties stopped this trend. In general, women have tended to fill lower status and men higher status service sector jobs. In 1976, approximately one in five men were professionals, employers or managers compared to one in twenty women. Over a much longer period than that covered by the chart, the growth of a managerial 'class' has been a feature of the British and other advanced economies. Whether managers have replaced owners as the dominant force in industry is a key issue discussed later.

Employees in employment: by industry

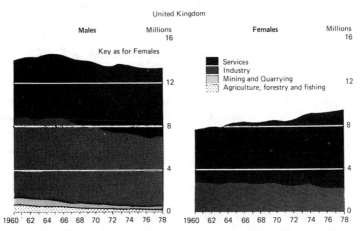

United Kingdom

Males   Millions 16   Females   Millions 16

Key as for Females

■ Services
▨ Industry
▤ Mining and Quarrying
▨ Agriculture, forestry and fishing

1 Includes manufacturing; gas, electricity, and water, and construction industries.

2 For females, also includes agriculture, forestry, and fishing, and mining and quarrying.

Source: *Social Trends,* 1980, p. 123.

Industry remains the major area of male employment, although to a somewhat lesser extent than previously. Between 1901 and 1978, the decline in the industrial sector was about 1½ million men. Female employment in industry fell by half a million over the same period. Partly because of technological advancement (it is largely unskilled jobs that have been lost) and partly because of the way industrial jobs have been regraded, the proportion of skilled to semi-skilled and unskilled occupations in industry has dramatically increased. Again, this applies much more to men than women.

1 Class and Change in Britain

Change in Class Structure and Culture

The Upper Class and the Managerial Elite
The upper class consists of the few thousand wealthiest and most

culturally privileged businessmen and property owners in the country. We also consider the very top of the upper middle class in this section because they often work closely with the upper class and are highly privileged themselves. By upper middle class is meant people like managing directors of large companies rather than middle level management; chiefs of staff rather than high ranking officers; top rather than middle level civil servants, and so on. The important issue is whether the wealth and opportunities of the upper class also give them much greater power and control over industrial, political, and cultural life than other groups.

A common culture is, as we have seen, an essential aspect of class. To a large extent, traditional landed and newer commercial wealth now share a similar background and cultural outlook. Their way of life is substantially different from that of most of the rest of the population (Chapter 3, partly illustrates this, pp. 61–8). Writing about upper class culture, Anthony Giddens says:

> The most striking characteristic of the British upper class in the latter half of the nineteenth century is the mutual penetration of aristocracy and those in commerce and industry . . . Certainly the dominant ethos (cultural tone) remained a 'gentlemanly' one, facilitated by the entitlement of industrialists, or at least of their offspring; but the very creation of the notion of the 'gentleman' was in substantial degree the product of the nineteenth century, and the rise of the public schools was the milieu (cultural context) for effecting this peculiar fusion of the old and the new. In this manner there came about that 'blend of a crude plutocratic (power based on money) reality with the sentimental aroma of an aristocratic legend' which R. H. Tawney described as the feature of the British upper class. *(All brackets author's)*.

We now consider the wealth and economic and industrial power of the upper class. The wealth of the upper class has diminished as a percentage of total wealth but remains formidably large. Wealth is much more unequally distributed than income, mainly because of the importance of inherited wealth. According to Lord Diamond's commission, in 1923 the top 1% owned 61% of all private wealth. In 1974, this had dropped startingly to 22% but, by 1976, had risen to 25%. The increase between 1974 and 1976 was due mainly to the rises in share prices during that period. It is probably a safe assumption that the policies of the Conservative government of 1979 onwards will not diminish the proportion of wealth owned by the richest 1%.

Not unexpectedly, the wealth of the very rich tends to be made up differently from that of other people. They are much more likely to own shares and sizeable amounts of property – including land – than others: they are also more likely to own art treasures, precious metals and jewels. The preservation and creation of substantial wealth gives the upper class a shared material basis for class identity and sets them apart from the majority. Upper class exclusiveness can be partly explained as an attempt to maintain and defend its common interest.

Few of the wealthy depend on earned income as a major source of their wealth. The share of all national incomes of the top 1% of income earners in 1976/77 was 3.5% – a small figure compared to the percentage of wealth owned by the 1% most wealthy. Many major shareholders draw salaries as directors of the company or companies in which they have holdings. Usually, however, the day-to-day running of large companies is in the hands of paid managers who are not usually extremely wealthy people in their own right. This raises the crucial issue of *where* industrial power lies in contemporary capitalism – with owners (or, at least, large shareholders) as Marx argues, or with managers. It should be noted that the new, managerial class, is just as well established in central and local government and in nationalised industries as in private enterprise.

Ralf Dahrendorf has made a significant contribution to the debate about where power lies in modern societies. He argues that with the development of large scale joint stock companies which enable the general public to buy shares in a company, much control is exercised by top salaried managers and less by capitalist owners. He refers to this process as the decomposition of capital. Following Weber rather then Marx, he goes on to argue that, in *advanced* industrial societies, power operates through large organisations rather than through a few very rich individuals (those who make up the capitalist class). Managers of organisations, unlike old-style capitalists, cannot pursue their own interest alone, but must answer to shareholders, perhaps government, and even the general public. According to Dahrendorf, this applies still more to the managers of publicly owned companies and to top civil servants. Dahrendorf, therefore, sees modern societies as 'managed' societies. To understand modern societies, 'capitalist' or socialist, it is necessary, therefore, to come to terms with their institutional (organisational) nature (see Chapter 15 for the development of this point). He further contends that the rise of managers has produced considerable potential for conflict within the economic elite (that is, between owners and management). He considers that whereas owners tend to be interested in profit, managers are more concerned with the long-term productivity and security of the corporation which they see both as in their own interest, and in that of its shareholders, small and large. Again, managers are regarded as more constrained (controlled) by the rules of the large organisations of which they are a small part than the tycoons of early capitalism ever were. It is part of Dahrendorf's thesis that management is also constrained by the powerful organisations of the working class, mainly unions, as well as, to some extent, by government.

Anthony Giddens criticises Dahrendorf sharply on two counts. First he points out that, even though the growth of joint stock companies has broadened the basis of ownership, profit remains the purpose of capitalist enterprise: thus, the system is still a capitalist one. In addition, only a minority still gains substantial profit from shareholdings. There is a huge difference between multi-millionaires, like Sir James Goldsmith, with majority holdings in several major companies and somebody who owns, perhaps, a few hundred pounds of shares. Giddens's second point is related to his first. He suggests that far from there being a conflict of interest between capitalists and top managers, there is more likely to be a *close identity of interest*. They are both primarily concerned with the success and profitability of the company. As far as companies having a public 'conscience' is concerned, there is no guarantee of this, although some do. We examined in Chapter 7 several examples in which companies put their own welfare before that of the general public, if the latter is considered to include workers (made redundant) and local communities (variously neglected or abused).

Giddens' contention that owners and top management – the economic elite – share common goals, suggests the important wider question of whether the upper and upper middle class dominate the other major institutional elites, as well as the economic elite, of the country. Drawing on a study of elites, carried out at Cambridge, he concludes that at least half the top positions in *all* major institutional sectors in Britain, including the economic, the military, the armed forces, the judiciary and the church, are filled by people from public school backgrounds (see Chapter 18 for details). In other words, a majority of those in top positions in this country come from a privileged and, more or less, wealthy upper or middle class background. Whether these people can be called a ruling class is an issue we also discuss in Chapter 18 pp. 514-19).

The importance of the Dahrendorf–Giddens disagreement bears emphasising. It is, after all, about who controls our society, how they do so and in whose interest. This must surely matter to all of us. Do capitalists manipulate our world in their own interest or is power mainly located in large organisations which, almost impersonally, run our lives? We can agree with Dahrendorf that we live in a society of large organisations run by 'experts' and with Giddens that there is still a rich and powerful upper class with a distinctive culture. How and to what extent these two points can be reconciled we leave for further consideration (see especially Chapters 15 and 18).

The Middle Class
The middle class is a huge group. Although some of the developments we discuss have affected the class as a whole, a preliminary distinction must be made between the upper and lower middle class. According to figures cited by A. H. Halsey in 1978, 20.1% of the population are upper middle (Halsey prefers simply to call them 'middle') and 24.9% lower middle class. The term 'white collar employee (or worker)' is sometimes used to refer to the salaried middle class in general, but we have tended to use it to describe the lower levels of this group.

a THE UPPER MIDDLE CLASS The upper middle class is composed of professional, managerial, and administrative occupational groups and higher technicians. Karl Renner first referred to it as the 'service class' and the term has been adopted by Halsey and others. Although the word 'service' is somewhat ambiguous, the term may well become standard. The very top of this group we considered in the previous section because of its links with the upper class. Most members of the upper middle class do not, of course, achieve any national power or prominence but, locally, many have significant influence and status. They often participate in voluntary organisations, become magistrates, or stand for local government. Comparatively speaking, they are well off. Typically, they might earn one and a half to two and a half times as much as the average national wage, and enjoy substantially more than average fringe benefits. They earn strikingly more than their lower middle class counterparts. In 1980, the average pre-tax wage of a doctor was well over twice that of a school teacher. Even so, their income has tended to decline relative to that of most other groups, particularly manual workers. Since 1913–14, higher professional workers' salaries have gone up 26 times, whereas those of unskilled manual workers have gone up 54 times – over twice as much.

The relative decline in the living standards of some of the groups that comprise the middle class has led them to take a more militant attitude towards their employers. This happened particularly among those, such as doctors, employed predominantly by the state. This same process has also occurred among lower middle class groups, such as teachers, social workers, nurses and, for that matter, clerical workers in the civil service. As far as this development is concerned, the middle class can be considered as a whole. There has been considerable recent sociological interest in this trend which is given full coverage in Chapter 14, pp. 374-7.

b THE 'WHITE COLLAR' CLASS: LOWER MIDDLE OR WORKING CLASS? Office workers and salespeople make up the majority of the lower middle class. This group has rapidly expanded during this century and in 1971 made up 24.9% of the working population of which rather more than half were clerks. At the top of the lower middle class are the so-called semi-professions of teaching and nursing. The 'typical' white collar figure is the clerical worker about whom there have been a series of studies since the war. The reason for this interest is clear and centres upon a disagreement about the class position of white collar employees. Marxists argue that their relationship to the means of production is that of wage-workers and that they are, therefore, part of the working class. Marxists, however, also recognised that they are non-productive workers whose class consciousness is likely to be less advanced, from a socialist point of view, than that of industrial workers. As we have seen, Weber regarded this group as middle class: he sometimes referred to it as 'the new class'. It was 'new' in that it was largely created by the needs of big business and central and local government for office workers and other white collar staff.

C. Wright Mills published the first major post-war analysis of the white collar employee, in 1951. He drew almost exclusively on American data but the basic developments he comments on are also a feature of British society. His work reflects the influence of both Marx and Weber. The influence of Marx is apparent in Mills' distinction between the old, *property owning* and *self-employed middle class* and the new, *salaried white collar class*. He includes in the latter group managers, paid professionals, salespeople, and office workers (a wider but comparable definition to our own). Even in 1940, this group outnumbered the old middle class and now does so overwhelmingly. Thus, the United States has gone from a nation of small capitalists to a nation of hired employees. A similar process has occurred in most advanced industrial countries. In this sense, what Zweig calls *debourgeoisement* has certainly taken place. Whatever we call the 'new class' it is certainly not identical with the old bourgeoiseie and petit-bourgeoisie.

Mills recognised that, in terms of their class situation, source and size of income (often relatively small), the white collar group could be considered working class – but he hesitated to classify them as such. In fact, he tended to refer to them as the *new middle class* for reasons which recall Weberian stratification theory. He claimed that the white collar group had higher *status* than manual workers among all sections of the public. Historically, this was largely because of the 'borrowed prestige' they acquired from working in close proximity to ownership and management. This 'reflected' status has become less common with the growth of separate, often relatively large-scale 'office areas', many of which seem closer to the factory floor than the boss's room. More recently, it is the better 'perks' associated with white collar work and the continuing belief that non-manual work is more prestigious than manual work that gives the white collar class a status edge over manual workers.

Mills observed that the white collar class is uncertain of itself and insecure about its future position relative to that of well paid manual workers. The high wages and comfortable standard of living of the affluent manual workers challenged its marginal superiority, sometimes causing what Mills referred to as 'status panic'. He saw several possible directions of development for the white collar class. These were:

It might become part of the working class

It might establish itself more securely as part of the middle class

As it increases in number and power, it might form a buffer between labour and capital and so blunt class conflict

It might become a distinctive class, separate from others

A study of clerical workers, published in 1958 by David Lockwood amply illustrates the 'ambiguity' of the work and status situation of clerks. Lockwood drew his material from Britain: he examined the social position of clerks under the model of stratification presented by Weber. He analysed their market position, work situation and status situation. It will be remembered that, according to Weber, the major indicator of class is market position. Lockwood was in no doubt that the market situation of clerks is substantially better than that of the manual worker even though the average wage of skilled workers is higher than that of clerks. Clerks have more job security, better prospects of occupational mobility (into management) and, generally, better pension rights and fringe benefits, such as cleaner, more comfortable work conditions and longer holidays. More recent data comes from Lord Diamond's Commission on the Distribution of Income and Wealth. In 1977, employee benefits added the equivalent of 20% of the value of their pay for white collar workers, compared to only 14% for the blue collar workers. The value of these benefits is, however, increasing fast for both groups. Lockwood also emphasises the higher wages of clerks as compared to manual workers although this is now less true than at the time he wrote.

Lockwood extends Weber's conceptualisation of class to include the work situation of clerks. Again, he argues that, historically, clerks have tended to be closer to, and more influenced by, management than labour. He points out, however, that in large, modern mechanised offices identification with 'the boss' is less apparent. Developments since Lockwood wrote show a furthering of this trend. In particular, a rapid unionisation among white collar employees hardly suggests either deferential or snug attitudes to employers. In 1970, white collar

240

union membership was 38%, an increase of one third over 1964. It is significant, however, that unionisation has been much more a feature of the public than the private sector. In 1970, the former was 80% unionised, and the latter only 10%. Willingness to organise for economic defence and advancement does not mean that public sector white collar employees are politically radical, but it is obviously a trend which might seem promising to Marxists as well as socialists of a milder ideological hue who wish to claim the political support of this group. A very much higher proportion of the lower middle class than the upper middle class vote Labour, though in no election has a majority done so.

Lastly, Lockwood examines the status situation of clerks. He remarks that the differences in class and work situations between clerk and manual worker continue to provoke status rivalry. At worst, clerical 'snobbishness' is answered by 'working class' contempt, although such stereotypical attitudes are probably less common now than at the time of Lockwood's research. Any clerical affectation is probably due as much to what Mills refers to as 'status panic' about the growing ambiguities of their social position than any real sense of superiority.

A third study we can briefly refer to is by David Weir. In the late nineteen sixties, he conducted a survey of 98 male clerks in large *private* sector firms. He tended towards the conclusion that clerks had a *distinctive* group consciousness. He contrasted their attitudes to social mobility with those traditionally associated with the middle class – that is, that society is a 'ladder' which anybody can climb up if they make the effort and have the ability. He summarises his findings succinctly:

> The replies . . . taken together indicate a pattern that seems incompatible with the perception of the class structure as an open one, affording opportunities to all who possess the appropriate motivation to move upwards!

Yet, despite this, clerks, particularly those in the private sector, are far less inclined to 'us and them' attitudes than the manual working class. A majority, however, do not *personally* expect to be upwardly mobile although most recognise the possibility of upward mobility in *general* terms. Weir has also commented interestingly on the position of female white collar workers who occupy a majority of the lower status positions of this kind of work. They often do routine jobs, such as filing or operating machines, which are quite similar to factory work. Yet they are less militant than men and more likely to think of themselves as middle class. They are also less likely to be union members although this is beginning to change.

Finally, Howard H. Davis's sensitive analysis of interviews with 19 senior clerks merits our attention. Although the clerks invariably call themselves 'middle class' they are, nevertheless, reluctant to define themselves as 'not working class' because many of them 'came up' from the working class and consider that opportunities of mobility still exist. To a much greater extent than the traditional working class they believe in the effectiveness of individual action in career terms and also in making social relationships not necessarily bound by ties of class.

In conclusion, the research evidence shows that the subjective class consciousness of white collar employees tends to be ambiguous in conventional class terms or, more precisely, in Weber's terms to show a distinctive awareness of their own interests. The increase in unionisation among this group, and the substantial minority of them that regularly vote Labour, gives some support to the hopes of Marxists, such as Westergaard and Resler, that they will eventually identify their 'true' proletarian interests. Meanwhile they use unions to pursue their own interests as they see them, not in the spirit of proletarian solidarity or, still less, as a means to achieve radical social change.

The Working Class

In the decade between 1961 and 1971, Britain employed 12.5% fewer people in the manufacturing sector. By contrast, Japan employed 21% more and West Germany 2% more. The British working class is shrinking in size. Nevertheless, it still remains the largest class. In 1972, 55% of adult males were working class. The total percentage of working class people was somewhat greater as working class men tend to have larger families, although this is now a diminishing trend.

a THE AFFLUENT WORKER: 'EMBOURGEOISEMENT' OR CONVERGENCE?
The 'embourgeoisement' hypothesis, first presented in the late

nineteen fifties, sparked off one of sociology's classic debates. The issue is about what is happening economically, socially, politically and culturally to the upper end of the working class. Are they, as Zweig suggested, becoming more middle class – that is, experiencing 'embourgeoisement'? Or, is what is happening more complex than this rather glib term suggests?

The 'embourgeoisement' hypothesis seemed particularly persuasive in the aftermath of the decisive defeat of Labour in the 1959 general election. As with the 1979 election, twenty years later, there was a swing against Labour among the working class. D. E. Butler and R. Rose suggested that Labour might be experiencing particular trouble in holding the affluent working class vote. The response of A. R. Crosland, a leading Labour politician, was to suggest that Labour should try to widen the basis of its political support to include as many middle class people as possible, rather than rely too exclusively on its traditional working class support.

In this atmosphere of rather speculative and politically charged debate, John Goldthorpe, David Lockwood and their collaborators decided to put the embourgeoisement hypothesis to empirical test. Their inquiry, which spanned several years in the early nineteen sixties, is considered something of a model of sociological research but is not beyond criticism. Their initial assessment was that the embourgeoisement thesis was probably an oversimplification. In order to avoid bias, however, they followed the scientific procedure advocated by Karl Popper and sought to *disprove* their own expectations. This meant choosing an area and sample as favourable as possible for the validation of the embourgeoisement thesis. (A *selected* sample of this kind is termed a *quota* sample.) Luton, a prosperous and expanding town, qualified well as a suitable locale. It had the particular advantages of having a substantially migrant labour force – clearly willing to move to find better paid work – and of being without a strong Labour tradition. The research was based primarily on 229 manual workers and, for comparison, 54 lower level white collar workers. The former were drawn from three high wage paying local manufacturing firms. They were also all married men, as the researchers had a particular interest in examining family life-style, although this meant that the sample was not representative in terms of marital status and age.

Goldthorpe and Lockwood questioned their respondents under

243

three major headings: economic, relational (community relationships), and normative (what their political behaviour was). They found that the high wages of the men in the sample did put a middle class standard of living within their reach. They shared many of the consumer items enjoyed by the middle class, such as televisions, refrigerators and automatic washing machines. Apart from this, their economic situation was largely different from that of the middle class. Firstly, their high wages were usually gained only at the cost of overtime: the average working week was 40 to 50 hours. Moreover, 75% of the sample were on shift work. A 'normal' background of overtime and shift work could put pressure on family and social life of a kind rarely experienced by the lower middle class. Secondly, promotional prospects were appreciably worse than for non-manual workers and this was fully realised by the majority of both groups sampled. The manual workers appreciated that any economic advances they made were likely to be *on the basis of their present economic role* and through collective bargaining, with the help of their trade unions. The non-manual sample typically entertained more hope of personal progress but they, too, have become more unionised, though less so in the private sector. Thirdly, as already mentioned, the lower middle class generally benefited from greatly superior fringe benefits. Fourthly, and perhaps more important, most of the manual workers expressed much lower levels of intrinsic satisfaction (pleasure in the job for itself) than did the white collar sample.

Goldthorpe and Lockwood's second category, relational aspects, may be thought of as cultural and community life. Not surprisingly, given the nature of the sample, few of the men studied shared the traditional pattern of community life often found among urban industrial workers and their families. Equally lacking, however, was any evidence that middle class company and life-style was sought, as might have been expected if 'embourgeoisement' had taken place. Kin still played a relatively prominent part in the social lives of the couples studied. This was particularly true of the (approximately) 50% of the sample whose kin lived mainly within a fifty mile radius of London, but it still applied to many of the rest. 41% of the former and 22% of the latter named kin in response to the question 'who would you say are the three people that you spend most of your spare time with?' (apart from spouse and children). Otherwise, *close neighbours,* rather than selected individuals from within the larger community, provided most friends. Interestingly, white collar couples had more contact with friends who were not neighbours, even though they also spent still more time with kin (probably because their kin were generally nearer).

Only 7% of the couples sampled deviated from the above relational pattern to the extent of having predominantly and unambiguously middle class friendship networks. Generally, affluent working class couples associated with those whose presence in their lives was largely 'given', such as kin, close neighbours and workmates. Relations were usually informal. They were, for instance, much less likely to have people round for dinner than the white collar groups. They were also far less likely to belong to formal organisations and those they did participate in, such as working men's clubs, tended to be solidly working class.

The changes in relational patterns that did typify the sample were not in the direction of embourgeoisement. The difference between them and the traditional working class could be explained by reference to major objective factors of their existence, such as work and geographical and residential mobility. Their relatively high level of consumption was explicable in terms of their hard work and relatively high pay. Their family *centredness* or *privatisation* can partly be explained in terms of new leisure facilities in the home and lack of traditional community links. In these limited aspects the life-style of the affluent worker *converges* with that of the lower middle class.

Goldthorpe and Lockwood's findings under their third heading, the normative aspect, are dealt with in Chapter 17, and we summarise them only briefly here. They concentrated particularly on the political norms of the main sample. On the basis of what they admit is limited data, they found a negative correlation between working class affluence and Conservative voting. In other words, the affluent worker is less likely to vote Conservative than less affluent workers. Again, they explain this by reference to the social, and not merely economic, realities of the affluent worker's life. Employment in large-scale industry, high union membership (87%) and frequent life-long membership of the working class are factors cited. It is interesting, however, that Goldthorpe and Lockwood make little of a *margi-*

nal trend away from Labour among affluent workers. This trend was apparent in their own data, assessed on the basis of the way members of the sample had voted in 1959 compared to their *intended* votes for 1964. Certainly, the *long-term* tendency since 1945 has been for the Labour vote to drop as a percentage of the total vote, and much more recent data than that available to Goldthorpe and Lockwood suggests that 'defections' among affluent workers have contributed to this trend. They themselves comment that the strong Labour vote among affluent workers was based on *instrumental* (practical self-interest) thinking rather than traditional emotional *solidarity* (identification) with the party. This important finding left open the possibility that they would change their vote if it seemed to suit their interests to do so.

We summarise the previous two sections from a comparative middle and working class perspective in the section immediately below.

b MIDDLE CLASS AND WORKING CLASS CONVERGENCE? In place of the 'embourgeoisement' hypothesis, Goldthorpe and Lockwood offer the observation that some *convergence* is occurring between the upper working and lower middle class. Instead of the upper working class becoming more like the middle class, both classes are *in some respects* developing a number of common characteristics. As we have seen, convergence is not much apparent in the political and social relational areas. It is, however, occurring in the field of economic *consumption*. Both groups seek a good standard of living, particularly in furnishing their homes with modern amenities. Given this, it is logical that *home and family centredness* should be a feature of members of both groups. Outside the family, their patterns of social life continue to be distinct. Money is the basis on which the consumer-family life style exists and it is not surprising that, in pursuit of it, *collectivisation* in the form of unionisation has been increasingly adopted by the salaried middle class as well as by the working class. The areas of convergence are, then, *economic consumption, family centredness and privatisation,* and *instrumental collectivism*. A. H. Halsey adds the observation that, in addition, status distinction between the middle and working classes has become less obvious and less important during this century and especially since the last war. He attributes this primarily to increased rates of

246

social mobility. With so many more first generation middle class people about, spotting the 'right' accent or the 'right' dress becomes a more precarious way of identifying status. But Halsey is aware of the relative superficiality of this. Just as important for him in making for a fairer and more equal society are the political and legal rights (mainly of association, such as the right to join a union) only acquired or consolidated by the majority during this century and discussed elsewhere in this book (see, especially Chapter 18). Even so, he cannot be accused of underestimating the extent of continuing inequality. The middle sections of society may have converged but the vestiges of status no longer cover the continuing huge discrepancies of wealth and poverty at the social extremes (see next chapter).

C THE TRADITIONAL WORKING CLASS AND ITS CULTURE: FRAGMENTATION OR RECONSTRUCTION? Before deciding whether the traditional working class is fragmenting or perhaps even disappearing, we need to know its composition. Defined most broadly, the traditional working class means manual workers, whether in or out of work, and their families. In addition, the term has special reference to workers in the now generally declining basic industries such as shipbuilding, mining, docking and heavy manufacturing. The phrase *traditional working class culture* refers to their way of life, based on work, community, a strong sense of solidarity and support for the union movement and the Labour party. (see Chapter 3 pp. 62-6, and Chapter 4 pp. 92-4 for further detail.) These people are the core of the working class, and it has been suggested, mainly by a number of liberal writers, that the working class is falling apart from the centre. In Ralf Dahrendorf's terms there has been a 'decomposition of labour' just as he believes there has been a 'decomposition of capital'. He argues that, in advanced countries, the working class has developed into three fairly distinct groups. First, are skilled workers such as miners – well paid and enjoying relatively high status and jealously ready to defend their position through their unions. All this is rather less true of semi-skilled workers such as bus conductors and they have something to protect and are generally organised through unions to do so. Much more precarious is the position of unskilled workers, such as kitchen hands. Because they are less well-paid, more easily replaced and usually less well organised, unemployment and poverty are often a real threat to them and they make up a relatively large proportion of the unemployed. Marxists would not deny that there is an empirical basis to the above description of the contemporary working class. As we shall see, however, they argue for a different *interpretation* of the facts from Dahrendorf.

Undoubtedly, certain developments have occurred which have greatly affected the traditional working class. First, because of the expanding service sector, more people of working class origins 'made it' into the middle class in the post-war period than at any previous time. Meanwhile, the manual working class itself declined in size, though it remains the largest class. Further, the decline of Britain's basic industries located in the inner cities, coupled with the housing clearance and renewal policy, and patterns of migration, have dispersed traditional, concentrated, working class communities. Now, a smaller working class is residentially more widely dispersed, and this has weakened community life. Few 'Bethnal Greens' remain, and if something like traditional community can re-emerge on public housing estates, patterns of privatisation and generally less intense neighbourhood relations militate against it. The continued popularity of 'Coronation Street' is probably as much an exercise in nostalgia as realism: or, if the characters are perceived as 'real', they are seen as part of yesterday's reality rather than today's.

Prosperity is a second development that is sometimes assumed to have eroded traditional, militant working class consciousness. Even if the word 'affluent' is too generous to describe the living standards of most of the working class, the vast majority are materially far better off than their counterparts of two or three generations ago. Although our analysis of the 'affluent worker' shows that new forms of militancy can replace the old, group self-interest expressed through unions falls short of traditional class solidarity. The Welfare State is also often considered to contribute to a more comfortable and therefore less discontented life for the working class. In 1980, however, there occurred significant reductions in real terms of welfare benefits to several groups and this served as a reminder that minimum standards can be lowered as well as raised. What effect this may have on working class attitudes is not yet clear.

248

The above developments have brought about a change in working class cultural life and attitudes. We can now see that the surge of interest in working class culture in the nineteen fifties and sixties was an attempt to capture in art a way of life that was already in retreat. A number of so-called 'Kitchen sink' novels, plays and films celebrated the toughness, humour, vitality and closeness of traditional working class life. The best of them such as *Saturday Night and Sunday Morning, Look Back in Anger, Chicken Soup with Barley* and *This Sporting Life*, still live on because they successfully convey aspects of this culture. Yet, for all their authenticity, they begin to seem positively nostalgic. Now, at a time when most own their own houses, many in suburbia, it is clear that these works describe times past.

What new norms, values and patterns of behaviour are replacing traditional working class culture? The liberal progressive view is that, just as the material standard of life has generally improved, so have levels of cultural opportunity and achievement. A much more pessimistic view is based on the theory of mass culture. Historically, elite-masses theory has had more appeal to conservative than to left-wing critics, but C. Wright Mills has given the concept a radical gloss. He agrees with liberals that affluence and consumerism have blunted material discontent but he savagely attacks the 'cultural trivialisation' of the media which he thinks distracts working people from seriously considering the nature of the society they live in and their own position within it. If they were able to do so, they would appreciate that they are still controlled and exploited at work and stunted in educational and cultural opportunity. Instead, he sees the majority of working and new 'middle' class people as processed mass. It may be remembered that we discussed Christopher Lasch's similar sentiments in Chapter 4, p. 92.

There is some similarity between Mills' observations and the cultural aspects of Goldthorpe and Lockwood's convergence thesis, but there is also a vital disagreement. They, like Mills, recognise the growth of consumerism and of privatised leisure across the classes, but whereas he sees little hope of a resurgence in working class consciousness and political activity, they are by no means so pessimistic. A basic difference of context is that Mills is writing of America where trade union activity has always been much weaker than in Britain, and which has never had an effective socialist party. Goldthorpe and Lockwood do observe a possible erosion in traditional working class support for the Labour party (see Chapter 18) and in active union involvement, but also stress that a new, if more critical and demanding, possible basis of support for the left exists among instrumentally oriented workers.

More orthodox Marxists than Mills, if, indeed, he can be called a Marxist, tend to reject the mass society model. They see culture in terms of classes, not masses. Thus, Raymond Williams states:

> There are in fact no masses: there are only ways of seeing people as masses.

He means that to lump people together as a mass is to miss the variety of individuals and groups. Nevertheless, Williams like other Marxists, is profoundly concerned that the media in capitalist society tends to make people passively satisfied with the mediocre. Remember, the Marxist ideal is fulfilment for all and they see little prospect of this in contemporary capitalist society.

Marxists analyse working class culture within the framework of the changing relations of the working class to the means of production. Richard Johnson makes the point in slightly broader terms:

> The conditions of existence of classes profoundly shape class cultures, less by specifying 'interests', more by supplying a kind of agenda with which the culture must deal. It is a matter of historical record that working class culture has been built around the task of making fundamentally punishing conditions more habitable.

The need to struggle for a comfortable survival through unions and political action, will continue to be 'on the agenda' for working class people in the foreseeable future. But Marxists recognise that in material terms the need for this struggle is not equally great throughout the working class. Dahrendorf's division of the working class into three broad groups —the skilled, semi-skilled and unskilled — is perhaps crude but some such distinction is necessary. At any rate, it clearly cannot be assumed that a skilled craftsman, say, a fitter, and an unskilled worker, will recognise much identity of interest even though Marxists consider that they share the common experience of exploited labour. Not only are there significant economic differences between such groups, but their social outlook or 'consciousness' varies considerably. The Weberian, David Lockwood, uses another term, 'social image', to describe general social attitudes and we have already met two of the major 'types' he finds among the working class. These are *proletarian* or *traditional* 'them and us' attitudes of groups such as miners and *instrumental* attitudes such as those exemplified by the affluent car-workers. He finds a second type of social image among the traditional working class which he terms *traditional deferential*. This attitude is common among individuals who work close to their bosses and involves respectfully 'knowing their place'. A considerable body of research on social images exists in addition to that of Lockwood. Howard H. Davis, amongst others, has pointed out that the social consciousness of craftsmen tends to be quite distinctive. The self and occupational images of the maintenance fitters of his own study were based on a strong sense of individual merit and achievement. It is worth remarking that these attitudes are not unlike those frequently attributed to middle class professionals! Serge Mallet, the French Marxist, has examined the attitudes of a quite different group of workers, those in automated industry. He finds evidence that they might unite with technicians and lower level management with whom they frequently deal against top management and ownership. Thus, he takes the view that developments in the occupational structure have created a 'new' working class with considerable potential for radical change. Certainly, we are beginning to build up a complex picture of social consciousness among the working class.

Marxists bring some order to the above complexity by reference to basic Marxist theoretical concepts and perspective. Firstly, they point out that, whatever their differences, the working class share a common relationship to the means of production. Braverman has made the more specific observation that capitalism has developed in a way that has progressively removed control of work out of the hands of more and more workers. Most workers – manual and non-manual alike – play small roles in large organisations. Secondly, and related to this, they argue that a common relationship to production is the basis of a common class interest. Thirdly, they contend that this common class interest can be best expressed in the socialist

251

movement aimed at stopping capitalist exploitation and establishing a more equal society. The fourth part of this chain of thought is *how* this change will happen. Here the link is uncertain because Marxists disagree on the matter themselves. Simplifying somewhat, structuralists such as Althusser contend that the working class in general will only become aware of, and energetically pursue, its common interest in socialism when capitalist society begins to collapse and ceases to produce prosperity. Other Marxists, notably E. P. Thompson, stress that, within limits, working people have made their own history, and will make their own future. This leads to an emphasis on the need to 'raise the level of consciousness' among the working class by socialist propaganda and organisation. Despite their disagreement, both Althusser and Thompson make the important point that social consciousness is not static, but open to change. Because the working class is divided and even fragmented today does not mean it will be so tomorrow. It is also relevant to point out here that if white collar employees are included within the working class, as they are by many Marxists, then the numerical strength of the working class is much greater and so, therefore, must be its *potential* political strength. It is likely that a revival of working class politics would be based on some sort of 'coalition' extending from white collar unionists, through the employed manual working class, and embracing many of the growing numbers of unemployed. Such a 'coalition' would be based not only on mutual interest but also on a sense of moral solidarity by which the stronger shoulder some of the burden of conflict for the weak.

There is a wide range of agreement among sociologists of various perspectives and ideologies that the contemporary working class is internally highly differentiated both in terms of living standards and cultural outlook. But whereas liberals such as Dahrendorf tend to regard such divisions as a fact with which it is futile to argue, Marxists point to the continuing underlying common structural situation of the working class and regard the varying, and in some cases 'low', level of socialist consciousness among different groups of workers as a 'problem' to be wrestled with rather than as an immutable reality. If this comment makes sociology seem uncomfortably close to politics, it does not mislead.

2 Social Mobility

Terminology and Factors Associated with Social Mobility
We have already defined the concept of social mobility as movement up or down the social class hierarchy. Mobility may be *long-range* (from social class v to social class I) or, what is much more common, *short-range*. *Individual* and *stratum* mobility can occur and the former is considered to be generally more possible in modern than in traditional societies. *Ascribed status* refers to social position which is predetermined by others and is usually acquired at birth on the basis of the social standing of the individual's parents. *Achieved status* refers to the social position individuals acquire in their own lifetime, whether higher or lower than the one they had at birth. Again, the possibility of achieving a change in social status is considered to be greater in modern than in traditional societies, although most people remain in the class of their birth. The word 'achieved' is slightly misleading in this context, because merit is not necessarily implied in a change of social status.

The terms *status of origin* and *status of destination* provide a more neutral alternative to describe the same phenomenon. *Status of origin refers to the status into which a person is born and status of destination to the one he or she acquires. Intragenerational mobility* describes the situation when an individual acquires a different social status from the one which he previously held. *Intergenerational mobility* describes social mobility between generations and it is our main concern here. Finally, the terms *vertical* and *horizontal* mobility are frequently used. Vertical mobility is simply another way of referring to upward or downward mobility and horizontal mobility involves a change from one occupation to another of equal status. Strictly speaking, horizontal mobility refers to occupational rather than social mobility as it involves no change of social status.

Status and class differences usually coincide, but rapid social mobility can cause them to be 'out of joint'. For example, a public school 'type' who finds himself having to do, say, a manual job may find the symbols of middle class status, such as accent and dress, something of an embarrassment. The same can happen to the working class 'lad' who suddenly 'makes it': he may appear to lack the polish of the more established rich. *Status dissonance* is the term used to describe this kind of occurrence.

253

It should be remembered that most people remain in the class into which they are born. This can be *partly* because their life-style effectively cuts them off from other groups. For example, the traditional working class were often culturally very 'inbred'. Parker has referred to this as *social closure*.

We now give a list of the major factors associated with social mobility – simply as a checkpoint: they are explained later in the section. It is scarcely possible to separate the overlapping factors affecting group and individual mobility. Broadly speaking, however, those affecting groups come first:

1 Substantial Change in Occupational Structure
2 Differential Fertility
3 Educational Opportunity (Qualifications)
4 Social and Cultural Factors
5 Intelligence and Talent
6 Marriage

All these are explained and illustrated below in our detailed analysis of social mobility in England and Wales.

Social Mobility in England and Wales: A Test of the Liberal Ideal of Equality of Opportunity

There have been few more important public issues in twentieth century Britain than that of equality of opportunity. For Britain to be the 'open society' of liberal ideals, a society in which equality of opportunity exists, a good deal of social mobility must take place. More precisely, people must be able to compete for occupational position, on equal terms, regardless of their social class background. Many liberals of various political persuasions have regarded equality of opportunity as a pre-condition of a fair society. Of course, equality of opportunity does not guarantee equality of outcome: it means that people will achieve jobs suitable to their intelligence and talents, regardless of social background. As we have seen, Marxists want a different kind of equality from this: they want resources to be distributed in terms of need rather than competition. Others, again, are influenced by both views. Here, however, we examine how far the classic liberal ideal of equal opportunity is achieved in Britain. To do this, we must analyse the extent of social mobility in this country.

254

a STUDIES OF SOCIAL MOBILITY IN BRITAIN There have been two major studies of social mobility in England and Wales, the first led by David Glass in 1949 and the second conducted by a team of sociologists at Nuffield College in 1972. The latter is known as the Oxford Mobility Study. Ideally, the findings of the two surveys would be directly comparable, and it was certainly the intention of the Oxford group to achieve this as far as possible. In fact, they do not attempt precisely to *replicate* Glass's methodology partly because of a number of criticisms that have been convincingly made against it. The major effect of the flaws in Glass's methodology is that he may have underestimated the rate of social mobility, particularly long-range upward mobility. As one of his important findings was that there was little long-range mobility, either upwards or downwards, the methodological criticisms are significant. Glass also found that family and social background had a major effect on social status and that most people remained at a similar level to their fathers.

Our analysis of the 1972 findings will be assisted by reference to the following table although by no means the whole of the following discussion emerges from the data presented there.

Inter-generational class mobility: adult males, England and Wales, 1972

Destinations (Ten years after entry to work)

Origins	Middle class %	Lower Middle %	Working class %	
Middle class	7.0	3.7	2.6	
Lower Middle	7.0	9.9	13.9	
Working class	6.1	11.3	38.5	
Total	20.1	24.9	55.0	100

Source: A. H. Halsey, *Change in British Society*, p. 114. (slightly adapted).

This table repays detailed study. The vertical readings of the grid describe inter-generational inflow to three destination classes. The horizontal readings describe inter-generational outflow from origin classes. The diagonal reading from top left to bottom right describes those who were still in their class of origin ten years after starting work. A further key piece of information is that in terms of their class of *origin*, 13.3% of the sample were middle class, 30.8% lower middle class and 55.9% working class. These figures contrast interestingly with their 1972 *destinations* which were respectively, 20.1%, 24.9% and 55.0%.

Broadly, the findings of the Oxford Study confirm two popular clichés. The first is that the chances of improving one's social status got better in the post-war period, and the second – perhaps more a sociologist's than a layman's cliché – is that is is still much easier to *retain* high social status once born to it than it is to *achieve* it in the first place. Let us take these points in order.

Because of the expansion of the middle or service class since the war, there has been more opportunity for the lower middle and working class to move upwards. John H. Goldthorpe, a major contributor to the Oxford Study, rejects the thesis that a significant degree of 'closure' exists at the higher occupational levels of British society. Writing of the upper end of the middle class (the top 8% occupationally) he argues that the survey data shows 'a very wide basis of recruitment and a very low degree of homogeneity in its composition'. In other words, people from a great variety of social origins are members of this class (recruitment), and by that very fact its members are in many ways dissimilar (lack homogeneity). A particularly interesting illustration of this is that, in 1972, marginally more members of social class 1 came from working class backgrounds than from upper middle class backgrounds. This shows a very much higher rate of long-range upward mobility than Glass found. If we return to Halsey's table, we can see that what Goldthorpe says of class 1 is true of the middle class as a whole. Indeed, in 1972, almost two thirds of it were made up of people of non-middle class origin.

The lower middle class, too, is highly penetrable from below. It contains more people of working class origins (11.3%) than of lower middle class origins (9.9%), although relatively few middle class people (3.7%) are downwardly mobile into it. Concluding this point, then, opportunity for upward mobility substantially increased in post-war Britain. There is, however, quite another way of looking at the findings of the Oxford Study and we must adopt this perspective now.

The chances of a class 1 son remaining in class 1 compared to the chances that a working class son has of reaching class 1 have changed little over recent generations. Again, referring to the table, the proportion of sons of middle class origin who

256

retained middle class status is more than 1 in 2, whereas only about 1 in 9 working class sons achieved this status. What has happened is that increased opportunities have been shared more or less equally between the classes: there have been rather more opportunities for all. But if the chances of upward mobility for working class sons have improved, the shrinkage of working class jobs and the expansion of middle class ones has protected the middle class against downward mobility. Overall, therefore, relative mobility rates have changed remarkably little. Goldthorpe concludes that the pattern of inter-generational mobility in recent decades has been one of stability or even marginally increasing relative inequality.

It needs to be said that the Oxford Study does not address itself directly to the Marxist concern with the upper class. Other data shows that there is much more self-recruitment to this group than to the much larger class 1 as a whole. It is also quite probable that those of non-upper class origins who do become members of it tend to adopt the values and attitudes of that class. Marxists are also able to interpret what is happening to the working class in a way quite consistent with their perspective. The working class is the most closed class and despite the differences between them, its members remain relatively disadvantaged. These factors may provide a sound basis for solidarity and collective action.

b FACTORS EXPLAINING THE RECENT PATTERN OF SOCIAL MOBILITY IN BRITAIN We now turn to discuss the factors that account for the pattern of social mobility described above. First, the increase in upward mobility has been largely due to a substantial shift in employment from the industrial to the service sector. Men have particularly benefited because lower status white collar jobs have been filled mainly by women, and men have been able to fill most of the new professional, technical, administrative and managerial posts. The increase has had little, if anything, to do with government policy. Indeed, in so far as the relative class rates of mobility have not changed, government policy to achieve greater equality of opportunity can be said to have failed.

Historically, differential fertility rates between the middle and working classes (that is, middle class families have produced fewer children) has created 'space' into which some working class people could move. Quite simply, the middle class did not produce enough children to fill all the middle class jobs available. This has been especially true in the rapid expansion of the service sector in the post-war period. Since the mid-nineteen sixties, there has been a tendency for family size to fall throughout the social classes, and although differences remain, differential fertility is now less important in explaining upward social mobility. The slight general increase in the birth rate in 1978 and 1979, even if sustained, is not likely to change this.

We have already examined the effect of educational expansion on social mobility and there is no need to rehearse the contents of this lengthy section here (see Chapter 5). In summary, Halsey *et al*'s research on the tripartite system and various less extensive studies of the comprehensive system show little *relative* change in the educational success and career achievements of children of different class origins in the post-war period. The middle class has taken as much, if not more, advantage of state education as the working class and has virtually sole access to the privileged private sector. Gamely, but not entirely convincingly, Halsey argues that a *further* expansion of educational opportunity must, by reduction, disproportionately benefit the working class. There may be no liberal alternative than but to try this, but history warns against excessive optimism about the likely results.

The influence of social and cultural factors on both educational and career opportunities does not need to be laboured here. It has been a constant theme in earlier chapters. The material disadvantages of a lower working class background are obvious, but the cultural disadvantages, if any, remain open to debate despite Halsey's sophisticated statistically-based attempt to show that they are much less than Bernstein and Bourdieu have argued.

However much intelligence may be helped or hindered by social environment, there is no doubt that the possession of high intelligence can be of assistance in upward mobility, and that low intelligence is a near fatal bar to it. Obviously, this factor applies virtually exclusively to the lower classes. It requires no intelligence at all to be born into the upper classes (although it usually requires, at least, the intelligence to appoint a good accountant to stay there). Lipset and Bendix have suggested that high intelligence may help working class children to recognise middle class attitudes and norms and to see the advantage of imitating them.

Traditionally, exceptional talent in either entertainment or sport has been an avenue to the top for a few working class people and, particularly in the United States, for some black people. But for most, this possibility is just a dream. There are not many Sophia Lorens or Muhammad Alis. A further miscellaneous group of factors, such as character, looks and luck can no doubt play a part in mobility but they are too unpredictable and personal to require more than brief acknowledgement here.

Of more sociological importance is the fact that women achieve upward mobility by marriage more often than men. This is a result of their generally inferior economic position and earning power. 'She's a gold digger' can be understood more sympathetically in the context of a society in which women depend heavily on men for material comfort and social status. This dependency is not the fault of individual women but lies in the nature of our sexually unequal society (see Chapter 11).

If the recent past is a good guide, the prospects for upward mobility in Britain depend on the further expansion of the service sector. In the early nineteen eighties, the medium term prospects are for less employment in this area. Clearly, expansion cannot go on for ever. If higher status and better paid jobs are not available, a better academically qualified population will go to waste at the dole queues. There has so far been quite remarkably little thought about this possibility and what is to be done about it.

Britain is still a class divided society. Wealth remains concentrated and relative poverty persists. Social mobility out of the working class has increased but middle class children have as good a chance as ever of maintaining the status inherited from their parents. Both of these factors are due to the expansion of the service sector and not to the success of government policies aimed at bringing about greater equality of opportunity. There is more 'room at the top' (or, more precisely, in the middle) but the class origins of those who 'make it' are roughly in the same proportion that they were fifty years ago. And in the future, it is quite possible that upward access will become more difficult. In 1980–81, for instance, thousands of civil service jobs were lost. Already the most rapidly expanding 'occupational' group in British society is the unemployed. Practically and culturally, the country is largely unprepared for this – that is, neither the policies, nor attitudes and ideas to deal with it are much in evidence.

For the working majority, however, a degree of *situational convergence* has occurred. White collar employees at all levels tend more frequently to work in large organisations and, like the manual working class, have to haggle in the market place to maintain and defend their pay and working conditions. To do so more effectively they have become more unionised. According to Goldthorpe and Lockwood, *instrumental collectivism* increasingly characterises the attitudes of most employees – whatever the colour of their collar. Whether common economic experience and response will ever provide a basis of a shared political approach among unionists is a matter for speculation. Union membership has become a *less* reliable factor in predicting voting behaviour. Specifically, a greater number of trade union members vote Conservative or Liberal than twenty years ago. It may be, however, that in a time of economic crisis in which white collar as well as manual working class security is threatened, a more unified political approach will emerge among unionised employees.

Convergence has also partly occurred at the cultural level, although what is said here must be balanced against the emphasis we have already given to cultural inequality and difference. Traditional working class culture has declined but so, too, has the aura of respectability and status that used to envelop the middle class. Certainly, the symbols of status have diminished in importance to the point where they can easily seem quaint or ridiculous – the cloth cap or 'plummy' accent of the comic's joke. People seem to value others and themselves in terms of *consumption* rather than traditional status. Yet, consumption is frequently not ostentatious: indeed, much of it is privatised and family based. One television set is much the same as another. The thrill of owning the first colour television among one's peer group can only be brief – the machinery of mass production sees to that.

Assessments of modern culture are too various to catalogue in detail here. For some, the cultural profile of corporate capitalist society is flat and uninteresting. Others, however, see a burgeoning of individual expression in increased leisure activity and regard the variety of electronic based entertainments now possible within the home itself as a great improvement in the quality of life. What cannot be doubted, however, is the privatised nature of our culture.

Guide to further reading and study

Ivan Reid's *Social Class Differences* in Britain (Open Books, 1977) is again recommended for the sheer volume of information it provides. More theoretically sophisticated, but nonetheless highly readable is A. H. Halsey's *Change in British Society* (Oxford University Press, 1978). J. Westergaard and H. Resler's *Class in Capitalist Society: a Study of Contemporary Britain* (Hutchinson, 1973) covers similar ground from a Marxist perspective. Gordon Rose's *The Working Class* (1970) and John Raynor's *The Middle Class* (1969), both published by Longman, are clearly presented and relatively undemanding, and useful for basic reading. Extracts from J. M. Goldthorpe *et al*, *The Affluent Worker in the Class Structure* and David Lockwood's *The Blackcoated Worker* are available in E. Butterworth and D. Weir, eds, *The Sociology of Modern Britain* (Fontana, 1977), together with other useful articles on stratification. On the cultural side, Richard Hoggart's *The Uses of Literacy* (Penguin, 1966), is interesting and, appropriately, highly literate. A book to which every teacher should have access, but which few sixth formers will read is John Goldthorpe's *Social Mobility and Class Structure in Modern Britain* (Clarendon, 1980). The introductory chapter contains a useful review of other literature on social mobility.

Past Questions

1 Consider the implications of the growth of white collar occupations for theories of social stratification. (AEB, 1976).
2 Describe and account for patterns of social mobility in any *one* society. (AEB, 1977).

3 What evidence is there for suggesting that Britain is a stratified society in the nineteen seventies? Explain the conceptual basis of your analysis of stratification (JMB, 1978).

4 Compare the relationship between education and stratification in Britain and *one* other society. (London, 1979).

5 'The thesis of the white collar worker becoming proletarian should be viewed as sceptically as that of the manual worker becoming middle class.' In the light of the available evidence, do you agree? (AEB, 1980).

10 Wealth, Poverty and the Search for Equality

The Issues

This chapter is about the extremes of inequality in Britain and in the contemporary world. Focusing mainly on Britain, it deals primarily with the brute facts of material inequality and attempts to explain them. Our brief consideration of poverty in the Third World should be considered as a supplement to the sections on Development and Underdevelopment and Population at the end of Chapter 7, in which the reasons for the relative inequality of the developed and underdeveloped countries are discussed. Inequality of cultural opportunity usually goes hand in glove with material inequality. We do not explore this matter here, as it was a major theme of Section B and appears again prominently in Chapter 19.

Material equality is a socialist and communist rather than a liberal ideal. Yet many holding these views would shy back from committing themselves to the principle of complete equality. It is worth recalling that even the Marxist ideal of a classless society does not necessarily imply *complete* equality even in material matters. Nevertheless, the majority of socialists and communists seek a much greater measure of equality than exists in Britain and the contemporary world. We briefly examine the search for greater equality in the case of four societies. Finally, and partly in view of the difficulties experienced by these societies, we ask whether equality is possible or desirable.

Wealth and Poverty: Some Facts

We can usefully begin our examination of the extent of inequality in Britain by looking at the distribution of income and wealth. This will give us a clear picture of relative inequality. The difference between income and wealth as economic assets needs to be made clear. Income is, generally, 'money in the hand' and, within the limits of a person's commitments, can be spent as he wishes. Wealth includes other assets besides cash savings. Income enables a person to consume, whereas wealth, as well as doing this, gives long term security and status. We look at income first.

Comment on the table is straightforward. There been relatively little overall change: what change has taken place has been notably at the expense of the top 1% and in favour of the group *between* the top 10% and the bottom 50%. The relative position of the bottom 50% has changed remarkably little.

The Distribution of Income in the U.K. after Tax

Income share of the	1949	1976/77
top 1%	6.4	3.5
top 10%	27.1	22.4
next 40%	46.4	50.0
bottom 50%	26.5	27.6

Source: *Royal Commission on the Distribution of Income and Wealth.*

As we saw in the previous chapter, wealth is much less evenly distributed than income. The very rich are invariably wealthy because of what they inherit, not because of what they earn. Despite the gradual trend towards a redistribution of wealth in the post-war period, the top 1% are still about 25 times richer than average, and the gap between the richest and the poorest is almost unimaginable. In concrete terms, it is the difference between sleeping in a louse-infested bed in an East End doss-house and sleeping in the world's best homes and hotels. It is the middle class that has primarily benefited from wealth redistribution – largely as a result of the increase in home-ownership. Statistical experts warn us against the incompleteness and inadequacy of official figures on the distribution of income and wealth. In particular, the exclusion of *non-marketable* assets, especially state and other pension rights, tends to exaggerate inequality. On the other hand, massive upper class family wealth is sometimes obscured in official figures (partly because of tax-avoidance strategies such as making 'gifts' to relatives). In any case, the pattern of fundamental inequality is clear.

Both the statistics and human reality of poverty in the Third World are a challenge to our imagination. In 1978, the world spent 120 billion dollars on arms while 17 million infants died of malnutrition, bad water or preventable disease before reaching their fifth birthday. As Westerners seek to make marginal economies to cope with the energy crisis, over 600 million families in the Third World struggle on incomes which would not pay half the cost of the average Western family's annual heating bill.

Finally, without being sanctimonious, a different kind of poverty should be mentioned. Cultural critic Jeremy Seabrook calls

265

it 'the poverty within us'. He means the constant obsession with material things that thinly obscures the lack of values and humanity in Western society. Things have become more important than people. The claim to be, if not poor, at least 'stretched' is common. Yet we live in a period of great wealth. Seabrook suggests that in the West, the common plea of 'poverty' is actually a cry from the impoverished spirit rather than the empty stomach. Of course, it cannot be suggested that this is true of those in genuine material need.

The Poor

This section examines the extent and causes of poverty in Britain and, more briefly, in the Third World. First, however, we consider what it is like to be poor.

THE MEANING OF POVERTY (A PHENOMENOLOGICAL PERSPECTIVE) Most people reading this book will not *know* poverty because they will never have experienced it. The poor do not, on the whole, go in for further education and read books like this. The stunting of educational and cultural opportunity is the consequence of poverty. Some who read this book will have *seen* poverty: some may have even seen the absolute degradation of poverty in, say, Calcutta. But seeing poverty is not the same as *being* poor. It is very easy to close your mind to poverty that is merely observed. In India, the visiting Westerner will, at first, often give to the poor, but endless requests for alms become an irritation. Excuses not to give come readily to mind: 'They're taking me for a ride'; '*This* one doesn't look hungry'; 'He'll spend it on drink'; 'They're using the baby to make me feel sorry for them'; 'Anyway, surely the abolition of poverty is the responsibility of the international community, not of an individual', and so on. In fact, neither personal charity nor the efforts of relief agencies have solved the problem, although that does not mean either should cease.

The main effect of poverty is to cause human pain and suffering. This may be physical, such as rickets or the failure of the brain to develop fully, or mental, such as demoralisation and despair. In so far as there is enough wealth in the world to abolish poverty we can say that this pain and suffering is needless. Let us look at two cases of poverty in Britain. Both involve children of single parents. They may seem slight in

comparison with starvation in the Third World, bu
imagination will show what distress underlies them. First.

> Being poor means being sad on the first day of school. My little
> girl shan't have a uniform. The head teacher says it won't be
> covered by the Department of Health and Social Security or the
> education authority as it is not compulsory. The fact remains
> that the only children without one are from families that can't
> afford it.

Second:

> Being poor meant finding a flat for £10 and having the DHSS
> refuse to pay more than £6, so your child is removed into care
> and you are lodged in a doss house with no bathroom.
>
> (*The Times*, 24th December, 1979)

Human statistics are meaningful primarily in terms of the personal experience they attempt to record. Think of the following
statistics in those terms. In Britain in 1978, 500,000 children
lived in families whose income was below the official poverty
line even though one or both parents were in full-time work.
Almost 1,000,000 lived in families dependent on supplementary
benefit because the head of the family was physically or socially
incapacitated in some way. Over 100,000 were in the care of
local authorities, and about 300,000 were left alone either after
school or during holidays, often because both parents worked.
It is not, however, only child poverty that should be perceived
in human terms but all poverty.

DEFINITION AND EXTENT OF POVERTY AND INEQUALITY Before the
extent of poverty can be estimated, we must define what we
mean by the term. Poverty can be thought of as either *absolute*
or *relative*. Absolute Poverty is insufficiency in the basic necessities of existence: in practical terms, this usually means being
without adequate food, clothing or shelter. Absolute poverty is
a rarity in Britain but commonplace in the Third World. In
Runciman's terms, relative poverty or *deprivation* is not being
able to afford what one's *reference group*, or group of comparison,
enjoys. In his recent (1979) authoritative survey on poverty,
Peter Townsend described relative poverty as the inability to
participate in the community's style of living. Thus, a person
who cannot afford the record player that all his friends have is
relatively deprived. Understandably, some social commentators

267

/ be taken too far. It is one thing to
.ck of a record player, but are these
respect of, say, coloured televisions or
principle, however, the concept of relative
olicable to any such situation.

we draw the poverty line as far as Britain is
oviously absolute poverty is a rarity although
at less well than they should and live in unhealthy
Peter Townsend offers several different approaches
to aring poverty. He starts with the government's own
definition embodied in the *supplementary benefit* scale. The
scale determines a minimum level of income for claimants who
are unable to work, and whose other sources of income, if any,
are inadequate to meet their needs. Supplementary benefits are
paid for out of general taxation and are quite separate from
contributory benefits such as old age pensions and unemployment
and sickness benefits. Supplementary benefits are *means tested,*
which is to say that they are given only to those whose own
resources are below a certain level. Means testing necessarily
involves an intrusion into privacy. The value of supplementary
benefits in real terms has tended to increase, but the value
relative to the average wage has not changed greatly.

In 1969, there were about 5 million people in Britain claiming supplementary benefit, that is 9% of families below the
official poverty line. Both J. C. Kincaid and Frank Field have
argued that this grossly underestimates the numbers in poverty.
There may be as many as 2 million people or more affected by
the non-taking up of benefits. This includes some workers
whose jobs pay wages that are below the income that supplementary benefits would provide for a worker's family. Aston-
ishingly, some have regarded this as an argument for reducing
benefits rather than raising the wages of the low-paid. To 'earn'
poverty is a grim irony and not exactly an incentive to work.
Some authorities have claimed that a realistic point at which to
draw the poverty line would be 20% or even 40% above basic
supplementary benefit rate. The Supplementary Benefits Commission does sometimes allow special grants to be made up to
this level, although discretionary grants may eventually be
reduced. 'The supplementary benefit plus 40%' point would put
12½ million in poverty.

The above definitions are all based on varying levels of material deprivation. Townsend's use of the concept of relative deprivation, which produces a total of 14 million in poverty (22.9% of the population), adds a consideration for how people feel when they lack the means to get what their friends and acquaintances have. People who are clearly unable to meet the demands and expectations inherent in their social relationships are relatively poor. We recall the child whose single parent could not afford a school uniform. In terms of sociological jargon, her distress was relative, not absolute, but no less personally felt for that. Some of the Conservative press attacked Townsend's broad concept of poverty as hopelessly unrealistic and there is no doubt that, a socialist himself, he sees no solution to poverty without a fundamental redistribution of wealth.

Townsend's massive empirical survey (1200 pages!) was carried out in 1968–69. We have to ask if his findings are still applicable. Writing in 1979, A. N. Atkinson, himself an expert in the area, argued that, during the decade between Townsend's research and its publication, the overall relative position of the poor was no better. For instance, the earnings of the lowest paid 10% of male workers improved by a mere 1% of the median between 1968 and 1978 (from 66 to 67%); unemployment trebled in that period, and there was a substantial increase in the number of one parent families.

Who, then, are the poor? This is an important question in itself but, as we shall see, the answer to it also indicates some of the causes of poverty. In 1978, over 60% of recipients of supplementary benefits were retired people; about another 20% were unemployed; over 10% were one parent families and about 2% were sick or disabled. Apart from those on supplementary benefit, we must include hundreds of thousands belonging to low wage families.

The Causes of Poverty and Some Policy Solutions

There is a variety of possible explanations of poverty. Not all are equally applicable to all groups. We discuss suggested causes and policy solutions of poverty together.

POVERTY AS MORAL INADEQUACY A popular nineteenth century view of poverty was that it was the result of laziness or even moral inadequacy. Hard work was considered to be the virtue that ensured prosperity and those who did not practise it were felt to deserve poverty. Few would see laziness as the major cause of poverty in contemporary Britain; the facts disprove this point of view. Over a third of the poor are old people, and almost another third are actually in work but are poorly paid. The occasional panic about social security 'scroungers', orchestrated by elements in the media, is disproportionate to the size of the problem. There are far more who fail to claim benefits to which they are entitled than who claim dishonestly. The small percentage (about 5% of claimants) who actually get more from social security than they would from work are generally unskilled workers with large families. This anomaly of the system perhaps reflects more discreditably on a society that tolerates such low pay than on the individuals concerned

POVERTY AS MISFORTUNE A second explanation of poverty is that it is often due to personal misfortune or need, rather than the result of individual moral failing. This view is associated with progressive liberal or social democratic political ideas, and it inspired much of the reforming legislation that set up the framework of the twentieth century Welfare State. First, contributory old age pensions and then insurance for employees against sickness and unemployment were introduced by government. The Welfare State was consolidated and extended by the first post Second World War Labour government. Two important measures were the setting up of the National Health Service, and of the National Assistance Board. The purpose of the latter was to provide help for those who remained unemployed after their unemployment benefit had been exhausted, or who were otherwise without income. The role of the NAB has since been taken over by the Supplementary Benefits Commission.

The reformer's view that poverty 'hits' certain identifiable groups, who must therefore be helped, is enticingly simple, yet poverty stubbornly persists despite the Welfare State. It is a severe disappointment to the many politicians and intellectuals, who hoped that the Welfare State would virtually abolish poverty, that millions are in receipt of social security in the early nineteen eighties. Such was certainly not the intention of Lord Beveridge whose official report was largely responsible for the structure of the NAB. He hoped that a low unemployment and high wage economy, coupled with a better system of unemployment insurance, would mean that the supplementary function of the NAB would substantially decrease rather than increase. There are other criticisms of the way the Welfare State operates. One is that it fails significantly to redistribute wealth from the better off to the poor. This is because the middle class make more use of the Welfare State than the poor. Thus, they keep their children in education for longer, and, often, use the health service more. Further, as middle class people, from clerks to Principal Secretaries (top civil servants), run the Welfare State, it is *in a sense,* an employment subsidy for them. Often, the bureaucratic way in which welfare is administered confuses or 'mystifies' those who need help. Long waits, form-filling and questioning may or may not be the norm, but they happen frequently enough – particularly in the administration of social security – to intimidate some.

Reformers still hope to improve and extend the Welfare State. Some, such as the late Richard Titmuss, would like to see the abolition of *means tested benefits* (those given after income and other support has been assessed) in favour of the universal right to a minimum standard of living for all – that is, the triumph of the principle of *universalism* over *selectivity.* More recently, Peter Townsend has been involved in campaigning to reduce the extent of dependency on supplementary benefits and the humiliating means tests that go with them. He was an influential figure behind the state pensions scheme introduced in 1978. This should gradually reduce the number of old on supplementary benefit. Others call for the improvement of administrative techniques and better co-ordination of public and voluntary welfare agencies. Marxists, however, believe that reform is not enough and, as we shall see in considering the fourth explanation of poverty, regard it as the inevitable product of capitalist society. In any case, it should not be assumed that the Welfare State will expand indefinitely, or even that welfare expenditure is never reduced. Indeed, after six years of Labour rule in which very little redistribution of wealth to the poor occurred, cuts in welfare expenditure were implemented by the Conservative government, elected in 1979. Social services had an effective 9% cut imposed on their projected expenditure for 1980–81 and, as a result, planned cuts in such services as home helps, meals on wheels and old people's homes.

THE CULTURE OF POVERTY THESIS A third explanation of poverty is that it is generated and regenerated by the cultural attitudes and life-style of the poor. This is the 'culture of poverty' theory, one which tends to be adopted by conservative social critics. It often involves 'trait analysis' of the life-style of the poor. These traits, or characteristics, are said to include present-centredness, a sense of resignation and fatalism, and a strong predisposition to authoritarianism. At its most extreme, this interpretation sees the poor as inadequate and pathological. Edward Banfield describes the 'lower class individual' as follows:

> Although he has more 'leisure' than almost anyone, the indifference ('apathy' if one prefers) of the lower class person is such that he seldom makes even the simplest repairs to the place that he lives in. He is not troubled by dirt and dilapidation and he does not mind the inadequacy of public facilities such as schools, parks, hospitals and libraries; indeed, where such things exist he may destroy them by carelessness or even by vandalism. Conditions that make the slum repellent to others are serviceable to him.

Given that Banfield regards the cause of poverty as rooted in psychological attitudes, he is dubious about easy solutions aimed at changing the way in which people live. Cultural attitudes tend to undermine imposed reform.

An earlier study by Oscar Lewis puts the concept of the culture of poverty in a wider context. The conditions in which it flourishes include a low-wage, profit-oriented economy and inadequate government assistance for the poor. These are frequently to be found in Third World areas which are undergoing 'development' by foreign capital and, more locally, in inner-city areas almost anywhere in the world. Given this wider context, the culture of poverty thesis loses its conservatism and becomes, generally, more useful.

Sir Keith Joseph's concept of the 'cycle of deprivation' has some similarity to the 'class culture' approach but it lays greater stress on the effect of material factors, such as poor housing and low income, in undermining prospects for self-improvement from generation to generation. Among cultural factors, he particularly emphasises the inadequacy of parental upbringing and the home background. The logical conclusion of this is to help and strengthen the family. Whether this can be done on a piecemeal basis is highly debatable. In any case, research, led by Michael Rutter, has shown that most poverty is not inter-generational. Even if the 'cycle' were broken for those who supposedly suffer from it, the majority of those who are in poverty would remain so.

STRUCTURAL EXPLANATIONS OF POVERTY Finally, we come to the analysis of those who regard the rough consensus of the major parties around the Welfare State solution to poverty as mis-guided. Most of these critics are socialist and some Marxist. They consider the cause of poverty to be in the structure of the capitalist system itself. Profit, not human need, is the basic principle of capitalism. The Welfare State merely patches up the wounds caused by exploitation and greed – and not very effectively at that. J. C. Kincaid concludes his influential book *Poverty and Equality in Britain* with the following remarks:

> Poverty cannot be abolished within capitalist society, but only in socialist society under workers' control, in which human needs, and not profits, determine the allocation of resources.
> For the immediate present, the urgently needed reform of the Welfare State remains contingent on the mobilisation of the working class as an independent force in British politics.

Kincaid's last sentence indicates that even within capitalism some reform is better than none. The alleviation of suffering and deprivation cannot be left to await 'the revolution'. The alternative to such a programme may be that a new 'under-class' of the poor and powerless will develop. A virtual halt to national economic growth, high unemployment, and a labour movement only half-heartedly committed to the needs of the poor, is the type of scenario that could enable this to happen.

Stratification in Socialist Societies: The Search for Equality

Convergence Theory

Stratification in Socialist societies is of interest for two major reasons. Firstly, a large number of societies, particularly in the Third World, have been so attracted to the ideal of socialist equality that they have based their socio-economic system on socialism. This is one of the chief world developments of this century. The second point is of more specific sociological interest. The socialist societies present us with an empirical testing ground of the practicality of social equality – as defined in socialist terms. We must be careful, however, not to reach simplistic and uninformed 'verdicts' on the practical possibility of equality on the basis of the experience of socialist societies so far. In the sheer struggle to survive, in a hostile world, many socialist regimes have pursued policies far from their own preferred ideals.

One of the most formidable criticisms of the efforts of the Soviet Union and other industrialised Communist countries to achieve greater equality than exists in the West, is implied in *convergence theory*. This view argues that the nature of modern industrial technology requires the same range of skills wherever it is used, and that people of different abilities and education will attract correspondingly different rewards. This classic functionalist argument was applied to the Soviet Union by American liberals Daniel Bell and Clark Kerr in the early nineteen sixties, partly to demonstrate that the egalitarian hopes of the Soviets were destined to flounder before the 'logic of industrialism'. J. H. Goldthorpe, in the spirit of diligent empirical research for which he is widely respected, decided to 'test' whether the system of stratification operating in the Soviet Union was in fact substantially similar to that of advanced capitalist countries. We consider his and other relevant findings on this matter in the context of a broad survey of stratification in the Soviet Union. We then move on to examine convergence theory as applied to Sweden, a socialist democracy. Finally, we briefly look at stratification in two Third World countries: China and Tanzania.

The Soviet Union: Equality or Convergence?

The first socialist society was the Soviet Union. After the Bolsheviks (Communists) came to power in 1917, vigorous efforts were made to reach a much greater degree of social equality than existed in Tsarist Russia. Wage differentials between blue and white collar workers were greatly reduced, and rapid expansion of the social services occurred. Further, from the nineteen twenties the Soviet Union provides us with a classic example of a society in which structural change opened up the opportunity for substantial upward social mobility. The change in this case was due to the rapid rate of industrialisation,

274

which provided higher status jobs for former peasantry. The expansion of administrative, managerial and political posts enabled a limited number to achieve mobility to a higher status range. No great credit redounds to government policy for the increase in upward mobility, although peasants and workers were favoured over the middle class. A rapidly modernising country tends to experience an increased rate of upward mobility – regardless of whether it is communist or capitalist. The same happened in the United States during a period of comparable expansion.

For a 25 year period, up to the death of Stalin in 1956, the process towards greater equalisation tended to be reversed, except in respect of increased social mobility and even this took place in a society that was becoming more and more stratified. This was due to Stalin's belief that the country needed firm leadership both for internal development and in foreign affairs – he feared Germany – and partly because of his own authoritarian personality. Liberty – civil, political and economic, such as workers' control of, or participation in industry – declined, as did equality, during Stalin's dictatorial rule.

More recently, there has been a partial return to the ideal of material equality in the USSR, although substantial differentials exist. What is important from the point of view of comparative stratification, however, is not the precise ebb and flow of inequality but *how* it is produced. On this basis Goldthorpe rejects convergence theory, and argues persuasively that the *underlying basis* of stratification is different in the Soviet Union and other centrally-controlled Communist countries from the capitalist West. He contends, that whereas market forces produce *class* stratificiation in the West, they are not allowed sufficient operation to do so in Soviet-type regimes. In Soviet society, Communist Party control produces a *politically based form of stratification*. Top politicians ultimately have the power to determine and to change the structure of status and rewards (that is, there is stratification hierarchy). Following the logic of Goldthorpe's argument, it is more precise to refer to this group of top people as a *ruling political elite* rather than a ruling class.

Goldthorpe is surely correct to see stratification in Soviet-type countries and the West as *generically* different (of a different type). Frank Parkin also makes a point based on the distinction between a market and a politically controlled economy, adopted by Goldthorpe. He is able to illustrate that the allocation of rewards, in the form of income and status, is somewhat different in Russia and other East European countries from that in the West. In particular, manual workers tend to be better paid than lower white collar workers, who also tend to receive fewer fringe benefits than in the West. In Marxist countries there is a tradition of allocating higher status to manual work whereas, in the West and perhaps particularly in Britain, the opposite tendency prevails (Chapter 9, p. 241). Nevertheless, an educated elite of much better paid employees also exists. Parkin found, however, a somewhat narrower range of income than in the West, though it has been argued that the privileges of politicians and top bureaucrats perhaps partly cancel this out. Parkin found a higher rate of social mobility in the East European countries than in the West and, significantly, more long-range mobility. He considers that the large number of recruits to the 'intelligensia' has helped to prevent the development of a distinct culture and style among this group comparable to that of the English upper class or French *haute bourgeoisie*. As Parkin is aware, the high rate of upward mobility in Russia was probably due more to the rapid expansion of that country's service sector than to deliberate policy (though this played a part). The same process has occurred in England in the post-war period. In both countries upward mobility will almost certainly decline if this expansion stops and in the absence of government policies to maintain it.

Although Goldthorpe and Parkin do make important distinctions about the causes of stratification in advanced Western and East European countries, they both recognise that substantial material inequality still exists in Russia. Speculatively, David Lane raises the possibility that this inequality *may* be part of a transitional phase after which true Communism will be achieved. This speculative optimism is not shared by Yugoslav former politician and writer Milovan Djilas, who was one of the first to offer a critique of the nature of stratification in Soviet and other East European Communist Bloc countries. He argued that a new ruling elite or class (the distinction is not always clearly made) of *political leaders* and *bureaucratic officials*, as distinct from an economic ruling class, had emerged in these countries. His thesis has become a familiar one and has, more recently, been applied to China and other non-European countries. Most socialist societies, European or otherwise, do produce a sizeable bureaucratic class which generally operates *under* the control of the political elite. History has shown that both politicians and bureaucrats can threaten the liberty and living standards (they are expensive non-producers!) of the majority of the people whose 'servants' they are supposed to be. The two groups are highly interdependent and it is not surprising that they sometimes have a sense of shared interests against 'the masses'. As Tom Bottomore suggests, the term *power elite* rather than *ruling class* better describes the political, rather than economic, basis of the power of the ruling minorities in the East European Communist countries.

Although Goldthorpe and Parkin undermine convergence theory, it remains possible that, as functionalists argue, there is a deeper *general* reason for the widespread, if not universal, occurrence of stratification, which neither convergence theory nor Goldthorpe or Parkin explore. We return to this issue in the next section. Yet, Goldthorpe and Parkin do open the door to the possibility that men can adapt systems of stratification to fit in with their own political and ideological beliefs. Alvin Gouldner, the American radical sociologist, goes further, and passionately argues that both Eastern Communist and Western capitalist countries could be both more equal and more democratic. With this in mind we now examine convergence theory in the context of Sweden.

Sweden: Corporatism and Convergence
The concept of the corporate state is often associated with convergence theory, though the concepts are distinct. Corporatism involves a high degree of co-operation and consultation between government, business and trade unions in 'managing' the industrial state and in reducing internal conflict between capital and labour. J. K. Galbraith has been a particular exponent of this concept and regards a degree of corporatism as necessary to the efficient running of an advanced society and implies, therefore, that some form of corporatism will be universally adopted in such societies. Sweden is often considered to be a prime example of a corporate state. We will give a brief description of Swedish society and then comment more theoretically.

Swedish socialism is of great interest because it is the only example of 'socialism' in an advanced Western society which

277

can be said to have gone 'beyond the Welfare State'. The well-funded and comprehensive Swedish Welfare state was largely the product of an alliance between the Swedish Social Democratic Party and the unions. The Swedish Welfare State has achieved a far higher degree of equality and security among the country's citizens than in Britain. Of course, the price to pay is a much more redistributive system of taxation (Sweden has the most redistributive system of taxation in Europe). The policies of the partnership between the Social Democrats and unions promise to breach the divide between capital and labour to the extent that, within half a century, the former may even be absorbed by the latter and one socialist community created. Already Sweden has an advanced system of industrial democracy (see Chapter 14, p. 392) and a proposal adopted by the LO (the Swedish TUC) for 'employee investment' within companies would, if accepted by the government, eventually result in the socialisation of the Swedish economy. Of course, this may not happen and, indeed, in 1979, the Social Democrats went out of office for the first time in 44 years. Nevertheless, Sweden provides a credible example for those who argue that socialism in advanced societies can be achieved via 'the long, hard march through the institutions', rather than through the frightening gamble of revolution.

The Swedish case suggests that convergence theory is both too generalised and based on highly elitist assumptions. Sweden combines a degree of equality as great if not greater than, that of Soviet-type societies and enjoys at least as much civil and political equality as Western, capitalist societies. Swedish society certainly has its problems but its achievements suggest that greater equality, democracy and participation are possible than convergence theory implies. It lends support for Gouldner's belief that to a significant extent men and women can 'run' society rather than 'be run' by it: neither technocratic nor undemocratic political elites are inevitable.

The Struggle for Equality in the Third World: Tanzania and China

Space does not allow for a detailed account of the struggle of many underdeveloped countries to achieve development through socialist means but the matter should at least be briefly dealt with here (see also Chapter 7, p. 200). We will make the tension between democratic and elitist tendencies within such societies our major focus for consideration.

The case of Tanzanian socialism provides an example of how the idealism of a leader and the enthusiasm of the masses can be frustrated by a gamut of problems including the emergence of an *indigenous* (home-produced) system of stratification. Here we only have the space to contrast the democratic and participatory ideas which Julius Nyerere, Tanzania's president, aspires to, with what several admittedly critical Tanzanian intellectuals argue has actually happened. Nyerere has said:

> Socialism is a way of life, and a socialist society cannot simply come into existence. A socialist society can only be built by those who believe in, and who themselves practise, the principles of socialism.

Critics point out that, in practice, the power of party and state officials has expanded rather than contracted since Nyerere made this statement in 1967. I. G. Shivji calls the rulers of Tanzania a 'bureaucratic bourgeoisie'. This includes the cabinet, top civil servants, industrial leaders, party officials and army officers. Meanwhile, he suggests, Nyerere's scheme of village democracy and economic development flounders. As Nyerere himself realises, his ideas are destined to survive only on the printed page until the industrial proletariat and much larger peasant class can learn to apply them. For him, this remains the full and, as yet, unachieved ideal of socialism. Nevertheless, he defends the take-over of power from colonial rulers, the control of the 'commanding heights' of the economy by the state rather than by foreign capital, and the (sometimes) democratic rural development schemes, as a start and as certainly better than the colonialism that preceded his regime.

China is, perhaps, the socialist country that has most consciously attempted to grapple with the problems of centralised political and bureaucratic power, and the threat to liberty and equality this presents. Its recent history shows the problems involved in that struggle. Commentators have generally been more favourable in their assessment of Chinese than of Soviet efforts in this matter although the balance sheet has varied at different times since 1949 when Mao's Communists took power. The trend towards greater popular participation and social equality in the late nineteen sixties was largely due to the convictions and leadership of Chairman Mao. Such *charismatic* (per-

279

sonal) interventions cannot, of course, be relied on, nor are they always successful in the face of the vested interest of privileged politicians and bureaucrats, and the sheer difficulty in making participation work effectively. After the death of Mao a trend towards elitism in government and organisation asserted itself, but whether this will threaten the democratic and participatory goals of the Chinese Revolution, it is still too early to say.

Is Equality Possible or Desirable?

In describing stratification in necessarily rather formal terms, we may have made inequality seem rather an abstract matter. The human realities associated with inequality are, however, not in the least abstract. They are concerned with great wealth and the life-style, power and opportunity that go with it; also with poverty and all that goes with that. In global terms, the gap between the rich and the poor nations is increasing. In Britain itself, great inequality persists despite a growth in the numbers of families within the middle income bracket. Is inequality, then, part of the 'nature of things' or can it be much further diminished or even abolished?

Let us begin to answer this question by examining the arguments of those who consider stratification to be inevitable. Within sociology, this view has always been associated with functionalist theory. The definitive functionalist presentation of this issue was by Davis and Moore (1956), but the roots of the functionalist position can be traced to Durkheim and Herbert Spencer. Both of them considered that as societies evolve and grow more complex a greater variety of social roles and functions develop. One of the first examples of role differentiation in the evolution of most societies is that of tribe or band 'leader' or 'priest', or perhaps a combination of both. Now differentiation need not lead to stratification if equal power, status and rewards are attached to all roles but, in practice, this rarely, if ever, occurs. Indeed, Durkheim and Spencer assumed the opposite – that key or particularly demanding roles, such as leader or chief, would be recognised as having more status than functionally less important and demanding ones. Since role differentiation, in a factory or bureaucracy, for instance, is so

280

much a part of modern life, so must stratification be. A complex system of stratification is seen by functionalists as a necessary product of a complex society.

Davis and Moore extend some of the arguments of earlier functionalists and add a number of their own. They contend that some positions in the social system are more important than others for the functioning and stability of society. Thus, the position of 'chief' or managing director are both relatively crucial in these respects. Functionally important positions require talented people to fill them and there are only a limited number of such people in a given population. Even talented people must undergo long periods of training if they are to execute such key roles as surgeon, air pilot or research scientist. In return for undergoing lengthy training and for the qualifications and skills thus acquired, they require more pay and 'perks' than less able and less well trained people. In addition, they would also expect their occupations to carry high status. The existence of a group with greater access to material and status rewards than others means, in effect, that a system of stratification also exists. As such a group is necessary to all societies, it follows that stratification must be inevitable as well as functional.

Marxist scholars have been notably energetic in revealing and attacking the assumptions behind the arguments of Davis and Moore. Recently, Bowles and Gintis have pointed out that, in the United States, intelligence is less associated with economic success (and thus with career success) than the socio-economic status of a person's parents (see Chapter 5 for details of this argument).

Tom Bottomore, writing several years before Bowles and Gintis, firmly refutes the contention that the occupational hierarchy is a true reflection of innate 'talent' or ability:

> The major inequalities in society are in the main social products, created and maintained by the institutions of property and inheritance, of political and military power, and supported by particular beliefs and doctrines, even though they are never entirely resistant to the ambitions of outstanding individuals.

Bottomore has further argued that this state of affairs is only mitigated, not abolished, by increased educational opportunity and more open competition in the job market.

Davis and Moore have also been attacked by Tumin for failing to appreciate the great wastage of talent and potential amongst the lower classes that stratification can cause. Because of social background disadvantages there is not, in his view, equal opportunity. Tumin also stresses the human cost of stratification in terms of the frustration and sense of failure that quite able, but less privileged, members of society can feel.

Marxists seem able to cite enough evidence to demonstrate that stratification benefits some at the expense of others and that it persists, not merely because it is useful, but at least partly because the rich and powerful wish it to. Marxists, however, tend to overlook the possibility that *as well as* benefiting the rich and powerful at the expense of the less advantaged (as most systems of stratification certainly do), stratification may exist for other, more necessary reasons. We will return to this point shortly.

Marxists themselves believe that stratification exists because of the unequal ownership of private property. They consider that if private property is abolished and communism established, class stratification will cease to exist. This is easier to assert than to prove: after all, historically and in the contemporary world few, if any, clear examples of non-stratified societies can be cited. Attempts to 'engineer' more equal societies have given doubtful cause for optimism. The communist revolution in Soviet Russia may have produced more economic equality than exists in most capitalist countries but few would deny that political power in the Soviet Union remains very highly centralised. There does seem to be a widespread, genuine commitment to equality in Communist China but the continuing ideological ferment there means that the principles on which the new social order rests are still not entirely clear. Stratification, therefore, seems so universal that as well as being seen as a frequent mantle for exploitation, it can also be argued that it must be functional.

The essence of the functionalist position, then, is that *somebody* must do the more difficult and skilful tasks and will, as a result, expect higher rewards and status. This argument could still be true, whatever the social origins of those who came to occupy the top occupational positions. It would be sustainable even if children of lower class origins were disproportionately successful (instead of the opposite). The Marxist reply to this would be that, *if* people were rewarded according to need rather than on the basis of the nature of work they performed, no material or status inequality would result from differences in occupation. In a communist society, all property would be held in common and the product of all human labour would be shared on a rough basis of equality, with variations depending on individual circumstances and requirements. In addition, as far as possible, jobs would rotate so that more people had an opportunity to do interesting work and escape being permanently trapped in boring and unhealthy occupations.

In an ideal sense, Marx's vision – for it is a visionary's dream – of a classless society is 'better' (if we may speak for a moment in moral terms) than the stratified societies that we are more familiar with. But is such a society possible? It is, perhaps, easier and more possible to answer this question in terms of 'degrees' of equality rather than in any absolute sense. Certainly, it is not beyond human imagination and ingenuity to construct more equal societies and a more equal world – even if complete equality remains elusive. It is merely very difficult. Perhaps, as Frank Parkin reluctantly accepts, a more equal world would be functionally less efficient. When the jealousy and the conflict that inequality causes is weighed in the balance, however, it may be that a more equal society would be less torn by strife, and less wasteful of human energy, than highly stratified societies are. Whether we shall ever know what the reality of social equality means is an open question, but it is an issue likely to remain alive for a long time yet.

Guide to further reading and study

Most of the books dealing with stratification in Britain mentioned in the *Guide* to Chapter 9 have sections on wealth and poverty. Notoriously, there are more sociological studies of the poor than the wealthy. By way of balance, I mention Frank Field *ed, The Wealth Report* (Routledge and Kegan Paul, 1979) even though the articles in it are aimed at an adult, academic audience. On poverty, J. C. Kincaid's *Poverty and Equality in Britain* (Penguin, 1973) is the best general introduction and is quite readable. Robert Holman's *Poverty: Explanations of Social Deprivation* (Martin Robertson, 1978) is also very useful. K.

Coates and R. Silburn's *Poverty: The Forgotten Englishmen* (Penguin, 1970), is a good account of a poor 'community'.

David Lane's *Politics and Society in the USSR* (Weidenfeld and Nicolson, 1970) is a standard reference. It is not easy to find material on comparative stratification at the right level. Frank Parkin's *Class, Inequality and Political Order: Social Stratification in Capitalist and Communist Societies* (Paladin, 1971) and John D. Stephens well-informed *The Transition from Capitalism to Socialism* (Macmillan, 1979) are useful, but are not really for younger students.

Past Questions

1 Is it accurate to see the poor as trapped in a 'culture of poverty'? (London, 1975).

2 'Inequality is both functional and inevitable for all social systems'. Discuss. (AEB, 1978).

3 Poverty, which used to be studied as 'social problem', has more recently been studied as an aspect of structured social inequality'. Describe this change of approach and explain its significance for our understanding of poverty. (AEB, 1980).

11 Gender

The Meaning of Gender

Ann Oakley makes a useful distinction between sex and gender. *Sexual differences* are biological in nature, whereas *gender differences* are culturally produced. This distinction has the further implication that sex differences are more or less unchangeable, whereas gender differences are very much open to change and adaptation. The definitive sexual difference between males and females is based on the parts of the body concerned with sex, procreation and nurture: the genitals and breasts. An example of a difference in *gender behaviour* occurs in Muslim society. Frequently women veil their faces, whereas men do not. Clearly, there is nothing natural about this. Because of the greater cultural influence of the West in Kuwait than in Saudi Arabia, this custom is somewhat less prevalent there.

The major preliminary problem in the sociology of gender is in deciding which aspects of male and female behaviour are biologically and which culturally based. Real behaviour cannot be separated out into two categories labelled 'biological' and 'cultural' – a fact which vastly complicates research into the matter. Authorities vary on whether, and to what extent, women are naturally (biologically) different from men, for example, more or less passive or more or less competitive than men. We cannot hope to solve this matter here although readers with an interest in biology or psychology may well wish to pursue it further using the recommended reading at the end of the chapter. Our perspective (and practical way of resolving the problem) will be to examine *particularly* major cultural influences on the behaviour of females and males. Comparative cultural studies of gender behaviour help here. They tell us that almost any kind of gender behaviour is possible. Witness, for instance, the following pattern in the Wahiba, a Bedouin tribe of central Oman in the Persian Gulf:

> The men live with their mothers, apart from their wives, whose huts may be as much as 50 miles away, and just visit them occasionally. Both men and women share the work of making the home but wives then have sole ownership.
>
> In general, work is equally divided, with goats and sheep being the responsibility of the women while the men tend the camels . . .
>
> One of the traditional tasks of the men is the cooking . . .
>
> (*Observer* magazine, 19 November 1978)

Examples of this kind which explode our assumptions about 'normal' gender behaviour are easily found. They make it clear that *gender identity* is more various, and, therefore, presumably, more adaptable to change than is often thought. This view is supported by various cross-cultural studies which show a wide range of gender behaviour. In particular, Margaret Mead's work demonstrates that there is no universal 'masculine' or 'feminine' personality. For example, in her fieldwork in the South Pacific she found that both sexes of the Arapesh conform roughly to our traditional stereotype of 'feminity', and both those of the Mundugumor to our 'masculine' stereotype. We will, therefore, assume nothing about supposed 'natural' differences between males and females, apart from the obviously physical, the most important of which is that *women bear children.*

Perspectives on the Origins and Nature of Gender Differentiation and Stratification

There are various theories about how the pattern of gender differentiation and stratification familiar in western industrial societies came about. Some critics stress the sexual basis of stratification, but others, mainly Marxists and socialists, see sexual stratification as very much within the context of class stratification. Most accept, however, that female subordination occurs within a class-divided society and the practical problem of analysis is largely in balancing the two elements of gender and class.

One of the first attempts at a general explanation since that of Engels in 1844, was Kate Millett's *Sexual Politics,* published in 1970. Theoretically, the book did little more than argue persuasively that the dominance of men over women occurs in every sphere of western social life. She contended that *patriarchy* (male dominance) is social rather than biological in origin, but did not really establish why, if this is the case, it is so widespread. Nevertheless, in her argument, Millett established the approach adopted by most later theorists of gender oppression, who pursued structural explanation in more detail. An exception, however, is Shulamith Firestone whose book, *The Dialectic of Sex,* was published about a year after Millett's.

Firestone finds the origins of sexual inequality in the basic reproductive unit of female, infant and male: in other words, in the family. The result of bearing and nurturing children is to make women dependent on men for the material necessities of life and protection. She, therefore, writes of 'sex class' as an additional category to 'economic class.' She argues that the liberation of women depends on the abolition of the family and the 'power' relationships and psychology that its unequal structure breeds. It is probably true to say that, as a result of Firestone's work, many feminists recognise more clearly the problems that can result for women from their reproductive roles, but rather than abolition of the family, they look for other solutions, including, more equal sharing of domestic work.

We now examine some feminist literature influenced by Marx and Engels (it is worth recalling Engel's analysis of the family at this point (Chapter 4 pp. 76–8).

Juliet Mitchell's *Women's Estate* (1971) is a Marxist-feminist attempt to analyse the nature of female oppression, particularly in capitalist society, and to explore how to combat it. She rejects a simple biological explanation of the sexual division of labour in the sense that women 'have to' bear and produce children. Instead, she points to the superior physical power and ability to coerce, of men. The point is that men have been able to make women do almost whatever they wanted. In her words 'Women have been *forced* to do women's work.' And 'women's work' can be almost anything. Thus, in many zones of tropical Africa women still perform many heavy 'customary' duties, such as carrying loads. The richness of Mitchell's analysis is, however, that she does not exclusively emphasise any one factor in explaining male domination. She considers that repression can operate in any of the three interconnected 'structures' of the family – the sexual, the reproductive, and the socialising – and also in the sphere of economic production. Accordingly, she urges that the 'fight' for liberation must be directed at all these structural levels, with particular reference to whatever is weaker at a given time. She considers that birth control has given women a basis of control over reproduction and sex – they are no longer 'slaves' to them – but her particular interest is in the area of gender socialisation. She seeks to explore how women come to accept, believe in and even want dependency and inferiority. She sees the production of *oppressive ideology* in structural terms:

> What does our oppression within the family *do* to us women? It produces a tendency to small-mindedness, petty jealousy, irrational emotionality and random violence, dependency, competitive selfishness and possessiveness, passivity, a lack of vision and conservatism. These qualities are *not* the simple produce of male chauvinism, nor are they falsely ascribed to women by a sexist society that uses 'old woman' as a dirty term. *They are the result of the woman's objective conditions within the family* – itself embedded in a sexist society. You cannot inhabit a small and backward world without it doing something to you.

In examining the ideological role of the family under capitalism, Mitchell calls upon Freud as much as Marx. Psychoanalysis helps to explain how children internalise notions of gender inferiority or superiority, and particularly the way in which *social* significance is given to *biological* differences. By being psychologically prepared for their different roles, girls and boys are predisposed to accept them. In an admittedly much simpler way than Mitchell, we will examine the process of the ideological reproduction of male domination or *patriarchy* in the next section.

Mitchell's general point about the importance of ideology has been taken up by D. H. Morgan. Just as in Marxist terms, the liberation of the working class is dependent on its members becoming conscious of their oppression, so too is the liberation of women dependent on their becoming conscious of their repression. Apart from a section on socialisation, we will not examine ideological oppression separately. Instead, we will analyse the relationship between structural and ideological oppression, particularly in respect of the family and work. In reality the two are inextricably woven together.

Another, more orthodox, Marxist should be mentioned. Sheila Rowbotham's *Woman's Consciousness, Man's World* (1973), studies the relationship of gender to class. She argues that gender oppression is distinct from class oppression but that in the case of working class women the two overlap. Their involvement she sees as essential to the creation of socialist feminism.

To summarise, then, feminist writers do not separate sexual and class oppression but try to understand how sexual oppression operates in a class structured society. It is not possible to quantify the relative effect of the two factors in any final way.

289

In technical terms, it could be argued that there is a major element of *status stratification* about sexual inequality just as there is about racial stratification, although feminist writers tend to prefer more Marxist terminology. Sheila Rowbotham usefully summarises the position held by most feminists, certainly by most socialist feminists, on the relationship between sexual and class stratification:

> More relevant to us are the consequences of opposing a form of oppression which has taken a specific shape in capitalism, which nevertheless existed in precapitalist society. In order to act effectively we have to try to work out the precise relationship between the patriarchal dominance of men over women, and the property relationships which come from this, to class exploitation and racism.

The above books usefully present various feminist perspectives. Since their publication a vast range of feminist literature has been produced. Of the sociological works, three of the best are Ann Oakley's *Housewife, Housework* and *Women Confined*. In the first of these works, she argues that gender inequality is culturally, not biologically produced. In the other, she too examines particular instances of female subordination in, mainly, British society.

Interest has also developed in *men's liberation*. Two aspects of this need noting. Firstly, men are seen to need liberating from their oppressive or chauvinistic tendencies towards women – the reverse side of women's liberation. Secondly, socialist writers argue that men are *in their own way* the victims of capitalism and need liberating from this.

Gender Socialisation: The Ideological Reproduction of Male Domination

Family and Education

Gender behaviour is first learnt through *primary* or basic socialisation within the family and is reinforced later in practically every sphere of social life and particularly at school and work. Socialisation refers to the various ways in which a child learns to act in a manner acceptable within a given society. Gender socialisation is part of this process. Traditional patterns of socialisation in most Western countries distinguish sharply bet-

290

ween male and female, although this has begun to change in the wake of the women's liberation movement. It is not too much to say that by the time they are 16, the majority of young men and women have been socialised into an ideology of male supremacy even if the forces of resistance to this ideology are stronger than they were. Broadly speaking, women are regarded as decorative, emotional and dependent, and men as practical, rational and dominant. Men are expected to earn a living and to support a family whereas women are expected to 'look after their men folk', and to produce children. Depending on its sex, a child is treated according to one or the other of these models and this prepares him or her for adult gender identity. Even before boys and girls can talk, they are spoken to in a different manner. Phrases such as 'he's going to be a big, strong boy' and 'isn't she a pretty little girl' trip easily off the tongue of family friends and relatives, and no doubt form the emerging self-identity of the child. Sue Sharpe quotes two classic examples of the sex stereotyping of males and females from birth congratulation messages:

Bet she's sugar and spice	A SON IS FUN!
And everything nice,	He'll keep you busy
A pink and petite little treasure	With blankets an' pins
Your new little 'she'	And charm your hearts
Who's certain to be	With his boyish grins!
A wonderful bundle of pleasure!	What's more he'll make you
	Proud and glad
	Congratulations mother and dad!

It is interesting that in parts of old Japan reinforcement of male children's sense of masculinity was even more extreme than has ever been the case in the West. The male child of four or five years old was allowed to treat his mother and other females more or less as he wished – even to the point of terrorising them. This was a rather crude preparation for male dominance in adulthood. It is less easy to find cultures which treat children of both sexes similarly and equally but in traditional Samoa this was substantially so until the age of five or six, when very noticeable differences in gender expectation did occur.

In most societies, as children grow older, they are increasingly type-cast into what sociologists term masculine and feminine *gender roles*. To play a social role is simply to act a given part. In contemporary British society, the role of house-keeping is still usually fulfilled by women, and that of main breadwinner by men. Boys and girls are prepared for future gender roles in a variety of ways. Boys are often given presents of cowboy suits, doctors' outfits and meccano sets, whereas girls are given dolls, nurses' uniform and cookery kits. The message could hardly be stronger. Jobs involving leadership and construction skills are for boys, whereas girls are expected to care for, assist and give service to others, either at home or at work. The basis of this division of labour is clearly laid down in childhood. This is most obviously so in families in which the jobs children are given to do around the house are based sex difference – say, cleaning and sewing for the girls, and mending broken plugs or furniture for the boys.

Some contemporary parents deliberately try to avoid socialising their children into traditional gender roles. One enterprising group of mothers in Liverpool, finding that the images of gender portrayed in available children's story books were too traditional, set about writing their own material. They rejected stereotypes in which the female is always weak and dependent and the male strong and dominant. Why shouldn't Princesses sometimes rescue Princes? If little Red Riding Hood had been trained in basic self-defence, perhaps she could have dealt with the wolf on her own account. Such notions may strike many as odd, but recorded interviews with some of the children who heard or read the stories showed they understood the point behind them. In small ways like this, social change can perhaps begin.

Gender socialisation within schools also plays a major part in conditioning males and females for future roles in the family and at work (see Chapter 5, pp. 133–5). When girls leave school at 16 or 18 they often get jobs that *are* as well paid as those held by boys of a similar age. Some office and secretarial work is particularly well paid, especially in central city areas. However, partly because women in general are less qualified than men and partly because they often leave work for several years to have children, opportunities for career advancement and salary increase are considerably less. The fact that almost as many females as males are involved in mainly part-time, *non*-advanced courses of further education rather demonstrates that females are expected and often expect themselves to do middle or low, rather than high, status work. As we shall discuss shortly this is, on the whole, an accurate impression of reality.

Gender Inequality and the Sexual Division of Labour

Gender, the Family and Work

So far we have described how gender identity is culturally created in advanced Western societies through socialisation and role-allocation. The question must now be asked why gender differentiation occurs at all. The answer is, as Mitchell and Oakley indicate, that a division of labour has developed in capitalist society by which women tend to be primarily involved in child nurture and domestic work and men in acquiring the basic means of livelihood. Socialisation prepares girls and boys for their future roles in the socio-economic system. Now, the only biologically inevitable feature of this particular form of sexual division of labour is that women give birth to children. The rest is open to gender adaptation. What follows, therefore, takes the broad perspective adopted by Mitchell and Oakley, rather than that of Firestone, that the sexual division of labour in capitalist society has taken a 'severe' form because this has been convenient for the capitalist system. The fact that in the last hundred years women have become increasingly involved in the economy illustrates rather than refutes the point – they have been needed in the expanding service sector. Nevertheless, the sexually based division of labour as described above is still powerfully entrenched in contemporary capitalist society, as was shown in the recession which began in 1979 when female labour was widely treated as more expendable than male. The sexual division of labour in capitalist society has resulted in a large degree of female dependency on males. This dependency has resulted in lower social status for women and correspondingly higher social status for men. As well as having less economic power and social status than men, women have also tended to be *politically* less powerful, because they are isolated and not organised. In short, although the social consequences of the sexual division of labour in capitalist society have tended to be disadvantageous to women and advantageous to men, this state of affairs is *not* inevitable. Both cross-cultural comparison and historical analysis of gender roles in our own society show that change is possible. We adopt the historical perspective next.

Changing Gender Roles Within the Family and at Work: Historical and Contemporary Perspective

Pre-industrial
It is not possible to understand the position of men, women and children within the family without discussing the relationship of the family to the economy. This is particularly obvious if we consider gender roles in the pre-industrial family. Broadly speaking, a water-tight division of gender roles and tasks existed in pre-industrial Europe. Wives were responsible for the three 'C's': child-rearing, cooking and cleaning. A man's task was to do agricultural work or, if he was a trader, to run his business. Men were not expected to perform any work in the house. Indeed, they would have been ridiculed for attempting to do so. This rigid division of labour at least meant that the woman was in fairly complete day to day control of domestic affairs. Some writers have stressed the authority of the woman 'within her sphere of influence' but this autonomy was within an overall context of male domination. The patriarchal or father-controlled family was the norm in pre-industrial Europe even before the Industrial revolution. The power of husband over wife extended to sexual intercourse at will. It seems that in those days sex was less associated with sentiment and romance than now, and must often have been a fairly empty experience for women. Indeed, the notion that women might enjoy sex was scarcely even discussed before the late nineteenth century.

The Nineteenth Century
Industrialisation disrupted traditional patterns of gender behaviour as it disrupted so much else. For a time, working class men, women and children worked together in industrial production and mining. Between 1802 and 1898, however, a series of Acts abolished child labour and gradually reduced female labour in these areas. Though many women found other work, often in the low-paid domestic service sector, a woman's place was increasingly considered to be in the home. In some

ways the position of the working class woman in industrial society was worse than that of the peasant wife. In pre-industrial society most families produced some of their own food and clothes – largely under the wife's organisation – whereas in industrial society the wife was often wholly dependent on what money her husband chose to give her to buy these things. This was a position of striking inferiority. No doubt some of the above legislation was passed in a spirit of paternalistic protectiveness but it was also notably convenient to have the labour force adequately catered for domestically, (for a specifically Marxist interpretation of this point see Chapter 4, p. 77). In this way, it was both healthier and more productive.

Although the economic situation of middle class women was much better than that of working class women, they were similarly dependent on their husbands for money. In a wealthy family, servants might free 'the mistress of the house' from domestic toil and child-care, but there were limits to what she could then do with her time. Most professions, apart from teaching, were barred to women. In practice, middle class women were likely to spend their often ample leisure time in socialising, improving the decor of their homes and, sometimes, in charitable works.

The law put the lid firmly on the trap of female subordination. As we have already observed women were debarred from the best-paying working class and middle class jobs. Worse than that, women had no legal existence at all in early nineteenth century Britain. Before marriage a woman was the responsibility of her father, afterwards, she and her possessions belonged to her husband.

By the end of the nineteenth century a series of Acts had partly improved this situation. One of these, the Married Women's Property Act of 1882, gave a wife the right to own property and to dispose of it to whom she wished.

The Twentieth Century: The Growth of Feminist Consciousness

The decline of the Victorian patriarchal family has been a major feature of twentieth century social history. *Contraception* (the control of fertility) undermined the Victorian family and the position of male as patriarch as much as anything else. Given the choice, most women preferred to have two or three children rather than six or seven. Traditional taboos against contraception did not die overnight and, in addition, some socialist women were suspicious that population control might be used as an alternative to social reform. Even so, the practical advantages of birth control were too obvious to miss. 'Having a family' of six or seven was a lifetime's work for many women, and could be physically ruinous as well as intellectually severely limiting. In any case, the beginning of a steady fall in the birth rate occurred in the late eighteen seventies and this correlates with an increase in propaganda in favour of birth control. Certainly, in the long run, women have overwhelmingly accepted that family planning is a pre-condition of their own independence. Decrease in family size coupled with the development of efficient, time-saving household technology enabled many women to spend much longer as part of the labour force. In turn, experience of work widened women's horizons, boosted their confidence and whetted the appetite of some for more freedom and equality. The massive involvement of women in production, service industries and administration during the First World War strengthened this new mood.

The fight for female political and civil rights was substantially a middle class led movement, although as historian Sheila Rowbotham says, the tendency of accounts of the suffragette movement to concentrate on the Pankhursts as personalities has meant a lack of detailed work on the social composition of the movement. There were certainly many working class women participants, including the doughty Hannah Mitchell, who criticised the 'talk' of some of the middle class radicals whom she found better preachers than practitioners of sexual equality:

> Even my Sunday leisure was gone for I soon found that a lot of
> the socialist talk about freedom was only talk and these socialist
> young men expected Sunday dinners and huge teas with
> home-made cakes, potted meat and pies, exactly like their
> reactionary fellows.

It would be absurd to underestimate the importance of the acquisition of the vote for women. The vote is a basic right of modern citizenship. Nevertheless, merely having the vote in no way solved the problem of sexual inequality at work and domestically. More recent legislation has, not very successfully, attempted to deal with the former (see Chapter 11 pp. 304–5) but the latter, perhaps because it concerns the 'private area of life' has not been seriously dealt with by legislation and government policy in Britain. In Sweden and the major communist societies, however, legislatively supported policies in this area have been both pursued and enforced more effectively (Chapter 4, pp. 84–5).

Inevitably, family relations were gradually affected by the backwash of these changes in the economic and political spheres. Separate gender roles within the family, or segregated conjugal roles as we can more precisely call them, began to break down somewhat. If women went to work, then, the onus was on men to knuckle down and do some of the housework, although many failed to do so. Willmott and Young have referred to the gradual blurring of task segregation between spouses as the development of *symmetrical* or *joint conjugal roles*. It initially developed among middle class couples, and particularly when both husband and wife worked as professionals. As Rhona and Robert Rapoport, (a dual-career couple themselves), point out it is still among dual career families that symmetrical roles most frequently occur. With more women of all classes working, however, *role sharing* is necessarily also increasingly common among working class couples. One survey, by Hannah Gavron, actually found that working class husbands shared housework more than middle class husbands, but this goes against other findings. Ann Oakley is, in any case, sceptical about whether there has been a marked recent trend for couples to share housework at all.

Work has given many women a broader experience of the world and, perhaps most importantly, it has given them an independent source of income. The Victorian period clearly showed that as long as a woman depended entirely on a man for income, inequality between the sexes was virtually inevitable. The shadow of patriarchy is still strong but there is now more equality and democracy in family life than previously. Decisions about family expenditure and leisure activities are more likely to be shared now than in the past. Couples often 'do' more together. These days, if the man does go for a drink in the evening, as likely as not his wife will want to go with him. If children prevent that, it is an easy matter to buy in a few cans of drink and watch television. The car has made the family outing a feature of post-war social life. In short, the home itself, with its battery of consumer durables, has become a basis of leisure and entertainment. Why go to the cinema when 'the movies' can come to you?

Recently, an interesting strand of opinion has become more noticeable in the feminist movement. It cannot easily be labelled but it involves a re-assessment and upgrading of the traditional role of women, and a better appreciation of its variety and necessity. While insisting on policies of equal opportunity in the job-market, those who share this emerging perspective reject the notion that the success of women should be judged merely or even mainly by their achievements in traditionally male dominated areas (such as warfare or banking). Instead, two things are stressed. Firstly, that some domestic and child-rearing work can be creative and humanly very rewarding – this carries the rider that men could beneficially involve themselves in it more. Secondly, historically, in any case, women have borne a heavy and necessary burden of labour. We will examine these points separately, but first it is worth repeating Sheila Rowbotham's warning that attempts to idealise 'women's work' are invariably 'reactionary.' Ideals of motherhood tend to collapse before the distasteful reality of changing nappies and scouring toilets.

Ann Oakley severely questions whether the way towards women's liberation is simply to compete with men in the employment market. Yet she despairs that men will ever recognise or allow proper reward for the work women do. As long as this is so, the prospects are that women will continue to depend materially and psychologically (for security and identity) on men. As she says:

> Men and women cannot be equal outside the home if they are not equal partners inside it.

Paid housework, or a guaranteed right to a proportion of the main breadwinner's salary, are possible solutions to material dependency (although they do not appear to have much support). In reality, however, Oakley is thinking mainly of the need for a change, indeed, *a revolution in attitudes* – of both sexes – to the quality, dignity and humanity of child rearing and domestic labour – whoever does it.

Virginia Novarra's book, *Women's Work, Men's Work*, forcefully asserts that women's work makes a vital contribution to the survival of the race. It does so in the following major ways.

Through

1 *Reproduction*
2 *Agricultural Production (globally, more women are involved in agricultural production than men)*
3 *Clothing the Family (often making or mending clothes)*
4 *Tending the Family and others*
5 *Cultural Transmission*
6 *Caring for the Home and Home Environment (unpaid or lowly-paid work)*

Some years ago, feminist literature was characterised by such titles as *The Second Sex* or *The Female Eunuch*. A sense of grievance was, and remains, justified but a growing appreciation of the extent and quality of female work historically may throw as much light on how matters can be improved.

Changes in family life and gender roles have not taken place without some stress and individual confusion and suffering. The ever increasing divorce figures are proof of that. By the late nineteen seventies, in England and Wales, the proportion of marriages to divorces was virtually 3 to 1. Annually, about 150,000 couples were deciding that their marriage partnership was not worth continuing. Mostly, it is women who take the formal decision to petition for divorce: 70% of divorce petitions are filed by them. If more women than men do find marriage a disillusioning experience, it may be because they approach it more romantically and with higher expectations of personal fulfilment and happiness. Advertising and the media still largely conspire to create these hopes. The reality of housework and bringing up young children can be a shock, especially if the personal and sexual side of marriage fails to compensate as expected. A survey of 40 women with children found that a majority regarded housework as tedious and often felt isolated in the home. 'Getting a job' may help, but equally it can increase pressure on a woman if her husband should fail to respond by doing his share of domestic work. There is some evidence to suggest that marriage and family stress punish women more than men. Whereas before marriage more men than women suffer mental illness, afterwards very much the reverse is true.

Men, however, have also had problems in adjusting to

299

changes in marriage and family. To lose control and privilege is rarely easy. However unreasonable it may be for a man to expect his wife to do for him what his mother used to, the tendency to make the comparison is understandable. Convenience foods probably do not compare very well to elaborate home-cooking, but this is part of the price both partners have to pay in a dual career family. Many men, too, must have found the anger and aggression of some women in the face of discrimination difficult to contend with. No liberation movement occurs without some explosion of rage against the dominant group, but this is little consolation to those in the firing line. On the whole, it is men who have benefited in economic and power terms from the sexual division of labour and it is inevitable that, sooner or later, female resentment should be expressed against them. There is no doubt that the sharp spur of female anger has stimulated many men to an appreciation of female exploitation. Of course, the sexual division of labour is not a product of a conscious male conspiracy but, historically, has been part of the way the basic functions of society have been fulfilled. Emotional rejection of what is now seen as an unfair and repressive division of labour will not in itself change things without the ultimate understanding and consent of both sexes.

In one very important sense, the sexual division of labour has affected men adversely and left them in need of a sort of liberation. The effort of working more or less continuously for forty or fifty years, which is the lot of many men, can take a tremendous physical and psychological toll. The health hazards of working down a mine or in a noisy, monotonous factory are well known. The fact that twice as many men as women under fifty have heart attacks may well be related to the demands of work. From the point of view of fuller self-expression, it is limiting for many men that their social identity and most of their time is so heavily bound up with their occuption. Given the variety of leisure pursuits available in the modern world, it is perhaps slightly ludicrous that for nine tenths of the average male's adult life he is thought of primarily in terms of his occupational identity. For the one tenth that he isn't, retirement, his physical and mental capacities are likely to be in decline. If this balance could be readjusted without significantly reducing their families' standard of living, many full-time working men would probably welcome it. The increase in female labour and in automation may make this increasingly possible. But for both sexes to make the most of these new developments, a change in traditional, rigid attitudes to gender indentity would also have to take place. The lyrics of the pop-group, the Kinks, may come to reflect a new social, though not, of course, physical reality:

> Girls will be Boys
> And Boys will be Girls . . .
> It's a mixed-up muddled-up
> Shook-up world . . .

Women and the Labour Market: 'Escape' or Exploitation?

So far, we have considered domestic and directly economic labour together because they are two sides of the same coin: one would not be possible without the other. It is necessary, however, to give a more detailed analysis of women's position in the employment market. Generally, increased job opportunities for women have been seen as part of their assumed 'liberation' and work has certainly often provided individual women with an escape from the tedium of domestic toil. Marxists and socialists point out, however, that there is considerable evidence of female 'exploitation' and accompanying underachievement in employment, and that female employment and unemployment has varied with the economic need for it. Women have been the most expendable of workers. The increased use of female labour has, therefore, been a double-edged sword.

Even in the mid-Victorian era, when working class women were legally banned from working in heavy industry and mining, and middle class women were denied the right to qualify for most professions, women were by no means entirely excluded from the labour market. Working class women were 'needed' as domestic servants and a certain number of middle class women worked in lower status professions. Working class women often *had* to find work to supplement the wages of their husbands. They frequently did so as full or part-time domestic servants of whom there were well over half a million at this time. Hundreds of thousands of others were employed in textile production, an area of traditionally high female employment and low wages. Middle class women who needed to work, perhaps because they were spinsters or widows, could earn a living as elementary school teachers. By the 1890s, there were almost 150,000 female teachers. Nursing was also a major area of female employment. The 'semi-professions' of teaching and nursing were of much lower status and pay than the major professions of law and medicine (for instance) from which women were excluded.

The situation of women at work began to change towards the end of the nineteenth century and even more so in the twentieth century. Even allowing for population expansion, the increase in the numbers of women at work has been massive. Between 1911 and 1974, four million more women were added to the total labour force of about twenty five million. Of the six million people in part time work well over half are women.

Although most women who work probably want to do so, it would be a mistake to assume that the increase in female labour has been an unmitigated boon for them. Women in full time work have for a long time been paid less than men, even though the gap has narrowed substantially in recent years. Yet even though the Equal Pay Act of 1975 established the legal principle of equal pay for equal work, the average wage of women is only about 75% that of men. In successive years, 1978 and 1979, the average female wage fell slightly as a proportion of the male wage, after rising gradually since the middle nineteenth sixties. This is largely because, historically, women have been concentrated in low paid jobs. Clerical and secretarial work which became increasingly available to women from the latter half of the nineteenth century was often poorly paid. Whereas, in 1977, 51% of employed women were in intermediate and junior non-manual work, only 5% were professionals, employers or managers. The latter figure compares to 21% of men in these occupations. Inequality of status between the two sexes is even more startling in the world of manual work. A majority of male manual workers is classified as skilled, whereas only 1 in 5 female manual workers are so classified. There is reason to believe that some jobs are classified as unskilled or semi-skilled precisely because they are generally done by women and not because of the real skill-content of the work. Throughout the occupational structure, then, men still tend to have more authority and status than women and to be better paid. Although there are more female accountants, police, barristers, doctors and even electrical engineers than ten years ago, in none of these occupations do women make up even 10% of the total, except in medicine where they represent 13.5% of the work force.

The areas of employment in which women are concentrated, cleaning, nursing, teaching and to a certain extent social work are the so-called 'helping' professions. It is almost as if the domestic role of looking after others is transferred into the work situation. Like domestic labour itself, work in these areas is comparatively poorly paid. The fact that teaching is sometimes said to be 'not badly paid for women' is perhaps more a reflection on the historically low wages of women generally, than on the great financial rewards offered by that profession. In any case, in teaching as in all professions, women tend to occupy lower scale, less well paid posts.

In addition to enjoying less authority, status and wages at work than men, women also tend to have less security. Although about 30% of female workers are now unionised, the majority still lack the strength and protection union membership gives. Part-time workers are in an especially weak position in the labour market. Of Britain's six million part-time workers, three and a half million are women. Part-time workers employed for fewer than sixteen hours a week are not entitled to redundancy payment, nor most other benefits under the Employment Protection Act. In effect, they can be hired and fired at the employer's wish. The traditionally weak position of women in the job market has led some commentators, including Hilary Wainwright, to suggest that women have been used as a 'reserve pool' of cheap labour in the expanding service sector. Women on the fringe of the job market could be employed when necessary in times of economic expansion and made redundant to save money in times of contraction. The law now protects women in full-time employment from this kind of treatment but those in part-time work are still vulnerable.

It would be superficial to suggest that employers alone have been responsible for the work situation of women described above. The fundamental weakness of most women as independent wage-earners lies in the fact that they also produce and are expected to bring up children. This means that they are not usually consistently involved in a career between, roughly, the ages of twenty-five and thirty-five, which is a crucial period for gaining experience and promotion. In practice, because of their dual commitments as housewives and workers, many women do not seriously attempt to compete effectively with men in the labour market. Many find 'temping' or part-time work fits in best with their domestic responsibilities. In addition, it is well established that large numbers of women welcome an 'escape' from the home, even into work that does not seem particularly fulfilling. Further, women who restart their careers at, say, thirty-five often do not have quite the same expectations as a similarly qualified man of the same age. In times of high unemployment, they are frequently glad to be able to get a reasonably suitable job at all. There is, too, a certain realism in the relatively low career expectations of many women in that the 'missing ten years' can constitute a severe disadvantage. On the other hand, those who have families and try to compete in career terms as well often put immense pressure on themselves – despite, sometimes, succeeding. A society which presents half its population with the above range of options seems to be profoundly flawed.

If, however, it would be wrong solely to 'blame' employers for the weak position of women at work, it would be even more short-sighted to suggest that lack of female ambition is the reason. The basic problem is that, as Hannah Mitchell put it, women compete 'with one hand tied behind their back' – the hand that 'holds the baby' and does the housework. That problem can only be solved either by relieving women of much domestic work or by rewarding them more substantially and securely for it. We now turn to the issue of policy and solutions.

Women's Liberation: Policy and Continuing Problems

We have seen the extent of gender inequality. We now ask what government has tried to do about it. The main measures of the 'equality package', as Ann Oakley calls it, are as follows. The Equal Pay Act (operative from 1975); the Sex Discrimination Act (1975); and the Employment Protection and Social Security Pensions Acts (1975). The 1967 Abortion Act and the

Divorce Law Reform Act implemented in 1971 also have profound implications for women, though they are not specifically part of the 'package'. The first two focus largely on employment. It is too early to say how effective they will be but they do nothing *positively* about the concentration of women in low-paid occupations. A more *interventionist* policy might, for instance, involve guaranteeing women a minimum number of top and middle level positions in business companies and professional establishments. Sometimes, to achieve *actual* equality more than *legal* equality is required: after all, we are all legally entitled to eat at the Savoy Grill . . . The terms of the Sex Discrimination Act are more easily enforceable in education, and there are more signs of greater equality of achievement in that area, but the gap remains wide.

The Employment Protection Act contains the first legal entitlement to *maternity leave* for women in Britain. It bans dismissal on grounds of pregnancy and guarantees mothers their jobs for within 29 weeks of childbirth. Circumstances (and there are potentially many: the death of the child is one) in which paternity leave rather than maternity leave might be desirable are not recognised by the Act, and to this extent it has an element of chauvinistic protectionism about it. Still, 29 weeks 'grace' is better than nothing, although it could hardly have been much less. Further, the Social Security Pensions Act puts women's sickness and unemployment pay and pension rights on an equal basis to those of men.

Despite the above legislation and the seemingly not very effective Equal Opportunities Commission, women's status at work relative to that of men has not much improved over the last decade. We have already seen why this is so. Neither does the future look entirely hopeful. Noticeably more women are being educated to a higher level than previously, but still predominantly in subjects likely to lead to traditionally low-paying, 'female' professions.

The extent of female participation in politics may be taken as one measure of their influence on national life. On this basis their influence is low – notwithstanding Mrs Thatcher. In August 1978, only 5% of MP's were women, and only 6% were ministers.

Despite, therefore, the existence of *formal* or legal equality between the sexes, substantial *actual* inequalities persist. In the

305

face of what are, from the feminist point of view, rather depressing facts, perhaps it is permissible to risk a note of optimistic speculation. It has occurred to some writers that certain qualities traditionally associated with women but which can occur in either sex – such as caring, gentleness and sharing – might provide a better moral blueprint for human conduct and survival than such traditionally 'masculine' characteristics as ambition, aggression and competitiveness. Ann Oakley, in the article quoted from above, cites a variety of feminist science fiction which speculates on precisely this possibility. Men are sometimes missing from this hypothetical future – their destructiveness is implicitly seen as both undesirable and dangerous. In the spirit of this literature, perhaps the nuclear bomb can be seen as a symbol of the male contribution historically: an achievement heavy with destructive potential. If so, it is perhaps time that the 'other' sex had a turn at, or at least more involvement in, the creation of a new social reality based on more positive and life-enhancing principles.

The issue of women's liberation is too urgent to conclude at the level of high speculation. At a more practical level, three positions on gender inequality can be distinguished. The first accepts an element of inevitability about gender roles but wants equality of status, rewards and security between them. A second viewpoint would like to see much more flexibility in the playing of gender roles. There would be more 'house-husbands' and more women operating as 'the main-breadwinner'. These two approaches are not incompatible, but to achieve either would require a massive change of outlook (among many women as well as men) and a substantial programme of legislation aimed particularly at improving the financial security of the houseperson. The third position seeks to abolish gender roles altogether. Instead, the two principles that would operate would be that people would do what they were best at and wanted to do and that, despite this, the needs of the community, and particularly children, should be met. It still seems a distant ideal.

Guide to further reading and study

The best way to learn about gender stratification is to adopt an aware and critical attitude of what is going on around you. Every day can be participant observation study day in gender stratification.

Tony Marks's article on gender in Meigham *ed., op. cit.,* is a good introduction to the topic. Volume 6 Number 4 (April, 1977) of *The Social Science Teacher* is devoted to gender roles, and is most useful. The gender pack published by Virago is aimed at a younger target group than 'A' level but contains much 'nitty-gritty' information: Jean Coussins, *Taking Liberties: An Introduction to Equal Rights* (Virago, 1979). Ann Oakley's *Housework* (Martin Robertson, 1974) is probably the best study of that area. Sue Sharpe's *Just Like a Girl: How Girls Learn to be Women* (Penguin, 1976) is an empirically based examination of the whole area of gender socialisation. Hilary Wainwright's chapter in Philip Abrams *ed., Work, Urbanism and Inequality* (Weidenfeld and Nicolson, 1978) is a well documented and a theoretically rigorous look at the position of women in the labour market.

Of the general literature on feminism referred to at the start of this chapter, perhaps Juliet Mitchell's *Women's Estate* (Penguin 1971), says the most in the shortest space. For a readable and thoughtful look at gender from a male, see Andrew Tolson, *The Limits of Masculinity* (Tavistock, 1977). But men have a good deal more thinking, writing and acting to do on this issue. Gender is a topic that lends itself to project-type work, especially as there is now a range of specialist studies within the area. Ann Oakley's *Women Confined* (Martin Robertson, 1979) is particularly commended for closer study.

Past Questions

1 '... teachers, parents and pupils themselves have notions of 'Femininity' which affect the treatment and expectation of girl pupils.' (Marks, P.) Discuss. (AEB, 1978).
2 Discuss, with examples, the view that sociology has focused upon the world of men, at the expense of the world of women (London, 1979).
3 Females and ethnic minorities are *generally* less 'successful'

than males and ethnic majorities in advanced industrial societies. Examine why this is the case in *either* of the two categories. (AEB, 1979).

12 Race

Basic Terminology

The state of research into race in Britain is sufficiently
advanced to allow us to approach this topic a little more
adventurously than previous ones. The Policy and Economic

Planning Report, published in 1977, is particularly authoritative and well researched; we will use its findings freely. Instead of merely presenting perspectives on racial stratification, we will attempt to test them more vigorously against empirical data. After all, if sociology is to progress as a discipline, it must be able to match the major theoretical elements of the perspectives against field research evidence, and decide which are more useful and precise in given situations. No perspective can be considered to be above this kind of rigorous testing.

There are two major analytical approaches to racial stratification: one has its roots in Weber, the other in Marx. According to the Weberian approach stratification distinctions made *purely* on grounds of racial differences, such as colour of skin or size of nose, are status differences. Thus, if a yellow person is treated as inferior or superior just because he is yellow, he experiences status differentiation. Marxists, however, have argued that racial stratification in the capitalist world, including Britain, is best understood as part of the structure of class stratification. We shall examine the evidence for these two views in the case of Britain in the following sections.

An important preliminary distinction between race and ethnicity must be made at this point. *Race is a matter of biology.* The major races are the Negroid, Mongolian and Indo-European, although many sub-divisions exist. *Ethnicity refers to cultural identity.* A person could be brought up in and fully share the culture of an ethnic group to which he does not belong racially. A further point about ethnicity must be made. Ethnic groups may live side by side in the same society without any sense of superiority or inferiority in relationship to one another – that is, without racial stratification. Percy Cohen refers to this as *segmentalism* and distinguishes it from racial stratification.

The Historical and Economic Background of Racism in Britain and the West

Race is a crucial contemporary issue both in Britain and internationally. South Africa is the major focus of racial tension in the world, for it is only there that race is openly, and even proudly, proclaimed as the very basis of stratification. This system is known as *apartheid*, although it has recently been presented as 'separate development'. Apartheid involves the legally enforceable separation of whites and blacks in a way that ensures far higher material and status rewards for the former. In certain other countries, the lines of racial stratification are less sharply drawn but are still quite clear. In Britain and the United States, coloured (or black) minorities tend to hold low-paid, low-status jobs, to live in poor housing and to be less well-educated than the white majority.

a **The Historical Background of Race Relations**
The roots of contemporary racial division lie in the expansion of European empires, particularly during the eighteenth and nineteenth centuries when these empires straddled the world. The British Empire extended to the Far East, but more significant from our point of view was the occupation of India, Pakistan, large parts of Africa, and several islands in the West Indies. It is from these areas that coloured immigrants came to Britain after the Second World War. A key factor in laying the foundations for later racial conflict in Britain, the United States, and parts of Africa was the exploitation of Africans, especially West Africans. The major element in this exploitation was the slave trade. Slave traders, mainly from Britain, France, Spain and Portugal, bought and kidnapped Africans, and transported them to the southern United States and the West Indies, where they were sold to work on plantations. In the southern States, a social structure based on slave labour developed, which left a legacy of bitterness, bigotry and exploitation, even after the formal abolition of slavery in the United States in 1863.

Between the two world wars, the major problem for Britain and other European imperial powers was to hold down discontent in conquered territories. By the early nineteen sixties, most British colonies had acquired independence, and already coloured immigration into Britain had begun. The focus of conflict shifted from the struggle for independence in the colonies to problems associated with the settlement of coloured immigrants in Britain itself. As early as 1958, race riots occurred in the Notting Hill area of London. After 1980, when Zimbabwe (formerly Rhodesia) became independent under majority rule, the only African country in which a minority of European extraction (in this case a large one) continued directly to dominate the black majority was South Africa.

311

The desire for economic gain is certainly a major motive for imperial expansion. The hope of acquiring political power and prestige, and of converting the conquered to, say, Christianity or Marxism, are others. Economic realities clearly underlie much twentieth century racial conflict – the spread of racial conflict in the United States is an example. From the late nineteenth century, there was a strong demand from Northern industrialists for cheap, black labour from the south. Later, this demand also occurred on the West Coast. As well as being cheap, black labour could be used to undermine the power of trade unions and to divide black and white working class people along racial lines. For their part, many black people were glad to leave the South, still darkened by the shadow of slavery, even though they encountered resentment and, sometimes, violence from the white working class in the urban areas of the North and West. In the early nineteen sixties, the big cities of the North and West were as torn by racial conflict and riots as the South.

b The Economic Background of Race Relations (with particular reference to Britain)

Economic factors also provide the major explanation for the pattern of coloured immigration in Britain and, to some extent, for the 'panic' about immigration in the late nineteen sixties and nineteen seventies.

Migration can be explained in terms of 'push' and 'pull' factors. The 'push' factors refer to conditions in the country of origin, such as unemployment and poverty, which persuade people to leave: the 'pull' factor is the demand for labour in the country of immigration. This is considered by Peach and others to be the dynamic influence behind British post-war immigration. A major personal motive for migration is, of course, to rejoin family and kin.

Immigrants to Britain went mainly into unskilled and semi-skilled jobs in industrial production. This enabled more of the indigenous population to move up into the expanding service sector – a fact which, at first, certainly sweetened acceptance of immigration. Not all immigrants, however, started at the bottom of the social hierarchy. Many thousands of doctors and nurses from India, Pakistan and the West Indies, were needed to support Britain's overstrained health system: even so, they tended to get the toughest and least prestigious posts, often in large, metropolitan hospitals.

In some areas where a shortage of labour existed, active recruitment occurred. London Transport recruited drivers in the West Indies and the Health Service also advertised widely. Official figures show that, in 1965 alone, Britain took 1,015 doctors from India, 529 from Pakistan and 182 from other Commonwealth countries. The Health Service is a striking, though not unique, example of Britain's dependence on the work of immigrants. In 1975, 35% of hospital doctors and 18% of family doctors came from outside Britain.

It is useful to draw a parallel between migrant workers in Europe and British immigrants. In the post-war period, the expanding economics of Western Europe needed foreign labour to increase production. Those countries which had colonies or former colonies, such as Britain or France, first recruited labour from these. Other countries which were without colonies, particularly West Germany, Luxembourg and Switzerland, had to recruit from elsewhere. They did so mainly from the poorer, non-industrialised countries of Eastern and Southern Europe – Greece, Turkey, Yugoslavia, Italy, Spain and Portugal. In 1974, it was estimated that 15 million immigrant workers and their families were living in Western Europe. A Common Market report for 1974 gives the proportion of immigrant workers in the labour force of the Western European countries as follows:

Luxembourg	35%
Switzerland	25%
France	11%
Germany	10%
UK	7%
Belgium	7%
Denmark	2%
Netherlands	3%

Source: *Our People,* Thames Television.

These workers are overwhelmingly concentrated in low-paid jobs with unpleasant and sometimes quite dangerous conditions (such as asbestos processing) and long hours (like the restaurant trade). They are also particularly vulnerable to redundancy during recession.

A vital difference, however, exists between Britain's immigrants and Europe's migrant workers. Immigrants to Britain who were Commonwealth citizens had a *right* to settle here with their families and to exercise full civil and political liberties, including voting. Most came believing that they would receive fair and equal treatment with white citizens. For many, these hopes have not been fulfilled.

Aspects of Racial Stratification in Britain

In attempting to assess the extent and causes of racial inequality, the workplace is an obvious starting point. Housing is perhaps the next most important point to consider. Racial inequality in education has already been considered in Chapter 6, and the relevant section might be read again, after those on employment and housing, as an example of inequality of cultural opportunity. The feelings and opinions of blacks and whites about one another are also presented as aspects affecting racial stratification.

a Race and Employment

The economic background to coloured immigration has already been analysed. Here, we look at the job levels of the major coloured minorities compared with those of whites. These are generally worse and the table below gives details of this. (What should be compared are the *percentage* figures, not the sizes of the unweighted and weighted samples.)

All the minority groups are disproportionately concentrated in the semi-skilled manual or unskilled manual categories. This is strikingly illustrated in the case of Pakistanis. Overall, representation in skilled manual work is comparable with whites, though somewhat lower for Pakistanis (33%) and substantially higher for West Indians (59%). The percentage of West Indian males in manual work, 91%, is startlingly high, even though the majority are in the skilled category. This may be partly explained by the fact that the educational levels of West Indian immigrants have tended to be lower, at the time of immigration, than those of Indians. Most had to get manual jobs and, if they sought upward mobility, to achieve it within the manual stratum. Indian and African Asians have, respectively, half and

314

three quarters of the proportional representation of whites in professional/management and white collar work whereas Pakistanis and West Indians have a fifth.

Job level analysed by country of origin — men

	White	West Indian	Pakistani/ Bangla- deshi	Indian	African Asian
Men in job market who have worked					
(unweighted)	996	634	495	508	226
(weighted)	1,594	2,896	1,391	1,867	1,050
	%	%	%	%	%
Job level (socio- economic group):					
Professional/ management	23 ⎫ 40	2 ⎫ 8	4 ⎫ 8	8 ⎫ 20	10 ⎫ 30
White-collar	17 ⎭	6 ⎭	4 ⎭	12 ⎭	20 ⎭
Skilled manual	42	59	33	44	44
Semi-skilled manual	12 ⎫ 18	23 ⎫ 32	38 ⎫ 58	27 ⎫ 36	24 ⎫ 26
Unskilled manual	6 ⎭	9 ⎭	20 ⎭	9 ⎭	2 ⎭
Not classified	1	1	1	*	*

Source: *PEP Report,* 1977, p. 73.

Since 1975, minority unemployment has tended to be proportionately higher than that of the general population (it is about 4% of the total). The proportion of unemployed blacks has tended to rise in times of economic recession. This gives weight to the theory that, to some extent, minorities serve as a 'reserve pool' or marginal source of cheap labour which, within the limits of law, can be cut during a slump, and re-employed when expansion occurs. Minority unemployment is a particular problem amongst teenagers. In some inner city areas it has been estimated at 30% of the total, or even above. The consequences in personal and social terms can be easily imagined.

What factors account for the unemployment distribution presented in the table? One theory is that the relatively low occupational status of blacks is a result of the fact that they are recent immigrants. It is argued that, in time, they will move up the occupational hierarchy. This view seems to be drawn largely from the experience of immigrant groups in the United

States. Each wave of ethnic immigrants into the United States took its place in turn on the bottom of the ladder and began to clamber up – sometimes on the shoulders of the next in-coming group. The British, Italians and Eastern Europeans have all done this. A version of the same process is happening now, as the American negro begins to edge significantly beyond the Hispanic elements (those of mainly Mexican and Puerto Rican origin) in the population. A problem in applying this model to British coloured immigrants is that no further wave of immigrants is likely to replace them on the bottom rung of society's ladder. In any case, it is doubtful if the post-war expansion of white-collar employment will continue: opportunities for upward mobility are, therefore, likely to be fewer.

Another explanation of the low occupational status of blacks, not wholly incompatible with the previous one, is that they are discriminated against in the employment market. This is certainly true. An objective assessment of the extent of discrimination in job applications was carried out by PEP. The job 'applicants' (some, in fact, were actors), were made up of West Indians, Pakistanis and a group of white immigrants, who were Greek. Their treatment by prospective employers was compared with that of a group of white British 'applicants'. The research is of great interest in terms of both its findings and method. Recruitment to unskilled and semi-skilled manual jobs was tested. The results of the various tests for discrimination in manual jobs are given below:

Discrimination against each minority group for four situations combined

	West Indians		Indians		Pakistanis		Greeks	
No. of cases	104		111		109		84	
	No.	%	No.	%	No.	%	No.	%
Net discrimination	28	27	31	28	25	23	9	11

Note: doubtful cases are here *not* treated as genuine cases of reverse discrimination.

Source: *PEP Report,* 1977, p. 111.

316

The tests for discrimination in manual jobs:

> ... show that there are still substantial levels of discrimination against Asians and West Indians . . .; that (they are) mainly based on colour prejudice rather than prejudice against foreigners; and that levels of discrimination against Indians, Pakistanis and West Indians are much the same.

Some further discrimination for white-collar jobs occurred against Asians and West Indian applicants in 30% of cases. At junior levels there was more discrimination against men than women. There was a high level of discrimination against applicants for management traineeships (42%). Thus, discrimination closed that gateway to possible promotion to really senior positions for two in five coloured applicants.

Given the above situation, there is an obvious role for trade unions, not only in improving the pay and conditions of coloured employees but also in seeking to cut down on job discrimination. Trade union membership is rather higher amongst the minority groups than amongst the white population. The faith of Asians and West Indians in trade unionism has not met a very positive response. The official and repeatedly reaffirmed position of the Trades Union Congress is, of course, strongly against racial prejudice and discrimination, but the actual conduct of unions at local level has failed to live up to conference rhetoric. The PEP report gives several cases in which the local union directly supported discrimination or allowed discriminatory practices to develop through failure to oppose them. The most common justification given by union officials for the lack of a strong lead against discrimination from the unions is that it would not meet with the approval of their members. In practice, it seems that the membership has not been properly asked what its opinions are on this matter. John Rex's observations on the relations of coloured labour and the unions support the analysis of the PEP survey. Reviewing research in the area he states:

> In the long run the picture which may emerge is that, despite their trade union membership and their loyalty to the unions, the immigrants may confront unions which at best ignore their grievances and at worst positively support more privileged native workers in preventing the immigrants from breaking out of replacement employment into the main parts of the labour market.

317

The extent of discrimination against coloured minorities in the job market is so great that it must be considered a large additional burden to the normal problems of immigrant adjustment. It is true that coloured working class people also share the inequalities experienced by the white working class, but racial inequality as well as class inequality defines their structural situation.

b Race and Housing

Black people suffer from poor housing more often than others. Again, the *PEP Report* summarises the situation succinctly:

> Although Asians and West Indians are more in need of council housing than the rest of the population, because their housing conditions in the private sector are much worse, they benefit from council housing less.

Let us first examine racial inequality in housing in the private sector. Superficially, the housing situation of Asians and West Indians may seem no worse than that of the general population. According to 1971 census figures, 50% of West Indian heads of household are owner-occupiers – the same as in the general population. For Asians, the figure is even higher – 76%. But owner-occupation performs a completely different function for the minorities than for the indigenous population. For the minorities, home ownership is frequently not a sign of status and material comfort, nor a secure financial investment. They tend to live in older housing which often lacks basic amenities. PEP data shows that the number of black people living in houses built before 1940 is 86%, and that well over a third lacked exclusive use of bath, hot water and inside toilet. Many coloured people, particularly Asians, live in this kind of housing because they have no alternative. They are often excluded from council housing because of length of residency requirements and can only afford the cheapest housing in the private sector.

The PEP report claims that there was a 'sharp decrease' in the levels of discrimination in purchasing and renting accomodation between 1967 and 1973, and implies that this may have been due, in part, to the Race Relations Act of 1968. Nevertheless, the figures presented on discrimination are disquieting enough. 27% of West Indian and Asian testers were discrimi-

318

nated against when telephoning for rented accomodation, 17% were discriminated against when attempting to purchase a house, and 12% received inferior treatment.

We now examine council housing. 28% of the general population, 26% of West Indians and only 4% of Asians live in council houses. The PEP findings on race and housing are carefully and fairly represented. Housing allocation systems tend to disfavour minorities for a number of technical reasons, even where no racial discrimination takes place. Even so, evidence is produced to show that discrimination in allocation has occurred and still does occur in some areas. One indicator of discrimination is the relatively long time blacks sometimes remain on some council waiting lists compared with the general population. Encouragingly, however, the report sees a recent decrease in the extent of discrimination, although no cause for complacency is implied, and the analysis of housing ends with suggestions for policy improvement. One recommendation, sensibly enough, is that more large houses should be built or bought to house the larger black families.

It is obvious that the position of the minorities in the housing market is a result both of their limited financial resources and of some discrimination. Class and racial factors are, however, less easy to separate than this statement implies. Personal finance is an indicator of class but the relatively low income of blacks is itself, in some cases, due to discrimination. A problem as complicated as this will find no easy solution.

c Prejudice, Panic and Racial Stratification

We have already discussed the role of prejudice in two central areas of social life: employment and housing. There is no shortage of supporting evidence that many white Britons are racially prejudiced. Studies by Daniel and by Jowell and Prescott-Clarke are major relevant examples. Abram's research of 1966 showed that, of a sample of 2,500, 10% were prejudiced, and 17% prejudice-inclined. For what it is worth, this author's own intuition is that in a situation of close personal involvement, such as whether or not to date or take home a member of another race, an uneasy awareness of race (prejudice is, perhaps, too strong a term here) might figure prominently in most people's calculations. We are still far from a relaxed acceptance of racial equality in everyday affairs.

Unease can turn to panic and hatred in times of stress. In such periods, racial minorities may become scapegoats for wider discontent. This happened to the Jews during the Depression – not only in Germany but to a lesser, although noteworthy, extent in parts of Britain, too. Jews were blamed for everything from international Marxism to capitalist world conspiracy! They were abused and victimised, not least among minorities of working class unemployed in parts of the East End of London. More recently, it is blacks who are the scapegoats of hard times. For some, they provide an outlet for frustration and an excuse to avoid analysing the real and complex causes of recession. As black sociologist, Stuart Hall, says with some irony:

> After all, who now wants to begin to explore and unravel the complex tissue of political and economic forces which have created and sustained the poverty of the inner-urban working class . . . Above all, is there a simple, obvious and more natural explanation at hand? Of course they are 'poor' because the *blacks* are *here*. That is not a logical proposition, but ideologists do not function by logic – they have a logic of their own. Race has provided, in periods of crisis and upheaval, precisely such a self-justifying circle of explanations.

Stuart Hall considers the tense national debate of the late nineteen-seventies about how many people of coloured descent there are in Britain and how many more might be allowed in as an irrelevance. In fact, in 1978 there were 1.9 million, out of a population of over 55 million. By that year, coloured immigration had been dropping continuously for some time and had reached a point where it was quite clear that fears of 'swamping' were completely unfounded; in fact more people were leaving Britain than arriving in it. It is difficult not to agree with Hall that continued obsession with immigration and further legislation to reduce it was more a symptom of panic and scapegoating than a measured attempt to deal with a real problem.

Prejudice and discrimination build barriers between people of different races. In Britain, these barriers have reduced the life-chances of members of minority groups. The result is racial stratification. We now discuss whether the position of black people in this country is such that they can be regarded as an 'underclass' beneath and adrift from the working class as a whole.

320

d Is There a Black 'Underclass'?

Defining the structural situation of the minorities is no mere academic matter. It is a necessary part of doing something about racial inequality. In summary, the evidence presented in this chapter shows that *the coloured minorities suffer from both status (racial discrimination) and class inequality.* It is easier to note the potentially disastrous convergence of racial and class inequalities than to disentangle the two. Probably, they cannot be fully disentangled.

In attempting to put a name to the distinct structural position of blacks, John Rex has suggested the term 'underclass'. The word recalls Marx's term lumpen proletariat which refers to the unemployed, and in some cases unemployable, mass beneath the proletariat. Marx's term, however, had no particularly racial connotation. We can see four arguments for using the term underclass, all of which differentiate blacks from the working class and therefore prevent them from being fully identified with it. Firstly, blacks are subject to racial discrimination and need to find ways of fighting it. Secondly, blacks as a group tend to be poorer than the working class as a whole: in that sense they are an 'underclass'. Thirdly, the trade union movement and, perhaps to a lesser extent, the Labour Party, has failed to adequately meet the needs of black people. Fourthly, blacks have produced their own cultural and, to some extent, political institutions, and it seems likely that these will be further developed. Self-help is, perhaps, the first and last line of preservation.

It may, however, still be premature to speak of a black 'underclass'. Matters may not yet be quite as clear cut as this term suggests. There are strategies for black advancement, other than black community politics, which involve co-operation with predominantly white organisations on a basis of *mutual* interest and which might improve the conditions many blacks live in. We examine the political solutions that may be open to blacks in the next section and this should be regarded as an extension of our discussion on whether or not blacks can be regarded as an underclass.

e Ethnic Community Politics and Class Politics: The Black Response to Racial Discrimination and Inequality

The data given in the previous four sections shows, in the

words of John Rex, that 'the situation of the blacks is structurally distinct from that of the majority of the working class.' Initially, the structurally inferior position of blacks reflected the problems of immigrant adjustment, but the *enduring reason* for it is the extent of prejudice and discrimination in British society coupled with the indifference and occasional hostility of the unions. Racial discrimination is essentially a form of status stratification and it represents the major immediate problem of blacks in Britain.

ETHNIC COMMUNITY POLITICS In the absence of substantial help from the British working class movement, coloured people largely rely on *family and community self-help*. The following quotation is a perceptive and articulate personal account of what many immigrants must have felt as 'strangers in a strange land':

> My position was that of a young black Jamaican woman – an immigrant. I was not able to act as a detached observer, maintaining a value-free stance, and with emotions under strict surveillance. English behaviour was often unusual, and sometimes decidedly hostile, and I reacted to it with powerful feelings and protective strategies. It is not easy at first to distinguish the unpredictable and harmless from the really unpleasant. I had little understanding of the heterogeneous English society, and when I met an unusual situation I turned to my relatives and friends for help. Their advice, although not necessarily well-informed, gave me the support I so often needed in making sense of my experience.

Ethnic cultural identity is generated by the natural social ties of the ethnic community. The American immigrant experience provides a parallel to that of British immigrants. For instance, the Irish, Italian and Jewish communities formed organisations to defend and advance themselves in all areas of American life. The Irish were famous for their political social welfare 'machines', the Italians for their clannish and secretive business-criminal Mafia organisations, and the Jews are still well-known for their sense of ethnic loyalty and identity. The basic cell in these sprawling ethnic structures was usually the extended family. The same is true in many of Britain's immigrant communities. In the early period of post-war immigration, the typical immigrant was, however, a single person – usually a man. Nevertheless, his major aim was often to bring over his family and he sent money 'back home' for this purpose. Once the family had arrived, the next important step for many was to buy a house. To raise the money for this – and a surprisingly large minority of immigrant houses are fully paid for – required financial co-operation between family and, possibly, friends.

The need for everyday mutual assistance and sharing among family, kin and friends as they settle into a new country and culture is obvious. Baby-sitting, gifts and loans assist over short-term crises, and friendly chats and advice are the stuff of daily life. Many immigrants are used to relying on family and friends for help rather than on the state, and may actually prefer to do so. A survey conducted in Birmingham, published in 1980, reported that elderly West Indians and Asians depend on state welfare less than elderly whites. Many, apparently, did not know of services like meals on wheels and home helps to which they were entitled, but most of those who did rejected them in favour of support from their families and neighbours.

Although much community life is informal, specific needs do produce the incentive to create more formal institutions. Some, of course, are more formal than others. At the humblest level is the ethnic shop or genuinely local ethnic restaurant. Beyond these are social clubs, discos and various places of pleasure and entertainment, with ethnic management and largely ethnic clientele. These may overlap, more or less, with the white world, although sense of separation is virtually inevitable.

Sometimes, particularly when an ethnic group feels threatened or spurned, ethnic identity expresses itself in political or quasi-military organisations. The core of the American civil rights movement of the nineteen-sixties was a coalition of black pressure groups. The Black Panther Party was, in part, a break-away from the non-violence of the civil rights movement into more aggressive, para-military politics. The Panthers explained their position partly in terms of the need to defend themselves against police victimisation of the black community. The immediate upshot was several bloody confrontations in which several Black Panthers were killed. In view of the American experience, what John Rex has to say about certain trends in black politics in this country deserves close attention: it is his second point that is significant: the riots of Bristol and Brixton already show him to be wrong on the first.

I think that street battles and riots provoked by blacks are
unlikely and I do not, though I am less sure here, think there
will be any literal application of the slogan 'Burn baby, burn' in
British cities . . .

I do think, however, that the black political movements are
moving toward a posture of defensive confrontation and that
they are quite realistic in doing so.

Rex concentrates particularly on ethnic community politics
although we can apply much of what he says nationally. He
suggests three types of black political movements: *issue-oriented*,
personality-oriented and *ideologically-oriented*. A major example of an
issue-oriented movement is the protest against the number of
black youths arrested on suspicion ('sus'). This a charge under
the 1824 Vagrancy Act which allows the police to arrest, without warrant, a person whom they reasonably suspect to be
'loitering with intent to commit a felonious offence.' Police evidence alone can be sufficient to convict. Estimates of the percentage of coloured people making up 'sus' arrests vary from
44% (Home Office) to 80% for certain inner urban areas (Law
Centres Working Group). The nature of the 'sus' law and the
manner of its application have caused widespread concern both
within and beyond the black community. Certainly, it has not
helped relations between the police and blacks.

Issues need not be of long standing to cause conflict. On the
contrary, those that suddenly arise are often the most inflam-
matory. Thus, the police raid on a restaurant in the St. Paul's
area of Bristol in April 1980 sparked off one of the country's
worst urban riots.

Education is another, quite different, issue which has provoked black action. In Redbridge and elsewhere, black parents
and teachers have very positively involved themselves in supporting the school curriculum, with additional schooling in the
evenings or at weekends.

We now consider Rex's second type of movement, the
personality-oriented. An example of a nationally-known (though
sparsely supported) personality-oriented movement in Britain
was the Black Power Group led by Michael X during the
nineteen-sixties. He was a mere shadow of the much better
known Malcolm X who led the Black Muslim movement in the
United States. Rex has in mind, however, local personalities
who can manipulate incidents sometimes to further a cause but

often for maximum personal publicity.

A more reliable basis for a political movement than the merely personal is ideological belief – Rex's third category. The American Black Panther Party, mentioned above, provides an example of this kind of movement. Within the British black community, there are a number of groups which are as much cultural as political, and which have distinctive ideologies. One example is the Rastafarian movement (see Chapter 13). Members of the group are disciples of the late former Emperor of Ethiopia, Haile Selassie, whom they believe to be divine. With varying degrees of conviction, Rastafarians subscribe to black separatism and some wed socialism to their religious beliefs. It has been said of this and of other 'back to Africa' movements that they represent an extreme defensive reaction by blacks against a white society which has already rejected them. A return to Africa is not, however, a realistic option, particularly as the majority of coloured immigrants have never been there in the first place. But the identity, confidence and expression that such movements provide should not be dismissed or underestimated. We develop this point at some length when discussing black and brown youth in the next chapter.

CLASS POLITICS Community politics alone are unlikely ever to be enough radically to change the position of Britain's black population. John Rex may virtually despair of an effective black and white working class alliance but he still recognises its ultimate desirability, if the massive governmental resources needed by inner city ethnic groups are ever to materialise. Community politics are necessary both to 'defend' and develop the community, but only government (arguably in combination with industry) can provide the means to lift 'ghetto' conditions – economic, housing and educational – much nearer to the acceptable national norm. In getting political support for such a programme blacks are not without some political muscle. At the lowest level, political parties need black votes just as unions require members. The Labour Party has already passed two important pieces of legislation, the 1968 and 1976 Race Relations Acts, attacking discrimination in major areas of life. They seem to have had some effect. Perhaps now the principle of *positive discrimination* on behalf of blacks – particularly in guaranteeing them adequate jobs and income – is an aim worth persuading the Labour Party to pursue. The 1968 and 1976 Acts seek to achieve equality under the law, but greater material equality is a harder ideal to attain and may require this different policy, which may *favour* black people. No doubt, too, many blacks will deem it expedient to continue to work in, and with the unions, in the hope of persuading them to support black interests more actively. Beyond this, there are, of course, other options open to blacks – from seeking succour from the Conservative Party to making common cause with the Marxist-Trotskyist left. It is not the business of the sociologist to dictate individual choice but to illuminate the social context in which choice is made.

Guide to further reading and study

Despite its importance this is not the best covered topic in sociological literature at our level. A good starting point for some useful articles and further references is Volume 8, Number 4 (April 1979) of *The Social Science Teacher*. If it is obtainable, *Our People* (1979), Thames Television Ltd., 306-316 Euston Road, NW1, is a very useful, fact-filled pamphlet. The Commission for Racial Equality's *Five Views of Multi-Racial Britain* (1978) gives much more theoretical and demanding coverage of racial issues. For a fuller treatment of the subject in a single volume, Sami Zubaida, *ed, Race and Racialism* (Tavistock, 1970) is worth mentioning although it does not cover recent developments. D. J. Smith's *Racial Disadvantage in Britain: The PEP Report* (Penguin, 1977), is an empirical survey perhaps best used as a book of reference. John Rex's work in this field requires no recommendation although his *Race, Community and Conflict* with R. S. Moore (Oxford, 1967) is quite demanding. An easier and much shorter read is his article 'Black Militancy and Class Conflict', in R. Miles and A.Phizacklea, *eds, Racism and Political Action in Britain,* (Routledge and Kegan Paul, 1967). Finally, for an alarming account of racial violence in East London read *Blood on the Streets* published by Bethnal Green and Stepney Trades Council and available from 58 Watney St, London E1.

Past Questions

1 'Despite the concentration of immigrants in certain areas, strictly defined ghettos have not been produced, but there is a growing indication that they may well appear in the future.' (Allen). Discuss. (AEB, 1975).

2 Discuss critically sociological explanations of racial conflict. (AEB, 1977).

3 Race relations are more akin to caste divisions than they are to class structure'. Discuss. (London, 1979).

13 Age, Generation and Class

The Concept of Generation Defined and Explored

Generation describes groups of individuals born within a few years of one another. Depending on which year is taken as base point, generations will overlap. Generation, therefore, refers to *contemporaries* or people in the same age group. The concept of generation has not been greatly employed by sociologists. The exception to this is the considerable attention paid to youth and adolescence, not only by sociologists but also by the media. Yet, even in the case of youth, sociologists have found it difficult to establish to what extent generation, as distinct from factors such as class and gender, influence attitude and behaviour. Until recently, very little systematic sociology has been written about the various stages of adulthood before old age. Old age itself has been treated more fully, but has often been labelled a 'problem' rather than explored as a category of social experience.

This chapter cannot hope to fill in the gaps of contemporary research. What it does attempt to do is to use the best of recent work to provide a clear framework of understanding of the concept of generation and, in particular, to examine the relationship between stratification by generation and stratification by class. It is essential to understand that the social significance attached to different age groupings varies from society to society: the obvious example here is old age. In most traditional societies, the old or 'elders' are regarded as having acquired much experience still likely to be useful to the rest of the community. Accordingly, they tend to play an important role in decision making and have high status. In modern societies, where the speed of change is much more rapid, 'the wisdom of the elders' becomes irrelevant much more quickly. Certainly, the old are not accorded the power and status in modern societies that they have in traditional ones. Similarly, Margaret Mead's *Growing Up in New Guinea* and *Coming of Age in Samoa* make it clear that adolescence in other societies is not regarded as a distinct and often problematic period of training and adjustment to the extent that it is in modern societies.

Just as the significance given to a particular age group varies from one society to another, so attitudes to an age group can change, sometimes considerably, within a single society. Thus, middle age (41–60) did not exist in Victorian Britain in the same sense that it does now. Because the period in which procreation and the rearing of children took place was longer, and life expectancy was much shorter, ageing and death tended to follow quickly upon the completion of family upbringing. Nowadays, after the last child becomes independent, up to twenty years or more of 'prime' adulthood may remain to any married couple: this may require considerable individual and pair bond adjustment.

Five age groupings can usefully be suggested as a frame-work for considering generation in modern society. There is no pretence of sophistication here and, indeed, conceptual refinement is not necessary because only youth and old age will be considered in detail and these are widely accepted as social and as biological categories. The age groupings are tentative and approximate: childhood (0–14); youth (15–20); young adulthood (21–40) (although the difference between the two ends of our groupings is particularly obvious here); middle age (41–60); and old age (60+ onwards). It is not biological age itself, but the position of an age group within the social structure and, in particular, the attitude of others to those within the age group that create its social identity. Thus, it is largely because the elderly retire at 60 or 65, become economically unproductive and, in many cases, dependent on government subsidies, that their social position is weak. Matters could be arranged differently; if they were, the position of the old would be correspondingly different.

We now briefly examine childhood, young adulthood and middle age, leaving youth and old age for more detailed consideration later. Childhood is, universally, a period of dependency and socialisation. In this sense, children probably have the most in common of all age groups. This is not on account of shared generational identity, however, but for what is virtually the opposite – the inability to think and fend for themselves. For this reason, it makes more sense to analyse childhood in the context of the family than by means of the concept of generation, although it should be noted that the peer group is a crucial formative influence on the behaviour, attitudes and self-image of the child. In addition, generation perhaps reminds us more vividly of the rights and needs of the child than merely considering him in the context of the family in which he is clearly in a relatively weak position.

330

Adulthood is rarely discussed conceptually by sociologists except in relation to the specific problems adults may have, but in theory there is no reason why it should be considered inferior to youth as a basis for understanding the experience of the relevant age group. Before using the concept in this way, it is important to make a fundamental qualification. There is little doubt that the major concerns of the majority of adults – family, work and leisure – are more affected by class than by age. Sooner or later, generally sooner for the working class and later for the middle class, the young adult will feel social pressure to get married. Partly because most young adults will have been socialised to accept marriage as their normal lot, this pressure will coincide with their desires, but it will be no less real for that. In addition, certain tax and other financial advantages, such as ease of acquiring a joint mortgage, are available to the married couple and not to a pair simply 'living together'. Once married, the young couple are likely soon to find themselves entangled in some of the more substantial financial commitments of our consumer society. Mortgage repayments are likely to be the major economic burden on a young, middle class couple and rent payments the major outlay of the working class pair. The feeding and clothing of a family, the running, repair and maintenance of a house, and perhaps a car, are further examples of economic pressure. All this, frequently in combination with the demands on time and energy of a young family, structures the social lives of young adults in a radically different way from their own adolescence a few years previously. The massive rise in divorce in the late nineteen sixties and seventies no doubt reflects the stress of this period of life.

The position of young adults in their work situation is also a possible further source of stress. They often experience the heavy weight of established, middle aged people who block their career and, consequently, their social advancement. This applies as much to the shop floor worker waiting to become foreman as it does to a social worker waiting to become a senior or team leader in his job. At best, the senior person may change jobs or retire; at worst, it may be a question of the younger workers hoping that their elders will be forced by sudden death or illness to vacate their positions. Where promotion depends greatly on length of service, as it does typically in modern bureaucratised professions and office work, underlying generational conflict may be strong, however much it may be veiled by prudence and necessity.

We will regard middle age as the period between approximately forty-one and sixty years of age. It is dangerous to make broad generalisations about age groups, and this is particularly true of middle age. By the time it occurs, class differences tend to be even more marked than in young adulthood. Middle class occupational incomes, which usually increase in measured annual increments, are generally substantially more than those of manual workers. In turn, this means that the standard of living of middle class, middle aged households is relatively higher than that of working class, middle aged households.

Although the cumulative nature of the material advantages of the middle class is perhaps at its most obvious in middle age, this period of life is similar in a number of ways, regardless of class. Family dispersal eases the financial position of working class as well as middle class couples. Many women of all class backgrounds choose this time to return to work, which further helps the economic situation of the household and can also provide personal fulfilment and companionship. It is at the psychological rather than the material level that the pressures of middle age can be strongest. For both male and female, the role of parent becomes of diminished importance and there is a need to develop new identities and roles if loneliness and boredom are to be avoided. This adjustment is made no easier by the fact that family dispersal coincides with a decline in physical powers and attractiveness. Women, especially perhaps those who do not return to work, may feel these pressures particularly acutely. Dependency, or at least partial dependency, on prescribed drugs can be the result of short-cut attempts to come to terms with these problems. Stress on males is more likely to be generated through work and, for them, alcohol is the conventional relief. It would be misleading, however, to give the impression that the majority of middle-aged people are, depending on their sex, either drug dependent or alcoholic: this would be an unkind reversal of the stereotype of youth held by some of the middle-aged. Many of the middle-aged make creative use of the extra time available to them, although arguably neither the leisure industry nor social policy makers have quite realised that this age group is more substantial, in terms of its size and the money and time at its disposal, than, for instance, the 'teen-age' market.

The remaining two groups, youth and age, we discuss in separate sections to follow.

The Social Formation of Modern Youth

A number of factors have come together to put modern youth in a socially distinct and prominent position in relation to the rest of society. These are the development of a system of compulsory schooling, the speed of change, the relative affluence of most (though not all) young people, and the related growth of a youth-oriented leisure industry. Sociologists of all perspectives agree that these developments structure the position of modern youth. They can be referred to as *generationally specific* factors. We will examine the factors that divide young people later.

Compulsory Education

The development of a system of compulsory education has been the major new influence on modern youth. The school provides the essential context in which large numbers of young people can share a collective experience. Just as the concentration of working people in factories was a precondition of the formation of an industrial working class, so the concentration of young people in schools was necessary for the formation of modern youth.

Before state education was established, 'youth culture' existed as a clearly identifiable phenomenon only in private schools and universities. These insitutions alone provided relatively large numbers of young people with the opportunity to become self-consciously aware, to some extent, of their common circumstances and identity. *Tom Brown's Schooldays*, set in the private school of Rugby, successfully describes an experience available almost exlusively to the children of the wealthy, and then only to male children. The better known private schools were forcing houses for the formation of leadership qualities. No margin was allowed for youthful rebellion other than high-spirited 'pranks and japes', but the companionship that often developed amongst pupils, and the variety of group and team identities and rivalries, showed how important the generational peer group could be in a setting where it was able to flourish. There is little evidence on which to build a picture of the peer group activity of adolescents of low social origins before the late nineteenth century, although the novels of Dickens tell us much about the very least fortunate. Indeed, in Fagin's gang of young pickpockets we catch a glimpse of a 'deviant youth sub-culture' almost fifty years before sociologists discovered the phenomenon. For the majority of young people, work and family took up most of their time. Leisure activities outside the family suggest no special age group interests apart from courtship, and even this was often hedged in by ritual and family concern.

It was, then, only the development of a universal system of schooling that separated off young people from the rest of the population for a large part of their daily lives. The school provided the context for common peer group experience and awareness. At first, it was compulsory to attend school only until the age of ten (Mundella's Education Act, 1880). It was not until after the Second World War, when the school leaving age was raised to fifteen, that adolescents, or 'teenagers' as they came to be called, made a social impact on the general public. In the post Second World War period, higher education also expanded greatly and, consequently, students became a larger and more prominent social group.

The Speed of Change

A second feature of modern society which explains the rise of youth is the speed of change. This is related to education in that it is partly because of the new developments in scientific, technological and professional knowledge that so many more young people receive higher or further education. This can create a gap of knowledge (if not necessarily one of practical competence) between the generations. Computer programming is an example of the new technology that has had an intake almost exclusively of young people, simply because training in the necessary skills was not available to older adults during their period of education, and they have rarely had the opportunity of retraining.

In the nineteen sixties, social critics often argued that the speed of change in norms, values and ideas contributed to a 'culture gap' between the younger and older generations. Such an assessment is not easily proven. We will return to the question of whether there is a distinct youth culture and consciousness in a later section and in this context also discuss the influence of the media on youth.

The Relative Affluence of Youth

A third factor associated with the social prominence of modern youth is its *affluence* (wealth) compared with that of previous generations of young people. The wealth of the young does not simply reflect the increase in total wealth, but, because wages paid to young employees have increased proportionately to those paid to others, their relative position in the market has improved. In addition, the money of the young is usually uncommitted: mortgages, rent, family and household expenditure take up little of their income. Although the spending power of youth is only a small percentage of total spending power, producers compete keenly for it through the advertising media. Entertainment, audio and audio-visual equipment, records, cosmetics and fashionable clothes account for much youthful expenditure and certainly much more in proportion to that spent on such items by the rest of the population. All of these purchases are associated with enjoyment, self-presentation or both.

Youthful Creativity and Idealism

Emphasis on social context should not be allowed to obscure the creative response of many of the young to the situations and opportunities with which they are presented. Evaluations differ of the quality of the contribution made by young people to areas of 'pop' culture, but there is no denying the importance of that contribution in the post-war world. Young people in colleges, universities and even schools have acted on a variety of social and political issues in a way that has attracted public attention to particular issues, and which has sometimes changed the course of policy and events. The best example of this is the protest against the Vietnam war, in which large numbers of students joined in the United States, France and Britain.

Psycho-Social Factors

A further factor needs to be mentioned in examining major

influences on youthful behaviour. How far is the behaviour of the young affected by adolescent psychology? A precise answer to this question depends on knowing what adolescent psychology is – if, indeed, it is the same universally. There is no clear agreement about this: what can be said is that the 'natural' adjustment to, and learning about, adult roles that occurs in all cultures during youth has been greatly extended in modern societies. The expansion of the educational system is the immediate reason for this but the underlying factor is the variety and complexity of the skills now required of a competent adult at work and in the home. Extended socialisation and education have brought new opportunities for personal development, but also new sources of stress. Public examinations and difficulties in obtaining a job are well-known areas of tension. Given that these occur at a time when the individual is experiencing great physical, mental and emotional change, it is not surprising that a variety of disorders show a sharp incline during the teenage years. According to data assembled by Michael Rutter, these include suicide, para-suicide (attempted suicide), alcoholism, schizophrenia, anorexia nervosa and depression. This must be kept in proportion, however, for only a small minority of teenagers suffer acutely from any of these illnesses.

It must be emphasised that the above factors are contextual and general in nature: they do not, of course, affect all young people in exactly the same way. There are, for instance, great differences in education and wealth amongst young people which greatly influence opportunity and experience. Class underlies these and other differences and it would be mistaken to assume common material interests or generational consciousness amongst the young. We now examine how class and generational factors interact to produce distinct and varied youth sub-cultures.

Youth

Terminology and Perspectives

The interesting aspect of the sociology of youth lies in analysing and interpreting what young people do, think and feel. For instance: what did the young radicals of the sixties want? Why do some young people dye their hair orange? (A genuine mystery to some older people). What does all that football chanting mean? Sociological perspectives are useful only in so far as they explain behaviour: we will, therefore, keep this theoretical section brief and let the perspectives speak for themselves in practical application.

Three major perspectives on youth can be described. These are *functionalist, generational 'unit' and class-structural*. There are, of course, variations of each. Talcott Parsons and S. N. Eisenstadt present functionalist models. For them, youth is a period of training and preparation for adulthood. Personal difficulties in 'growing up' and even group rebellion are seen as dysfunctional, if predictable. Even so, they note that most young people do, in fact, successfully negotiate the transitional phase of adolescence. This functionalist model is not ahistorical (it does not lack historical awareness). Functionalists fully recognise that in modern society the period of youthful socialisation tends to be longer and that particular stresses accompany it. Weber's concept of the status group is also sometimes used in functionalist analyses of youth. Young people are considered to share the same pre-adult status and also to share similar problems of adjustment. Identity, security and much personal 'problem solving', as well as leisure activity, are based on the peer group.

Karl Mannheim's concept of the generational 'unit' lies between functionalist perspective and the concept of separate generational consciousness that was popular in the nineteen sixties. Mannheim appreciated, as functionalists do, that the educational system cuts young people off from the work-centred life of adults. Within generational groups, particular units sometimes form. Thus, in higher education student movements emerge in certain circumstances. This is because students are frequently together and, as a result, are able to discuss and organise their response to major issues such as wars and racial discrimination. Sometimes their response takes the form of protest. No doubt because the nineteen sixties was a period of exceptional student activism, some commentators tended to overstress the separateness of the generations and the extent of generational conflict. Charles Reich in his book, *The Greening of America*, wrote as if a 'new consciousness', inspired by youthful imagination and idealism, was about to engulf America. He forgot that this radical consciousness was largely confined to middle class students in higher education, and was by no means adopted by all of them.

More recently, British sociologists, particularly the mainly Marxist group at the Centre for Cultural Studies in Birmingham, have argued that youth should be analysed in the specific class context of particular youth groups. Thus, student protest movements should be seen not just as the action of young people but of young, *middle class* people. Again, 'slum' gangs should be analysed not merely as 'young delinquents', but in relation to their class, neighbourhood and family environments, including the culture of working class adults. This approach, therefore, allows for the operation of generational factors within a broad framework of class, and we use it more than any other in this chapter.

Although we have already explained the meaning of the terms culture and sub-culture (see Chapter 3), it is appropriate to expand the definition here. *Culture refers to the way of life of a given group, for instance, of a particular society or class. Sub-culture refers to those aspects of the life of a group which distinguish it from the main or dominant culture.* Thus, we can speak of West Indian or Jewish sub-culture in Britain. *A counter-culture or contra-culture describes a sub-culture which is opposed to the dominant culture.* The term was widely used of the new radical life-style of the nineteen sixties.

Youth Conformity and Sub-Cultural Non-Conformity

Most young people conform, more or less, to society's norms. For them, peer group identity *complements* rather than *conflicts* with their roles in the family and at school or work. We explore *conformity* among youth shortly. Immediately, we examine the minority sub-cultures of non or less conformist young people. The only reason for preferring the term *non-conformity* to *deviance* here is that much youthful sub-cultural activity only *borders* on the deviant. (The explicitly deviant we examine in Chapter 17.) We have already explained how young people tend to be 'set apart' from the rest of society and we have mentioned some of the influences and stresses upon them. This section is more interpretist in that it analyses how certain minority groups of young people respond to their own experience, including the pressures of the media and the educational systems and, in doing so, often create original and interesting life-styles. We can roughly categorise these responses into three types: delinquent, pleasure seeking or political. Response is, however, mediated or influenced by social context – to express it crudely, either middle class, working class and/or ethnic culture. Differences in family, neighbourhood and educational experience deeply divide young people. We can put the above points in simple, diagrammatical form:

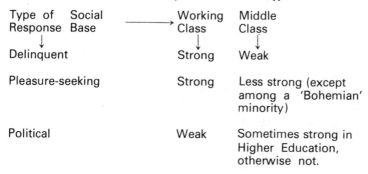

Youth (Minority) Sub-cultural Types

Type of Response	Social Base	→	Working Class	Middle Class
Delinquent			Strong	Weak
Pleasure-seeking			Strong	Less strong (except among a 'Bohemian' minority)
Political			Weak	Sometimes strong in Higher Education, otherwise not.

We will use these three types of sub-cultural response as a general guide (but no more than that), first to examine working class youth, then middle class youth. It must be noted that many young people opt in and out of sub-cultural activity and that between conformity and non-conformity there is a considerable 'grey' area.

Working Class Youth Culture and Sub-cultures

Working class youth culture is concentrated in areas such as the inner city and, more recently, public housing estates. It is a field of research that has been well studied both in Britain and the United States. The Chicago School of urban sociologists began the serious sociological study of this topic (see Chapter 17). Much of the best contemporary material has been published in Britain. Peter Willmot in *Adolescent Boys in East London* (1966), takes care to put the delinquent activity of a minority of working class adolescent boys within the context of working class youth peer group activity in general. We will examine working class youth in terms of activities rather than values.

Nevertheless, it is worth listing some major underlying values as a reference point for what follows. These are: anti-authoritarianism; pleasure-seeking ('fun'); a strong sense of territory; masculinity and an admiration of physical strength and skill.

80% of Willmott's sample belonged to peer groups and enjoyed, with their friends, a variety of leisure activities such as dancing, going to parties and motor-bike riding, for instance which did not include their families. Significantly, though, the majority disapproved of gang violence and 'taking and driving', and it would be quite wrong to think of them as delinquents. The kind of things they 'get up to' – playing football (sometimes in the streets), watching football (with an eye to opposition supporters and the police), drinking and going to parties – can easily lead to 'scrapes with the law'. This is not the main point, however, as far as 'the lads' are concerned. Their aim is 'to have fun' and to 'get kicks'. It is mainly in terms of pleasure-seeking, therefore, that we analyse further working class youth culture.

One of the best ways of 'having fun' is to annoy authority. The artful mocking of it is a constant theme in the now vast literature on the activities of working class youth. Teachers, policemen and youth club leaders are the frequent butt of their ridicule and, less often, of their practical jokes. In an observational survey of a group of working class youths, Paul Corrigan found that a large number thought of teachers as 'big-heads'. We saw similar antagonism reported by Hargreaves and Willis (Chapter 5). Social workers and probation officers possibly escape more lightly because they usually work on a one to one basis with 'clients' rather than as obvious representatives of large and dominant institutions such as schools or the police force. At school, fun often takes the form of a rearguard action against being bored. The ultimate resort is to 'bunk off'. In all inner city areas, there are always a few working class 'kids' on the streets or at home during school time. They might be playing football, listening to records or just 'waiting for something to turn up'. In more official jargon, they might be referred to as 'at risk'.

It would be misleading to suggest that working class youth culture is exclusively or even mainly concerned with taking a rise out of authority. Much of it is positively motivated and

340

energetically pursued. Mending, painting and decorating motor-bikes and scooters, playing football and being a football supporter, 'chatting up girls' can all involve great commitment and skill. There are many middle class teenagers relatively deficient in these areas compared with the working class. A minority of working class 'kids' play music and write songs, and many more take an intelligent interest in music, although the research of Murdoch and Phelps suggests that, for the boys, music is largely a matter of background noise or 'aural wallpaper'.

It is obvious that young working class people like spending time together away from adults. Nevertheless, they *are* working class and this shows in their activity. The skinheads of the middle and late nineteen sixties exemplify this point. Like other groups of young lads, no doubt the aggressive and occasionally violent behaviour of the skinheads can be explained in terms of a pursuit of excitement, but John Clarke, in a contribution to the collection of writings, *Resistance through Rituals* (edited by Hall and Jefferson), offers additionally a more thought-provoking explanation. He suggests that the behaviour and style of the skinheads, far from being random and irrational, closely reflects the realities of their lives. He points out that many features of the skinhead style – the short haircut, the wearing of braces over shirts, turning trousers up inches above the ankles, the wearing of cheap, heavy boots – were only slightly exaggerated and dramatised versions of traditional working class dress. Clarke suggests that, by dressing this way, the skinheads were, perhaps unconsciously, reasserting traditional class and community identity. This interpretation gains credibility when we remember that East End working class communities have been damaged and destroyed in the post-war period. Decline in employment opportunities, housing clearance programmes, near-chaos in parts of the Inner London Education Service must have caused disorientation, anger and despair in many lives, not least in those of the young. It is perhaps not surprising – although deplorable in itself – the skinheads frequently turned their aggression against immigrants rather than on the investors, developers and planners who were more responsible for their grievances and fears. Clarke, therefore, sees skinhead aggression and violence as largely defensive. He explains their behaviour as 'a symbolic defence of (threatened) territory' and

341

as 'a magical attempt to recover community'.

Sociologists cannot locate all youth sub-culture so convincingly in class context as Clarke does the skinheads. This is partly because the media tends quickly to take up and popularise stylistic and creative sub-cultural aspects. Thus it may be that Punk music and style of dress was originally the product of unemployed, working class youth but, within a few months, the movement was being commercially exploited in the youth market generally. The Punk clothes worth hundreds of pounds, which were advertised in *Vogue* magazine, illustrate the point. In adopting sub-cultural forms, such as Punk music, for mass consumption, the commercial enterprises involved, and the media, both attempt to adapt the product for maximum acceptability and consumption. Thus the attempt to 'devulgarise' the Sex Pistols was rightly seen by the group as an attack on their freedom to produce and perform the material they wanted. When a sub-cultural symbol, like Punk rock music, is commercialised, instead of providing a long-term focus on which the movement can coalesce and identify, the symbol is 'stolen' by the pop industry, reprocessed and presented to a wider audience which does not seriously associate it with the protest and rebellion it may have originally represented. In contrast to the Punks, the skinheads did not produce anything saleable on the mass market, although some London and fashionable provincial boutiques attempted to market skinhead style clothes.

As well as providing ideas for the pop industry and media, youth sub-cultures also borrow freely from them and from other sources. The Teddy Boys of the nineteen fifties combined features of the style of London upper-class 'toffs' and American 'movie' gangsters to produce their own distinctive, swashbuckling, rather status-conscious style.

Underlying the above rituals is the desire to assert masculinity, often in a physical way. This is not exclusive to the working class, but it is chiefly in manual labour that working people have expressed themselves and physical toughness is particularly respected among them.

In the hard world of working class youth sub-cultures, the position of the female is very much that of pillion-passenger. Motor-bike 'burn-ups' and gang fights (real or mock) are forms of display, and all the better if girls are there to observe closely. As a *Sunday Times* newspaper analysis of a gang fight wryly states: 'excitement is heightened if police, press, TV – and girls – are in attendance'. The women's movement has, as yet, made few inroads into working class youth gender relations. It would be a mistake, however, to see the girls as mere status symbols and prizes in the social game-playing of the boys: the female peer-group has a distinct and important existence within the larger teenage peer group itself. Girls share much leisure activity. They are more likely than the boys to know details of the top twenty, to read teenage magazines, and to be familiar with the latest dance routines – which they perform, usually in protective togetherness, at discos. 'Going steady' is what detaches working class girls from the sex-based peer-group. If they can, they tend to marry early and their career aspirations, if any, are low. We reviewed these matters in our chapter on gender.

Working class youth sub-cultures are not usually consciously political. Nevertheless, when an issue affects their own interest closely, working class youth sometimes respond in a more or less political way. Two such issues are race and unemployment. Occasional clashes between groups of white and black youths have been a feature of urban life in this country since the nineteen fifties. A minority of white working class youths have reacted to what they see as the black 'alien' presence in or near their own communities with hostility and aggression. A number associated themselves openly with the fascist movement which underwent a revival in the late nineteen seventies. We examine the response of black youth to this in a separate section. In the late nineteen seventies and early eighties, unemployment was experienced by increasing numbers of young people, black and white. More and more sixteen year olds left school for their first year of 'non-work'. 'Dole-queue rock' – full of strident protest and youthful disillusion – was one response. What the long term result of large scale youth unemployment will be, is a matter for speculation. No doubt some public figures hope that competition for jobs will force young people to conform and 'smarten up'. What seems more likely to develop among the unemployed is apathy and, among the employed, a determination to hang on to the jobs they have, whether they like them or not. There is also the possibility that this situation will prove fertile soil for the development of radical feeling among the young.

Two important groups of working class young people have received little attention so far. We may term these the 'respectables' and the 'real delinquents'. About one fifth of Wilmott's sample were ambitious to leave the East End and, if possible, obtain non-manual jobs. In addition to these, the majority of the rest had satisfactory relations with their families and, to a lesser extent, with their teachers. Only a hard core of about 10% were 'delinquent'. We study these in Chapter 17. They are an interesting group and you may wish to read the relevant section of that chapter now.

Middle Class Youth Culture and Sub-Cultures

Most middle class young people, like most working class people, more or less conform. They do not, however, conform to the same way of life. After all, they come from different backgrounds. A young middle class person of sixteen is much more likely to receive further formal education than his working class counterpart, and this is even more true of young males, than of females. Homework takes up much of the time of young middle class people. Even if they had the inclination, they would seldom have the opportunity to 'mess about' on the streets of their neighbourhood. Research by Murdoch and Phelps, on the other hand, shows that by no means all middle class teenagers spend most of their out-of-school time doing homework. In addition to the more academic ones, Murdoch and Phelps observed a group of young, middle class males who, as well as doing their academic work adequately, found time to pursue an interest in 'progressive' pop music. Their taste was much more likely than that of working class youth to include some folk and pop music protest songs.

We will defer until a later chapter our consideration of delinquency among middle class youth and concentrate here on pleasure seeking and political sub-cultural activity. Their pleasure seeking is rather different from that of working class youth. It needs to be understood in the context of higher education because it often occurs on or near college or university campuses. These campuses, particularly the residential ones, concentrate students, relatively free from financial worries, in a cloistered and tolerant situation. In Kenneth Kenniston's phrase, they are allowed a 'period of extended youth' which enables them to experiment with, and test, various values, attitudes and life-styles, as well as to acquire advanced formal education and training. Kenniston refers to this further as 'youth as a stage of life' which, for some, can continue into their late twenties. During these years, a minority of students sometimes adopt life-styles which may involve certain modes of dress, drug-taking, 'getting into' music, a free attitude to relationships and other behaviour foreign to the majority of the population.

We will examine a study by Jock *Young of psychedelic drug-taking as an example of a mainly middle class youth sub-cultural form of activity. Of course, from a legal point of view, such activity is delinquent. Here, however, we are viewing it from the perspective of those involved, who see it as a way of acquiring desired experience. Over the years, members of such groups have been described as 'bohemians', 'beatniks' (or just 'beats'), 'hippies', or simply 'student-types'. We will tend to use the term *bohemian* for general reference. Following Matza, Young describes the pleasure-seeking, bohemian life-style in terms of *subterranean values*, although he is careful to point out that the use of psychedelic drugs is only one aspect of this way of life. Other subterranean values are short-term hedonism, spontaneity, excitement, and dislike of conventionally organised work. These contrast with *formal* values such as deferred gratification, planning future action, predictability and acceptance of productive work as virtuous. Broadly, subterranean values are concerned with pleasure and self-fulfilment for its own sake, and formal values with work and the necessary control that goes with it. Herbert Marcuse has seen the same contrast between subterranean values and formal work values in Freud's pleasure and reality principles. He expresses this as follows:

Pleasure Principle Values	*Reality Principle Values*
Immediate Satisfaction	Delayed Satisfaction
Pleasure	Restraint of Pleasure
Joy (play)	Toil (work)
Receptiveness (to pleasurable stimuli and experience)	Productiveness (in work)
Absence of Repression	Security (in return for self-repression/control)

Source: Herbert Marcuse, *Eros and Civilisation,* 1956, p. 12.

345

We will not argue the merits of the pleasure and reality principles here, but simply note that the former rules in the bohemian world, and the latter in the world of organised work.

Bohemians sometimes take psychedelic drugs, such as cannabis and LSD, because they believe that these improve their moods, and even enhance their perception of the world. Cannabis is a relatively mild psychedelic and is taken for its relaxing 'mellowing' effect. LSD is stronger, and some claim that under its influence new insights may be realised and joyful and profound states of awareness achieved. We must add that *any* psychedelic drug may also produce the opposite effect, especially amongst inexperienced or 'naive' users. Young suggests, however, that experienced users can often exercise considerable control over the effects of psychedelics, and the drug then becomes part of the whole way of life of the sub-culture rather than its main dominating influence. Psychedelic drug-taking may fit in with the kind of music, literature, leisure style and even personal relations preferred by the group. To get a 'feel' for bohemian sub-culture, it is best to read the novels of, say, the American 'beat' of the fifties, Jack Kerouac, or to listen to the 'sixties' music of the Grateful Dead or Jefferson Airplane. Of course, these artists belong to different 'moments' in the history of 'bohemia', but they are, nevertheless, part of the same broad tradition.

In general, political opinion amongst the young, including students, presents similar aspects to that of the rest of the population. Family and class are better indicators of a young person's political views than age. Two minor qualifications must be made to this. First, young people in Britain are somewhat more likely to prefer the Labour Party than other age groups, particularly the very old. This is usually attributed less to youthful radical idealism and more to the fact that post-war generations have been socialised in a period when the Labour Party has been well established: for pre-war generations it was less a 'natural' alternative. Secondly, radical, usually socialist or communist groups, do attract a small minority of students. Others may join in when important issues, such as the Vietnam War, arouse their concern. As we shall see in the next section, however, neither the political nor the pleasure-seeking activities of a privileged minority of middle class young are likely, in themselves, to 'change the world'.

346

Middle Class Youth, 'Generational Consciousness' and Change

The idea that a new 'consciousness' or awareness was developing amongst the young was generated largely by the student movements of the nineteen sixties, and already it seems conceptually inadequate and dated. Young prophets of change advocated a heady mixture of bohemian alternative life-style and political idealism, as a recipe for improving what they saw as a corrupt world. Ironically, the notion of an alternative consciousness reached the height of popularity in such books as Charles Reich's *The Greening of America* and Theodore Roszac's *The Making of a Counterculture* when most of the student movements, including those in the United States, were in decline. The stated values underlying the 'new consciousness' were commitment to openness in interpersonal communication, and a willingness to share emotional, spiritual and physical experience generously. 'Ours is the radicalism of love', said a female student activist, in a phrase which sums up the idealistic aspirations of the movement. Charles Reich, in particular, argued that these values were beginning to dominate over the more conformist, work-based values of mainstream society – especially amongst the young. The 'pop' media, especially progressive music and underground newspapers, were the means by which the new values were disseminated. As well as citing the growth of youth 'pop' culture to support his case, Reich adduced the spread of the commune 'alternative society' movement and the emergence of less inhibited life-styles. This was to make great claims on the basis of slight empirical evidence, and sweeping conceptualisation. More measured analysis of the youth culture of the nineteenth sixties established that the 'new consciousness' existed almost exclusively amongst middle class youth, generally in higher education. Only the young in universities and colleges had the education and the time to reflect critically on American society at a period when racial tension and the Vietnam war provided serious cause for concern. But to move from disillusionment with American society to founding an 'alternative society' was a large step. In fact, few went so far as to set up new communes or to join existing ones, although several hundred of them, reflecting many different beliefs and values, mushroomed in the late nineteen sixties. Some failed rapidly although others have continued to exist. For most of the young,

347

the 'new society' amounted to no more than a liberalisation of opinions and behaviour which manifested itself in style of dress, patterns of music-listening and reading, and a more open attitude to human relationships.

A survey by *Fortune* Magazine in 1969 showed, however, that a *large* minority of students identified to some degree with the progressive attitudes and behaviour associated with the 'New Left', a term which broadly covered the youthful cultural and political radicalism of the period. But, like the books which eulogised this new radicalism, the survey reflected a movement at its height and not, as the editors of *Fortune* thought, the beginning of a new, potentially dominant trend.

In retrospect, it is obvious that the middle class, frequently liberal and permissive background of the young radicals, and their privileged educational experience and leisure opportunities, deeply influenced the nature of the student movement. To speak of a 'generation in revolt' and of 'generational consciousness' on the basis of the behaviour of this limited group – as many contemporary commentators did – was to disregard the majority of youth who were at work or unemployed. These young people did not have then, any more than they have now, the opportunity to experience a 'stage of life' in which personal and intellectual development is a priority nor, as we shall see, do they share common cultural pursuits with those who do.

It would be a mistake to dismiss the bohemian life-style and political idealism of some middle class young as irrelevant self-indulgence. In a period of rapid technological and socio-economic change, they have more time and leisure than most to make sense of what is happening. Most importantly, they can contribute to the way change is interpreted and perhaps controlled in moral and human terms. This brings us back to the issue of the social effects of the new technology, and particularly its influence on the relationship between work and leisure (see Chapter 15). The ideal of a freer and more fulfilling society is as much that of Marx as that of youthful radicals. The difference is that he argued that the exploited and deprived, rather than the privileged, should be both the prime creators and the beneficiaries of such a society. Certainly, those that have borne the hardest burden of labour have as much right to enjoy such a society as those who have not.

Black and Brown Youth

Although most black and brown youths are working class as measured by parental occupation, it is not appropriate to treat them exclusively under the heading of working class youth because of the importance of racial and cultural (ethnic) factors. As we saw in Chapter 12, the same argument applies to coloured adults. All young people have the problem of forging a workable identity, but for black and brown youth it is particularly acute. They are presented with two potentially conflicting adult models. First is that of the British citizen, sharing equal rights and duties with whites: second is that of the black person, visibly distinct and with a cultural heritage that goes back to, say, the Punjab, Nigeria, Barbados or Hong Kong. Achieving a workable balance between these identities is possible but often difficult. There are two major reasons for this. Firstly, as we have just mentioned, it is bound to be difficult to bring into focus two separate national, historical identities. Secondly, the problem is made much worse by the experience of *prejudice* or *rejection*, since self-identity partly depends on what others think of you. Coloured immigrants and their children cannot avoid seeing themselves in the mirror of white people's eyes. What they often see there is suspicion and resentment, if not downright repugnance and hatred. (We studied this more empirically in Chapter 12.) The cultural life of immigrant groups, and particularly of the young, cannot be properly understood without bearing in mind the hurt and anger that racism can provoke. Equally, it must be remembered that Britain's minorities, including second and third generation 'immigrants' are proud of, and attached to, their ethnic cultural heritage. This is obvious in many ways such as literature, language, dress, food, religion, family tradition and so on. The phrase 'black is beautiful' captures both the pride and defensive self-assertion that has notably characterised ethnic groups in America and Britain since the nineteen sixties.

We will take West Indian youth sub-culture for more detailed analysis here. Love of music, religion and a liking for street based social activity are well known aspects of West Indian culture. Unemployment, or irregular employment, is also part of the familiar background of life, and young blacks, both here and in the Caribbean, are accustomed to dealing with it. The West Indian hustler in Britain has his parallel in the

Jamaican 'rude boy' or 'rudie'. Rudies cope with the indifference of the job market by 'hustling' a living out of dealing in drugs, gambling, pimping or stealing. As a last resort, some may 'play the welfare system', but they have little taste for the bureaucratic 'hassle' this can involve. Often they live in some style, sporting smart cars and well-cut clothes with an easy air. Not altogether surprisingly, some 'rudies' prefer this life-style to the lower-level manual work that might occasionally be offered them. Still, we must be careful not to suggest that the 'rudie' is the typical figure of West Indian youth sub-culture. Many young blacks look hard for work and are demoralised and embittered if they do not find it. We simply do not have the empirical data available to say what is typical. All that we are doing here is describing some options available to West Indian youth.

The cool, worldly image of the rudie contrasts sharply with the religious fervour of another major West Indian youth sub-cultural figure, the Rastafarian. The 'Rasta' movement illustrates the defensive, retreatist trend which is an almost inevitable part of the cultural tradition of a group actually or potentially oppressed. Rastafarians trace their spiritual roots back to Africa: their plaited hair and, sometimes, their dress styles imitate African originals. They believe that the late Emperor Haile Selassie of Ethiopia will be reincarnated and will lead them out of 'Babylon' – a biblical reference to capitalistic society. From Kingston to Brixton, Reggae is the music of Rastfarianism. Reggae lyrics are heavy with biblical references, and the music's slow, moody rhythms reflect the influence of the 'sacred' drug, ganja (a type of marijuana).

Political movements are rarer than cultural ones among black youth; yet the politics of race, however simply they may be conceived, can hardly fail to be part of every young black person's consciousness. To be black in Britain is to risk prejudice and discrimination. That experience, or the possibility of it, unites black youth – rudies, Rastas and just boys and girls on the street – in a defensive awareness that can be broadly termed political. A single issue can suddenly kindle smouldering resentment into active hostility. In a time of rising unemployment among black youth, that possibility seems likely to be with us for a long while to come.

Is There a Generation Gap?

When discussing the question of whether there is a *generation gap*, the sociologist is frequently left with the feeling of grasping at empty air. All the detailed empirical evidence points to the conclusion that there is no wide gap between the generations. Yet, when talking to adolescents about this issue, one senses their mild discontent and feelings of being misunderstood by adults – even though they may be unable to cite substantial grievances. Similarly, adults are often inconsistent in their comments on 'the young', either over-praising or over-criticising. Such attitudes may mask uncertainty, and even insecurity, in relation to 'the coming generation'. After reviewing evidence about generational attitudes and behaviour, we will make an attempt to explain this latent antagonism in social structural terms.

We have already stated that a number of relatively small scale surveys stress that most young people, of whatever class, are fairly conformist and get on quite well with their parents. A well known larger survey confirms this. The National Children's Bureau conducted a survey of more than 13,000 sixteen year olds, in 1974. These teenagers were all those still able to be contacted who were born in a single week of March, 1958. Questions were asked on a wide variety of aspects of behaviour and attitude, but sex and drugs were excluded as topics, because answers were considered likely to be evasive. On questions relating to marriage and the family, teenagers emerged as thoroughly traditional. Only 3% rejected the idea of marriage and most wanted to have children. Four out of five respondents said that they got on well with both their parents. The main areas of conflict with them were over dress and hair, although in only 11% of homes was this a frequent source of friction. Stylistic conformity is a sign of peer group identification and some tension with parents might be expected in this area. Research carried out by Michael Schofield on the sexual behaviour of young people confirms the overall picture of relative conformity on the part of adolescents. Most young people associate sexual intimacy with personal, emotional involvement and do not regard sexual pleasure as an end in itself. Although Schofield's evidence and that of others shows a tendency for more young people to be willing to consider sex before mar-

351

riage, this is in line with the growth of permissive values in society generally.

Another large scale social survey published by the National Opinion Polls (NOP) in 1978 confirms the broadly conformist pattern revealed by the NCB data. 66% of a sample of young people between the ages of 15 and 21 cited one or both parents as the most influential person, or persons, in their lives. Although listening to pop music was the most frequent non-energetic pastime for 85% of those questioned, pop musicians had fallen from favour compared with 1967, when NOP had conducted a similar survey.

There is no evidence that illicit drug taking, except drinking alcohol in pubs, is widespread among teenagers, although within specific sub-cultures certain drugs are sometimes used. It is arguable that this is a more intelligent, if still potentially dangerous, use of drugs than that of many adults who become, to varying degrees, dependent on medically prescribed drugs in order to 'cope with life'. In the nineteen seventies alcohol related offences, including drinking and driving offences, have increased among teenagers of both sexes; yet the flouting of the law prohibiting the drinking of alcohol in public places by those under 18 is widely tolerated by many sections of the community. It may be more useful to ask why this adult/teenage 'conspiracy' to ignore the law exists than simply to condemn those teenagers who drink while under age.

The suggestion that young people tend to be politically radical usually refers to the age group two or three years older than that surveyed by the National Children's Bureau – and even then it refers only to those within higher education. In fact, class and family correlate far more reliably with political identity than does youth, which provides no basis of prediction whatsoever.

Young people differ from adults to some extent in personal style and leisure pursuits, but tend to have similar attitudes of acceptance towards the family, marriage, and the social and political order. It is not surprising, then, as Smith points out in his book on adolescence, that most young people are ultimately successfully socialised into adulthood in the areas of work, family and citizenship. In a sense, Smith sees the problems that accompany adjustment to adult roles as adolescent 'teething pains'. This, is however, rather an *adult-biased* view. From the point of view of the young, perhaps an essential aspect of their experience is a sense of *powerlessness*. Weber has emphasised that power is a major aspect of stratification. Young people notably lack it – at school, at work and in the family. It is true that positions of power and authority exist within the 'alternative' world of the peer group, but this may not compensate for powerlessness in the 'real' adult-controlled world. Support for this interpretation comes from the National Children's Bureau survey. Far more resentment of school and teachers was expressed than of family and parents. 11% thought school was largely a waste of time; 15% said they never took school work seriously; 29% said they did not like school (a further 14% were unsure), and 54% found homework boring. Although some of this discontent may have been due to resentment at the raising of the school leaving age to 16, which this group of teenagers were the first to experience, a wider explanation is required.

The answer may lie in that being educated in modern society also requires being organised in terms of the allocation of group (academic and pastoral) membership, which classrooms a pupil is expected to be in, and the structuring of rest-break time. All this is done to achieve prescribed goals, notably examination success, which pupils may regard as necessary but often find irksome to pursue. In contemporary secondary schools, it is not so much resentment at traditional discipline but alienation at being a small part in predetermined and often impersonal organisation that may be the cause of pupil disillusionment and restlessness. Eagerness to earn money may be seen partly as a compensatory wish for independence.

Structural conflict between the young and adults occurs in other situations: with the police, for instance, who are required to enforce a large body of legislation restricting the activities of young people who, in the absence of family commitments, are precisely that group in society which has the leisure time to pursue many courses of behaviour, some of which are destrutive. The family, too, is sometimes the focus of generational power struggle even when, as in many homes, family relationships are basically happy and reassuring. Conflict over such matters as personal style, pocket money or when to be back after an evening out, can cause tension in the home which in some instances can become chronic. Particularly unpleasant atmospheres can be created when parents use the financial

353

dependency of a teenage son or daughter as a means of securing conformity.

Survey evidence on the attitudes of young people can be misleading. Frankly, one would not expect teenagers to have radically different attitudes from adults about politics, sex, and so on. But in terms of their everyday lives they are constantly in a position of subordination and, consequently, of low status. To explain the resulting friction as part of the syndrome of problematic adolescent behaviour smacks of psychological determinism and ignores real social structural tension and conflict.

In addition, the impact of various youth sub-cultures on the adult world should not be underestimated as a source of intergenerational tension. These sub-cultures, as presented by the media, are often seen by adults as representative of the young in general. Indeed, many young people not involved in them directly nonetheless pick up their fashions, language, attitudes and behaviour. Whereas youth often views such groups as the hippies, mods and punks with an eye to imitation, adults, especially parents, tend to regard them with strained tolerance, if not downright unease. Parents know that such sub-cultures provide models that may cause their children to stray from conformity into political protest, delinquency or bohemianism. In some ways, the straight and narrow road from youth to adulthood is the least interesting. It is not surprising, therefore, that a large minority occasionally deviate onto more adventurous and dangerous terrain. In doing so, some lose their way, but others acquire knowledge and experience that may be both personally valuable and of use to society.

Old Age, Population and Social Policy

We introduced the basic principles of demography in Chapter 7 (pp. 201–4). That discussion provides a useful basis for understanding the position of the old in society. So far in this century, there has been a steady increase in the number of old people, both absolutely, and as a percentage of the total population. In 1901, the number of men over 65, and women over 60, was 2.4 million, and in 1976 it was 9.6 million. The figures, as a percentage of the total population, are 6% and 17% respectively. For a variety of reasons, mainly relating to the birth rate at particular times, this trend is not likely to continue much beyond the end of the nineteen seventies – but it will not go substantially into reverse, either. As a result, the working population must expect to have to maintain, for the foreseeable future, a largely dependent retired population of upwards of 15% of the total population. Within this group, it is projected that the very old, those aged 75 or over, will grow as a total percentage of the retired. For instance, the number of 85 year olds is expected to increase by 50%, up until 1995, to 700,000.

It is not surprising that concern for the elderly tends to be intermingled with an uncomfortable awareness of cost: care of the very elderly is the most costly. Inevitably, the old have been allocated a growing proportion of public expenditure, despite the claims of other needy groups. Yet the standard of living of pensioners, as a group, has declined relative to the rest of the population. Nicholas Bosanquet gives impressive evidence of this in his book, *A Future for Old Age*. As real incomes rise, people tend to spend more on transport, services and leisure, and less on food, shelter and heating. More is also spent acquiring cars and certain other consumer durables. Apart from a minority of old people who do have quite a high standard of living, the expenditure patterns of the elderly do not reflect these changes. In fact, they are much as they were twenty years ago. A proportion of 43.4% of income is spent on food, housing and heat by all households, whereas married pensioner couples spend 52.8% of their income on these three necessities, and single women pensioners 60.3%. Bosanquet gives a detailed picture of the relative poverty suffered by the old which reflects this basic inequality.

The economic situation of the old suggests the low social status they have in our society. Yet, contrary to the still popular myth, the British are not flagrantly neglectful of their elderly. Surveys by Townsend and others show that the majority of them are actively involved with relatives and friends: even among the bedridden, over half are looked after outside hospitals. In fact, only 5% of all old people are in residential institutions – about the same figure as in the early 1900's. Arguably, however, this is not the most telling statistic. An Age Concern survey of old people outside institutions found 38% living with just a spouse and 28% living with others. The fact that over 70% do not live with their children reflects the dominance of the nuclear family. In practice, this means that

355

many old people are often lonely, even if they are seldom genuinely neglected.

Yet, in addition to relationships, and activity based on the family, old people, like other age groups, seem to prefer the company of their own generation. Many churches have old age pensioner clubs or other associations or activities, such as whist evenings, 'suitable' for old people. Most local political clubs and working men's clubs make similar provisions. Small groups of old people appear to meet frequently and informally at times of day when most of the rest of the population are at work. Old women are preponderant in these groups since women out-live men, on average, by about five years. In the post-75 year old population, the proportion of women to men is about 2 to 1. In addition, women are able to retire on a state pension at 60, whereas men work to 65. Amongst these facts is, perhaps, the basis of a case for an old men's liberation movement.

It is, perhaps, because modern societies value work so highly that the retired population suffers in status. Traditionally, a person's social identity has been derived mainly from his work and, implicitly, the old often seem to be regarded primarily as 'spent' workers. It is possible that if, as a result of unemployment, enforced leisure increases further, assumptions about the relationship between work and leisure and their relative value will change – and the status of worker, non-worker and past worker will change with them. These changes would, in turn, depend on the continuing substitution of machine labour for human labour, not only in the production of goods but also of services. Possibly, the working positions of the old and other generations will not be so different if more people experience periods of non-work, enjoy even shorter working weeks and generally perhaps come to regard work less and less as the centre of their lives.

It is debatable, however, whether even a change in cultural attitudes of this kind would mean that 'the wisdom of the aged' would be more appreciated in contemporary society. By contrast, the old of 30 or 40 years hence will all have experienced mass education and will have been brought up in a technological society. Margaret Mead's statement, that in a post-figurative or fast-changing, future-oriented society, the knowledge and skills of the old become quickly dated, may no longer apply so forcibly to the old of 2000. All this is speculative and, for the present, the immediate issue is to help the elderly to deal with their material and human problems without patronising them, or seeming to regard them as a 'problem' in themselves. Christopher Lasch has suggested that the tendency of America to regard old age as a 'problem' reflects the selfish *individualism* or *narcissism*, as he calls it, of American society. We can entertain the same possibility of Britain. Lasch argues that the decline of belief in an after life and the identification of youth with beauty and success makes us dread old age. We push the thought of it to the back of our minds, just as we push old people into the sidings of society. When we do confront it, we often try to explain it away. Some pretend old age is exclusively a social category when clearly it has its roots in biological decline; others try to arrest the biological process itself by pills, potions or jogging. The refusal to face old age is a refusal to come to terms with our own mortality. Lasch, a radical and severe critic of American culture, offers no easy solution to what amounts to a national neurosis about old age. He insists that nothing but a re-ordering of work, education, the family and other major institutions will bring the old out of their redundancy and isolation back into the mainstream of society. For this to happen, we would need to believe that it is valuable for the old to be involved with us, and we with them. This would have to include a willingness to face with them the problem that ultimately comes to all – our own deaths.

Guide to further reading and study

There is no shortage of literature in this area, but the topic cries out for a more imaginative and participatory approach than exclusive reliance on teaching notes and reading lists.

Changes in generational attitudes of youth can be effectively studied by means of records or cassettes. No present-day teacher who went through the sixties even half awake will need to be told that Bob Dylan had a lot to say about most things. His songs have a better chance than academic analysis of explaining to the present generation of young 'why it all mattered'. The records of a number of 'sub-Dylan' singer-writers, such as Phil Ochs, are worth chasing up, to illustrate the protest phase of the sixties youth movement. The psychedelic and counter-cultural influences of the late sixties are apparent in the recordings of The Grateful Dead, Jefferson Airplane (later Starship), The Beatles and The Rolling Stones. For those who have lost touch since, Simon Frith's *The Sociology of Rock* (Constable, 1978) will be helpful. For recent developments, students themselves should be encouraged to be their own 'experts'.

The media, particularly the press, provide an excellent 'free' resource for this topic. A content analysis of how a newspaper or newpapers (why not a comparative analysis?) present, say, young or old people over a period of time can be educational. The extent to which stereotypical images prevail is something to look for. Football 'hooliganism' is a topic that some students might want to study (over the years *'New Society'* has published several articles on it). An analysis of advertisements can also be revealing – particularly in terms of how styles and patterns of consumption may be manipulated.

All this may leave relatively little time for traditional academic study. For once, this may be no bad thing. There are several books, however, which will give more sophisticated perspective to what is learnt through the above approach, although it is hoped that this chapter will achieve the same end. Mike Brake's *The Sociology of Youth Culture and Youth Subcultures* (Routledge and Kegan Paul, 1980), is comprehensive but is more a teacher's than a student's book. *Resistance Through Rituals* (Hutchinson, 1976), edited by Stuart Hall and Tony Jefferson, provides an excellent, but by no means easy, collection of readings on youth subcultures, from a generally interactionist-cum-Marxist viewpoint, with gender aspects well covered. Paul Corrigan's *Schooling the Smash Street Kids* (Macmillan, 1979) is in a similar vein, though more simply written. Anthony Smith's *Adolescence* (Longman, 1970) gives a thorough presentation of functionalist analysis, although Smith himself is not a slave to this perspective. Finally, Margaret Mead's *Coming of Age in Samoa* and *Growing Up in New Guinea*, published in paperback (Pelican), are fascinating anthropological studies. Both in method and content they are the match of more recent work.

Past Questions

1 'To use the term 'sub-culture' is to exaggerate the different life-styles of adolescents, delinquent or otherwise.' Discuss. (London, 1975).

2 'There has been little evidence of students and other sections of youth developing a generation consciousness.' (D. Lynne in Meighan *et al*, *Perspectives on Society*). Discuss. (AEB, 1979).

3 Explain and discuss the argument that youth represents a class or stratum with interests of its own in opposition to those of adults. (AEB, 1980).

Section D **Work, Organisation and Alienation**

How to Use this Section

The pairing together of the themes Work, Leisure and Organisations is common enough not to require extended explanation. It is important, though to relate these matters to others of central concern. Above all, work and organisations are to be linked with stratification. Indeed, in an earlier draft of this book these two chapters were part of what was envisaged as a large central section on stratification: they are now separated out of convenience rather than theoretical conviction.

Whatever definition of class is accepted there is no doubt that work greatly affects it. Industrial conflict is a major dimension of class conflict and alienation at work is regarded by Marxists as a product of the capitalist division of labour. That there is a relationship between work and cultural and leisure activity will already be obvious to readers and this is examined in more detail in Chapter 14. It is only recently that organisational analysis has been rigorously related to stratification – yet to make this link is vital. Organisations are the practical, day-to-day context in which class and, for that matter, gender and racial inequality, are expressed and regenerated. Of course, organisations must be understood partly in terms of the useful functions they perform but they must also be seen as systems of power and potential conflict which benefit some more than others.

14 Work and Leisure

Themes and Definitions

This chapter covers three major themes. It deals with the quality of people's *experience of work*, whether satisfying or otherwise.
Secondly, it discusses *how working people organise themselves at work
to pursue, mainly, better pay and conditions*. Finally, it examines *the
relationship between work and non-work* and, in particular, how
automation may be revolutionising our ideas about the normal
and proper nature of that relationship. We look in detail at the
organisational structure of work in the following chapter. It is
enough to say here that the organisations people work in –
factories, offices and farms – are by far the most important
public institutions that affect their lives. Socialisation at work
has an immense influence on values, attitudes and behaviour.
   In addition to the above themes, we begin by again stressing

362

the relationship of work to class. Stratification (the major social divisions) was the central theme of Section C, and class is the major example of it. Work and class are inseparable: the one produces the other (though this statement does not do full justice to the Marxist definition of class).

The Experience of Work

Broadly, there are three possible responses to work: *alienation, neutrality* and *satisfaction*, and we study these below. Beyond mere satisfaction lies the prospect of *genuine fulfilment* at work and we also consider what this might mean.

1 Alienation

It may seem unduly negative to begin our analysis of the experience of work with alienation but most sociologists seem agreed that work is not a very fulfilling experience for the majority. Mary Weir's remarks are representative in this respect:

> For millions of people work is the least rewarding aspect of life. The hours spent at the work bench or in the office are more likely to be hours of endurance than enjoyment, when people do jobs which provide few opportunities to use their skills and abilities. A sense of personal satisfaction and achievement is more likely to be associated with their lives outside work than within it.

Perhaps the central problem of work in this century is not physical exploitation but the sense of personal uselessness and meaninglessness produced by routine, repetitive work.

Marx and Weber
Two accounts of alienation must be distinguished. First is that of Marx: *he considered that workers in capitalist society are alienated from work because they own neither what they produce nor the means by which they produce it.*

363

He is quite clear about this:

> Finally, the alienated character of work for the worker appears
> in the fact that it is not his work but work for someone else,
> that in work he does not belong to himself but to another
> person.

A further aspect of alienation is apparent in the quotation.
Because of the need to sell his labour, the worker loses his
independence in work; he becomes alienated from his own
activity and thus from himself. The contemporary Marxists,
Bowles and Gintis, have attempted to relate the nature of the
division of labour in capitalist society to the need of the ruling
class to maintain control over the workforce. By daily repeating
the same limited task(s), workers are prevented from understanding the whole of the process of production. What they do
not understand they can hardly aspire to control. Bowles and
Gintis do not, of course, regard the capitalist mode of production and the resultant alienation and mystification of the workforce as inevitable.

A second definition of alienation is widely used. To understand it we must first briefly describe what *bureaucracy* is.
*Bureaucracy is a form of organisational structure characterised by a vari-
ety of roles, some of which have more authority and status than others.*
Nearly all large-scale organisations in modern societies are
organised in this way and we are so familiar with this form of
organisational structure that we tend to think (wrongly) that it
is the only type possible (for alternatives see the next chapter).
This approach to understanding alienation rests on the work
of Weber, although he himself seldom used the term.
In this definition, *alienation is seen as caused by the effect on the
work situation of the bureaucratic division of labour.* Weber considered
that working particularly at the lower levels of bureaucracy,
such as in a factory or an office, is alienating for two basic
reasons. Firstly, doing the same thing over and over again, say,
filing invoices, is boring to most people. Secondly, bureaucratic
employees have little control over their work situation, and this
is unsatisfying. Woodward, Touraine and Blauner have applied
Weberian-type analysis specifically to industrial work and we
examine their conclusions below. Weber himself was probably
the first sociologist to appreciate that lack of identity, control
and a sense of meaninglessness, in short, alienation, can equally

affect the clerk, the typist, the soldier or anyone who fulfils a small role in a large, bureaucratic organisation. He stressed that alienation can occur as easily in state bureaucracies as in privately owned ones. Indeed, he anticipated that alienation would be a particular problem in socialist societies because of their inevitably (in his view) bureaucratic nature.

Despite the above major differences, Marx and Weber described the *psychological consequences of alienation* very similarly. The phrase 'feelings of alienation' refers to the same human experience for both. Writing of the industrial labourer, Marx says:

> He does not fulfil himself in his work but denies himself, has a feeling a misery, not of well-being, does not develop freely a physical and mental energy, but is physically exhausted and mentally debased.†

Etzioni summarises Weber's view and, usefully, links it with that of Marx:

> . . . the worker, soldier, and researcher – and by implication all employees of all organisations – are frustrated, unhappy . . . When asked, 'all said and done, how satisfied are you with your work?' about 80% of American blue-collar workers answered 'not satisfied'. Alienation is a concept that stands for this sentiment and the analysis of its source in Marxian-Weberian terms.

Despite their common understanding of what it means 'to feel alienated', Marx and Weber's difference over the origin of alienation is highly significant. Differing diagnoses lead to differing prescriptions. For Marx, the ultimate solution to inequality and alienation at work is to abolish capitalism and establish a communist system in which the means of production and what is produced are the common property. What is produced is then distributed on the basis of need, not purchasing power. This is a road down which Weber had no wish to travel – as we have noted, he anticipated that, whatever the theoretical ideal, communist societies would be very bureaucratic. He offered no solution to bureaucratic alienation, but regarded the march of 'rationality' as inevitable in all modern societies whether capitalist or socialist. He saw practical advantages in bureaucracy but feared its potential to alienate. Perhaps this accounts for the occasional pessimism and faint sense of regret for more romantic and less 'rational' times past in Weber's work.

Blauner, Touraine, Woodward and their critics

About the early nineteen sixties, a succession of books appeared which examined *the relationship between technology and work satisfaction*. Notable among these were works by Touraine, Blauner and Woodward. The findings they presented were very much in accord. The French sociologist, Touraine, summarised three recent historical stages in production technology and worker involvement: flexible machines/craftworkers; standard machines/unskilled workers; automation/superintendents. He associated the first and third of these with relatively higher levels of satisfaction. Blauner's typology is similar though slightly more complex.

Technology and Alienation

Type of Work →	Craft	Machine Minding ↓	Assembly Line ↓	Process ↓
Type of Production/ Product	No → Standarised Product	Mechanisation and standard- isation	Rationalisat- ion Standardised Product	Rationalisat- ion Uniform Product
Level of Skill →	High	Low	Low	Responsibility & understand- ing needed
Level of Alienation	→ Low	High	Highest	Low

Blauner's model is virtually self-explanatory. Machine-minding is usually required in *batch* production which is technically less efficient than assembly line *mass* production, but usually involves the worker in a slightly more varied way. Although the empirical basis of his work has been criticised as not very adequate, his conclusions find support not only from other sociologists but from common experience. Many artists have preferred the creativity and fulfilment of craft-work to the humdrum security and financial rewards of a safe but boring job. At the other end of the satisfaction-alienation spectrum is assembly line work. Of course, as we shall see, workers find ways of surviving and coping, but the phantoms of monotony, repetition and sheer tedium are never far away. In process work, by contrast, the worker is 'freed' from the machine. He oversees much, if not all, of the process of production and therefore has a closer involvement and identity with the whole. The brutal fracturing of the division of labour is partly healed.

Woodward's terms – unit, batch, mass and process production – cover the same area as Blauner's typology – craft, machine, assembly-line and process production. Like Blauner, she sees mechanisation as causing an increase in alienation until the onset of process production, which would show on a graph as the upside-down 'U curve' of alienation, takes a steep plunge. She also notes that in unit and process production, the dividing line between workers and technical and supervisory staff tends to be more blurred than in the case of batch and mass production. The situation was closer to what Burns and Stalker call the *organic model of organisation* involving more communication and democratic decision making. Thus, less alienation occurred through powerlessness.

Blauner's optimistic view of the effect of automation on work satisfaction has been sharply criticised by Duncan Gallie. He notes pointedly that the size of Blauner's sample of process workers was only 99, of which 78 were sampled in 1947 and 21 in 1961. Gallie himself, however, did not choose a sample survey method. Instead, he made four detailed case studies of workers in automated oil refineries, two in France and two in Britain. The point of this was to supply a *comparative cultural* frame of reference which he felt was missing in Blauner's work. In both cases Gallie found that *indifference*, not satisfaction, was the most frequently expressed attitude to work. On a whole range of other matters mainly affecting industrial relations, however, he found substantial differences between the French and British workers. He concludes that broad generalisations about workers' attitudes and about industrial relations, should consider variables relative to given cultures and not simply technological change. We can accept this basic point of Gallie's but it should be said that other work, including that of Wedderburn and Crompton, tends to verify Blauner, Woodward and Touraine's conclusion that automated labour is *in itself* relatively more satisfying than other forms of mechanised labour.

We earlier made an important distinction between Marx's and Weber's understanding of the major cause of alienation.

367

Blauner, Woodward and Touraine are closer to Weber in that they analyse alienation in terms of the technical organisation of production rather than in terms of the private ownership of the means of production. Blauner suggests four dimensions of alienation, which he contrasts with four non-alienative states:

Alienated States	Non-Alienative States
1 Powerlessness	Control
2 Meaninglessness	Purpose
3 Isolation	Social Integration
4 Self-estrangement	Self-involvement.

There is no need to explain the use of these terms at length. A little thought will make it clear why a fragmented, partial relationship to production tends to lead to alienation, and a fuller one to a more satisfied set of responses. 'Self-estrangement' can be regarded as the final stage of alienation in which the individual begins to lose self-respect and motivation. Blauner's list is a useful summary of what has already been said or implied about the psychology of alienation.

One point of Blauner's can usefully be taken further here. It is the contrasting conceptual pair of *self-estrangement* and *self-involvement*. The notion that work can alienate a person from himself is common to both Marxist and Weberian inspired literature on alienation. The idea presupposes that there does exist a self to be alienated from. The humanist psychologist, Abraham Maslow, has, as we have seen, attempted to define broadly what the fundamental, common properties of human nature are (see Chapter 6). He argues that whereas practically all jobs provide the means to satisfy basic social needs (food, shelter), fewer satisfy *egoistic* needs (status), and fewer still allow for relatively full *self-actualisation* (self-fulfilment, creativity). Others have elaborated on Maslow's simple scheme, but as a clear statement of the root social-psychological cause of alienation it is difficult to improve. *Alienation is the frustration of human potential as a result of unfulfilling work.*

2 Work Satisfaction and Neutrality: A Social Action Approach to Work Experience

Blauner's analysis of alienation has received criticism from

Goldthorpe and Lockwood in addition to that offered by Gallie. Goldthorpe and Lockwood's social action approach to this issue also leads them to reject the Marxist analysis of alienation. They point out that many of the workers in their sample did not have high expectations of work and were not therefore disappointed by their experience of it. They worked not for satisfaction, still less for fulfilment, but for money. Goldthorpe and Lockwood call this an *instrumental orientation* to work (the term orientation is preferred to attitude): it is used as a means or instrument to get something else – money. Their sample was mainly of young, married workers who, mindful of family commitments, may have been particularly 'money conscious', but other research bears out and extends this finding. Dubin shows that, for many industrial and white collar employees, work is not a major area of interest and self-expression. In a generally more representative sample of the male manual workforce than Goldthorpe and Lockwood's, Wedderburn and Crompton nevertheless confirm the latters' findings. The cumulative implication of these findings is that the workers are neither consciously alienated from, nor satisfied with, work but accept it *neutrally* as a means to an end. They work largely to finance their family and leisure life which does have personal meaning to them.

Another way of explaining this is to distinguish between *intrinsic* and *extrinsic* orientations to work. A person who works for intrinsic reasons does so for the satisfaction the job gives. Such people include craftsmen or vocationally motivated nurses. In this context, extrinsic means the same as instrumental. Most people appear to work for predominantly extrinsic reasons, and to have low expectations of what the job offers in itself. If dissatisfaction is the difference between expectation and experience, then, most are not dissatisfied, because they expect little in the first place. Thus, surveys suggest that women in routine office work are more satisfied than men doing work of a similar level of skill. A possible reason for this is that work is less of a central life interest for them than for men and so they are more easily 'satisfied' with it.

We seem, then, to have two almost contradictory perspectives on work experience: on the one hand, certain kinds of work are considered alienating and, on the other, the people who do these kinds of work may regard them as neutral but not alienating experience. We can easily reconcile the two views if we extend our understanding of alienation. Alienation is not just a description of *subjective* (personally experienced) feelings of many workers; it is also a more *objective* (more widely generalisable) statement about the waste of human potential that certain kinds of routine work, both manual and white collar, involve. In this sense, alienation is about lack of fulfilment, not just actual feelings of misery. It is quite possible to have many unfulfilled capacities without knowing it. Such a grossly unfulfilled person is alienated from his or her true potential. Marx argued that fulfilment at work is generally possible in socialist, but not in capitalist society. Weber thought fulfilment at work for the majority was incompatible with the extreme division of labour of large scale organisation, whether in capitalist or socialist societies. We need to look at the concept of fulfilment in greater detail because its use does imply the value judgement that some kinds of activity, including varieties of work, are more or less better (in the sense of more fulfilling) than others.

3 Fulfilment in Work

Abraham Maslow's theory of human needs can be usefully applied to the concept of fulfilment at work. Nearly everybody will expect to meet their basic needs of food and shelter through work, and most, too, will hope for some pleasant social interaction while at work. Fewer will acquire substantial esteem or prestige for the work they do though only the most humble will be outside the positive status hierarchy altogether. Only a tiny minority achieve self-actualisation or self-fulfilment through work. Very few are allowed to perform at a level of personal excellence that brings their best creative skills and abilities into play. Examples of some who can are people at the very top of our occupational elites, such as managing directors of large companies, star sportsmen and entertainers, and creative academics. Many others are perhaps haunted by what Gouldner calls 'the unemployed self' – a sense of potential under-developed and a life wasted in senseless work.

We have noted that Marx did not consider fulfilling, non-alienating work to be generally possible in capitalist society. Some Marxists regard with suspicion the limited industrial participation or *power-sharing* schemes involving workers, which have been adopted in Germany and Sweden, but others consider them a step on the road to a more socialist and less alienating society. Those who, unlike Marx, see alienation primarily as the result of technological and/or organisational factors, naturally look for solutions within these terms (we exclude of course, those who ignore the problem or believe it to be insoluble). We examine a variety of attempts to achieve relatively more 'human' systems of organisation and technology both later in this chapter (pp. 391-4) and Chapter 15 (pp. 410-3).

Informal Attempts to Deal with Alienation: An Interactionist Perspective

Reform and revolution aside, those who have to work in boring jobs are faced with the day-to-day need of 'getting by'. Here are some of the ways they use to do so.

The interactionist concept of *managing* self and others provides a helpful perspective on the many people who 'survive' monotony at work (and school). Apart from snatched conversational exchanges, day-dreaming is perhaps the most universal 'strategy', as Jason Ditton remarks in his participant study of work in a factory bakery:

> Although the workers looked as if they were doing the work automatically, one man, who had worked for twelve hours a day for two years in the 'dough' . . . pointed out that, underneath this, the mind never stops. Though giving the impression of working without thinking, he said that 'you think of a hundred subjects a day' . . .

Doubtless his 'hundred subjects a day' cover a similar range of musings as those in which you and I indulge.

Next to 'escaping into your head', the most common way of dealing with stress and monotony is probably by humour – 'having a laff'. In his authentic description of nineteen fifties working class life in Nottingham, *Saturday Night and Sunday Morning*, Alan Sillitoe gives us more than a few examples of 'laffs' through the actions of the novel's anti-hero, Arthur. Here is one:

> At a piecework rate of four-and-six a hundred you could make your money if you knocked-up fourteen hundred a day – possible without grabbing too much – and if you went all out for a

thousand in the morning you could dawdle through the afternoon and lark about with the women and talk to your mates now and again. Such leisure often brought him near to trouble, for some weeks ago he stunned a mouse – that the overfed factory cats had missed – and laid it beneath a woman's drill, and Robboe the gaffer ran out of his office when he heard her screaming blue-murder, thinking that some bloody silly woman had gone and got her hair caught in a belt (big notices said that women must wear hair-nets, but who could tell with women?) and Robboe was glad that it was nothing more than a dead mouse she was kicking up such a fuss about. But he paced up and down the gangways asking who was responsible for the stunned mouse, and when he came to Arthur, who denied having anything to do with it, he said: 'I'll bet you did it, you young bogger!' 'Me, Mr. Robboe?' Arthur said, the picture of innocence, standing up tall with offended pride. 'I've got so much work to do I can't move from my lathe'.

A tough sense of the ridiculous is at the heart of traditional working class life. In part, it is a way of coping with the absurdity and tyranny of work. We discussed working class humour and other cultural attitudes earlier (Chapter 9).

The ultimate escape at work is going to sleep. Quite often, night-shift workers are 'allowed' an informal 'kip' after they have finished their quota, but the British Leyland worker who was dismissed after bringing a bed to work was obviously considered to be taking things too much for granted. Apart from such arrangements, many workers have some recollection of occasionally going to sleep while working, either through monotony or fatigue, just as most students do.

An experienced foreman or sympathetic floor manager will not attempt to stop harmless attempts by workers to 'kill time' or, at least, make it pass more quickly. He may even extend a tea-break or stop to chat with an obviously tired, sick or stressed worker when the occasion seems to demand it.

All the daydreams, 'laffs', 'kips', and 'tea and sympathy', however, cannot make fundamentally boring work interesting. As we shall see, alienation is arguably the underlying cause of much industrial conflict and discontent as well as the milder, improvised 'escape attempts' described above.

The real escape, though, is *leisure* time. It is then that workers, starved of meaning and expression at work, can hope to 'do their own thing'. If, to use C. Wright Mills' image, people sell little pieces of themselves for money during week-days, they attempt to reclaim themselves in the evenings and at weekends with the coin of fun. Mills' tart irony rightly suggests that the problems of personal freedom, pleasure and leisure are more complicated than this simple division of time into 'work and fun' suggests. We examine these issues after the following section on industrial interest groups and conflict.

Industrial Interest Groups and Conflict

Industrial interest groups are formal organisations concerned with the interests of their members. There are two broad types, *employers' associations* and, for employees, *trade unions* and *professional associations.* In practice, employees make much more use of formal interest group organisations than employers. This is partly because employers are supposed to be in competition with each other and, indeed, the law discourages co-operation that might restrain trade or raise prices artificially. It is also because it is often easier and more convenient for employers to consult informally and in private. Both employers and trade unions are represented by national bodies, the Confederation of British Industry (CBI) and Trades Union Congress (TUC) respectively.

The Growth of Unionism

While the total number of union members has grown spectacularly since the last war, from 7.83 million to 11.51 million, the number of unions has declined from 186 unions affiliated to the TUC in 1951, to 112 in 1980. The net result has been the development of much bigger and, generally, stronger unions. As Jenkins and Sherman point out this trend to 'concentration and enlargement' matches the same process in industry itself.

The traditional and still the main purpose of trade unions is to protect and improve the pay and working conditions of their members. Recently, unions have frequently brought issues of job security, participation in management and even environmental and social policy issues within their range of concern. Nationally, the TUC is a powerful pressure group on major matters of economic and social policy. It was the trade unionist, Jack Jones, who thought up 'the social contract', on the basis of which the Labour government and unions attempted to co-operate for over two years. At the local level, it is the increase in the influence and power of shop stewards, who are the immediate representatives of unionised workers, that has been the striking development in the post-war period. Shop stewards have often taken the immediate responsibility for taking industrial action, although their decisions are usually ratified by national leadership. Undoubtedly, there is some disagreement between those who support the 'shop steward movement' as being both democratic and sensitive to the needs of local unionists, and those who would prefer national union leaders to have more power over union members as they do in Sweden and Germany. This tension remains unresolved.

White Collar Unionism: Reasons for Growth

The growth in the unionisation of non-manual employees is the major explanation of the recent increase in union membership. In 1967 there were 2.5 million non-manual workers in TUC affiliated unions. In 1977. there were over 4.6 million non-manual members (this includes a minority in basically manual worker unions). This increase exaggerates the extent of recent white collar unionisation as several non-manual workers unions had sizeable membership before affiliating to the TUC in the late sixties or seventies. Of the white collar unions, the National Association of Local Government Officers (NALGO) is the fourth largest union in the country (709,000 members). The teachers' unions, including polytechnic and university teachers, and the Civil Service unions, both have well over half a million members. In all, the percentage of white collar membership of the TUC was 38% in 1977, and has been estimated at a possible 50% in 1985.

We now examine the reasons for the increase in white collar unionism. These are: the increasing concentration of employees in large buildings such as office blocks; the willingness of major employers to recognise unions; government (mainly Labour) promotion of union recognition; and, most importantly, the desire to improve wages and other conditions of work. Writing before the rapid increase of the nineteen seventies, George Bain emphasised the first three factors at the expense of the fourth.

As most of the increase in white collar union membership has occurred in the public sector we would expect these three factors to be strongly apparent there. Both before and since Bain wrote, public sector employment has been becoming more concentrated and bureaucratised. Interestingly, Bain suggests that, as a result, white collar workers have been increasingly bound by rules made by remote management and that, in order to claw back control over their work situation, they join unions and indulge in collective bargaining. In explaining white collar unionisation, Bain puts the desire to be able to control their work situation more effectively ahead of the wish to obtain economic benefits. The evidence of the late nineteen seventies contradicts this assessment. Several white collar unions took industrial action in pursuit of (relatively) high wage claims during that period. In particular, Civil Service unions pursued a long and effective strategy of industrial action in 1979.

Writing almost a decade later than Bain, Jenkins and Sherman agree with his second point – that recognition of unions by employers is central in providing the stable and legitimate conditions in which they can develop. Above all, has been the ready acceptance of the *closed shop* by senior management. *A closed shop means that union membership is made compulsory for all employees*. Where it exists, it necessarily increases union membership. By 1979, over 65% of white collar workers belonged to closed shops (not much less than the percentage for manual workers). It may seem odd that management should actively promote union power, but there are good reasons for this. The closed shop brings stability and representativeness to collective bargaining. Simply, management knows who it is dealing with and that management-union agreements can usually be 'sold' to workers by union representatives. There are now 3,800 full-time shop stewards (representatives of the unions in places of work), paid by employers – more than full time trade union officials (about 3,000). Companies with closed shops normally pay individual union dues to the union before the worker receives his wages.

We now turn to the third factor accounting for the growth of white collar unionism. In addition to Bain's research, study at the Industrial Relations Research Unit at Warwick University further confirms that government policy has tended to stimulate union growth. The Trade Union and Labour Relations Acts of

1974 and 1975 provided statutory assistance to unions in securing recognition and collective bargaining rights. Partly as a result, a big growth in the closed shop took place in 1976–1977, though the trend was, in any case, well established.

The fourth factor, the economic, seems the most important. Whatever government and employers do, a white collar employee will not join a trade union unless he or she sees it to be in his own material interest to do so. White collar employees expect the same kind of services out of unions as do manual workers. Jenkins and Sherman picturesquely refer to the following as 'the recruiting sergeants': reduced pay differentials (the difference between high and low paid jobs), compared to manual workers; redundancies and the effects of inflation on the purchasing power of wages, in addition to the facts already mentioned.

Simply because most people join unions for economic reasons does not mean that all unions, whether manual or white collar, will behave entirely similarly, or that all their members are suddenly 'working class'. David Lockwood, using Weber's concepts, has pointed out that the *work situation* (authority, independence) *market situation* (qualifications, experience) and *subjective* class consciousness of white collar workers vary enormously. As the lower level white collar employee finds work increasingly bureaucratised, and as he becomes more remote from employers and management, he will define his own interests as distinct from theirs and look to his union to defend them. It may be that as the status rewards for white collar work diminish, the monetary and other material rewards associated with such employment will come to seem still more important. Kenneth Roberts suggests that white collar unionism means not that the white collar group are joining the working class, but that they are trying to stay ahead of it. We have already seen that instrumental collectivism is not in itself a sound basis for class solidarity (Chapter 9). Indeed, it could be regarded as institutionalised selfishness. At a higher level, although some staff associations involving more senior white collar staff adopt union membership, they may still perceive a harmony of interest between themselves and their employer. Such attitudes are perhaps especially strong in the private sector. Rosemary Crompton, from a specifically Marxist perspective, has stressed the variety of white collar unions and

376

the motives of their members. In her view, this reflects the ambiguous class position of many white collar workers. They are neither productive workers nor do they control the means of production and profit. They stand between labour and capital and their behaviour at work reflects this ambiguous position.

The Professions

The expansion of professions is a further feature of the growth of the service sector characteristic of modern societies. In addition to managers and administrators, professionals make up a large proportion of what Halsey refers to as the 'service class'. Higher professionals include lawyers, scientists, engineers, doctors and dentists. Their market position is significantly stronger than that of lower professionals such as teachers, social workers and nurses and this shows in the much higher salaries they tend to command. Most lower professionals work for the government. Among higher professionals, private practice is becoming more rare and employment in the service of industry or the government increasingly common. This change in the market position of professionals has increased the possibility of conflict with other groups.

Until quite recently, sociological writings on the professions tended to assume both their high social status and that the contribution or 'service' of professionals to the community was qualitatively superior to that of 'lower' status workers. Marxists are an exception to this, as they have always placed the highest value on manual labour. Current analysis of the professions is much more inclined to use the concept of conflict in interpreting their relationship to society. This is apparent in two main ways. First, no necessary 'community of interest' is assumed between client and professional. On the contrary, their interests tend to be seen to be in *structural conflict*, regardless of the 'goodwill' of individual professionals. Secondly, because most professionals are now *paid employees*, their relationship to their employers is also regarded as a potential source of conflict similar to that experienced by other employees. Both are part of the general process by which work has become increasingly bureaucratised.

The Functionalist Approach and 'Trait' Analysis Approach

The work of functionalists such as Bernard Barber and Talcott Parsons, typifies traditional sociological analysis of the professions. Quite simply, this perspective sees the professions as fulfilling useful social functions. They provide necessary medical, legal, architectural or religious advice and service based on specialised knowledge and competence. The key attribute of professions is considered to be a primary commitment to community rather than self-interest. Terence Johnson distinguishes between functionalist analysis of professions and 'trait' analysis though the two approaches are highly compatible. *'Trait' analysis is based on an attempt to list the basic characteristics of professions.* 'Trait' analysis has proved to be something of a blind alley. On the basis of his own survey of the relevant literature, Millerson points out that no two authorities agree precisely on what the basic traits of a profession are. The following, however, are frequently mentioned: professional authority (over the 'layman'); the sanction by the community of the power and privilege of professionals; the confidential nature of the professional client relationship; a code of ethics (rules) regulating the profession; a theory of knowledge underlying the practice of the profession (such as medical research/theory); and the existence of a professional culture. A professional culture involves broad consensus about how to behave as a professional, and is said to be passed on to new recruits. Even today, barristers can still participate in a quite ritualised common culture.

The 'trait' approach is so uncritical of official professional ideology (the views professionals hold of themselves) that it is almost 'pre-sociological'. Client response is assumed automatically to 'fit in' with the expert's view and the possibility of conflict between professionals and other individuals and groups is unexplored. The functionalist approach is hardly more sophisticated. Johnson charges that they do not examine the historical development of professions and so fail to appreciate that professional practice is deeply involved with power relations in society, including those based mainly on money. Consistently enough, he illustrates his argument by reference to various historical stages in the development of professions, and, in particular, stresses changes in the professional-client relationship. In the sixteenth and seventeenth centuries, professionals were typically answerable to wealthy patrons. The professional's freedom was limited by this dependence and he certainly did not serve the majority of the community. Industrialisation changed the status of the professions. Their members and independence increased. The technical expertise of, for instance, engineers and specialist lawyers, was formidable and professionals achieved new status and power. Leading professions were able to persuade the general public of their own ideology – their own assessment of their skill and importance. It was at this time that professions developed into self-regulating organisations which were able to control their specialist areas of work, including the standard of entry to them. Control of entry enabled them to regulate the supply and therefore the price of professional services. Obviously, this was a very desirable position for professionals to be in. Medieval craftsmen similarly attempted to regulate occupational entry and the supply and price of services. No doubt members of most occupations would wish to do the same. The difference between professions and other occupations is that they have succeeded in convincing the public of their special skills and importance and of their need for corresponding privileges, whereas others have not.

A Power-Conflict Analysis of Professions

In contemporary society the traditional high status and autonomy (freedom) of professionals is less taken for granted, though they remain a relatively wealthy and privileged group. Modern professions can be usefully understood in terms of power-conflict. By analysing their position in the market and in the work place, we can get a better idea of their power and prestige relative to other groups. We consider professions in relation to three centres of power and control: central and local government, the client, and other colleagues. These centres of control apply somewhat differently to different professions.

a GOVERNMENT CONTROL During the course of the twentieth century, the government has become a massive employer of professional as well as lower white collar and manual employees. Government has not only become the paymaster of the great majority of 'semi-professionals' such as teachers, social workers and nurses, but also of doctors, dentists and various other specialist professionals. To a greater or lesser extent this has

379

caused 'a crisis of identity' within these areas. The issue has been whether to respond to the power of government by organising as a union, or whether to maintain a more traditional professional image, even if this involves a less robust approach to industrial bargaining. The various industrial interest groups representing teachers illustrate the dilemma. Some, like the NUT, call themselves unions, and others, like the Assistant Masters Association, prefer the more professional sounding term Association – a preference that does indicate a more traditional and conservative attitude to their occupation, and industrial bargaining. Nevertheless, like other major groups employed by government, professionals have generally opted to use some of the means employed by unions to protect and promote the interests of their members even if they have not adopted the title of union. The British Medical Association is a good example.

As a result of the nationalisation of the health service most doctors and dentists became employees of the government. Both the British Medical Association and the British Dental Association have increasingly adopted the approach of trade unions in defending the pay and conditions of their members whilst still attempting to retain a professional ethos. The BMA ultimately altered its rules so that it could legitimately act as a trade union (even though it had actually been doing so for many years). On the other hand, professional aloofness was maintained by not affiliating the association to the TUC. The militancy of some junior doctors, which has included demonstrations, strikes and other forms of industrial action, suggests that the future of the BMA will be no less militant. Even so, it will continue to fulfil the traditional functions of a professional association as it has done since it was founded in 1851. This 'dual functioning' as both a professional association and as a trade union is not unique to the BMA. A number of other small professional associations, including the Council of Engineering Institutions, also operate in this way. This is a pattern that authors and trade union activists, Clive Jenkins and Barrie Sherman, dislike. They would prefer professional associations exclusively to carry out their traditional functions and, in addition, to leave their members to join large, national unions which would look after their interests as paid employees. The complex historical heritage, however, makes the achievement of so tidy a solution unlikely in the near future.

b CLIENT CONTROL It is helpful to divide client control of professionals into two categories depending on whom they work for: *control exercised by large scale organisations*, whether public or private, which employ professionals and *control exercised by the individual client largely through choice*. We will take the first type of control to begin with, as it closely relates to our previous discussion. Many professionals, including accountants, lawyers, engineers and scientists, are now directly employed by business corporations and so are also part of the new salariat. In organisational terms, this is often very similar to being employed by the state. The professional in this situation loses the freedom associated with independent practice and, usually, the opportunity to employ a broad range of expertise. He tends to do highly specialised work (in a sub-branch of law or accountancy) and, although his professional judgement is usually accepted within a limited area, has to submit to the overall authority of management. Several more recent commentators have rightly observed that Weber overlooked the potential for conflict between professional experts and management – whether in the public or private sector. In general, professionals are better qualified than management but have less authority within organisations. As Burns and Stalker point out, some managers deal with this situation by adopting more flexible, open-ended and democratic modes of decision-making. They use the term 'organic' to describe this tendency. A large-scale empirical study of the same issue led Peter Blau to conclude that this is, indeed, often the approach taken by management who have well qualified professionals on their staff. As Etzioni points out, however, professional and management functions are different, and the possiblity of conflict cannot be entirely removed. In ideal-type terms, professionals make recommendations on the basis of what seems 'right' by professional principles, whereas managers look for solutions that 'work' in terms of the rules and goals of the organisation. Stewart Clegg and David Dunkerly have commented interestingly on this issue and suggest that in practice, organisational and technical development have reduced the authority of professionals anyway:

> Increasing standardisation has taken place in the legal and accounting professions. The popularity of 'do-it-yourself' house

purchase and divorce is evidence of such routinisation; accountancy, largely through the effects of computers, has become more and more codified, standardised and routinised. In other words, not only clerical work but professional activities as well appear to be subject to an increasing division of labour characterised by routinisation.

Marxist Herbert Gintis, goes further and suggests that highly fragmented (specialised) and, therefore, alienated labour is as much a characteristic of bureaucracy as of industry. He adds that the division of labour in a hierarchical way ultimately favours those at the very top. These are not professionals, nor even managers, but members of the capitalist class.

It is not surprising that in the face of the above trends, many professionals 'hang onto' traditional notions of their status and power. The logical alternative might simply be to accept that they are merely very well paid workers. Most Marxists would argue that this is, indeed, so. From an action perspective it is easy to see that this ambiguity in the work situation of the salaried professional can produce a real personal dilemma. A corporate lawyer may be required to pursue a case by his employer-client which in his professional, personal and even moral opinion is a waste of time. But 'he who pays the piper calls the tune' – professional judgement can be overridden by top management. A teacher who is genuinely committed to his subject and education 'for its own sake' may find that 'exam pressure' forces him to teach in a way he dislikes. 'Exam pressure' is a term that can cover active control from the hierarchy and pupils in his own institution and, more remotely, parental, community and governmental opinion.

We now turn to the relationship of professionals to individual clients. If we except semi-professionals, the majority of professionals are still not employed by large institutions although a growing number are. In any case, the relationship between the professional and individual client continues to be of great importance. A frequently debated issue is the extent to which the professional can use his specialist knowledge to manipulate or 'mystify' the client (perhaps to 'get rid' of him quickly, avoid questions, or simply hide his own ignorance), and whether he should be prevented from doing so. We need to clarify this with an example. Some commentators feel that many doctors prescribe drug treatments too easily. This is felt to be particularly true in respect of psychological 'ailments' including, for instance, depression. The result is that, without proper counselling the client may think of the drug as a 'cure' rather than merely a treatment of symptoms. There is also the possibility of dependency. The real cause of depression is likely to be personal or social in origin and is likely to go undiscussed. To this extent the client's need is not met. Those who make these criticisms offer a number of related solutions, all of which involve the education of the public. If the client is to be recommended drug treatment, then he or she should be told more about what the drug is, how it works, and what its limits are. In addition, he or she should be told what positive steps can be taken to deal with the problem by means of, say, diet, exercise, or the handling of his personal and work relations. Given the limited time of doctors, the educational system and the media might be expected to play a role in this. Thus a culture in which people cared for their own health rather than relied on 'the expert' could further develop. The 'jogging' movement, and greater awareness of diet, suggest that this is already beginning to happen

Ivan Illich is one of the leading critics of 'professionalised knowledge'. He considers that often professional ideology functions primarily in the interests of professionals despite its supposed concern with standards and quality of service. He reacts against the wrapping up of knowledge in parcels labelled 'expert' because this produces a passive and even timid attitude to learning and makes the client unnecessarily dependent on the professional. He believes in as much open access to information as possible whether it be about medicine, the law or whatever. Underlying his suggestions is a belief that education, formal and informal, should be an active process in which the teacher or expert advises rather than dictates, participates rather than controls.

c PROFESSIONAL CONTROL OF PROFESSIONALS The third form of control, that of professionals over themselves continues to be important even though today it is often 'major' clients or employers who wield decisive power over the professional's life. Professional associations continue to regulate entry and, though they may often mean little in an everyday sense to their members, they can be a source of advice, support or, sometimes,

383

censure, if things go wrong. They can also be a basis of leisure activity. Finally, because of the hierarchically organised division of labour, professionals themselves are frequently organised hierarchically in given organisations. A specialist surgeon or senior consultant is very much 'the boss' of 'his team' of junior doctors, various medical auxiliaries and nurses. In turn, these also occupy varying positions in the hierarchy. Thus, differential power and control manifests itself in the professional's working situation.

Recent analysis suggests that for the public to hold professionals in awe serves only to perpetuate the myth that their work is incomprehensible to most and deserves unquestioning respect. This sense of mystery serves as an ideological cloak beneath which professionals can pursue their own interests which need not coincide with those of others. Increasingly, clients are bringing professionals to account on the same practical basis as other occupations, that is, in terms of the quality of their work. Nevertheless, professionals do remain relatively wealthy and privileged partly because there is an objective basis to their claims to be especially competent in difficult skills. As far as professional power is concerned, we have noted several developments which challenge, even if they do not undermine, it.

Industrial Conflict

There are numerous forms of industrial conflict, of varying degrees of severity. The most important is the *strike*. Associated with striking is picketing – trying, within the limits of law, to persuade other workers to join a strike. Another form of action often used as an alternative to the strike weapon in industrial conflict is 'working to rule'. The sit-in involves the occupation or take-over of a factory by workers and is often a reaction to large-scale redundancies or closure. It usually occurs as a last resort but sometimes leads to a positive attempt by the workers to save the factory themselves.

Another form of conflict, industrial sabotage, can occur for a variety of reasons, from personal boredom or malice to opposition to management policies or even the capitalist system in general. Minor acts of sabotage sometimes have a comical aspect which helps to release tedium and frustration, as when a distinguished foreign client was delivered a new Mercedes complete with six coca-cola bottles clanking deep within its bonnet. Huw Beynon tells of the response of a line worker, who was prone to absenteeism, to the question of what it felt like to come into work on a fine, bright Monday morning. The answer was that he didn't know! The implication is, of course, that the worker found better things to do than work on fine, bright Monday mornings. Certainly, children 'bunk off' school because they find it 'boring' and 'a drag'. (see Chapter 5). Presumably some of 'the dads of the lads' indulge in similar practices for much the same reasons. Beynon also gives a number of examples of industrial sabotage which contain a serious message to perhaps otherwise inattentive management. Thus, workers who felt they were undermined or expected to work too quickly sometimes sabotaged cars to make their objection known. As Taylor and Walton imply, sabotage is a somewhat primitive method of communication, and it has been largely, though not entirely, superseded by trade union negotiation. Absenteeism is a form of escapism or even of rejection, rather than conflict. It mostly occurs in industries which take a severe physical and mental toll.

The damage that strikes do or do not do to the economy of Britain is a matter of recurrent controversy in this country. This often bitter debate is frequently conducted with only scant attention to relevant facts. The diagram below presents some data on strikes which we can use as a basis of our own discussion.

The graph shows that the general level of strike activity in the nineteen seventies was much higher than in any period since the last war. Between the wars only the short period between 1919–22 produced a higher average level. It is the *length* not the *number* of strikes that has increased.

Compared with other industrialised western societies, however, Britain's recent strike record is *moderate* rather than exceptional. Between 1968–77 the average number of working days lost in Britain was 452 per 1000 workers, compared with 1187 per 1000 in Australia, 1893 in Canada and 1500 in the United States. Some of Britain's more immediate competitors did lose markedly less: West Germany, 24; Sweden, 18 and Holland, 36. Italy, one of Europe's weaker economies, is an exception (1433 days lost per 1000 workers). Overall, Britain is about half way down the international strike table.

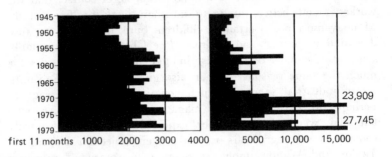

Number of Strikes (1945–1979)   **Days Lost in Strikes (1945–1979)**

Strikes (all industries and services)   aggregate number of working days lost
numbers of stoppages beginning in year   in stoppages in progress in year (000's)

Source: *New Society,* 10 January, 1980, p. 66.

Industrial Conflict: Factors Associated with Strikes

The Economic Motive

The most commonly stated motive for striking is *to improve pay* though we must immediately point out that research frequently demonstrates important non-economic underlying causes. Between 1965–74, 56.1% of disputes and over 80% of working days lost were the result of conflicts over pay. Most of the strikes during the so-called 'winter of discontent' of 1978–79 were mainly about pay, and were all the more intense as a result of the previous period of voluntary wage restraint. Between 1965–74, 80% of stoppages were about economic issues, and these involved 90% of the days lost. Even the steelworkers strike of 1980 was superficially about pay; relatively little was said about the British Steel Corporation's plan to reduce its workforce by approximately a third over a period of years – a strategy that might have been expected to result in industrial

386

action. It may be that in times of high inflation unions feel they have to concentrate on pay in order to maintain, if not improve, the real value of wages. Sometimes strikes also concern working conditions or other matters affecting workers' welfare. The miners threatened to strike in early 1977 if the National Coal Board refused to implement early retirement plans for them.

Why has the importance of the economic motive apparently increased? Firstly, because of the growth in unionisation, people are better organised to take industrial action, including striking, than ever before. Secondly, rampant inflation has provided a persistent motive, or, at least, a justification, for strikes. Finally, there seems to have been a growth in consumer values the satisfaction of which requires high wages.

Underlying Motives (Non-economic): Control and Independence

The rather quantitative approach to explaining strikes in the previous section should not be taken entirely at face value. There is evidence that even though pay claims are the immediate cause of most strikes, other factors operate at a less obvious level. Here we cite two case studies to illustrate the point. First, is Alvin Gouldner's *Wildcat Strike: A Study of Worker-Management Relationship*. He finds that a strike for higher wages is just one event in a long chain of conflict between workers and management. The conflict stemmed from a change in management at the plant. Traditionally, worker-management relations were informal, friendly and based on trust. The new manager, an outsider, introduced new machinery and attempted to 'rationalise' the administration of the plant. This limited the independence and offended the pride of the workers, particularly the miners. The relationship between workers and management was redefined in terms of conflicting interests, rather than a sense of mutual understanding and interest. It was in this context that the wildcat strike 'for higher wages' occurred, but to see it simply in terms of money would be sociologically unsubtle.

Lane and Roberts make a still more fundamental point than Gouldner about strikes. In their own case study of a strike at Pilkington's glassworks, they found that a strike occurred at the end of a period of quite good industrial relations in which most workers expressed no major grievances about pay or other matters. A strike also occurred in similar circumstances at the Vauxhall car assembly-line plant at Luton shortly after Goldthorpe and Lockwood completed their 'affluent worker' study. Lane and Roberts conclude that *strikes should be regarded as 'normal', in the sense that they are an accepted 'weapon' in the bargaining process between management and labour.* Their use in the context of industrial bargaining is not exceptional and usually requires no special explanation.

The desire of workers for some control and independence of their work situation and the need for effective power in industrial bargaining falls far short of a wish to 'take over' industry. Political motives of this kind are very rarely behind strikes although before the first world war they helped to inspire the syndicalist movement. Syndicalists took the view that revolution could best be achieved by a general strike followed by a seizure of power by the workers. More recently, politically motivated strikes have been rare. As Turner says, where an industrial conflict occurs, left wing activists may often take a lead in organising the workers but their ability to 'stir up' conflict that does not already exist seems marginal.

Structural Conflict between Capital and Labour

The previous points assume a certain 'in-built' conflict between capital and labour. Marxists stress this conflict particularly strongly. Hyman makes the general point:

> the confrontation within the workplace of two bases of control provides a constant source of instability and conflict.

Given that owners and management, on the one hand, and the labour force, on the other, want as large a share as possible of the profit of their mutual toil, disagreement and friction is virtually inevitable. Even the most optimistic personnel manager would hardly expect to do more than 'regulate' it in the context of modern large-scale industry. It is because they, too, see a day-to-day conflict of interest between capital and labour, that Lane and Roberts claim that strikes should be seen as 'normal' rather than labelled a 'problem' (once the public is presented with a 'problem' the next stage is often to look for the 'culprit' – not the most fruitful approach in industrial relations).

Marxists see a final solution to class conflict in industry only in the introduction of a socialist society. Others see a functional need to make the capitalist system operate more effectively. Thus, human relations theorists, Scott and Homans, argue that better communications between management and workers – for instance, through trained personnel managers – can provide a more constructive atmosphere and reduce disruption. Marxists consider this approach to be biased towards management and manipulative of workers. At worst it passes off deep problems of structural conflict and exploitation as personal or even psychological difficulties.

Causes Related to Specific Industries

So far, we have talked about the general causes of strikes. The extent to which strikes occur, however, varies between industries and between societies. We now attempt to account for these variations. We start by examining the strike record of different industries. James Cronin finds that highly unionised workers in industries crucial to the national economy, which tend to use incentive schemes to increase production, and which are subject to economic fluctuation, tend to be prone to strike. A recent study showed that, on average, miners, dockers, car workers, shipbuilders and iron and steel workers accounted for a quarter of strikes and a third of working days lost, even though they only cover about 6% of employees. With the possible exception of mining, these industries have tended to fluctuate within a spiral of decline and this may have contributed to their strike record. A second point is that the production technology in some of these industries is particularly alienating – for instance, the car industry – or the work is extremely hard and wearing as is mining and dock-work. In a sense, a strike can be a needed break or, to use Kenneth Boulding's words, it acts as a 'catharsis' and 'a release of tensions'. Finally, traditional industries such as these are often situated in areas with strong working class communities. Union strength and militancy and class solidarity are often the norm in such occupational communities. In some respects, however, this picture of the typical strike-prone industry is ten years out of date. Firstly, these kinds of communities are now in decline, and some of the workers involved in these industries conform more closely to the 'privatised' pattern of living observed by Goldthorpe and Lockwood, rather than the more open community life-style of the traditional working class. Secondly, the relatively strike-prone seventies saw a wider range of workers of all kinds and, not least, non-manual workers, using the strike weapon. Almost everybody, from civil servant to sewage worker, seems to have realised that union membership and action are the best way of maintaining or improving wages. This is true not only in Britain but also in many other countries.

It is, in any case, unwise to generalise too much about the strike records of particular industries because variations between societies are substantial, although the above pattern has some basis in international as well as national statistics. We turn now to this broader issue.

Industrial Relations Systems Analysis Applied to Different Societies

Although industrial relations systems analysis particularly reflects the sociological perspective of Talcott Parsons, its basic principles are more generally applicable, and need not embody his own conservative values. This approach links the particular factory or industry to the wider society. Strikes are seen in the context of the total national system of industrial relations, including workers and unions; management and government agencies especially concerned with the work place; the work community and, finally, the tradition of industrial relations in a given society. Industrial law is an important part of the 'environment' of industrial relations in most advanced countries and has often been a cause of dispute between labour and government in Britain. In the space of two years, between 1969 and 1971, both major parties attempted to introduce substantial legal changes in the position of the unions. Both failed, mainly because of the strength and effectiveness of union opposition.

Britain's system of industrial relations, once widely admired, has been traditionally conducted in an *informal* way without great reliance on the law. Undeniably, it has not stood up well to the economic stresses of the nineteen sixties and seventies. By contrast, the German system which is based on a more detailed structure of law, has recently enjoyed greater harmony, though this may have been as much due to economic prosperity as to their industrial law. In the Soviet Union, industrial peace is achieved by legal compulsion – a generally unpopular means in the West. Theirs is a system of industrial relations in which power is concentrated in the Government's hands. The opposite approach would be to adopt a system of real industrial democracy, that is, union participation or control. We consider this option after concluding our discussion of strikes, and that section can be regarded as a more detailed analysis of industrial relations systems in practice.

Multiple Motivations for Strikes

The major *stated* motive for strikes is the economic one. We have also suggested a range of other important contributory factors. As Hyman points out, however, it is a false dichotomy to assume that the causes of a given dispute must be either economic or *non-economic*. He adds that the relative importance of the various causes that contribute to the start of a strike may change as it goes on, and new reasons for continuing it may appear. The sheer determination 'not to lose' may increase as a strike goes on. Lane and Roberts point out that strikes can snow-ball. New grievances may become apparent as the strike continues and support may come from the previously uncommitted at the prospect of a good settlement. As the interactionist Silverman succinctly puts it, industrial relations must be seen as a changing *process* and not merely in structural terms. We must also reiterate that the broad social, political and legal structure within which a strike occurs (or is prevented from occurring) is of fundamental importance in comparing the strike profiles of different countries.

Beyond Industrial Conflict? Workers' Participation and Control

Most people do not control their work situation. Not only are their work roles defined by others, but they play no part in determining the goals and policies of the organisations for which they work. In Britain this statement is true not only of privately owned businesses but also of state run enterprises. Broadly, there are three opinions on this situation. The first is that the hierarchically (top downward) organised division of labour is inevitable and that 'both sides of industry' must accept their different roles and get on with the job of producing goods or services. This view accords with functionalist assumptions. A second view is that workers can usefully participate in some management decisions by means of elected representatives. Thirdly, is the view that the divide between ownership/management and labour must be removed by the introduction of socialism. We discuss these views more theoretically in Chapter 15 (pp. 425-9) but a few words are appropriate here.

The first view is probably the most commonly held. Rightly or not, most owners and managers think they should continue to 'run' industry and most workers, whether through lack of confidence and experience or otherwise, seem content to agree. A particularly conservative variation of this approach is to hold the view that the unions have become too strong and have 'upset the balance' of British industrial relations, and must therefore be curbed. This view inspires the suggested industrial legislation of Margaret Thatcher's government.

High hopes are often attached to the principle of participation. Worker participation in management and ownership (by having shares in the company) occurs in Sweden and Germany, and is said by its supporters to raise productivity and to improve industrial relations. It is true that industrial relations in these countries are the most trouble-free in Europe. It must be stressed however, that other factors, not least growing prosperity, may be causal here. A further aspect of industrial relations in Sweden is that labour and government have consistently 'struck deals' involving, for instance, wage-restraint, on the one hand, and government commitment to social reform on the other. In any case, Swedish unions tend to be more restricted by law than are British. The arrangements broadly described in this paragraph are referred to as 'corporatism' and Sweden, in particular, is often cited as a corporate state. The German scheme received a positive assessment by a government commision in 1970. Most of the fears of German management about sharing responsibility and authority with labour had proved groundless and co-operation, not obstruction, had been the net result. In his thoughtful book *The Politics of Industrial Relations,* Colin Crouch argues that Britain would benefit from adopting a system of industrial relations similar to, though somewhat more flexible than, the German and Swedish models. He calls this approach 'bargained corporatism'. He sees a possibility that such a system might heal the divide in British industry:

It is usually employers' representatives who bemoan the idea of 'two sides of industry' and who call upon workers to co-operate in the common good. But it is not workers who instituted the rigorous distinction between those who make decisions and those who receive instructions. Or, to put it another way, how can responsibility be demanded from those to whom responsibility is not given? The changes needed to induce more co-operation in British industry will have to be at the level of power and structure before they can be expected in workers attitudes.

Some socialists see participation as a 'half-way-house' to collective ownership and the running of industry. Others, however, consider that participation still leaves the balance of power and decision making too firmly in the hands of ownership and management, and are reluctant to see any change that would undercut the independent power to act of shop stewards. Some of these – particularly Marxists – favour a system of *workers' control* of industry rather than participation, and ultimately want the collective ownership and operation of industry in a classless society. No fair test of workers' control has yet occurred in Britain. Three of the best known cases – at Fisher Bendix, Meriden, and the *Scottish Daily News* – have been typical in that they were all 'taken over' by workers as a last ditch alternative to closure. Not surprisingly, they continued to struggle afterwards, particularly in terms of raising development capital. It is not easy to find a society in which workers' control has had a reasonable chance to operate. Clegg and Dunkerley argue that only a socialist society would provide the conditions that would enable worker-controlled enterprises to avoid the kind of isolation and difficulties experienced by British attempts. They dismiss the Soviet Union as too centralised in its economic management, and see the involvement of workers in Yugoslavia as participation rather than control. They settle on China during the cultural revolution phase as a closer example. For a time, many factories did operate with a high level of workers' involvement and in an anti-hierarchical way. Role-rotation symbolised in the slogan 'from the masses, to the masses', occurred widely, as did group-based methods of management decision making. Of course, such evidence is too scant to base any generalisation on, especially as more recent events in China have reversed the above trends. Equally, however, the ideals of socialism as applied to the organisation of work need not be shelved simply because they remain unachieved. If the principles of workers' participation or control become generally seen as humanly desirable, they would then be seen as humanly possible.

As far as Britain is concerned, such genuine commitment to industrial democracy does not exist, even within the mass of the Labour movement. Tom Forester is aware of this in the four reasons he gives for the failure of the movement towards industrial democracy in this country. These are lack of agreement on the precise definition and scope of industrial democracy among its supporters; inconsistent support from the trade unions and Labour party; employer hostility, and apathy among the rank and file. We can add the opinion that these attitudes reflect a culture that still socialises the majority to conform to authority rather than participate in policy and decision making. A. Halsey has said, the British are a deferential (awed by authority) nation. For the working class it is easier to obey or oppose capital and management than actively to share or take over responsibility, because most of them have never been educated otherwise. Still we concur with Forester's realistic rather than defeatist conclusion:

> To re-work a famous phrase, the spirit of man *is* straining to be free, but only after the mortgage has been paid. It will require a great deal more theoretical and propagandistic groundwork before the ideal of industrial democracy becomes a reality.

Work, Leisure and Culture

Sociologists normally distinguish between work and non-work as well as between work and leisure. Work is essentially a matter of necessity. It is primarily concerned with acquiring the means to live. Whereas work time is governed by need, leisure is 'free time'. It is the individual's own, to use as he wishes. Not all non-work time is leisure time. People have demands on their time such as certain family and domestic responsibilities which are concerned with duty rather than pleasure.

An interesting literature exists on the relationship between work and leisure. Its basic assumption is that certain kinds of leisure patterns can be associated with certain kinds of work. We will summarise some of this research critically. The age we live in, however, begs for a broader treatment of 'the leisure problem' than this rather narrow perspective might suggest. New technology; levels of unemployment unthought of since the nineteen thirties; the decline of the industrial labour force relative to that of the service sector, taken collectively, have profound social implications. We use the concept of culture to analyse the effects of these developments. Substantial changes in work and leisure patterns throughout the social classes mean changes in *our way of life as a whole* (of our culture) though, of course, these will show themselves differently in different groups and social classes. We will examine the issue of cultural change, particularly in the context of automation, after an analysis of the relationship between work and non-work and, briefly, family relations.

Work, Leisure and Family Relations

Stanley Parker has presented a widely used ideal type to clarify the relationship between work and leisure. He describes three patterns:

1 *The Extension Pattern*
2 *The Neutrality Pattern*
3 *The Opposition Pattern*

Parker's findings are based on his own original work, and the research of others.

In the *Extension Pattern* work and leisure overlap, often to the point where they are not clearly distinguishable. The central life interest tends to be in work rather than in family or in leisure activity distinct from work. The pattern is more likely to occur among the middle class because only their work is generally interesting enough to stimulate near 'total' involvement. The attitudes to work of academics often exemplify this pattern. Thus a professor of medieval history may take a 'holiday' visiting castles or cathedrals built during his favoured period. His 'hobby' may be architecture – again, especially of his 'own' period. To those who do not share his obsession, the 'absent minded professor' type can be irritating, not least to his family. Parker's own examples of people who take care of children and youth employment workers are perhaps less extreme examples of those who have careers characterised by the extension pattern. Careers that are associated with this pattern tend to be *intrinsically* interesting (interesting in themselves), to draw

395

considerably on the ability and talents of those who do them and, often, to be vocational in nature. In Maslow's terms, such work is 'self-actualising' (see Chapter 5 pp. 158-9).

A quite different variation of the extension pattern is the case of somebody who may not particularly like their work but is so ambitious that 'they never leave work behind'. Where a 'work-aholic' attitude becomes compulsive (out of control) it can be regarded as a mental pathology (illness). Edgell has noted that families in which the male is very oriented to career success ('spiralist') tend to be husband dominated.

In the case of the *neutrality pattern*, there is no strong relationship between work and leisure of either a positive or negative kind. Leisure is 'a change' from work without being the necessary 'escape' it often is in the oppositional pattern (see below). The following are examples of work associated with this pattern: clerical work, semi-skilled manual work, semi-professional work, such as insurance or real estate selling. Parker's own example is bank employees. This level of fairly routine work is not likely to be of compelling personal interest, nor is it likely to draw greatly on the ability and talents of those doing it. In leisure time, they may look for more expressive alternatives to work. Very often, the family is a strong focus of interest and leisure activities may include family outings or DIY projects, often with involvement of the other partner.

With the *opposition pattern*, work and leisure activities are sharply separate and central life interest is in the non-work sphere. Yet, separate though the work and leisure spheres are in the mind of the worker, the sociologist can see a strong oppositional link between them. The worker is so physically drained or psychologically alienated by work that he seeks refuge in 'recuperative' leisure activities. Assembly line work, mining and deep-sea fishing and similar, so-called *extreme* occupations, are examples of this kind of work. Sometimes more than just 'repair' (Parker's word) or recuperation seem to be sought. The heavy 'boozing' associated with a minority of manual workers in tough jobs is perhaps an unconscious attempt to obliterate from mind the tedium of work as well as being a straightforward pursuit of pleasure and fun.

In Marxist terms, the denial of self expression at work creates strain and builds up frustration. The daily treadmill of alienating work cannot but cast a distorted shadow across the rest of our culture. Repressed anger and resentment can explode, usually legitimately, but sometimes criminally in the pub, at football and other sporting 'contests' (the word is deliberately chosen) or, occasionally, even in the streets. It hardly needs to be added that people usually do this kind of work for extrinsic or instrumental reasons. The predominant motive is money. It is easy to see why this pattern has often been associated with *segregated conjugal roles*. Tired miners and assembly line workers no doubt often feel they have 'earned the right to be looked after' by their wives when they get home from work. The assumed justice of this attitude, however, becomes wholly inappropriate when both partners work.

As Parker fully acknowledges, there are other ways of looking at the relationship between work and leisure than those proposed in his framework. He himself was reacting to the oversimplification of previous schemes which he felt tended to fall into two schools: the *segmentalists* – who believe that society is divided into fairly self-contained areas (work, leisure, education, religion) and the *holists* who argue that work and leisure are beginning to merge together. Wilensky is one observer who sees a trend towards segmentalism. Not only manual work but much white collar and even professional work has become routinised. As a result self-expression and creativity find an outlet mainly in leisure pursuits. Certainly, there has been an expansion of leisure time but the quality of that leisure is hotly debated. The passive and manipulated 'mass society' of Mills and Marcuse, is hardly recognisable as the slowly blossoming liberal culture of Shils (see Chapter 9, p. 553). Parker also cites several examples of the holistic approach: play encroaches upon work in the form of the long coffee break, the business lunch, and the card games of night shift workers; work encroaches upon play in do-it-yourself and spare-time jobs. The growth of 'flexitime' is a further relevant example of the fusion of work and leisure. Parker is right to see the segmentalist-holist polarity as too simplistic but it is a useful starting point for analysis and there are signs of its influence in his own model.

Other factors, besides work, may influence leisure. Not least, people's leisure style and taste reflect their own personalities. We examined style among youth in some detail in Chapter 13. As we also indicated in that chapter, age has a great effect on choice (and capacity for) given leisure activities. A person's education will effectively limit leisure opportunities. An individual is unlikely to read poetry or drama unless he or she has been 'taught to appreciate' them. Geographical location is another influential factor. Countrymen are much more likely to do certain things, such as hunt and fish, than are urbanites, whatever their respective social backgrounds. Peter Hall points out that leisure patterns follow life cycle. Physical recreation is very important for the young unmarried, whereas the middle aged and elderly, especially men, are more likely to prefer gardening. Yet, despite differences in extent and choice of watching, television is the most popular leisure activity for all ages and both sexes. Car ownership, a factor so obvious it can be easily overlooked, has a major effect on leisure possibilities. Car ownership is higher among the middle class and no doubt contributes to their greater tendency to have *extended* friendship networks.

In the view of this author the above models, designed to illuminate the relationship between work and leisure, whilst informative, are inadequate. Changes in patterns of work and leisure need to be seen in a much broader context of technological and cultural change.

Culture, Class and Change

The debate about the relationship between work and leisure has perhaps imposed too narrow a focus on the whole matter of cultural attitudes and pursuits whether at work or otherwise. Most critics would accept the observation that the quality of work and leisure life are both profoundly affected by technological change and by the nature of control and subordination at work and in society as a whole. The relationship between social control and culture is examined in detail in Chapter 19, and we have already raised important related issues in Chapters 3, 4, and 5. Here we will concentrate on technology and culture and, in particular, the effect of automation, including the influence of micro-chip technology, on social life as a whole, rather than on work or non-work taken separately.

Cultural change is, of course, not new, although the speed at which it occurs has increased since the industrial revolution. Some aspects of cultural change to which we have already

398

referred are the break-up of traditional working class community, the forging of a common outlook between the surviving aristocracy and industrial elite, and the development of privatised nuclear family living among the majority of the working and middle class. The cultural effects of micro-chip technology are likely to be of comparable significance with these developments.

In the following analysis, it is important to remember the relationship between work, class and culture. This is a general, not rigid, relationship, but it is one which will help us to distinguish which groups are likely to benefit from the new technology and which not.

Automation: Opportunity or Disaster? An Exercise in Policy Speculation

We will follow Lilley's definition of automation which considers it to be the introduction of highly automatic machinery, or processes which largely eliminate human labour *and* detailed human control.

Optimists see a great potential for liberation from labour in the new micro-chip technology, whereas pessimists see it mainly in terms of the unemployment and accompanying social problems they believe it will produce. There is a further school of thought, expounded by thinkers like Hermann Kahn and Daniel Bell, which considers that as new technology replaces human labour, other jobs will be created that will not only absorb those who have been displaced but will also service a higher standard of living. Even the last alternative, however, tends to assume a reduction in the working week and an increase in annual holidays. All these opinions relate to the future and all are sufficiently realistic to have a chance of being proved correct.

We will discuss the pessimistic view first. The major problem forseen is high unemployment (perhaps 5 million unemployed in Britain) coupled with psychological and practical failure to make the necessary social and economic adjustments. Already the word-processor has reduced the secretarial staff by half in some places in which it has been introduced, and large automatic warehouses need only one or two supervisory and technical staff. Michael Young's magnificent piece of sociological fiction, *The Rise of the Meritocracy*, first published in 1958, seems even more relevant now than then. Young did not regard his description of the future as inevitably destined to come true, still less, did he want it to. He merely warns us that it might. Young foresaw the emergence of a new elite of top scientists, technologists and professionals – men who have necessary *specialised* skills and reap high financial and status rewards as a result. This would happen together with a large mass of unemployed, or people employed in low grade work, such as domestic service or cleaning large buildings. He argued that the new 'masses' would include not only unemployed industrial workers but hundreds of thousands of clerical and office workers also 'laid waste' by new technology. Young pretends to be writing in 2034 but most of his projections appear to have already happened, or to be ominously close.

> More and more was demanded of the skilled men, less and less of the unskilled, until finally there was no need for unskilled men at all. Their work was merely routine, and so it could by definition be progressively taken over and performed by mechanical means. The more simplified a job became, the more easily could it be done by a machine which would feed itself with material, press the lever, and extract the finished article. Semi-automatic became fully automatic. Displacement of low-grade labour became very rapid after the Hitler war with the development of electronics, and especially of servo-mechanisms well-suited to direct industrial processes broken down into their simplest components. So marked was the progress that a new word – 'automation' – was coined for the old business of mechanisation in the new form it was taking ...
>
> Many for whom there was no place in industry came to rest in routine clerical work, or in distribution. That was a happy solution, though not a permanent one. Mechanisation, starting in the factory, did not end there: offices and shops were also invaded. In the middle of the century book-keepers and typists were still common in offices; by the last quarter they had almost disappeared.

Though unnervingly right in his basic scenario, Young was wrong on an important point. He assumed for the purposes of his book, that educational reform would take the best to the top of society (his 'meritocracy') and ensure that the unintelligent would be left at the bottom. We have seen that social mobility patterns have not produced such a neat result. But it may well be a worse situation than even Young half-jokingly envisaged, to have large numbers of intelligent as well as less intelligent people unemployed or poorly employed and, perhaps, with little prospect of a better future.

Those who take what we have labelled a more optimistic view of the effects of the new technology usually do so on the basis of two qualifications. Firstly, they argue that the *social* effects of economic change must be planned for. Secondly, they contend that attitudes of guilt and humiliation associated with unemployment and 'the dole' must gradually disappear. Given this, the possibility of a much freer and more personally fulfilling culture can be built on the basis of the material affluence provided by technology. A number of socialists have been associated with this view, including Herbert Marcuse and Clive Jenkins. Marx himself must be counted among the optimists. He considered that technological invention provides the means of human liberation *if* it is collectively owned, controlled and used. This is what he said about automation and the social possibilities it creates:

> The human factor is restricted to watching and supervising the production process ... The counterpart of this reduction is that all members of society can develop their education in the arts, sciences, etc., thanks to the free time and means available to all.

The material and the cultural aspects of 'liberation' are, in fact, closely linked. Socialist 'futurologists' like Marcuse and Jenkins, look forward to a time when wealth will be allocated by government on the basis of personal need rather than by the market on the basis of competition. This goes well beyond current conceptions of the welfare state. It means that people will have stopped thinking of wage-labour as the only generally respectable means of obtaining an income and accept that other bases of distributing wealth (such as need) are equally legitimate. In other words, a decline in commitment to the 'work ethic' must occur. The work ethic is based on the value that work is virtuous and should be rewarded and that, by corollary, unemployment is a sign of poor character. The point is that, in a time when there is not enough work to go around, this attitude itself becomes redundant. Nevertheless, it will not change easily. Those who are employed may well continue to pursue whatever rewards they can get, regardless of the needs of others. But it may be, as Jenkins suggests, that the power of the unions has a better chance of forcing through more egalitarian policies in the coming age rather than a more general appeal to charity and the goodwill of the community. Nevertheless, as he realises, they too, would have to be persuaded to act beyond their own immediate sectional interest and on behalf of the unemployed.

It is scarcely possible to exaggerate the change in cultural attitudes required before the liberated society envisaged by Marx can come about. In addition to the material rewards and sense of 'virtue' associated with work, it is also a prime source of *identity* and *status*. A society of greater leisure might offer, as Marx implies, a whole range of new identities and perhaps, instead of status, various forms of self-fulfilment. All this assumes that the new technology will be used substantially, if not exclusively, to create socially constructive commodities and services, and not destructively in, for instance, an expansion of armaments production. To hope for this is optimism in the extreme. It may be that our species will prove too afraid to make the most creative and liberating use of the new technology. To do so would require an unprecedented level of national and international trust, co-operation and sharing of resources.

It is possible that the ideas of hard-nosed liberal realist, Daniel Bell, will prove closer to the truth than those of socialist Clive Jenkins. Bell's idea of post-industrial society is not greatly different from what Young foresaw, except that he is confident that continued expansion in the service sector (including personal and social services) will provide both employment and the conditions of a better, more humane life than previously. He does not appear to share Young's concern with the possibility that post-industrial society will be sharply divided into meritocrats and masses or, simply, 'winners' and 'losers'. James Robertson sums this up well and puts the matter in to global context:

> It is best to be blunt about it. This approach to the future implies an ethic of elitism and domination in a class-divided world. Internationally it implies that, by becoming super-industrialised as the less developed countries become industrialised, today's industrialised countries will maintain their economic superiority. It implies that within each super-industrialised country there will be two sharply polarised classes – a responsible technocratic elite in charge of every important sphere of life, and the irresponsible unemployed masses . . .

Guide to further reading and study

Tom Burns *ed, Industrial Man* (Penguin, 1970) contains a wide-ranging collection of shortish articles on work. So does S. R. Parker *et al, eds, The Sociology of Industry* (Allen and Unwin, 1972). On industrial relations and conflict Richard Hyman's *Strikes* (Fontana, 1972) and Colin Crouch's more recent *The Politics of Industrial Relations* (Fontana, 1979) are recommended. A useful reader on trade unions – most of the contributions from a distinctly left-wing standpoint – is Tom Clarke and Laurie Clements *eds, Trade Unions Under Capitalism* (Fontana, 1978). Stanley Parker's piece on work and leisure in *The Sociology of Industry, op. cit,* (George Allen and Unwin, 1972), remains a standard introduction. Clive Jenkins and Barrie Sherman's *White Collar Unionism: The Rebellious Salariat* (Routledge and Kegan Paul, 1979), covers leisure and quality of life issues as well as the subject indicated in the book's title.

Further relevant literature – much of it interpretist – is listed at the end of Chapter 15.

Past Questions

1 Can the whole of social life be explained primarily through the economic relationships characteristic of a society? (JMB, 1977).

2 Assess the impact of technology on work satisfaction (AEB, 1976).

3 Offer a sociological explanation of industrial conflict (AEB, 1978).

4 Striking represents one form of industrial conflict. What other forms are there and how can the varied levels of conflict in different industries be explained? (AEB, 1980).

5 Examine the relationship between work and *two* of the following a) family life b) leisure c) political beliefs. (AEB, 1976).

15 Organisations, Class and Power

Organisations are a personal issue as well as a public reality. The problem is, people often fail to see the personal importance of organisations. Students often profess boredom at the thought of studying them; yet, no topic has more to offer in the way of practical understanding. Most of us will spend our working lives with large or medium-size organisations and if we do not learn to 'manage' them, they will certainly manage us. Perhaps the feelings of alienation that many students experience at the very thought of studying organisations is a symptom of the fact that they can only conceive of being controlled and manipulated by them, and not vice-versa. This quiet desperation was given a voice by the nineteen sixties student radical, Mario Savio, when he urged fellow rebels at Berkeley, California, to stop the bureaucratic machine of the university by 'laying' their bodies on it. Partly to combat this pessimism, we will examine not only the structure and functioning of organisations but who has power and control within them, and also whether more democratic organisational systems are possible.

Both Weber and Marx were fully aware of the importance of the concepts of power and control in analysing organisation. They agreed that organisations are the instruments which 'run' modern life but disagreed about which groups had real control of them. Weber's organisational theory is linked closely to his analysis of the 'new class'. He had no doubt that top organisational officials had great power both in private industry and government departments. He anticipated the dictatorship not of the proletariat, but of the official. He felt that as bureaucracies expanded they would develop vested interests, and argued that even a democratically elected Parliament would have problems in controlling top civil servants and their departments (although he believed it should try). Marx, however, contended that in capitalist society the capitalist class controls the bureaucrats and uses them for its own ends. He argued that this was true not only of the salaried officials of private industry but, ultimately, of state bureaucrats as well, because he considered that the capitalist class also controlled the state. We have already met a modern version of this argument in the work of Dahrendorf and Giddens (Chapter 9, pp. 235-7) and will return again to it in this chapter.

Durkheim was not primarily interested in class control of organisations: rather, he took it for granted, as natural. He was more concerned with how a society, made up of complex organisations and characterised by an advanced division of labour, could hold together. As we have seen, he believed that this was possible because of organic solidarity – the interdependence of people and organisations in modern societies (see Chapter 7). Durkheim's point was a general one: later sociologists have had much more specific interests in the field of the sociology of organisations than he did.

Formal and Informal Organisations: A Preliminary Distinction

Formal organisations are operated by special officials on the basis of established rules, to achieve certain goals. Practically all the large organisations of modern society such as factories, office complexes, super-markets and schools, are formal structures. Their respective officials, rules and goals are familiar to us all. Although formal organisations are a particular feature of urban, industrial societies, certain examples such as armies and monasteries have existed for centuries. To an extent, formal organisations in modern societies have taken over or *supplemented* functions previously performed by family, kinship and community groups (see Chapter 4, pp. 87-8). Thus, state welfare as well as family help is available to the sick and needy through various organisational channels.

Informal organisations develop within all formal organisations. *Informal organisations are freely created social group relationships, not formally part of organisational structures.* It is difficult to imagine that even the most rigidly run prison or concentration camp does not have some form of 'underground' system of communication. The achievement of formal goals may depend on whether informal groups operate 'for' or 'against' the formal organisation. To put it in functionalist terms, they may be functional or dysfunctional. Thus, anti-school peer-groups are an example of informal organisations which are dysfunctional to the achievement of formal educational goals.

It would be misleading to leave the impression that informal organisations exist only within formal structures: friendship groups of peers and gangs occur outside them. Typically, perhaps, people find more meaning in their informal relation-

406

ships than in their formal ones. The reservation widely felt about the 'over-organised' quality of modern life is partly based on the feeling that formal organisations seem to be intruding more and more into the private area of life. Even though more leisure time exists, it is largely 'organised' for us by the mass media rather than used imaginatively and intelligently. Obviously, this view is controversial and we assess it critically in Chapter 19, pp. 53-65.

Theoretical Perspectives on Organisations

Although there are many organisational theories that the student might come across, we can conveniently divide them into four main groups. *These are the bureaucratic or mechanistic; systems theories – particularly organic systems theory;* theories based on the concept of *interaction;* and *conflict theory.* Although these perspectives are frequently contrasted they are by no means wholly exclusive in all respects. Indeed, we will consider the bureaucratic and organic approaches together as much to show their complementary as their contradictory aspects.

We make no analytical distinction between industrial and other kinds of formal organisations in this section. The types of organisational structures described below can occur in both the industrial and non-industrial sectors such as central and local government departments.

1 Bureaucratic and Systems Theories

Bureaucratic or Mechanistic Theory and Organic Systems Theory

Max Weber laid down the classical or bureaucratic model of organisational theory. His model is a functionalist one. *He maintained that bureaucracy is the most functionally efficient form of organisation, even though it can sometimes operate in a rather 'inhuman' way.* Bureaucracies are formal organisations generally recognisable by certain characteristics. He constructed an ideal type of bureaucracy to show what these characteristics are. We can summarise them as follows:

407

1 *The existence of different offices (or positions) governed by rules the purpose of which is to fulfil a specific, given function or functions*
2 *The hierarchical organisation of offices – that is, some positions have more authority and status than others*
3 *Management based on files and records used with the assistance of office staff*
4 *The appointment of trained officials to occupy roles in the bureaucracy*

Weber saw the growth of bureaucratic organisation as a major example of the application of rational thought to practical problems. He regarded the triumph of rationality as a characteristic feature of the modern world. Another of its manifestations was the massive development of science and technology. Weber also described the nature of an official bureaucratic position. Above all, it involves a commitment to performing the functions the official is appointed to do and not to any powerful person or patron who might wish to interfere with the official's course of duty. It was necessary for Weber to make this point because, in the middle ages, this principle did not apply. When a king or lord appointed someone to a high position of service within his household, he expected his appointee to be loyal to him *personally* rather than merely to perform pre-determined and agreed functions. By contrast, a modern bureaucratic official is expected to do the job described in the terms of his *contract*. The contract defines his duties, establishes his salary scale and gives security of tenure subject to an agreed period of notice and good conduct. Most people reading this book will eventually take up a position of this kind. We live in a bureaucratic world! A classic example of a modern bureaucracy is the civil service. A pupil leaving school with a clutch of 'O' levels may begin as a clerical officer. In time, he or she becomes an Excutive Officer and then, perhaps, a Senior Executive Officer: more remotely, the office of Principal Secretary beckons. Each office has its own functions and the further one progresses up the hierarchy, the more power and status accrue.

Criticisms of Weber's bureaucratic model will become apparent as we examine alternative organisational theories, and some dysfunctions of bureaucracy. One point is worth making immediately, however. There is an implicit contradiction in Weber's bureaucratic functionalism, and his more usual emphasis on conflict. Oddly, Weber did not fully develop the perspective that as well as fulfilling useful functions, organisations are also frequently the focus of conflict between groups. We develop this issue later in this chapter.

The organisational type that most obviously contrasts with the bureaucratic is what Burns and Stalker (1961) termed the *organic system*. They contrast organic systems with what they call *mechanistic systems* but, as the latter are in no way distinguishable from bureaucracies, this need not detain us.

Organic systems are characterised by a less rigid division of labour than mechanistic ones; they are less rule-bound, less hierarchical and more open to the influence of the informal group. The last point is crucial. The skill and experience of the individual can be communicated *laterally* (sideways) across the network of those involved in the task. The *team* as a whole shares power and responsibility. Overall, the organic approach shows a more subtle awareness of the complex nature and effects of interaction, formal and informal, than does the bureaucratic. Such an approach is often considered appropriate for relatively high level technical or scientific employees in, say, the electronics industry – for example, a team of computer programmers. Nevertheless, it has also been successfully tried with manual workers. At their Kalmar plant, Volvo broke down assembly work into 20 different functions. Each one is performed by a team of 15 or 20 workers. The cars pass from team to team on trolleys, allowing the worker considerable freedom of movement. The teams are not hierarchically organised, and solutions to problems are supposed to be reached through co-operation and not by authoritarianism.

Although the bureaucratic or mechanistic and the organic systems models of organisations are, to some extent, in competition with each other, there are circumstances in which one model may be more appropriate than the other. Burns and Stalker suggest that bureaucracy is often suitable for the pursuit of clear goals in stable conditions, such as producing a commodity for a safe and established market, and that an organic system is appropriate to less stable conditions in which precise goals may still be developing, such as electronics research.

Scientific Management, Human Relations Theory and Socio-technical Systems Theory
Frederick W. Taylor's theory of scientific management reflects

409

the same principles as Weber's bureaucratic theory, and, to a lesser extent, human relations theory and socio-technical theory bear comparison with organic systems theory.

Taylor, an American contemporary of Weber, reached his conclusions independently of the Austrian social scientist. Taylor was specifically interested in industrial organisations and particularly in developing ways to improve production. What he said about the role and function of the industrial worker was comparable with Weber's comments on the lower level white collar employee. Further, both recognised that higher level bureaucrats and managers had relatively more power. Like Weber, Taylor decided that efficiency was best obtained by task specialisation and standardisation, and the centralisation of decision making power at the top of the hierarchy. He argued that all mental work should be removed from the workshop, and put in the hands of management. He presented his ideas in a book entitled *Scientific Management*. An unadmitted guiding principle seemed to be to treat the worker as an extension of the machine or organisation and, indeed, this notion is, more or less, implicit in all bureaucratic structures. Among the advice he offered was that 'the two hands should begin and complete their motions simultaneously' and that 'proper illumination increases production'. In addition, he recommended that pay levels be closely tied to productivity. It seems appropriate that Taylor's approach is often referred to as *mechanical* or *mechanistic* theory.

Human relations theory originated as a reaction against Taylor's scientific management theory. From 1927 to 1932, a series of studies was mounted into worker productivity at the Hawthorne Works of the Western Electricity Company in Chicago. Initially, the researchers, led by Elton Mayo, were positively influenced by Taylor and their area of enquiry was actually suggested by his work. They wanted to find out the optimum level of illumination and other environmental factors to maximise production. There is more than a touch of comedy about the way they arrived at the 'results' of their research. They 'found' that the relation between the variables of illumination and production was virtually non-existent. In one of the studies in which the workers were placed in a control room in lighting conditions equivalent to moonlight, they still maintained a reasonable level of production: it fell off only when illumination was so reduced that they could not see properly!

Ultimately, the Hawthorne experiments were of outstanding importance both because of the new theory of industrial relations they suggested, and by virtue of their contribution to a better understanding of social scientific method, specifically that of observation. We have already discussed the second of these, the effect of the researcher on the behaviour of the subject of research, in Chapter 2. We concentrate now on the first, the content of their findings. To put it simply, they found that *the productive performance of the workers was affected by social factors,* as well as material ones such as the level of illumination. The social factor at work in this case was the interest of the research team in the workers. Unexpectedly, this seemed to stimulate them to greater efforts than otherwise. The presence of researchers in a factory is, however, rare.

Follow-up studies by the Mayo team showed that the informal relationships of the workers themselves constitute the most important social variable affecting production. The role of informal groups was established by the notable Western Electric Company Bank Wiring Room experiment involving the wiring of switchboards. A group of 14 workers was set up separately and observed for six months. It was found that, although they were paid on the basis of a productivity bonus scheme, the men did not respond to this by individually trying to maximise their production, but established their own production norms as a group. Group disapproval was equally the fate of those who produced either more or less than the agreed norm.

Underlying the human relations approach is a more complex and more humanistic theory of human needs than that implied by classical theory. The latter assumes that *individuals* will work harder in improved material conditions and if they are given higher material rewards for more work. *Human relations theory argues that people also need the security, companionship, identity and guidance of the informal peer group.* These psychological needs are only capable of fulfilment with others. Taylor's attempt to treat the work-force as isolated individuals was based on the misleading fiction that workers are, in fact, isolated. In modern, large-scale organisations work is a collective experience.

The socio-technical systems theory attempts to combine both the technical and social factors affecting work so as to bring about the most effective overall performance. Mary Weir summarises three major points suggested by socio-technical system theorists to achieve this end: the individual must have some power to control and regulate his work; he should be able to adapt his own standards of work both to the expectations and demands of others and to the changing work situation generally; and the job should be both varied and have a coherent pattern. Finally, it should be linked meaningfully to the rest of the production process. It should also provide the worker with status in the community.

Both the human relations and socio-technical systems approaches have been criticised as merely 'making exploitation more bearable'. In a challenging critique of management theories the Marxist, Harry Braverman, attacks both Taylor's theory, and human relations and similar schools. He suggests that Taylorism did not last because it was too obviously crude and insensitive. The 'softer' theories provided the necessary ideological fig leaves to cover the still basically exploitative nature of capitalist production. But they fail to confront the private ownership and control of industry which Marxists traditionally regard as the root of alienation. Even given Braverman's premise, however, there remains the argument that it is better to be exploited in comfort than discomfort!

The Dysfunctions of Bureaucratic Organisation: Breaking the Rules

The arguments in favour of bureaucracy are considerable. Firstly, the bureaucratic division of labour combined with technological innovation has greatly increased the production of goods and services: to that extent it is efficient. Secondly, a bureaucracy usually ensures a degree of predictability: production quotas are pre-determined, people know how they are likely to be treated. Thirdly, partly because of its very impersonality, bureaucracy is often a condition of fairness. People are appointed to offices on the basis of qualifications and merit rather than patronage. Further, clients are dealt with by bureaucrats on the basis of equality and need, not favouritism. That, at any rate, is the theory, although several sociologists have criticised and modified it.

Arguing within a functionalist framework, Robert Merton points to several dysfunctions of bureaucracy which can lead to inefficiency. First, rigid adherence to bureaucratic rules may prevent an official from improvising a necessary response to unexpected circumstances. Thus, to offer our own example, a secretary in a production company, in the absence of superiors, may happen one day to find herself having to deal with an important client. Conceivably, by retreating behind her official role – 'I'm sorry, I'm only the secretary. I don't have the authority to deal with business matters' – vital orders may be jeopardised or, at a minimum, the client may feel he or she has not been well treated. In such a case, initiative, confidence and some imagination are needed. Bureaucracy does not always teach these qualities and can actually smother them. The results can be 'passing the buck'. Secondly, there is a danger that those rigidly trained to obey rules rather than to consciously achieve goals will become what Merton calls *ritualistic*. This means that they attach more importance to observing rules and procedures than in achieving the purpose for which they exist: this is referred to as goal displacement. As lower level bureaucrats are often not kept informed about general organisational goals, ritualism must be considered a potential fault of bureaucracy, rather than an individual failing. Merton classifies ritualism as a form of anomie (see Chapter 16, pp. 442-3). Finally, Merton argues that the sometimes alienating effect of bureaucracy on both bureaucrats and the public with whom they deal can be dysfunctional. Bureaucratic or ritualistic characters are not the most adaptable and efficient of people, and clients who have to submit to long bureaucratic procedure before, say, they can receive needed social security are unlikely to be very co-operative.

Merton argues within functionalist assumptions but, as we have seen, Burns and Stalker suggest that in certain circumstances it is more efficient to break with the bureaucratic method of organisation altogether. Broadly, this is when co-operative and organic rather than competitive and hierarchical structures are more suitable to organisational goal attainment. Arguing along similar lines, Peter Blau gives a number of examples in which formal bureaucracy proved inappropriate. One such instance occurred in an isolated American navy island base. Virtually cut off from external control, the formal organisation of the base broke down and natural leaders, who worked effectively but within an informal framework emerged. A better known study by Blau is of an American state employment agency. He compared two groups of job placement interviewers who operated on different organisational principles, the one highly bureaucratic, the other much more informal and co-operative. On balance, the second approach proved more effective in placing clients in jobs. Blau did not over-generalise from this case-study to the point of concluding that informal organisation is more efficient. Indeed, he found evidence to suggest that it sometimes operated in a biased manner as there were fewer bureaucratic checks to prevent officials favouring some clients at the expense of others. Rather, he suggested that what is often needed is balance, varying with circumstances, between formal and informal methods.

It is worth recalling two studies that we have already met which point to the limits of a rigidly bureaucratic approach. First is the pioneering Hawthorne study presented earlier in this chapter which established the importance of the informal social group in production. Second is Alvin Gouldner's case-study of a wildcat strike which showed that unrest can occur when workers, used to informality, responsibility and independence, have a bureaucratic regime imposed upon them.

Finally, there can be no clearer demonstration of the limited effectiveness of rigid rule-following in achieving goals than the fact that workers use the strategy of 'working to rule' (doing all tasks by the book) in the industrial bargaining process.

Refusing to work overtime is a common example. The result is often inconvenience to the public. Thus, transport workers can make chaos out of timetable schedules merely by working a 'normal' day. Strict and time-consuming adherence to safety check rules or a rigid refusal to allow more people on a bus than is officially stipulated can also be used as pinpricks in industrial campaigning. Put negatively, working to rule can be presented as a 'withdrawal of goodwill'. The National Union of Teachers (NUT) adopted this approach in their industrial action of 1979. In particular, lunch-time supervision of children was suspended. This was hardly lethal in its effect but it did result in a number of 'mad hatter's dinner parties' here and there. Clearly, then, relationships and goodwill, as well as rules are a part of organisation.

Talcott Parsons' Functional-Systems Theory

Parsons' organisational theory is interesting in that it combines elements of Weberian functionalism with those of systems theory. He retains the notion that organisations have goals, but describes them as potentially much more flexible and capable of adaptation than does Weber.

Parsons treats organisations virtually as though they are small-scale societies, and his organisational analysis strongly recalls his social systems theory (see Chapter 3, pp. 57-9). The various parts of organisations are seen as interdependent; they have certain needs that have to be met for survival; they have goals; the whole is something more than the sum of all the individuals who are members of the organisation. The organic analogy is clearly apparent in all this; even so, there is nothing so far mentioned that adds substantially to Weber's analysis of bureaucracy. Parsons, however, goes beyond Weber in two important ways. Firstly, he pays more attention to the capacity of organisations to interact with one another and with the environment in general. The notion that, in order to function effectively, organisations must adapt their structure and goals to changes in the environment has certainly been of influence in modern management. In a fast-changing age the possiblity of 'being left behind' is ever-present. An organisation that cannot adapt is not likely to survive. An example of an organisation that has adapted to change is the House of Commons, a very different body now from that of several hundred years ago. British Leyland is an example of an organisation that is finding adaptation – particularly in its response to foreign competition and new technology – a struggle.

Secondly, Parsons recognises that organisations must, in some way, meet man's expressive as well as his instrumental needs. Even so, it is clear that he considers these needs are to be accommodated within the terms of the organisation's pre-set goals and certainly not as ends in themselves. This seems a deterministic and unconvincing way of reconciling personal needs with rational organisational goals. In reality, the individuals and groups that make up organisations often disagree much more than Parsons is willing to concede.

A well known application of functionalist systems theory is Peter Selznick's analysis of the Tennessee Valley Authority, set up in 1933 by President Roosevelt to help the region combat the effects of the Depression. The Authority was set up with the intention of involving local people in policy making. In practice, this did not happen and instead powerful local farmers were the major effective interest group consulted by the Authority's officials. Selznick suggests that the reason why this occurred was that for the organisation to 'survive' and its officials to retain their jobs, compromise had to be made with the major local power group. This may have been so but it is just as easy to see these developments in terms of interest group or class conflict as organisational survival.

2 Social Action and Interactionist Theories

Social Action Theory

David Silverman describes the meanings that individuals attach to, and find in, organisations, to be the major concern of action theory. People, not organisations, have goals. He is, however, appreciative of Parsons' attempt to conceive of organisations in terms of change and development, and he himself contextualises action within a wider institutional and social environment. He cites the previously mentioned study of Gouldner as an excellent example of an analysis that combines a sense of historical and institutional context with an understanding of the meaning actors attach to their behaviour (see Chapter 14, pp 387).

Another excellent example of the importance of understanding how human behaviour, particularly in its emotional rather than its rational aspects, can affect organisations, is given by Ralph Glasser. In a television documentary (1980), Glasser tells how the olive producers of the Italian rural village of San Georgio refused to use a co-operative olive press – even though there existed good 'rational' economic arguments for doing so. Instead, they preferred to take their olives for pressing to the owners of private presses who were usually wealthy. Glasser suggests that the olive farmers acted in this way because they had a traditional relationship, based on established expectation and *fiducia* (trust) with the private press operators. By contrast, as Glasser points out, 'You can't have a relationship with a co-operative'. In fairness, it should be said that co-operatives do sometimes work well, and people do have relationships within them. Nevertheless, it is obvious that the producers did not *feel* that they could relate to the new situation. This feeling became the major operative factor in the above situation and accounts for the failure of the co-operative. Glasser indulges in some conservative romanticism, but underlying this is a wise awareness of the texture of relationships and feelings woven over time, and a fear of what the brutal blade of technology and bureaucracy might do to them in the name of progress and rationality.

A better known example of a piece of research utilising action perspective, is Goldthorpe and Lockwood's affluent worker study. It will be recalled that they studiously avoided attributing motives to the workers but took the trouble to ask them what their motives were. It turned out that a majority had an instrumental orientation to work, or, simply, they worked for money, not satisfaction. (Chapter 14, p. 369).

Total Institutions: Interactionist Analysis of the 'Ultimate' in Bureaucracy

Social action theory and symbolic interactionism are compatible theoretical approaches, but whereas the former has been developed mainly in Europe, the latter was founded in the USA, and has its own characteristic concepts and vocabulary.

We may live in an increasingly bureaucratic world, but most of us can escape from it into our private lives and personal relationships. Most of us think of these 'escapes' as necessary to a balanced life and even to sanity itself. There are, however, some who live all the time, and for a long period, in highly bureaucratic organisations, in *total institutions*. How does the self – to use the interactionist term – adjust to omnipresent and 'permanent' bureaucracy? Before answering this question, we must briefly examine some different types of total organisations.

A major distinction between different types of total organisations is whether membership is *voluntary* or *compulsory*. Monasteries are an example of the former, prisons of the latter. Whether members belong to an organisation by choice or not will tend greatly to affect the quality of life within it – as a brief consideration of the difference between a monastery and prison should show. The voluntary-compulsory membership distinction does not, however, apply in every case: the members of some institutions, old people's homes and mental hospitals, for instance, may contain both types. A further way of categorising total institutions is simply in terms of the *purposes* they serve. Thus, goals may be *custodial* (prisons), *protective* (mental hos-

417

pitals), *retreatist* (monasteries), or *task-oriented* (armies, boarding schools). Often a total institution may serve several purposes, for example, prisons protect the public and, sometimes, seek to reform their inmates.

Erving Goffman's *Asylums*, based on a field study carried out in a hospital in Washington in 1955–56, remains the best known study of a total institution. In order to see at first hand the personal and psychological effects on the patients of life in an asylum, Goffman undertook a participant observational study, playing the role of an assistant to the athletic director. We can divide what Goffman refers to as the *career* of the mental patient into two stages, the breaking down of the old self and the construction of a new self. Part of the second stage is the adoption of *modes of adjustment* which enable the individual to 'get by' on a day-to-day basis and perhaps to salvage some of his sense of individuality.

The first blow to a person's old or established sense of identity is when someone – often a close relative – complains of 'abnormality'. Identity is further broken down during the inpatient phase. Not all mental hospitals are equally bureaucratic, but the admission procedures Goffman mentions include photographing, finger-printing, number assigning, listing personal possessions for storage, and undressing. Not surprisingly, he refers to this as the process of 'mortification' of the self. In the second stage referred to above, the inmate attempts to build a new self centred on the institution. The system of privileges and rewards operated by the institution in return for obedience or, perhaps, for doing work around the hospital, focus the individual's attention and energy, and may give a sense of meaning and purpose and so help to reintegrate the personality. Despite the fact that total institutions are geared to standardise behaviour, inmates manage to adopt individual modes of adjustment. *Withdrawal* or *retreatism* is an extreme and often irreversible adjustment. Two forms of adjustment in which the institution tends to 'take over' the inmate are *conversion* and *colonisation*. Conversion is when the inmate accepts the institution's definition of himself as, say, 'emotionally immature' and tries to conform to the pattern of 'perfect inmate'; colonisation occurs when the institutional regime so engulfs the individual that it comes to seem preferable to the world outside. Prisoners, as well as mental patients, who prefer to have their lives 'run for them' sometimes adopt this mode of adjustment. Goffman uses the term, *playing it cool*, to describe a general posture of strategic adjustment. The mental patient may adjust to the bureaucratic power structure, and to other inmates largely as an attempt to improve his chances of discharge. In prisons, a similar adjustment is often rewarded with a remission of sentence. Goffman considers playing it cool to be the most common form of adjustment.

Some inmates *rebel* or, to use Goffman's precise term, take an 'intransigent line' rather than genuinely adjust, although he says relatively little of this possibility. The film, *One Flew Over the Cuckoo's Nest*, based on a novel by Ken Kesey, was a dramatised version of the rebellion of McMurphy, a patient in a mental hospital. McMurphy simply refused to accept the total planning and routinisation of his life. For him, the officially pre-programmed and controlled time-table – meal times, basket-ball games, television watching, lights out and, above all, day trips – provide opportunities for anarchic self-assertion. One episode in the film in which a bus-load of mental patients, led by McMurphy, take over a ship is a classic of comic absurdity. Finally, McMurphy ends up subdued by a brain lobotomy – the ultimate form of control. Lobotomies may be rare but electric shock treatment, the use of drugs, and manipulation of privileges, rewards and punishments to achieve conformity are common. The film does not moralise but, in the end, McMurphy's madness compares well with official thought and personality control. We are reminded that when 'society' defines someone as deviant, the consequent loss of that individual's freedom, and the tools used in reforging acceptable behaviour are formidable. Still, the film ends optimistically with McMurphy's friend, a previously subdued Indian, breaking out of the hospital in a bid for freedom.

A book very much in Goffman's style (although not uncritical of him) is *Psychological Survival: The Experience of Long-Term Imprisonment*, by Stanley Cohen and Laurie Taylor (1972). The authors frankly proclaim that one of their purposes is to provide a 'manual of survival' for long-term prisoners. Accordingly, they devote one chapter to 'making out and fighting back'. They find much more evidence of resistance in Durham prison – where they did their research – than Goffman did among patients in the Washington hospital. Accordingly, they write of *modes of resistance* rather than *adjustment*. They list five types of resistance: *self-protection, campaigning, escaping, striking* and *confronting*. Self-protection and campaigning are individual types of resistance. Cohen and Taylor spend little time on the material side of self-protection, for example getting more and better food. They concentrate on the protecting of self-image. They stress how prisoners reject the most damning 'labels' – 'killer', 'thug', 'brutal psychopath', – sometimes humorously and sometimes in anger. Campaigning, the most popular form of which was sending letters to MPs, was more often done as a way of 'getting back' at authority, rather than in any real hope of progress on given issues. Escaping, striking and confronting all involve a high degree of collective effort or connivance. The term 'confronting' needs to be explained. It describes any major collective effort to force the prison authorities, and sometimes a wider audience, to listen to the prisoners' complaints and opinions. There could hardly be a more conspicuous example of trying to draw public attention to grievances than, for instance, occupying a prison roof for a period – as has sometimes happened.

Cohen and Taylor show typical interactionist awareness that the differences between 'normals' and 'deviants' is generally one of degree rather than of kind. In a later book, *Escape Attempts: The Theory and Practice of Resistance to Everyday Life* (1976), they extend their concept of resistance to more conventional, as distinct from totally bureaucratic, situations. We have already seen how, at work and in schools, people attempt to 'manage' their own situations, despite the constraints imposed by the organised environment. In the first two chapters in the next section we examine further the tension between the demands of society for order and conformity, and the frequent tendency of individuals not to 'fit in'.

3 Conflict Theories

This section should be regarded as a direct continuation of the opening part of this chapter, in which the conflict perspectives on organisations of Marx and Weber were introduced. Whereas Parsons tends to see power as being used for 'necessary' purposes in the common interest, for example, in maintaining law and order. Marx and, to some extent Weber, sees it as being used by groups or classes mainly in their own interests. Thus, Weber feared the abuse of power by bureaucrats on their own behalf, and Marx on behalf of the capitalist class.

Clegg and Dunkerley remind us of what should really be obvious – that the reason for the existence of most organisations is the need to organise the labour process, and that this involves the control of workers by employers. Like Bowles and Gintis, they regard the extreme fragmentation of the labour process in industrial and office work as one means of controlling the working force, because it prevents them from understanding the nature of the whole production process. They differentiate not only between buyers and sellers of labour but also between working groups of different power in the market. Thus, they explain at length the reasons for the particular exploitation of female labour, as we also did in Chapter 11. Their discussion leads naturally to the question of different forms of organisational control (see next section), and to whom the product of labour rightly belongs, and how it should be shared. As they point out, their perspective is pertinent to organisations in both communist and capitalist societies. The most obvious difference between organisations today and in Marx's time is that many are now operated by the state. They show that a 'them and us' feeling in the workforce can occur in undemocratically run state enterprises such as those in the Soviet Union, as well as in capitalist ones. A state that simply gathers in profit or surplus value and redistributes it unequally is hardly likely to be perceived as any improvement on a capitalist entrepreneur.

Wallerstein's comments on organisations are comparable with those of Clegg and Dunkerley. He gives the broadest dimension possible to organisational analysis. He suggests that national societies are inadequate units for economic and social analysis and that they should be seen as only one organisational level within the *capitalist world economy*. Specific organisations, like the nation state or multi-national corporations, operate within the capitalist world system. This is generally true, but it should be realised that the political and organisational influence of the Soviet Union has provided an increasingly powerful challenge to capitalism since the war. We have examined this issue in the context of development (see Chapter 7, pp. 194-201).

One matter on which Clegg and Dunkerley say relatively little is how private troubles arising in organisations can be related to 'public issues'. An obvious example is how a corporation's policy of plant closures or cut-backs – perhaps the result of recession – can cause the personal misery of unemployment (Chapters 7 and 10). There is need for much more analysis of how individual and, indeed, national experience is formed by organisations operating in an unpredictable world system.

A number of liberal structural sociologists have applied Weber's concepts in a way that emphasises the functional aspect of organisations but shows an awareness of conflict. We have already seen that Weber considered that socialist societies were likely to become as bureaucratic, if not more so, than capitalist ones. More recently, this view has been presented as part of the broader, more controversial *convergence* thesis. In this context, convergence means that the economic and organisational structure of advanced societies, whether capitalist or socialist, are becoming increasingly similar. The view that such societies need central economic planning and large governmental bureaucracies to implement decisions is crucial to this idea. Another aspect of this thesis appears in the work of Daniel Bell and Ralf Dahrendorf. They argue that the complex problems of advanced societies require advanced management techniques. Political argument will not solve essentially technical problems, and may make them worse. Thus, national investment in energy may need to be planned years ahead, regardless of which government is in power. In their view, top managers and their technical advisers are vital in giving long-term continuity in both advanced capitalist and socialist societies. Dahrendorf, and, particularly, Bell, consider this new class of experts to be a highly influential elite (see Chapter 14, pp. 399–402 and this chapter). They see potential for conflict between this high status and well paid elite and the less privileged and well-off. Nevertheless, they consider this inequality to be inevitable and as much a feature of communist as of capitalist societies.

As we have seen, Marxists do not consider that managers have as much power as Bell and Dahrendorf suggest. In the West there is also the power of capital to consider and, we must add, in the Soviet Union, that of top communist politicians. Nevertheless, the massive extent of bureaucracy and the power of top management to use bureaucracy as their instrument are noteworthy and quite recent features of modern society.

Marxists can certainly learn from Weberian-inspired organisational analysis. Two points are apparent. Firstly, the 'new managerial class' is both highly paid and relatively powerful. In their eagerness to establish the primacy of capitalist power, Marxists tend to disregard this even though it is a fact that can be easily accommodated to Marxist theory and policy. Secondly, as Weber realised, the power of large organisations to control and alienate is immense because of their very size and of the remoteness of those who control them. The novelist, Kafka, caught the sense of how in modern societies organisations seem to 'run peoples' lives' almost without personal direction. This description is at least as applicable to the Soviet Union as to the West. Clegg and Dunkerley appear to have integrated this important insight into an essentially Marxist framework. They recognise that bureaucratically run organisations tend to produce alienation not only among lower level workers but even among professional employees as well. Crucially, however, they insist that it is still necessary to locate and analyse the major source of control behind organisations, whether it be capital or a political elite. Only then does it become possible adequately to relate organisational analysis to the issues of inequality of power and wealth. The basic question remains 'in whose interest is this organisation run?'

Control and Involvement, Oligarchy and Democracy in Organisations

We have already seen that Weber considered that modern organisations are best run along bureaucratic lines. For him, bureaucracy meant hierarchy and hierarchy meant oligarchy, that is, that power and control are concentrated at the top. More recent theorists have examined the issues of control and involvement in organisations and, as we shall see, have produced a more complex picture. The organic systems theory, mentioned above, has already introduced the notion that organisations can be run on somewhat more democratic lines than the bureaucratic model suggests. We now examine this matter more directly.

Etzioni takes three of Weber's major concepts, *power, authority* and *legitimation*, and applies them to the understanding of the way organisations work. Etzioni starts with the basic problem of how the majority of people, workers and employees, can be persuaded or forced to do what they might not freely chose to do – work for others. To understand Etzioni's answer, we must first know what Weber's three terms mean: *power is the ability to impose one's will* (for example by brute force); *legitimation is the acceptance of power because it is considered to be rightly exercised* (for example that of a king); and *authority is legitimate power*. Weber offered a three-part ideal-type model of authority: *traditional, charismatic*, and *rational-legal*. Traditional authority is 'hallowed with time', like that of a king, an established dynasty or a pope. Charismatic authority is generated by the personality of the individual, like that of Hitler or Martin Luther King. Rational-legal authority is established in law or written regulations. We have already said that it is this type of authority that characterises modern bureaucratic organisations.

Why is it that individuals accept the control and power of organisations and, specifically, of top organisational officials over their lives? Etzioni presents in turn, an explanatory typology of control: *coercive, utilitarian* and *normative* or *social*. Coercive power is control based on physical means, such as brute force. Utilitarian power is based on the use of material means, such as money payments: it embodies an element of positive incentive to conform, in the form of a reward. Normative power is based on morality and social conscience. When people conform for normative reasons they do so because they believe they *ought* to. Normative power and conformity are associated with legitimation because they occur when people accept that a given power is legitimate. Thus, a Catholic who accepts the authority of the Pope does so out of normative conviction. A citizen may obey the law from normative conviction although, for others, the threat of coercion may be necessary. Likewise, employees in an organisation, say a commercial one, may feel normatively disposed to accept its authority even though they originally joined it for ultilitarian reasons (to make a living). Bureaucracies are largely based on rules and often create an atmosphere of normative conformity. A little thought will make it clear that in many types of organisations, such as schools, two or even three kinds of control operate.

Etzioni matches three types of *involvement* with his typology of control. Coercion tends to produce *alienation*, utilitarian control is based on *calculative commitment*, and normative control on *moral commitment*. Calculative and moral commitment have, in effect, already been explained. Alienation is the opposite of commitment: it is the rejection by the spirit of what the body has to do, such as to serve a life-sentence in prison or to do endlessly repetitive and boring work. In part, Etzioni sees it as a leadership problem to decide what kinds of incentives are necessary to involve members in the organisation's goals. He also recognises, however, that workers and employees are likely to have their own ideas about the nature of their involvement, and that these will affect the running of the organisation. As we shall now see, there is perhaps more to this issue than Etzioni himself allows.

Is Democracy in Organisations Possible?

The most uncompromising statement of the inevitability of managerial elites is the so-called 'iron law of oligarchy' of Robert Michels. With the German Socialist Party chiefly in mind, he argues that popularly representative parties and unions, whose aim is to replace autocracy with democracy, are forced by necessity to develop a 'vast and solid' bureaucratic organisational structure themselves. In due course, the party bureaucracy itself becomes centralised and undemocratic. The vested interest of the organisation's elite rather than the needs of the people at large effectively becomes the most important consideration, despite professed democratic and socialist ideals. Ordinary people acquire no more power or control as a result of these movements. One set of masters replaces another. In that sense, Michels' 'law' is similar to Pareto's theory of circulating elites.

Alvin Gouldner criticises Michels' account as unbalanced. Michels emphasises only the ways in which organisational needs work against democratic possibilities. Tellingly, Gouldner suggests another need – ignored by Michels – that of the consent of the governed (or employees), to their governors. He sees a certain *recurrent* tension between the need for central leadership and authority and the desire of many people for more power, satisfaction and involvement at work than a rigid bureaucratic regime might allow. He says, with some poetic finesse, 'if oligarchical waves repeatedly wash away the bridge of democracy, this eternal recurrence can happen only because men doggedly rebuild them after each inundation'.

Gouldner's thoughts conveniently bring us to the nub of the debate about organisational oligarchy and democracy. Both democracy and oligarchy are possible in organisations and, for that matter, in the political system. What people get depends on what they want, and their power to obtain it balanced against that of others. Power-conflict is a process not an outcome. Thomas Jefferson, the second American President, counselled the people to be ever vigilant in the protection of their democratic rights, lest they be whittled away by central government.

Gouldner has rough words for Selznick (see pp. 415–6) as well as Michels. He refers to Selznick's 'dismal' catalogue of organisational needs. These are 'needs' for security; stable lines of authority; stable relationships, and homogeneity (similarity of parts). Gouldner, maintaining his emphasis on democracy, juxtaposes what he sees as an equally important set of needs: needs for challenge, for lateral communication, for creative tension, for heterogeneity (diversity) and the consent of the led. We return to the oligarchy-democracy debate shortly in the context of union organisation.

Gouldner, therefore, sees neither oligarchy or democracy as 'inevitable' but as alternatives to be championed and contested. Similarly, Rensis Likert offers a model of control-involvement which is more representative of the full range of possible management-worker structures than is Etzioni's. He identifies four important systems of organisation: *exploitative/authoritative; benevolent/authoritative; consultative* and *participative group management.* We can add a fifth: the *democratic/egalitarian* system of management favoured by some contemporary socialists but probably not fully achieved in any socialist regime.

In exploitative/authoritative systems, power and control are centralised and workers are treated exclusively in terms of their productive capacity. In the early stages of industrialisation in both Britain and America, powerful industrial moguls, such as Ford and Rockefeller, ran their industrial empires in this way. Frequently, this pattern became modified to the extent that the entrepreneur did begin to develop an interest in the general welfare of his workforce – the benevolent-authoritative pattern. Often this was for ulterior motives: a healthy workforce was a

426

better workforce and, in any case, entrepreneurs often wanted to 'spike the guns' of unions which built up on the basis of working class discontent. Frederick Taylor was the theoretical philosopher of authoritative or, perhaps more accurately, authoritarian style of management. The consultative approach recognises that the workforce may have something to offer the management, at least in certain areas, in the way of experience and advice. Even where regular consultative meetings are established, however, ultimate decisions remain in the hands of ownership or management. Again, this system can become little more than decorative diplomacy. The concept of participative group management has had considerable support and success in parts of Europe in the post-war period. In Scandinavia and West Germany, workers have had substantial representation on the management boards of large companies for many years. In Britain, the Bullock report of the late nineteen seventies recommended that Britain's nationalised industries should implement a similar system of participation. The report's recommendations were rather complicated and their partial application to British Leyland and the Post Office petered out. The participation 'debate' continues, however.

The democratic-egalitarian model goes beyond the concept of the participation of 'both sides of industry' to that of abolishing the notion of 'sides' altogether. For a Marxist, this would first involve the abolition of class inequality. This does not, of course, mean that separate roles, such as manager or production worker, will cease to exist; rather, it is a question of making management democratic. Perhaps managers could be elected for a term of some years, as MP's are now, and positions on the board could rotate (as the American Presidency does in the sense that it can only be held for two four-year terms – for good democratic reasons!). To be genuinely egalitarian, this system would also involve a reduction, if not the abolition, of the differences in reward and status between management and workers. Obviously, this model would be barely acceptable within the limits of capitalist economic and social belief. The implementation of a democratic-egalitarian system would probably require socialism. We discussed this matter in some detail in Chapter 14, pp. 391-4.

It is appropriate at this point briefly to discuss whether, regardless of their capacity to participate in industrial democ-

427

racy, unions can be successfully democratic themselves. This returns us to Michels' thesis. Lipset, Trow and Coleman, on the basis of a study of a printers' union in the United States, found that in certain circumstances democracy is possible. The printers' union had a thriving two party system. They put this down to the fact that the long and odd hours worked by the printers produced work-connected leisure organisations which, in turn, provided a basis of communication for, and involvement in, union politics. But Lipset's broader conclusion is more pessimistic. In most industries, the majority of workers quickly leave work for home, and it is only a minority which actively involves itself in union politics. This is certainly the case in Britain, where seldom more than a third of workers vote when given the opportunity to do so. Allen, however, points out that the formal machinery of union democracy is time-consuming and cumbersome to operate. In practice, the way union leaders are kept in check is more simple. If the workers disapprove of what they are doing, membership declines. Allen's argument is not entirely convincing. As early as 1949, C. Wright Mills pointed to the communication gap between national union officials and branch officials and between both these groups and the mass membership. These problems are by no means resolved today.

Gouldner perceives oligarchy and democracy as matters of preference and belief rather than 'inevitabilities'. This is not to deny that certain circumstances tend to promote oligarchy and others democracy. Professor Schumacher's book, *Small is Beautiful*, made the point that large organisations tend to require centralised power and that smaller ones can be democratically run. Nevertheless, given the intent, a measure of democracy is possible even in large organisations. At root, preference for organisational oligarchy or democracy depends on a view of human nature. Those who consider that people work best in a highly regulated structure will prefer classical or bureaucratic models: those who consider that people best express themselves in freer contexts will tend to support more democratic organisational structures. Even where democratic systems may be more time-consuming and less efficient, they may still be preferred, for human and moral reasons. But to leave the matter thus would be to mislead. Might, not right or need, usually determines the way organisations operate. Historically, there are almost no examples of democracy being achieved without struggle.

Towards a More Unified Sociological Theory of Organisations

A unified theory of organisations should not be attempted at the expense of ignoring significant theoretical differences between scholars of different perspectives. Nevertheless, several contributors to organisational theory have suggested that a framework of overall analysis, capable of sustaining certain differences in perspective, does now virtually exist.

Amitai Etzioni, who adopts a conflict structural approach, considers that it embodies the essential elements of both the classical and human relations perspectives. He clearly considers these to be two sides of the same coin – the rational and the personal-social. He also observes that conflict is a normal and, sometimes, a useful, feature of organisational life. For instance, a strike involves conflict, but it can lead to a settlement of differences and to a new period of organisational stability.

Etzioni is pursuing a promising approach in bringing together conflict-structuralism and micro-level sociology. However, Clegg and Dunkerley's more recent work, *Organization, Class and Control*, is a still more impressive attempt at synthesis. Whereas Etzioni draws mainly from Weber in presenting structural-conflict, Clegg and Dunkerley lean heavily towards Marx. They see class domination and conflict as *endemic* in both capitalist enterprise and state bureaucracy. They consider that the state bureaucracy in Russia is even more an 'engine' of repression, than the state in capitalist society, and in this analysis Weber's understanding of the oppressive burden of state bureaucracy is apparent. Yet they create no sense, as the structural-functionalists do, that the men and women who occupy small roles in large organisations are for that reason powerless. They understand that workers interpret and respond to their conditions and sometimes organise to change them. In this way conflict-structural theory and interactionism seem to complement each other in their work. Of course, Marxists appreciate with functionalists that organisations can function without conflict for long periods and sometimes almost indefinitely. The difference is that Marxists consider that structural division and, therefore, potential conflict is a permanent feature of capitalist society, whereas functionalists consider basic harmony and consensus quite possible. For Marxists such consensus is the result of the ideological conditioning of the working class to conform to a social and organisational order that exploits them and drastically limits their self-expression.

Guide to further reading and study

Diagrams of bureaucracies, including schools, are easily obtainable or, alternatively, can be drawn up. A contrast between bureaucratic goals and 'actual' complex interaction can be made by asking students to compare the formal goals of educational establishments with what they, individually and as a group, 'get up to' at any given time. This can include daydreaming, 'bunking off', or whatever.

'Organisations' is not a topic well-loved either by teachers or students and, in general, the literature lives down to expectations. Among the general introductions, David Dunkerley's *The Study of Organisations* (Routledge and Kegan Paul, 1972), is brief, and simply presented. David Silverman's important work, *The Theory of Organisations* (Heinemann, 1970), is for teachers rather than students. Much interactionist material in this area manages to be both readable and theoretically interesting. Erving Goffman's *Asylums* (Pelican, 1968) and Stanley Cohen and Laurie Taylor's *Psychological Survival: The Experience of Long-Term Imprisonment* (Penguin, 1972) are especially recommended. Those who are prepared to range more widely will profit from E. F. Schumacher's *Small is Beautiful* (Abacus, 1974). Recommendations of literature with a more structuralist bias in respect of industrial organisations is made at the end of Chapter 14.

Past Questions

1 In order to 'get things done' rules in bureaucratic organisations frequently have to be broken. How does this come about? (AEB, 1976).
2 Can organisations be democratic? (AEB, 1977).

430

3 Outline the main features of Weber's ideal-type of bureaucracy. What are the dysfunctions of bureaucracy? (AEB, 1980).
4 What is a 'total institution'? Does this concept enhance our understanding of prisons *or* boarding schools *or* mental hospitals *or* shops? (AEB, 1980).

Section E **Social Order, Public Power and Personal Potential**

How to Use this Section

The central theme of this section is the relationship between social order and individual potential and expression. This relationship is complex and contradictory. Social order normally ensures a stable context within which the individual can pursue his own ends, but this secure frame-work constricts as well as protects. The law itself embodies this ambiguity. Positively, it does establish some of the more important, formal rules of social order within which social interaction can take place. Negatively, it prevents individuals and groups from doing some of the things which, left to their own devices, they might want to do. The first chapter in this section describes *the nature of social order* and the various means of social control, such as the armed forces, the police and the courts, which may be used to enforce it. This chapter also introduces the concept of *deviance:* the term sociologists use to describe the breaking of social rules as norms. Chapter 17 is substantially a detailed examination of various types of deviance. It concludes, however, with a general review of theories of deviance and social order and suggests that the various sociological perspectives are more complementary in this area than is often realised.

Chapter 18 begins by examining more explicitly a concept that underlies the previous two chapters, that of *power*. Power, the ability to make someone behave as *you* want regardless of *their* will, is an aspect of all social relationships and institutions though those who have power may not always choose to use it. In this sense power operates, for example, in the family, the classroom and the workplace. The most familiar public context in which power-conflict takes place is politics. Laws are made by individuals or groups that have power. Marxists, however, consider that 'real' power in capitalist societies lies with big business, and not with political parties and government. The nature and distribution of power is an issue about which sociologists sharply disagree. In many ways this disagreement is a logical extension of the sociological debate on stratification discussed earlier (see Chapters 8, 9 and 10).

Chapter 19 discusses *ideology, culture and creativity*. This may seem an abrupt change from the central focus on the previous chapter, power. This is not so, however. There is no more important form of power than ideological power, the ability to influence and even control the ideas and beliefs of other men. We begin our analysis of ideologies or systems of belief by examining the social functions of religion. As it happens, this is an area in which Marx and Durkheim are in considerable agreement. We also examine the rather different perspective of Max Weber on religion. Despite the decline of traditional religion, there is no sign of an end to ideological belief in today's world. Communism is an example of a secular (non-religious) ideology. An analysis of the interests that control the media and the effects of the media on its audience continues the theme of ideological power.

The last section of Chapter 19, on the fulfilment of personal potential (self-actualisation), attempts to redress the structuralist bias of the preceding cultural analysis. The point is emphasised that the individual can interpret, change and even, in part, reject the culture he inherits. Though most people do not 'make history' in any public sense, many live their personal biographies much more originally and creatively than some arm-chair critics of popular culture suggest. Nevertheless, there is a real danger that 'mass culture', piped into the home and passively received, will undermine intellect and spirit. The final section of the chapter discusses this possibility.

16 Social Order, Social Control and Deviance (Theory 6)

We have made the problem of stratification and equality the central pivot of this book, but the related issues of social order, social control and deviance can hardly be considered of less importance. Indeed, for functionalists, social order is the crux of sociological theory. As explained in Chapter 1, they regard social order as a precondition of the survival of society. Marxists treat this view with great suspicion. They consider that the relevant issue is not the necessity for social order, but the question of who benefits from such as does exist. In their view, social order in most societies does little more than provide opportunity for the powerful to exploit the weak. Despite these apparently incompatible starting points, we shall see that there are complementary as well as contradictory aspects in the way in which major structuralist theories treat this topic.

Neither symbolic interactionists nor ethnomethodologists have produced a distinctive general theory of social order, control and deviance. The macro-level has not primarily been their scale of concern. Instead, they have concentrated on the various 'actors' involved in behaviour 'labelled' as deviant. Some interactionists, particularly a number of British sociologists, have, however, attempted to link micro-level research with structural perspective.

Perspectives on Order, Control and Deviance

Functionalism

Social Order: Durkheim, Parsons and Shils

Functionalists regard social order as more normal and natural than disorder. Society, like the human body, depends for survival on the orderly functioning of its various parts. To understand this is to appreciate the fundamental point of the organic analogy.

The tradition which sees social order as natural goes back to Durkheim. Underlying social order was what he called social solidarity: we described what he meant by this term in Chapter 7. In essence, social solidarity depends on basic moral consensus. In turn, morality exists primarily to keep society together, Durkheim himself is quite clear on this point and it is the basis of his whole sociology:

> Society is not a simple aggregate of individuals who, when they
> enter it, bring their own intrinsic morality with them; rather,

435

> man is a moral being only because he lives in society, since morality
> consists in being solidary with (at one with) a group and varies with
> this solidarity. Let all social life disappear, and moral life would
> disappear with it, since it would no longer have any objective.

The final sentence of this quotation makes it clear that, for
Durkheim, morality is a *human* not a *divine* reality. Its purpose
is to exercise control on man's instincts and wayward will.
Durkheim does not trust human nature and sees a fundamental
need for a system of moral order to constrain it:

> The totality of moral rules truly forms about each person an
> imaginary wall, at the foot of which the flood of human passions
> dies without being able to go further ... if at any point this
> barrier weakens, (these) previously restrained human forces pour
> tumultously through the open breach; once loosened they find no
> limits where they can stop.

No less than Durkheim, Talcott Parsons sees a need for a system of norms and values to provide a framework of social
order. He prefers the more neutral term *values* to morals (that
is, he wishes to avoid any suggestion that given values are
good or bad). (We examined his social system theory in some
detail in Chapter 3.) For Parsons, underpinning the whole
social system and providing the ultimate basis of all social
integration are the fundamental values of society.

Edward Shils's thinking on the problem of social order is
also well worth mentioning. He, like Durkheim and Parsons,
stresses the role of values in creating coherent social order:

> The existence of a central value system rests, in a fundamental
> way, on the need which human beings have for incorporation
> into something which transcends and transfigures their concrete
> individual existence. They have a need to be in contact with
> symbols of an order which is larger than their own bodies and
> more central in the 'ultimate' structure of reality than is their
> routine everyday life.

This passage typifies the almost reverential attitude of many
functionalists to what they regard as the moral nature of society and, particularly, order and authority. A slightly more original feature of Shils's analysis is his emphasis on the role of the
central elite in maintaining social order and consensus. The elite
can do this only if its authority is generally accepted. Shils, like
all major functionalist thinkers, appreciates that acceptance of

436

central authority and values does not occur equally in all parts of society. His interest, however, is in explaining the functional necessity of consensus, authority and order rather than in analysing why they are barely accepted or even rejected by some individuals or groups. As we shall see, Marxists and interactionists have far more to say on these matters and their views can be cited in criticism of functionalist theories of social order.

Social Control and Conformity

Before dealing with specifically functionalist thinking on social control, it will help to introduce the concept briefly in more general terms. Social control refers to the means and processes by which individuals and groups are persuaded or forced to conform to dominant norms. We can divide social control into *formal* and *informal* control. Formal means of control are the courts, the police and armed forces. Usually, these are subject to the major overall source of social control: the state. It is enough just to stress this essential point here, as we deal fully with the state later. On a smaller scale, specific organisations may have their own means of control. Thus, corporal punishment, 'lines', expulsion or detention may be used in schools. Informal means of control consist of less organised but often very powerful pressure to enforce conformity. Because functionalists consider that informal social control must be effective for society to work, we deal with it first.

Informal social control occurs largely by means of socialisation. We have examined in some detail how functionalists consider that the individual is wedded to the norms and values of society by means of socialisation within the family, educational system and in other ways. It is universally accepted by sociologists – not just functionalists – that socialisation is the major means by which moral and psychological commitment to society are brought about. By psychological commitment we mean that people become mentally predisposed to conform as a result of socialisation. The significant difference between functionalists and Marxists on this matter is that the former tend to emphasise the necessity of socialisation whereas the latter frequently stress its exploitative and repressive aspects.

Although functionalists prefer conformity to be underpinned by *moral consensus*, they accept that formal control, supported, if necessary, by coercion, must be the ultimate means by which it is enforced. That is why the courts, police and armed forces exist. Even so, when moral consensus breaks down, the problem of social order and control becomes much greater. In practice, elements of formal and informal control often operate together. The quotation below illustrates a combination of informal moral and more formal coercive persuasion of a kind more commonly found in traditional than in modern societies:

> The traditional community was able to compel individual family members to follow collective rules through a disciplinary technique called the charivari . . . The charivari was, in its essentials, a noisy public demonstration to subject wayward individuals to humiliation in the eyes of the community. Sometimes the demonstration would consist of masked individuals circling somebody's house at night, screaming, beating on pans, and blowing cow horns (which the local butchers rented out). On other occasions the offender would be seized and marched through the streets, seated perhaps backwards on a donkey or forced to wear a placard describing his sins . . .
> (In France) sexual offenders were often the targets of charivaris, such as married men in the village of Vaux (Oise) who got single women pregnant.

Contemporary Europeans rarely resort to such elaborate ritual to censure and control others; with the decline of traditional moral standards there is more tolerance of a variety of behaviour. Nevertheless, informal psychological coercion can be exercised against an individual who offends people morally or otherwise even if force, or the threat of force, is now less easily used outside a legal context. Consider, for instance, how it may be practised against someone who is known to be having an affair with a popular colleague's wife. He may suddenly find himself not invited out for 'a drink with the lads', to dinner parties, or to weekend sports outings. The 'atmosphere' may quickly change when he sits down with his colleagues for a chat or a game of cards; customary banter may begin to take on the quality of personal antagonism; those who already dislike the individual concerned, recognising the way the wind is blowing, may adopt an openly aggressive attitude . . . the list of possible censorious responses could be continued almost indefinitely. At some time or another, most people will experience

438

some of the above forms of social disapproval. The psychological effect on the censured individual is not pleasant and, of course, is not intended to be. Feelings of tension and pressure indicate that social constraint is biting. The need for group acceptance and approval is often enough to bring the individual 'back into line'. Although the above analysis of psychological coercion in a small group context is quite compatible with functionalist assumptions, there are few examples of such micro-level work in functionalist writing. Instead, functionalists tend to concentrate on the social system as a whole, leaving the understanding of small group behaviour to interactionists.

Deviance

We must begin by giving a basic functionalistic definition of deviance, to be qualified, it must be stressed, by other perspectives. Deviant behaviour occurs when an individual or group behaves in a way contrary to the normative consensus. Some authorities suggest that the term 'deviance' be reserved for those acts for which moral disapproval is likely to be generally felt, and that the term 'non-conformity' be used to refer to normative breaches which do not arouse moral censure. Whilst it is useful to bear this distinction in mind, it should not be regarded as rigid. Often behaviour which offends custom or polite practice is referred to as deviant even though no obvious immorality has occurred. There are a number of terms and analytical observations employed by functionalists which are also in general sociological use. We will deal with these before presenting some more controversial elements of functionalist deviancy theory.

a THE RELATIVE NATURE OF DEVIANCE Deviance is both culturally and historically *relative*. We will examine the cultural relativity of deviance first. An act can be judged deviant only by reference to a specific standard – usually the norms of a given group, and these vary from one group to another. Thus, to consume alcohol would be deviant in an orthodox Muslim community, but not in most Christian ones. To take another example, it is a Sikh tradition always to wear a turban in public, a practice continued by many Sikhs in Britain. Needless to say, within the general British population such an attitude to headgear is entirely foreign, and anyone other than a Sikh who

439

adopted it would be considered highly abnormal. Deviance, therefore, is relative in that what is considered deviant changes from one cultural group to another.

The historical relatively of deviance merely means that definitions of what is deviant can change within a given society or group over a period of time. Changes and developments in normative attitudes towards deviance are part of what is meant by the term 'cultural change'. Changing attitudes to divorce and divorced people in Britain illustrate the point. In the Victorian period, divorce was generally strongly disapproved of, and virtually impossible to obtain except by the wealthy few. In contemporary Britain, divorce has become so common that the stigma attached to it has inevitably diminished greatly, and we would not now consider divorced people as deviant.

b THE VARIETY OF DEVIANCE A consequence of the relative and changing nature of deviance is that the variety of deviant behaviour is immense: this is easily demonstrable by reference to the field of deviant behaviour in just one society – Britain. In modern British society, deviance includes the following varied forms of behaviour: murder; having sexual intercourse under the age of sixteen; appearing nude in a public place; playing football in the outfit of a clown; wearing the clothes normally worn only by the opposite sex; attempting to fly without artificial aid. *All that the above factors have in common is that they contravene accepted norms.* We cannot even add that they all provoke moral censure. Some, such as attempting to fly without artificial aid, are likely to provoke amusement or pity depending on how seriously the intentions of the would-be aeronaut are taken. Finally, the variety of deviance is illustrated by the fact that any man or group is capable of taking an alternative 'deviant' position to the accepted one, although he may have to suffer unpleasant consequences for doing so.

c DURKHEIM AND DEVIANCE Our treatment of functionalist deviancy theory proper begins with Durkheim. He observed that deviance is *universal, normal* and *functional.* There is no problem in accepting the universality of deviance. No society can command total conformity from all its members. That Durkheim should consider deviance to be normal might seem a contradiction in terms: in fact, such a conclusion is implicit in the universal nature of deviance. If it occurs everywhere, it must in that sense be normal, even though the precise forms deviant behaviour takes in a given society are regarded as abnormal in that society. The functionality of deviance raises more serious problems. How can socially destructive behaviour, such as vandalism or murder, be in any way functional to society? Actually, *it is not deviance itself but the reaction of others to it that Durkheim sees as functional.* Deviant behaviour gives society an opportunity simultaneously to condemn the type of behaviour in question and to reaffirm collective moral unity (remember, Durkheim was insistent on the reality of society as a moral entity and he considered any behaviour that focused moral sentiment as functional to the extent that it did so). Perhaps Durkheim's analysis of the social functionality of deviance caused him to ignore the stress, inconvenience and suffering that some deviant behaviour causes. In this instance, abstract functionalist argument formulated in social systems' terms seems to obscure the more urgent reality of human experience.

A highly controversial aspect of Durkheim's thought is his tendency to equate deviance with 'social pathology'. By this he means that deviants must be sick in a way comparable to, though obviously not identical with, the physically sick. In fairness, this exaggerated comparison is only really apparent when he adopts a strict version of the organic analogy. Consistent with his appreciation of the relative nature of deviance Durkheim pointed out that social normality and social pathology or deviance vary from society to society. He was in no doubt that social pathology tended to increase during times of great social change. In such times people are often left without clear rules or normative guidelines, and so become more prone to deviance. In particular, the decline of religious certainties could undermine security and confidence in traditional morality. Durkheim referred to this state of 'normlessness' as *'anomie'*. We analyse his detailed application of this concept to suicide in the next chapter. He considered that the rapid change of the late nineteenth century generated a climate of anomie characterised by increasing rates of suicide, homicide, drunkenness and other signs of pathological desperation. He believed that the major problem in modern society is to find a new basis of moral solidarity. He did not believe that overlapping self-interest, the basis of organic solidarity, was quite enough.

d ROBERT MERTON Robert Merton, writing just before the Second World War, made the most significant contribution to functionalist deviancy theory since Durkheim. Merton used the term 'non-conformity' instead of deviance, but we may assume that what he is talking about is, in fact, deviance. As can be seen from the diagram below, Merton juxtaposes conformity and four types of non-conformist adjustments.

	Culture goals	Institutionalised means
1 Conformity	+	+
2 Innovation	+	−
3 Ritualism	−	+
4 Retreatism	−	−
V. Rebellion*	±	±

* This fifth alternative is on a plane clearly different from that of the others. It represents a *transitional* response which seeks to *institutionalise* new procedure-oriented toward revamped cultural goals shared by members of the society. It thus involves efforts to *change* the existing structure rather than to perform accommodative actions *within* this structure, and introduces additional problems with which we are not at the moment concerned.
Source: Taken from Peter Worsley, ed, *Modern Sociology*, 1978, p. 619.

For him, conformity lies in accepting the 'culture goals' of society – material success is such a 'culture goal' in the USA – *and* in pursuing them by legitimate 'institutionalised means' – that is, within the limits of normative and legal acceptability. Correspondingly, three of the four forms of adjustments lie in rejecting either or both culture goals and the institutionalised means by which they can be pursued. The fourth, rebellion, involves both a rejection of the goals and means of the old order (− −) and an attempt to assert new ones (+ +).

There is much to quarrel with in Merton's model, as we shall see when we examine his analysis of 'innovation' (his major concern) as applied to criminal deviancy, but he does map out the chief areas of deviancy in a way that is interesting and suggestive of possibilities for further research. Merton himself has developed the concept of ritualism as applied to bureaucratic work. He points out that people involved in such work can become so dominated by rules of procedure and routine that they lose sight of the purpose of their work. Thus, a social security official who delays urgently needed assistance until every bureaucratic check has been made on a client is indulging in ritualistic behaviour. Merton feared that such 'bureaucratic characters' might become something of a plague in large-scale, highly organised modern societies. Merton's retreatist category provides a useful perspective. It is arguable, however, that the retreatists he mentions – such as some outcasts, vagrants, chronic drunkards and drug addicts – *drift* into deviancy for a variety of complex reasons. Generally, Merton's plus and minus signs tend to oversimplify the complexity of real life, although his model has some value as a basis of departure for classifying deviancy.

Marxism: Social Order, Control and Deviance

Social Order

There is good reason for making this section shorter than the one which preceded it. Marxists do not 'see' society in the way suggested by the group of concepts with which this chapter is concerned. They understand society in terms of conflict rather than order. Marxists barely pause to acknowledge the practical necessity of social order. Where order exists, they see it in terms of the control of one class by another, not as the product of genuine consensus. They primarily concern themselves with capitalist society but recognise the same principle – class domination – in other, more traditional societies. The dominant class seeks to establish and maintain a social order based invariably on its own interests, at the expense of others. Class conflict is always likely to undermine order imposed by the ruling class.

It will be remembered that, when analysing social stratification and conflict, we spent longer on the Marxist than the functionalist perspective. Now, in dealing with social order and control, we make the reverse emphasis. Seen from the Marxist perspective, the law and the various control agencies that enforce it are tools of class exploitation rather than bulwarks of justice. The law is not regarded as a neutral instrument that provides equal justice for all, but as something protecting the property rights of the wealthy few at the expense of the rest. The law is certainly functional, but for the privileged minority, not the majority. *Individual* property rights are seen as much more firmly established in law than, for instance, the *collective* rights of the trade unions. These are regarded as insecurely established, and always likely to be whittled down by government or disadvantageously interpreted by the courts. Marxists virtually turn the concept of legal justice in capitalist society on its head. The fact that the statistics appear to show that proportionately more working class people than middle class people commit crime is taken to illustrate the biased, class nature of bourgeois justice, rather than greater working class criminality. To take an extreme example – if someone in poverty steals from a wealthy person or institution, the injustice is seen to lie with the society which tolerates poverty, not with the individual.

Marxists argue that not only does the law protect inequality but that people have unequal access to the law. Having money to hire a good lawyer can mean the difference between being found innocent or guilty. At a more subtle level, the ability to present a respectable image in court might appeal favourably to the sentiments of predominantly middle class magistrates, judges and jurors. These points may well explain why there is some evidence to suggest that working class people are more likely to be found guilty than middle class people for the same offence.

By citing such examples, and there are plenty of them, Marxists are able to throw back the ideals of liberal justice at those who profess them. Does freedom under law simply mean freedom to be unequal? Can freedom exist without a much greater degree of equality? Does equality under the law really exist when the content and operation of the law seem to favour the middle class? Of course, these are Marxist questions based on controversial Marxist assumptions, but they are serious enough to warrant consideration regardless of personal ideology.

Social Control, Ideology and Repression
Marxists agree with functionalists that socialisation plays a crucial part in social control, but whereas functionalists tend to accept the necessity of this, Marxists are highly critical of the dominant values and norms of capitalist society which they equate with 'capitalist ideology'. They consider that the working class is often ideologically deluded or 'mystified' into conforming to a social order that is against its 'true' interests. Marxists generally regard in this light attempts by sections of the media to persuade the working class that strikes are irres-

ponsible and 'bad for the country'. Similarly, Marxists are much more critical than functionalists of the role of the ruling class in formulating central values and ideas. They would agree with Shils that the ruling ideas of a society are those of the ruling class (Shils prefers the term *elite*), but they stress that these ideas benefit those at the top of society rather than those at the bottom. Thus, if the working class practises the values of hard work and conformity to the law, the bourgeoisie will be able to enjoy its wealth, power and status in peace. Working class people who avidly pursue personal success (a 'bourgeois' value in the Marxist view), weaken the collective strength of the working class while not seriously challenging the power of the bourgeoisie which, in any case, can usefully absorb a limited number of able working class people. So what is called by functionalists the 'central value' of economic individualism, is, in Marxist terms, an example of some members of the working class being misled by bourgeois 'individualistic' ideology.

If socialisation is the soft edge of social control, the hard edge is represented by the army, police, courts and custodial system – what Althusser calls the 'repressive state apparatus'. Marxists see these as instruments of class rule. Some also consider that teachers, probation officers and social workers play a similar role: 'soft cops' is how they are sometimes described. Members of these professions or semi-professions are largely concerned with persuading frequently rebellious or alienated youth to conform to what, in the Marxist view, is an exploitative society.

'Deviance': a 'dirty word'

Because Marxists do not recognise the legitimacy of capitalist social order, they generally have little use for the concept of 'deviance'. The response of the majority of Marxists to working class deviance amounts to 'Well, what can you expect? Some might have more than a sneaking sympathy for, say, the working class thief: a few might even regard his theft romantically as a form of property redistribution – incipient socialism! But no Marxist would regard crime as a substitute for organised economic and political action by the working class, or even as a significant form of support for it. In any case, Marxists condemn explanations of working class crime based on assumptions of inferiority or pathology. For them, blame lies with the sys-

445

tem and, perhaps, those who benefit from it, not with its victims.

Those Marxists who have taken a more active recent interest in deviancy theory have tended to focus their attention on the upper end of the class system. Frank Pearce's book, *Crimes of the Powerful*, is a notable contribution of this kind (see Chapter 17). Pursuing a different theme, Colin Sumner has suggested that Marxists try to analyse how definitions of normality and deviance in class-divided societies are produced, and how they serve the system. This could be a very interesting line of analysis. To what extent, for instance, do the media form standards of normality and deviance? Who controls the media and in whose interest? Sumner leaves us with a strong sense that these and related questions are well worth pursuing.

Interactionism: Deviance, Social Order and Control

It might seem perverse, at this stage, to depart from the order in which we have been considering the topics of this chapter. The nature of interactionist theory, however, demands a quite different treatment from that given to functionalism and Marxism. Historically interactionalists have been much more interested in deviance than in social order. Interactionist research on social control has been more vigorous, and since the late nineteen sixties several major studies of specific agencies of control have been published. Yet, these studies reflect the characteristic interactionist assumption that those who control deviance must first define what it is. It is, therefore, with deviancy theory that we can most logically start our analysis. For reasons given there we reserve detailed consideration of interactionist social control theory until the next chapter.

Primary and Secondary Deviance – Labelling
Whereas functionalists stress normative consensus, interactionists argue that modern societies are characterised by a great variety or *plurality* of values and norms. This diversity of attitude exists in most areas of human activity, including religion, sex, politics and race. Conformity to the law is seen not as a product of moral consensus but either as the ability of some groups to impose rules or, as a matter of practical necessity.

446

Until recently, interactionists have paid more attention to *how rules are applied and the effect of their application or non-application on the deviant person*, rather than why and how some groups and individuals, such as employers and headmasters, make the rules and others, such as employees and pupils, have to obey them. We return to this issue, essentially one of power, shortly. On the practicality of rules, Lemert points out that much modern legislation is justified in terms of organisational requirement, rather than morality. For instance, many traffic offences are not immoral in themselves. Travelling at 32 miles per hour in a 30 mile per hour zone would not cause genuine moral indignation in any but the most authoritian personality: even so, the practical necessity to enforce the speed limit remains.

Interactionists do not, then, analyse deviance simply as rule breaking, but equally in terms of how and to whom the rules are applied. This is the basis of Lemert's distinction between *primary* and *secondary deviance*. According to him, primary deviance is the initial commission of a deviant act. Secondary deviance is the effect that 'societal reaction' has on the conduct of the deviant subsequent to the commission of the initial deviant act. 'Societal reaction' means the reaction of society, or specifically of any group within society, such as the police, the courts, the family and acquaintances of the deviant, the media and, through the media, the public. Lemert's relative silence on primary deviance is a matter we will return to, critically, later.

Primary and Secondary Deviance

Primary Deviance (Rule Breaking) for example, Speeding	Label (Societal Reaction)	Secondary Deviance That is,
	→ Charge, Conviction ↓ *or*	→ Deviant Status In this case, 'Traffic Offender' (Minor Criminal)
	No Label for example, Ignored, Not Noticed Rationalised (Seen as a 'Mistake')	

He and other interactionists have overwhelmingly given their attention to secondary deviance. If, as Howard Becker claims, 'an act is deviant when it is so defined', (an act is deviant when societal reaction declares it to be), then it is what happens in the life of the deviant *after* the social definition has been made that is the focus of interactionist analysis. We can illustrate the distinction between primary and secondary deviance in schematic form.

Learning, Meaning and Societal Reaction

We can use Howard Becker's study of marijuana users to illustrate two further points about interactionist deviancy theory. These are that deviant behaviour, like most other human behaviour, including conformist, is *learnt,* and that people become deviant partly because they find such behaviour meaningful that is, to oversimplify somewhat, *they become deviant because they want to.* Becker also explores the labelling process or societal reaction in some detail. The idea that deviant behaviour is learnt is implied in the title of Becker's key essay 'Becoming a Marijuana User', and is consistent with Mead's theory of socialisation. Becker points out that to smoke marijuana enjoyably, first, the technique has to be learnt; then it is necessary to learn how to perceive the drug's effects and, finally, the user has to learn to enjoy them. It perhaps needs to be explained that, without this learning process, taking the drug can be both unpleasant and, seemingly, without effect. (We gave a fuller account of the meaning of psychedelic drug use in pleasure-seeking sub-cultures in Chapter 13.) Learning and meaning are linked in Becker's analysis. *People only voluntarily learn what seems meaningful to them.* Like Mead, Becker fully allows for the influence of 'significant others', in this case dance musicians who use marijuana, on the individual. Using it is part of their way of life; it fits in with their style and they naturally offer 'established newcomers' the opportunity to try it. Becker notes that the individual is likely to drop or cut back on marijuana smoking when he or she leaves this environment, and the habit ceases to have much cultural meaning.

Becker introduces a concept termed *deviant career,* which he relates to societal reactions. Like any career, that of a deviant is affected by a variety of unpredictable factors which he calls *career contingencies.* The first contingency, a precondition of a deviant career, is that the action or actions of the individual be labelled as deviant. To draw examples from beyond Becker's particular study, labels such as 'mentally ill', 'socially handicapped' and 'juvenile delinquent' may trap a person within an identity from which it may be difficult to escape. Thus, a *stigma* is attached to him which may damage his self-image and affect the response of others to him. For example, a person labelled 'mentally ill' or 'criminal' may be discriminated against when trying to get a job, or rent lodgings.

Social Order and Control

Interactionists reject the functionalist theory that order rests on a consensus of values. Instead, they offer a *power model* of conformity and deviance. *The norms and laws of a society are invariably the product of conflict between groups.* Becker is quite clear on this:

> People are in fact always *forcing* their rules on others, applying them more or less against the will and without the consent of those others.

He goes on to give several examples of this. Rules are made by the old for the young and, to a great extent, by men for women, and by whites for blacks. To take the last example, in the southern States of the USA, the segregation laws preserved the interests and prestige of whites, and subjugated and exploited blacks. But Matza, in particular, has recognised that in reality norms and values are more changeable and ambiguous than either the functionalist or a simple power-conflict model might imply. We can illustrate this from our previous example of black-white relations. For over a century, and particularly in the last 25 years, race relations in the United States have been changing and legislation has fully reflected this. Normative change always brings ambiguity: people don't quite know where they stand. Thus, as segregation in the southern states was challenged and increasingly discredited, the laws upholding it were increasingly ignored in 'liberal', often urban areas. Normative change and ambiguity also illustrate the relative nature of social norms and values which interactionists fully accept. They are not timeless commandments etched in stone, but matters that may be contested, changed, undermined or even ignored.

Matza has further pointed out that the deviant's self-definition might not accord with the neat categories of law and convention and that definitions may be contested. For instance, what is the 'correct' label for women or, for that matter, men, who receive 'gifts' from those with whom they have more or less casual sexual relations? Some might readily call them 'prostitutes', but it could be that the individuals concerned have taken great pains to preserve their self-respect by not behaving precisely as they think prostitutes do. Perhaps the gifts are meant to be occasional, and not thought of as payment for favours given. In this way, personal acceptance of the identity of a prostitute can be plausibly resisted. Difficult though it may be to appreciate this distinction, as far as interactionalists are concerned, if a distinction genuinely exists in an individual's mind, it exists as a fragment of reality.

We examine interactionist analysis of social control in the next chapter. Here it is enough to say that interationists do not consider that agencies of control simply enforce the will of successful interest groups as expressed in the law. They, too, have their own interests and ideology which prevent them from being neutral instruments of enforcement. We will consider this proposition in relation to both the police and the courts.

An Assessment of the Interactionist Theory of Deviance
Two major criticisms of the interactionist approach can be made. Firstly, it does not offer an explanation of primary deviance. Secondly, it is said, particularly by Marxists, that it fails to explain adequately the relationship between power, especially class power, and deviance. We take these points in order. Even Lemert hurries past primary deviance on his way to analysing secondary deviance which is clearly his main interest. Becker, with engaging frankness, agrees that 'stick-up men' do not 'stick people up' simply because somebody has labelled them 'stick-up men', but he still leaves unexplained why some men and women behave in this way whilst others do not. It is true that interactionists do not claim fully to explain why deviance occurs in the first place, but this does result in certain weaknesses in their general theory. In particular, the notion that certain social environments – perhaps those which are in some way 'deprived' – may be associated with certain sorts of deviant behaviour is, apparently, of little interest to them. Yet, this view is not necessarily incompatible with interactionist perspective and, if it were explored by interactionists, might even be found complementary to it.

We now turn to the second criticism commonly made – that it deals inadequately with the relationship between power and deviance. More precisely, this is a specifically Marxist criticism that most interactionists do not sufficiently link their analysis of law and deviance to class theory. In the Marxist view the law and the state ultimately operate in favour of the ruling class. Marxist sociology of deviance is, therefore, concerned with showing how this is so. Many interactionists do not subscribe to a Marxist class conflict theory of society. Rather, they see the power structure in terms of a contest between all sorts of groups – including ethnic, religious, feminist – as well as classes which seek to establish their own interests and moral values. Becker's own case study of the interests behind The Marijuana Tax Act of 1937 (aimed at stamping out use of the drug) does not mention class at all, but concludes that the Federal Bureau of Narcotics was the major influence or 'entrepreneur' in getting the Act passed.

The above Marxist-interactionist disagreement in no way invalidates basic interactionist labelling theory nor its associated concepts. Indeed, many Marxists, particularly younger ones, are freely using interactionist concepts and notably so in the area of sub-cultural analysis. We have already come across examples of this in the work of Paul Willis and Jock Young. Further, when interactionists deal with class and power, they often reach conclusions compatible with Marxism. Thus, the proposition that white collar crime might be under-recorded in official statistics because of police and judical bias in favour of the middle class is commonly found in Marxist and interactionist literature.

Guide to further reading and study

The subject of this chapter is complex and this is more than reflected in the literature. The second year student, however, will find that the problem of social order is well covered from the functionalist and conflict structuralist points of view in Cuff and Payne, eds, *Perspectives in Sociology*, (Allen and Unwin, 1979). The first two chapters of Anthony Giddens' *Durkheim*, (Fontana, 1978) give a clear account of his thought on this matter. (This book is aimed at a general audience and should be within the range of the more advanced student.) A straightforward, well-presented and comprehensive survey of deviancy theory is Charles S. Suchar's *Social Deviance: Perspectives and Prospects* (Holt, Rinehart and Winston, 1978). It deserves a place in, for instance, a college or sixth form library. So, too, does Howard S. Becker's seminal work *Outsiders* (The Free Press, 1963). This work is still as clear a statement of the interactionist theory of deviance as any. Just within our range is Stanley Cohen's *Folk Devils and Moral Panics* (Martin Robertson, 1981). As well as providing a readable account of the 'Mods and Rockers' phenomenon of the sixties, it can serve as an introduction to interactionist deviancy theory. Paul Rock's *Deviant Behaviour* (Hutchinson, 1973), is a readable but quite demanding textbook written from an interactionist perspective. Several books dealing with particular areas of deviant behaviour are recommended at the end of the next chapter where past questions can also be found.

17 Types of Deviance

Students are often disappointed when they come to study deviance. The topic promises more than it seems to deliver. Crime, sexual deviance, drug addiction – the labels all sound enticingly sinful. In practice, the topic is so theoretical that the appealing decadence of these activities becomes lost. Immersion in theory seems to smother the initial, exciting whiff of evil and, sometimes, student interest in the topic, too. This chapter is, in part, intended as a sympathic response to this problem. By now a certain knowledge of theory can be taken for granted; thus we can look at a specific area of deviancy in more detail without becoming too involved in abstractions.

1 Crime and Delinquency: Theories

What causes crime? This question has become increasingly urgent as far as Britain and most Western European countries are concerned, because of the large officially recorded increase in certain kinds of crime since the end of the Second World War, and particularly since the late nineteen sixties. The rise in the number of *indictable* (more serious) offences known to the police has been greatest in the areas of violence against the person (1969 – 37,800; 1977 – 82,200), and in various forms of stealing. We will question the precise accuracy of official criminal statistics, but clearly recorded increases of this size are likely to be correct at least in the *trend* they indicate. (See table below).

Six broad explanations of crime are considered below: the urban sociological; the functionalist and strain perspectives; the biological; the interactionist; the Marxist; the multi-factoral. These perspectives need not be regarded as mutually exclusive, though some obviously are. There is no real distinction between the terms crime and delinquency: both refer to the breaking of the criminal law. The term juvenile delinquency, however, describes violation of the law by someone less than seventeen years old.

a Crime as 'Inbred'

The view that some individuals are psychologically predisposed to crime as a result of their biological inheritance is not, of

INDICTABLE OFFENCES RECORDED BY THE POLICE

England and Wales   Thousands

	1969	1970	1971	1972	1973
Total (1)	1,498.7	1,568.4	1,665.7	1,690.2	1,657.7
Violence against the person	37.8	41.1	47.0	52.4	61.3
Sexual offences	23.5	24.2	23.6	23.5	25.7
Burglary	420.8	431.4	451.5	438.7	393.2
Robbery	6.0	6.3	7.5	8.9	7.3
Theft and handling stolen goods (2)	911.5	952.6	1,003.7	1,009.5	998.9
Fraud and forgery	78.9	89.5	99.8	108.4	110.7
Malicious and criminal damage (1) (3)	14.7	17.9	27.0	41.9	52.8
Other offences	5.5	5.4	5.6	6.9	7.8

	1974	1975	1976	1977
Total (1)	1,963.4	2,105.6	2,135.7	2,636.5
Violence against the person	63.8	71.0	77.7	82.2
Sexual offences	24.7	23.7	22.2	21.3
Burglary	438.8	521.9	515.5	604.1
Robbery	8.7	11.3	11.6	13.7
Theft and handling stolen goods (2)	1,189.9	1,267.7	1,285.7	1,487.5
Fraud and forgery	117.2	123.1	119.9	120.6
Malicious and criminal damage (1) (3)	67.1	78.5	93.0	297.4
Other offences	8.2	8.4	10.1	9.7

Source: *Home Office*

455

course, sociological, although sociologists must consider its validity against sociological explanations. The recent origins of this view are traceable, in crude form, to Cesare Lombroso, an Italian doctor whose ideas were influential around the turn of the last century. Lombroso believed that certain 'primitive' physical characteristics, including large jaws, acute sight and a love of orgies(!) indicated a criminal type, but empirical research by Charles Goring established no such correlations. More recently, it has been suggested that men possessing an extra male sex chromosome (Y) are more likely to commit violent crime than others. This is so, but such men still account for a very small proportion of all violent crime.

Hans Eysenck is the champion of the hereditarian argument in this as in other fields. He claims to have established a link between certain genetically based personality traits, such as *extroversion,* and criminal behaviour, although he prudently describes this as a *predisposition,* not a necessarily causal factor. Sociologists tend to react sceptically to such arguments. It can never be finally proved that a given action is primarily the 'result' of genetic predisposition rather than either the influence of social environment or individual choice. Sociologists are, however, more favourably inclined to psychological arguments which explain behaviour as a response to social or, for that matter, physical environment, rather than heredity. Thus, the Chicago school of sociologists, whose work we discuss next, appreciated that the material deprivation, physical decay and tough cultural environment of the inner city influenced children in such areas towards delinquency. Sociologists also accept that extreme conditions of this kind might produce mental illness, including criminal pathology (acute material or mental deprivation, or both, could make someone criminally insane). Nevertheless, few sociologists, if any, see such unusual circumstances as the basis of a general explanation of crime. What they do accept is that certain social conditions might produce a given kind of response, such as delinquency, but such resultant activity is certainly not regarded as mentally abnormal. Some sociologists are occasionally accused of being sympathetic to deviants. If true, this is perhaps less dangerous than regarding them as mentally aberrant, for what solutions to crime does this explanation lead to? Drug treatment? Brain surgery? A course of behaviourist psychotherapy? To some, these treatments seem more insane or, to be consistent, more criminal than the behaviour they seek to control.

b Urban Ecology and Crime

The inner city is the major location of crime associated with deprivation, and the *Chicago school attempted to establish links between environment, deprivation and crime, both theoretically and empirically.* Mainly by the use of official statistics, they attempted to demonstrate empirical correlation between high rates of crime, numerous other forms of deviancy, such as alcoholism, mental illness, prostitution and suicide, and the conditions of life prevailing in what Burgess called the 'zone of transition' of the urban area. Both the transience of the inner urban population (that is, its unsettled, mobile nature) and the physical decay of the environment were conditions conducive to deviance. The Chicago sociologists, when referring specifically to the physical environment, tended to use the terms 'zone of deterioration' or 'twilight zone' and when referring to population mobility, 'zone of transition'. Decaying conditions helped to create stress on the family, to weaken community relationships, and to isolate the individual, thus giving rise to anomie. Such circumstances could predispose individuals towards deviant behaviour. The fact that these areas were already generously populated by more than their share of assorted crooks, pimps and conmen made the possibility of 'picking up' a criminal 'trade' all the more likely.

The Chicago theorists, like Durkheim before them, contrasted the high crime rates of the inner city with the much lower crime rates of rural and suburban areas. They found an explanation for this, to some extent, in the thinking of Durkheim and Tönnies on the break up of traditional community and the growth of anomie. Small, rural communities can 'police and protect' their own, but in cities, both property and people become impersonal. Cars and luggage, for example, can be stolen in full view of the public who may have no idea of what is going on. Related to this is the vast growth in the *amount* of property, both personal and public, during this century and particularly since the war. When 'nobody' seems to own, say, a lamp-post or a telephone kiosk, it becomes, psychologically, easier to hurl a brick at it. A further point is that the sheer mass and variety of conflicting interests in the city makes

457

community control difficult, and generates friction conducive to crime.

An overview of studies of delinquency in Britain by John Barron Mays seems to support the conclusions of American research. Studies in Liverpool dockland, in Croydon, in a mining town in the Midlands, and in old and new areas of Bristol all appear to agree that delinquency is a larger part of the way of life of such areas than elsewhere, and has survived the coming of greater prosperity. Mays' work, however, is more contemporary by some 30 years than that of the Chicago school, and he considers more recent explanations of deviance in the urban context. The Chicago school itself did little more than develop that part of Durkheim's anomie theory dealing with social disorganisation in modern urban society.

c The Functionalist and Strain Perspectives

The functionalist, Robert Merton, concentrates on the effect of the social system on the deviant, rather than the way in which immediate physical environment influences behaviour. He emphasises how the potential criminal is excluded from the legitimate opportunity structure (conventional career success), and so is pushed towards crime in order to get what he wants (desired goals). A reference back to Merton's model of conformity and non-conformity will show that he contextualises non-conformity within the normative structure of the *social system as a whole*. He classifies criminal deviance under 'innovation', that is behaviour which accepts socially prescribed goals (+), but which uses normatively unacceptable means (−) to obtain them. Specifically, in the USA the culture goal of material success is accepted by some who nevertheless lack the legitimate means – for example, skills, qualifications and connections – to obtain it. Crime provides a major alternative means by which material success may be obtained; so much so, in fact, that Daniel Bell entitled an article 'Crime as Part of the American Way of Life'. Because the dominant norms that guide and constrain people in pursuits of material success are of little use to those excluded from the legitimate opportunity structure, Merton refers to their situation as anomic. This is a valid, if somewhat elastic, application of Durkheim's term.

Underlying Merton's analysis is the assumption that the desire for economic gain lies behind much crime. This view was held, albeit in much simpler form, by Victorian social reformers such as Charles Booth who believed that once poverty had been abolished there would be no 'need' for crime. In fact, relative (or comparative) deprivation continues, even though extreme poverty is rare in the West. Although thieves may have 'enough', they steal because, like the rest of us, they want *more*. Crudely, greed has replaced need as a dominant motive. The strain theorists, to whose work we now turn, develop these notions to a more sophisticated theoretical level.

Sociologists who have followed and extended Durkheim's analysis have sometimes been referred to as 'strain' theorists, no doubt because Merton's model poses a strain between the goals of the potential criminal and the structure of the legitimate opportunity. Whilst generally agreeing with Merton that the desire for economic gain motivates such crime, Cloward and Ohlin (1960) make a more detailed analysis of the possible forms of criminal reaction to lack of legitimate opportunity. Some criminals may adjust with spectacular success and rise to the criminal world's equivalent of the top managerial level: the 'godfather' figures of the Mafia are an example. At a lower level is the 'skilled craftsmen' who may work for himself, or for an organised gang. In the latter instance, he would expect high 'wages' or a substantial 'cut' from the job. Less organised crime provides an alternative for those without access to the criminal elite: haphazardly planned and sometimes risky street crime is a common example. Perhaps the near-pointless violence sometimes associated with this type of crime reflects the sense of 'double failure' of the low-grade criminal, a 'loser' in both the 'straight' and criminal worlds. Another group still, 'the retreatists' (see Merton's model) seek to negate their sense of failure by taking drugs.

Albert Cohen, another strain theorist, emphasises the 'status frustration' felt by lower class youths in explaining their delinquent behaviour. As we have seen, they tend to 'fail' at school and often drift in and out of unsatisfying, low-status work. He uses the term 'reaction formation' to describe how delinquent gang members rebound from conventional failure and seek to create their own alternative status hierarchies based on their criminal achievements. Committing a daring offence or even having a criminal record may become matters to boast about. Yet the desire for status is not, in itself, deviant. Thus, delin-

459

quent behaviour is seen as a distorted mirror-image of normal behaviour – an unpleasing glimpse of what anyone might do in the absence of legitimate alternatives of self-expression and esteem. A. K. Cohen provides a link between functionalist-strain and sub-cultural theory (discussed below). The latter approach, however, tends to see deviant sub-cultures not so much in reactive terms but as a positive assertion of lower working class values.

d Sub-cultural and Interactionist Theories

SUB-CULTURAL THEORIES We discuss the sub-cultural and inter-actionist perspectives together, although they are distinct, because an increasing number of authors use concepts and insights from both.

The sub-cultural theorist, Walter B. Miller, reacted against the analysis of the strain theorists, discussed above. He was the first to make a clear analysis of gang delinquency in terms of positive lower class values such as toughness, smartness, excitement and freedom from authority. It is this conformity to lower working class culture rather than rejection of middle class values that is the key to understanding delinquency. A very similar analysis to this was independently adopted in Britain during the nineteen fifties by both Terence Morris and J. B. Mays. Lower working class kids were often free to roam the streets in search of 'kicks' and were inconsistently, and there-fore ineffectively, punished by their parents if their 'fun' happened to break the law. Indeed, their parents might well be criminal themselves. In a study of East London in the early nineteen sixties, David Downes noted relatively little difference between the values of youthful delinquents and those of the adult lower working class. A study by Willmott of the same kind of area suggested that about 10% of working class youth were delinquent-inclined and that this inclination was formed by social environment. (See Chapter 13, pp. 339–40).

In part, the work on sub-cultures of Downes and others, provided the basis on which the Birmingham Centre for Cultural Studies has produced an impressive body of work analysing youth, particularly working class youth sub-cultures. It needs to be clearly stated that most of this research is not concerned primarily with working class juvenile delinquency as such, because most working class juveniles are not delinquents.

Nevertheless, there is often a thin line between legitimate excitement on the streets and breaking the law: the search for fun does not necessarily stop at the point of illegality. On the contrary, the enjoyment of motor-bike 'burn-ups', soccer 'hooliganism', and minor acts of vandalism is probably sharpened by the fact that they involve cocking a snook at law and authority. *Delinquescent* (delinquency prone) behaviour is not too strong a word to describe the tendency of much working class youth sub-cultural activity. We described these sub-cultures at some length in Chapter 13 and the student should re-read the relevant section (pp. 339–44), bearing in mind that there our concern was with pleasure-seeking, whereas here it is with delinquency. As was also pointed out in Chapter 13, some black youngsters also have life-styles that border on the delinquent. A 'black' song expresses the point more eloquently than a sociologist could, although the words lose much without the music:

> Many rivers to cross
> But I can't seem to find my way over
> Wandering, I am lost
> As I travel along the white cliffs of Dover
>
> Many rivers to cross
> But where to begin ... I'm playing for time
> There've been times
> I find myself thinking of committing some dreadful crime.

The interactionist, Matza, has criticised sub-cultural theorists for over-stressing the difference between sub-cultural and dominant values. Instead, he sees adolescents, particularly from the lower class, as drifting into crime out of a sense of fatalism and lack of something else to do. More recent sub-cultural theorists have accepted that this can often happen, but they still maintain the importance of distinct sub-cultural identity and values.

INTERACTIONIST THEORIES In the previous chapter we highlighted, mainly through Howard Becker's analysis of marijuana users, three major elements of 'labelling' theory: its explanation of deviancy as learnt; the stress given to the meaning of deviant behaviour by the actors involved; and the role of societal reaction. We pursue these points further here.

The American sociologist, Edwin H. Sutherland, insisted that delinquent behaviour is learned. Sutherland can be seen as an intermediary figure between the Chicago school of the inter-war period and modern interactionists on both sides of the Atlantic. Like the urban sociologists, he recognised that a socially disorganised environment is conducive to delinquency, but he wanted to understand more about the personal and psychological experiences that lead an individual into delinquency. After examining virtually all possible explanations, Sutherland arrived at the hypothesis that people commit crime because they learn to do so. He refined this into the theory of *differential association*. The difference between those who do, and those who do not, commit crime is that the former have been associated with criminals and the latter have not (or not to the same extent). In support of his thesis, Sutherland pointed out that crime is often concentrated in particular areas, streets and even families. This fitted in well with the ecologists' emphasis on the adverse influence of deteriorating neighbourhoods on children's behaviour. On the other hand, Sutherland's emphasis on the role of 'significant others' (in this case, criminals) in deviancy socialisation shows the influence of the symbolic interactionist, George Mead, on his ideas.

Undoubtedly, differential association is the joker in the pack of theories of crime and delinquency. As a statement of the obvious it is not easily matched, even in a discipline noted for such pronouncements. It is, of course, true that all social behaviour that is not entirely instinctively preprogrammed involves some element of learning and habituation. What Sutherland fails to explain convincingly is why only *some* individuals with apparently the same 'associational' experience of crime become criminals. We are back where we started! On the credit side, he did help to undermine crude explanations of delinquency as *merely* unsocial or maladjusted behaviour and, instead, explained it as 'normal' *within the context of the deviant's own experience and environment.* This approach has influenced both policy and theory. Practically, it directs the reformer's attention to changing the social situation rather than the individual – a common enough approach in Europe but one which, perhaps, needed more vigorous assertion in individualistic America. Theoretically, Sutherland's admittedly schematic attempt to understand delinquency from the delinquent's point of view has been fully shared by modern interactionists. We have already analysed how Becker describes the regular use of marijuana as a learned habit. David Matza incorporates the same idea into his concept of *affiliation*. Deviants drift, but they drift towards activities that interest them and about which they want to know more. Both Becker and Matza seem to allow for rather more choice in the matter than Sutherland, as Becker's example of marijuana *use* (a positive emphasis) shows.

There is no need to expand here on the importance of the meaning attached by actors – in this case delinquents – to their behaviour: that point has been frequently made already. In particular, the sub-cultural studies of the Birmingham group, presented in Chapter 13, show a strong interactionist influence in their concern for the feelings, motives and experience of 'the kids'.

MORAL PANICS, MORAL CRUSADERS AND THE MEDIA The insight that deviance is 'constructed' by a combination of individual action and societal reaction is central to interactionism. We use Stanley Cohen's book, *Folk Devils and Moral Panics* to provide a detailed analysis of this process which rests squarely on Lemert's concept of secondary deviance.

Interactionists frequently argue that societal reaction can actually increase or 'amplify' the deviant behaviour of the labelled individual or group. Stanley Cohen has used the example of the rival 'Mod' and 'Rocker' youth factions of the mid nineteen sixties to illustrate the point. The dramatic pre-publicity given to their expected confrontations almost certainly attracted many more young people than might otherwise have been present. In this way, the media helped to create the events it anticipated or, as Cohen says, 'these predictions played the role of the classic self-fulfilling prophecy'. Similarly, over-reporting of what did (or did not) happen at a confrontation could help attract more people on another occasion (don't we all like 'being in the papers'?) In turn, over-reporting could provoke excessive public reaction. Once a 'spiral of amplification' of this kind is generated, it can acquire an artificial momentum of its own: when this happens, what is 'real' and what is imagined is not easy to disentangle.

Given that the media does not consciously seek to popularise deviant activity, why does this over-reporting take place? There is, of course, the sound commercial reason that deviancy stories make good copy and sell newspapers. A more sociological explanation is offered by Cohen. It is suggested in the title of the book itself: *Folk Devils and Moral Panics: The Creation of the Mods and Rockers*. In what sense, then, were the Mods and Rockers 'devils' and what was the nature of the 'moral panic' they precipitated? To answer this question, Cohen uses the concept of 'boundary crisis'. Post-war Britain was relatively affluent, but the majority had not yet adjusted psychologically to the new prosperity. The frank pleasure-seeking and instrumental attitude to work of some groups of young people seemed to undermine the work ethic in a dangerous and uncomfortable way. Although most people had experienced a shift in the balance between work and leisure in their own lives, commitment to the values of hard work and self-discipline prevented them from entering the newly-discovered pleasure gardens with the gay abandon of the Mods and Rockers. The activities of the latter could be tolerated to a greater degree than would have been imaginable in the thirties, but even so morality dictated that 'there had to be limits'. The press presented 'the need for limits' as 'self-evident' and a matter for 'common sense', but such terms should not be taken at face value by the sociologist. Whatever their moral validity, their effect is to tend to close down a debate in favour of the dominant consensus. No doubt this is partly because an open discussion on some of the issues raised by the behaviour of the Mods and Rockers, including attitudes towards drugs and sex, would by definition bring into question majority consensus on such matters.

Those who seek to organise and orchestrate ritual condemnations of 'folk-devils' are referred to by interactionists as 'moral crusaders' or 'moral entrepreneurs'. They 'make it their business' to see that morality is defended and that justice is done to those who offend it. Often, some of the more popular Sunday newspapers take on this task, although perhaps they do so because deviancy stories boost sales, rather than as a result of deep commitment to traditional morality. Lord Longford and Mrs Mary Whitehouse have been more obviously sincere moral crusaders in what they sometimes call 'the fight against pornography', and Mrs Whitehouse, as chairperson of the pressure group, The National Viewers and Listeners Association, has opposed the way sex and violence have been presented on radio and television.

e Marxism, Crime and the Law

In *Crimes of the Powerful,* Frank Pearce offers more than a critique of white collar crime. He outlines and, in part, empirically illustrates, a full Marxist theory of the law, crime and power of what Marxists call the ruling class. Central to his argument is the concept of 'ideology' which he treats, in traditional Marxist terms, as the ideas of the ruling class (which are sometimes also believed in by sections of the working class). To a large extent, the idea of 'law and order' in capitalist society is regarded by Marxists as simply as an ideological tool of the ruling class, intended to make sure that the working class conform. Public moral concern with lower class crime and the money, time and energy spent on controlling it diverts attention from the exploitative activities of the ruling capitalist class, whose leading representatives would not creditably survive close legal scrutiny of their own business or professional lives. Generally, they have the wealth and power to ensure that such examination seldom occurs, but gradually a body of research on upper class crime is being produced. Pearce himself quotes a American Federal Trade Commission estimate that *detectable* business frauds accounted for over fifteen times as much money as robbery. William Chambliss' detailed study of organised crime in Seattle, Washington, reached the conclusion that leading figures in the business, political and law enforcement fields made up the city's major crime syndicate and worked together for massive criminal gain in gambling, prostitution and drug trafficking. Much illegally made profit was then ploughed back into legitimate business. Chambliss contends that crime occurs among all classes, but that the types of crimes committed and the extent to which the law is enforced varies between classes. The crimes of the powerful are likely to be more lucrative and to escape prosecution. It is important to get Chambliss' work in perspective. He does not show that the majority of the local upper class in Seattle is criminally corrupt, and still less that the majority of the upper class in the United States is corrupt. Nor does he or any Marxist have to do so to prove that capitalists control the capitalist system. They do this, according to Marxists, whether they break the law or not. If the rules of the game are weighted in their favour, they may not need to break them. Perhaps the point of Pearce and Chambliss' research is that if the needs or convenience of the upper class require criminal behaviour, then it is often forthcoming.

Just as Marxists do not accept the law in capitalist society at face value, neither do they accept the categories of crime and deviance as fair or objective. On the contrary, many so-called criminals and deviants in capitalist society are seen as 'victims of the system'. Yet the plight of the lower class criminal and deviant has never concerned Marxists to the extent that it has liberals. This is because Marxists see the hope for social change in a revolutionary movement of the 'solid' working class, certainly not in the criminal fraternity. By contrast, it is central to liberal philosophy to seek to 'reform' and improve the conditions of marginal groups, including criminals and deviants, rather than to wait for social transformation brought about by a revolution they neither want nor expect.

Two aspects of the Marxist analysis of criminal deviance are of great interest. Firstly, there is a considerable need for the general public to be more precisely informed about the 'crimes of the powerful' and particularly about the relationship between powerful economic interests, the law and political power. The Watergate scandal and aspects of the Jeremy Thorpe 'affair', concerning the relationship between business and politics, hardly fill the public with confidence. Similarly, the large sums shown to have been illegally paid by many international companies to help create favourable trading relations with given countries make petty theft look very petty indeed. To what extent do these cases, however extreme they may seem, throw light on what is typical? Here is a tangled but fascinating web for researchers to trace and explain. Secondly, the Marxist analysis of law as a form of ideology is also of immense potential interest. David Gordon argues that *'selective'* enforcement of the law which penalises the working class and favours the upper class creates a misleading impression of who is 'guilty' in capitalist society. As Frank Pearce and Jock Young point out, a full analysis along these lines would require careful qualification. It is undeniable that many laws do work for the day-to-day convenience (traffic laws) and protection (laws prohibiting violence against the person) of most citizens. Despite this, the thesis that the powerful few are able to use the law as an ideological smokescreen to confuse the majority whilst they themselves get on with the business of business, is certainly worth further exploration.

466

f The Empirical Approach: An Example

The final approach to criminal and delinquent behaviour considered here is empirical rather than theoretical in nature. It is an attempt to establish what social facts or factors correlate with criminal and delinquent behaviour. Of course, neither facts nor factors can exist in a theoretical vacuum, and must be presented within some structure of meaning; nevertheless, the multi-factoral approach is noted for producing profuse data rather than profound theory. Explanations are offered in a piecemeal way, which may be termed pragmatic, and with careful reference to the empirical findings which are considered to substantiate them. Often, the theoretical perspectives that are adopted tend to be interdisciplinary or taken from other, more conceptually grounded work. The empirical, pragmatic and interdisciplinary approach is typical of traditional British criminology and has found a major expression in the work of the Cambridge Institute of Criminology and particularly in the writings of D. J. West. Research at the Institute predates the development of interactionist and Marxist deviancy theory in Britain, and still continues vigorously. The major, if somewhat remote, intellectual influence on the Institute is Durkheim.

Perhaps West's best known work is his contribution to a longitudinal study of delinquency. The original sample was 411 eight year old boys from 'deprived' urban backgrounds. The third report of the study team, *The Delinquent Way of Life*, written by West and Farrington, was based on interviews with 389 of the original group, then in their mid-teens, between 1971 and 1973. 101 of these youths had official convictions by the time of the interview. The content of the previous two reports is well summarised by West and Farrington:

> Our previous work demonstrated that a constellation of adverse factors present at an early age, notably large families, low intelligence, poverty, unsatisfactory parental child-rearing behaviour and criminality, increased very significantly the likelihood of a boy acquiring a juvenile delinquency record.

It is probably correct to say that the average newspaper reader would be well aware of all this – certainly, the Chicago urban sociologists of the inter-war period were. To spend large sums of money 'demonstrating' the above perhaps does little more than suggest that sociology is, indeed, sometimes the science of the obvious.

467

In its analysis of the boys' behaviour at primary school, the report claims that 'troublesome' behaviour is seen as 'a particularly powerful indicator of future juvenile convictions'. In a review of the book, Laurie Taylor, a leading interactionist, wrote of this particular 'finding':

> Being called 'troublesome' (or 'intelligent' or 'queer') has social and cultural consequences. It may actually impel individuals towards particular cultural groups with specific values, ideas and behaviour'.

In other words, the label 'troublesome' may push a child into becoming a 'trouble-maker' whereas another label – let us say a more positive one – might affect his behaviour quite differently. For West and Farrington to fail at least to mention this is, as Taylor points out, to by-pass a considerable body of research relevant to their conclusions.

In the third report, West and Farrington's main 'finding' is that certain 'antisocial characteristics' tended to occur together in the delinquent. Here, their work depends on psychological as well as sociological perspectives. The antisocial characteristics are 'self-reported aggression, unstable work record, anti-establishment attitudes, driving after heavy drinking, heavy gambling, drug use, involvement in antisocial groups, sexual activity, immoderate smoking, hanging about and being tattooed.' Again, none of this is surprising. West and Farrington conclude by claiming that they have clearly demonstrated 'the close connection between officially recorded delinquency and particular attributes of character and life style – the delinquent way of life'. Whether these 'attributes of character' are considered by the authors to be inborn or to be the result of the deprived childhood experience of most of the delinquents described in previous reports, we are not told. The former – in effect an argument that there is a criminal personality-type – would align West and Farrington with the behavioural psychologist, Eysenck. The latter – that it is social environment or even a repressive social system that 'causes' lower class crime – is a radical, if not revolutionary one, and might lend support to policies of massive social reform. The conclusion is inescapable that a fuller theoretical contextualisation of West and Farrington's work is necessary. A purely empirical approach is impossible because both the selection and interpretation of facts require a theoretical framework. We return to the general problem of criminal and deviancy theory at the end of this chapter.

g Crime Perspectives

It is necessary to be sensible about interpreting crime. Clearly, some interpretations and factors can be used in explaining some kinds of crime, but not others. Thus, material or status deprivation might help explain the crimes of the poor but not those of the rich. Further, certain theories are more compatible than others. Again, in explaining the crimes of the poor, socioeconomic, urban ecological and Marxist interpretations cover common ground in a similar way: so, too, do the interactionist and Marxist interpretations of white-collar crime. In so far as the empirical approach is theoretically 'neutral', the data it produces can be interpreted variously. In practice, however, this approach is frequently linked with reformism – for the 'help' or 'correction' of deviants – and steers clear of the criticism of the system employed by Marxists and some radical inter-actionists.

We now examine two other major types of social deviance: suicide and political deviance.

2 Suicide

Suicide occurs when a person intentionally kills himself. Suicide in Britain has declined since the early nineteen sixties, when over 5,000 suicides per annum were regularly recorded. In 1976, 4,300 people committed suicide. The suicide rate showed a slight upturn in 1979.

The best starting point for the study of suicide is still Durkheim's *Le Suicide*, first published in 1897. Although recent sociologists have convincingly criticised Durkheim's statistical method, his typology of suicide remains fruitful ground for analysis. He divided suicide into *altruistic, egoistic* and *anomic*.

Altruistic suicide occurs when an individual sacrifices his life for what he believes to be a higher cause. This type of suicide has much in common with martyrdom; indeed, it might be considered as self-inflicted martyrdom. The most spectacular recent example of altruistic suicide is the action of the Japanese pilots who dived their planes into enemy shipping, thereby committing *kamikase*.

It is best to think of egoistic and anomic suicide together, as opposite sides of the same coin. If we explain anomic suicide first, it will become clear how egoistic suicide fits into Durkheim's general pattern of explanation. *Anomic suicide occurs in its typical pattern when economic change so disrupts the fabric of society that the norms and beliefs by which people once lived no longer seem to apply.* We can illustrate the point by taking an example which, again, occurred after Durkheim's own death in 1917. The Wall Street Crash of 1929 caused an outbreak of suicide among the American rich or, more precisely, the previously rich. It can be argued that they were driven to suicide not only by material loss but also because of stress in the face of the psychological and normative adjustment to the different life style that loss demanded. Durkheim's own nineteenth century research substantiated the view that economic change, whether for better or worse, tended to increase the suicide rate.

Viewed in a wider theoretical context, Durkheim's research into suicide should be regarded as an attempt to illustrate that social facts (in this case, economic change) explain individual behaviour (suicide). It is the major example of his use of the positive method. More recent work by Henry and Short has provided qualified support for this approach. They showed that business cycles could be correlated with suicide rates. Unlike Durkheim, however, they use psychological as well as sociological theory and data in their analysis. This is a welcome recognition of the complexity of the issue.

Ervin Stengel goes too far when he says that 'Durkheim's concept of the collective state of society and its suicidal inclination is only of historical interest', but there are various emotional and personal factors invariably involved in the committing of suicide which cannot be adequately explained and understood as mere correlates of social facts 'measured' by statistical trends. The ethnomethodologist, Jack Douglas, goes further, and insists that suicide must be understood as an act fraught with personal *meaning*. That personal meaning, he considers, can never be understood in statistical terms. We return to his criticisms of Durkheim in a slightly different context later.

We now explain egoistic suicide. This is more likely to occur *when a society is so unstable that the individual may be unable to find meaningful guidance and security in times of moral uncertainty.* Durk-

470

heim cited evidence to show that Catholic communities provided a stronger focus for personal identity than Protestant ones, and therefore tended to have lower suicide rates. It is also in the absence of stable identity and social conditions that anomic suicide occurs. In practice, modern sociologists have tended to use the term anomic suicide to describe *suicide occurring in unstable or fast-changing social conditions, whether these are caused by economic change or other factors. Thus, the term anomic suicide can cover egoistic suicide as well.*

It is worth including in this brief survey of suicide a reference to P. Sainsbury's study of suicide in London (1955). This work is theoretically unsophisticated, but it makes the important point that suicide can occur for a variety of different reasons and not always simply because of strictly social factors. The following illustrates the point. As Stengel points out, Sainsbury's categories and his allocation of individual cases within them are 'somewhat arbitrary and artificial', but some such distinctions are necessary if the various factors contributing to suicide are to be understood.

Causative factors in 390 cases of suicide in North London 1936–8. Modified after P. Sainsbury, *Suicide in London,* 1955

Factors	Contributory in % of cases	Principal in % of cases
Social factors	60	35
Personal	20	14
Physical illness	29	18
Mental disorder	47	37
Personality abnormal	17	17

Source: *Stengel,* 1977, p. 47.

We now examine suicide and parasuicide in contemporary British society. Parasuicide is a broad term which describes attempted suicide, or apparently attempted suicide. It is necessary to include apparently attempted suicide within the meaning of the term because every year many hundreds and even thousands of people, particularly young people, use a suicide gesture as a thinly veiled cry for help. By the late nineteen seventies, the annual parasuicide rate in Britain was well over 100,000 – about 20 times more than the figure in the early nineteen fifties. What has caused this spectacular rise? No doubt the

471

increased availability of drugs, both on prescription and on the black market, has something to do with it, but for a more convincing sociological explanation, it is helpful to refer again to Durkheim's concept of *anomic suicide*. Anomic suicide is only one example of anomic behaviour which is caused by anomie. Durkheim defined anomie as feelings of normlessness or rootlessness due to social change and instability. Other examples of anomic behaviour besides suicide are crime and drunkenness. Durkheim argued that as society changes from the traditional to the modern, anomic behaviour would increase. There is considerable evidence to support his case. In particular, the high rate of parasuicide among the young indicates a sense of meaningless and despair. In the comments of social workers and of young parasuicides themselves are to be believed, this is certainly true. 'A feeling of absolute loneliness' often inspires parasuicide, according to one involved observer. Other signs of anomie among parasuicides are drug-taking, high rates of venereal disease, illegitimate pregnancies, abortions, and frequent address changes. Even Durkheim did not foresee problems of this scope, but his concept of anomie does enable us to understand social change, fragmentation and decay much more profoundly than might otherwise have been possible.

3 Political Deviance

We end our discussion of deviance and social control with a brief analysis of political deviance, partly in order to conclude on a note of optimism. In certain cases, though by no means all, political deviance can be an expression of great personal idealism and morality. It is this aspect we wish to stress here. Firstly, however, it is necessary to explain what political deviance is. *It is political action or belief which goes beyond the limits of political behaviour allowed by the existing regime.* Examples of political deviants are the Russian dissidents against the Soviet Regime, of whom the author, Solzhenitsyn, is outstanding. The generals who conspired to overthrow Hitler in 1944 are another example. Closer to home, the IRA provides a less comfortable example. The issue of the individual or group versus the state which is raised by the question of political deviancy is of general social interest. We began our analysis of order and deviance by talking of the practical necessity of norms, and the various ways, including socialisation, by which people are taught and persuaded to observe them. We have suggested all along, however, that the individual may use his own will and imagination to negotiate and adapt society's rules. In rare instances he may reject them altogether. This may happen where an individual considers that it is his moral duty to do so. Thus, a pacifist who refuses to accept call-up papers is pitting the authority of his own conscience against the authority of the state. In many lesser instances, an individual may feel that he must at least protest before obeying a particular rule. Of course, this is unlikely to occur with most day-to-day norms; yet, bearing in mind the apparent ease with which people can be persuaded to follow evil and destructive authority, it is worth ending with the observation that each individual has the option of trying to change or, in the last instance, even of rejecting, the norms and rules that frame his life – as well as obeying them.

Power, Social Control and The Definition of Deviancy

By now, the reader will be aware that defining who is deviant is no simple matter. It is true that functionalists see the matter as fairly unproblematic: for them, deviants are those who break society's rules. The state makes the formal rules of society, and various control agencies, such as the police and the courts, enforce them. Interactionists and Marxists see the matter in more complex ways. From what has already been said, it will be clear that they both consider that agencies of control implement rules that favour some at the expense of others, although this is not equally true of all rules. We can take this as our starting point for more detailed analysis.

Interactionism
Recent interactionist deviancy theory has tended to concern itself particularly with the way agencies of social control process potential deviants and administer or withhold labels. Not only have the police and courts been scrutinised, but also probation officers, teachers and social workers. Ethnomethodologists have

473

been especially active in studying social control. They even go beyond interactionists in searching out the *meanings* that social actors give to the events. To understand why a policeman arrests a 'suspect' or why a magistrate convicts on given occasions, *situationally specific* studies of each case must be made. Motives for action vary and although observation may show that consistent patterns exist, no absolute generalisation about conduct is possible, because people change.

Paul Rock offers a model of the police as a law enforcement agency. He bases his analysis mainly on American material because the sociology of the police has been largely an American pursuit. Four related issues underlie his model:

1 *The Police as Inhibitors (Preventing/Controlling) of Deviancy.*
2 *The Police as Transformers of Deviancy*
3 *The Police as Translators of Definitions of Deviancy into Enforcement.*
4 *The Police as Creators of the Reality of Deviancy in the Public Mind – that is, how the public perceive deviancy.*

Before explaining what the above issues mean, it is worth pointing out that Rock brings them into a common focus by envisaging the police system as an organisation which interacts with society. This study is, therefore, an example of an interactionist organisational analysis. The police must achieve, or at least appear to achieve, the primary and externally prescribed goal of enforcing law and order, but they also have certain secondary goals which relate chiefly to maintaining themselves as a strong, efficient, respected and well-paid organisation. To a great extent, the achievement of primary goals depends on the achievement of secondary ones. Thus, a poorly paid police force with a low morale would not be expected to be very successful in the enforcement of law and order.

We turn to Rock's four issues. There is no difficulty in understanding the role of the police in inhibiting deviancy. This is not an impartial activity, however, as they have to *select* which areas of deviant behaviour merit most skill, effort and resources. A drive against vandalism may mean that less manpower is directed towards, say, stopping business frauds. Decisions of this kind *transform* deviancy: crudely, the pattern of deviant behaviour is, to some extent, structured by what the

474

police 'allow' to happen or not happen. In turn, this may be affected by police manpower and resources as well as decisions about which crimes are more, or less, important. This leads us to the issue of the police as *translators*. They translate the law into action (or not) partly on the basis of the content of the law itself, partly in response to variations in public opinion and partly in terms of their own understanding of the importance of a given law. Thus, a certain stand in public opinion favouring community policing seems to have contributed to its adoption in some areas, such as Devon and Cornwall. Skolnick particularly stresses the power of the police to define the 'operative legality of the system of administering criminal law' that is, to choose which laws to enforce. An excellent example occurs in the Manchester area. There, Chief Constable Anderton has proclaimed freely that he finds prostitution and pornography repugnant. Undoubtedly, he has required the law to be enforced against them much more rigorously than is usual elsewhere. Of couse, he has a legal right to do this, but his decision is (inevitably) political in the limited sense that he is enforcing principles clear to himself though not necessarily to everyone else. Finally, we consider the police as creators of the 'reality' of deviancy as perceived by the public. This is a result of their power to operate certain policies of enforcement both at a senior level, and on the beat. To a greater or lesser extent, such policies *may* involve real discrimination as well as necessary selection. Thus blacks, the working class or young people *may* be relatively discriminated against. Skolnick also points out the relevance of practical and routine factors in affecting police behaviour. A policeman may decide that it is 'about time' he made an arrest, or he may believe that it will help his career to achieve 'a high score'. The result of all this is that statistical 'facts' about deviancy presented to the public are, in ways both profound and trivial, created by the police. We examine this point in more detail in the next section.

The same essential argument that the agency of control itself partly determines who is labelled deviant applies also to the judicial system. Pat Carlen's aptly titled book, *Magistrates' Justice*, shows the magistrate to be as impressionable and even as partial in judgement as others.

THE COURTS – MAGISTRATES AND JURORS Carlen's study, and a number of other interactionist and ethnomethodological ones concentrate on the actors in the courtroom drama itself, usually with due attention to what happens 'behind the scenes'. The variety of accidental contingencies that can affect the outcome of a trial is striking. The kind of support a defendant gets from key figures, such as probation officers and social workers, can often greatly influence and even determine the nature of a sentence. If, for instance, a probation officer decides that a client has finally 'gone too far' (admittedly a crudely unprofessional response) and makes this clear in his report to the court, a harsher judgement may be likely. The 'plea-bargaining' system, prevalent both in Britain and the United States, is a practice which would seem to lend itself to abuse. Plea-bargaining involves the accused obtaining more favourable treatment in return for an admission of guilt. Firstly, the interrogation of suspects in police custody can involve 'deals' in which, say, a lesser charge is 'traded-off' for a statement admitting an offence. Secondly, judicial officials sometimes give more lenient sentences in return for guilty pleas. When justice is put into the market place like this, the possibility of a 'bad deal' for the poor and less well-informed seems correspondingly greater. Needless to say, this trade-off process can facilitate police and court business and sometimes gains prestige for the police and prosecution; that is, presumably, the justification for it.

The kind of detailed, closely observed study we have been describing is frequently favoured by the ethnomethodologists, although such an approach is by no means their monopoly. Harold Garfinkel, one of their chief exponents, was led to his conclusions partly by his attempts to analyse the deliberations of a group of jurors. In the following taped comment, he appears to be saying that the jurors used their own common-sense knowledge of society to arrive at what seemed to them a fair verdict:

> What I mean is that it was for them a matter that somehow or other in their dealings with each other they managed, if you will permit me now to use it (commonsense), to see. (*Author's brackets*).

Garfinkel further suggests that it is the job of sociologists to describe and understand what this commonsense knowledge is and how it is applied in a particular context. The application of this view to control theory is that jurors arrive at verdicts not merely on the basis of legal considerations but by calling upon a much wider fund of general knowledge, including an acquired idea of justice. Functionalists tend to consider that the process of legal enforcement is relatively unbiased. Ethnomethodologists make the point that even though people are, to some extent, guided by mutually accepted standards of conduct, behaviour is diverse, different and not wholly predictable. This includes the process of normative and legal enforcement. To put the matter extremely, in a given case justice can be what jurors and judges decide it is, rather than something more objective.

Marxism, Social Control and Deviancy Definition

We can deal briefly with the topic indicated under this heading because the concept of social control summarises and focuses all that we have said so far about Marxist theory in the last two chapters. Ruling class control of the social order and of definitions of deviancy is the crux of Marxist analysis in this area.

Capitalist ideology affects the various agencies of social control as it does all other institutions in capitalist society. The police 'automatically' concentrate on working class rather than middle class crime because this is what they have been taught to look for and expect.

Stuart Hall has made an interesting Marxist analysis of what he calls 'policing the crisis' of contemporary British capitalism. He considers that British capitalism is experiencing severe difficulties. In order to divide and distract the working class from criticising and organising against capitalism, the capitalist media and leading politicians create a 'panic' about immigration and immigrants. This has the effect of putting working class whites at odds with working class blacks (nearly all blacks in Britain are working class) and obscuring from both that the real cause of unemployment lies in the nature of the capitalist system itself. The generally racist climate affects the police. Assisted by increased government expenditure on law and order, they concentrate more attention and resources in black areas and particularly against black youth (see Chapter 12). This has the result of ensuring high crime figures for blacks and stigmatising the black community further in the eyes of the public. This brief summary inevitably fails to do full justice to Hall's argument, but his analysis amounts to a very comprehensive structural explanation of how one ethnic group comes to be defined as 'deviant'.

Control Agencies and the Social Creation of Statistics

So far, we have quoted official statistics with the occasional hint that they may not be quite as 'factual' as they appear. We will now explore this possibility further. Criminal and suicide statistics are those chosen for discussion here, although similar considerations apply to court and government statistics generally.

What are criminal statistics? Or rather, what do they purport to be? Two main units are measured: the offences and the offenders. Given that not all offences known to the police and officially recorded as having been committed are solved, the figure for offences is always larger than that for offenders in any given year. Thus, in 1976 the total number of all recorded offences in England and Wales, indictable and non indictable, was 3,792,000 and the number of persons found guilty of offences was 2,072,000.

Some of the inadequacies of official statistics are of a technical nature and are not a matter of controversy. First, there is a 'dark number' of undiscovered crimes. There are various possibilities that explain why a crime might go undiscovered: a victim of blackmail may be afraid of his blackmailer; a shoplifter may persuade the shop management not to prosecute; a neighbourhood quarrel involving minor crime may be adequately controlled without calling the police; a victim of assault who knows his assailant might block legal proceedings for friendship's sake. An accurate estimate of what the sum total of such 'offences' might be is impossible, but few criminologists would be surprised if they exceeded the number of recorded crimes. One Chief Constable has 'guestimated' that crime reported to the police is only 10% of all crime, although a very much higher percentage of serious crime does come to police attention.

Several other variables can affect the accuracy of official statistics. Updating of police equipment, especially in communications and in information filing and retrieval methods, and improvements in training would be expected to increase detection rates. Expansion of the police force should achieve the same result. Between 1974 and 1978, the police force in England and Wales increased by 7,000, and it may be that the apparent 'increase' in crime during this period was in some part actually an increase in the *detection* of crime. If the police decide to 'crack down' on a particular kind of crime, then the statistics for that crime would be expected to show an 'artificial' increase during the relevant period. For example, in November 1978, the Tokyo police made a massive temporary switch of manpower and resources to achieve the arrest of members of motor bike gangs who had previously been able to break traffic laws with near impunity. Clearly, traffic offences involving motor bikes would go up for November of that year though, if the policy of deterrence worked, not for December. Similarly, when the police respond to 'moral panics' by concentrating more effort to combat 'the evil' in question, fluctuations in the statistics relating to that crime correspondingly occur.

Statistics can be made to seem misleading simply by being used badly. The selective use of statistics to support subjective generalisations is a particularly common form of misuse. Vague statements referring to 'the increase in sexual crimes and crimes involving violence' are an example. Sexual crimes actually decreased between 1969 and 1977 – (see the table on p. 455). There had, of course, been a massive increase in crimes of violence in that period, but it does not include murder and the non-indictable offence of assault (a less serious category of crime than violence against the person). Confusion also sometimes occurs because the statistical implications of legislative change is not always properly appreciated. For instance, as a result of the Theft Act of 1968, the figure for theft and the handling of stolen goods before and after the Act's implementation are not comparable.

The queries so far raised in relation to the validity and use of official statistics have been mainly technical and, as such, are amenable to technical solution. A number of interactionists and ethnomethodologists, however, have raised a more fundamental question about the accuracy and meaning of official statistics. It is best to approach their argument through a specific case: that of juvenile delinquency. In his book, *The Social Organisation of Juvenile Justice*, ethnomethodologist, Aaron Cicourel examines how two towns, with almost identical

479

populations, experience quite different rates of juvenile crime as recorded in official statistics. He gives two explanations: the different organisational policies pursued by the police in the two towns, and the different way police policy towards delinquency was interpreted *via the background expectancies'* of officers dealing directly with juveniles. In the first town, a loose attitude to recording delinquent acts and an informal approach to dealing with delinquents made the problem *appear* small, and vice-versa in the other town where much 'tighter' practices and stricter assumptions prevailed. In the first case what came to be regarded as a small problem seemed to require progressively fewer officers to deal with it, whereas in the second case the problem became amplified and so more manpower and resources were deployed to 'solve' it. All this, of course, affected the statistics of delinquency in the two towns in opposite ways, decreasing them in the first instance, and increasing them in the second. Cicourel's general conclusion for sociological research is:

> A researcher utilising official materials cannot interpret them unless he possesses or invents a theory that includes how background expectancies render everyday activities recognisable and intelligible.

Cicourel's point that statistics are partly created, and not simply collected, has been applied in much wider contexts than his own limited comparative case study. In particular, the validity of the statistically 'typical' criminal – the young, urban working class male – is considered as a partly misleading abstraction by some interactionists. It is worth noting that in a number of self-report studies of young people (that is, research based on descriptions by young people of their own conduct), the ratio of working class to middle class delinquent activity drops from the 5 or 6 to 1 of official statistics to about 1.5 to 1. Further, in 1977 and 1978 a relatively large proportion of black youths were arrested on 'suspicion' or 'sus' as the youths called it. Many felt themselves to have been discriminated against. Clearly, this is a sensitive area and not one about which to make wild generalisations, but on the basis of television investigations alone there is evidence that sometimes this is so. Perhaps this adds a further characteristic to the criminal stereotype in inner urban areas – colour.

It is not only the young working class male who may be

grossly over-represented in criminal statistics. We have already cited a range of studies by both interactionists and Marxists which seek to demonstrate an in-built (though not necessarily always conscious) bias of the social and legal systems in favour of the upper and middle classes and against the working class. As early as 1940, Edwin Sutherland produced evidence that white collar crime might be substantially under-estimated in official statistics. He found that often the petty crimes of pilfering or major crimes of bribery passed unnoticed or, were dealt with 'within the firm'. Even the flouting of commercial and industrial law was more likely to be the subject of governmental reprimand than legal action. A study by W. S. Carson of 200 firms in south east England, some 25 years later, found similarly that only 1.5% of officialy detected breaches of factory legislation were prosecuted. To these we must add the more far-reaching allegations, made by those Marxists to whom we have already referred, of crime involving local ruling elites and, internationally, large corporations. (pp. 465–6).

The work of Anne Campbell on female juvenile delinquency goes some way towards undermining the statistical basis for the view that far more males commit crimes than females. Official statistics put the ratio of male to female crime at about 7 to 1 – the precise ratio varying with age groups. In a self-report study of 105 adolescent girls, Campbell found that in an overall average of offences, the male to female self-admission rate was 1.12 to 1. She attributes this to paternalism on the part of the police who favour what they consider to be 'the gentle sex' in matters of law enforcement. As a result, they issue far more informal and unrecorded cautions to females than males. Campbell's research cannot be considered conclusive, although other evidence also exists to suggest that female crime is under-represented in official statistics. Certainly, the view that men are 'naturally more aggressive' than women and, consequently, more prone to crime needs to be treated with caution. As more women have moved into the labour force and have received 'tougher' socialisation, the ratio of female to male crime has tended to narrow – even as measured by official statistics.

The views put forward by Cicourel and other ethnomedologists and interactionists have not gone without criticism. Barry Hindess has made a sharp analysis of their critique of official statistics. He comments in turn on two possible versions of their position, both of which he finds supported in their writings. The first position is that because we can never 'ultimately' know precisely why and how individual policemen, magistrates and others select the causes that 'make up' official statistics, these statistics are virtually useless. This is because although the individual cases may appear in the same statistical category, they may not in fact refer to the same phenomenon. Hindess refutes this conclusion whilst agreeing with the observation that provokes it. He argues that this kind of 'ultimate' uncertainty is a feature of all aspects of life and not just a problem for sociologists. They, like the practitioners of other disciplines, must simply make sure that, as far as possible, their data, including statistical data, is representative and internally consistent (that is, that each unit that is supposed to refer to a given phenomenon actually does so). Admittedly, this is more easily said than done, but it *must* be done if sociology is to be practised at all. The second or 'weak' version of the interactionist position as construed by Hindess is that because the 'everyday understandings' of police, magistrates and others help to 'create' official statistics, these must be taken into consideration when evaluating and interpreting a given set of statistics. Hindess agrees with this but considers it to be a statement of the obvious. In effect, it is the position he himself takes in refuting the first, and in his view more typical, version of the interactionist position. In putting forward the view that the 'everyday misunderstandings' of those who create statistics must be considered in this way, Hindess also refutes the simplistic positivistic position: that official statistics can be used unquestioningly to 'prove' a given case.

The same issues about the use of official statistics are at stake in two well known interactionist critiques of the statistical basis of Durkheim's analysis of suicide. Both Maxwell Atkinson and Jack Douglas criticise Durkheim for assuming that all coroners used the same criteria in deciding what was or was not suicide. They are easily able to give evidence to the contrary. Douglas points out the example of one coroner who would decide that suicide had occurred only if the evidence of a suicide note could be produced. Other coroners accepted less conclusive evidence. Ultimately, this meant that different coroners were contributing a different range of 'facts' to the 'same' statistical category, with the result that 'statistical reality' could be imprecise and misleading. Let us take a more serious example of this point: the validity of the statistical basis supporting Durkheim's claims about the distribution of egoistic suicide. Durkheim explains the relatively 'low' rate of suicide in Catholic societies as compared to Protestant ones, in terms of the greater integration of the former. But another explanation can be given for the differences in the recorded rates of suicide between the two types of society. The Catholic religion condemns suicide as a mortal sin, something which merits eternal damnation. In many cases this cultural attitude towards suicide might very well influence coroners to return a verdict other than suicide. Pressure of this kind would not generally be put on coroners in Protestant societies where moral condemnation of suicide tended to be less. In view of this, uncritical acceptance of official suicide statistics for the purposes of comparative social analysis would be poor methodology.

Making Sense of Deviancy Theory

The various theoretical approaches to social order and deviance are often presented as mutually exclusive. Certainly, it would be ludicrous to imagine that 'sticking them all together' would somehow result in a complete theory satisfactory to all parties. Nevertheless, in some ways the major theories can be seen as complementary rather than contradictory. Further, in some instances, differences in terminology obscure a larger measure of agreement than might at first be apparent.

Even on the subject of social order, control and integration, it is possible to uncover elements of agreement between the two major structural theories about how society functions. Functionalists argue that conformity and consensus are necessary for the orderly functioning of society, but Marxists, too, need to explain why, in many capitalist societies, the majority accept the system, and appear to have no taste for revolution. Marxists believe that the many working class people who accept and even support the capitalist system have been deluded by 'bourgeois ideology' into a state of 'false consciousness'. Both theories are describing the same phenomenon: what differs is the terminology and the underlying political values: functionalists tend to support and want to conserve bourgeois, liberal society, whereas Marxists do not. Not surprisingly, these preferences often seep into their theoretical analyses.

There is also a considerable measure of unstated agreement between Marxism and functionalism about social deviance. Merton thought of criminal behaviour as a result of exclusion from the legitimate opportunity structure of society, and strain theorists examined what this meant in terms of economic and status deprivation. There is a clear implication in all this that 'society' bears at least some responsibility for crime simply because the gateways to legitimate achievement are wide open for some and almost closed for others. Marxists observe the same unequal access to material and status reward hierarchies but condemn it more comprehensively. To them, theft is just the distorted mirror image of capitalism's already ugly face. The convergence between the two perspectives is even apparent sometimes at the level of moral evaluation. The Marxist 'what can you expect?' response to the high crime rate in Western Europe and the USA expresses a sentiment comparable with that of the liberal, Daniel Bell, when he refers to crime as 'part of the American way of life'.

The major achievement of interactionism has been to rediscover for sociology the notion that the central social reality is individual meaning and experience. In view of the tendencies towards determinism within both structural theories, this is a crucial contribution. As an account of how people behave in everyday life in relation to the legal and normative order, interactionism seems closer to what actually happens than the functionalist conformity-deviance model. Life is more complex than the functionalists allow. Marxists argue, however, that interactionism is inadequate in its analysis of how the power of institutions and the class interests behind them affect and even control individual lives (see Chapter 15). The laws, rules or norms of institutions are powerful means of regulating behaviour, and this is notably true of the institutions that constitute the 'bourgeois' state. Moreover, institutional frameworks often survive the coming and going of individuals. In their different ways, Marxists and functionalists appreciate better than interactionists that it is the institutional structure of society that both limits and provides opportunities for individual and group action.

Perhaps interactionism would be more effective if, as well as concerning itself with individual meaning, its protagonists also attempted to develop it more vigorously as a 'linking theory' between the concept of the 'creative' individual, and the 'formative' institutional structure of society. We have already noted some efforts in this direction, though these have been more a matter of Marxists using interactionist perspective than the other way around. Despite the limits of the interactionist approach, many would feel that amidst such abstract concepts as order, social control and deviance, individual meaning and reality should be retained. If that makes sociological generalisations more difficult, then so be it.

Deviancy Perspectives, Methods, Policy and the Future

Having examined some similarities between the various perspectives on deviance, here we briefly explore the practical consequences for policy formation of the different approaches. The functionalist stress on the need to control deviance leads to superficially uncomplicated solutions: control requires punishment or treatment or, at least, a warning.

Both Marxists and interactionists have been 'accused' of sympathising with deviants, rather than the social order against which they offend. Young sociologists, alienated from society to various degrees, may, indeed, find it easy to identify with 'outsiders', such as juvenile delinquents, who are more obviously at odds with 'the system' than themselves. Certainly, the choice of observational or participant observational methodology brings close involvement with groups studied. Jock Young, Paul Willis, Paul Corrigan and, before them, William Foote Whyte, chose this method. Becker himself shows how close to the point of identification deviancy researchers sometimes get:

> To develop and test my hypothesis about the genesis of marijuana use for pleasure, I conducted fifty interviews with marijuana users. I had been a professional dance musician for some years when I conducted this study and my first interviews were with people I had met in the music business. I asked them to put me in contact with other users . . .

It would be a mistake, however, to lump together interactionist and Marxist sympathy for the 'underdog' without reference to their broader positions. The American Marxist, Gouldner, has attacked interactionists sharply on the grounds that they approach deviancy in a spirit of sentimental romanticism. Practically, they accept that there must be limits to deviance, but emotionally they are attracted by it. They incline to favour more tolerance to deviants or even to 'turn a blind eye'; hardly a comprehensive programme. It is certainly true that Marxists have recently made more strenuous efforts than interactionists to envisage a wholly different approach to deviance from that generally adopted in Britain and America. Ultimately, they hope for a society in which freedom and justice will combine to make the category of deviant obsolete. As Ian Taylor, Paul Walton and Jock Young state:

> The task is to create a society in which the facts of human diversity, whether personal, organic or social, are not subject to the power to criminalise.

Perhaps, after all, this is simply a more organised way of saying what many interactionists feel but do not believe is possible. Will there not always be rules and, if so, will there not always be some who break them?

Speculation aside, both Marxists and interactionists stress the need for a fairer system of law and order. The concept of *community justice* in which the law is interpreted and administered by local people has had some currency but, as Stanley Cohen has pointed out, there is no guarantee that such justice would be any more humane than at present, and some chance that it might be less so. The policy of expanding free legal aid and advice is widely acceptable to radicals. For the Marxist committed, such policies would also provide a basis to educate clients about the nature of justice in capitalist society and could be linked, tactically, to the more distant goal of bringing about the fundamental change necessary to achieve a just society.

Guide to further reading and study

In addition to the more general works mentioned at the end of the last chapter, the following are useful in specific areas. John Barron Mays' *Crime and its Treatment* (Longman, 1975), develops some policy issues only suggested here. Perhaps the best general suicide is Erwin Stengel's *Suicide and Attempted Suicide*, (Pelican, 1977). Durkheim's *Suicide*, (Routledge, 1970), is worth sampling, though more for its methodology than its findings. It is in Part II that Durkheim explains his three-fold typology of suicide. Chapter 6 of Jock Young's *The Drugtakers* (Paladin, 1971), is an excellent account of the values and life-style of a deviant, hedonistic sub-culture, but it requires concentrated reading. An assorted collection of interactionist and Marxist articles is contained in Paul Rock and Mary McIntosh, *eds*, *Deviance and Social Control*, (Tavistock, 1974). Again, the student must expect to work hard to absorb the best from them.

Past Questions

1 Delinquency appears to be a disproportionately male and urban phenomenon. How would you explain this? (AEB, 1975).

2 Critically assess sociological accounts which attempt to explain different rates of conviction for crime between *either* social class groups *or* gender groups. (AEB, 1978).

3 'Durkheim was not interested in individual cases of suicide . . . Rather he wanted to show that the cause of rates of suicide was wholly social.' How far was he successful? (AEB, 1978).

4 Many cities have 'problem areas' near the centre. Why is this? (AEB, 1979). (See also Chapter 7).

18 Power, Politics and People

Power and Authority

According to Max Weber, power is 'the probability that one actor within a social relationship will be in a position to carry out his own will despite resistance, regardless of the basis on which this probability rests'. In more ordinary language, power is the ability to get one's way – even if it is based on bluff.

Although we think of *power* as being associated particularly with politics it is, in fact, an aspect of all, or nearly all, social relationships. As Weber writes, positions of power can 'emerge from social relations in a drawing room as well as in the market, from the rostrum of a lecture hall as well as the command post of a regiment, from an erotic or charitable relationship as well as from scholarly discussion or athletics'. We can add that power plays a part in family and school relationships also. If Weber's sociology has a single central concept, it is that of power. It is as important in his perspective as is conflict in that of Marx, and order in that of the functionalists. He considered that economic and social goals as well as political ones are achieved through power-conflict. People compete for limited resources and status: for every one who achieves fortune and fame, there are thousands who do not. Nevertheless, it was characteristic of Weber that he stressed the importance of the political sphere. Political decisions, such as changes in taxation

489

or social welfare, could be taken, and these could have great effect on the economic and social life of a country.

Weber distinguished *authority* from power. Authority may be thought of as *legitimate power* (power that is accepted as being rightfully exercised). He divided authority into three broad types: *traditional, charismatic* and *rational-legal*. We have already examined authority in the context of organisations. Here, our interest in it is as a form of political power: accordingly, we choose our examples from the political sphere. The sense of the inevitability of traditional political authority is well illustrated by an established dynasty, such as the centuries-old Habsburgs of Austria. By contrast, charismatic authority is generated by personality and the myths that surround it. Hitler, Martin Luther King and the Cuban revolutionary leader, Che Guevara, are all examples of charismatic leaders. The fact that they are all recent figures shows that charismatic authority is still a feature of modern politics. In advanced industrial countries, however, rational-legal authority tends to be the predominant type and has, in particular, replaced traditional authority. This type of political authority tends to be the predominant type and has, in particular, replaced traditional authority. Rational-legal political authority is established in law. The American system of government provides the best example of it because, unlike Britain, it has a written constitution (articles of government). This establishes the relationship between the legislature (which passes laws), the judiciary (which can determine if these laws are constitutionally allowable), and the executive (which, under the law, runs day-to-day government). Britain is often considered to have an 'unwritten' constitution but this has never been codified in a single, rational-legal document.

Politics: Power, Policy, the State

Politics is about power and purposes. It is the struggle to achieve the means to do certain things or, more precisely, to implement policies. Sometimes, what politicians want to do becomes obscured in the struggle to get the power to do it, but we must recognise, at least analytically, both these aspects of political activity.

Firstly, we deal with the means of power. The major means of political power is government and we can conveniently discuss the chief types of government here: *democracy, oligarchy* and *dictatorship*. We will consider each in turn.

Democratic systems can be divided into three broad types: *representative* or indirect democracy; *participatory* or direct democracy, and *delegatory* democracy. In representative democracy, the people do not rule directly but elect representatives to rule for them. Representative democracy is associated with parliamentary institutions to such an extent that it is often referred to simply as parliamentary democracy: Britain and America are major examples. In addition, representative democracies tend to be characterised by what are termed *civil liberties*. These include freedom to organise politically, freedom of speech and of the press, and the equal status of citizens under the law. In practice, these freedoms except – arguably – the last are not absolute. They are established in, and limited by law. Thus, freedom of the press in Britain is limited by the laws of libel and contempt (which cover what can legally be written about other people), and the Official Secrets Act. In the USA the comparable legislation is less strict and, to that extent, it has a freer press than Britain. The principle that freedom, like anything else, has to be balanced against other principles, applies in both countries.

The crux of our concern with democracy is the debate between liberals and Marxists about the nature and extent of democracy in advanced capitalist countries. Liberals consider that, for instance, Britain, West Germany, Italy, Australia and the United States are *genuinely* democratic. Marxists disagree: they argue that, at best, these countries are 'bourgeois democracies' which deny 'real' freedom to the majority of their population. For Marxists, a greater degree of freedom depends primarily on greater equality. For instance, freedom under the law may not seem very meaningful to someone who cannot afford a lawyer. This liberal-Marxist debate is the main recurrent theme of this chapter.

Participatory or direct democracy strictly means that people represent themselves and take their own decisions. The term 'participatory', however, is often used to mean some degree of personal involvement in decision making, short of direct democratic control. It has been in small communities, such as ancient Athens and medieval Geneva, that something approaching direct democratic self-government has proved most feasible. Nevertheless, in modern Tanzania and China, both large countries, popular involvement in day-to-day affairs has been found possible at the local or village level. In neither country has this replaced central government and bureaucracy (such as the civil service), often of a rather authoritarian kind, at the national level. The Russian revolutionary, Lenin, hoped and believed that a socialist revolution would replace the capitalist state with a proletarian state largely run by, or at least answerable to, direct democratic institutions called *soviets* or *communes*. At first, there were some signs that this might happen during and after the revolution of 1917. The fact that it did not, and that an authoritarian government developed instead, poses problems for modern socialists, who continue to seek more direct forms of democracy than are common in parliamentary democracies.

Delegatory democracy is a form of 'half-way house' between direct and indirect democracy. *Delegates are mandated (told) by those who elect them to carry out specific orders and are, therefore, much more 'tied' to the wishes of their constituents than are undelegated representatives.* In the late nineteen seventies and early eighties there was a fierce debate in the Labour Party which focused on the extent to which MPs should be representatives or delegates.

Oligarchy is government by the few: the term is usually used to describe government by an unrepresentative few. Frequently, the basis of oligarchical power is military. Thus Greece, the ancient home of democracy, was recently ruled by a junta (group) of colonels for several years. Although it is theoretically possible to talk of representative oligarchy, different terms are usually preferred. Liberal political theorists use the terms 'representative elite' or 'democratic elite'. Marxists deny that what liberals call democratic elites are, in fact, genuinely democratic; instead, they use the term 'ruling class'.

Dictatorship is government by a single individual responsible only to himself. Hitler and Stalin were dictators, each man professing different political ideologies, Fascism and Communism, respectively. Yet it is for the similar *way* in which both concentrated total power in their own hands, and the great inhumanity with which they exercised it, that they are remembered. rather than for their ideological differences. The term 'totalitarianism' is often associated with dictatorship, but has a rather wider usage. Totalitarian regimes are those in which power is wholly concentrated in the hands of a few people or

492

of a single person.

The State

At this point, the important concept of the state must be more fully introduced. Governments, whether democratic, oligarchical or dictatorial, generally exercise power through the state. The state includes the government itself – of whatever kind – both in its capacity as the maker of law and of policy. It also includes the civil service – a vast bureaucracy of many thousands of people. The judiciary and magistracy are also part of it. Local government is, by definition, not part of the central state apparatus but is often greatly influenced and, in some respects, even controlled, by central government. Local government can, therefore, sometimes be a powerful arm of central government: (The Labour governments of the nineteen sixties and seventies persuaded most local authorities to accept and implement some form of comprehensive education.) In addition, local governments have their own bureaucracies. As we have seen already, when referring to the work of Althusser, Marxists have a much more extensive conception of the state than the minimal description given here. Their view will be fully discussed shortly.

Politics is not only about power struggle. It is also about *policies, or the purpose to which power, once attained, can be put.* We will say something of the general beliefs and goals (or ideologies) of the major parties in Britain and the United States shortly. Here, it is enough to indicate the wide range of issues that can become questions of political conflict. In Third World countries, these could include starvation, land reform, population control and literacy; in Western countries, women's rights, immigration, taxation and public spending policy have been recent issues. It is worth noting that the political struggle does not always take place *within* the existing political system. For instance, totalitarian regimes do not allow organised opposition to exist: those who oppose the government are virtually forced to establish illegal political groups to have their opinions heard, and to achieve their goals. Such groups existed in both Hitler's Germany and Stalin's Russia, as they do in present day South Africa and Czechoslovakia.

493

People

The struggle for power and the implementation of policies come to little if they do not benefit people. Politics and history no longer merely concern the exploits of famous men if, indeed, they ever really did. Modern politicians have to occupy themselves with the public good and to respond to the promptings of the public itself. How 'the people' are organised and how they organise themselves in the form of parties and national and local pressure groups is discussed below, as is the extent and limits of popular political participation.

Voting Behaviour and Political Socialisation

The Labour and Conservative (Tory) Parties have dominated British politics for most of the period from 1918 until the present day. In 1918, the Representation of the People Act was passed, which extended the vote to all men over twenty-one and all women over thirty. The act enfranchised millions of working class people and helped to make it possible for the Labour Party to take over from the Liberals as one of the two major parties. A majority of the working class increasingly saw the Labour Party as their 'natural' representative political organisation. The key questions in this section are, therefore, 'Who supports the two major parties, and why?' The answer to the first question is a matter of empirical fact, but the answer to the second requires theoretical explanation. We now examine the two questions.

Class and Voting

OBJECTIVE AND SUBJECTIVE CLASS The major variable associated with voting behaviour is *class*. Most working class voters vote Labour and most middle class ones Conservative: in fact, a consistently higher proportion of the middle class votes Conservative than those in the working class who vote Labour. Only about one fifth of the middle class vote Labour, whereas about one third of the working class now vote Conservative. Because the working class is larger than the middle class, the working class Conservative vote is about half of the party's total vote. Obviously, all the proportions given in this paragraph tend to vary up or down depending on who wins a given election. For instance, working class support for the Conservatives increased in 1979 when they won the election, and decreased in 1964 when they lost.

The above broad correlations between class and voting patterns are based on generally accepted definitions of class, such as that offered by the Registrar General. Widely used definitions of this kind are referred to as *objective*. Objective class may or may not coincide with *subjective* class, the class that a person *thinks* he belongs to. The distinction between objective and subjective class is of great interest to us here because the relationship between *subjective* class and voting behaviour is even stronger than that between *objective* class and voting behaviour. Evidence from a number of sources, including Butler and Stokes, has shown that about 80% of those who are both objectively *and* subjectively working class vote Labour, whereas the objective working class vote *as a whole* never rose above 67% between 1952 and 1962. The strength of subjective class image and voting patterns is further illustrated by the behaviour of the minority of unskilled workers who, for some reason, think of themselves as middle class. According to Butler and Stoke's data, 55% of this group voted Conservative in 1959. The tendency for those at the top of the occupational hierarchy who see themselves as working class to vote Labour is not quite as marked, but is still statistically very significant.

It should not surprise us that people behave consistently with their own view of things (subjective class self-image) more than in accordance with how some external indicator might lead us to expect they would behave (objective class). Weber was right to insist that the sociologist must seek to understand the subjective motives for action. Translated into the terms of this discussion, the insight that what people *believe* to be real becomes real in its consequences, means that if people believe they belong to a given class, they tend to vote for the party normally considered to represent that class. Nevertheless, we still seek an answer as to why people's subjective class, especially that of the working class, should so frequently vary from what might objectively be expected. Firstly, however, we briefly explain 'normal' or conformist voting behaviour.

CONFORMIST VOTING BEHAVIOUR Conformist voting behaviour is

defined as voting for the political party that, by general agreement, most represents the given voter's class interests – that is, the Conservative party for the middle class and the Labour party for the working class. Put this way, conformity is what is to be expected: most people vote in terms of class and self-interest (which are perceived as generally coinciding). To vote in this manner is considered to be politically *rational* behaviour although the actual variety of voting behaviour makes the definition seem somewhat arbitrary. It is, however, highly significant that Labour voters tend to hold *images* (impressions or views) of both society and the political parties as *more divided along class lines* than do Conservative voters. This is clearly apparent from the diagram below which is worth detailed study.

Party images in Bristol North East, 1955 (percentages)

	Images of the Labour Party	
	by Labour supporters	by Conservative supporters
For the working class	68	32
For the Welfare State	18	12
For the country as a whole	5	4
For full employment	4	2
For nationalisation, controls	4	32
Impractical, extravagant	1	18
	100	100

	Images of the Conservative Party	
	by Labour supporters	by Conservative supporters
For all classes	6	30
For free enterprise, for business	7	26
For the rich, big business	85	8
For individual freedom	—	14
For denationalisation	1	5
For full employment	—	9
Capable, experienced leaders	1	8
	100	100

Source: Jean Blondel, *Voters, Parties and Leaders*, 1969, p. 82.

Thus, 68% of Labour voters of the Bristol North-East constituency thought of Labour as 'for the working class' and 85% of them thought of the Conservatives as 'for the rich, big business'.

Frank Parkin has written with great illumination on working class voting patterns, and his work helps to explain the strong element of class awareness in the *traditional* working class Labour vote. He suggests that, given the generally Conservative nature of British society, what is surprising is that a majority of the working class *do* consistently vote Labour. He contends that the traditionally dominant institutions of our society – the established church, the monarchy, the military, legal and civil service elites, the public schools and ancient universities, the institutions of private property and the media – embody values which are both middle class and closely in accord with conservatism. Conservatives have for a long time appealed to communal values, such as nationalism, monarchy, religion and imperialism to 'unify' the country. It would seem almost inevitable that this powerful and pervasive conservative influence would encompass all classes. How is it, then, that a majority of the working class resist its full import? Simply, various 'shields' or 'barriers' exist against it, which allow socialist values to be fostered. These protective barriers are formed by working class sub-cultures which generate different values from the dominant culture. The major source of these values is the work-place. There, the working man may experience both the collective strength of his peers, and conflict with his employer. Thus, the work-place is the cradle of socialist values. Parkin also sees the traditional working class community as an additional basis of working class and socialist solidarity. Where occupational communities such as mining towns and dock areas exist, solidarity is likely to be especially strong. These areas, however, are on the decline (see Chapter 7, p. 191).

Goldthorpe and Lockwood have reached similar conclusions to those of Parkin. They divide the working class into two groups: *traditionalists* and *instrumental collectivists*. The former is divided into *proletarian* traditionalists and *deferential* traditionalists. The proletarian traditionalists are more radical and class conscious, and correspond to the socialist-inclined group described by Parkin. The more conservative, deferential working class need not concern us here. The instrumental collectivists are, however, of immediate interest. These are workers who are committed to a collective approach to unions and the Labour party, not out of loyalty or solidarity but because of what they can get out of them. In a quota survey that is now almost twenty years old, Goldthorpe and Lockwood found that affluent workers tended to support Labour, to an even greater extent than the working class as a whole, for precisely these instrumental reasons. This analysis does, however, allow for the possibility that instrumentally motivated workers will switch their vote if it seems in their interest to do so. More recent evidence suggests that this is exactly what some of them do.

With reference again to the figure, we now discuss the 'normal' middle class Conservative vote. The fact that Conservative voters entertain a wider variety of predominant images of their own party and of the Labour party must be carefully interpreted. It needs to be reconciled with the fact that the middle class votes Conservative *more solidly* than the working class votes Labour. The explanation is that Conservatives tend to believe that they vote Conservative not for class reasons, but because they consider that the Conservative party is 'better for the country' or is the party which 'governs in the national interest'. These motives are only implicitly apparent in the figure, but further evidence for them can be derived from a recent study of the social and political attitudes of farmers, a traditionally-minded group, in Newby *et al.*, *Property, Paternalism and Power* (1978). The farmers interviewed claimed to dislike class conflict, but voted and generally behaved in other ways very much in terms of their own class interest. They regarded their support for the *status quo* (society as it is) as in everybody's interest, not merely, or even particularly, in their own. No doubt they were sincere in this, but given that their income is typically five or six times greater than that of farm labourers, it is legitimate to ask whether or not they are 'right'.

DEVIANT VOTING BEHAVIOUR

a MIDDLE CLASS DEVIANT VOTERS There are fewer middle class than working class deviant voters, both absolutely and as a proportion of their class. Raynor suggests that the relatively few middle class Labour voters can be divided into two extreme groups, and we will add a third that recent research at Oxford has uncovered. The first group is those with considerable experience of higher education: these can be referred to as the 'intellectual left'. They include, particularly, some academics, journalists and 'media people' and members of vocational or 'helping' professions, such as social work or teaching. Slightly controversially perhaps, it can be argued that the wide education and knowledge of these people enables them to see beyond their own interest and to sympathise with the disadvantaged. They vote Labour because they see it as the party which better represents the disadvantaged.

Raynor's second group is those with low status within the middle class. Unlike the first group, they do not vote Labour for idealistic reasons, but more out of pique and insecurity. Typically, they rank higher in education and qualifications than in social status: they find outlets for the resulting resentment in the phlegm of radical politics. (It is worth noting that the analysis of radicalism in terms of status deprivation has been influential in recent American sociology and history, where it has been criticised as both conservative and speculative.) Certainly, this approach employs a highly cynical interpretation of motive. In refuting it, Frank Parkin argues that low status jobs are a *result* of radical ideals and not vice-versa. He suggests that the political attitudes of middle class radicals are formed before they start work, and that they choose work which is most compatible with their radical values. This tends to be vocational and of relatively low pay and status.

The third group for consideration are numbers of first generation white collar employees, or 'the sons of affluent workers' as John Goldthorpe calls them. It seems that some of these continue to support the Labour Party even after their rise in socio-economic status. No doubt this partly reflects loyalty to their 'roots' but it also suggests that, as the traditional working class shrinks, the Labour Party may have succeeded in presenting policies that potentially widen its basis of support.

b WORKING CLASS DEVIANT VOTERS The number of non-Labour working class voters is so large that it is almost misleading to categorise them as 'deviant'. It is certain that there must be profound reasons to account for so substantial a phenomenon. The most convincing explanation of the large working class Tory vote, and one which is echoed in most writings on the subject, is that the dominant institutions of our society embody conservative and middle class values. As a result, the working class as well as the middle class becomes socialised into conservative values *unless* more radical socialisation cuts across this central flow of influence (see Parkin, above). In functionalist terms, this simply means that a 'consensus around the central value system' is created by institutions such as the monarchy and the church, which exist partly for that purpose. Marxists agree, but consider that this process misleads or 'mystifies' the working class into conforming, sometimes enthusiastically, to a social system that exploits them.

Detailed study of the working class Conservative vote supports the above analysis. As we have seen, Goldthorpe and Lockwood have given the term deferential traditionalists to one group of working class Tories. Referring to the same group, McKenzie and Silver use the term 'deference voters'. These are people who prefer ascribed 'socially superior' leaders to those who have risen by their own efforts. McKenzie and Silver found these attitudes among some of the urban proletariat, although they are more usually associated with farm labourers. Often it seems that isolated, individual workers, such as caretakers of prestige, private establishments or personal and domestic employees of the wealthy, adopt deferential attitudes.

McKenzie and Silver suggest that what they term secular voters may be superseding deferential voters as the major working class basis of Conservative support. Compared to deference voters, secular voters are young and well-paid. In general secular voters seems to describe the group referred to by Goldthorpe and Lockwood as instrumentalists. The latter, of course, deny that this group is tending to become more Conservative and, in doing so, refute the embourgeoisement hypothesis. Nevertheless, the strong swing (11.5) of affluent workers from Labour to the Conservatives in the 1979 election suggests that the embourgeoisement hypothesis may have more long-term mileage in it than Goldthorpe and Lockwood suspected. In any case, they themselves point out that instrumentalists are more likely than traditionalists to change their voting habits to suit their perceived interests – a point also made by McKenzie and Silver. The latter also point out that instrumentalists tend to be less attracted to Labour by socialist values than of the benefits of practical policies. If such benefits are not apparent they may change their vote.

Variables other than Class Associated with Voting Behaviour

Besides class, other variables which correlate with patterns of voting behaviour are age, region, gender, religion and race. All of these are, in some measure, class-related. Thus, young people and women vote more according to their class background than any other factor: a young working class person will *tend* to vote Labour and a middle class woman will *tend* to vote Conservative. Nevertheless, these and other factors mentioned above seem to exercise a certain effect on voting behaviour relatively independently of class. We will briefly discuss these factors now, taking age first.

There is a tendency for the old to vote Conservative and for the young to vote Labour. Whilst most middle class young voters vote Conservative and most working class old voters vote Labour, in neither case is the normal class pattern of voting reflected *quite* as strongly as in the rest of the population. Why is this? The view that it is because the old are 'naturally' more Conservative and the young 'naturally' more 'left' or radical has been convincingly queried by both Goldthorpe and Lockwood and Butler and Stokes. The alternative explanation is made in terms of 'political generations'. Anthony King summarises this research succinctly:

> On this view, the preponderance of Conservatives among the over 65s is the result not primarily of their being old as such but of their having matured politically at a time when the Conservatives were the dominant party, and when Labour was only beginning to emerge as a political force (that is, in the first 20 years of this century – *author's brackets).*

Equally, young people since the Second World War have seen Labour either in government or as the major opposition party. What is true, however, is that the old change their vote, whatever it is, much less easily than young people. This difference in political constancy is well illustrated in the following diagram:

Voting Constancy and Age

Time when first able to Vote	Pre 1918	Inter- War	Post War	Post 1951
% Supporting the same Party in 1959 and 1964	86	81	79	58

Source: Anthony King, 'A Sociological Portrait of Politics,' in *New Society*, 13 January, 1972, p. 58.

Change is particularly likely to occur when a young person's parents vote contrary to their class and he reverts to class-party allegiance, but the best general explanation may be that young people simply take time to make up their minds and to develop settled patterns of political allegiance.

Support for political parties varies widely from region to region even *within* social classes. Thus, a manual worker in the south west is twice as likely to vote Conservative as one in Wales. The 1979 election was particularly notable for the strength of regional voting trends. For instance, the depressed north remained generally Labour whereas the affluent south eastern commuter zones swung strongly towards the Conservatives. The general principle seems to be that in regions in which one class and party is predominant, members of the other class tend to be more easily drawn away from 'normal' class-party allegiance towards the majority. The same is often true of towns and neighbourhoods of this kind.

Women are more conservative than men. If men alone had the vote, Labour would have been in power virtually all the post-war years. Research in this area is limited, but one line of speculation is that women are less likely immediately to experience the radicalising effects of industrial conflict than men and are, consequently, less likely to develop the related political affiliation to the Labour Party. Second, in an ageing population, there are more old women than men (over 1½ million more over 65 in 1977) and the old, as we have seen, are disproportionately conservative.

'Even religious history still matters in politics', Anthony King tells us. He goes on to say that 'the Church of England is still, to a most remarkable degree, the Tory party at prayer'. Surveys consistently show that Anglicans are much more likely to vote Conservative than members of other major churches. Butler and Stokes found in 1963 that, among Anglicans who went to church at least once a week, 72% were Tories. Interestingly, church attendance is, in general, associated with conservatism but this association is particularly strong among Anglicans. Catholics provide an exception to this trend in both Britain and America where, historically, they have favoured the more radical of the two major parties, the Labour Party and the Democratic Party, respectively. In Britain, the link between religion and politics is now on the wane, and is difficult to distinguish at all in younger voters. Northern Ireland, of course, is a complicated exception to this trend. Further afield, the 'Muslim revolution' in Iran suggests that, in the more traditional Third World, religion can be as powerful a source of political motivation as any other. Race is now an issue of considerable importance in British as well as in American politics (see Chapter 12). In both countries coloured ethnic groups have tended to vote left of centre.

All the above factors tend to correlate with class and, in some cases, with one another: even gender and religion correlate. Women are more religious than men, and both factors correlate with voting Conservative. Where two or more predisposing factors occur together, as in this case, the tendency they are associated with is more likely to occur. But it is crucial to note that it *may not* occur. There exist Conservative miners in working class areas and Labour company directors who regularly attend Anglican services. As political behaviour cannot be wholly predicted, this presumably indicates that it has an element of individual choice about it. It might be thought that this would be most apparent in the case of 'floating' or uncommitted voters. The evidence is, however, that this group is amongst the least educated and worst informed part of the electorate. They often appear to vote almost at random rather than after profound consideration. Nevertheless, the point stands. The possibility of political choice is real, and its likelihood is increased the better educated and informed the electorate is. Bryan Heading interprets the recent erosion of the reliable basic support for both major parties as an indication that more of the electorate are choosing to vote for whichever party seems to offer them most at a given time rather than simply to follow traditional allegiance. Perhaps prematurely he associates this apparant decline in the class basis of party support with increased affluence and applies it particularly to better-off Labour voters.

Parties, Pressure Groups and Government: The Liberal Model of the Democratic Society

Those who contend that liberal democracy 'works' argue that parties and pressure groups effectively represent people and influence government. Further, they believe that political government, reflecting the will of the people, is the supreme state power. The civil service is seen as the 'servant' of government: the judiciary is regarded as independent of government, but is not expected to concern itself with political matters. The liberal model of democracy is examined below. In addition to the term 'liberal democracy', that of 'liberal pluralist' or, simply, 'pluralist' is often used. Pluralist refers to the many groups – notably parties and pressure groups – that liberals believe participate meaningfully in democratic politics.

Parties, Political Elites and the State

Political parties existed in Britain well before universal manhood suffrage (that is, the right of all males to vote). Parties, therefore, predate democracy. Nevertheless, the party system has adapted well to the demands of liberal democracy. The major parties attempt to appeal consistently to certain broad groups of people. The Labour Party seeks support mainly from the working class and certain sections of the middle class, such as members of the new professions. The Conservative Party is traditionally the party of the middle and upper classes. There is, however, as we have seen, much overlap in the class basis of party support and, in particular, among the upper working and lower middle classes. Even so, a major party seems to require a solid basis of class support to survive. The Liberal Party rapidly declined as a major party when it ceased to appeal to an identifiable section of society. The suitability of the two party system to liberal democracy is further suggested by the American example. Two competing parties quickly established themselves after the Americans had won their independence from Britain. In time, these developed into the present day Democratic and Republican parties. Like the chief British parties, these also tend to represent major sectional interests, although not to the same extent.

Political parties have ideologies or certain principles and beliefs which usually reflect quite closely the values and material interests of those groups and classes from which they draw most of their support. The British Conservative Party is strongly committed to capitalism, whereas the Labour Party believes in socialism – although the majority in neither party would wish to fundamentally change the 'mixed' nature of the

504

economy. It is still probably true that the Conservative Party is the party of tradition, whereas the Labour Party identifies with progressive change and reform. For liberal-democratic theorists these are very significantly different ideological positions, but Marxists argue that, rhetoric aside, *the two major parties actually behave rather similarly when in government.* By contrast, liberal-democratic theorists consider that philosophical differences can lead to *practical policy differences.* Thus, various measures of the Labour government of 1945–50 would be considered distinctly socialist, and in sharp contrast to the clearly pro-free-enterprise policies of the Thatcher government elected in 1979. In fairness, this example is selected to suit the argument and most Labour and Conservative governments have been more similar to one another than these. In any case, it is a tacit assumption of liberalism that no major party will seek to overthrow the basic social and political 'consensus'.

Liberal democracy is, in part, a theory about the *the relationship between the majority of the poeple and their leaders, the political elite.* This relationship has balancing elements: the elite is *representative,* and yet it also *leads.* We will deal with these two aspects separately.

Historically, elite theory has tended to be undemocratic. Of the two major early twentieth century elite theorists, Pareto and Mosca, it was the latter who argued that the political elite *could* be generally representative of the people or 'masses', to use the term preferred by elite theorists. The party system, free elections and pressure group activity were means to ensure representativeness.

An important related issue to the representative nature of elites is the extent to which, once elected, they remain under democratic control. Is democracy 'real' only once every five years when people cast their vote? Robert Dahl believes that elections play an important part in controlling government and he also cites a second major means by which leaders are made answerable to the people:

> The election process is one of two fundamental methods of social control which, operating together, make governmental leaders so responsive to non-leaders that the distinction between democracy and dictatorship still makes sense. The other method of social control is continuous political competition among individuals, parties or both. Elections and political competition . . . vastly

505

increase the size, number and variety of minorities whose preferences must be taken into account by leaders in making policy choices.

Above all, elections, or the certainty that an election must come, means that a governing party must always conduct itself in a way that will ultimately appeal to the majority of the electorate. There is evidence that widespread retrospective voting does occur: many voters do remember major features in the overall performance of administration and this acts as a check upon it. As Dahl points out, however, many particular policies may be concerned with the interest only of a minority, such as farm subsidies for the agricultural interest, though this does not necessarily mean that they therefore alienate the rest of the electorate. Many policies which please a minority are non-contentious to the majority. When the election comes, nevertheless, the government knows that, to win, it must have the backing of a 'majority of minorities'. This, according to Dahl, keeps it in check.

Liberal elite theorists have stressed the necessity of *leadership* by the political elite almost as much as its representative nature. In large societies, only a minority can be involved in leadership. Further, competitive political selection should ensure that the elite leads on merit. The prime general function of leadership is to create social consensus and establish social order. Edward Shils believes that, in doing this, the elite protects its own interests, as well as those of the majority. Whilst agreeing that the process of consensus production does occur, Marxists deny that in capitalist society it works for the common good. On the contrary, it merely misleads the working class. Class conflict tends not to be stressed by democratic elite theorists. The alternative term to classes, 'masses' – which obscures classes and class conflict – sounds too contemptuous to modern ears to be used by liberal theorists. Instead, they stress the need for the political elite to weld these into a working consensus.

We can link Dahl's democratic theory with the functionalist view put forward by Talcott Parsons of how power operates in a democracy. Parsons argues that leaders *use* power for the general good or, more precisely, for collective goals. Leaders are 'honest brokers' in power. Defence of the country and maintenance of law and order are two examples of the necessary use

506

of power for the general good. It is crucial to Parson's theory that *how much* power political leaders use ultimately depends on the will of the people. In war-time, the representative of the people in Congress or Parliament may sanction the use of greater powers by the government. Emergencies aside, the use of power is controlled by the processes described by Dahl. Parsons, therefore, conceives of power rather as economists think of money: more or less can be created as the situation demands.

The Liberal View of the State
Liberal theorists tend to regard the relationship between government and the rest of the state as relatively unproblematic. The government rules and the civil service implements its policies. The Marxist idea that the capitalist class is the 'real' controller of the state is simply not taken seriously. Weber, however, raised an important question in relation to the civil service. He considered that, like all bureaucracies it created its own vested interests and tended to be slow-moving. Civil servants, for reasons of their own, *may* give partial advice to ministers or take too long in producing it. Weber regarded a powerful Parliament as the best protector against an oppressive civil service bureaucracy.

Pressure Groups
Pressure groups, as well as parties, are parts of the liberal-democratic model. If parties are the bulwarks of democracy, pressure groups are the supports and buttresses. They are an essential part of the pluralist vision in which power is seen as widely shared and exercised. Like parties, pressure groups predate democracy but like them they have become part of liberal democracy. Jean Blondel, who shares the pluralist perspective, sees parties and pressure groups as equally involved in the democratic process, although in different ways:

> Interest groups differ from political parties by their aim, which is not to take power but only to exert pressure. They differ from parties by their objects, which are usually limited in scope. They differ from parties by the nature of their membership, which is often limited to one section in society.

There have always been groups sharing a common interest which have collectively pressed their case to the powerful. The

Wolfenden Report states that in the period since the war the number of pressure groups has increased considerably. From the liberal point of view, pressure groups provide a *necessary* means of *limited* conflict on specific issues but this takes place within a *context of fundamental consensus*.

We can classify pressure groups into two broad types: *sectional* (or protective) and *promotional*. Sectional groups are those whose membership has some common factor, such as occupation. It is to defend the common interest of their membership that such groups exist. Trade Unions and professional associations provide the best known examples of sectional pressure groups. The biggest union is the Transport and General Worker's Union (TGWU), and a well known professional association is the British Medical Association (BMA). Sectional groups are usually economic but can also be produced by, for instance, religious and ethnic divisions. The National Association for the Advancement of Coloured People (NAACP) and the Congress of Racial Equality (CORE) are two traditional Black Rights pressure groups in the United States.

Promotional groups seek to promote a cause. One example is Amnesty International which seeks to aid and assist political prisoners throughout the world. Political prisoners are, roughly, prisoners of conscience as opposed to ordinary criminals. Amnesty International is an organisation for which there is likely to be a long-term need. By contrast, other promotional groups achieve their aim, and can then disband. For example, a variety of anti-Vietnam war groups sprang up in the nineteen-sixties but dissolved when the war came to an end.

We need to distinguish between pressure groups in terms of the time-span of their existence, as well as on the basis of their interests or the causes they champion. The anti-Vietnam war groups were examples of *ad hoc* groups, formed to contest a specific issue, whereas Amnesty International and, still more obviously, the Trades Union Congress (TUC) are *permanent* groups. (see diagram). Blondel also makes the important point that certain organisations which are not strictly speaking interest groups may occasionally use their *influence* in the political process. Thus, the Catholic church makes its official (though not necessarily representative), opinion felt on such matters as divorce and abortion legislation.

	Sectional Groups	Promotional Groups
Permanent	Trades Union Congress	Campaign for Nuclear Disarmament
Ad Hoc	Archway Road Campaign	Various Anti-War Groups

Pressure groups use a variety of means to influence public opinion, such as advertisements, demonstrations and meetings. Sometimes they focus more directly on Parliament or the executive government. Often this means lobbying a powerful or influential individual such as an MP. Our interest, however, is less in the detail of the methods of pressure group activity than in whether or not the results of this pressure are effective. Pluralists would say that they are, Marxists that they are not. At least, that is the essence of the argument, although both positions require some qualification. Christopher Hewitt has attempted to test which of these two cases is more correct by reference to empirical data. He examines the roles of a variety of interest groups in relation to twenty-four major post-war crisis issues which cover the area of foreign, economic, welfare and social policy. The issues he analyses include the debate and struggles over the Suez crisis, the nationalisation of steel, the National Health Service Act and the Commonwealth Immigration Act of 1962. He includes interest groups from all major sections of national life in his study, including trade unions (blue and white collar); business organisations; religious organisations; local government bodies; research organisations and various promotional groups. He concludes that policy making in Britain is not elitist in the sense that any single elite or interest is dominant, but that different interests succeed at different times. Statistically, the unions are particularly successful in that issues are most frequently resolved as they wish. The Marxist response to this argument is that issues dealt with in national politics are within the national consensus and that genuinely alternative (Marxist) principles and policies are not discussed. This view is examined in the next section.

There are other arguments put forward by liberal democrats in support of the pressure group system. Pressure groups provide an accessible, day-to-day means by which popular opinion and influence can be expressed. They act upon political parties but are not necessarily part of the party system. In practice, however, the two major industrial interest groups tend to be tied into the party system. The unions and the TUC, and business and the CBI tend overwhelmingly to support, respectively, the Labour Party and the Conservative Party. It is significant, although seldom stressed by pluralists, that in a society noted for its class system, the two major parties and the two major interest groups should divide along class lines. Nevertheless, the major groups which support and, in part, finance the political parties exact a 'price' for loyalty: in return, they expect their interests to be protected and advanced. If, in their opinion, this does not occur, then, on a given issue, they may oppose the party they normally favour. Thus, the proposals to change the legal position of the unions, put forward by the Labour government of 1966–1970, were opposed with great determination by the union movement.

A further criticism of interest group politics, in addition to that put forward by Marxists referred to above, is that it tends to leave out or, at least, to leave behind, those who are least able to organise themselves: these people are found in the overlapping categories of the poor, the old, and the chronically sick and disabled. Immigrant groups also have tended to be less organised than their needs require. This is partly because they are financially and materially disadvantaged, and therefore have difficulty in affording the cost of organisation, and partly because it takes time for a group to accumulate the knowledge and experience to deal with the complex structure of institutionalised power in this country. It is a feature of British and American politics that, in the nineteen sixties and seventies, the disadvantaged have become increasingly organised and vociferous. Instead of assuming that the welfare state will 'take care of them', the deprived have formed groups such as Claimants Unions (concerned with supplementary benefits) and Tenants Associations and squatters rights aimed at *obtaining* what they see as their rights. Even pensioners have been seen to converge on Parliament Square to lobby MPs. Often the deprived have been assisted in pursuing their interests by community social workers or radical professional people and, occasionally, students. Sometimes this link has taken an institutional form. Des Wilson and Frank Field, the charismatic former directors of Shelter (the pressure group concerned with housing) and The Child Poverty Action Group, respectively, exemplify this kind of alliance. Of course, the involvement and concern of radical intellectuals with the poor is by no means new, but it did receive fresh stimulus in the nineteen sixties, and this impetus remains apparent even in the early nineteen eighties. The increased number of pressure groups, particularly among the disadvantaged, may suggest that pluralism works; equally, however, the need for these pressure groups may indicate that the way liberal capitalism functions fails to satisfy the wants of large numbers of people.

It is not easy for people living in a Western democracy to evaluate the extent and quality of the political and civil 'freedom' that liberals claim exists in these countries. This freedom is manifestly not absolute. Freedom of speech and freedom of the press is limited by law. The party-pressure group political system seems to favour the loudest voices: certainly political rights have not led to a radical reduction in material inequality. But it would be very foolish to undervalue the freedom that does exist. Within broadly defined limits, people can speak their minds, even if some have far easier access to a public audience than others. People *are* able to organise for a cause even though some, by virtue of greater knowledge, wealth or influence, can do so more easily than others. Private lives are largely left private by the State – in their own homes, at least, people can 'be themselves'. These freedoms might not seem so substantial or so precious if we did not have before us the bloody alternative of totalitarianism practised in Germany and Russia in the nineteen thirties. Perhaps the major argument in favour of liberal democracy is that attempts to improve on it have usually resulted in something much worse and in the reduction of political, civil and personal freedom. In the post-Second World War period a cautionary, even defensive, note has characterised liberal statements about democracy. Ageing liberals remember pre-war Germany and Russia as far worse than any liberal regime and are now inclined to settle for and defend what they know and value rather than to experiment and try to improve. By contrast, socialists and Marxists argue that a fundamentally freer, more equal and more just society than exists in liberal democracies is possible. While legitimately disagreeing with liberals, they can learn from them that creating such a society is fraught with dangers and that, if the attempt fails, far more may be lost than gained. To regard liberal warnings of this kind as 'mere moralism' is to show a gross ignorance of the failures and cruelties of recent European history.

Representative Political Elite or Ruling Class?: The Liberal/Marxist Debate

The Marxist View of the 'Capitalist State'

Most Marxists would deny that the model of democracy described in the previous section represents 'real' democracy. For them, it is merely 'bourgeois democracy', a smokescreen behind which the capitalist class pursues its own interests. Parliament and political government are not considered to be the major source of power. *Capitalists make the important decisions: economic man rules political man.* Although many contemporary Marxists would modify this view, many also retain a firm commitment to it in its classic form.

We have discussed in sufficient detail already Marx's view of society as fundamentally divided by class conflict. Of more relevance here is the issue of *how* Marxists consider that the ruling class rules. Both Tom Bottomore and Anthony Giddens make the point that, if capitalists do rule, they do so indirectly. They cannot do so directly as they are in a minority, both in the legislature and the executive in most capitalist countries. In feudal society, there was a much more precise correspondence between economic and political power. The feudal lords were the ruling class in the sense that they occupied the major political as well as economic positions. The landed nobility fulfilled the most important positions in central and local government. That is not true of capitalists today, although they are well represented in politics. If capitalists rule at all, therefore, they do so indirectly. Because of this, Marxist attempts to 'prove' the existence of a ruling class have often tended to be either circumstantial (relying on suggestive rather than conclusive evidence), or rather abstract and theoretical. Ralph Miliband's book, *The State in Capitalist Society*, appears to fall into the first group, although Miliband himself would claim that he more than demonstrates his case. As the title of his book suggests, he is concerned with the control and operation of the state in capitalist society. He considers the state to be made up of the following institutions: the government, the administration (the civil service), the judiciary and parliamentary assemblies. State power lies in these institutions. In addition to what Miliband says, it is useful to bear in mind Althusser's concept of state apparatuses. The capacity of the state to control the armed forces and police as well as the major means of communication, notably the media, is crucial to its power. This control is open to challenge and, in any case, it is fiercely argued between liberals and Marxists precisely how much power the state in capitalist societies has over the ideological state apparatus. Obviously, the relationship between the government and media differs somewhat in different capitalist countries but, generally, Marxists argue that there is relatively limited freedom of expression, whereas liberals take the opposite view.

The Upper Class Background of Occupational Elites

A major part of Miliband's book examines two related questions whose answers, taken together, determine whether or not there is a ruling class in British and other European capitalist societies. Firstly, is the state actually operated by people from the same upper class social background? Secondly, if so, do these people run the state in their own interest and at the expense of other classes? Miliband's answer to both questions is 'yes', although he has an easier time answering the first than the second. On the common social background and experience of those who dominate the command positions of the state, Miliband is unequivocal:

> What the evidence conclusively suggests is that in terms of social origin, education and class situation, the men who have manned *all* command positions in the state system have largely, and in many cases, overwhelmingly, been drawn from the world of business or property, or from the professional middle classes. Here, as in every other field, men and women born into the subordinate classes, which form of course the vast majority of the population, have fared very poorly . . .

Although Miliband is primarily concerned with Britain, he cites considerable empirical evidence to show that the same situation prevails in other Western European 'democracies'.

Miliband's book was published in 1969, but substantially the same argument was presented in 1979 by Anthony Giddens who, in fact, makes a broader claim than Miliband – that there is *no* major institutional sector in Britain where less than half of those in top positions are of public school background, and, by implication, also of upper or upper middle class background. (For details, see Chapter 9.) Drawing on a study of elites carried out at Cambridge, Giddens concludes that over 80% of Anglican bishops, of principal judges and of army officers over the rank of major-general were from public schools, as were 60% of chief secretaries in the civil service, and 76% of Conservative MPs (1951–70). In contrast, only 26% of Labour MPs had a public school background.

Giddens emphasises especially the upper class dominance of industry, which, from the Marxist point of view, is particularly important because the economy is seen as the ultimate basis of power. In a sample taken from the Cambridge survey, 73% of the directors of the industrial corporations and 80% of the directors of financial firms proved to be of public school background.

Giddens cites other work which shows that directors of industrial and, especially, financial companies very often have kin 'within the trade'. The phenomenon of interlocking directorships is a point emphasised in both British and American literature on industrial elites. The term 'industrial elites' refers to the way in which various individuals hold directorships in more than one company so that the same individuals may sit together on several different boards. Accordingly, they may influence and even co-ordinate the policy of two or more companies: indeed, this is often precisely the intention of interlocking directorships. The Cambridge study showed an increase in directional connection between large companies. At the beginning of the century, fewer than half of the 85 corporations studied were linked by shared directorships, whereas in 1970, 73 out of 85 organisations studied appeared in the network of connections. Potentially, this provides an impressive basis for control of industry.

Is the Upper Class also a Ruling Class?

We come now to Miliband's second area of enquiry. Does the upper class rule in its own interest, and at the expense of others? As Miliband and Giddens are well aware, to demonstrate upper class dominance of major elites does not prove either that the upper class is the 'real source of political power' or, still less, that it *rules in its own interest*. In particular, the powerful position of the upper class in industry does not automatically mean that it can control the political process or that, 'in the last resort', its economic power is more decisive than the political power of government. These issues require further examination.

In attempting to determine whether the upper class is also a ruling class, it is helpful to establish what links exist between business and politics. If these are considerable, we can conclude that there is at least the *potential* for business to influence the political process and, perhaps, even to *control* it in its own interest. A study by Roth and Kerbey shows that, between 1960 and 1966, MPs held, in total, 770 directorships and 324 positions as chairmen, vice-chairmen or managing directors. It is highly significant that 90% of these positions were held by Conservative MPs. Insofar as the economic-political flow of influence does express itself through personal links of this kind, it is, therefore, far more likely to be found in the Conservative Party than in the Labour Party. The upper class is well represented in both industry and the Conservative Party. As we have seen 76% of Conservative MPs over the period 1951–70 went to public school, a major purveyor of upper class culture, compared with only 26% of Labour MPs. Few Marxists, however, regard the Labour Party as the likely means by which capitalism will be abolished and socialism established. Why is this so?

Marx himself held out little hope that socialism could be successfully introduced through Parliament, although there is evidence that he thought that the arrival of universal male suffrage (voting rights) might make the system more responsive to socialist demands. In the event, Marxists are able to point out that, despite seventeen years of Labour government, since 1945, the fundamental facts of inequality have not changed very much. Everybody has become better off, but the relativities have not changed significantly. Marxists tend to consider that the welfare state has partly 'humanised' but not fundamentally changed the position of the working class and the poor. Writing in the late nineteen-sixties, but expressing a perennial mood among Marxists, Miliband says:

515

Social-democratic parties (Labour parties) or rather social-democratic leaders, have long ceased to suggest to anyone but their most credulous followers (and the more stupid among their opponents) that they were concerned in any sense whatever with the business of bringing about a socialist society. (author's brackets).

In qualification of Miliband's remark, it should be said that there is still a sizeable socialist, if not Marxist-inclined, group within the Labour Party, which continues to work for fundamental change through the parliamentary system, despite its dissatisfaction with the performances of the Labour government of the nineteen sixties and seventies.

Nicos Poulantzas

Further analysis of the role of the ruling class in capitalist society is presented by Nicos Poulantzas, a French Marxist. In a celebrated exchange with Miliband, Poulantzas criticises him for concentrating too much on details about the social background of various occupational elites and of the ruling class as a whole. For Poulantzas, these factors are not particularly crucial. In his view, it would be possible for large numbers, even a majority, of people of quite humble social background to administer capitalist society – *but it would still be capitalist society* and therefore run in the interests of the capitalist class and not the proletariat. This brings us to Poulantzas's central point and the one on which he considers that he differs, at least in emphasis, from Miliband. Poulantzas contends that it is the structure of the capitalist system and not the social background of the various elites which is the major factor for Marxists to consider when analysing the state. According to him, what matters is the relationship of the parts, including the state, to the social totality (the whole of society). Thus, it comes as no surprise to Poulantzas that socialist parties with a wide basis of popular support and even, perhaps, with leaders of working class origins, should find it difficult to implement socialism when, supposedly, 'in power'. The British Labour Party might be elected 'to power' but what it can actually do is limited by the rest of the system. It would almost certainly be afraid to introduce policies that would lose the confidence of international financiers and stock exchange investors. To do so would probably cause a major economic crisis. There might even be the possibility that radical policies would turn the military against the government. This threat, however, is most easily demonstrated in relation to underdeveloped countries. Thus, the popularly elected (although not with an absolute majority) President Allende of Chile, a Marxist, was overthrown by a conspiracy involving some of the parliamentary opposition, members of the armed forces and the American Central Intelligence Agency. The implication is that when legality fails to protect the interests of capital, then illegal means may be used.

The above does not mean that Poulantzas dismisses the state as unimportant – far from it! Some years after his debate with Miliband, he wrote: 'The state plays a decisive role in the relations of production and the class struggle'. But Poulantzas warns that what a socialist party could actually *do* with state power, if it were to obtain it, would be conditioned by the relationship of the state to the rest of the system at that time. This would include such matters as the strength of capital and the extent of socialist support among the working class.

There is a element of 'shadow boxing' about Miliband's and Poulantzas's disagreement, because the former insists that his work is a structural critique of the state in capitalist society and not just a collection of loosely interpreted empirical data. In any case, Poulantzas's point that an adequate *theory* of the state must relate coherently to the rest of the social system is valid.

It is worth briefly exploring the wider implications of Poulantzas's remark that 'the state plays a decisive role in the relations of production and the class struggle'. In saying this, he is rejecting the deterministic interpretations of Marx's base-superstructure model of society. He denies that capitalism will inevitably collapse as a result of its inherent economic 'contradictions' as some Marxists still believe. (Whether Marx himself ever believed this, in any simplistic sense, is debatable.) For Poulantzas, the capitalist nature of society and class relations arising from relations to the means of production do *structure* class conflict – both in the economic and political context – but they do not pre-determine its outcome: socialism has to be achieved through political struggle. With some reservations, the American Marxist sociologist, Erik Wright, supports this position in his book, *Class, Crisis and the State*. In particular, he offers a sensitive discussion of the issue of whether socialism

517

can be achieved through the "bourgeois' democratic system or whether it requires violent revolution. We have already referred to some of the problems of the former approach: the difficulties in relation to the second are perhaps greater. Firstly, the human cost of violent revolution needs to be profoundly considered. Can it be justified? Secondly, modern governments have at their disposal such powerful and centrally controlled arsenals of destruction that they seem virtually unassailable.

Ideology and Power

A crucial question that Marxists need to explain is why the majority, who are not the prime beneficiaries of capitalism, do not oppose the system more vehemently. Miliband and Poulantzas are agreed that the dominant ideology plays a vital role in securing the compliance of the majority to the power and position of the ruling class. We have already discussed how the educational system can teach people to conform – even to a society in which they have relatively little material stake – and the role of the mass media in this respect is worthy of much more space than we can give it here. For the moment, a single quotation from Miliband will serve to represent the Marxist perspective:

> Given the economic and political context in which the mass media functions, they cannot fail to be, predominantly, agencies for the dissemination of idea and values which affirm rather than challenge existing patterns of power and privilege, and thus be weapons in the arsenal of class domination.

Ideological control involves power over men's minds. As Bachrach and Baratz point out, an aspect of this is the ability to decide which issues should be allowed to become publicly debated and which should not be, for instance, control of the press. Steven Lukes takes this point further by frankly recognising that the values, attitudes, and even wants of the majority can be moulded by the power of a few. Marxists are unimpressed by exercises such as that carried out by Hewitt (discussed earlier) which seem to support a pluralist model of power, because they argue that the issues that really matter are seldom discussed publicly, anyway. For Marxists, such issues would include whether a society based on private property (including that of the ruling class) *can* be socially just, whether violence is necessary to destroy the capitalist system and what a 'liberated' socialist culture might be like. The limits of the political debate are reflected in decisions taken and not taken (for example, issues of pollution and poverty may be disregarded and defence-law and order and immigration policy vigorously pursued). Marxists, then, agree with functionalists that ideological consensus can be achieved in capitalist society: the difference is their evaluation of it. Functionalists see it as necessary; Marxists regard it as an element in class exploitation. For them, there is no more telling illustration of the power of the ruling class than their ability to persuade the working class to accept and even morally approve of their own subjection. The consolation for Marxists is that they see the possibility of an end to inequality and the power of the ruling class.

Power Elite versus Ruling Class Theory: A Radical Disagreement

Before summarising the merits of the pluralist and Marxist views of democracy, we must briefly analyse the power elite theory of the American radical sociologist, C. Wright Mills. Mills was a conflict theorist but was much less of a Marxist than the other authors so far discussed in this section. He probably owed more to Weber than to Marx. He was a severe critic of post-Second World War American society. His fierce but measured language broke across the bland face of functionalist orthodoxy like a fire-cracker. A startled Talcott Parsons compared him to a gun-happy outlaw, free with the trigger but not very accurate in his aim. It is true that Mills began more than he was able to finish, but by the time of his death in 1962, he had sown the seeds of a radical revival in American sociological scholarship, and provided an intellectual starting point for the emerging political radicalism of the American New Left. His best known and most influential work is *The Power Elite*, first published in 1956. It is typical of Mills's intellectual inventiveness that he reworked traditionally conservative elite theory within a radical perspective. He argued that there are three popularly *un*representative elites at the top of American society: the political elite, the military elite and the industrial elite. Together, these made up the power elite. The relative power of the three elites could vary. In his own time, when the Cold War was at its height, he believed that the military was the most powerful of the three. He insisted, however, that members of the elites shared common material interests as well as, frequently, a common upper class background. Individuals such as President Eisenhower moved easily between the elites, and thus helped to fuse more closely identity of ideology and interest. Mills was in no doubt that the power elite 'ran' America to its own benefit and against that of the majority of people. He considered that the American Congress operated only at the middle level of power and was unable to check the power elite. It was influential mainly on those issues that did not fundamentally affect the structure of society or the essential interests of the power elite. Thus, it might legislate for a little more or a little less welfare aid but not for a fundamental redistribution of wealth. Below the power elite was what Mills did not hesitate to describe as 'the masses'. They comprised the middle and working classes and the poor. He regarded the middle class as fragmented and generally concerned with its own various sectional interests, and the working class as sufficiently 'well-fed' to be thoroughly deradicalised and uninterested in change. Mills's comments on the working class had plausibility in relation to the relatively unorganised and non-socialist American labour force but they were rejected by European Marxists as much less applicable to that continent. The poor consisted of such groups as the unemployed, the old and disproportionate numbers of coloured minorities. Mills saw little prospect that this group would become an effective agency for change, but he did refer, in passing, to the 'moral idea of a counter-elite' and to 'images of the poor, the exploited, and the oppressed as the truly virtuous, the wise and the blessed'.

As we shall shortly describe, this notion had considerable appeal to the young American radicals of the nineteen sixties to whom Mills became something of a folk hero and intellectal father figure. In turn, Mills regarded young, radical intellectuals as the best, if still unlikely, chance for change in America.

Liberal Pluralist and Marxist Theory: Summary
Pluralist theorists take liberal democracy more or less 'at face value'. They believe it works, and consider that political parties and interest groups adequately represent the people. Marxists present a variety of arguments to demonstrate that pluralist claims are incorrect and that power in capitalist societies is, in

reality, in the hands of the ruling class. They point to the dominance of the upper class in various major elites and, in particular, to the overlap between Parliament and industry. Even Labour governments have been seen to pose only a minimal threat to the ruling class and to have made no fundamental change in inequalities of power, wealth and prestige. The power of the ruling class in the area of ideological control helps to explain, for Marxists, the acquiescence of large sections of the working class in their own 'exploitation'. Mills's mixed legacy defies categorisation, but he caught the ascendant mood of the emerging American and European New Left of the nineteen sixties. The popular slogan of that decade 'Power to the People,' is not so distant an echo of Mills's inspirational rhetoric.

People, Participation and Power

Pluralist democratic assumptions, as well as being attacked from a Marxist point of view, have received criticism from another perspective. The phrase 'participatory democracy' describes this perspective which was presented particularly forcefully by radical American activists in the early nineteen sixties, although the concept has deeper roots both in America and Europe. The terms 'position' and 'perspective' perhaps suggest more precision and sophistication than actually existed in the thinking of those who supported participatory democracy in the sixties. The concept represented a commitment to the idea that people should have some control and involvement in the organisations and decisions that affect their lives. It was as much a matter of sentiment as of ideology, of action as of theory. In the late nineteen fifties and early sixties a strong feeling had grown up among some students and intellectuals, both in Europe and America, that power had become remote from ordinary people who typically played out their working lives in small roles within large organisations run by the powerful few. Groups of young radicals began to try to change this state of affairs by working with the poor and deprived in various community action projects. At first, the student activists were not clear about the relationship between their own local efforts and the change they hoped to effect in the central power structure of American society. As we shall see, ideas about this eventually did develop.

Although the new radicals were not very precise about their own theoretical position, they were able to articulate their criticism of pluralism. Firstly, they regarded power and inequality as issues that went far beyond merely *formal* political processes and institutions into every part of American life. They wanted to make participatory democracy real in every major institutional system from education to welfare organisations. Secondly, they considered that the poor were handicapped within competitive, pluralist democracy, as they have fewer resources and less knowledge than other groups to publicise and achieve their aims. Therefore, they needed help in these matters.

The practical expression of the new radical sentiment took the form of a 'return to the people'. An American student organisation, Students for a Democratic Society, established several community development projects in a number of depressed urban areas. It was hoped that, with help, the poor would begin to control the organisations that presently controlled them. The immediate purpose was to educate the poor in dealing with the power structure as well as to win specific 'battles' over such matters as welfare claims, housing conditions and official 'neglect' of the environment. The resolution of one such issue in Newark, New Jersey – putting a traffic light at a dangerous point on a road – took several months, but those involved learned much about the functioning of local government and administration. In Britain, two officially funded ventures, the Community Development Projects and the misleadingly named Young Volunteer Force Projects, to a certain extent pursued a simiar philosophy to the SDS.

Many of those involved in such schemes soon began to feel that their effectiveness was likely to be very limited. They realised, too, that in trying to help the poor in this way they were tacitly accepting the pluralist assumption that the poor really can compete successfully with other groups even in unequal, capitalist society. They began to appreciate that, in practice, their efforts were likely to make little difference to the fundamental causes of inequality and powerlessness. John Benington of the Coventry CDP expresses an opinion commonly arrived at by radical community organisers in Britain and America:

> A growing awareness of 'the flaw in the pluralist heaven' has forced a number of the CDPs towards a structural class-conflict

model of social change. This is based on the assumption that social problems arise from a fundamental conflict of interests between groups or classes in society. The problems are defined mainly in terms of inequalities in the distribution of power and the focus of change is thus on the centres of organised power (both private and public).

Benington's emphasis on fundamental as opposed to reconcilable conflict puts him firmly in the socialist camp. Indeed, the concept of popular participation, especially in industry, has long been a theme in socialist thought. Because of this, some critics, such as Tom Bottomore, do not regard participatory democracy as a new idea at all and would certainly deny that it provides the basis for a new political ideology. The fact that this principle of participation has also been enthusiastically accepted by the British Liberal Party as well as by many socialists, indicates that Bottomore is correct in regarding it as an inadequate basis for a distinctive political philosophy. Equally, it might be argued that any political philosophy that does not encourage and develop participation is itself inadequate. There is an increased awareness of this point among contemporary Western Marxists: they frequently argue for the development of socialist *and* democratic practice on the left, even 'before the revolution'. Genuinely democratic socialism will not suddenly appear without such practice.

To a limited extent and, often, grudgingly, the principle of participation has gradually gained more acceptance in British society. In the past twenty years, participation in education, planning, housing, transport and, marginally, in industrial decision making has tended to increase. The process, however, is slow and uncertain. Raymond Williams was right when he wrote of the emergence of democracy as 'the long revolution'. For this 'revolution' to be successfully established, democratic participation and (to accept the full logic of democracy) control, must exist in all major areas of social life. This includes the economic and social as well as the political. Democracy at work will probably affect the daily lives of people much more profoundly than do present political rights. Indeed, democracy cannot be properly understood in merely political terms. Families, peer groups and relationships can be more or less democratic. We saw earlier that power exists in virtually all social interactions. Democracy means sharing power by popular

involvement and, by involvement, generating meaning and identity.

Power, People and Sociological Theory

In this final section we examine more deeply the underlying
principles behind the theories of power and politics to which
we have already referred: liberal democratic, Marxist and
Weberian. Finally, we make a point which is inspired by
American populist or popular democratic tradition.

Liberal-democratic theorists, such as Robert Dahl, believe
that power is much more diffuse or 'spread out' than Marxists
believe. The political elite, according to them, is ultimately
answerable to the people and this is a constant contraint on its
actions. Yet the belief of liberals in *popular sovereignty*, that
power comes from the people *is* simply a belief. This idealism
is tempered by a recognition of the need for leadership. Finally,
political power is regarded by liberals as generally dominant
over the power of economic groups. To a large extent, liberals
echo Weber in this point of view. The implication of this belief
is that political rights, especially the right to vote, are very
important.

Marxists, on the other hand, argue that power is primarily a
function of the control of resources. To explain this, let us first
take an example from outside the political arena. As a rule,
large, athletic people have more physical power than small,
unathletic people. This is the direct result of the physical
resources at their disposal – their bodies. Similarly, rich people
have more power than poor people because they control more
economic and, therefore, other resources. Power might extend
as far as 'buying the time' (employing) of poor people and, to
that extent, controlling part of their lives. Even ideological
power involves the control of the means of communication –
such as the mass media or, historically, the pulpit. To put the
matter more technically and specifically, the roots of power
relations are in the relations of classes to the means of production (whether the production of things or ideas). In capitalist
society, the bourgeoisie own the means of production and are
therefore the most powerful class. This does not mean that the
proletariat is without power; it, too, has a relationship to the

means of production. After all, it operates them! This gives it a strategic advantage in class conflict. The collective withdrawal of labour is an immensely powerful weapon. Indeed, syndicalists, though not Marxists, have argued that a general strike is the most effective means of bringing down the capitalist system. Marxists consider that this could not happen and that a transition to a communist society could not take place without the guidance of a Marxist political party.

Marxists assume, then, that power will normally be exercised for self or *class* interest. This is to see power in terms of conflict rather than as a resource for *general* use, as the functionalists tend to see it. Even the pluralists who stress the existence of many 'mini' conflicts pay service to the ultimate predominance of basic consensus. Weber recognises both these elements but inclines towards a conflict view of power. In his distinction between power and authority, however, and in his organisational theory, he moves us on to the *institutionalisation* of power. 'Rational', institutionalised power he considers to be a dominant feature and, to some extent, a plague of modern times. Even so, he seems to bow before the necessity and inevitability of such power – a typically functionalist posture.

A less reverent view of power suffuses the American political tradition, even if this attitude has not appeared in functionalist sociology. Modern America was founded upon revolution against British imperialism. Americans have tended to remain watchful and, often, distrustful of their own leaders – sometimes with good cause. It was because Thomas Jefferson believed that politicians should be subject to the people that he, an American President, said 'God forbid we should be twenty years without a rebellion'. Jefferson exaggerated to make a point – which was that, left to themselves, those in power will probably try to acquire more power, and possibly abuse it. The more power they acquire, the greater the abuse can be. Democracy is largely about preventing this from happening. Modern examples of totalitarianism have re-emphasised Jefferson's wisdom. In this view, democracy is part of a process, almost cyclical in nature, in which government becomes over-powerful and is then brought down to size and shown to be the servant, not the master of the people; at least, for a time. And then the process begins again. For Marxists, a major challenge is to achieve a much greater degree of equality than exists in capitalist societies and to combine it with real democratic freedom. That this is possible still requires to be convincingly shown, both theoretically and practically.

Guide to further reading and study

Jean Blondel's *Voters, Parties, and Leaders* (Pelican, 1969) covers most of the ground dealt with in this chapter, from a generally liberal point of view. There is no comparably simple and comprehensive text written from a Marxist position. Ralph Miliband's *The State and Capitalist Society* (Quartet Books, 1969) is too specialised for 'A' level needs, but is not beyond the intellectual reach of a good second year sixth former. A more practical proposition is Anthony Giddens's article 'An Anatomy of the British Ruling Class', *New Society*, 4th October, 1979, but it is not enough in itself. Selectively used, C. Wright Mills's *The Marxists* (Pelican, 1963) provides a useful guide to Marxist political thought. It is more valuable as a work of classroom reference than either his influential *The Power Elite* (OUP, 1959) or his quite difficult collection of essays, *Power, Politics and People* (OUP, 1970). A more recent book which reviews and examines both liberal and Marxist political perspectives is Thomas R. Dye's *Who's Running America? The Carter Years*, (Prentice Hall, 1979). It is lucidly written and clearly presented. Its aggressively empiricist approach would not appeal to all, particularly theoretical Marxists, but it is a useful and readable contribution to the political elite – ruling class debate.

Past Questions

1 Examine the power of pressure groups in any society with which you are familiar (AEB, 1976).
2 Given that advanced industrial societies have, on most criteria, working class majorities, how is it possible for 'conservative' parties to win elections? (AEB, 1977).
3 Examine the view that power is increasingly diffuse in modern industrial society. (AEB, 1979).

4 'The concentration of power in early capitalist society has given way to a contemporary diversity of competing pressure groups among which none is supreme'. Examine and evaluate the evidence for this proposition. (AEB, 1980).

19 Culture and Ideology: Religion and the Media

Culture and Sub-cultures

The concept of culture has been used repeatedly throughout this book. Perspectives aside, it is a central concept of all sociology. If social structure is the skeleton of society, culture is its flesh and blood. Perhaps because culture is partly concerned with understanding people in creative interaction, many find it the most interesting area of sociology. Cultural analysis is the ground on which sociology meets several other disciplines. You cannot understand the culture of a society unless you know something of its history, literature and folklore. For example, probably the longest quotation in this book is from a novel, *Saturday Night and Sunday Morning* (Chapter 14, pp. 371–2). The passage was selected because it brings to life the human reality of assembly line work just as effectively as any sociological study.

Our working definition of culture has been 'a way of life' or, more fully, the relationship between various elements in a whole way of life. This definition is intentionally broad and encompasses all meaningful human action including that involving conflict. *Culture includes the expression of ideas, feelings or values, or combinations of the three. Communication is an essential characteristic of culture.* The forms of cultural expression are innumerable: language, mathematics, music and football are all cultural forms. So are bingo, hop-scotch, tiddly-winks and tribal dances, political meetings, pop concerts, religious services and the symbolic body-scars of certain social groups. Any consciously directed form of communication is a cultural activity – though the activity can be emotional or rational, or more, likely, both, in nature.

The precise content of various cultural forms is potentially infinite. Painting embraces both the controlled classicism of Michaelangelo and the free-wheeling abstractions of Jackson Pollock; music includes both the sounds of Sibelius and of Sid Vicious; linguistic expression is as much about working class or ethnic dialect as about 'Oxford' English.

In total, the myriad forms of meaningful human expression make up the whole of human culture. Few sociologists, however, take the whole of human culture as their unit of analysis! A society or nation is usually considered quite large enough. Nevertheless, it is important to be aware that the scope of the modern communications media *is* global and that, in some senses, we must, therefore, already have a global culture. Countries, such as Iran and Cambodia, once heard of only through travellers' tales, are now pictured daily in the privacy of our homes. This is a profound and fascinating change, and was encapsulated in Marshall McLuhan's famous phrase 'the global village'.

Functionalist Cultural Analysis

Sociologists of differing perspectives give their own twist of meaning to the term culture. As we have seen, functionalists stress the need for individuals to learn society's cultural norms and values in order for it to function in an orderly manner. Parson's own definition of culture in *The Social System* is too jargon-ridden to merit quoting but it does insist on a rigid 'fit' between individual action and social expectation and demand. In Parson's cultural scheme, people act according to almost predetermined patterns prescribed by society (see Chapter 3, pp. 47–50). For him the essence of national culture is the maintenance of value-consensus. We described specific reference to political socialisation and culture in the last chapter. In summary, the family and educational system convey values of patriotism and loyalty to the nation and teach conformity to its laws and norms. As we shall shortly see, the church and media also play a role in the socialising process.

Marxist Cultural Analysis

The essential point that national cultures do exist would, with qualification, be acceptable to most Marxists. The major qualification that Marxists make to the above proposition is that class-based cultures or sub-cultures also exist. For the ruling class, which generates the national or (to use Marxist terms) the dominant culture, there is a close correspondence between their own class culture and the dominant culture. This is to be expected. For instance, the values of loyalty and obedience to legal overlords, professed by the feudal nobility, were, on the whole, practised by them, and were all the stronger among the mass of society as a result of this consistency. But such correspondence between professed cultural ideals (ideology) and practice was not complete. Thus, although the church and nobility generally preached sexual fidelity in marriage, many did not practise it with much success. Yet, they continued to preach it, partly to encourage the masses to restrain and control themselves, partly to appear worthy of respect and obedience themselves, and, in some cases, no doubt, because they believed in it. In addition, this served as an ideological cover to their actual behaviour. Of course, when 'the cover is blown', then credibility tends to disappear with it. This happened towards the end of the middle ages, when many ordinary people began to feel that the nobility and, particularly, the church, had become corrupt in not 'practising what it preached'. Such a gap or discontinuity between cultural ideology and practice invariably portends great change.

It is usual for the subordinate class to create cultural forms distinct from, and sometimes in conflict with, the dominant culture. In the previous chapter, we referred to Frank Parkin's analysis of how the experience of the workplace and the solidarity of local community life can shield the working class from the otherwise overwhelming influence of the dominant culture. This was true, if to a lesser extent, of the medieval peasant. It did not take great wit or judgement to decide that working for as much as three or four days a week on the land of a feudal lord in return for little or nothing was neither pleasant nor just. Some peasants decided precisely that. No doubt their 'culture' in the form of daily conversations and behaviour, to some extent, expressed this. Certainly, the following rhyme, popular before the Peasants' Revolt of 1381, expressed frankly egalitarian attitudes:

When Adam delved
And Eve span
Who was then the gentleman?

In other words, when it comes to basics, we are all much the same – a potentially revolutionary sentiment in such a hierarchical society. Even the powerful propaganda of the church and nobility which stressed both the necessity and virtue of conformity to the peasants could not delude all of them about their harsh and unequal lot. Indeed, there were occasional rebels among the clergy and gentry themselves. A number of Franciscan friars condemned the luxury of the privileged and the poverty of the poor, and Robin Hood, who may once have been a well-to-do squire, (so the legend goes) romantically 'robbed the rich to give to the poor', and attracted some followers, and much sympathy in doing so.

531

Disagreements within Marxism on Culture

Though most Marxists would subscribe to the above, there have been disagreements among them about how best to analyse culture. On the one hand is the thought of Althusser and his followers, and, on the other, are the ideas of a number of British Marxists such as historian, E. P. Thompson and cultural critic, Raymond Williams. It helps to put the debate in terms of the base-superstructural framework explained in Chapter 8. We can regard the superstructure as the area of cultural activity and, of course, the base is the economic relations and resultant class system. Althusser argues that *in the last instance* culture is determined by productive relations (the base). Ideas, education and even most art are controlled by the ruling class so as not to threaten its power. Culture is not, therefore, an area of free self-expression although a *limited* amount of freedom of thought may exist among a few intellectuals (even so, they are severely limited in what they can actually *do*). We saw that Bourdieu applied and developed Althusser's ideas to education. Thompson fully accepts that productive relations 'largely determine' class experience, but allows a much greater margin for variation in the ways in which different individuals and groups respond to their class-based and other experience. His major work, *The Making of the English Working Class*, is substantially about the rich complexity of working class life at work, in leisure and in trade unions and other organisations. For Thompson, 'in the last instance', people make history, not the other way round. He is clearly angered by Althusser's contempt for historical analysis. Althusser's perspective is apparently based on the view that Marx (as 'read' and interpreted by Althusser) has provided a model of sociological analysis which explains the functioning of society and which therefore renders the less theoretical recording and analysis of events by such as Thompson naive and unnecessary. 'Historicism' is the term with which Althusser dismisses Thompson's approach. Thompson and Williams find, however, that a knowledge of cultural detail can change theoretical constructs and believe that Marx himself took this view. Further, as Marxist humanists, they consider that the way men make history is worth understanding for its own sake. To acquire this understanding it is necessary to study culture. Because culture is essentially creative and unpredictable, Williams defines it broadly as 'a whole way of life'.

He refuses to see it as overwhelmingly the product of the base. To this author, it seems clear that whilst the base structures cultural experience including class cultural experience, it is possible for groups and individuals consciously to think beyond the immediate material context of their own existence. Imagining what a socialist society might be like is just such an example. There seems to be a balance that Althusser and Thompson might yet strike. It would be sad if, amid their thunder, they failed to hear a call to parley.

Cultural Communication and Symbols

Any adequate new theory of culture will have to accomodate the basic insights of symbolic interactionism even if it does so under some other theoretical label. Understanding symbols is the key to understanding culture. *Symbols are the means by which cultural communication is brought about.* They are message carriers: they *mean* something. Language is the most important cultural symbol: flags, traffic lights, radio time-pips and morse-code are other examples. What symbols mean or 'stand for' does not depend on the symbol itself, but is determined by human beings. Thus, various national flags symbolise particular nations only because it has been decided that they should. The same principle applies to language: different languages use different words to mean the same thing. To understand a language or any system of communication (such as algebra), it is necessary to understand the meaning of its symbols. To the extent that meaningful communication is part of social life, then, the study of it must be of concern to sociologists.

Within the major sociological perspectives, it is mainly symbolic interactionists who employ symbolic analysis as a cornerstone of their approach. They emphasis the role language plays as a medium of *shared meaning* and so as a means of inter-subjective communication (see Chapter 3). They have particularly analysed the process of verbal labelling, notably in deviancy theory, but they also stress the inventive potential of language. People create new words and linguistic structures with which to express and share experience. The nineteen sixties was a particularly creative period as far as 'American-English' was concerned. This is particularly true of the radical youth movement which produced a vocabulary of what David Lodge the novelist has called 'psycho-babble'. Words such as

533

'hassle', 'far-out', and 'hang-up' were generated to describe seemingly new attitudes and states of mind some of which had their origin in drug experience, but which were to acquire more generalised meaning.

It is not only symbolic interactionists who study symbols. *Semiotics* – the study of signs or symbols – is a budding discipline in its own right. Its founder was the French cultural critic, Roland Barthes. He believes that every human phenomenon has a symbolic meaning even if that meaning is hidden. Thus, the high chair can symbolise authority, the heavy arm round one's shoulders comfort, or, in other circumstances, patronising control. In Britain, the study of symbols has been effectively pursued within a class analysis of society by scholars from the Birmingham Centre for Cultural Studies (see Chapter 13).

It is obvious that to have a very limited vocabulary or to be unskilled in the use of the spoken or written work is to be at a severe disadvantage in communicating. Marxists do not agree about whether the working class is at a disadvantage in comparison with the middle class because of its relative lack of skill in formal linguistic expression. Bernstein's hypothesis of restricted and elaborated codes has come in for some fairly effective criticism. It can be safely said, perhaps, that in so far as working class children are not exposed to as wide a range of words and expressions as many middle class children, they are deprived in a purely technical sense. Education should remove this disadvantage by improving the quality and use of language. In doing so, it need not employ literature that seems exclusively to embody middle class values and describe a middle class way of life. Material closer to the experience of working class children would be more meaningful to them. The problem of cultural deprivation should not, however, be conceived of simply in class terms. It can partly be thought of as lack of the technical ability to use a given symbolic system. It is a common experience to be cut off from an area of knowledge, such as French culture, mathematics and geometry by lack of competence in its symbolic medium. It may be that in the cumputer age, those who do not, in some measure, master the languages of computers will feel this kind of deprivation sharply.

Cultural Transmission and Record

Cultural transmission is the passing on of values, attitudes and information from one individual to another, and within a culture over time. The latter is done mainly through the socialisation of one generation by another, but also by the creation of formal and informal cultural records. Raymond Williams puts the point well:

> The history of the idea of culture is a record of our reactions, in thought and feeling, to the changed conditions of our common life.

The 'record' that Williams refers to is partly contained in writing, music and painting, but also, and increasingly in modern society, on film and audio, video and computer tape. In pre-literate societies ballads, myths and stories play a larger part in cultural transmission than in modern ones. The accumulation of cultural information through the generations might seem to provide the basis of social progress. In so far as scientific and technical matters are concerned this may be so. Certainly, the growth and development of science and technology has largely been cumulative and gradual. Whether human culture has progressed morally and aesthetically (in its appreciation and understanding of beauty) is more open to doubt. Even science itself, 'the tool of progress', can be, and is, used for evil purposes. There is no certainty that man's wisdom and humanity have evolved to the same extent as his scientific knowledge and material achievements. In that sense, there is a question mark over the cultural record of our species.

Sub-cultures

The concept of sub-culture, already fully introduced, is only mentioned here by way of a reminder that it is applicable to contexts other than class. We have already used it in analysing generation, delinquency and ethnicity. Religion is another major basis of cultural experience. Although, in the West, we tend to think of religion in terms of minority sub-cultures, such as English Catholics or Jews, it can play a part in national or even transnational culture, as in medieval Christendom and the contemporary Muslim world.

Culture and Ideological Control: Religion and the Media

There is no more powerful weapon than influence over men's minds. To influence thought is the surest way of influencing behaviour. Such influence depends on access to the communications media. In the past, the church was the major public means of ideological communication. The local gentry also played an influential role in the community. Their message to the people was generally to conform and to obey.

The modern mass media has largely replaced the church as a form of cultural expression and communication. Sociologists, however, find it far less easy to generalise about the influence of the modern media than about that of the medieval church. Politicians, on the other hand, have been less uncertain. Hitler and, his henchman, Goebbels, were convinced that control of the mass media by the state would provide a major means of establishing their ideas and securing their rule. They secured similar control over the educational system. Other totalitarian rulers have equally taken it for granted that social control can be achieved partly through control of mass communications.

The issue of ideological control is the major theme in our discussion of religion and the media. It is not, however, the only aspect of these matters explored. People are certainly not passive receptacles of centrally produced and administered ideas. Many interpret religion and the products of the media in a lively and creative way and we will attempt to do justice to this in what follows.

Religion

a RELIGION AS IDEOLOGY The most frequently observed function of religion is that of *integration*. In their different ways, both Durkheim and Marx were agreed on this. We are familiar, by now, with Durkheim's belief in the need for moral consensus in society. In traditional societies, religion was the major means by which this was achieved. For Marx religion is 'mere' ideology. For centuries it had misled and 'mystified' ordinary people into conforming to social orders in which the majority were exploited by the few. Happiness eternal was the promised reward for accepting their lot in the here and now. The following few lines from a well-known popular hymn, illustrate the kind of religious sentiment scorned by Marx:

The rich man in his castle,
The poor man at his gate,
God made them high and lowly
And ordered their estate.

Marx himself referred to religion as 'the opiate of the masses' and latterday Marxists have pilloried it as 'pie in the sky when you die'. Neither description could possibly be taken as a compliment. It is worth including a quotation from Durkheim at this point, which shows just how close he is to Marx on this matter:

Religion instructed the humble to be content with their situation, and, at the same time it taught them that the social order is providential: that it is God himself who has determined each one's share. Religion gave man a perception of a world beyond this earth where everything would be rectified; this prospect made inequalities less noticeable, it stopped men from feeling aggrieved.

Whereas Marx saw this as repressive, Durkheim saw it as necessary.

Both Marx and Durkheim used 'primitive' religion to illustrate their analyses. Durkheim wrote a major work on the topic, *The Elementary Forms of Religious Life*. In particular, he examined the significance of religious symbolism. He regarded the totem pole as a focus of collective tribal unity. Religious worship and ritual provided occasion for the reaffirmation of community. We can see similar symbolism in some contemporary religion. Catholics sometimes refer to their church as 'the body of Christ on earth'. There could be no more powerful image of collective unity than that: Marx's examination of 'primitive' religion goes straight to the heart of what he regarded as its ideologically exploitative nature. Priests and witch-doctors conspired to relieve ordinary tribal members of their surplus wealth by claiming that they needed to be supported in order to practice magic and to communicate with the gods. Often contributions were such that they were able to do so in some style.

One of the most interesting and challenging applications of Marx's analysis of religion as ideology was to the role Protestantism has played in justifying capitalism. Marx argued that

537

merchants and industrialists of the sixteenth century and later, preferred the Protestant to the Catholic religion because the former satisfied their commercial requirements more than the latter. Whereas Catholicism forbade usury (lending money at exorbitant rates), it was acceptable under Protestantism. Whereas Catholic theologians regarded great interest in acquiring wealth as greedy, Protestants, and particularly Calvinists (members of a Protestant sect) looked upon material success as a sign of God's grace and favour. Protestant philosophy offered a further bonus to practical minded capitalists. Hard work and industry were at the core of Protestant moral practice and these virtues applied as much to the working class as to the bourgeoisie. Credit in the heavenly bank account rather than a hefty wage-packet was to be the reward of labour. This view had much to commend it to industrialists concerned with profit, accumulation and investment rather than the standard of living of the working class.

b RELIGIOUS IDEAS: CAUSE OR CONSEQUENCE OF SOCIAL CHANGE? In one of the most celebrated of historical-sociological encounters, Max Weber took issue with Marx on his analysis of religion as ideology. Superficially, the debate is about a question of empirical fact, but at a deeper level it concerns the cause and nature of historical change. The factual issue is itself profound enough: was Protestantism primarily the product of capitalism or did it, on the contrary, help to produce capitalism? Marx takes the former view, Weber the latter. Marx's position has, in effect, already been explained. He argued that, like other forms of religious ideology, Protestanism helped to justify certain social relations – in this case the exploitation of the proletariat by the bourgeoisie. For Weber, the matter was less simple. He argued that Calvinism, a particular form of Protestantism, had played a major role in creating a cultural climate in which the capitalistic spirit could thrive. It would be too crude to say that Weber thought that Calvinism 'caused' capitalism, but he did consider that there was a certain *correspondence* between Calvinist ideas and the qualities required to be a successful capitalist. Calvinism provided favourable conditions for the development of capitalism. For instance, Calvinism preached hard work and frugality, the Protestant ethic – very useful virtues to a businessman. Weber cited many examples of Calvinists who became businessmen, while, however, fully recognising that factors other than the spiritual content of Calvinism contributed to the rise of capitalism. An important one was the development of new machine technology which massively increased production potential. We are not here concerned with the detail and precise accuracy of Weber's argument (though, commendably, many historians have been) but with his general explanatory approach. At this point we must make explicit the wider issue of which the 'capitalism/Calvinism' argument is one example.

Weber's major point here is that ideas can change history, and in so doing, can contribute to changes in the material context of life. It will be remembered that the whole trend of Marx's analysis of religious ideas is in the opposite direction. He sees them primarily as justifying existing social and economic circumstances, and certainly not as providing a major source of historical change. On the contrary, religion was an ideological pall intended to obscure new and different ideas. But Marx did recognise that new ideas *could* be developed. Man's consciousness is able to react thoughtfully and creatively to experience, particularly everyday work experience. Socialism itself had to be 'thought of' before it could become a reality. However, for Marx, ideas are formed within, and structured by, socio-economic material reality. Socialism only becomes possible or practically 'thinkable' when society is economically and socially developed to the point where socialist ideas are seen to be realistic.

C THE 'DECLINE' OF RELIGION IN MODERN SOCIETIES (SECULARISATION)
Following David Martin, we can distinguish two complementary aspects to *secularisation*. Firstly, it refers to the decline in voluntary involvement in formal religious activities such as church attendance or regular worship at home, and to any decline in the power, wealth and influence of the church as an institution. Over the centuries this decline of the church's wider influence has been apparent in, for instance, politics, the arts, medicine and social welfare. Secondly, secularisation applies to thought and attitudes and we examine this matter in the next section.

S. S. Acquaviva has charted the decline of Christianity in a wide range of countries, and the corresponding emergence of a more secular way of life. This has been nowhere more marked than in Britain now, reputedly, 'the most secular nation in

Europe'. The decline in formal religion has been comprehensive This has been especially true of the Church of England. The number participating in the rites of passage – baptism, confirmation and church marriage – has declined, as has that of Easter communicants. In 1950, two thirds of the children born alive in England were baptised in the Church of England; in 1973 the figure was well under half. In 1953, some 6.5% of the population took Easter communion in the Church of England. In 1973, fewer than 4% did so. In 1976, only 120,000 marriages were solemnised in the Church of England, compared with 194,000 in registry offices. The Church of Scotland and the Roman Catholic Church were both growing in membership in the nineteen fifties, but have both gone into decline since. The same story is true, to varying extents, of Methodists, Baptists, Congregationalists and Presbyterians.

The decline in institutional prestige of the church is well illustrated by Bryan Wilson in his article 'How Religious are we?' Half humorously, he remarks that religion 'is no longer news, except when a clergyman commits a moral misdemeanour'. He sees the role of religion in school and at the workplace as now almost negligible. Religious instruction in schools has often become a travesty: many teachers using the periods for current affairs. He suggests that the workplace is perhaps the environment 'most alien' to religious values. Mechanical principles of organisation, whether in factory or office, seem almost the antithesis of religious myth and values. The remoteness of contemporary religion from political life is worth more space than Wilson gives it. In the reign of Henry II, the major political opponent of the King was the Archbishop of Canterbury. Recently, we have seen the occasion when the Prime Minister was too busy to see the Archbishop.

The irrelevance of religion to practical and political affairs is, however, only generally true of the *internal* life of advanced, historically Christian nations. Religious issues often remain of major importance elsewhere and particularly in the relations between traditional, but modernising Muslim states, and advanced, western countries. The religious element in the conflict in Northern Ireland, with its various international ramifications, reminds us that religion can still fuel the fires of political and social conflict and that secularisation is by no means a universally accomplished fact.

Still, the process of secularisation has been steadily progressive in what was once Christendom. We must now explain why Weber's thoughts on the matter are an informative starting point. For him, secularisation was an aspect of the wider process of *rationalisation*. He considered that the underying principle behind modernisation is rational, scientific thought. Applied to technology and to organisation, rational thought has restructured the social world. Equally to the point, applied to man's understanding of himself and his place in the universe, rational thought has undermined religion and replaced it with various secular and, largely, materialistic explanations of his existence and relationship to nature. Darwin, Freud and Marx were major contributors to the replacement of religious explanations of human behaviour by scientific ones. Loss of intellectual authority and status helped to erode the moral authority of the church. Further, the urban, industrial proletariat was physically as well as spiritually more cut off from the church than the rural peasantry had been: the mill-tower rose larger than the church steeple. Although there were religious responses to the new industrial age, such as Methodism, the long term movement was away from religion. Partly in material consumption men found other sources of comfort and consolation, as well as other explanations of the meaning or lack of meaning of life.

d DESACRALISATION, 'DISENCHANTMENT' AND SPIRITUAL SURVIVAL
Desacralisation is the loss of the capacity to experience a sense of sacredness and mystery in life. In its way, it is quite as important as the more practical process of secularisation to which it is related.

The medieval world in which God was Creator, 'His' mother a virgin, and in which spirits, good or evil, were believed to intervene in everyday life must have been perceived in a qualitatively different way from that in which secular man sees the world today. Belief in mystery and miracle has largely gone, apart from the imaginings of children. 'Disenchantment', to use Weber's term for this, has set in. The triumph of science and reason has been at the cost of myth, fable and spiritual romanticism.

Yet there is ample evidence in the modern world that man's spirit or emotions, if that term is preferred, continue to demand a kind of satisfaction that neither science nor material prosper-

541

ity can bring. This can be illustrated by the undoubted fact that religion as a *source of personal meaning and fulfilment* survives much more widely and with greater vitality than institutional religion. Interestingly, Thomas Luckman considers that the primary function of religion is to give personal meaning to life. Although few in Britain go regularly to church, the vast majority believe in 'something', even if no more than a vague force behind the universe. What is more, according to David Hay, 'well over a third of all women and just under a third of all men in Great Britain claim to have had some sort of religious experience'. To use Hay's own terms, almost half of these 'wouldn't touch the church with a bargepole'. It is worth giving a brief extract from one of the examples of 'mystical' experience cited by Hay:

> Then it happened. 'I lost all sense of time, of my own body and 'ego'; it was as if I became one with the natural world . . . for an unthought passage of time I was filled with the certainty and knowledge of the meaning of life'. Previously he'd been cynical about religion . . .

It is surely beyond the scope and means of sociology, however defined, to understand and explain such experiences, but it is essential to acknowledge them as profoundly meaningful in human terms. There is a vast amount of creative art attesting to this, including the writings of poet-mystics, such as Blake and Coleridge, and some of the music of such groups as The Grateful Dead. Controversially, some of this work has been influenced by drugs. Psychedelic drugs are sometimes considered to be a short-cut to mystical experience, but others take the view that the dangerous and usually uncontrolled nature of the experience they induce amounts, at best, to 'counterfeit infinity'.

The yearning for spiritual and emotional fulfilment beyond everyday reality is further evident in the popularity of religious sects, particularly apparent since the nineteen sixties. These have included such movements as the Jesus People, the Divine Light Mission, the Moonies and the Scientologists. Some sects have contained elements of the crackpot and the exploitative, if not the downright sinister. Nevertheless, their considerable appeal, especially to the young, indicates that they do answer a real need – however, inadequately. One organisation, the Transcendental Meditation (TM) movement, has helped to spread the practice of meditation to many individuals and groups throughout the world. TM and other quasi-religious movements have been notably popular in the United States. It is worth remarking that religion has, in any case, declined less in the United States than in most European countries. This may be because religion there has never been as formal and institutionalised as in, for intance, Britain; nor has it been as closely identified with an upper class establishment. It has been rather more a matter of personal experience and expression.

Even those countries which have adopted communist or Fascist ideologies have not entirely escaped from the shadow of religion. For instance, the virtual deification of the Chinese leader, Mao, in his own life-time was a semi-religious phenomenon. Perhaps, the same can be said of the worldwide adulation among radicals of the 'martyred' Cuban revolutionary, Che Guevara – adulation that was sometimes given on the scantiest of knowledge of his achievements and beliefs. It may be that both Mao and Che provided a focus of identity and unity that many need. If so, their role in this respect is very similar to what Durkheim described as the social function of religion.

The Structure of the Media

Before presenting the sociology of the media, it is helpful to know what it is and how it is controlled. *The media consists of printed, audio and audio-visual systems of communication.* Major examples of each are, respectively: books, newspapers and magazines; records, radios and audio-tapes; the cinema, television, and video. The broadcasting media, particularly television, has replaced the press as the major media.

The media can be roughly divided into non-commercial and commercial. The non-commercial media is almost entirely publicly operated. The commercial broadcasting media and, to some extent, the press are also subject to public regulation. There is debate about the degree of public involvement that there should be in the media. Peter Golding divides publicly regulated media into three types. Firstly, is the goverment controlled media, whose explicit function is to convey government information (propaganda). This form of media organisation is associated with modern totalitarian states, but often occurs in

543

poorer countries in which the government is the only body capable of finding and organising a national press or broadcasting service. The second type of public mass media organisation is the semi-official statutory (established by Parliament) body. The BBC is a non-profit-making corporation which comprises a Chairman, Vice-Chairman and Governors. The Corporation is not directly responsible to a minister, but its members are, in effect, appointed by the government. The closeness or otherwise of the BBC to the government has always been a matter for dispute. The third sort of public regulating agency is concerned with allocating contracts for programmes and, unlike the BBC, only minimally with making them. The major body of this kind is the Independent Broadcasting Authority which oversees both commercial television and radio. The commercial press includes the 'quality' newspapers – the *Guardian, Times* and *Telegraph,* the 'middle-brow' *Daily Mail,* and the 'mass' circulation, *Express, Star, Sun* and *Mirror.* To these must be added many scores of magazines and journals.

Who, then, controls the mass media? For the moment, we will say no more about the BBC than that, under the Board of Governors, it is run by salaried professionals. The commercial media presents a quite different picture. The press is, in effect, run by those who can afford to buy and keep going a newspaper or magazine. 'Afford to' is an operative phrase as newspapers are often money-losers rather than money-makers. They are often *status* rather than economic investments, as the *Times* and *Sunday Times* were to Lord Thompson. The situation in respect of the commercial broadcasting media is slightly more complex. Groups or consortiums of people put in offers or *tenders* to run a local station as it becomes available, and the IBA decides who is sucessful.

Three points can be made about the commercial media. First, it *is* commercial. This means it is run for profit, even though an element of public service may also be involved. Later, we ask what effect commercial motivation has on the content of broadcasting. Secondly, is the extent to which the media in Britain is *concentrated* in a few companies. The following table, from Peter Golding, shows this very clearly. Thirdly, is the process of diversification which is characteristic of media-oriented companies. This means that they often have many other investment interests besides those in the media or are themselves part of larger companies. Thus, the International Publishing Corporation (IPC) which owns the *Daily Mirror*, *Sunday Mirror* and *Sunday People* is part of a larger company, Reed International which has interest in wallpaper, paints, DIY products, fabrics and building products, as well as publishing.

Proportion of total market accounted for by the five leading companies in each medium, 1972

	%
National morning newspaper circulations	86
National Sunday newspaper circulations	88
Commercial television: % television homes served	73
Paperback books: % domestic production (estimate, 1971)	86
Mid-price LP records: % market	69
Cinema: % box office takings (top four circuits)	80

Source: Peter Golding, *The Mass Media*, 1974, p. 49.

Theories of Media: Control and Effects

In order to understand a topic it is often helpful to give an historical summary of research in the area. The history of research on a given area can amount to a précis of the consensus of knowledge about one topic. Because of the perspectives division this is sometimes less true of sociology than of the natural sciences. In the case of media-research, however, it is hardly true at all. Past and current research trends frequently have little connection with each other. This is largely because media research in the first twenty post-war years tended to ask questions that were too limited in scope. Further, the answers to many of the questions that were asked often depended on the answer to other questions that were not asked! Thus research into media effects on audiences was sometimes conducted with little regard for those that the programme makers intended to produce. In addition, the part played by the owners of the commercial media in attempting to influence audiences was seldom considered. As a result of this piecemeal approach, much of the best media research in the last ten years has been concerned to find a new, more comprehensive framework for analysis. This has meant building better models and constructing more far-reaching hypotheses about how the media operates in a wider social context.

a LIBERAL OR LAISSEZ–FAIRE PERSPECTIVE The view that, within

545

generous legal limits, the media in capitalist democracies is free is widely held. Certainly, those commentators, such as Robert Dahl and Jean Blondel, who believe that liberal democracy 'works', consider that the media does provide access to a wide range of opinion. Perhaps because this is the dominant view in Western societies it tends to be assumed rather than proved. It is part of 'taken for granted' ideology. It has, however, been strongly criticised from Marxist perspectives. We will set aside these criticisms until later, and present only the liberal case here.

What, then, is the basis of the view that the media is 'free'? First, is the argument that freedom to set up newspapers, magazines and other publications ensures that a wide range of opinion will, in fact, be represented, even though not everybody can *afford* to establish a publication. Secondly, the principle that editors and, under them, journalists, rather than proprietors, decide the content of a newspaper is considered to be generally effective. Thirdly, the public has access to print through letters and, occasionally, through more substantial pieces. Fourthly, the broadcasting media ensures a wide and balanced expression of opinion by providing access to or, at least, fairly representing the opinions of, all major groups, including significant minorities. It will be remembered that freedom for minorities – as long as they stay within the law – is equally a principle of political liberalism. Groups that are so far beyond the social consensus that they wish to overthrow the existing order of society are less likely to have access to the media or to obtain favourable media coverage than other groups. 'Freedom within consensus' is perhaps a fair summary of the liberal view of the media. Fifthly, is the argument that the public can control the media by using its market power; it can refuse to buy or switch off and thus force the particular media enterprise to change or go out of business.

Journalists often hold a liberal or *laissez-faire* view of their own activities. In stereotype, they are tough, independent-minded people determined to 'get the facts'. The media audience appears in the liberal picture via free-market economics. Audience response is considered to have a major effect on whether a programme continues or not, and on the content of future programmes. The belief that the media is responsive to public opinion is crucial to the liberal view of the way it operates.

b MARXIST PERSPECTIVE *The strength of Marxist analysis of the media is that it puts the media in socio-economic context.* Its weakness derives from the fact that this context is so huge that it becomes difficult to prove conclusively any significant proposition made.

Marxists generally consider that the media operates in a way that helps to maintain the capitalist system. Althusser's notion of the ideological state apparatus which includes the media is not, perhaps, the best way of conceptualising the issue. After all, the state has relatively little directly to do with the running of the commercial media. The BBC would claim virtual autonomy from the government in most matters, although in France, Althusser's own country, the relationship between government and the media is closer. Herbert Marcuse, the American based Marxist cultural critic, provides a different, and perhaps more subtle, framework of analysis of the relationship between the media and the socio-economic system. He considers that the media diverts the masses away from an awareness of their *true* exploitation, just as religion did in the past. In this view, the source of this exploitation is the inequality of the work situation. Trivial but amusing entertainment, the prospect of consumer satisfaction that advertisements forever promise, dull the edge of any doubt about the social order. As Marcuse sees it, the message of the media is that all can hope to achieve material success and should strive to do so. He considers this message to be *illusory*, a form of ideological mystification. For him, cultural exploitation of this kind is as much part of the capitalist system as economic exploitation and social inequality.

Writing in similar vein Pierre Bourdieu criticises the liberal view that freedom of choice exists in media consumption. He says, in essence, that choice comes only with understanding. The majority cannot *really* choose to listen to, say, difficult programmes on philosophy or sociology, because they lack the linguistic means (or *interpretive codes* as Bourdieu calls them) to understand them. Only a minority are educated to be able to interpret this kind of material and, as long as this is so, the majority will not have access to it. Frank Parkin comments similarly on differential aesthetic or artistic appreciation. Manual labourers whose experience is of practical situations and who have little formal education may well be intellectually cut off from much worthwhile cultural achievement. It is simply not part of their

547

experience or world view. But this should not produce contempt for working class culture. In fact, some of the most appreciative and affectionate descriptions of working class culture have come from socialists such as Richard Hoggart, Raymond Williams, (both of working class origins), and the historian, E. P. Thompson. These pen-portraits are often tinged with nostalgia, because the culture is dying along with communities that produced it. Population dispersal and the emergence of the mass media are major causes of this decline (see Chapter 9, pp. 247–52). Later we briefly look at what Marxists think might replace both working class culture and the largely commercially inspired culture of the mass media. Although Marxists, in principle, therefore, prefer non-commercial media, they are critical of how it actually works in Britain. BBC1, they say, has to compete effectively with ITV, and consequently produces a similar range of programmes. If BBC 2 is able to be more adventurous, it is before smaller and usually more privileged audiences. As well as having to live with market forces, the non-commercial media sometimes has to respond to government pressures as well. Even in Britain overt political involvement sometimes occurs. This happened in the case of the programme 'Yesterday's Men' which was radically critical of a number of politicians. Reflecting on the experience, its producer said:

> I would never try to do it again . . . Better to be safe than imaginative.

Still, it is the economic system rather than the intervention of politicians that influences the content of the media. In a comment on 'Yesterday's Men', Philip Abrams puts the point well:

> Actually 'Yesterday's Men' was something of an exception in that it evoked control through political power. The more normal constraint is economic. As Eliot concludes, the typical situation, in Britain anyway, is not that variation occurs within a context of political toleration but rather that such variation as there is 'takes place against a ground base provided by the commercial logic necessary for the economic survival of (the) organizations of cultural production'. It is after all a market society.

Two largely empirical studies, *Bad News* and *More Bad News*, must be added to the more theoretical Marxists' works referred to above, although it cannot be assumed that all those involved in the research are Marxists. Their evidence is that the media

548

is far from unbiased and objective in its presentation of news. In particular, they found that the language used by newscasters and reporters in describing situations of industrial conflict reflected favourably on employers rather than employees. Thus initiatives of the former tended to be termed 'offers' or 'pleas', whereas those of the workers were described as 'threats' or 'demands'. A substantial body of quantified evidence of this kind suggested not conscious conspiracy, but systematic bias reflecting pre-existing attitudes.

c INTERACTIONIST PERSPECTIVE Compared with the broad views of the liberal and Marxist perspectives, interactionist analysis is less complete but more detailed. It attempts to tell us rather less about the role of media in the total social context but more of the day-to-day processes involved in the production of media material and of the variety and complexity of response to it. Three major strands of recent interactionist work in the area have been chosen for presentation. These are *the consensus-producing role of the media; the production of media material, by particularly, 'news people', and audience response.*

Interactionists have frequently illustrated the consensus-maintenance role of the media by reference to its treatment of deviance. We analysed this approach in some detail in Chapter 15. Content analysis of popular newspapers such as the *Sun* and the *News of the World* does show an extraordinarily high average of deviancy stories. These are reported against a background assumption that the majority are normal and moral, thus making the supposed abnormality of the stories' characters appear sensational and worthy of condemnation. Stanley Cohen gives a very useful ideal type model of how the process of deviancy selection, condemnation, and consensus-affirmation can occur. He titles the model, the 'signification spiral' (that is, the labelling of deviance) and it is only slightly adapted here.

The Signification Spiral

1 Identification of specific issue: eg, student political 'extremism'.

2 Identification of culprits: eg, 'subversive minority', 'lunatic fringe'.

3 Convergence: Linking of issue to other problems eg, lack of discipline and control of the young.

4 Notion of thresholds – once they are crossed, further escalation must result – 'slippery slope to anarchy'.

5 Explaining, warning and prophesying – 'Look what happened elsewhere'.

6 Call for firm steps – clamp down hard leads to the effect of reinforcing consensus.

Interactionists also link the production of media material with consensus reinforcement. They certainly see the restrictions on the freedom of journalists, broadcasters and others creatively involved in the media as much more considerable than do the more simplistic versions of the liberal model. Some of these are of a practical, organisational nature. When deadlines have to be met, it can be easier to go to an 'official' or 'accredited' spokesman, or 'expert' on a topic, rather than others who may be equally involved. The Glasgow Media Group established in their book, *'Bad News'*, that during a strike of Glasgow garbage collectors it was Council representatives rather than the strikers who appeared in the media, though political bias as well as organisational convenience must be considered as a factor in explaining this. At the most mundane level, a politician who has the sense to give a speech in time for the main editions will be likely to get more coverage than one who does not – even though his speech may not be 'worth' more reportage space.

We now discuss the third point, audience response to the media. From what has already been said, it will be clear that many interactionists share with Marxists the view that the media tends to produce consensus and conformity. But they also observe that a genuine *interaction* between individuals and the media can, and often does, take place. We examined this in the context of youth culture, when we saw that members of youth groups sometimes borrow and adapt styles of dress and behaviour that they see on the media. Equally, the reverse sometimes happens. The folk and rock musical revival of the nineteen sixties began at the grass roots before it happened on the media. It should be noticed that these points are further examined in the next section which reviews a wide, but not easily categorised, range of media research.

Functionalists

d SOME EMPIRICAL WORK ON MEDIA EFFECTS Much quantitative
work on media effects is fragmentary, lacking in adequate
theoretical conceptualisation, and contradicting other similar
research. The following is a brief attempt to summarise the
more interesting issues raised by this body of empirical work
and its more coherent findings.

A repeated finding is that the media *reinforces* already existing
attitudes and patterns of behaviour rather than causes entirely
new ones to be formed. Work by Klapper and by Winnick
established that audiences tend to *select* programmes or parts of
programmes that confirm their established preferences. Thus
Winnick showed a film about drugs, 'The Man with the Gol-
den Arm', to a group divided between those who favoured
drug-taking and those who did not. Both groups tended to find
that the film confirmed their existing views. A further aspect in
selection is the role of *reference group*. Few programmes attract a
blanket audience. Age, sex and class are factors that affect
selection. The media rarely seems to uproot the effects of primary socialisation by family and peer group but is itself 'mediated' by these agencies and the social context of which they are
a part.

Work by Dr William Belson, by H. J. Eysenck and D. K.
Nias largely contradicts the above findings on the specific question of the effect of violence on the media (Eysenck and Nias
also examine the effect of sex on the media). Belson compared
the behaviour and viewing habits of 1565 London boys aged
between 13 and 16, between 1959 and 1971. Markedly less violence was admitted by those who watched less television. Of
those who had watched a lot of violence on television, 7.5%
confessed to having engaged in serious violence themselves. Belson's findings clearly need to be taken seriously, but they are
certainly open to criticism. It cannot be proved that watching
more violence on television was the factor that 'caused' more
violence. Other variables may have been operative. Watching a
lot of television is itself associated with lower socio-economic
status. Perhaps it is some other factor or factors associated with
lower class culture that produces violent behaviour. It is almost
impossible to separate the effect of television from other variables affecting behaviour.

Eysenck and Nias, in their own laboratory research into violence
and the media, attempt to isolate the effect of violent films on

551

behaviour from that of other factors. Groups – both adult and children – exposed to televised violence consistently behave more aggressively than control groups. If – and they do not show this – these effects were duplicated in real life then they would have proved their case. But before rushing to conclusions, it is prudent to mention some critical comments on Eysenck and Nias' work. As Anthony Smith points out, comparative cultural data complicates the apparently simple truth of their findings. Japan, for example, has a very substantial degree of violence in its television, but a very low level of social violence. It seems that the Japanese emphasise the suffering caused by violence, rather than the aggression that caused it. This observation leads Smith on to a wider point. He suggests, in effect, that society gets the media it deserves. A violent society will tend to produce violence on the media – no doubt many will even *want* violence on the media. Though Smith does not say this, he seems to imply that what first needs reducing is real violence, then, perhaps, people will want less violent make-believe. This is not at all the conclusion of Eysenck and Nias, who ask for a degree of censorship of media violence and pornography. In so doing, they have the support of the National Viewers' and Listeners' Association, the 'brainchild' of Mrs Mary Whitehouse. Liberals and radicals alike tend to resist this. If entertainment, even art, can be censored today, perhaps news will be tomorrow. The issue is important enough in itself but, for our more immediate academic purposes, it is worth noting how social scientific research can easily become a part of political and social policy debate. So much for the ivory tower!

e MEDIA: CONTROL AND EFFECTS: SUMMARY There is agreement among liberals, Marxists and interactionists that the media must be seen in the context of the rest of society. To varying degrees it is also accepted that the media tends to reflect and uphold the *status quo*. Marxists see the *status quo* as an exploitative capitalist one, whereas liberals consider that both majority consensus opinion, and a considerable range of minority opinion is expressed on the media. The range of views expressed helps to form and change opinion. Marxists see commercial control of much of the media as an illustration of ruling class power, whereas liberals regard it as essential to the preservation of a free media. Interactionists also stress that the media tends to reinforce consensus, but are less specific about which group or groups consensus benefits. Much interactionist and straight empirical work illustrates the active role of audiences in selecting from the media. Selection seems to reinforce existing attitudes and preferences which further suggests that the key to understanding media lies in analysing its relationship to the social system as a whole.

Culture: Society and the Individual

The purpose of this section is to engage in a little, tentative 'futurology'. We try to imagine what sort of society Britain might become, seen first through liberal, and then through Marxist eyes.

The view that many liberals share of the future can be easily grasped and fairly stated. After all, Britain and the United States are liberal societies now. The future is conceived in terms of continuity and evolution, not radical change. Writing of liberal societies in general, Edward Shils argues that the life of the mass of the people has already improved compared to the past. He has no time for historical sentimentality:

> The proletariat of these past societies, except for a few skilled occupations with elaborate traditions of their own, were a poor, besotted lot; the peasantry were clods, sometimes woodenly pious, sometimes simply woodenly dull.

Things have got better, but Shils is moderate in his claims:

> A significant proportion of the population in every society lives in a fairly vegetative routine, withdrawn and unresponsive except for occasional patches of harsh aggressive expansiveness. In the mass society of the present century, the proportion seems smaller, the period of sensitivity in the individual's course of life longer.

Other liberals are more positive than Shils. The welfare state has improved the material side of life, provided free education, and raised the general level of culture. Equality is regarded as neither practical nor desirable but these improvements can be built upon providing that the economy produces the wealth to pay for them. Further progress must occur only within a framework of authority and order. Change must not be allowed to jeopardise civil and political liberties as it did in inter-war Germany. The spectre of totalitarianism has tempered liberal reforming idealism to the point where liberal ideology has become tinged with conservatism.

In contrast to the qualified and cautious idealism of liberalism, Marxism is unashamedly an ideology of liberation. Communist society requires a 'new man'. We have already met, in the work of Abraham Maslow, the idea that it is only when man's basic material and psychological needs are assured that self-actualisation can occur. The social dimension of this is that a society which provides this funadmental security for all will have a framework for cultural advance. Marxism goes further. It *insists* that capitalism cannot provide a framework for the full expression and development of human potential because it treats human beings; as commodities (in the 'free' market) and alienates them from the product of their work (through wage-labour). Only when collective ownership of the means of production is established and when the product of labour is shared more fairly will men identify with work and gain the confidence and self-respect to develop their potential. Until greater equality and fairness exist, conflict, not community, will characterise our culture. But if collectivisation simply means that the state takes over the operation of industry from capitalism, then little will change in the day-to-day life of ordinary people. In comparison with liberal capitalist societies, they may gain a little materially and lose some freedoms. Socialism without democracy is simply another form of tyranny. So what is the necessary democratic element needed in order for a democratic socialist society and culture to flourish? Democracy involves the individual having the power to participate meaningfully in the decisions and processes that affect his or her life, whether at work, in the family, at school, in respect of the media, and otherwise. That might seem to some to be almost too much democracy . . . But let us hold criticism of this view for a moment and explore it further. To those Marxists, socialists and others who favour a more participatory society, the alternative seems to be more alienation. To have no more power at work than to be hired or fired, for a woman always to have to see 'her man as boss', for pupils always 'to have to be told what to do', for the so-called 'masses' to sit passively 'watching the box' – rarely even stirring to change channels – is repressive. These situations prevent the

554

development of intelligence and personality. Only through participation can these qualities develop more fully. Participation is, then, a learning process but it must be based on a reality (people learn better in 'real' situations), a reality in which power is *genuinely* shared. Men and women must have more involvement in work than that of expendable wage-labourers (here today, gone tomorrow, but the computer goes on the same). Women must no longer be dominated by men. That requires economic equality between the sexes. For children, it is slightly different. They are not fully mature and need adult protection and guidance. But within a secure framework they can learn better by *doing* than by being told what to do. Further the media should be more accessible to the people and localities it is supposed to serve.

It is, of course, easy to outline blueprints. To make the, perhaps unavoidably, large-scale institutions of advanced society more democratic requires great imagination and effort. It requires the imagination to envisage how it can be done, and the effort to do it. Some Marxists, probably a small minority, say it requires violent revolution. The vast majority of Marxists and many other socialists and radicals disagree and settle for change by means of 'the long, slow march through the institutions'. The best way to change people's minds is not, after all, to chop off their heads! Open-minded debate and persuasion is the alternative course. The fact that the organs of opinion are generally on the side of the *status quo* makes the task difficult but, perhaps, not impossible. Further, the nature and outcome of ideological clash is greatly influenced by the economic and social context in which it takes place and to which it must be addressed.

It is not a purpose of this book fully to explain Marxist policy except in so far as Marxism, as well as being a sociological perspective, is also a political belief. Marxism remains the major ideological carrier of ideas about a possible alternative or 'new' culture and society. We have touched on this already in many contexts including the family, work, and stratification. Here we provide a final illustration of the link between Marxist sociology and politics by reference to the work on broadcasting of Raymond Williams. He starts from the belief:

> that men should grow in capacity and power to direct their own lives – by creating democratic institutions, by bringing new

555

sources of energy to human work, and by extending the expression and exchange of experience on which understanding depends.

These values guide his suggestions for change. He argues that the commercial media and, in his view, the too centralised and paternalistic BBC, should be dismantled. Instead, four or five independent, publicly funded, regionally dispersed corporations should be set up. *Publicly representative* intermediate bodies with powers to grant money to make programmes should be established. Groups and individuals who want to produce programmes should within the limits of scarcity, be given the means to do so. Williams is aware that allocation of resources must not be used as a form of control:

> it is of the nature of democratic culture that it keeps the
> channels of growth clear. It is a public duty to see that
> individuals or groups offering new kinds of work are given at
> least a fair chance.

In any case, he says, there should be no ban on people raising their own resources to make programmes. Now, these suggestions, even in the much fuller form they are given in Williams' book *Communications*, do not amount to a complete blueprint for a democratic socialist media. But they perhaps show that such a thing is possible.

Guide to further reading and study

After a brief general introduction, the study of culture is probably best approached through specific issues. John Berger's *Ways of Seeing* (Penguin, 1973), could, perhaps, provide the basis of a 'different' start. It challenges taken-for-granted notions of culture and perception. A wide selection of readings on religion and belief is provided in Kenneth Thompson and Jeremy Tunstall, *eds., Sociological Perspective, (Penguin, 1976)*. Another useful collection is R. Robertson, *ed., The Sociology of Religion,* (Penguin, 1969). New material, including textbooks, on the media seem to come out by the month. For a basic introduction at the right level, Peter Golding's *The Mass Media,* (Longman, 1974), remains hard to equal. Len Masterman's *Teaching About Television*, (Macmillan, 1980), is aimed mainly at teachers of under sixteen year olds, but the introduction provides a useful discussion of the 'ideological' content of television, and how to present this in the classroom. Neither the established 'What are the effects of?' media sociology, nor the new trend of analysis concerned with power and control, are easily translated into 'A' level terms. Of the former, H. J. Eysenck and D. K. B. Nias' *Sex, Violence and the Media* (M. T. Smith, 1978) is a comprehensive summary of existing material and of the latter, James Curran *et al.*, eds., *Mass Communications and Society*, (Arnold, 1977), is a useful reader. Finally, the last chapter of Raymond Williams' *Culture and Society* (Penguin, 1961), is still worth anybody's attention as a review of cultural issues.

Past Questions

1 Rituals, ceremonies and other public displays are devices by which the fabric of social life is established and maintained.
How far can the persistance of society be explained in terms of such 'devices'? (JMB, 1977).
2 Discuss the relationship between ownership, control and production in the mass media (AEB, 1977).
3 What do sociologists mean by 'secularisation'? Examine the extent of the process of secularisation in any one society. (AEB, 1977).
4 Give a critical analysis of *either*: (a) the usefulness of labelling theory in the sociology of deviance, or (b) the role of the mass media in the amplication of deviance. (AEB, 1980).

Section F
20 Sociology and Knowledge (Theory 7)

Is Sociology a Science?

We have already examined this question in the first two chapters of this book, and before adding further comment we will summarise what was said there. If science is defined broadly as the accumulation of verifiable knowledge, then sociology is a science. If it is defined narrowly as the testing of hypotheses by positivistic methodology, then sociology can hardly claim to be a science. (See Chapter 1, pp. 24-31). Such a definition would also exclude much observational work in other disciplines. It is true, however, that sociology rarely produces results that are as precise and repeatable as those produced by the natural sciences. Nevertheless, Durkheim, Marx and Weber never stopped trying to be as scientific as possible and their work laid a rich theoretical and methodological basis for the further development of the discipline along scientific lines. More recently, the complex and rigorous empirical research of professional sociologists, such as John Goldthorpe and A. H. Halsey, goes far beyond the competence and commonsense understanding of the layman in its methodological basis and findings.

In contrast to self-consciously scientific approaches to sociology, interpretive sociology is often less concerned with causal explanation or factual description than with human understanding. Perhaps such work is closer to the humanities than to sciences. This does not make it *un*scientific but, perhaps, it is essentially *non-scientific*. *Unlike functionalists and many Marxists, interpretive sociologists have often shown no great desire to have their work classified as scientific.* C. Wright Mills, a sociologist who does not admit to a simple label himself, refers disparagingly to the 'cook-book' appearance of some scientifically oriented sociological text-books. Erving Goffman compares traditional positivist methodology to the instructions on a child's chemistry set: 'follow the rules and you, too, can be a real scientist'.

Interpretive sociologists willingly embrace what embarrasses the positivists: the subjective element in society and in sociological research. Subjectivity cuts two ways. Firstly, the researchers have their values: secondly, those being studied behave individually and therefore in a way that cannot be precisely predicted. Ethnomethodologists, such as Cicourel and Garfinkel, claim that it is impossible for sociologists to be passive observers of 'truth'. What they 'see' is bound, in some sense, to be the result of the interaction between themselves and what they study. Yet ethnomethodologists *also* claim to be in the business of discovering and describing how people act and interact. Given their emphasis upon the subjective element in perception, how can they be confident of the accuracy of their own observations and reports? The answer seems to be that they, at least, are aware of the problem and so better able to deal with it than positivists, who may naïvely believe that they can 'phase themselves out' of their work. On the matter of the individuality of the subject of social research, Schutz, the phenomenologist, is relevant, and goes further than the eth-nomethodologists. He points out that, whereas the natural sciences have concepts about objects, the social sciences have concepts about objects which have concepts about objects (including, perhaps, the researcher himself). In other words, people can think and, we must add, choose. They may even decide deliberately to mislead the researcher. Because of this, the level of accurate prediction in the social sciences can never be as high as in the natural sciences. Schutz, however, also points out that groups of people share common patterns of thought and behaviour, and that the researcher is able to check his descriptions of these with those of other observers. If there is agreement about what is observed, this, perhaps, is as close to achieving objectivity as is possible.

So much for what sociologists themselves think about the nature of their discipline. We now examine the opinions of two major philosophers of science upon the same issue (a philosopher of science is somebody who systematically attempts to clarify the principles underlying science). On the whole, these commentators from outside sociology have tended to take a reproving tone. Karl Popper's particular 'bogey man' is Marx. It is, however, Marx 'the prophet of revolution' that Popper admonishes – not Marx the sociologist – although, in fairness, Popper's argument is that the two are inseparable. He says that in 'prophesying' proletarian revolution, Marx is essentially unscientific in taking as given something that has not yet happened. In Popper's view, 'prophecy', religion and ideology have no place in science and, therefore, he declares Marxism to be unscientific. We do not have to accept Popper's conclusion to agree that Marxists' sociological theory and concepts must be open to the same criticism and testing as those of other perspectives. The fact that a Marxist sociologist is likely to be politically Marxist does not free him from the constraints of the discipline. No sensible Marxist sociologist would want the kind of illusory freedom in which mere assertion replaces argument based on reason and evidence. It is Popper's soundest and central point that social science, like natural science, must constantly test and re-test its theories. The most rigorous way to do this is for the researcher to attempt to *falsify*, rather than verify, his or her own hypothesis – Popper's famous principle of falsification. He argues that Marxism cannot be scientific because many of its major theories refer to the future and are not, therefore, open to falsification. It is impossible to prove definitely that there will not be a proletarian revolution because the future is unknown. Such a statement is, therefore, unscientific. In their own defence, many modern Marxists would argue that their immediate concern is less with proving or falsifying propositions than with providing a theoretical critique of capitalist society and with developing theoretical alternatives to it. Most of them would also dissociate themselves from the supposed prophetic element in Marx's writing and, to that extent, Popper's criticisms become redundant.

A further point made by Popper is of particular interest to sociologists. It is that no hypothesis can be considered finally proven. For example, although thousands of white swans have been sighted, there remains the possibility of coming across a black one. Similarly, to do the same experiment 999 times with the same result may *seem* to prove something, but the thousandth experiment *may* produce a different result. The practice of science involves a sort of industrious scepticism and Popper would frankly like to see more evidence of it among social scientists. More research and less theorising seems to be his advice. In view of how difficult it can be to 'set up' sociological research, this is perhaps not an encouraging view.

Ernest Gellner is a recent writer in the tradition of Popper. His particular objection is Garfinkel's ethnomethodology. He condemns its obsession with subjectivism as mere romanticism and, like Popper, he advocates a staunchly empirical approach to the understanding of society. Although the Marxist, Barry Hindess, has little else in common with Popper and Gellner, he also attacks extreme ethnomethodological subjectivism in his critique of statistics (Chapter 17, pp. 481-2).

There is much commonsense – if this is not too odd a word to use of such sophisticated work – in the thought of Popper and Gellner. Theoretical cloud castles in the sky must be brought to earth and examined for substance and content, a comment that applies to functionalism as much as to Marxism. Similarly, those who are so 'hung up' on subjectivism that they allow lit-

561

tle hope of meaningful sociological discourse hardly help to further the development of the discipline as a collective enterprise. (For a further discussion of this point, see later in this chapter, p. 581).

Until now, we have tended to regard science as a standard by which to take the measure of social science. Apart from a simple distinction between a broad and narrow definition of science, we have assumed the concept of science itself to be unproblematic. In so doing, we are in danger of giving it the status of a sort of sacred cow, divine and inscrutable. The work of Thomas Kuhn, however, attempts to 'debunk' such a reverential view of science and to ask not only how true it is to its own professed principles of empiricism and objectivity, but also whether these principles are the ones by which the natural sciences actually operate. Subjectivity may be a spectre that haunts science as well as social science.

What is Science?
Kuhn dismisses the notion that science is merely a collection of theories, methods and factual findings. Instead, he suggests the view that scientists, like sociologists, make use of *paradigms* or perspectives about their specialist fields which influence the *direction* and *nature* of their experimental research. Thus, Einstein's theories can be said to have provided the basis of a new working paradigm for astro-physics. Many of his ideas were speculative, partial and unproven, but they have since *inspired* more detailed research into problems concerning space and time. To this extent, Einstein's thought seems to provide much the same function as a sociological perspective.

A central feature of Kuhn's argument is that scientific paradigms change radically at given periods in history. Thus, his book is entitled *The Structure of Scientific Revolutions*. This revolutionary change occurs when a discovery cannot be made to fit into the dominant paradigm. We need an example here. For centuries, it was believed that the earth was the centre of the universe and that the sun revolved around it. This paradigm survived despite the increasing difficulty of accomodating newly discovered facts to it. Eventually, Copernicus produced evidence that overturned it. A new paradigm, that the earth revolves around the sun, became accepted.

Given paradigmatic changes and revolutions within the sciences, similar disagreements in sociology, expressed through the perspectives, appear less crippling to the claims of the subject to respectability and even scientific status. It is true that the natural sciences generate a greater 'sense' of consensus about theoretical and methodological approach than sociology does, but it is still a young discipline and it is possible that greater 'paradigmatic unity' may yet develop.

A further criticism may be offered against the notion of science as a monument to objectivity. Science, too, is haunted by the problem of subjectivity. First, a relatively minor point. Heisenberg's *uncertainty principle* points out that the light required to observe tiny particles will affect the way they behave. Thus, to a small degree, the scientist causes the behaviour he observes! That is a classic example of the dilemma of subjectivity. Second, a serious ethical point. Scientific research, like social research, takes place *in* society. Research provides knowledge which may be used constructively or destructively. Scientists who allow their skills to be used in a cause they believe to be morally wrong are in the same position as soldiers, administrators and others who do the same. Research findings do not exist in a social vacuum – some power is likely to use them. Einstein believed passionately that scientists should take responsibility for the work they do and its possible application to human life.

What is Sociology?

By way of a long detour, we come again to this question. Sociology is the study of human social life by any means that are effective. These may be more or less scientific, depending on how that term is defined, or even non-scientific. *All that is necessary is that their application contributes to our knowledge and understanding of social life.* To do this, 'findings' must be presented sufficiently intelligibly to be communicable to the body of professional sociologists (and, ideally, via them to the interested public). C. Wright Mills is surely correct when he argues that sociology is better practised with imagination and flexibility than with rigid adherence to the models of natural science. *Sociology is a craft to be judged by its product: what works best is best.* Whilst not rejecting the broadly scientific basis of sociology, Nisbet caps Mills in stressing the role of the creative imagination in sociology. This, he says, gives it the quality of an art form. Nisbet's observation brings the wheel full circle: *sociology is both science and art*. Given the complexity of its subject matter, it needs to be.

The Sociology of Knowledge

We said in the first chapter that there can be sociology of everything. Perhaps this statement receives its most demanding application in respect of the sociology of knowledge. Actually, the matter is much simpler than the phrase 'sociology of know-ledge' might suggest. This branch of sociology seeks to study the influence of social context on ideas and beliefs. *Why* is it that people become, say, Communists, Catholics or Muslims?

Although the emphasis of the sociology of knowledge is on the ideas and beliefs of groups, it is helpful to begin our expla-nation of it by reference to the individual. The concept of indi-vidual socialisation is a particularly useful starting point. We saw in Chapter 3 that the norms, values and beliefs of a per-son are greatly influenced by the childhood socialisation she receives. What a child comes to *know* is largely the product of the particular society she is born into. A child brought up in a strongly Muslim culture will have a Muslim outlook, and one brought up in a communist culture will perceive life from a communist point of view. Yet both are likely to insist that *their* way of seeing things, their 'knowledge', is closer to 'the truth' than that of others. The sociologist of knowledge will not take sides in this dispute. His purpose is to establish why people come to believe what they do believe.

It is a simple matter to make the transition from the analysis of the social basis of individual knowledge to that of group knowledge. The same process of socialisation is at work in help-ing to create the outlook of groups as of individuals. *Educational systems, the culture of the workplace and the media all generate or rein-force values, beliefs and normative attitudes which contribute to the gen-eral stock of assumptions or knowledge, as we are calling it, of given societies or groups.* Thus, we would expect the media in commun-ist societies to present a different view of the world from that in liberal Western societies, both in its selection of facts and in its processing and treatment of them. The way 'the world' is presented will obviously affect the consciousness of the receiving

564

audience (though this does not imply that people cannot and do not resist the influences and interpretations that may be dominant within their national media).

Two concepts are especially important in the methodological armoury of the sociologist of knowledge: *relativity* and *ideology*. *In order to establish the social influences on cultural knowledge, the sociologist must proceed on the assumption that such knowledge is relative, not absolute.* *Relative* means, therefore, that the knowledge of, say, a Christian, Hindu, or whoever, owes something to the social context in which the beliefs developed. It is the sociologist's business to explore this connection. Thus, as we have seen, Weber explianed the growth of Calvinism in terms of its 'fit', or compatibility, with capitalism. To overstate the case slightly, people believed in Calvinism at least partly because it suited their economic interests to do so, whether they realised this or not. Now such a proposition may seem directly at variance with the claim of Calvinists that their beliefs represented the will of God. If we generalise the point to the effect that *all* religions or other systems of belief are, in part, socially (including economically) rooted, the potential for conflict between the sociology of knowledge and such religions appears to be very great. This should not be so, however. Sociologists may observe, with Pascal, that truth on one side of the Pyrenees is falsehood on the other, but they are not competent to deliver a final verdict on competing claims. They should not play God nor, *as sociologists*, should they deny God, (though their personal beliefs are, of course, their own business). They are concerned with the much more humble and limited task of *tracing the social links between systems of knowledge and the societies in which they develop.*

The second concept referred to above, that of ideology, has already been frequently used in this book and requires only brief reference here. The term refers to *ideas* and carries the particular implication that *the ideas people hold serve the purpose of justifying their own interests, even though they clothe them in the language of idealism.* The specific use of the concept in the sociology of knowledge will become apparent shortly.

So far, we have demonstrated that systems of knowledge do, indeed, differ and we have also shown how they are introduced (through socialisation and communication). We have not yet clearly stated what the social functions of knowledge systems

565

are. We can do this best by referring to various perspectives on the sociology of knowledge: the functionalist, Marxist, Mannheimian, and the phenomenological. Again, despite the vocabulary, it is all much simpler than it sounds.

Curiously, *functionalist* contributions to the sociology of knowledge are seldom referred to. Yet it is in this area that Durkheim's insight was perhaps at its greatest. He dismissed from consideration the claims to objective truth of competing religions and argued that *the major function of all religions is to integrate people into particular societies by creating moral consensus.* For him, this is the hidden or *latent* purpose of the passion, commitment and intolerance that often accompany religion itself, or any other powerful system of belief. The disbeliever in the creed, whether political or religious, is seen as a potential threat to social solidarity. It is for this reason, no doubt, that nonconformity is so harshly treated in totalitarian communist and fascist societies. Durkheim particularly stresses the importance of the educational system as a purveyor of knowledge (in the sense of moral values and attitudes as well as facts and skills). He perhaps overestimated the value of teaching conformity at the expense of the development of an independent and critical outlook.

In *Marx's* writings, the sociology of knowledge is subsumed into his concept of ideology. In turn, his use of ideology is firmly located in his class analysis of society. This contrasts with the funcionalist emphasis on the general belief system of a given society. Dominant classes produce ideologies – which they may or may not believe themselves – which justify or obscure their domination and mislead the exploited classes. Put into different words, dominant ideology legitimates the position of the ruling class. Marx argued that, in any age, the ruling ideas are the ideas of the ruling class. Thus, in a capitalist society, capitalist ideas prevail. We have studied many applications of Marxist approaches, particularly in the context of politics, religion, the media and education. (see, especially, the contribution of Marcuse, Chapter 19, p. 547 and Bourdieu, Chapter 5, pp. 110-14). Marx argued that only one form of knowledge is scientific, as opposed to ideological: the theory of *scientific socialism.* *As a materialist, however, he insisted that its truth could become apparent solely through practical application and the eventual creation of a classless society in which self-interested ideology would be unnecessary.*

Karl Mannheim, in his influential work, *Ideology and Utopia,*

566

extended Marx's analysis of ideological knowledge to Marxism itself, and to other revolutionary traditions. For him, there was no escape for Marxism from relativism into 'scientific objectivity'. The Marxist 'utopia' was no different in kind and no more historically inevitable than any other dream of the future. *Mannheim, however, did distinguish between bodies of ideas that support the status quo, which he called ideologies, and those that seek to change it, which he termed utopias.* He included Marxism among the latter. Both ideologies and utopias reflect historical circumstances. Thus, Marxism itself was generated by the realities of capitalist industrial society. Mannheim also related intellectuals' ideas to the social climate. Rather like Kuhn, he considered that the direction of development of knowledge in the natural sciences and mathematics, as well as other academic areas, was subject to social influence, although he did consider their content to be more objective. Less controversially, he pointed to the self-interested basis of much professional ideology (an issue we have discussed in some detail in Chapter 6). Yet Mannheim allowed that intellectuals have a greater range of awareness than others and thus are in a favourable position to develop alternative ideologies or utopias. This idea was adopted by C. Wright Mills in the nineteen fifties, who argued that intellectuals and students, not the proletariat, offered the best hope for change.

All the sociologists referred to above recognise that the religions, ideologies and subject disciplines that form men's minds and shape their knowledge are also created by men. Their emphasis, however, is on the former, rather than the latter, aspect. *Phenomenologists*, likewise, recognise both the socially formative and humanly created aspects of knowledge, but they begin their analysis with the latter. Arguably, the key emphasis in the title of Berger and Luckman's book, *The Social Construction of Reality: A Treatise on the Sociology of Knowledge* is on the 'construction'. *As far as they are concerned, all social reality, including knowledge, begins with subjective experience of it. Knowledge is not something that exists 'out there' that 'happens to' people.* The major means by which people communicate is language. In the last chapter, we saw that interactionists, with whom phenomenologists have much in common, stress the flexibility and developmental potential of language and, consequently, of knowledge. The exchange and development of knowledge occurs as much,

567

indeed more, in everyday communication than in academic environments. Berger and Luckman stress that it is the understanding of everyday life that is the major focus of sociology: virtually all spheres of human life involve the communication of information, attitudes or values and, in that sense, the sociology of knowledge is an aspect of all sociology.

We conclude by returning to the problem of relativity and knowledge. Perhaps it is not quite so clear cut as we indicated above. There are two contrasting traditions within sociology which claim to be able to achieve rather more than to lay bare the relative aspects of knowledge. The first is the *positivist tradition*. Although positivism is based on the principle of relativity, it aspires to such a definitive statement on the nature of knowledge that it can be regarded as a distinct theory of knowledge. Going back to Comte, this tradition contends that scientific knowledge is 'truer' than theological (religious) or metaphysical (idealistic in the sense of purely philosophical) knowledge and will, indeed, replace them. Comte argued that scientific or 'positive' sociology would eventually provide a complete explanation of human existence. Ironically, this was to claim the sort of absolute status for positivistic sociological knowledge that he denied to religion and philosophy, although it is doubtful if he was aware of this paradox. Durkheim also believed that although primitive societies were characterised by myth, legend and religion, modern society might achieve a truer understanding of social reality through scientific sociology. As we have seen, this belief is also present in Marx's thought. The two, however, did not agree about the nature of the 'reality' they perceived. *'Scientific' sociology, like traditional religion, has become pluralistic* – it offers no one version of the truth and can hardly, therefore, claim to be the key to it. Further, apart from the disagreements among positivists, there remains the possibility that there are other kinds of knowledge about social life than that based on the analysis of cause and effect, the fundamental principle of positivism. Berger's analysis of 'meaning' is one such example, and we give another below.

The second tradition within sociology that aspires to offer something approaching a comprehensive account of the basis of knowledge is the critical sociology of *the Frankfurt school of Marxists* (although Marx is only one, and perhaps not the greatest, influence on them). The best known critical theorist is Jurgen

Habermas (1929–). In his work, *Knowledge and Human Interests*, Habermas has argued that there are three forms of knowledge, the *empirical-analytic* (positivist), the *historical-hermeneutic* (interpretist), and *self-reflection* (a form of philosophical knowledge). In other words, Habermas accepts that the two forms of knowledge studied, respectively, by scientific and interpretive sociology are both valid but, interestingly, he adds a third. We can discern two elements in self-reflection, or critical, knowledge. Firstly, man uses his unique attribute of self-consciousness to examine critically his own social life. Unlike positivistic or interpretist knowledge, this involves consciously going beyond what is actually 'there' in external social reality by commenting critically upon it. Secondly, *Habermas suggests that there actually is an 'ideal' or objective standard by which we can criticise social reality – otherwise, what would the meaning be of such words as 'exploitation' or 'cruelty'? The basis of this standard of objective criticism is man's awareness of truth and this comes from within himself, not from society.* Truth involves saying what we 'really' mean and expressing what we 'really' feel. Societies often *repress* (a key concept in critical theory) our freedom to do this by making us afraid of the consequences (a form of control), Habermas wants to move towards a freer and more truthful society. But can we accept his 'objective' criteria for truth and freedom? They are remarkably attractive. We must extend to them, however, the same scepticism that the sociology of knowledge applies to all religion and social philosophies whilst recognising that, at some higher idealistic, or even human, level, Habermas may be right.

Does this sociological scepticism mean that there is *no* reality out there', or merely that, for some reason, people disagree about what it³ is? Karl Mannheim offers a helpful, if limited, suggestion on this matter. It is that *people's different perspectives on society (or on anything else, for that matter) are often complementary in nature. They can be used together to build up a fuller, more precise version of the object of study (in our case, society).* This comment has particular application to contemporary sociology, given its fragmented state. Of course, there is no guarantee that a more *unified sociological paradigm* – perhaps based on an integrated and developed structural-phenomenology – will more closely reflect 'social reality' than do any of the present perspectives. But perhaps the time is ripe for sociologists to make this constructive effort. The insights of phenomenology should be used to enrich sociology, not to destroy it. Admittedly, a collective enterprise of this kind would be painful and would involve laying to rest numerous sociological fables and exorcising not a few sociological ghosts.

Is a Unified Sociological Paradigm Possible?

Limited Perspectives?

Sometimes students express impatience with 'the perspectives approach' to sociology. Their impatience is based not only on the growing number and complexity of the perspectives themselves but also on the feeling that there ought, after all, to be more agreement on the nature of social life and how to study it. Reflecting on the disagreements among sociologists, a distinguished non-sociologist once remarked sardonically that sociology is a sub-committee set up by philosophers which has not reported back yet. I have some sympathy with the sentiment behind this jibe. As I have been writing this book, the sense has increasingly grown on me that there is an element of shadow-boxing about many of the sociological fisticuffs I have described, and that there is a much greater measure of potential agreement amongst sociologists than they have yet learnt to admit. Here, in a creative spirit, I want to suggest some elements of common, or complementary, ground between the perspectives and, unavoidably, to indicate certain approaches which no longer seem very useful. Ironically, this means that I must relax my text book writer's attempt to hold the ring neutrally between contesting perspectives and adopt for myself the sharper weapons of commitment.

Concern that sociological theory has become excessively fragmented has been widely expressed by sociologists themselves in recent years, despite a passive and often uncritical acceptance of 'the perspectives approach' within teaching circles. The functionalist, Ronald Fletcher, has been forthright in attacking this approach to teaching sociology: indeed, he refers to it as an 'entirely fallacious orientation' that is 'being imposed on each new generation'. He believes that there are certain fundamental principles accepted by the founding fathers which pro-

570

vide a sound basis for the study of society and, presumably, that the elucidation of these principles is what the teaching of sociology should be about. We will return to this shortly.

The Marxist, Anthony Giddens, likewise refuses to accept that the discipline of sociology is no more than a collection of differing perspectives. He explains the current 'seemingly disoriented situation of social theory' in terms of the post-war breakdown of the consensus around functionalism. He discerns three tendencies within sociology which have emerged during the 'post-consensus' period. First is the *perspectives approach* itself: an enthusiastic, 'Let the thousand flowers bloom' attitude to the subject. Second is a return to a would-be 'purely empirical' orientation to sociology which dismisses, or disregards, larger issues of theory in favour of *'getting on with research'*. Third is *a reversion to rigid orthodoxy*. Giddens has in mind crude Marxism, but crude functionalism represents the same search for simple certainty. Acually, Giddens' list is hardly exhaustive, and his selection of current trends a little pessimistic. As he is aware, other tendencies, including ethnomethodology and less crude varieties of Marxism, have emerged besides those he mentions. I agree, however, with his statement that 'social theory stands in need of systematic reconstruction'. We will now look at the various sociological perspectives with this need in mind. It should be said that what follows assumes that the major theoretical points made elsewhere in this book have been substantially absorbed by the reader.

Functionalism: How Adequate is the Organic Analogy?

In the first chapter, we introduced the functionalist comparison of society to a biological organism. In later chapters, we examined several applications of the organic analogy. The application examined in greatest detail was the way in which societies are considered to develop from the simple to the complex, just as growing bodies do. This approach stresses the evolutionary aspect of the analogy, and is apparent in the work of Durkheim and Parsons, but can be traced back to the British sociologist, Herbert Spencer (1820–1903), who was substantially influenced by Darwin's theory of biological evolution. We will consider shortly whether the concept of evolution manages to provide an adequate basis for understanding social change.

Apart from applications of the organic analogy based on

571

evolutionary perspective, others reflect the view that society is structured and functions like an organism. This emphasis finds its strongest expression in the writings of the British anthropologist, Radcliffe-Brown, (1881–1955), but it also partly underlies the more sophisticated social systems theory of Talcott Parsons. The basic notion here is that the various parts of society work in relation to one another (see the family-society model, Chapter 4, p. 75) and that society can best be understood by analysing these interrelations (see Parsons' social systems model, Chapter 3, pp. 280-3). Functionalists consider that just as some parts of the body are functionally more important than others so, too, must society be hierarchically arranged for functional purposes. This view is apparent in the work of Davis and Moore (Chapter 10, pp. 282-3) and Michels (Chapter 15, pp. 425-6). Another major functionalist concept is that of social equilibrium by which society is assumed to seek balance and orderly functioning in the same way that the body does. Consensus on norms and values is considered a necessity for healthy functioning, although the analogy is rarely pursued as literally as this. Deviant behaviour, however, is often compared to physical 'pathology' by functionalists, not least by Durkheim himself.

We now turn to a critical appraisal of functionalism. *Firstly, organs do not think, whereas people do, or, to put it more technically the organic analogy contains no parallel for intentional social action. Biological processes are not achieved through the use of will, reason and imagination but invariably take place below the level of conscious awareness.* Although Talcott Parsons claimed to have developed a 'theory of social action', he has been widely and effectively criticised for failing to do so. As Giddens remarks, with some elegance, 'recognisably human agents seem to elude the grasp of his scheme: the stage is set, the scripts written, the roles established, but the performers are curiously absent from the scene'. The result of this is that functionalism presents what Dennis Wrong calls an oversocialised conceptualisation of man. We, too, made this very point in Chapter 3 and used symbolic interactionist theory to balance functionalist analysis of socialisation.

A second criticism frequently made of functionalism is, as we have seen, that *it exaggerates the role of consensus and underestimates that of conflict in the functioning of society*. It should be added that the concepts of consensus and equilibrium are linked, in that functionalists regard the former as a precondition of the latter. This emphasis on stability and order is reflected in the organic analogy itself, although functionalists stress these as much because they accord with their conservative political views, rather than in slavish imitation of the analogy. It is true that organic bodies, particularly animals, strive to maintain internal balance (partly through an often complex process of homeostasis or adaptation) but there is no proof – indeed, it is most unlikely – that societies as entities are inherently endowed with similar adjustment mechanisms. Social order and equilibrium may be maintained through the conscious action of individuals and groups, but that is a different matter. Although consensus does contribute to social order it, too, must in part be intentionally created and maintained. It certainly cannot be regarded as automatically self-regulating or perpetuating. In other words, *social equilibrium and consensus occur in a different way from organic equilibrium.* There is no adequate explanatory parallel between the organic and social fields. Again, the biological analogy breaks down in practice.

A third criticism of the organic analogy is that *it produces a misleading separation of structure (society's parts or institutions) and system (society's functioning).* In particular, it leads only to a partial conceptualisation of the problem of social change. By contrast, this division seems to work well in the natural sciences. In biology, it helps to examine the structure of a plant or animal (anatomy) and then to describe how the various parts function in relation to one another and the whole. In a limited descriptive sense, the same approach is useful in sociology although, significantly, society cannot be similarly 'laid out' anatomically for examination. In real life, society 'functions' through the more or less organised actions of individuals and groups, not in the manner of an unreflecting organism. Nor does change occur solely through evolution and adaptation, although it may to some extent. Equally important in the history and development of nations and cultures are revolutions and drastic breaks with the past. Parson's notion of dynamic equilibrium, by which social balance adjusts to accomodate new phenomena within the system, still stresses continuity at the expense of change and severance. It also woefully underestimates the role of people in making history. For him, systems change and almost 'make' people, not the other way around. (See also p. 589).

In retrospect, Robert Merton's attempts to use the concept of function to embrace a wide variety of social events looks like the death throes of a theory stretched beyond its inherent capacity. In particular, his concept of *manifest* function which he uses to describe intended, as opposed to unintended (*latent*) consequences of institutional functioning is a notably impoverished attempt to allow for the role of choice in social life. The basic problem is that it is not possible to provide an adequate account of consciously directed action within a framework that takes as its model the unconscious functioning of the organism.

A final criticism of functionalism is that it is teleological, or tautological, as Chris Brown has called it. In other words, *because functionalists see certain functions being performed by given institutions, they conclude that there must be need for these functions* — that is, they explain causes by their consequences. Actually, many institutions exist, the 'need' for which can be doubted. Inevitably, opinions will differ as to which institutions qualify: some will suggest the House of Lords, others the trade unions. Further, men create organisations and institutions not only to fulfil social needs but to pursue their own purposes and interests — sometimes at the expense of others. As far as 'needs' are concerned, beyond basics, 'one man's meat is another man's poison'.

Finally, although nobody can take exception to a descriptive account of the functions institutions perform, including those many of us may not be aware of, this is only an aspect, and a rather obvious one, of sociological analysis. *Who made things as they are, and in whose interests,* are equally important questions which functionalists tend to ignore.

The issue is not whether functionalism is an 'incorrect' perspective but whether it is the most useful and illuminating available. It is certainly helpful as a descriptive, if uncritical, account of what institutions 'do' — and, as such, it has some appeal to students. Further, the functionalist analysis of socialisation warns us, usefully, of what is 'done' to us individually in order to make us conforming members of society. Both these aspects of sociological analysis, however, are fairly obvious and well dealt with in other perspectives. Functionalism must stand or fall on the fruitfulness of its central concepts as presented in the biological analogy, or in Talcott Parsons' more recent, and, admittedly, more sophisticated systems theory. Assessed on that basis, I suggest that functionalism is an outmoded, essentially nineteenth century perspective which is likely soon to be superseded.

Criticisms of 'Crude' Marxism and the Revival in Marxist Thought

The criticisms of structural-functionalism are persuasive enough to recommend a search for an alternative sociological paradigm. Marxism comes to mind although it, too, has been the subject of serious criticisms. We need to examine these before we can assess the merits of Marxism as a convincing basis for a unified sociological paradigm. I have taken the view that Marxist sociological theory is informed by, or learns from, Marxist political practice and, therefore, I have not rigidly separated the two here. The Marxist heritage is profoundly ambiguous: Marx has left two legacies, although it is unlikely that he intended to do so. The first is based on the belief that class conflict and socialist revolution are historically inevitable, and the other is based on the view that, to achieve a social revolution, it is necessary to work for a change in the consciousness of the working class. (As they come to realise the nature of capitalist exploitation, they will surely organise to end it). It is the first of these two legacies of thought which has been the most severely criticised.

The belief that a revolution of the proletariat is inevitable on account of certain economic 'contradictions' in capitalism, has been criticised repeatedly as crudely deterministic. This means that its adherents consider that 'the future is known from the past', and, they state, certain major future events are bound to happen because of 'the laws of history'. We have examined Karl Popper's comments on this issue earlier in this chapter. Marx's application of dialectical theory to historical change is sometimes cited as an attempt to uncover such laws. The principle of the dialectic is that opposite elements (thesis and antithesis) combine to produce a synthesis (new phenomenon). The concept comes from natural science, but as applied by Marx to recent history, it means that the clash of the capitalist class with the proletariat will produce a new synthesis: the classless society. It is doubtful whether Marx intended this model to be accepted as rigidly inevitable, but if he did, it is, indeed, an example of crude determinism. Perhaps Marx has suffered as much from the ideas of some of his followers as from his critics. No wonder he once said 'I am not a Marxist'. The major refutation of determinism, which modern Marxists do generally accept, is that, *within the structural realities of their time, men make their own history and, for that reason, the future cannot be predicted.*

A second criticism of Marxism is that it is *idealistic in theory and cruel and repressive in practice.* When commentators say this they have in mind primarily the example of Soviet totalitarianism and imperialism. They argue that the Russian record of human rights and foreign policy is not attributable simply to the wickedness of the Soviets, but is a basic feature of Marxist 'dogma' itself. They contend that 'in the real world' it is not possible to combine material equality with a high level of personal freedom and expression. When the state is controlled by an unrepresentative group, it may use its power to repress not only political opposition but also to organise, control or repress a wide range of other activities, not least those of a cultural kind. Many European and American Marxists accept these criticisms, but deny that the Soviet regime represents a fair picture of Marxism. We now examine some of their ideas on the subject.

First is the trend towards *Marxist humanism.* This aspect of Marxism concentrates on the repression of human potential in capitalist society and the prospect of its release in communist society. The sources of humanism within Marx's own works are his early writings on human potential and his analysis of alienation, discussed in the last chapter. In Britain, Raymond Williams and E. P. Thompson are major representatives of Marxist humanism (see Chapter 19), and in the United States C. Wright Mills and the German exile, Herbert Marcuse (see Chapters 9 and 19 for both) achieved international influence.

At the risk of oversimplification, we include critical theory within the broad trend of Marxist humanism (see pp. 568-9 of this chapter). Critical theory, as its name suggests, raises the possibility of criticising the way things are from another point of view. Marcuse himself was a critical theorist until his death in 1979. He attacked capitalist 'reality', particularly from the point of view that it is culturally repressive – especially, although not exclusively, of the working class (see Chapter 19, p. 547). Before fleeing to America from Nazi Germany, Marcuse worked at Frankfurt University, the 'home' of critical theorists. Like other philosophers and sociologists of the Frankfurt school, Marcuse was greatly influenced by Freud as well as by Marx, and effected a synthesis of the two that captured the imagination of many student radicals of the nineteen sixties. He took Freud's concept of psychological repression and applied it to capitalist society. He argued that capitalism is not interested in full human expression and development, but primarily in exploiting labour. In doing this, it represses human potential and reduces people to the level of a machine. Because, like Habermas, Marcuse holds out the possibility of more liberated human life, we class him as a Marxist humanist. His work, as well as that of Williams, Thompson and Mills, shows that the interest of Marxist humanists is not narrowly sociological but extends to the whole range of cultural expression.

A second contemporary trend in Marxism is *Marxist structuralism*, associated particularly with the French Marxists, Althusser and Bourdieu. We discussed their thinking in the context of socialisation, especially education, and referred again to Althusser in Chapters 18 and 19. Structuralists tend to see a rather tight fit between the base and the superstructure. In other words, they see culture less as free expression and more as an area in which ideological conformity to capitalist society is created. In this sense they are rather like structural functionalists, although whereas the latter generally approve of conformity to capitalist society, Marxist structuralists certainly do not.

Thirdly, developments in Marxist thought have also been forged in *political practice* as well as in the studies of academics. Lenin, Mao and the Cuban revolutionary, Che Guevara, were men of action as well as intellectuals. They were all successful revolutionaries and it is not surprising that they emphasised the need for Marxists to organise in order to create the change they wanted rather than to assume that history was inevitably on their side. They stressed the role both of the revolutionary party and of committed leadership in helping to bring about revolution. The danger in this was that the leadership would lose touch with the majority of the people on whose behalf revolution was supposed to take place. Having 'imposed' revolution, post-revolutionary change might also have to be imposed on a population whose 'consciousness' might be far from communist. Marxists differ on whether such imposition is justifiable. The alternative is to seek fundamental change only with mass support, either gradually or through revolution. The difficulty here is that the forces of the system preventing the growth of such support are immense; one way of measuring support is through the ballot box. Zimbabwe has an elected Marxist government, but it remains to be seen whether it can survive the opposition of the powerful countries and international business interests ranged against it. The elected Marxist government of Allende in Chile was prevented from doing this.

It is not easy to classify neatly the theoretical contributions of Marxist activists. The three revolutionaries mentioned above all stressed the need for men to force the historical issue in order to bring about socialist change. To that extent they were humanists. Whether the violence they used in pursuit of change contradicts their humanism is a point that could long be debated.

Contemporary Marxism is in a ferment of debate; yet some issues are becoming clear. Few Marxists now are historical determinists, although a case could be made that the French structuralists have merely substituted cultural mechanics for economic. But the broad trend to reconcile the immense power of social structure to form people with their capacity ultimately to change the repressive nature of their own social environment is extremely positive. We return to this theme in our final section which deals with the possibility of a unified sociological paradigm.

Interpretive Sociology: Is it Compatible with a Structural Perspective?

Since Mead, symbolic interactionism has progressed theoretically as much through practical application as through abstract thought isolated from research. Accordingly, we have been able to examine in some detail recent interactionist analyses of work, deviance and organisation. There is no need to review this research now. Instead, we will discuss the criticism frequently made of interactionism – that it lacks a structural dimension. In particular, we will assess Tom Goff's comparison of Mead's sociology to that of Marx. In his book, *Marx and Mead*, Goff attempts to show that the work of Marx and Mead is, essentially, complementary rather than contradictory. To the extent that he is successful, his analysis has profound implications for the theoretical reconstruction of sociology called for by, among others, Anthony Giddens. In what follows, I will not attempt to prove propositions already extensively discussed earlier, but will simply restate them in order to outline a fuller argument. Firstly, both Marx and Mead emphasised that the individual is formed in society, and give comparable emphasis to the influence of social structure on people. Mead went into far greater detail of how this takes place and his social psychology has been very useful in much practical interpretist research. Recently, Marxists such as Jock Young and Paul Willis appear to have been influenced by it or, at least, by other compatible currents within phenomenology. Secondly, both Marx and Mead describes people as conscious beings with the potential to change and recreate their own social environment: neither the individual human being nor the group is ever 'reduced' to society. If Mead conveyed much more of the psychology of individual choice and understanding than did Marx, Marx presented a much more urgent message of emancipation from social repression and an alternative and freer way of life. A third point of convergence can be derived from the other two. For both of them, social structure and human creativity are not separate, but dialectically related – that is, man and environment interact with each other and can change each other. This leads to the fourth agreed point – that human thought is located in a social context, and informed by experience. In that sense, it is practical in nature and, for Marx at least, can be directed most rationally towards radically improving the quality of human life.

Goff has indicated Marx's concept of alienation as a major possible area of difference between him and Mead. Certainly, Mead had no particular sense that the division of labour in capitalist society was especially alienating: in fact, he was inclined to argue that the process of productive fragmentation was likely to continue and seemed none too distressed by it. He did, however, have a vivid appreciation of the way social institutions can smother individuality – a sentiment which accords with a Marxist-Weberian notion of alienation (see Chapter 15, pp. 363-6). The following quotation shows this:

> Oppressive, stereotyped and ultra-conservative social institutions
> – like the church – . . . by their more or less rigid and inflexible
> unprogressiveness crush or blot out individuality or discourage
> any distinctive or original expressions of thought and behaviour
> in the individual selves or personalities implicated in and
> subjected to them . . .

It is not too much to conclude, therefore, that Mead's framework of social analysis can be adapted to accommodate the concept of alienation.

Although the above considerations indicate that Mead's social thought is compatible with, and even complementary to, the structural aspects of Marxist theory, it remains true that the former is more suited to the micro-level of analysis and the latter to the macro-level. It is unquestionable that Mead developed the more detailed conceptual tool-kit for small-scale interaction and Marx the more detailed one for institutional analysis and class conflict, although in so far as these two levels inevitably overlap there is room for synthesis. But accepting that different levels of social analysis exist, and that theory and research will reflect this, it is objectionable to present the two perspectives as radically opposed: the above shows that they need not be.

Whether ethnomethodology is inherently compatible with structural perspective is open to more doubt and depends on how exactly it is defined. In the first chapter, ethnomethodology was referred to as an attempt to describe how individuals make sense of, or give explanatory accounts of, their experience. We need to extend this point here before returning to the broader issue of the relationship between ethnomethodology and structural perspective. Two concepts used by ethnomethodologists need to be introduced. Unfortunately, both reflect the extreme verbosity with which ethnomethodology is commonly associated, but they are capable of simple definition and illustration. The terms are the *documentary method* and *indexicality*. The documentary method is employed by all of us and involves the assumption that a given event or occasion can be made sense of by seeing it as just one example, or document, of a general type. Thus, to take Cicourel's previously cited study of delinquency, a police officer may see a particular youth with *what he regards* as delinquent characteristics and accordingly place him within the general category of delinquent, that is, he reacts to the 'documentary' evidence, perhaps a skinhead haircut and tattooed arms. He could, of course, be mistaken. The concept of indexicality means that sense can only be made of any object or event by relating it back to its context, or the circumstances of its occurrence. Thus, the word 'five' makes sense as an answer to the question,'What time is it?' but not as an answer to

'How many players are there in a cricket team?' Similarly, to continue with the kind of example that appeals to Harold Garfinkel, the founder of ethnomethodology, a policeman in the outfit of a clown would make sense in the context of a fancy dress ball but not in the context of a drugs raid. We can agree, then, that meaning depends on context. The interrelatedness of meaning and event – almost to the point of equation – is referred to as *reflexivity* by ethnomethodologists, and is a third key concept of the perspective. Because of their respect for the uniqueness and unpredictability of personal meaning, ethnomethodologists examine social activity with careful reference back to context and the various verbal descriptions (conveyors of meaning) given of it by social actors. Study in this depth of detail has, necessarily, to be on a small scale, as was Cicourel's study of the social organisation of juvenile delinquency, and Atkinson's research into coroners' definitions of suicide.

Both structural perspectives and symbolic interactionism offer theories of social order and structure. For the former, order and structure lie in the institutional framework which constrains members of society, and for the latter order is negotiated and structure created through interaction. Ethnomethodologists go a stage further back, as it were, by examining *how individuals cope with, and make sense of, existing situations* (whether 'orderly' or not). This interest need not, in my view, be incompatible with structural perspective. Presumably, it is not unlikely that the underlying patterns and taken-for-granted assumptions which individuals seek and find reinforced in experience (reflexivity) can be widely *shared*. If so, this fact structures interaction. Otherwise, there would be chaos. Yet some ethnomethodologists seem to object to the concerns of other perspectives. Perhaps this is partly a territorial dispute which will be resolved once ethnomethodologists have defined their areas of research interest in a way that is more comprehensible to other sociologists.

Towards a Unified Sociological Paradigm

In this section, I want to make three major points in support of the thesis that I have consistently urged in this book – that sociology has, and needs to have, an essential underlying theoretical coherence and unity. The first point is that *the*

581

methods of sociology, although highly diverse, can be regarded as a unifying factor in that they are the common property of all practitioners of the subject. The second point is that the *major concepts in sociology provide a basic sub-structure to the discipline* (Nisbet's term) despite differences in definition and usage within perspectives. The third point is that, leaning heavily on Anthony Giddens, I want to explore briefly some emerging possibilities for the *systematic reconstruction of sociological theory* that he deems necessary. Such a reconstruction, however, is likely to be a matter of synthesis rather than complete innovation.

The first point is perhaps the least important and can be briefly made. I differ from what still seems to be a prevailing assumption of some sociologists that qualitative methods are overwhelmingly associated with interpretist theory and quantitative methods with functionalist theory (and perhaps, too, mere empiricism). Clearly there are substantial links of this kind – some of which we pursued earlier (Chapter 2, pp. 24-40). However, I believe that these were stronger, say, fifteen or twenty years ago than now. Today, sociologists seem increasingly to use whatever method suits their purpose best, and this is not always 'one or the other type'. Stan Cohen, David Hargreaves and many feminist sociologists have used a wide variety of methods in the course of a single piece of research. As the work of these authors suggests, sociological methods are perhaps better thought of as a varied tool-kit of analysis rather than ideological appendages of various perspectives.

The second point is also a relatively simple matter. It is not difficult to study sociology with the help of a more explicit emphasis on concepts, even though this approach to teaching the discipline appears to have declined in recent years. Witnessing chaos in the subject, sociologists have sometimes apparently mistaken the subject itself for chaos and have conceived of it almost exclusively in terms of disagreements between the perspectives. Indeed, some teachers of sociology go to great lengths to invent differences that they imagine may exist between perspectives, presumably because they think either that by doing so they are practising sociology, or because they believe it is a stimulating intellectual exercise. Using the major concepts as a framework of presentation provides a way out of this confusing sophistry and fragmentation. It is true that a given concept may carry a variety of interpretations and meanings, but these are usually logically compatible and often complementary. We will briefly recap on some of the major concepts used in this book. They are self; socialisation; culture; ideology; structure; stratification; power; order; change; agency and community. The above do not make up a complete list of all the major concepts I have used here: still less do they comprise all the major concepts in sociology. The point is, however, that the systematic exploration and application of such concepts can provide a coherent basis both for sociological teaching and, to some degree, research, which is certainly not achieved by excessive and exclusive emphasis on the perspectives. The perspectives are usually taught in relation to topics (often in no particular order) with theory and method slotted in somewhere. An alternative approach is to use concepts or, better, clusters of related concepts, which have a particular relevance to a given topic or series of topics as more explicit tools of analysis. Thus, the concepts of socialisation and culture have special application to the topics of family and education and can provide part of the focus for studying these topics. Similarly, stratification is a concept that applies to the topics of class, race, gender and generation. It is not, however, necessary to fit topics into clusters of concepts to give them due importance – this is merely a method of approach. Concepts do, of course, recur throughout topics: my point is that giving more weight to the basic concepts of sociology and rather less to the perspectives can produce a more coherent basis for approaching sociology and give a truer reflection of the fundamental concerns of the discipline than simply pursuing topics via perspectives. Looking beyond 'A' level sociology, I would also argue that an approach to social science which stresses concepts and methods will have more to contribute to a core curriculum than one based primarily on the perspectives. The proof of the pudding must be in the eating, however, and I want to illustrate my point about the importance of concepts by referring to some detailed examples – most of them used earlier in this book.

First are the concepts of self, socialisation and culture which we treated as a cluster in Chapter 1. For several reasons these related concepts are an excellent vehicle for presenting sociology to 'A' level beginners. Firstly, they are not too abstract and can easily be given personally meaningful illustration. The basic idea that the self or individual is socialised into a given culture can be explained by reference to any student's own biography. Secondly, the concepts lend themselves to cross-cultural comparison. Margaret Mead's work can be used to show just how much of what is taken for granted in a given society is, in fact, culturally influenced. Thirdly, they can be used as a natural platform for coming to terms with the basic ideas of Parsons and Mead in a way that does not make their thought seem confusingly contradictory (as it is frequently made to appear). Conflict theory can also be initially approached by linking the concepts of socialisation and class culture. Early in an 'A' level course, it is enough to appreciate the 'them and us' attitudes of the traditional working class and the more individualistic 'society as a ladder' orientation of the middle class. Admittedly, this is a sparse introduction to conflict theory, but in the first month or so of a course it is enough. Perhaps the above example shows that giving due emphasis to fundamental concepts does not involve disregarding the perspectives. On the contrary, it helps to establish them on a sound and comprehensible academic basis within the discipline.

Before turning to other concepts, it is worth dwelling further on the central importance that culture should have in the theory and teaching of sociology. Culture is an analytical tool too important ever to have gone out of usage, but it has recently been given particularly powerful application by leading Marxists on both sides of the channel. For Raymond Williams and Pierre Bourdieu, it is the focal concept around which they organise much of their material, although they do so in different ways. Further, culture defined as the transmission of values and norms has always been central to functionalism (reflecting particularly the influence on the perspective of anthropology through Malinowski and Durkheim). Whereas functionalism stresses the apparently 'neutral' but essentially conservative concept of socialisation, Marxists extend cultural analysis into the area of ideology – another concept used recurrently here. No sociologist would argue that social structure and culture are separate entities: on the contrary, the point is that they fuse and interact. To analyse structure and ignore culture would be to perform an autopsy on the corpse of society. That is why cultural themes flow through our treatment of class, gender, racial and generational stratification. Nevertheless, a specific concept may be particularly appropriate in the analysis of a given topic. Thus, culture is especially applicable to topics involving socialisation and communication, such as education and the media.

I want now to turn to the concept of social structure, possibly the most important in sociology. I shall link structure with a number of other concepts, including power. I hope to show that the somewhat different ways these concepts are treated within given perspectives need not preclude a coherent analysis and understanding of their meaning and application. Marxism, functionalism, and social action perspective are all broadly structural. George Mead also fully recognised the powerful influence of social institutions, although he staunchly resisted the idea that this is a totality. Stratification is the major structural concept and is most commonly applied to class, gender, race and generation (although, in theory, it can be applied to any form of distinction which results in social inequality). I don't deny that, in the analysis of stratification, emphasis must be given to the *various perspectives. Equally, however, there is a great deal of common ground* – acknowledged and partly unacknowledged – between them, particularly between the conflict structuralism of Marx and Weber. Take the examples of racial and generational stratification: racial and generational groups often experience status stratification on the basis of, say, colour and age, as a Weberian might contend. This approach, however, can be accommodated within a broader theory of class conflict in a way acceptable to Marxists. Although age groups may share a common generational experience, class is probably a greater influence on young people's lives. Similarly, most blacks are members of the working class as well as of a racial group and therefore the concept of class as well as status is important in understanding their structural position. Many sociologists, of course, prefer to recognise these complexities rather than try to live within some rigidly orthodox version of a perspective. John Rex, for example is prepared to work with both Weberian and Marxist concepts, even though it is also obvious that he has no relish for the more obscurely theoretical Marxist formulations. A similar open-mindedness seems to characterise the work on stratification carried out by John Goldthorpe. The conceptual framework of the *Oxford Mobility Study* may be broadly Weberian, but Goldthorpe's own comments on class inequality and conflict should please any Marxist.

The links between the concepts of stratification and power are too well-known to require pursuing in detail here. Broadly, Marx located the source of power in class relations and Weber saw it more diffusely as the possible product of class, political, military, personal, ideological or other factors. For some sociologists, that is that: never the twain shall meet. Yet, under the guise of a very different terminology from Weber's, Marxists as different as Althusser and E. P. Thompson have argued that power is generated not exclusively at the economic level, but also, to a significant degree, at the political and superstructural level. Of course, there are important qualifications to be made, but that position does not seem to be basically incompatible with what Weber says.

It will not have escaped notice that I have said nothing so far of functionalist analysis of stratification. I do not wish to pursue my case beyond reason, and the fact is that functionalist and Marxist stratificational theory are in contradiction. Functionalists regard stratification as inevitable, whereas Marxists consider that, in certain circumstances, class inequality – the major form of stratification – could be abolished. I object, however, to the current sociological vogue of regarding this and similar differences as primarily ideological. Unless sociology is to be regarded as a mere mish-mash of personal opinion, these issues need to be treated as theoretical differences which require to be tackled and, as far as possible, resolved at the theoretical and empirical level. That is what sociology is supposed to do. We all know that personal values and ideology play a role in scientific and social scientific inquiry, but that should not preclude professional communication and co-operation in developing theory among sociologists of different political viewpoints.

My examination of the concepts of culture and structure should have given a clearer idea of the basic point I am trying to make here. I am not attempting to sweep the perspectives under the carpet in a stubborn attempt at achieving sociological unity nor, indeed, am I denying that it is partly in treating concepts differently that differences in the perspectives show themselves. The issue is one of emphasis and approach. First things first: concepts should have a larger share in the presentation of sociology than they usually do, and explanation of them should, if possible, be handled in a way that avoids logically contradictory notions of what the concepts mean. The perspectives ought not to involve such radical contradiction or, if they do, something is badly wrong somewhere, and students would have every right to be sceptical of, if not downright disillusioned with, the subject.

I want, finally, to examine the question of whether the development of a unified sociological paradigm is desirable or possible. Given that the theories which help to make up a paradigm are built upon concepts, the issue of a unified sociological paradigm is an extension of the problem of conceptual analysis. However, the scale and complexity of the matter is unique in sociology – it is very much the $64,000 question of the subject. Perhaps it is sensible to think in terms of paradigmatic unity as a useful *ideal* to focus constructive work rather than as some sort of static and stultifyingly final theoretical consensus. At best, the alternative to this seems to be to accept several partly contradictory sociological paradigms as a permanent feature of the discipline and, at worst, to consider that these various paradigms or perspectives can reasonably be based on mere ideology or personal opinion. In my view, neither of these positions is logically or scientifically tenable. Perhaps a third position is that, in Althusserian terms, the various perspectives are concerned with different 'problematics'. I take this to mean that they pose different questions, and so examine somewhat different areas of social inquiry. I can accept that sociologists will pursue distinctive interests using methods of their own choosing, but I can see no reason why their analyses should not be accessible to the comprehension and criticism of others.

It is only possible here to examine one or two theoretical issues of relevance to the question of paradigmatic unity. I must, however, first briefly outline the scope of the problem. I suggest that two major theoretical areas on which 'paradigm building' requires to concentrate are those of *structure, change* and *agency* (who or what causes change) and *culture* and *community*. The last two are paired because the understanding of community as shared culture is recurrent in sociology, not least in functionalism and Marxism. What we have already said about structure and culture can be considered to support what follows. Firstly, then, we review some problems that the concept of structure currently presents in sociological theory. I agree

587

with Giddens that conflict structuralism, particularly Marxism, provides a better basis for understanding how social groups, including classes, relate to one another than does consensus structuralism. In particular, the organic analogy applied to society as a whole obscures more than it illuminates. But it can be added that the assumption of stable social and political consensus and equilibrium in the West made by intellectuals, including leading sociologists, in the nineteen fifties, was thoroughly undermined by the turbulence and conflict of the next decade. Still more decisively, consensus assumptions should never be applied to the cauldron of world politics or to understanding the emergence of Third World countries; in fairness, they seldom were. As well as Marxists, labelling and interactionist theorists have produced a whole range of arguments against a simple consensus-deviance model (see Chapters 16 and 17, especially pp. 473-7). At this stage, it hardly seems premature to declare broadly in favour of the conflict theorists on the long post-war debate about the balance of conflict and consensus in modern societies. The notion of consensus must, however, retain a major place within sociological theory, but it requires to be linked to the concept of ideology (and, via ideology, to culture). When national consensus does exist, the questions to ask are why and how it was brought about and, particularly, in whose interest it operates. In other words, consensus must be viewed in ideological terms. Simply to assume value consensus as 'normal' misses important issues, and reduces the sociologist's role to attempting to describe the processes by which conformity is achieved or not (an essentially conservative contribution).

On matters of structure and power Marxists can learn much from Weber. Exploitation and domination are not exclusive features of capitalist society: indeed, the most totalitarian of power structures probably lie outside capitalist societies. Weber's analysis of power and bureaucracy helps to explain why. (See Chapter 15, pp. 407-8). I would argue, nonetheless, that Weber's assumption of the inevitability of bureaucratic hierarchy and elitism needs to be balanced by a more positive sense of democratic alternatives.

Probably more sociological brawls have occurred over the issue of social change and agency than over any other. There is no need to repeat in detail our review of the Thompson-

Althusser debate (Chapter 19, pp. 532-3) or the remarks about historical determinism made earlier in this chapter. What I conclude, optimistically, from these discussions is that there is an emerging consensus that regards both traditional structural-functionalism and crude Marxism as unacceptably deterministic. The alternative is to see man as the agent of his own destiny, despite the obstacles he places in his own path.

Anthony Giddens has pointed out a theoretical issue of considerable interest concerning structure, agency and system. He remarks that functionalism tends to collapse the distinction between structure and system to the point where the two terms are used interchangeably. This is the result of regarding the operation of the social system as merely the functionings of social structure (the fundamental functionalist tautology) and, in the process, disregarding the contributions of social actors. It becomes impossible, however, to amalgamate the two if we take the contrary view that people, not institutions or structures, are the dynamic agents of social systems. In order to 'bridge the gap' between structure and system, Giddens proposes that the term *structuration* be used. If I understand him correctly, he intends to use it to synthesise two elements: (1) *that people – individually or in groups – are the active forces in social systems and* (2) that *they work within structured (or normatively defined) situations.* Thus, structure and system meet dynamically at the point of social action. Most illuminatingly, Giddens compares structuration to the process of linguistic communication of meaning (systems operation) and, in the process, it (language) can be changed and expanded (agent activity). It is not difficult to imagine how the concept of structuration could be applied to the analysis of normative structures and creative activity within organisations and social situations. It seems to go some way towards reconciling the two sides of the agency-structure debate within sociology.

We now finally examine the problem of culture and community with a view to showing that both concepts are at the heart of all structural sociology. It is sometimes said that community is of concern to functionalists but not to Marxists. Functionalists regret the 'loss' of traditional community whilst Marxists invest too much hope in the future to idealise the past. Further, functionalists often seem to be concerned to 'preserve' whatever remnants of community that do survive in modern society whilst Marxists want to drive a wedge between any 'false' solidarity of the classes. This radical difference conceals an even deeper shared concern. Marxists, too, desire community, but whereas functionalists seek for it in the past, Marxists project it into the future and, specifically, see it as a feature of 'classless' society which will be achieved sometime after the demise of capitalism. At least this suggests a common goal of social harmony and thus provides a starting point for theoretical dialogue. The concept of culture is relevant here because, without shared values, the basis of community does not exist. What functionalists have steadfastly failed to accept is that, as long as society is deeply divided along class lines, culture and community will reflect this fracture. The material and cultural inequalities that class systems produce fuel conflict and discontent. They preclude stable community (assuming that the enforced 'community' of totalitarian societies, which represses class conflict, is unacceptable).

As I begin to conclude, I recall a lecture delivered in September, 1979, by Ronald Fletcher. His thesis was that there is a 'shared universe of discourse' within sociology – substantially arrived at by the founding fathers – which is merely obscured by the current over-emphasis on perspectives within teaching circles. There is a case for this view. Even functionalists accept, in theory, the possibility of creative social action and, further, have made attempts, however cumbersome, to build the concept of conflict into their theoretical framework. Unlike Fletcher, however, I consider neither functionalist theory based on organic analogy nor Parsons' social systems model adequate to the task of utilising the concepts effectively either in empirical research or theoretical exposition. That said, his fundamental premise stands – that the founding fathers conceived of the social world in a broadly complementary and compatible way, rather than a contradictory one. Enough is shared in the way of basic concepts and categories to make progressive discourse possible. All the better, if, within a coherent framework, great diversity exists. It is intriguing to find Marxist, Tom Bottomore, and functionalist, Robert Nisbet, displaying a similar sentiment to that of Fletcher in their preface to a book which they jointly edited, *A History of Sociological Analysis* (1979). They, too, suggest that sociology is bigger than, and something more than, the differences that occur within it. Particularly arresting is the notion that Marxist sociology can be more positively viewed as a movement *within* sociology in general, rather than as alternative to it:

> But there is today no Weberian nor Durkheimian sociology, and even in the case of Marx a considerable gap exists between Marx's own theory of society and the various forms of present-day Marxist sociology, with the development of the latter, we would dare to suggest, embodying advances in, 'sociological' rather than 'Marxist' thought.

Despite the sense that a broad sociological framework does exist, Bottomore and Nisbet recognise that modern sociology contains a variety of different strands of interest, including a vital phenomenology of interaction. They are certainly a long way from concurring with Comte's narrowly positivistic ambition that sociology should develop the means 'to know in order to predict, to predict in order to control'! Yet they are also far from uncritically according equal status to all perspectives. To do so would be virtually to accept that sociological research is simply the organised presentation of subjective feeling, and the teaching of sociology merely the purveying of this indulgence to a wider audience. On the contrary, sociological research, like the perspectives themselves, must be assessed on the soundness of its theoretical and empirical content. Analysing the influence of personal or political ideology on research is simply one factor in this task and not, as has sometimes seemed to be the assumption, the major concern of teaching sociology. All disciplines finally face the problem of whether we can objectively 'know' anything, but some sociologists have tended to revel in this essentially philosophical problem at the expense of the pursuit of more practical matters of theory and method. I might add that such metaphysical obsession is particularly inappropriate for offering at 'A' level.

Happily, there is a growing body of sociological research that is well able to bear scrutiny in terms of rigorous standards of assessment. As we have seen, given that the methodological basis of quantitative and qualitative research is different, the basis of assessing it varies accordingly. The upsurge in highly empirical work, such as Townsend's *Poverty Report* and the *Oxford Mobility Study*, and the burgeoning of Marxist phenomenology are contrasting examples of current trends. Yet, there is no reason why this work should not be broadly complementary rather than contradictory. Despite its variety, it should produce a sounder basis for building general sociological perspective than mere speculation and subjectivism. Perhaps there is a new Marx or Parsons waiting in the wings who has the capacity to extract pattern and form from amongst the detail. If so, and if he or she can bring some harmony to the current cacaphony, we will all have cause to be grateful.

Guide to further reading and study

The reader is referred back to the end of Chapter 2, where several suggestions are made for further reading. In addition, the following may be within the range of students well into their course. David Berry's excellent *Central Ideas of Sociology* (Constable, 1974) is wide-ranging and not slavishly tied to a perspectives approach. Stephen Mennel's *Sociological Theory: Uses and Unities* (Nelson, 1974), is a succinct summary of a wide range of sociological theory, but is weak on Marx. Tom Bottomore and Robert Nisbet's *A History of Sociological Analysis* (Heinemann, 1979) is best used for reference; Most of the contributions are demanding. Finally, Durkheim's *The Rules of Sociological Method* (The Free Press, Macmillan, 1966) still repays a critical read.

Past Questions

NB In addition to the following, questions involving stimulus material should also be used as these are becoming increasingly a part of sociology exams at advanced level. It would be quite possible to use some of the quotations in this book to construct such questions.

1 Is a science of human behaviour possible? (AEB, 1978).

2 Men have purposes and motives; it is not possible therefore to be scientific about human behaviour.' Discuss. (AEB, 1976).

3 'Sociology frequently produces a new methodology but never any results.' Is this a valid comment on the contribution of sociology? (JMB, 1978).

4 With reference to one particular area of social life, compare the usefulness of *participant observation* and *survey work* to sociologists. (AEB, 1978).

5 Sociologists frequently use a variety of secondary sources such as literature film, journalism, and statistics produced by government and institutions. What are the limitations of such sources for sociological research? (AEB, 1979).

6 Participant observation is a method of research which has aroused considerable controversy. Examine the arguments *for* and *against* participant observation as a method of research. (AEB, 1980).

Bibliography of Books and Articles
from which quotations have been taken

ABRAMS, P. (1979) 'A power within a world of power,' in *Times Higher Educational Supplement*, September 2, 1977.

BANFIELD, E.C. (1977) 'The imperatives of class' in J. Raynor and E. Harris *eds, Urban Education: The City Experience*, Ward Lock.

BECKER, H. (1963) *Outsiders: Studies in the Sociology of Deviance*, The Free Press.

BENINGTON, J. (1977) 'The Flaw in the Pluralist Heaven,' in J. Raynor and E. Harris *eds, Urban Education: The City Experience*, Ward Lock.

BLONDEL, J. (1969) *Voters, Parties, and Leaders: The Social Fabric of British Politics*, Penguin.

BOTTOMORE, T. (1964) *Elites and Society*, Penguin.

BOTTOMORE, T. and NISBET, R. (1979) *A History of Sociological Analysis*, Heinemann.

CHEVANNES, M. and REEVES, F.W. (1979) 'Footprints in the Sand' in R. Meighan, I. Shelton and T. Marks *eds, Perspectives on Society*, Nelson.

CICOUREL, A. (1968) *The Social Organisation of Juvenile Justice*, Heinemann.

CLEGG, S. and DUNKERLEY, D. (1980) *Organisations, Class and Control*, Routledge and Kegan Paul.

COOPER, D. (1973) 'Being Born into a Family,' in Phil Brown *ed, Radical Psychology*, Harper Colophon Books.

CROUCH, C. (1979) *The Politics of Industrial Relations*, Fontana.

DAHL, R. (1968) *A Preface to Political Theory*, University of Chicago Press.

DELMAR, R. (1977) 'Looking Again at Engels's 'Origins of the Family, Private Property and the State,', in Juliet Mitchell and Ann Oakley *eds, The Rights and Wrongs of Women*, Penguin.

DITTON, J. (1972) 'Absent at work: or how to manage monotony,' in *New Society*, 21 December, 1972.

DOUGLAS, J.W.B. (1968) *All Our Future*, Panther.

DURKHEIM, E. (1972) from Anthony Giddens *ed, Emile Durkheim: Selected Writings*, Cambridge University Press.

ETZIONI, A. (1964) *Modern Organisations*, Prentice-Hall.

FORESTER, T. (1980) 'Whatever happened to industrial democracy,' in *New Society*, 17 July, 1980.

595

GARFINKEL, H. (1974) 'The Origins of the Term 'Ethnomethodology',' in Roy Turner ed, *Ethnomethodology*, Penguin.

GIDDENS, A. (1977) *The Class Structure of the Advanced Societies*, Hutchinson.

GIDDENS, A. (1979) *Central Problems in Social Theory: Action, structure and contradiction in social analysis*, Macmillan.

GOLDTHORPE, J.H. (1980) *Social Mobility and Class Structure in Modern Britain*, Clarendon Press.

GOULDNER, A. (1965) 'Bureaucracy is not Inevitable,' in Peter Worsley ed, *Problems of Modern Sociology*, Penguin, 1978.

HALL, S. (1978) 'Racism and Reaction' in *Five Views of Multi-Racial Britain*, published by the Commission for Racial Equality.

HALSEY, A.H. (1979) 'Bernstein on the block,' in *The Times Educational Supplement*, 16 December, 1979.

HALSEY, A.H. (1978) *Change in British Society*, Oxford University Press.

HAY, D. (1979) 'The Spiritual Experiences of the British' in *New Society*, April 12, 1979.

HYMAN, S. (1972) *Why Do Strikes Occur?*, Fontana.

JENCKS, C. *et al.*, (1977) 'Schooling and cognitive inequality,' in P. Raggat and M. Evans eds, *Urban Education: The Political Context*, Ward Lock.

JOHNSON, R. (1979) 'Three problematic elements of a theory of working-class culture,' in J. Clarke *et al*, eds, *Working Class Culture: Studies in history and theory*, Hutchinson.

KINCAID, J.C. (1973) *Poverty and Equality in Britain*, Penguin.

KING, A. (1972) 'A Sociological Portrait: Politics,' in *New Society*, 13 January, 1972.

LAING, R. (1973) 'The Mystification of Experience,' in Phil Brown ed, *Radical Psychology*, Harper Colophon Books.

MARX, K. (1844) in T.B. Bottomore and M. Rubel eds, *Karl Marx: Selected Writings in Sociology and Social Philosophy*, Penguin, 1967.

MARX K. (1859) in David McLellan ed, *Grundrisse*, Macmillan, 1971.

MEAD, G.H. (1934) *Mind, Self, and Society*, The University of Chicago Press, 1962.

MILIBAND, R. (1969) *The State in Capitalist Society*, Quartet Books.

MILLS, C.W. (1956) *The Power Elite*, Oxford University Press.

MITCHELL, J. (1971) *Women's Estate*, Penguin.

NISSEL, M. (1980) 'The family and the welfare state,' in *New Society*, 7 August, 1980.

NYERERE, J. (1979) 'The Rational Choice,' in A. Coulson *ed, African Socialism in Practice: The Tanzanian Experience*, Spokesman.

OAKLEY, A. (1979) 'The failure of the movement for women's equality,' in *New Society*, August 22, 1979.

PARSONS, T. (1959) 'The School Class as a Social System: Some of its Functions in American Society,' in *Harvard Educational Review*, XXIX (Fall, 1959).

POULANTZAS, N. (1978) *State, Power and Socialism*, New Left Books.

REID, I. (1977) *Social Class Differences in Britain: A Sourcebook*, Open Books.

REX, J. (1979) 'Black Militancy and Class Conflict' in R. Miles and A. Phizacklea *eds, Racism and Political Action in Britain*, Routledge and Kegan Paul.

ROBERTSON, J. (1978) 'Technology-master or servant,' in *New Scientist*, 23 November, 1978.

ROWBOTHAM, S. (1973) *Women's Consciousness, Man's World*, Penguin.

ROWBOTHAM, S. (1977) *Hidden from History: 300 Years of Women's Oppression and the Fight Against It*, Pluto Press.

SHILS, E. (1961) 'Centre and Periphery' in Peter Worsley *ed, Modern Sociology*, Penguin, 1978.

SHILS, E. (1963) 'The Theory of Mass Society,' in Philip Olson *ed, America as a Mass Society*, Collier-Macmillan.

SHORTER, E. (1977) *The Making of the Modern Family*, Fontana.

SILLITOE, A. (1958) *Saturday Night and Sunday Morning*, W.H. Allen.

SKOLNICK, J. (1966) *Justice without Trial*, John Wiley.

SMITH, D.J. (1977) *Racial Disadvantage in Britain: The PEP Report*.

STENGEL, E. (1977) *Suicide*, Penguin.

TAYLOR, I., WALTON, P. and YOUNG, J. (1976) 'Towards a New Criminology' in Paul Willis *ed, Crime and Delinquency in Britain*.

TAYLOR, L. (1977) 'No More Flags' in *New Society*, 31 March, 1977.

THOMPSON, E.P. (1968) *The Making of the English Working Class*, Penguin.

WEBER, M. (1920) *Economy and Society*, Bedminster, 1968.

WEIR, D.J.H. (1977) 'Class Consciousness among Clerical Workers,' in E. Butterworth and D. Weir *eds, The Sociology of Modern Britain*, Fontana.

WEIR, M. (1976) from the Introduction of Mary Weir *ed, Job Satisfaction: Challenge and Response in Modern Britain*, Fontana.

WEST, D.J. and FARRINGTON, D.P. (1977) *The Delinquent Way of Life*, Heinemann.

WILLIAMS, R. (1961) *Culture and Society*, Penguin.

WILLIAMS, R. (1968) *Communications*, Penguin.

WILLIS, P. (1978) *Learning to Labour*, Saxon House.

YOUNG, M. (1958) *The Rise of the Meritocracy*, Penguin.

Author Index

Dahl, Robert, A., 505-6, 546
Dahrendorf, Ralf, 235-7, 247, 248, 250, 252, 422
Daniel, W.W., 319
Darwin, Charles, 541
Davis, Howard, H., 242, 251
Davis, Kingsley, 220, 280-2, 572
Delmar, Rosalind, 77
Ditton, Jason, 371
Djilas, Milovan, 276
Dore, R., 124
Douglas, Jack. D., 470, 482
Douglas, J.W.B., 17, 79, 107, 122, 132
Downes, David, 460
Driver, Geoffrey, 136
Dunkerley, David, 381, 393, 421, 429, 430
Durkheim, Emile, 5-7, 31-4, 52, 109-11, 170-6, 178, 183, 194, 211, 219-20, 225, 282, 406, 433, 435-6, 440-1, 457, 467, 469-70, 472, 482, 487, 559, 536-7, 566, 568, 571, 584, 592
Dye, Thomas, R., 526

Eggleston, John, 147
Eisenstadt, S.N., 337
Engelmann, S., 149
Engels, Friedrich, 76-8, 83, 287, 288
Etzioni, Amitai, 365, 381, 424-5, 429
Eysenck, Hans, 120, 122, 456, 468, 551-2, 557

Farmer, Mary, 104
Farrington, D.P., 467, 468
Field, Frank, 139, 268, 283
Firestone, Shulamith, 288, 293
Fletcher, Ronald, 89, 104, 570, 590
Floud, J.S., 145
Ford, Julienne, 147-8
Forester, Tom, 394
Frank, Gunder, 199
Frankenburg, Ronald, 38, 204
Freud, Sigmund, 49, 50, 541
Frith, Simon, 358

Galbraith, J.K., 191, 194, 277
Gallie, Duncan, 367
Gans, Herbert, J., 179, 185, 192
Garfinkel, Harold, 476, 559, 581
Gavron, Hannah, 35, 42, 297
Gellner, Ernest, 561
Giddens, Anthony, 228, 234, 236-7, 451, 512, 513-14, 526, 571, 572, 578, 588, 589
Ginsberg, Allen, 101

Gintis, Herbert, 121-2, 124, 281, 364, 382
Glasgow Media Group, 550
Glass, David, V., 255, 256
Glasser, Ralph, 416-17
Goff, Tom, 578, 579
Goffman, Erving, 56-7, 418-19, 430, 559
Goldthorpe, John H., 27, 62-3, 91, 242-6, 249-50, 256, 257, 260, 261, 274-6, 277, 369, 388, 390, 417, 497, 499, 500, 501, 559, 585-6
Gomm, Roger, 161, 167
Goode, W.J., 85, 88
Gordon, David, 466
Goring, Charles, 456
Gorz, André, 204
Gough, Kathleen, 80
Golding, Peter, 543-4, 556
Gouldner, Alvin W., 277, 278, 370, 387, 414, 425-6, 428, 485

Habermas, Jurgen, 569
Hall, Stuart, 320, 358, 477
Hall, Peter, 398
Halsey, A.H., 19, 113, 116-18, 122-3, 139, 143, 145, 150-2, 158, 227, 237, 238, 246-7, 255, 256, 258, 261, 377, 394, 559
Hargreaves, David, 129, 340, 582
Harris, C., 86
Harris, Elizabeth, 204
Harvey, David, 185
Hay, David, 542
Heading, Bryan, 503
Heath, A.F., 116, 132
Heller, T., 162
Henry, A.F., 470
Heraud, B.J., 182-3
Hewitt, Christopher, 509, 518
Hindess, Barry, 481-2, 561
Hite Report, 89
Hoggart, Richard, 92, 261, 548
Holman, Robert, 283
Homans, G., 389
Hoyt, Homer, 177-8
Hunt, J., 149
Husserl, Edmund, 16
Hyman, Richard, 388, 391, 403

Illich, Ivan, 156-7, 165, 383
Jackson, Brian, 117, 145
Jefferson, Tony, 358
Jencks, Christopher, 107, 151
Jenkins, Clive, 373, 375-6, 401, 403

602

Subject Index

Private schools, 67-8, 333-4, 514
Professionals
  income of, 238
  'knowledge' of, 156-7, 162, 381-2
Professions, 377-84
  and trade unions, 380-1
  functionalist theory and, 378
  power-conflict analysis of, 379-84
  trait analysis of, 378-9
Proletariat, 211
Protestant ethic, 538-9
Public schools. *See* Private schools
Punks, 218, 342

Qualitative research, 35-8
Quantitative research, 27-31
Questionnaires, 28-9

Race
  and class, 310, 321
  and crime, 324, 461, 477-8, 480
  and education, 135-8, 149, 324
  and employment, 314-18
  and housing, 318-19
  and imperialism, 311-12
  and moral panics, 319-20
  and politics, 321-5, 343
  and stratification, 310, 320, 321
  and trade unions, 317
  and youth, 324, 341, 343, 349-50
  definition, 310
  riots, 311, 312, 323-4
Race Relations Acts, 325-6
Rastafarians, 325, 350
Rationalisation, 366, 408, 541
Reference group, 267
Reflexity, 581
Regularities, 32
Relations of production, 212, 214
Relative deprivation. *See* Poverty
Religion
  and ideology, 530, 536-8
  and social control, 172, 531
  and social change, 538-9
  and the sociology of knowledge, 565
  and voting, 502-3
Restricted codes, 111-12
Revolution, 5-6, 214-15, 573, 577
Ritual, 52, 113, 538
Role, 21, 22, 48-9, 56, 57, 174
  gender, 91, 291-2, 297, 397
Ruling class, 277, 514-21
Rural-urban continuum, 175

Sampling, 27-9
Science
  sociology as a, 6-7, 35, 558-64, 566-8
Scientific method, 24-5, 562-3
Secondary contacts, 176
Sects, 542-3
Secularisation, 539-43
Segmental, 171, 176
Self, 53-7
  -actualisation, 158-9, 368, 370-1
  -involvement, 368
  management of, 371
Self-fulfilling prophecy, 130, 463
Sex Discrimination Act, 133, 304-5
Sexual division of labour, 293-4, 300
Shareholders, 235, 236
Significant others, 54, 448, 462
Signification spiral, 549-50
Skinheads, 341-2
Social action theory, 8, 13-15
  examples, 243-6, 416-17
Social change, 5-6, 8, 12, 14. *See also*
  Revolution and Evolutionary
  change.
  and technology, 215, 233
  and urbanisation, 169-94
  economic context of, 231-3
  functionalist theory and, 172-6
  in Britain, 234-53
  Marxist theory and, 214-15
  Weber and, 538-9
Social class. *See* Class
Social closure, 254, 256
Social control
  and culture, 536-53
  formal and informal, 437
  functionalist theory and, 437-9
  interpretist theory and, 499-50, 473-7
  Marxist theory and, 444-5, 477-8
Social differentiation. *See*
  Differentiation
Social facts, 11, 32, 34, 482
Social images, 251
Social mobility
  and education, 118-26, 158, 258
  definitions, 209, 253
  factors affecting, 257-60
  in socialist countries, 274-5, 276
Social order, 8
  functionalist theory and, 10, 172,
  435-7
  interpretist theory and, 14, 56, 449-
  50
  Marxist theory and, 12, 443-4
Social pathology, 441, 572

609